BEYOND THE TEXTS

BEYOND THE TEXTS

An Archaeological Portrait of
Ancient Israel and Judah

William G. Dever

SBL PRESS

S|B|L PRESS

Atlanta

Library of Congress Cataloging-in-Publication Data

Names: Dever, William G., author.
Title: Beyond the texts : an archaeological portrait of ancient Israel and Judah / by William G. Dever.
Description: Atlanta : SBL Press, [2017] | Includes bibliographical references and index.
Identifiers: LCCN 2017033562 (print) | LCCN 2017042027 (ebook) | ISBN 9780884142171 (ebook) | ISBN 9780884142188 (hardcover : alk. paper)
Subjects: LCSH: Excavations (Archaeology)—Israel. | Israel—Antiquities. | Palestine—Antiquities. | Palestine—History—To 70 A.D. | Bible. Old Testament—Antiquities. | Jews—History—1200-953 B.C. | Jews—History—953-586 B.C.
Classification: LCC DS111 (ebook) | LCC DS111 .D56 2017 (print) | DDC 933—dc23
LC record available at https://lccn.loc.gov/2017033562

Printed on acid-free paper.

With profound gratitude to an anonymous benefactor
whose generosity is outstripped only by her modesty.
Without her unwavering encouragement and support,
I would never have been able to undertake this project.

Contents

Contents

Foreword

This book has been in the making for nearly sixty years, at least in my mind. It began in 1958, when as a young seminary student I discovered Ernest Wright's *God Who Acts: Biblical Theology as Recital*. Wright had declared, "In biblical faith everything depends upon whether the central events happened" (1952, 126–27).

I still remember the thrill I felt upon reading that declaration. I had been reared in a southern fundamentalist preacher's home, and at twenty-five I was an ordained minister myself, now enrolled in a liberal seminary and in an identity crisis. How could I reconcile the higher learning to which I was committed—preparing for an academic career—and my Christian faith? Ernest Wright, a prominent Christian clergyman, and also America's leading scholar at the time in both the fields of Old Testament theology and biblical archaeology at Harvard, had shown me the way.

I finished my BD degree (now an MDiv), and then in 1959 I submitted an MA thesis on the "revival of Old Testament theology," a movement in which Wright had been a leader. And since Wright had moved from McCormick Theological Seminary to Harvard in 1958, I resolved to pursue my studies with him. I was going to show that the "central events"—patriarchal migrations, the promise of the land, a unique monotheism, Moses leading an exodus and conquest—that these events had actually happened.

Unfortunately, at Harvard I soon discovered that, while I may have had the necessary dogmatic temperament for theology, I had little talent. Nevertheless, Wright, who knew me better than I knew myself, steered me into archaeology at Shechem in the summer of 1962. I never looked back.

After finishing my doctoral dissertation in 1966, I moved on to the Directorship first at the Hebrew Union College in Jerusalem (1968–1971) and then of the W. F. Albright Institute of Archaeological Research (1971–1975). For the next twenty years I concentrated on fieldwork in Israel and the West Bank. Most of my publications during that period dealt with the Bronze Age and increasingly with issues of theory, method, and mounting critiques of traditional biblical archaeology.

At the University of Arizona after 1975 (until 2002), I continued with efforts to foster a newer, more secular and professional "Syro-Palestinian" archaeology, employing explicitly socioanthropological approaches and training a generation of graduate students who would embody the departure. For many years I had advocated a dialogue between archaeology and biblical studies, but not until the mid-1980s did my interests turn to the biblical period: the Iron Age.

By 1987 I had read Robert Coote and Keith Whitelam's *The Emergence of Early Israel in Historical Perspective* and Thomas Thompson's *The Origin Traditions of Ancient Israel: The Literary Formation of Genesis and Exodus 1–23*. Then at the 1987 meetings of the American Schools of Oriental Research and the Society of Biblical Literature in Boston, I convened a plenary session on "Earliest Israel." The invited speakers were Whitelam, Norman Gottwald, Lawrence Stager, and Israel Finkelstein, in addition to me. Thompson and Diana Edelman, in the audience, rose to confront us. The battle was joined.

Finkelstein's *The Archaeology of the Israelite Settlement* appeared the next year, but the seminal papers at the Boston meetings were never published. In 1991, I published papers on historicity in Edelman's edited volume of seminar papers, *The Fabric of History*, and in a Festschrift for Gottwald. The gauntlet was thrown down the following year by Philip Davies's *In Search of "Ancient Israel."* Then 1994 turned out to be a pivotal year for me: papers at symposia in Bern, Rome, and Pisa, as well as contributions to the Neil Richardson and Philip King Festschriften, all in one way or another on the interaction between text and artifact.

In 1996 the issues were sharpened with the publication of papers from a Jerusalem symposium volume edited by Volkmar Fritz and Davies, *The Origins of the Ancient Israelite State* (I was invited but unable to attend), in particular by Whitelam's provocative *The Invention of Ancient Israel: The Silencing of Palestinian History*. I recall reading Whitelam's diatribe against Israeli and American archeologists as "Zionist" ideologues with dismay and growing anger. By now I knew who the ideologues really were.

The next year (1997) I published nine chapters in various volumes, seven of them on the specific topic of how to write better, more archaeologically informed histories of ancient Israel and Judah. The same year there appeared Lester Grabbe's edited volume *Can a 'History of Israel' Be*

Written? I critiqued this volume in a session at the ASOR/SBL Annual Meetings. Grabbe, in the audience, introduced himself and insisted that my skepticism about the members of his European Seminar on Method in Israel's History was misplaced. But it was not: neither he nor his colleagues ever subsequently produced any history of ancient Israel (see below and excursus 1.1). It was then that I resolved that I would do so. In the previous decade of this controversy, I had been in my fifties and sixties. It was now time, but I was not yet ready.

From the late 1990s on, I thought about a new, revolutionary archaeological history of Israel. But not until the turn of the millennium, in retirement, did I resolve to undertake the task. Now in my mid- to late seventies, I had the necessary gravitas and nothing to gain, nothing to lose. The result is this volume.

I am indebted to many along the way, although it was lonely at first—colleagues, friends, family without whose encouragement I would never have had the temerity to undertake such a daunting task, one that others thought impossible or at best undesirable. I would single out Larry Stager, a staunch defender of sound historical method and an unfailing supporter of my work. Other colleagues who inspired me were Susan Ackerman, Beth Alpert Nakhai, and Carol Meyers, who helped me to be more sympathetic to the lives of women in ancient Israel. Ron Hendel and Ziony Zevit have shown me more sophisticated ways of reading the biblical texts.

Two recent works have had an immediate impact on me during the writing of this history. Lester Grabbe, originally an adversary, became a model with his *Ancient Israel: What Do We Know and How Do We Know It?* (2007). This work provided me with a prolegomenon, and my employment here of a *continuum* from proven to disproven is borrowed from him. Avraham Faust, an innovative younger Israeli archeologist, gave me a draft of his 2012 *The Archaeology of Israelite Society in Iron Age II*, a harbinger of things hopefully to come.

I am also grateful to my thirty-one PhD students, with whom I explored many trial runs in graduate seminars in Jerusalem and at the University of Arizona in the 1970s–1990s. They are my real legacy, and I dedicate this book to them with affection and esteem.

Most of all, I acknowledge an incalculable debt to my wife Pamela, who believed confidently in this enterprise (and me), even when I thought it might be folly. She saw me to the finish. I am also indebted to Norma Dever, my first wife, who is unique in being able to turn my handwritten manuscripts into print suitable for publication.

I am also indebted to Nicole Tilford and Bob Buller of SBL Press, who with great skill and patience turned a cumbersome manuscript and illustrations into a real book.

Finally, I owe more than I can say to an anonymous benefactor who coaxed me out of "retirement" in my late seventies and made me believe that I had one more work in me—as it turned out, my magnum opus.

This book is intended primarily as a handbook for biblical scholars, historians of the ancient Near East, and nonspecialists interested in the biblical world. In order to keep the narrative flowing, I have confined the discussion of some controversial issues that could not be avoided to endnotes for each chapter, where references to a full bibliography will be found. I have tried to cite all major works that I think relevant, as well as offering reasons for my preference where sharp disagreements are apparent. I am not defending any particular "school," only trying to provide a reasonable, balanced view of what really happened in the light of the best current archaeological evidence we have. This is *a* history of ancient Israel, not *the* history. Other histories should be and will be written in due time, but we do not need any more paraphrases of the Hebrew Bible. Future histories will likely be largely archaeological histories—advancing on this one—because archaeology is now our only source of genuinely new data.

The main text is deliberately written in the third person, in the interest of a dispassionate style of inquiry. In the notes to chapter 1 and in the conclusion, however, I use the first person because I happen to know almost all of the scholars whose views are discussed, and I have often been involved in the controversies and in all honesty cannot always separate the individual from methods and aims. I can only hope to have been fair, despite some sharp disagreements. In the conclusion, I step beyond fact to some personal convictions, and for these I take full responsibility.

On a few practical matters, I note that discussions of sites with no specific reference depend largely on Stern's edited five-volume *New Encyclopedia of Archaeological Excavations in the Holy Land* (Stern 1993, 2008), which can be supplemented by entries in the *Anchor Bible Dictionary* (Freedman 1992); the *Oxford Encyclopedia of Archaeology in the Near East* (E. Meyers 1997); and *Civilizations of the Ancient Near East* (Sasson 2006). Where final report volumes published after these works are available, they may be cited. A recent and valuable resource is *The Oxford Handbook of the Archaeology of the Levant c. 8000–332 BCE* (Steiner and Killebrew 2014). Several chapters in *The Oxford History of the Biblical World* (Coogan

2001), although brief, are written by archaeologists or biblical scholars familiar with the biblical data. Finally, a definitive corpus of pottery was published after this book was ready for press, a two-volume work edited by Seymour Gitin: *Ancient Pottery of Israel and Its Neighbors from the Iron Age through the Hellenistic Period* (Jerusalem: Israel Exploration Society, 2015). This is a magisterial work by numerous experts and should be consulted to supplement the necessarily brief discussions of pottery here.

The bibliography contains mostly English-language works. That is because the international dialogue is most often in English, and all the basic Israeli archaeological publications (even doctoral dissertations) have long been published in English.

Biblical chronology follows Cogan and Tadmor 1988 and Cogan 2001. For Egypt, dates are those of Shaw 2000. For wider ancient Near East chronology, Rainey and Notley 2006 is taken as authoritative.

All dates are BCE unless further specified. The term *Palestine* is used only for ancient Canaan (although Roman in origin) and has no implications for the modern situation in the region.

Since this is a history of ancient Israel, not that of either the biblical literature or the history of Near Eastern archaeology, the reader is simply referred to other discussions. Few biblical commentaries are listed, for reasons elaborated below; the biblical text is what it now is, and the historical claims that the narratives are making are clear enough to be tested critically. Later interpretations—"cultural memories"—are irrelevant for our purposes.

Most of the histories of ancient Israel written over the past fifty years or so are cited. But no attempt is made to compare them to the history offered here, because ours is quite simply unique. Readers will have to judge which histories are more satisfactory, more in keeping with what we now know and may want to know in the future.

No literature after mid-2015 could be cited, although many discussions are ongoing, and there is a constant flow of new archaeological data. That is why this is a provisional history—and perhaps more a "phenomenology," a "portrait," as the title has it.

Alambra, Cyprus
Spring 2016

Figures

Abbreviations

AASOR	Annual of the American Schools of Oriental Research
AAT	Agypten und Altes Testament
AB	Anchor Bible
ABD	Freedman, David Noel, ed. *Anchor Bible Dictionary*. 6 vols. New York: Doubleday, 1992.
ABRL	Anchor Bible Reference Library
ABS	Archaeology and Biblical Studies
ADAJ	*Annual of the Department of Antiquities of Jordan*
ADPV	Abhandlungen des Deutschen Palästinavereins
AHUCBASJ	Annual of the Hebrew Union College Biblical and Archaeological School in Jerusalem
AJA	*American Journal of Archaeology*
ALASPM	Abhandlungen zur Literatur Alt-Syrien-Palästinas und Mesopotamiens
ANEM	Ancient Near East Monographs/Monografías sobre el Antiguo Cercano Oriente
ANESSup	Ancient Near Eastern Studies Supplement Series
ANET	Pritchard, James B., ed. *Ancient Near Eastern Texts Relating to the Old Testament*. 3rd ed. Princeton: Princeton University Press, 1969.
ANGSBA	Annual of the Nelson Glueck School of Biblical Archaeology
AOAT	Alter Orient und Altes Testament
ASOR	American Schools of Oriental Research
ASORDS	ASOR Dissertation Series
AWE	*Ancient West & East*
AYB	Anchor Yale Bible
BA	*Biblical Archaeologist*
BAR	*Biblical Archaeology Review*
BASOR	*Bulletin of the American Schools of Oriental Research*

BJS	Brown Judaic Studies
BLS	Bible and Literature Series
BZAW	Beihefte zur Zeitschrift für die alttestamentliche Wissen-schaft
CANE	Sasson, Jack M., ed. *Civilizations of the Ancient Near East.* 4 vols. New York, 1995. Repr. in 2 vols. Peabody, MA: Hendrickson, 2006.
CBQ	*Catholic Biblical Quarterly*
CHANE	Culture and History of the Ancient Near East
ConBOT	Coniectanea Biblica: Old Testament Series
CRB	Cahiers de la Revue biblique
CurBS	*Currents in Research: Biblical Studies*
EB	Early Bronze Age
ErIsr	*Eretz-Israel*
ESHM	European Seminar in Historical Methodology
FAT	Forschungen zum Alten Testament
GBSNT	Guides to Biblical Scholarship: New Testament
HANES	History of the Ancient Near East Studies
HSM	Harvard Semitic Monographs
HSS	Harvard Semitic Studies
HUCA	*Hebrew Union College Annual*
IDB	Buttrick, George A., ed. *The Interpreter's Dictionary of the Bible.* 4 vols. New York: Abingdon, 1962.
IEJ	*Israel Exploration Journal*
JANER	*Journal of Ancient Near Eastern Religions*
JAOS	*Journal of the American Oriental Society*
JBL	*Journal of Biblical Literature*
JEA	*Journal of Egyptian Archaeology*
JESHO	*Journal of the Economic and Social History of the Orient*
JETS	*Journal of the Evangelical Theological Society*
JFA	*Journal of Field Archaeology*
JHS	*Journal of Hellenic Studies*
JMA	*Journal of Mediterranean Archaeology*
JNES	*Journal of Near Eastern Studies*
JSOT	*Journal for the Study of the Old Testament*
JSOTSup	Journal for the Study of the Old Testament Supplement Series
JSSEA	*Journal of the Society for the Study of Egyptian Antiquities*
LAI	Library of Ancient Israel

LB	Late Bronze Age
LC	Late Cypriot
LHBOTS	Library of Hebrew Bible/Old Testament Studies
LM	Late Mycenaean
MB	Middle Bronze Age
MMA	Monographs in Mediterranean Archaeology
MPP	Madaba Plains Project Series
NEA	*Near Eastern Archaeology*
NEAEHL	Stern, Ephraim, ed. *The New Encyclopedia of Archaeological Excavations in the Holy Land.* Vols. 1–4: Jerusalem: Israel Exploration Society and Carta; New York: Simon & Schuster. 1993. Vol. 5: Jerusalem: Israel Exploration Society; Washington, DC: Biblical Archaeology Society, 2008.
NGSBA	Nelson Glueck School of Biblical Archaeology
OBO	Orbis Biblicus et Orientalis
OBOSA	Orbis Biblicus et Orientalis, Series Archaeologica
OJA	*Oxford Journal of Archaeology*
Or	*Orientalia*
OrAnt	*Oriens Antiquus*
OTS	Oudtestamentische Studiën
PEQ	*Palestine Exploration Quarterly*
RSR	*Recherches de science religieuse*
SAHL	Studies in the Archaeology and History of the Levant
SBLMS	Society of Biblical Literature Monograph Series
SBT	Studies in Biblical Theology
SBTS	Sources for Biblical and Theological Study
SHANE	Studies in the History of the Ancient Near East
SJOT	*Scandinavian Journal of the Old Testament*
SO.S	Symbolae Osloenses Fasciculi Suppletorii
SWBA	Social World of Biblical Antiquity
SymS	Symposium Series
TA	*Tel Aviv*
UF	*Ugarit-Forschungen*
VT	*Vetus Testamentum*
VTSup	Supplements to Vetus Testamentum
WAW	Writings from the Ancient World
ZAW	*Zeitschrift für die alttestamentliche Wissenschaft*
ZDPV	*Zeitschrift des deutschen Palästina-Vereins*

CHAPTER 1

"History from Things": On History and History-Writing

Any attempt to produce a history of ancient Israel must begin by asking what we mean by *history*. What is history? Who writes it, how, and why? What are the appropriate sources, aims, and methods?

One way of defining history is to compare it with antiquarianism. For our purposes here, that means asking whether the writers and redactors of the Hebrew Bible were purporting to recount actual events for which they had evidence or were simply antiquarians uncritically collecting, preserving, and handing down older traditions, perhaps both oral and written.

One of the great historiographers of our time, Arnaldo Momigliano, has made the distinction clear. Antiquarians are engaged in "erudite research," although not necessarily critical in treating their sources. Historians, on the other hand, from the time of Thucydides and Herodotus onward have attempted to place great historical events in chronological sequence to make sense of them and to explain these facts in order to instruct their readers. The distinction is partly the difference between description and explanation, between simple narrative and didactive purposes.[1]

Historian Robert F. Berkhofer has stated:

> History, historical fiction, fictional history, and fiction all exist along a spectrum ranging from supposedly pure factual representation of literal, historical truth to pure nonliteral invented fictional representations of fantasy. No work of history conveys only literal truth through factuality, and few novels, even science fiction ones, depict only pure fantasy.... But even realistic novels, like fantasies, create the worlds their characters inhabit. Thus the issues of differences and similarities among these literary genres center upon both the actual existence of the characters and the reality of their larger contextual world, hence upon what readers expect from each genre.[2]

A recent work by a well-known historian, John Lewis Gaddis, is entitled *Landscape of History: How Historians Map the Past* (2002). The metaphor of "mapping" is apt: we cannot reconstruct the past; we can only draw a provisional portrait of it. In attempting this, Gaddis says, the historian must recognize the elements of multiple choices and of personal subjectivity, the risk of oversimplicity, the illusion of "laws of the historical process," the necessity of being satisfied with proximate causes, the role of speculation, and the need for the most parsimonious explanations. Finally, it must be acknowledged that there are multiple ways of knowing the past.

In passing, Gaddis has some acute observations about postmodernists and history, especially their relativism. The fact that our findings inescapably reflect who we are does not mean that one interpretation is as valid as any other. Nor can we escape moral responsibility for our statements evaluating the lessons of the past.

Gaddis cleverly paraphrases Machievelli on the purpose of history-writing: historians "interpret the past for the purpose of the present with a view to managing the future."[3] That is what we shall attempt here. In trying to negotiate between the controversial and extreme views that plague our branch of archaeology, I will steer a rational, middle-ground course. In particular, we will utilize the principle of Occam's razor: seeking the most parsimonious explanation that satisfies the evidence that we happen to have.

Another model for history-writing may also be worth considering, drawn this time from jurisprudence. The similarities of the two approaches to evidence are striking.

Jurisprudence	History-Writing
Purported event	Purported event
Witnesses: persons	Witnesses: texts
Court: place of trial	Court: historical inquiry
Basis: jurisprudence	Basis: method
Principle: "innocent until proven guilty"	Principle: "innocent until proven guilty"
Attorneys: prosecuting, defense	Attorneys: skeptics, synthesizers
Jury: one's peers	Jury: the larger community

Judge: elected by a majority	Judge: history itself
The decision: True beyond a reasonable doubt; "the preponderance of the evidence."	The decision: "In the lack of positive evidence, possibly true."

Before proceeding, we may note that both of the above models incorporate a notion that is current in today's presumably postmodern intellectual and social world: probability or possibility in place of certainty, in this case in attempting to know anything about the past.

Sources

Virtually all histories until the modern era were based on surviving written texts as sources, whether or not they incorporated older oral traditions. There were, of course, monumental remains: sculptures and other data ("antiquities") that were known particularly in the classical era (perhaps also in ancient Israel). But these material remains were not usually taken into account as historical evidence of any value, except anecdotally. Not until the rediscovery of the long-lost worlds of antiquity in the medieval period, and especially of the ancient Near East in the archaeology of the modern era, were monumental and artistic remains conceived of as significant historical sources.

For our history here, the major textual source is obviously the Hebrew Bible. For the early period, the so-called patriarchal era, we have the narratives in Genesis. These stories, however, are part of the J and E sources of the Pentateuch, which most scholars would now date quite late in the monarchy, not earlier than the eighth or seventh century. They were probably then reworked extensively in the exilic or even the postexilic era in the sixth century or later. This date contrasts with that of an earlier generation of biblical scholars, who dated J as early as the tenth century, E as early as the ninth century.[4]

In any case, the Genesis narratives are some thousand years later than the time frame that the events described in the patriarchal era would require if read in a straightforward manner. The question of whether these stories preserve any genuine historical information will be addressed when we come to chapter 2, on the prehistory of ancient Israel.

For the settlement horizon in the twelfth–eleventh centuries and the monarchy in the tenth–early sixth centuries, we are dependent first on the pentateuchal books of Exodus, Leviticus, and Numbers, dealing with the exodus from Egypt and the wandering in the wilderness, containing material that will be regarded here as legendary. Leviticus deals mostly with priestly legislation that seems highly artificial, at least for the preexilic period, and it will generally be disregarded here.[5]

The so-called Deuteronomistic History (Dtr) is a composite literary work extending from Joshua through Kings, plus the book of Deuteronomy. Most scholars date the first compilation late in the monarchy, with extensive additions and revisions in the exilic and postexilic period. Not only is the Deuteronomistic History a relatively late work, but scholars differ widely as to its value as a source for history-writing.[6]

It is obviously a didactic work that describes the past not only in order to teach its lessons to the writers' contemporaries but primarily as a method of imparting the religious and ideological messages that reflected the writers' worldview. Nevertheless, there are "enough elements in these stories that may be used in a historical reconstruction."[7]

Finally, some of the prophetic literature may be relevant for the preexilic history of Israel. For the eighth century that would include Amos, Hosea, Micah, and Isaiah; for the seventh century, Jeremiah and Ezekiel. The books bearing the names of individual prophets are undoubtedly partly the work of later scribal schools and are thus elaborate literary productions. Nevertheless, these works may provide some reliable historical information if they are used with caution and adequate critical controls.[8]

Some generalizations about these literary sources are in order. (1) First, these sources are all relatively late, none even near to being an eye-witness account, except possibly the last portions of Kings that narrate the fall of the southern kingdom. That does not mean, however, that these sources are useless for historical reconstruction, but it does require at every point that they must be subjected to careful scrutiny. These stories cannot be read at face value as history. The accounts are most reliable when they can be corroborated by external evidence such as extrabiblical texts or, in this case, by archaeological data.[9]

(2) Not only are the biblical texts late, but they are highly selective, reflecting almost exclusively the worldview and the interests of the elitists who produced them. It must be remembered that the Hebrew Bible was written by a handful of intellectuals, religionists, and professional scribes

affiliated with the court and temple in Jerusalem.[10] They did not represent even 1 percent of the population of ancient Israel and Judah throughout their history. It is only archaeology that can give a voice to the anonymous masses of ordinary folk, all those who "sleep in the dust" (Dan 12:2).

(3) Finally, the Hebrew Bible does not pretend to be history, if by that we mean a disinterested report of what really happened. There is, in fact, no word for *history* in the Hebrew Bible. There are, to be sure, genealogies ("x begat y") or stories about certain events ("these are the matters [*haddibrê*] pertaining to..."), but there is no interest whatsoever in what we would call an objective factual history based on empirical evidence. The Hebrew Bible is *theocratic* history—a story combining fact and fancy in a self-conscious attempt to legitimate and enforce the authors' orthodox theological views.[11] Their tendentious narrative portrays an "ideal Israel" in their ideal world, not the real Israel of history. That character obviously limits the potential of the Deuteronomistic literature as a source for history as we would see it today.

"History from Things"

One aspect of the postprocessual archaeology that has characterized the last twenty years or so has been a renewed interest in archaeology and history-writing. This was partly a reaction against New Archaeology's vulgar materialism and its depreciation of ideology and especially of the role of the individual in shaping history.[12]

One result of the more recent focus on history is the notion that artifacts may be compared with textual facts and thus can be "read" in a similar fashion. The impact of this insight, which in retrospect seems rather obvious, has been the redefinition of the archaeologist as "a historian of things." That may seem not only a repudiation of New Archaeology and its rapprochement with anthropology but a return to the much-maligned "culture history" approach of the previous era. The implications of the new focus on *material culture*, however, are revolutionary (below).

The seminal development of the new approach was Ian Hodder's 1986 *Reading the Past: Current Approaches to Interpretation in Archaeology*. Hodder had moved from structuralism to poststructuralism, then to postprocessualism, and finally to what he and others came to call "cognitive archaeology" or sometimes "the archaeology of mind." In keeping with postprocessualism's emphases, however, this approach is concerned with establishing "the meaning of things," events as well as material culture remains. As Hodder put it, "to study history is to try to get at purpose and thought," at "the inside of events."[13]

This approach eschews both the determinist notion that meaning is external and functionalist (a mere "epiphenomenon"), as well as the postmodernist motion that all assignments of meaning are arbitrary and equally valid. It willingly confronts, however, the subjective mental processes of both actor and observer, thus "cognitive archaeology," or, as often described, "contextual archaeology." For Hodder and others who followed, this was a play on words: con-textual, artifacts *with* texts.[14]

Hodder's metaphor of reading artifacts like texts was taken to its logical conclusion when he and others began to speak of the language, grammar, and syntax of artifacts, the mastery of which is essential to all critical reading. These are among the *hermeneutical principles* of postprocessual and cognitive archaeology, and they obviously invite comparison with the hermeneutics of textual reading, in this case the much-debated principles of biblical hermeneutics (below).

The cognitive archaeology of Ian Hodder, Michael Shanks, Christopher Tilley, and others seems at first glance a refreshing change from the New Archaeology's functionalism and reductionism. It looks like a step in the right direction, toward finding *meaning in things*. But however promising, it may be a step too far—further than we can actually go.

The cognitive archaeologists are still largely influenced by postprocessualism. They repudiate any notion of regularities of cultural laws in favor of what Renfrew calls scathingly a meta-archaeology. They are strongly influenced in some cases by Marxism, by critical theory, by postmodern preoccupation with politics and power, and in their historiography by idealist historians in the grand tradition of R. G. Collingwood (1946) and Benedetto Croce (1921). Renfrew finds their emphasis on hermeneutics—on "interpretive" archaeology—too ambitious, too unrealistic. We cannot find the Truth of things, only an understanding of how things work in a particular social context. We cannot "reconstruct" the past, but we can make and test inferences (see further below on pragmatism).

Renfrew's is thus a more modest cognitive, yet still processual archaeology. It is also realist in that one conceives of the past as really existing in a physical world, much like the present, with human individuals living their lives and interacting with each other and with their environment very much as we do today. This realism is not, however, extreme empiricism or positivism, because it acknowledges the subjectivity of all our interpretations. Renfrew's cognition tries to embrace the "cognitive map" of the ancients, based on what is preserved of their culture in material remains. The crux of the matter is to make explicit the inferences that sustain our arguments.[15]

Another departure from Hodder, Shanks, and Tilley and their idealist or interpretive archaeology is that of Robert W. Preucel and Stephen A. Mrozowski (2010) in their model of the "new pragmatism." They also espouse finding the meaning of things. For them, however, the question of meaning is inseparable from the question of what things do, or of what can be done with them. In keeping with the traditional epistemology of the uniquely nineteenth-century American philosophical movement called pragmatism, they argue that the meaning (i.e., the truth) of any thing or idea can be determined only by considering the consequences it routinely generates. When taken to the extreme, this practical approach can lead to relativism, even expediency. But like Renfrew's approach, its realism may be an antidote to extreme idealism. Finally, its focus on the real world leads to relevance, to social action rather than philosophical musings. It also recovers history-writing as a primary goal of archaeology.

The kind of history that archaeology can now write is cultural history—not the now-discredited *Kulturgeschichte* of New World archaeology up to about 1960, but a new comparative history of various cultures that moves beyond materialist causation to broader explanations of change and to the exploration of meaning. As Ian Morris puts it in the conclusion of his magisterial *Archaeology as Cultural History: Words and Things in Iron Age Greece*: "I have argued for a particular approach to archaeology, seeing it as cultural history. I suggested that such a historical view of the field is best developed through very concrete empirical work rather than abstract theorizing."[16]

This approach reflects disillusionment with postmodernism's "linguistic turn" and a reembodiment of a "historical turn" in mainstream archaeology since the early 1990s. This new cultural history largely abandons forty years of experiments in abstract, ideological theories borrowed from other disciplines, elevated to all-encompassing dogmatic schemes, as largely useless. It embraces instead an archaeological *practice* that is eclectic, data-oriented, empirical, inductive, and realistic. It addresses

epistemological issues openly, but it does not shy away from generalizations, and it is willing to formulate arguments even if probabilistic when
there are correlations between our textual and archaeological records
when critically examined. That is, in fact, the method that the best historians and archeologists (including classical and Near Eastern) have always
practiced. This method also characterizes the best science, which as Bintliff
(a former advocate of theory) points out "was democratic and arose from
the physical skill and high craftsmanship of experimenters finding practical meaning in real-world, hands-on encounters with matter."[17]

Influenced by Hodder's cognitive archaeology, some have tried to
show that the hermeneutics, the principles of interpretation for both texts
and artifacts, are necessarily similar. Thus one can demonstrate the existence of parallel schools of interpretation in both disciplines over the past
several generations (although not always contemporary).[18]

If there is merit in trying to read artifacts as texts, this has enormous
implications for an archaeologically based history of ancient Israel. It
means, at minimum, that new and better histories are now possible, if the
historian can take advantage of the mass of new information now made
available by the progress of modern archaeology. Maximally, archaeology
becomes not only a source but a *primary* source for history-writing. That is
the presupposition here, and it is what makes this history of ancient Israel
and Judah different.

Material Culture Studies as an Independent Discipline

Archaeology is obviously a discipline that deals primarily with material
culture, or with human culture as it is reflected in artifacts. By definition,
that has usually meant studying artifacts from the remote past. But in the
last two decades or so there has developed a discipline that studies more
recent and even contemporary material culture—not relics, the artifactual
remains from extinct societies, but objects from living cultures. Here the
objective is to write recent or contemporary history largely *without* texts.

Two volumes that appeared in 1993 signaled the growing maturity of
a real discipline of material culture studies. Both were published, significantly, as the results of conferences held at the Smithsonian Institution
and its Museum of Natural History. One volume is a series of essays edited

by the distinguished historian of technology W. David Kingery: *Learning from Things: Method and Theory of Material Culture Studies* (1996).

Its methodological approach was ably summarized by Kingery in the preface:

> At the heart of the conference was the conviction that the things human-kind makes and uses at any particular time and place are probably the truest representations we have of the values and meanings within a society. The study of things, material culture, is thus capable of piercing interdisciplinary boundaries and bringing forward meaningful discussions and interactions among scholars in many disparate fields.[19]

Kingery calls this enterprise a relatively new and distinct discipline. In his own essay Kingery speaks of "the grammar of things," noting that artifacts are signals, signs, and symbols. However, he warns that much of their meaning is subliminal and unconscious. Thus "objects must also be read as myth and poetry."[20] That may sound daunting, or even illegitimate to some. But if we have learned anything from postmodernist and New Critical readings of texts, we must realize that all history-writing is affected by such subjective factors. They cannot be denied, only accounted for, since we are the subjects doing the reading.[21]

A prior volume, under the same auspices, was co-edited by Steven Lubar and Kingery, Curator of Engineering and Industry at the Smithsonian's National Museum of American History. It is a series of essays entitled *History from Things: Essays on Material Culture*. One of the most provocative discussions is that of Jules David Prown, "The Truth of Material Culture: History or Fiction?" That question has astonishingly close parallels to the question that biblicists, always logocentric, have been asking of their texts since the dawn of modern critical scholarship. Biblical and Levantine archaeologists, on the other hand, always pragmatic and often inimical to theory—to epistemology—have tended naively to avoid the issue.[22] The chapter by Prown would be an eye opener to scholars in both disciplines, and it should be required reading.

Several authors in these two volumes expand on the potential of artifacts as a primary source for history-writing, applauding archaeologists for being "unfettered by textual evidence." Revolutionary as this may seem, the presupposition goes back to Aristotle's views of sculpture, for instance, which does not necessarily place a value judgment on the sculpture but ranks *mens* above *manus*. Indeed, the history of Western civilization can be seen as mind over matter.[23]

Prown argues that the potential of objects in providing an entré into cultural beliefs lies in the universality of many human experiences. "In the end, reality rests on the vision seen through the culturally conditioned eyes of the analyst." Nevertheless, philosophers and historians of technology have too often worked in isolation, the latter usually dismissed as inferior in their grasp of reality.[24]

Lubar expands on the idea of artifacts as a primary source. Because cultural meaning is carried by a variety of vehicles, all of which must be expressed in words to be understood, objects have "an inescapable textuality." Historians of technology are distinguished by the texts they read: objects. This follows Geertz's argument that a technological artifact should be regarded as a "cultural phenomenon," which is like any other cultural phenomenon but can make for better historical explanation. Objects then, like texts, must be deciphered. What is required is "research outside the library, the hands-on scrutiny of three-dimensional objects."[25]

That is precisely what we archaeologists do and have long done—but without adequate training in history or any self-conscious historiographical focus.

Among the few archaeologists in these two volumes is Michael Schiffer, a well-known New World archaeological theorist. He acknowledges that the past is past. It no longer exists as part of the phenomenological world, and thus it can never be fully known. Nevertheless, "the study of the human past is made possible by the fact that some objects made and used long ago survive into the present and so can serve as evidence." That evidence can be interpreted by inferences we make about past human behavior. Depending upon the weight of the evidence and of the relevant generalizations, this process of archaeological reasoning can be not only systematic but even scientific.[26] This "positivist" claim for archaeology may seem astounding to many text-based historians, but it is tacitly assumed by most archaeologists, because otherwise their enterprise is little more than treasure hunting.[27]

The key to the interpretation of archaeological evidence is what Schiffer and others have long called "formation processes of the archaeological record." This entails not only the recovery and description of material culture remains but the inquiry into the past thought and behavior that produced these things. Formidable as that goal may be, I would argue that it is no more formidable than the task that text-based biblical historians take on. It all depends on adequate hermeneutical principles that enable us (1) to sift out from a mass of data reliable and relevant facts and (2) to place these facts in a larger cultural context that gives them meaning. The fact that absolute Truth is not obtained does not imply that all history-writing is futile—mere fiction, as biblical revisionists and other postmodernists assert (below).

Prown, whom we have already quoted, is perhaps the most positivist of all the contributors to the above volumes. For him artifacts are "historical evidence," uniquely so because, unlike other historical events that happened in the past, "artifacts constitute the only class of historical events that occurred in the past but survive into the present. They can be re-experienced: they are authentic, primary historical material available for firsthand study."[28]

Furthermore, objects are in some respects "truer" than texts, since "the questions that artifacts pose are authentic" ones, and they "do not lie." To put it another way, artifacts are indeed fabrications, but they are not fictitious in the same way that texts may be.[29] Objects can communicate to us directly, unedited, if we come to understand the universal beliefs, emotions, and values that they connote. Artifacts, like texts, are thus metaphysical expressions of human culture.

Maquet in the above volume addresses the obvious question here: What hermeneutical principles does "reading artifacts" demand? (1) The first interpretive method is inference. Meaning is no more directly available in the material object than it is in a text. (2) Meaning must be supplied by us as observers, as readers. Maquet stresses the need to look at groups of objects—precisely what we archaeologists call an "archaeological assemblage," our basic unit of analysis. (3) While we cannot approach the object as cultural insiders, we can draw upon timeless multicultural and universal human experience, on what one might call common sense.[30]

The latter may be dismissed by some as an improper analytical tool, as no method at all. But it is in fact what both archaeologists and textual scholars often employ. Biblicists fall back on "the plain meaning of the text." Archaeologists typically utilize analogy as their essential even if subconscious method—working from the known to the unknown. To postmodernists all this becomes merely a narrative (or a metanarrative). But so is theirs, and why is theirs any better than ours?[31] All claims to knowledge may indeed be social constructs, but some constructs are better than others, that is, truer to the evidence that we have, ultimately more sat-isfactory as an account of how it actually may have been in the past.

History, by broad consensus today, is an attempt, not only to describe what happened in the past in the light of the limited evidence that we have, but also to chart and explain changes over time. We archaeologists seek to find the causes of events and their consequences over very long time spans, both collective and individual. And even though we may not be able to offer final causes, we can plausibly suggest what are called proximate causes. That may not seem like much, but it is far better than the current revisionist nonhistories of ancient Israel (below).

John D. Hunt explores the potential of reading objects as "a battle of things against words," in which we can prevail only by deciding what *kind* of history we want and think possible. Having long thought and written about this, I can only concur with Hunt that "a new history must find a new discourse, not just a new set of materials to work with."[32]

Kinds of History

In the late 1990s some had distinguished several kinds of history, in keep-ing with the Annales school then in vogue in some circles:

La longue durée The "deeper swells"	(1) Natural history, or a description of the changing environment; similar to Pliny's *de rerum naturae*
Évenements	(2) Narrative history, or the connected story of ordinary events
	(3) Political history, an account of the deeds of great people and public events
Conjunctures	(4) Cultural history, or the history of culture as adaptation of cultural institutions
	(5) Socioeconomic history, or the history of social and economic institutions, of social strati-fication, of trade and commerce
	(6) Aesthetic history, or the history of art, archi-tecture, music, and ideal values

Mentalités	(7) Intellectual history, or the history of ideas, including religious ideas, of the development of literature
	(8) Technological history, the history of things, of technological innovations and material culture

In distinguishing these different histories, one may compare our two sources for history-writing as follows.[33]

Texts	Artifacts
Writing system	"Language" of material culture
Vocabulary	Artifacts of all types
Grammar	Formation processes
Syntax	Ecological, sociocultural context
Author, composition, date	Date, technology
Cultural context (*Sitz im Leben*)	Overall historical setting
Intent	"Mental template" or markers
Later transmission, interpretation	Natural-cultural transformations
What the text symbolizes	What the artifact symbolizes
How its meaning is relevant today	How its meaning is relevant today

Archaeology alone cannot, of course, write all of these various histories, since texts are essential for doing intellectual, religious, or political history, where the principal actors must be named and their thoughts discerned, if possible. It is also obvious that the various histories distinguished here are largely for heuristic purposes. Several of these categories overlap, so much so that an ideal history might combine all these approaches. That would, however, be unwieldy, impossible in practice. But archaeology is not mute, as some biblicists and even a few archaeologists have asserted, simply because it usually cannot attach an individual name to an event. Archaeology—the study of things—can speak volumes, but all too often historians have been deaf.[34]

Different Histories?

Let us give a few examples of how archaeological data might be superior to the textual data in the Hebrew Bible in writing new and different histories of ancient Israel.

The book of Kings gives only nine verses (1 Kgs 16:17, 21–28) to the reign of Omri. A thorough analysis of the text, which presents no lexical problems, yields only the following information. (1) Omri laid siege to the previous capital of Tirzah. (2) He had enough popular support to succeed Tibni at Tirzah and then reign there for six years. (3) He purchased the hill of Samaria as a new capital and reigned there for another six years. (4) His deeds were more evil than those of all his predecessors, a record of which was left in a book that we do not possess. (5) He died, was buried in Samaria, and was succeeded by his son Ahab.

A critical analysis of these statements suggests that some are so biased that they are meaningless (Omri did "evil"). Others are subject to doubt (half or more of the population supported Omri). Still others are reasonable but cannot be confirmed (the purchase price of Samaria was two talents of silver). Finally, other statements are probably factual but banal (Omri died and was buried at Samaria).

The discernible facts are bare-bones, obvious. Further, there is no attempt here at explanation, which is the essential element of history-writing—not even an explanation of the fact that the name Samaria is significant because it means something like "watchtower." (The writers attribute the name only to the name of the former owner, probably a folk etymology.) In short, early or late, there is little or no real history to be found in the biblical narrative, even though the establishment of the Omride dynasty at the new capital of Samaria was surely a pivotal event.

There then is no hint in this cryptic account of Omri and Ahab's extraordinary planning and construction of a royal city at Samaria, of the wealth and sophistication of life there, of the overriding Phoenician influence in the north, and, most significantly, of the fact that Omri was so successful in holding off the Neo-Assyrian advance in north Syria that for more than one hundred years after his death the northern kingdom appears in cuneiform annals as "the house (dynasty) of Omri."

The archaeological data, by contrast, would allow us to write a substantial volume on the reign of Omri and its significance on the larger stage of ancient Near Eastern geopolitics. We could write a full chapter on the Phoenician-style ivory carvings alone, another on the derivation and significance of the fine ashlar masonry. Archaeology is *mute*? We are missing only the name of Omri in the archaeological data, but even without that detail the evidence would be sufficient to paint a portrait of a truly royal establishment in the north in the ninth century.

The picture we can now draw of some of Israel's neighbors and rivals is even more instructive. Take the Philistines, for instance. If we were confined to the Hebrew Bible alone, we would gather that these peoples were (1) non-Semitic invaders from the islands of the Mediterranean; (2) their appearance in Canaan was roughly contemporary with that of the earliest Israelites; (3) they were governed by a military aristocracy, grouped in a pentapolis along the southern coastal plain; and (4) their military superiority posed a threat to the tribal league, and in time it became a pretext for appointing the first Israelite king.

All this is niggardly information, although it turns out to be largely correct (except that the Philistines probably invaded from Cyprus rather than "Caphtor," i.e., Crete). Yet today we have excavated four of the five cities of the Philistine pentapolis (all but Gaza). Accordingly, we have such a wealth of archaeological data that we know almost more about early Philistine history than early Israelite history.[35] Which source is mute: archaeology or the biblical texts?

Would it help if we had the names of the Philistine kings? Or another "Goliath"? If the old canard that archaeology is mute, mindlessly repeated now for two generations, means only that the principal actors were anonymous, that counts for very little. But in fact the extrabiblical texts recovered by excavation, legal or illegal, do supply many of the actual names—and with them dates far more precise than these we have in enigmatic notices in the Hebrew Bible.

Archaeology as a Primary Source

In stating that archaeology is now a primary source for writing ancient Israel's history, we are presupposing the following.

(1) Archaeological data, compared to textual data, are a primary source because they are prior in time, almost always contemporary. It is agreed by critical scholars that the texts of the Hebrew Bible are almost all later than the events that they purport to describe, in most cases centuries

later. Thus our accounts of the earliest kings of Israel in the book of Kings belong to the seventh–sixth century at the earliest, some four hundred years after the events in question. By contrast, at least 99 percent of all archaeological artifacts are contemporary with the events that they reflect. There are almost no archaeological heirlooms, or what we call "curated artifacts." Artifacts come instead directly from the time and circumstance that produced them.

(2) The archaeological data are unedited, a direct witness, frozen in place and in time until the moment that they are brought to light once again by the archaeologist. The text can only refer to the reality; the artifact is the reality. Of course, there are some natural processes of degradation and sometimes perturbations caused by later occupants of a site (what are called N-transforms and C-transforms).[36] But it is important to note both that these alterations are almost never the result of deliberate human bias and that we can control quite well for whatever biases there may be. Even allowing for the fact that artifacts must be interpreted after they are found (a banality of which some never seem to tire), it is still possible to preserve the objects and regard them again in their pristine state. Sometimes it is said that "archaeology is an unrepeatable experiment," that is, that an object excavated and recorded badly cannot be excavated again with improved methods. But that refers only to field methods, not to *interpretative* methods, which can always be repeated—and we still have the object itself available for renewed analysis. It may be thought that the original context, always so important in archaeology, has been lost. But with today's much more detailed three-dimensional recording and the possibilities of computer simulation and manipulation, the context can be restored, even enhanced.

Contrast the situation with ancient texts in general. We do not have the original text or the original context, much less any possible oral tradition. We have copies of copies of copies, and even an understanding of these in their later context may not bring us very close to the presumed original. To be sure, the text is still available, even if misread. But it is not an eye-witness report in the same sense that an artifact is.[37]

In particular, let us look at the biblical texts. We do not have and never will have the *editio princeps*. What we do have is a textual tradition that has been deliberately edited and reedited over more than a thousand years, as well as in a secondary process of transmission that usually cannot be reconstructed. What we confront in the Hebrew Bible is thus a version of a version of a version in an endless hermeneutical chain. That is why it is pointless to insist on "what the Bible says." *Which* Bible? *Whose* Bible?

Archaeology, on the other hand, is a superior source in that it allows us to leap over the intervening centuries, as it were, to come face to face with the primary data, the realia of the past. The interpretive task is indeed just as essential as it is with texts. However, one can argue that it is not more difficult but rather simpler. Certainly the task is more immediate, and it has the advantage of being more faithful to the original (without altering it beyond all recognition).

(3) Archaeological data are also primary, more importantly, because they are more varied. The data provide a sort of "cross-cut" through the everyday life of the masses of ordinary folk, who after all do have a role in shaping history. Given our sophisticated methods of modern retrieval in the field today, there is almost no limit to the variety of information that archaeology can and does yield. In Israel today we have what is arguably the largest archaeological data base in the world. In the "debris," formerly discarded but now subject to laboratory analysis, we have revelations of past lifeways that were undreamed of a generation ago. Archaeology's aspirations to be scientific may be dismissed by uninformed critics as pretentious, but the hard sciences are now on the verge of transforming our discipline.[38] Can textual scholars make such a claim about any of their new analytical methods?

(4) The biblical texts are fixed, their potential for information predetermined by the limited perspective and deliberate selectivity of the few elites who wrote and rewrote the Bible. We can never ask of these texts more than they want to tell us. But we can always ask more of the archaeological record, which has no cultural bias in what it conveys to us. In theory, it is mostly still there, frozen in time, and once we move beyond the so-called accidents of discovery (much overstressed) to deliberate, systematic large-scale excavation, which we are doing, we are almost unlimited in what we can learn.

(5) Archaeological data are primary because they are dynamic, not static. Just as the variety of our information is expanding exponentially, so is the overall amount of information. For example, archaeologically we know today at least ten times more than we knew a generation ago—and Albright's "archaeological revolution" has only begun. By contrast, there is likely to be little if any genuinely new information to be gleaned from the

biblical texts, even with the most determined and ingenious winnowing. That fact seems not to be recognized by most biblicists, but it is obvious. The canon is closed, and the texts we have are as clear as they are ever likely to be.[39]

(6) Finally, archaeological data are primary because an *external* witness is required to confirm the historicity of the biblical narratives, if possible, and archaeology is, by definition, the only candidate (including, of course, the texts that it may recover). Archaeology is primary because it provides an independent witness in the court of adjudication, and when properly interrogated it is often an unimpeachable witness.

Case Studies

Let us take two case studies, one textual and one archaeological, drawn from one of the most mundane aspects of daily life, cooking and preparing food. In the biblical text there are several descriptions, of which 2 Sam 13:3–14 is one of the more detailed. Amnon, one of David's sons, was attempting to seduce his half-sister Tamar. As a device, he feigned illness and asked her to feed him in his room. The text goes on to describe how Tamar took flour, kneaded it into dough, baked cakes in his sight, and served them up in a pan.

What does this story tell us about actual food preparation in the tenth century, which we now know would have been the historical setting of this narrative, if a reliable report? Not very much, it turns out. Grinding grain and baking in primitive societies of all times is well known, and similar processes can be assumed here. The one detail that the text does add is dubious. The Hebrew work for "pan" (*maśrēt*) does not fit any of the Iron Age ceramic vessels that we actually have.[40] Furthermore, what we know of baking shows that it was normally done not in a portable brazier of sorts but in a large permanent outdoor oven (a *tannûr*).

For those who know little about archaeology, a tenth-century ceramic vessel that we call a cooking pot will tell them nothing, no matter how they manipulate it and use all their senses. They cannot "read" the pot (or hear it), because for them it is mute: they do not know its language, the language of material culture. For the specialist, however, the pot speaks loudly. An archaeologist, depending on modern analytical techniques, could easily tell us where the clay came from, how the pot was formed, the temperature of the kiln in which it was fired, why it is likely the product of a women's domestic workshop, something of the foodstuffs cooked in it, its lifespan within a margin of a few years, and exactly what its predecessors and its successors looked like. All this is an explanation of change, and there it provides a history of these typical cooking pots, as well as a clue to the *mentalité* of those who made and used them. With the typological and comparative methods of modern archaeology, we have here a "mental template" on which the pot was based, that is, a clue to its symbolic and cultural role.[41]

To underscore the significance of this point, we should note that the cooking pot cannot lie. It is exactly what its makers and users intended it to be. It thus has an intrinsic meaning, not one that we arbitrarily supply. Today we are fortunate to have the techniques that enable us to discern much of that original meaning, even though archaeologists cannot actually read the mind of the ancients. As Louis Binford puts it, "archaeologists are poorly equipped to be paleopsychologists."[42]

By comparison, what about the biblical texts? These texts, unlike our cooking pot, can and do lie; that is, they may mislead. Critical scholars recognize this fact, that the biblical texts are largely propagandistic. They are not entirely fictitious and thus may be based on authentic sources here and there. But by and large the intent of the biblical authors and redactors is not to tell it as it was but rather to tell it as they wished it had been. Thus the Hebrew Bible is widely regarded today as historicized fiction or fictionalized history, not only by revisionists but also by the majority of mainstream scholars.[43] That leads to our next question.

Can a "History of Israel" Be Written?

There can be no doubt that the field of biblical studies (at least of the Hebrew Bible) has faced a historiographical crisis for a generation or so. Already in the 1980s there was a dissatisfaction with conventional histories of ancient Israel. Van Seters initially raised the general issue of ancient Near Eastern historiography in 1983, followed by critiques of biblical histories by Halpern (1985) and Garbini (1988). More radical scholars later known as revisionists (below) were soon repudiating all conventional text-based histories, but in some cases looking toward archaeology as a potential alternate source. As Thompson put it in 1987:

> It is … the independence of Syro-Palestinian archaeology that now
> makes it possible for the first time to begin to write a history of Israel's
> origins. Rather than the Bible, it is in the field of Syro-Palestinian archae-
> ology, and the adjunct field of ancient Near Eastern studies, that we find
> our primary source for Israel's earliest history.[44]

Thompson's sanguine view of archaeology (even his name for the discipline) was based on the newer, more secular, and professional archaeology
that had gradually been replacing conventional biblical archaeology in
the work of Dever and others of his generation since the mid-1970s.[45]
It is a shame that these early insights were not followed up, because the
opportunity for the first real dialogue between archaeology and biblical
studies—our two sources—was lost (below).

In 1992 Thompson did attempt his own "secular history" of ancient
Palestine, as did Ahlstrom the following year (1993). Both invoked
archaeological data wherever possible, even though they were not specialists. Neither of these novel histories of Palestine by biblical scholars had
much impact, however, and they remain largely curiosities in the history
of scholarship. The problem, unseen at the time, was that the complex
archaeological data now being amassed by the increasingly mature, professional discipline of Syro-Palestinian archaeology (now the preferred
name) was burgeoning to the point where no nonspecialist could deal with
it competently. Meanwhile, the historiographical challenge, not successfully met, was now becoming more urgent.

Matters quickly came to a head in 1992, when Philip R. Davies at Sheffield University published a brief, deliberately provocative book entitled
In Search of "Ancient Israel." Davies's contribution was to distinguish three
Israels: (1) a historical Israel, about which little could be said, since the biblical narratives dated after the Palestinian Iron Age in question, that is, to
the Persian era; (2) a biblical Israel, which the sources make a late literary
construct removed from historical reality; and (3) an ancient Israel, again
a construct, this time of modern scholars (particularly Israeli and American, Davies implied). Here the biblical texts were largely discredited, and
Davies referred to the mass of Iron Age archaeological data in a single
footnote, only to dismiss it as irrelevant to his Persian-period Israel.[46]

In 1997 Lester L. Grabbe of Hull University responded to the growing
frustration by founding the European Seminar on Methodology in Israel's
History, which met regularly thereafter for some fifteen years. Originally

there were twenty-one members, all biblicists from Europe. There were no archaeologists among them, however, although Helga Weippert had produced a handbook that is in fact still useful (1988) and could have been included.

The Seminar's initial publication in 1997 was entitled, not surprisingly, *Can a "History of Israel" Be Written?* Grabbe, the editor, called for a lessening of rhetoric and more attempts at dialogue. In his introduction he argued that "our goal as historians is to find out 'what actually happened.'" This echoed, of course, von Ranke's famous positivist notion of "wie es eigentlich gewesen war." But the term *minimalist* now seems first to appear, and most of the authors in this volume were skeptical, particularly Carroll, Davies, Lemche, and Thompson, whose discussions are heavily ideological and often acrimonious.[47]

The archaeological data were rarely invoked in this volume, usually only to discredit them and archaeologists. Carroll, identifying himself with "postmodernist questioning of the project of modernity," envisions only a "fictional" Bible and a "bogus history." As for archaeological artifacts, Davies asserts that these are made to conform to an imagined narrative constructed from the biblical text.[48]

Barstad does envision a sort of "narrative history" based on some reliable information to be derived from the biblical texts. But if "verifiable truth" is our objective, he declares that a history of ancient Israel would be not only short (he says ten pages or so) but utterly boring. Archaeology is mentioned only in one footnote, and then simply to assert that in interpreting material culture remains "we apparently encounter insurmountable methodological difficulties" in attempting to relate archaeology to biblical texts.[49]

Several things strike one in reading this first deliberate, concerted effort by European biblical scholars at writing new and better histories of ancient Israel. First, by the late 1990s the battle lines that would determine the debate thereafter are already drawn. The real issues, however, are poorly defined, even obscured (they are not "theological"), and the rhetorical character of the subsequent discourse is already evident. Here for the first time we encounter the concept of postmodernism, with Carroll embracing it and Barstand acknowledging its reality but warning of its danger.

Above all, one is struck by sincere concerns with historiography and efforts to grapple candidly with differences of opinion, but this is a monologue. Only Grabbe betrays any understanding of the progress of Israeli or American archaeology by this time, and that is minimal. "Very little about matters of society and religion can be gleaned from artifactual evidence alone."[50] Nowhere in the entire volume is any of the extensive literature of the 1970s–1980s on the transformation of "biblical archaeology" cited, not even citations of the several handbooks and multivolume encyclopedias readily available at the time.[51] In short, the proposed *dialogue* between archaeology and biblical studies was compromised before it had even begun, and nothing more than vague notions for any *new* histories of Israel were offered here (see further excursus 1.1).

Prolegomena: 2000–2010

Having surveyed the literature on the prospects for writing new histories of ancient Israel from the early 1990s to the turn of the millennium, let us look briefly at further developments.

Noll's *Canaan and Israel in Antiquity: An Introduction* appeared in 2006, but it made no first-hand use of archaeology, did not address the revisionist challenge, and broke no new ground. In 2004 Day edited a volume of essays by mainstream scholars, *In Search of Pre-exilic Israel*, which was obviously a response to Davies's 1993 volume. Here there are several valuable discussions of the biblical literature as possible preexilic sources for history-writing.

Two years later, Banks's *Writing the History of Israel* (2006) gave a general summary of the history of the discussion, but it offered little guidance except to note that a history of Israel "without reference to the Bible" might be written, and if written "would have significant implications for the study of the Hebrew Bible."[52]

The same year Moore's *Philosophy and Practice in Writing a History of Ancient Israel* (2006) appeared, ostensibly as a response to minimalism, but it made little impact. Later she collaborated with Kelle to produce *Biblical History and Israel's Past: The Changing Study of the Bible and History* (2011), presumably a guidebook. The citation of the literature, however, is quite selective, and the authors' evaluation of the archaeological data is minimal and often lacking in discrimination. They align themselves with Davies's (2008) and Lemche's (2008) nonhistories but do mention Grabbe's (2007b) more positive evaluation of archaeology.[53]

In 2007 three books appeared that marked a breakthrough: Williamson's edited volume of essays *Understanding the History of Ancient Israel*; Grabbe's *Ancient Israel: What Do We Know and How Do We Know It?*; and the Finkelstein–Mazar volume edited by Schmidt, *The Quest for the Historical Israel: Debating the History of Early Israel*.

The essays in the first volume covered a broad array, including chapters by Mazar and Ussishkin. The third volume consisted of a series of public debates between Finkelstein and Mazar, which, while brief and lacking documentation, marked the first steps toward a real history of ancient Israel based largely on the archaeological data (still contested, however). Grabbe's volume, building on long personal involvement in the discussions in Europe and Israel, was the first recognition by a biblical scholar that archaeology was now a primary source for writing any history of ancient Israel and Judah. This work was a breakthrough in progress toward a true dialogue between archaeology and biblical studies, rather than the monologues that had for so long dominated both disciplines.[54]

Grabbe's tactic was to compare the textual and the archaeological data, then rank the results of what we could learn along a continuum of information from left to right—proven "wrong" to proven "correct"—the middle ground being the most reasonable. This deceptively simple device was similar to the "convergences" that Dever had sought in a previous book with a similar title (*What Did the Biblical Writers Know?* [2001]). Grabbe surveyed the textual and the archaeological data period by period, his archaeological coverage as competent and his judgment as balanced as one could hope for from a nonspecialist. What is pertinent here is Grabbe's explicit recognition that henceforth the archaeological data will constitute our primary source. That is because these data alone can serve as an external witness to critique, complement, and correct the biblical texts with their limited potential as a source for reliable facts. Grabbe acknowledges that this work is only a prolegomenon, but it is the prolegomenon for which we had been waiting.

By 2008 Grabbe had edited the first of two volumes entitled *Israel in Transition: From Late Bronze II to Iron IIa (c. 1250–850 B.C.E.)*, the initial one on archaeology, the second (2010) on the biblical texts. Here, for the first time, the discussions of the European Seminar (above) included several archaeologists. One of the key members, Barstad, also offered the same year a volume of essays that moved beyond his somewhat earlier works, entitled *History and the Hebrew Bible: Studies in Ancient Israelite and Ancient Near Eastern Historiography* (2008). He now acknowledged that a "history of events" like ours here had become problematic. But he argued that one cannot and must not give up on new histories and that only interdisciplinary projects offered any hope. Moreover, he opined that "cultural memory" would mean the end of history-writing, just as we have argued here (2012).

Apart from the brief sketches of history by Finkelstein and Mazar in Schmidt's edited 2007 volume (above), Israeli biblical scholars and archaeologists remained generally aloof from the discussion of biblical historiography. They typically had no training in critical biblical studies, any more than as historians, and they tended to remain distant from questions of biblical historiography in Europe and America, as though these were problems of Christian theology. Moreover, they were generally hostile to religion due to conflicts in Israel. Always secular, as their counterparts in America had become by the 1980s–1990s, they were ambivalent about how, or even whether, to use the Hebrew Bible. By now Israelis were characterizing their own style of "biblical (yet secular) archaeology." They had become good field technicians; they were publishing widely; and they controlled most of the fundamental data. But only gradually did they address the larger historiographical and epistemological issues. Yet the brief chapters by Mazar and Finkelstein in Schmidt's 2007 edited volume marked a beginning.

Finkelstein had tried to characterize Mazar, Dever, Faust, and Stager as "Bible archaeologists" between 1995 and 2007, but he avoided the issue posed by the biblical revisionists (who by now had naively adopted him and his "low chronology" as suitably minimalist).[55]

Then in 2006 Faust became the first Israeli archaeologist to confront revisionists such as Davies, Lemche, Thompson, and Whitelam directly, in the last pages of his *Israel's Ethnogenesis: Settlement, Interaction, Expansion and Resistance*. The following year (2007), in an issue of *Near Eastern Archaeology*, Faust responded to Finkelstein (and Herzog) to defend himself against the charge of being a "biblical archeologist." In the same issue, Grabbe sided with Finkelstein, but he concluded that the crucial methodological issues had been ignored. Joffe tried to resolve some of these issues, concluding that Faust's and Finkelstein's "studied indecision presented here is unlikely to satisfy anyone.[56] Here the discussion, begun in the early 1990s, remained until about 2010: a few tentative prolegomena; virtually no new histories.

Readings and Reality

Can we move ahead by going back to our earlier notion that artifacts are similar to texts and can be read with similar methods of interpretation? If so, that invites further comparisons of the basic character of both before moving on to methods of interpretation. Before we ask the essential question of *meaning*, however, let us look more closely at texts. The salient features of texts in themselves can be readily identified.

(1) A text is indeed a construct, as postmodernists insist. But contrary to their notion, a text is a *deliberate* construct, unless one assumes that the authors were merely doodling or too confused to know what they really thought (which is absurd).

(2) A text, therefore, is an encoded symbol that has a referent, an inherent meaning, even if that meaning is not self-evident. Meaning is not supplied; it is discerned, at least wherever possible. A text may be *only* a symbol, but that does not mean that it does not point beyond itself to some reality.[57]

(3) A text, however, may have more than one meaning if the author is ambivalent, a careless writer, or intends to obscure rather than to clarify. A text may thus be a form of propaganda (postmodernists would say that it always is). A text can lie; it can deceive or mislead us. That may be due to the author's intention, the interpreter's incompetence, or even his or her deliberate ideological manipulation. Nevertheless, there is such a thing as authorial intent, although many postmodernists would deny that. If such were not the case, no rational inquiry or credible conclusions would be possible; the result would indeed be nihilism.

(4) If a text is a construct, of whatever sort, it can and should be deconstructed. But the intent should be not only to reveal its supposed contradictions or to unmask its ideological biases, ultimately to discredit it as believable. The purpose of our interrogation of the text should be rather to reconstruct the text after critical analysis. The intent is to recover its own meaning as far as possible, whatever the interpreter's ideology may be. It is a truism that absolute objectivity is impossible, but some objectivity is better than none.[58] Likewise, to offer some sense of the meaning of a text is better than falling back on the lame declaration that there is none.

(5) Finally, although the meaning of a text is sometimes not transparent and our interpretation is simply a mere translation, we must develop some hermeneutical principles that are promising. But in the end, these

are always subjective. There is no alternative: we are the subjects. This is not a counsel of despair, only the recognition that knowledge is a social construct. Claims to knowledge of natural or cultural phenomenon are made possible, however, by appealing to universal human experiences of which we are a part.

All archaeological arguments are arguments by analogy. For example, a text that seemed to be about parental love would be impenetrable had we not experienced such love, and furthermore assumed that the essentials of human nature have not changed substantially over time. That is often derided by the theorists as "essentialism," but unless there are some essentials, no common knowledge is possible.

Let us now look by comparison at an artifact in the quest for *meaning*, in this case a tenth-century cooking pot, such as we have seen above.

(1) Our cooking pot is also a construct. It was made by someone, sometime, somewhere, with deliberate intent. It was meant to serve as a pot for cooking, not a store jar or a lamp. Here the intent is more manifest than it may be with texts.

(2) The cooking pot is also an encoded symbol, one that has a referent, in this case clearly food preparation. That part of the code is easily decipherable. But archaeologists assume that artifacts point further beyond their surface meanings, that they reflect the behavior and potentially the thought of the makers. Their manufacture and intended use reflect *mentalitiés*, or cultural norms. That is why archaeologists universally presume that a typology, the classification of artifacts by descriptive categories, works. It works because a *type* may be an abstract concept, but it cannot fail to have cultural significance.[59]

A ceramic type, such as our cooking pot, is a *mental template*, an embodiment of a conceptual world that is somehow related to the real world. Again, this is an argument from universal experience, from analogy. It is in that sense that archaeologists often call their data *realia*. A text, of course, is also tangible, an object written with something on something. But its ontological character is more ambiguous. Noth spoke long ago of the "plasticity" of archaeological remains, an apt phrase: malleable but real.

(3) Unlike a text, which may be ambiguous, our cooking pot has only one meaning. Texts can and do lie; that is what propaganda is. But an artifact cannot lie. It could mislead us, but only because we might misinterpret it. If we are sophisticated enough to go beyond functional and determinist explanations, however, we will understand that cooking is not just about

food; ultimately it is about lifeways, foodways—cuisine—which looms large in every culture's self-understanding. Again the particular cultural manifestation may be unique, but the cultural phenomenon is universal.

(4) Deconstruction may be a useful technique with a text, but it is useless with artifacts. Although we could do so, we do not need to take our cooking pot apart, even for laboratory analysis, in order to interpret and understand it. Deconstructing a cooking pot would leave only a pile of sherds. We need not unmask the cooking pot's inner contradictions, reveal its lies, because there are none. The cooking pot is exactly what it appears to be. It does reflect an *ideology*, if by that we mean the maker's intent. But that is discernible on quite objective grounds, and it is so fundamental that it is unexceptionable.

(5) Finally, a hermeneutical principle for artifacts is similarly based on some subjective elements, but it is based also on the reality of human experience, on analogy, in the end literally on common sense.[60]

The above comparisons of texts and artifacts are based on mainstream textual scholarship, in this case predominantly biblical. If we were to take into account postmodernist interpretations of texts, noted above, the picture would be quite different. Most biblical scholars are not postmodernists, of course, at least of the more extreme type, but the comparison is still pertinent. The postmodern challenge cannot be ignored, tempting as that may be.

In typical postmodernist discourse, paraphrased only slightly, everything is a text; there is nothing outside the text; texts refer only to other texts, in an endless circle; metanarratives must be challenged; all claims to knowledge must be viewed with incredulity; "facts" based on texts are simply social constructs; ideology is everything; all readings are based on race, class, gender, power, and, ultimately, politics; meaning is arbitrary, culturally conditioned, so it can be structured to suit the observer; in the end, there are no facts, only assertions.

If all this is not nihilism, it is relativism taken to its limits (an oxymoron). It is evident to most that such a minimalist approach to texts and their interpretation precludes *any* history-writing—at least if the biblical scholars have no recourse to any other source, such as archaeology. It is not a coincidence that the biblical revisionists, having discredited their textual sources and lacking the will or the ability to tum to archaeology, have given up their early, tentative attempts at writing new histories of ancient Israel (below).

What would a "postmodern archaeology" look like? Our cooking pot above would be an isolated example that does not refer to any other cooking pots, much less a larger assemblage of objects. It would be only a social construct, an abstraction. It would have no inherent design or function. Analyzing it by deconstructing it (dismantling it) would undermine any credibility or usefulness that might have been presumed. The cooking pot is all about power and politics. That is what a postmodern cooking pot would look like. All of this is patently absurd, so irrational that it defies reason. But for postmodernists, that means nothing, since the whole enterprise is about the rejection of reason, of the Enlightenment ideal (i.e., of modernism, the Western cultural tradition). Henceforth we shall regard postmodernist readings as futile, mainly because they cannot deal with the essential dimension of both texts and artifacts—*meaning*.

Back to Basics: Hermeneutics

The biblical revisionists and other skeptical scholars were right, however, in one respect: the Hebrew Bible *in itself* is no longer an adequate basis for writing a satisfactory history of ancient Israel. At best, here and there, it is a secondary source. That leaves us largely dependent on external sources, of which archaeology is the most obvious. Thus one must ask: Why did the biblical revisionists (and others) not pursue their original, intuitive appeal to archaeology? Why did they continue to ignore the accumulating data finally being well published and readily accessible? Why did they repeat the old canard that American and Israeli archaeologists were driven by a biblical agenda when the literature showed that they had not been for at least thirty years? Why revive "biblical archaeology" as a whipping-boy— unless one were simply hostile to writing any history of ancient Israel? (Confusing it with the history of *modern* Israel?)

These are lingering, troublesome questions. Whatever the case, we seem to live in an atmosphere of radical skepticism, of cynicism about any Truth, of cultural relativity. Many scholars focus on what we do not know, rather than on what might be (and is) known. Both biblical/historical and archaeological scholarship center today on the "new pragmatism"—on doing what works. But how do we determine what "working" *means*.[61]

The fundamental question here is about epistemology: How can we determine the meaning of texts and artifacts? Is our notion of meaning discerned (inherent), or is it supplied (constructed)? The answer may lie in defining the term *meaning* more precisely, then recognizing that there are several legitimate levels of meaning.

The category of meaning has to do essentially with intent, so that a text means is what its author intended, what was actually said (unless the author was schizophrenic, incompetent, or deliberately obtuse). That can be understood as the original meaning. Yet there are obviously other levels of meanings that may be considered equally legitimate, such as later inter-pretations or secondary meanings. Krister Stendahl long ago suggested these two levels of meaning in his classic analysis of the Biblical Theology movement. As he put it, there are two questions in our inquiry: (1) What *did* the text mean? (2) What *does* it mean?[62] As archaeologists, we would add: (3) What happened?

This poses another question, one that most biblical scholars have taken to be fundamental: How are we to read texts? Responding to the way we are reading biblical texts here, with regard to finding out what really hap-pened in the past, many biblicists will declare: "But that's not the way to *read* texts!" These critics overlook the fact that there are many ways to read a text (their own inner disagreements illustrate that). It all depends on the questions one is asking of the texts; that, in turn, depends on what is meant by history and what kind of history one wants.

Here it may be helpful to compare ways of establishing the meaning of the biblical texts in several different approaches, as outlined above in discerning different kinds of history.

Type of History	School or Method
1. A history of events	archaeology
2. A history of traditions	form and redaction criticism
3. A history of the literature	literary and source criticism
4. A history of ideology	history and philosophy of religion
5. A history of institutions	political history
6. A history of interpretation	exegesis; reception history; theology

In the history of ancient Israel and Judah here, it is obvious that we are taking the first approach almost exclusively. That does not imply that the other approaches—the alternate readings and derived meanings—are not

legitimate and important. It means only that we are leaving those questions to those who are more competent, more interested in those issues.
Our approach here to the biblical text is (1) that it must be accepted for
what it is, in its present form, however complex the formation processes
may have been; and (2) what it says in its narratives about supposed past
events is clear, and our task is only to test the validity of those claims on
the basis of external data, the only relevant evidence we have. When, how,
and why the textual tradition developed, who transmitted it—these are all
questions of secondary significance to the archaeological historian, and
archaeologists *are* historians—not literary critics, much less theologians.

Turning now from the meaning of texts to the meaning of artifacts, the
same interpretive principles apply. Our cooking pot above means what its
maker intended: it is about cooking. That is the original meaning. Presumably its subsequent owner agreed and so used it. Nevertheless, a cracked
cooking pot might have been used secondarily as a flower pot, a new yet
authentic level of meaning. Later still, a modern archaeologist may use
the cooking pot as a "type fossil" to help reconstruct an entire historical
and cultural system. Here we shall try to separate and clarify these levels
of meaning.

Toward Two Hermeneutics

Thus far we have looked closely at our two sources for history-writing,
texts and artifacts. Both sources can theoretically produce useful data,
but both obviously require interpretation, that is, hermeneutics. The word
hermeneutics derives from a Greek word meaning "interpretive art" and
refers to a systematic strategy for interpretation, for discerning or assign-
ing meaning, particularly with texts. Ever since the beginning of modern
textual (or source) criticism in the nineteenth century, biblical scholars
have struggled with this problem, which is obviously fundamental. The literature is vast and bristles with both historical and theological issues, so it
cannot be surveyed here, even if one were competent to do so. For our purposes—evaluating the biblical texts as historical but secondary sources—it
will suffice to offer some general, practical principles that would probably
find widespread agreement.[63]

(1) The biblical texts must be approached precisely as any other texts
that happen to have survived from the ancient Near East.

(2) The first task is to establish the genre of the text, which will have much to do with its historicity. Prose, that is, narrative history, will probably be more useful than epic, myth, poetry, and the like.

(3) All the tools of critical scholarship and textual analysis must be employed in order to establish the date, authorship (if possible}, sociocultural content, audience and authorial intent, and redactional history of the text. Postmodern interpretative methods that bypass these traditional methods are useless and should be repudiated.

(4) Texts must be approached as objectively as possible, so as to allow them their own voice. All interpretations are, however, subjective to some degree, so our own presuppositions should be stated clearly and justified at the outset.

(5) Analysis should begin with an attempt to isolate problems inherent in the text, such as omissions, inconsistencies, contradictions, anachronisms, and incongruencies with facts known from other sources.

(6) Appeals to miracles or divine intervention as explanations of events must be dismissed by the modern historian as unsatisfactory.

(7) Stories that are simply fantastic cannot be credible, even if that judgment may appear subjective.

(8) Finally, the meaning of texts, whether discerned or possibly inferred, is legitimate only to the degree that it is consonant with the author's (and tradent's) intention, even if one repudiates that. An additional level of meaning that few Syro-Palestinian or biblical archaeologists have even addressed is the issue of hermeneutics. They have been overwhelmingly pragmatic, regarding theory as irrelevant, "mere speculation." That has been especially true of Israeli archaeologists, at least until very recently, and few American archaeologists have dealt with theoretical discussions in other branches of archaeology, advocating some rapprochement with anthropology in particular. The New Archaeology of the 1970s–1980s, with its emphasis on theory building and testing of hypotheses, came and went with barely any notice in our field.[64]

One exception among American archaeologists is David Schloen, who has advocated a deliberate "archaeological hermeneutic," something that he thinks has not really been attempted. He is particularly dismissive of what he calls "objectivism." It is not clear, however, what objectivism is (positivism?). Hodder had read artifacts as texts, but Schloen strangely characterizes this as a "text-free archaeology," whereas Hodder emphasizes the wordplay *contextual*, that is, "*with* text." Schloen's own view is that "archaeology itself is not history.... archaeology is the prehistory of facts and not the history of symbols." But what does this statement mean?[65]

One could analyze the remaining literature of archaeological hermeneutics, except for the fact that there is none. The few discussions of theory in our discipline either mention socioanthropological models in order to discard them or simply allude to the disagreements over interpretation that plague our discipline. Most discussions seem to assume that interpretive theories are all borrowed from other disciplines and can be dismissed as inappropriate to ours, and further that a properly *archaeological* hermeneutic is either impossible or unnecessary.

Archaeological Theory, Practice, and Hermeneutics

Given this impasse, we may offer our own tentative suggestions for an archaeological hermeneutic that would cover both field methods and interpretation of the data.

(1) Methods, aims, and presuppositions must be specified up front.

(2) On principle we must strictly separate artifacts and textual facts, in the interest of an independent and honest inquiry. In particular, the biblical texts, however they are to be understood, must be held in abeyance. They cannot be allowed to influence the archaeological agenda initially. Only later can they (like other texts) be taken into consideration. Archaeological method is archaeologically based on the analysis of material culture remains.

(3) "Facts" are not facts until established as such by empirical investigation and confirmation. Even then, these facts do not constitute data unless they are converted into useful information in the context of meaningful questions.

(4) Stratigraphy and field recording—determining the facts on the ground—are the fundamental considerations, the source of any reliable data. Artifacts carelessly excavated, torn out of context, poorly documented, or published selectively or not at all can never yield reliable information on any topic. There are innumerable, tragic case studies to illustrate this problem.

(5) Chronology is essential. An artifact that cannot be dated with some precision is useless for historical reconstructions, indeed a hindrance and a cruel illusion. Again, examples are legion.

(6) Context in archaeology is everything. It is only context—the physical in situ context, as well as the larger social and cultural context—that can give an artifact meaning. Isolated from that context, the artifact is little more than a curiosity, interesting but enigmatic.

(7) A single artifact, even in a good context, may be misleading. It must be seen as an integral part of a representative assemblage of artifacts, both onsite and in broader comparative studies.

(8) Statistics based on too narrow a sample are meaningless. Even at best, they are only probabilistic arguments.

(9) Arguments from analogy are fundamental in archaeology, but they require the broadest cross-cultural comparisons. Yet in the end they may be dependent on experiential wisdom, or self-referential knowledge (i.e., common sense).

(10) Assertions must be supported by evidence. Invoking various authorities may be evidence of a consensus, but it does not constitute prima facie evidence.

(11) Theories, that is, models, are only heuristic devices; they do not lead to truth. When there is little or no evidence, speculation may be legitimate, but it, too, is justified only as a heuristic device.

(12) Extreme views to the right or left—"contrarian" arguments—should be dismissed as a distraction. The truth is more likely to lie in the middle, in mainstream or consensus scholarship, in a balanced "sweet reasonableness."

(13) The essence of sound scholarly method in archaeology, as in other disciplines, lies in rational, honest, dispassionate, competent analysis. Absolute objectivity is impossible, but some objectivity is better than none.

(14) All evidence pro and con must be evaluated and all of it argued.

(15) There is no such thing as archaeological proof, except perhaps in terms of negative evidence. Proximate explanations are more likely to be defensible than supposed ultimate explanations. The principle of Occam's razor should always be kept in mind: the most parsimonious explanation that will account for the data is the one to be preferred.

(16) There is no substitute for long experience in the field and hands-on familiarity with material culture remains. The opinion of nonspecialists is largely irrelevant and can safely be disregarded. The views of experts in related textual evidence can be considered, but not when it comes to a definitive *archaeological* interpretation.

(17) Finally, it must be borne in mind that archaeology, like all the humanistic disciplines, is not a science but an art. The essential challenge is the why and how of human behavior, and that can never be fully fathomed.

Toward a New Paradigm: A History of Israel without the Bible?

The idea broached here that archaeological data now constitute a primary source for writing a history of ancient Israel may suggest to some that the texts of the Hebrew Bible have become dispensable, no real source at all. Already in 1991, as the archaeological data began to mount in quantity and quality, Miller asked a question at an international symposium that was not necessarily rhetorical: "Is it possible to write a history of Israel without relying on the Hebrew Bible."[66] His answer was that it might be but that it would not be desirable. Yet the question did not go away.

Miller was a mainstream biblical historian, although he had had some archaeological experience. A few years later the European revisionists had burst on the scene, most admittedly radical leftists (above). Not surprisingly, their rejection of the Hebrew Bible altogether as history led them to propose new histories of ancient Israel that took up Miller's question and answered yes. It is possible, indeed necessary, to eliminate the Bible as a source. Thus Thompson had advocated a sort of secular history of Palestine as early as 1987 (above), and by 1985 there had been calls for just such a secular discipline. Thompson, to his credit, followed up his prospectus with a massive 1992 publication, *Early History of the Palestinian People: From the Written and Archaeological Sources.* Unfortunately, this was an idiosyncratic work that made only amateurish use of the available archaeological data, and it attracted little attention.

Thompson's work was followed the next year with another effort at a sort of secular history, Gösta Ahlström's *The History of Ancient Palestine from the Paleolithic Period to Alexander's Conquest* (1993). This was an ambitious and in some ways learned work. But it, like Thompson's effort, demonstrated that a nonspecialist simply could not master the burgeoning archaeological data.

No one seemed to grasp the obvious. New histories of ancient Israel would have to be undertaken either by biblicists teaming up with archaeologists, or possibly by archaeologists themselves. In that formative period of research, archaeologists apparently did not yet see themselves as historians, "historians of things." A few programmatic essays appeared in the following years, but little was done to show that archaeology might supplant or even complement the typical logocentric approach of biblical historians. Archaeology did indeed appear to remain mute.

A German scholar sometimes mistakenly lumped with the European revisionists, Ernst Axel Knauf, made an astute observation at the same symposium that raised Miller's question noted above. In response to Noth's old dictum about archaeology, Knauf pointed out that, for those who do not know Hebrew, the *Bible* is mute.[67] Neither he nor the others in the symposium, however, followed up on this insight. But the notion that archaeology could perhaps speak up was broached. Its language was simply not yet deciphered.

Some years later Knauf (2008), although an extremely skeptical scholar, stated on the subject of extracting information from the biblical texts: "I think, with the majority of historians past and present, that it can be done. Data from literary sources though, have to be sifted as rigorously as data from archaeology; some are useful and others are not."[68] He went on to say that we all need to demonstrate that "history can be written on the basis of archaeology, and, if need be, on the basis of archaeology alone; and also [to demonstrate: WGD] what kind of history would emerge from such an endeavor."[69] Knauf did not note Dever's discursus some years prior on kinds of history that had become part of the issue.

Few other biblical scholars had been as bold or prescient as Knauf. But already as he was writing, Lester L. Grabbe, founder of the European Seminar on Methodology in Israel's History, to which many of the revisionists belonged, published the work referred to above, *Ancient Israel: What Do We Know and How Do We Know It?* (2007b). This work was a breakthrough in the progress toward a true dialogue *between* archaeology and biblical studies, rather than the monologues that had for so long dominated both disciplines.[70] Grabbe's *continuum* was quite similar to the *convergences* that Dever had sought in a previous book with a similar title (*What Did the Biblical Writers Know?* [2001]). Grabbe surveyed the textual and the archaeological data period by period, his archaeological coverage as competent and his judgment as balanced as one could hope for from a nonspecialist.

What is pertinent here is Grabbe's explicit recognition that henceforth the archaeological data will constitute our *primary* source. That is because these data alone can serve as an external witness to critique, complement, and correct the biblical texts with their limited potential as a source for reliable facts. Grabbe acknowledged that his work was only a prolegomenon, but it is the prolegomenon for which we had been waiting.

Meanwhile, a recent survey of the historiographic issues over the last generation or two by Diane Banks did not show much grasp of the potential or archaeology. But nevertheless, she concluded that a history "without reference to the Bible would be desirable." Furthermore, "should such a history be written, it would have significant implications for the study of the Hebrew Bible."[71]

The following is an attempt at just such a new and different history, even if in the end it is only a prolegomenon. It will be largely a history from things, and it must be judged a success or a failure by how well it integrates and interprets things, artifacts, and texts. One postmodern scholar—a New Testament specialist—opines that what we academics do is "rub texts together" to see if we can create sparks.[72] Surely it is preferable to create *light*, light that may illuminate the human past and point the way to a better future.

Notes

1. Momigliano 1966, 217, quoted in Kofoed 2005, 213. See further the discussion in Kofoed 2005, 214–34, with full references.

2. Berkhofer 1995, 67.

3. Gaddis 2002, 10 and passim. On postmodernism, see further below and n. 31; see also excursus 1.1.

4. For general orientation to the Hebrew Bible as a potential source for history-writing, see Friedman 1987; Barton 1996; McKenzie and Haynes 1993; Schniedewind 2004; Tov 2012. For J, E, and P specifically, see Baden 2009, 2013. For the revisionists' negative view of source criticism generally, see Whitelam 1991, 1996; Thompson 1999; Lemche 1998b; 2010b; Davies 2007, 2008. For critiques of them, see Provan 1995; Barr 2000, 103–80; Dever 2001, 4–52; Brettler 2003, 2007; Uehlinger 2005; Barstad 2007, 2008, 2010; Albertz 2010.

5. See references in n. 4 above; see also further discussion in ch. 2.

6. On Dtr especially as a historical source, see Weinfeld 1972; Mayes 1983; Halpern 1988; Knoppers 1993; Nielsen 1997; Knoppers and McConville 2000; Na'aman 2006. For summaries and critique, see the essays in Halpern and Lemaire 200, with full bibliography; add the essays in Davies and Edelman 2011; Grabbe 2011.

7. These views, published in Hebrew in 2002, are quoted in Amit 2006, 5–7, whose succinct summary of the problem is one of the most useful. She opts for an eighth-century date for the earliest edition of Dtr (2006, 11).

8. For a convenient summary of the prophetic literature, see Coogan 2006, 229–336. For critical scholarship, see Wilson 1980; de Moor 2001; Petersen 2002 and references there. The prophetic will be sifted through in succeeding chapters on the monarchic period, using, however, the archaeological and extrabiblical data as a criterion to establish how much material may be early and reliable.

9. Virtually all scholars would give assent to this principle of critical scrutiny, even those of conservative and evangelical persuasion. See, for instance, the numerous essays on pertinent topics in the dictionary of Arnold and Williamson 2005, published by Intervarsity Press, an arm of the Intervarsity Christian Fellowship. The present work differs from the broad consensus chiefly by taking the archaeological data, often treated minimally as the primary data and the most reliable criterion for establishing the historicity of the biblical narratives. See further below.

10. Biblical scholars recognize this fact, of course, but nevertheless most continue to write "histories" that are little more than histories of the literature *about* the history of ancient Israel, such as Garbini's "paraphrase of the Hebrew Bible" (1988). As a recent example, see Kessler 2008, which scarcely make any use of archaeology and deals not with the real "social history" of Israel but only with that of the handful of elites who wrote and edited the Hebrew Bible. The author is a Marburg professor, but he does not seem to be aware of the disconnect. By contrast, see now Avraham Faust's social history of ancient Israel (2012a), based almost exclusively on the rich archaeological data. Others who do not see archaeology as an effective source include Miller and Hayes 1986; Davies 1992; Lemche 1998c; Cogan 1998; and Thompson 1999. Even Banks (2006) and Moore and Kelle (2011)—both presuming to be "guidebooks" for the future—barely appreciate the potential of archaeology as a source for history-writing; their summaries and critiques are superficial. Moore and Kelle propose that the revisionists are really "plausibilists," which gives them the benefit of the doubt. But they remain minimalists; and even if they are "plausibilists," one cannot write history on the basis of possibilities (see Moore and Kelle 2011, 54–56).

11. Again, this view reflects consensus scholarship, although many historians do not carry it through to a logical conclusion. As McKenzie puts it, "Whether the events that the Bible relates as past causes or explanations actually took place as described was not the ancient historian's primary concern.... in the Bible, history was written for an ideological purpose" (2005, 420). The revisionist's claim to be the only proper skeptics is fatuous. Here all critical scholars are minimalist. See further below on postmodernism.

12. For orientation for the New Archaeology and subsequent postprocessualism, see the surveys in Renfrew and Bahn 1991, 9–49; Preucel 1991; and the essays in Whitley 1998. See also Hodder 1986, 1999; Trigger 2006, 1–3; and cf.

Hodder 2012. I have evaluated these trends in several publications, especially Dever 2003b, 515–19 (see in particular the full bibliography).

13. Hodder 1986, followed up by later works such as Hodder 1987; Hodder and Hutson 2003; and, of course, the works cited in n. 12 above. On cognitive archaeology and the quest for "meaning in things," see other seminal works such as Shanks and Tilley 1987; Tilley 1990, 1991, 1993; Renfrew and Zubrow 1994; Preucel and Hodder 1996. Postprocessualism has been the general paradigm for at least twenty years now in world archaeology. Israeli archaeologists, however, typically pragmatic and opposed to "theory," until recently paid little attention to this trend any more than they did to New Archaeology. Virtually the only discussions are Bunimovitz 1995a and Faust 2007a, both aligning themselves with Dever 1993a. See further Dever 2003b, 515.

14. Hodder 1986, 90–97, 118–46, especially 91. See also Dever 2003b, 516–17. See further below.

15. A comparison of the views of Hodder and Renfrew (as well as other contemporary theorists) can be found conveniently in Hodder's revised edition of *Archaeological Theory Today* (2012). Hodder remains a postprocessualist cognitive archaeologist, Renfrew a processualist cognitive archaeologist. But in *practice*, both scholars employ a blending of the two approaches—in other words, the diversity and eclecticism, the pragmatism, that characterizes much of mainstream archaeology today. See n. 16 below.

16. Morris 2000, 309. See also the résumé of trends in theory over the past sixty years or so, as well as a more detailed definition of the "new" cultural history (2000, 1–28, 66–78). As for the historical turn that Morris documents, he says: "I argue that we are now entering a new phase in archaeological scholarship, when historical archaeology in the traditional sense of texturally documented periods, should displace prehistory as the central arena for debating new concepts.... Archaeology as a whole will become more historical, in the broader sense of thinking historically about people in the past" (2000, x). On the new pragmatism, see Preucel and Mrozowski 2010.

17. Bintliff 2011, 20. See also similar practical observations on "correlations" between sources by Flannery and Marcus (2011, 29 and passim) and Morris (2000, 24–27). These correlations between texts and artifacts are equivalent to Dever's "convergences" between some biblical texts and material cultural remains (Dever 2001, passim) that lead to judgments beyond reasonable doubt.

18. Thus Dever 1997a; 1997e; 2001, 65–68, although little noted. Perhaps the only other Syro-Palestinian archaeologist to react to Hodder's notion of reading artifacts like texts is David Schloen. However, he simply dismisses such an enterprise as "positivism." It is fundamentally "objectivist and antithetical to hermeneutics ... quite brashly imperialist." See Schloen 2003, 291. For Schloen, "The State is a state of mind." This is a typical postmodern half-truth elevated into an absurd proposition. Renfrew's "cognitive map" is quite similar to that of the historian Lewis Gaddis, discussed above.

19. Kingery 1996b, ix; see the adaptation of this model already in Dever 2003b, 520. Kingery was my colleague at the University of Arizona until his untimely death.

20. Kingery 1996a, 1.

21. Lubar and Kingery 1993. On the postmodernist challenge, see further below.

22. Prown 1993. On the hermeneutical impoverishment of most archeologists, see n. 10 above. Prown states with no hesitation that "any artifact—and the inclusive view would mean any works of art as well—is a historical event" (1993, 2). Perhaps the artifact is more properly speaking a reflection of an event or events, or as Prown states in the same paragraph, "artifacts are historical evidence" (1993, 3). That is the basic presumption throughout this work, which is what makes it different. It is also the assumption of the "Fribourg school" of art history. For an introduction to this school—often ignored by text-oriented scholars—see conveniently Uehlinger 2005; see also Keel and Uehlinger 1998; Schroer 1987.

23. Kingery 1996a, 2, 3, 4. Hodder's early work agreed with this insight, but in his later works such as Hodder and Hutson 2003, he backed away to some degree from getting at "the inside of things, of history" toward a more modest "cognitive archaeology." He now thinks that "reading text is not an appropriate analogy for reading material culture because text is a different sort of sign." Nevertheless, "text is a better metaphor for material culture than language." And material culture can be read easier and better than texts, because texts are already interpretations. See Hodder and Hutson 2003, 168, 204, 205.

24. Kingery 1996a, 4.

25. Lubar 1996, 32–35.

26. Schiffer 1996, 73. Schiffer, a leading New World archaeological theorist, was, like Kingery, my colleague at the University of Arizona for nearly thirty years.

27. As for science in archaeology and the way in which the natural sciences will impact archaeology now and in the future, note the multimillion dollar project of Israel Finkelstein and other Israeli archaeologists and scientists (see Shanks 2010). This is the outgrowth of nearly forty years of movement in archaeology in the direction of what may be called, with the influence of natural sciences, archaeometrics—the ability at last to measure and quantify material cultural remains and even cultural phenomena.

28. Prown 1993, 3.

29. Artifacts may deceive us if we misunderstand their meaning, but they do not intentionally deceive, as texts may do. Thus their essential "truth." See Prown 1993, 5.

30. Maquet 1993, 32–40. On analogy—"common sense"—see further below.

31. The term "incredulity toward all metanarratives" is that of Jean Francois Lyotard, one of postmodernism's principal gurus, in *The Postmodern Condition* (1984). This extreme skepticism toward texts and their interpretation underlies almost all of postmodernism's pronouncements (one cannot say "epistemology"),

not to mention the agenda of the biblical revisionists. The result is multicultural-
ism—a form of cultural relativity in which one "reading" is as valid as any other,
in effect, anarchy. That means the end of any rational discourse and obviously
any history-writing. See the scathing denunciation of postmodernism in Keith
Windschuttle's *The Killing of History: How Literary Critics and Social Theorists
Are Murdering Our Past* (1997); and John M. Ellis, *Against Deconstruction* (1989).
For how recent anthropology, ethnography, and psychology have tried to combat
postmodernism, see the trenchant analysis of Greenfield 2000. The threat in these
disciplines is the same as it is for history and archaeology. As Greenfield puts it:
"'Truth' has been radically deconstructed" (2000, 570). For devastating critiques
of postmodernism from leading archaeologists, see Morris 2000, 12–17, 66–79;
Bintliff 2011, 1–21; Flannery and Marcus 2011, 23–24. The latter raise the question: "Is it really the case that theory has died, or simply that Post-modernism
will be the death of archaeology?" They conclude that "only if Post-modernism
were to endure forever—which we do not expect—will be cause for a memorial
service" (2011, 23, 29). See also the about face of Terrence Eagleton, a prominent
postmodernist (1996). For the devastating effect of postmodernism on the arts,
see Roger Kimball, *The Rape of the Masters: How Political Correctness Sabotages
Art* (2004). For a critique from a Levantine archaeological perspective, see Dever
2001. The response of the biblical revisionists has been to demonize Dever, *never*
to look honestly at the archaeological data that he commends to them. See further
below and excursus 1 below.

34. Hunt 1993, 294. Cf. Dever 1997a (discussed above, on "reading" artifacts).

33. Dever 1997b, 17, 21. Obvious as these above categories of different histories may be, or taking artifacts as sources, there is not much awareness among
archaeologists—perhaps because few self-consciously define themselves as historians.

34. The pejorative term "mute" apparently derives from Noth's *History of
Israel* (1960), although his actual appreciation of archaeology was somewhat more
positive. For its perpetuation by biblicists, see Herrmann 1975; by revisionists, see
Carroll 1993; see even some archaeologists such as Finkelstein. Ernst Axel Knauf,
himself usually a skeptic, had the perfect comeback for this mindless assertion:
"For those who don't know Hebrew, the Hebrew Bible is mute" (1991, 41). He advocates, as Dever does, learning the language of both texts and artifacts.

35. For Philistine history and culture, see the full discussion in chapter 2. For
the biblical memory of the Philistines, see Machinist 2000; Stager 2006; Gitin 2010.

36. See Schiffer 1987 on those "Natural" and "Cultural" transformation processes that shape the archaeological record.

37. The endless process of textual and intertextual interpretation of the biblical texts, the "idealization"—or recently, "cultural memory"—tends to obscure the
reality of the text itself. More recent narrative criticism has made a point of focusing more on the literary quality of the biblical text, quite apart from its potential
as data for history-writing (or for theology). The archaeological data, in any case,

retain their tangibility more readily. On recent cultural-memory studies, see ch. 2, n. 42; ch. 3, n. 2.

38. See n. 27 above.

39. Many biblical scholars thus now appeal to archaeology intuitively but hesitantly, perhaps because of their uncertainty about the primacy of their own data. Their canon is closed, however, and ours is not. See n. 10 above.

40. The only ceramic vessels that would seem to suit the meaning of a frying pan are found not in the Iron Age but in the Persian–Hellenistic period. Other Hebrew terms for similar vessels—*marḥešet* (Lev 2:7; 7–9), *maḥăbat* (only in Lev 2:5; 6:14; 7:9), and *pārûr* (only in Num 11:8; 1 Sam 2:14)—reflect mostly late P material, of Persian-period date. For further discussion and illustration of typical Iron Age forms and their presumed biblical names, see Dever 2001, 230–34, with reference to R. Amiran's fundamental 1970 work.

41. Contrast this admittedly positivist reading of our cooking pot with an imaginary postmodern or New Critical reading. In that approach, the cooking pot would be only a "signifier," but signifying nothing. It is "self-contradictory"; it appears to be for cooking, but it may just as well be a lamp.

42. Binford 1982, 162.

43. See Dever 1997d, 20 and references there to such terms as *theocratic history, historicized myth* or *mythologized history, rationalized myth,* a form of *historicality, history-like, tradition, narrative history, story, prose fiction,* or *simply fiction.*

44. T. Thompson 1987, 39.

45. See Dever 1974, 1981, 1982, 1985b.

46. Davies 1992, 24 n. 4, with reference to A. Mazar 1990. He simply ignores the other handbooks: H. Weippert 1988; Ben-Tor 1992; and Levy 1995. Altogether, there are some two thousand pages of data there. As for Davies's "Persian-period Israel," he cites no archaeological evidence for that either.

47. Quote from Grabbe 1997, 14; see the list of Seminar members on p. 12. It is evident that the polemics, now appearing for the first time, are directed mainly against Dever 1995a and 1995d, which was a critique of Davies 1992 and T. Thompson 1992. But these articles dealt with historiography and ethnicity from a mainstream perspective. The term *minimalist,* which soon came to dominate the discussion, was never used (although *nihilist* was, and clearly defined).

48. Carroll does not share the notion "that archaeology can make good the defects of the Bible in historical construction" (1997, 88), which he attributes to Dever. He also asserts that "shards lacking writing are harder to interpret and less interesting than shards with writing on them" (1997, 99). To the question "Can a history of ancient Israel be written?" Davies says: "I am inclined to say 'No,' unless it is allowed that a bogus or unreliable history is still an adequate account of history" (1997, 101).

Davies writes that archaeologists like Dever, who "construct an Israel in detail equal to biblical detail," are working with an impossibility and are really theists in disguise (1997, 108, 117). He himself remains "skeptical, minimalist and negative."

"The invention of history will never cease" (1997, 122). The imagined "theism" is an ad hominem argument without any basis in fact.

Lemche acknowledges Dever's plea for an independent, secular discipline of Syro-Palestinian archaeology but claims that his actual work betrays "a remarkable influence from biblical studies" (1997, 125). He agrees with Whitelam (1996) that "ancient Israel" is a scholarly construct, a creation of "Zionist ideologies" (1997, 138). The Dan inscription is dismissed as probably a forgery.

T. Thompson launches a twelve-page attack on Dever for presuming that we can identify any ethnic "Israelites": all his archaeological "ethnic markers" are false (1997, 166–78). As for his own 1992 "secular history of Palestine," he now declares that it "was after all hardly history, critically speaking, but rather just another rationalistic paraphrase for biblical Israel" (1997, 179).

These references are cited not to engage in polemics but to show that the first Seminar volume in 1997 threw down the gauntlet and thus unfortunately set the parameters for much of the subsequent discussion of "archaeology and the Bible" for more than a decade. See further below; see also Carroll 1997, 88, 101–3; Davies 1997, 105–8; and excursus 1.1.

49. Barstad 1997, 49, 64. Barstad seems to be the first to see in the views of others in this volume how postmodernism is becoming an issue. See further below and excursus 1.1.

50. Grabbe 1997a, 30. Grabbe argues further that "a good deal of the interpretation of archaeology depends directly or indirectly on the text" (i.e., the biblical text). No one who had an honest, searching look at the basic handbooks such as H. Weippert 1988, Mazar 1990, Ben-Tor 1992, or Levy 1995 could have made such a statement. That kind of old-fashioned "biblical archaeology" had been defunct for at least fifteen years when Grabbe 1997b was published.

51. See Grabbe 1997b, passim. Mazar 1990 is mentioned once, in a footnote by Davies, only to be dismissed as irrelevant (see n. 46 above). Ben-Tor 1992 and Levy 1995 are never mentioned, nor are Stern 1993 and 2008. Even H. Weippert 1988 is only mentioned twice in passing.

52. Banks 2006, 223, 234.

53. As an example of Moore's and Kelle's indiscriminate judgments, they label Dever a "maximalist" (2011, 34), despite the fact that his publications have undermined all of Albright's notions of a patriarchal era, the exodus and conquest, Moses and monotheism, and so on.

Elsewhere they simply quote both sides of a conflict as though they were equal (as on the idiosyncratic low chronology). This is an unreliable "guidebook"; the same can be said of Moore 2006.

54. See the laudatory review of Grabbe 2007b in Dever 2010b. Grabbe's prolegomenon helped to inspire the present work.

55. *Ideology* has become a catchword in current discourse, particularly in biblical studies, as Barr observes (2000, 102, quoting Clines). Yet the term has a bewildering array of meanings, mostly negative (i.e., your ideology is bad; mine

is good). Ideology is neither necessarily good nor bad. It is, like all representations of reality, a form of propaganda, the advocacy of a cause. It all depends on the cause. Ideology becomes problematic only if it is a detriment in evaluating the evidence critically or if it is concealed and seeks to deceive. Barr's extended discussion of ideology, with full references, is a judicious analysis (2000, 102–40). He argues that revisionist ideology is problematic for both reasons noted above. The ideology of the revisionists does distance them from our data, particularly the archaeological data, and it does so deliberately to obfuscate rather than to enlighten. See Barr 2000, 141–78; Dever 2001, 23–52 and passim.

56. See Faust 2007a; Grabbe 2007c; Joffe 2007.

57. If a symbol does not point to some reality, it has no significance, no power. A stop sign is only a symbol, but a driver who ignores where it points and routinely runs through it will turn out to be wrong—dead wrong.

58. See n. 55 above.

59. On the fundamental method of typology in archaeology, see Renfrew and Bahn 1991, 104–8.

60. Biblical scholars have accused archeologists of falling back on common sense—no "method" at all. Thus M. Smith 2006, 276–77. Yet the interpretation of both artifacts and texts depends ultimately on common sense (now sometimes returning as "self-referential knowledge"), that is, upon an intellectual framework that is derived from one's existential participation in human experience, assuming that it is universal and timeless. Without that frame of reference, our perceptions could not refer to anything. Postmodernists, of course, must deny that there is any such frame of reference, since their incredulity toward texts and artifacts requires that there be none. Thus their tirade against essentialism. See Lemert 1997, 40–43, for postmodernism's "critique of the cultural ideal which holds that social differences are at best incidental variance on one, universal, true and essential nature." For an eloquent defense of essentialism in the interpretation of material culture, see Prown, who states: "Although commonality of sense perception cannot be proven either empirically or philosophically, certain conclusions can be drawn on the basis of the shared neuro-physiological apparatus of all human beings, which is not culturally specific and has evolved only slowly over time, and also from the inescapable *commonalities of life as lived*" (Prown 1993, 17, emphasis added).

61. On the new pragmatism, see Preucel and Mrozowski 2010; cf. Levy 2010b. On the recent emphasis on the meaning of things, see Hodder 1987, 2012; Shanks and Tilley 1987; Tilley 1990, 1991, 1993; Renfrew and Zubrow 1994; Hodder et al. 1995. See also above and Lubar and Kingery 1993; Kingery 1996b.

62. Stendahl 1962, 1:419.

63. For basic literature on biblical hermeneutics, see mainstream works such as Van Seters 1983; Barton 1996; Brettler 1995; Barr 2000; Knoppers and McConville 2000; Kofoed 2005; Collins 2005. For narrative criticism, less radical than Frei 1974, and New Critical approaches (below), see, e.g., Alter 1981; Berlin 1983; Sternberg 1985. For postmodern and New Critical hermeneutics, see nn. 39, 43,

44, 55 above; for conservative views, see the essays in Millard, Hoffmeier, and Baker 1994; Provan 1995; Baker and Arnold 1998.

64. See Dever 1981, 1988, 1989, 1993a. The first Israeli critical discussion on theory was that of Bunimovitz in 1995a—a good twenty-five years after discussions of theory became prominent in archaeology elsewhere in the world. There have been few follow-ups; see, however, Bunimovitz and Faust 2010.

65. See Schloen 2003, 291. Schloen has called for an explicitly archaeological hermeneutic, which he attempts in the one hundred pages of his 2001 work on "the house of the father" and a far-ranging model of patrimonialism. Here one may count more than thirty "–isms," mostly in philosophy and sociology, that Schloen discusses at length and then rejects. His own preference seems to lie in Ricouer's and Weber's "interpretation theory," in a sort of phenomenology that relies on "lived experience." He espouses Ricouer's inclusiveness and eclecticism as providing a theoretical middle ground. It is noteworthy, however, that when Schloen finally comes to discussing the real houses of Iron Age Palestine (only 40 out of 360 pages), he abandons even his own minimalist hermeneutics altogether. He falls back, as we all do, on (1) ethnographic parallels, i.e., analogy; (2) elementary spatial analysis and statistics; (3) common sense (his lived experience) when available; and (4) textual evidence. In sum, Scholen's is nothing like a useful archaeological hermeneutic.

66. Miller 1991.

67. Knauf 1991, 46.

68. Knauf 2008, 82.

69. Knauf 2008, 85.

70. Grabbe 2007b; see the review of Dever 2010b.

71. Banks 2006, 334–35.

72. Adam 1995, 60.

EXCURSUS 1.1

A Critique of the European Seminar on Methodology in Israel's History, 1998–2010

The European Seminar was presumably the principal showcase for European Old Testament historical scholarship. Thus it may be worthwhile to digress a bit to chart developments after its initial volume was published in 1997. Subsequent volumes of the European Seminar on Methodology in Israel's History (by 2007 the title had become simply "European Seminar in Historical Methodology," no "Israel") were disappointing. The 1998 volume, on "the exile as history and ideology," questioned whether there had been a historical exile (the soon-to-be theme of "the empty land"). Again, this volume featured no archaeologists, nor were there any attempts to deal with the extensive archaeological data on the relevant late seventh–sixth centuries (Late Iron II–III). Barstad, the most positive, never even mentions archaeology, nor does Thompson. Grabbe's section on "external sources" deals exclusively with extrabiblical texts. He thinks that a tentative "history of the exile" might be written and that archaeology might possibly play some role, but he cites no data and gives no specifics.[1]

In 2001 two Seminar volumes appeared, one, not unexpectedly, on whether the Hebrew Bible was at least a product of the Iron Age or was rather Persian (Davies) or Hellenistic in date (Becking, Carroll, Lemche, and Thompson). Only Albertz and Barstad demurred (Becking and Grabbe to some degree). The argument that the biblical texts were "too late" to be regarded as historical sources was gaining ground.[2]

The other 2001 Seminar volume dealt with biblical prophecy and a presumably urban context. But here, too, the focus was almost exclusively on texts (many of them regarded as post–Iron Age), and the discussion of sites was largely theoretical. The real sites of ancient Israel in the Iron

Age, brilliantly illuminated now by archaeology, were discussed only by Grabbe.[3]

The Israeli archaeologist David Ussishkin was now listed as a Seminar member, but not until 2008 would there appear any contributions by him (or any other archaeologist). By now Grabbe, the Seminar's founder, was defensive about the Seminar's alleged minimalist or "postmodernist" stance or about its being labeled a school at all.

The 2003 volume *"Like a Bird in a Cage"* dealt with the well-known invasion of Judah by Sennacherib in 701. In his introduction, Grabbe did cover some of the archaeological data, and with commendable skill for a nonspecialist. Yet inexplicably, no archaeologist was among the contributors, despite the fact that by now there was a wealth of relevant data—especially from the renewed excavation of Ussishkin and others at the key site of Lachish. As Grabbe himself acknowledged, "none of the participants devoted much space to the questions of archaeology."[4]

The 2005 Seminar volume was ostensibly devoted to Israelite-Judahite kings, but only Josiah and Manasseh were treated. In general, the historicity of Josiah's "cultic reforms" was doubted, with only Uehlinger citing the considerable archaeological data on "popular religion" in the late seventh century (describing his position as a "well-grounded minimal view").[5]

The 2007 volume dealt with the Omride dynasty of the ninth century. Niemann's discussion of Samaria, dependent now on Tappy's authoritative two-volume survey, was supplemented by the paper of Ussishkin (the first in any volume by an archaeologist). Grabbe, however, made a considerable step forward in advancing the notion of archaeological data as "primary," above all by proposing to use those data to confirm or contest the picture in the biblical text. Here he deliberately steers a middle course between minimalism and maximalism, foreshadowing his own 2007 volume, *Ancient Israel: What Do We Know and How Do We Know It?*[6]

In 2008 and 2010 there appeared two Seminar volumes, both entitled *Israel in Transition: From Late Bronze II to Iron IIa (c. 1250–850 B.C.E.),* the first volume on archaeology, the second on texts. Now, at last, archaeology plays a major role in the Seminar's addressing the historiographic issues.[7]

We have devoted considerable space to the publications of the European Seminar because it should be one of the best showcases of changing scholarly fortunes in attempting to write new histories of Israel over a period of nearly twenty years. During this period, however, there were, to be sure, developments elsewhere in historiography, as well as the appearance of several actual histories of ancient Israel and Judah.[8]

Oddly enough, Israeli archaeologists and biblical scholars (with the exception of the distinguished historian Nadav Na'aman) remained largely aloof from the discussion of "Bible and history" until the late 1990s, apparently regarding this as a European and North American intellectual (and theological) dilemma. The archaeologists, none trained either as critical biblical scholars or as historians, much less anthropologists, eschewed theory and remained engrossed in data-gathering. Only in a few popular "post-Zionist" publications did some of the issues surface. Finkelstein and Silberman's *The Bible Unearthed: Archaeology's New Vision of Ancient Israel and the Origin of Its Sacred Texts* (2001) became a best-seller. But apart from its idiosyncratic "low chronology," it was simply a well-written summation of commonly known data. It provided no documentation, and it by-passed the historiographical crisis that revisionism had brought to a head since the mid-1990s. This was despite the fact that by now Finkelstein had allowed himself to be co-opted by the European biblical revisionists, even though he was no radical skeptic.

One element in the antipathy of revisionist members of the European Seminar toward archaeology in Israel is clearly related to their charge that it is Zionist archaeology. In their view, it is dedicated to establishing the legitimacy of the modern state of Israel by "constructing a past" in the land. That explains the ferocity of Thompson's original attack on Dever (1997), which focused on several of his previous publications (Dever 1991a, 1992c, 1993a, 1995a, 199bd) on ancient Israelite ethnicity. This was in spite of Thompson's admission that his own 1992 *Early History of the Israelite People* had seen pottery and other material cultural traits as "ethnic markers."

If there were any doubts about the impetus, they would be removed by looking at Lemche's contribution to the 1997 Seminar volume, where he declares that "the Hebrew Bible ... is not really talking about a real society (nation)." He applauds Whitelam's *The Invention of Israel: The Silencing of Palestinian History*, published the year before, whose project he declares "a pioneering one and polemical in its planning and execution."[9] Whitelam had argued that Israeli and American archaeologists affiliated with them (Albrightians) had collaborated to dispossess the Palestinians from their land. Histories of ancient Israel were not only flawed; they were illegitimate in principle.

In the same volume (1997), Carroll attacked the Israeli archaeologist Nahman Avigad (the most benign of men) for his publication of a group of seventh–sixth-century bullae with biblical names because "from such bits of baked clay he reconstructs the world." Further: "I suspect that ideology is behind such reconstruction." Avigad, and even Finkelstein, "is tending towards an indulgence in the production of ideological literature (propaganda in other words)."[10]

When Dever responded to these and other of Whitelam's and Lemche's publications (1996, 2001), he became the principal target of the polemics, although he could hold his own in rhetoric. In 1997 Lemche had compared Israeli nationalism with nationalism in twentieth-century Europe, specifically with the Nazi movement, that co-opted archaeology in trying to create a super-state. Later (1998b, 2000a, 2008) Lemche likened Dever's attempt to define *ancient* Israelite ethnicity with both Israeli and Nazi propaganda.

It is in the light of all the above that Dever (and others) suggested that some revisionist works bordered on anti-Semitism. At best, they have consistently resisted writing the new, archaeologically based histories of ancient Israel that some of them once envisioned, almost always when they are undertaken by Israeli or American scholars. An explanation is needed if we are to get beyond the current impasse.

The Postmodern Challenge to History

In the background of all the above discussions from the early 1980s onward, there lurked the specter of postmodernism, although the phenomenon was rarely acknowledged (or even recognized by most observers). Postmodernism is notoriously difficult to define, largely because its fundamental impulse is to defy all categorizations. It is more readily characterized by what it is against rather than what it is for.[11]

Postmodernism rejects all that "modernity" is assumed to have stood for, essentially the Enlightenment tradition of reason, science, individualism, progress, and, eventually, capitalism and the modern industrial state. In postmodernist discourse, these are all "social constructs," that is, fictions, false ideologies. Thus there is no absolute knowledge of anything.

In the words of a principal spokesman of postmodernism, Jean Francois Lyotard, one's attitude must be "incredulity toward all metanarratives." Obviously *the* great metanarrative in the Western cultural tradition is the Bible. And since texts are constructed and must thus be "deconstructed," the Bible's claims to historicity and authority are to be rejected. For biblical studies, this critique mostly took the form of New Literary criticism. For many of its practitioners, what the text is thought to say is immaterial (i.e., not available). We must ask only how the text is *able* to say what it says, that is, how it functions conceptually and in what cultural context. According to various postmodernist theorists, "there is nothing outside the text" (Derrida). A text is a "signifier," even a "zero-signifier" (Barthes, with other advocates of semiotics). A text "is not an aesthetic structure"; it is a "signifying practice," not an object but "a work and a game" (Lévi-Strauss). "Textual meaning is not an objective property, but it is rather a product of the interpretive strategy brought to bear on it" (Fish). "We need to suspend our assumption that our words refer to things" (Derrida). In semiotic readings we have only "the endless slippage of meaning and interpretation" (Ward). Deconstruction ("close reading") reveals that "the text always undoes the argument it is ostensibly making" (Adam). The purpose of deconstruction is "through and through a messianic affirmation of the coming of the impossible" (Adam). The concept of an "author" no longer exists; he or she is dead (Barthes). "There is no 'the' text" (Adam).[12]

The latest device of the biblical revisionists is to deflect the discussion from history to what is becoming the newest fad: cultural memory. Lemche, for instance, is forthright in stating how this works:

> Cultural memory is not history—a mistake often made—but rather deals with the way people construct their history. It is a different matter whether or not this construction has much or little to do with what actually happened, something of little interest to students of cultural memory.[13]

In the same collection of essays in which Lemche's quote appears (ironically titled *The Historian and the Bible*), Hans Barstad observes that cultural-memory studies really mean the end of history. As he puts it, "If we want to retain the term 'history' at all, we cannot refrain from discussing whether or not past events are 'true' in a positivistic sense."[14]

In whatever guise—postcolonialism, postmodernism, deconstruction, ideological criticism, New Literary criticism, semiotics, New History,

radical feminist readings, or reception history/cultural memory studies—
the fundamental presuppositions about how to read texts are virtually
identical (politically correct). (1) There is no external reality to which the
text refers. (2) Texts refer only to other texts in an endless hermeneutical
circle. (3) There is no intrinsic meaning in texts, no discernible authorial
intent. (4) All meanings are subjective inferences, culturally conditioned
(i.e., constructs). (5) There are no facts, only interpretations.

These assertions appear so extreme that we might be accused of caricaturing postmodernists and biblical revisionists. Yet all these and similar
statements are typical of recent discourse and can easily be documented.
The challenge for history-writing, which cannot be avoided, is whether
such skepticism toward reading texts makes *any* history possible, at least
a history of events. The answer is that it does not. As Thompson put it in a
moment of candor:

> There is no more "ancient Israel." History no longer has room for it. This
> we do know. And now, as one of the first conclusions of this new knowl-
> edge, "biblical Israel" was in its origin a Jewish concept.[15]

Those who think this is nihilism have a point. If there are no facts, there
is no history of events to be written. This is ideology, not honest, critical
scholarship.

New Literary criticism and similar postmodernist approaches to reading texts did not make many inroads in biblical studies until the 1990s.
But their radical skepticism developed at the same time that a number of
biblical scholars were embracing what came to be called minimalism or
revisionism (below). A heated exchange of views in 1995 in the prestigious
Journal of Biblical Literature between Davies, Thompson, and Provan can
now seen to be a bellwether.[16]

The same year there appeared a long two-part review article by Dever
severely critiquing several biblicists for what he saw as antihistorical
trends. Then there were published in short order Whitelam's *The Invention of Ancient Israel: The Silencing of Palestinian History* (1996), Lemche's
The Israelites in History and Tradition (1998a), and Thompson's *The Mythic
Past: Biblical Archaeology and the Myth of Israel* (1999).[17]

In 2001 Dever launched a full-scale attack on these works, arguing
that the impetus lay in a thinly disguised postmodern agenda, that is, an
extreme skepticism that amounted to nihilism with regard to writing any

history of ancient Israel. The poorly informed and heavily ideological attacks on archaeology in Israel and on Israeli and American archaeologists were seen as particularly ominous. The biblicists of the Copenhagen and Sheffield schools (all members of the European Seminar and beginning to be known as revisionists) retaliated in Fritz and Davies's 1996 volume and Grabbe's 1997 volume.[18]

As an example of how some revisionist biblical scholars have attempted to discredit the archaeological evidence and the archaeologists who have produced it, one may note Lemche's book *The Old Testament between Theology and History* (2008). The title and the reputation of the author would lead one to believe that this work would focus on a nontheological approach to a new history of ancient Israel. The allegedly minimal evidence of the biblical text might be supplemented by archaeological data, which all agree is our only other source. Instead, we find in the text a caricature of only a few pages, citing Dever once only to dismiss him as an old-fashioned "biblical archaeologist" and citing Finkelstein four times in passing. No other archaeologist is cited, and nowhere does Lemche cite any of the primary archaeological data, even that readily available in numerous handbooks. Then he appends an amateurish sixty-page "archaeological history of Palestine" that reads like a term paper, again without a single archaeological reference.

One wonders why a reputable biblical scholar, but who has no archeological training, no relevant field experience, no firsthand acquaintance with the material culture data, would presume to write such a history. This only obfuscates the issues, and it is precisely the kind of monologue that prevents us from moving on to a dialogue and *real* histories of ancient Israel. Does this little exercise reflect willful ignorance, hostility to new data, simply a misguided ideology? Unfortunately, this is not an isolated case, and the misuse of archaeology is one of the reasons why works like the present one must be undertaken.

That little has changed can be seen in Lemche's recent return to the topic of ethnicity, where it all began in the early 1990s. Here (2012) he claims that the Hebrew Bible is our only source for defining "Philistines," and the evidence there is niggardly. He completely ignores that fact that *volumes* have been written in the last twenty years defining Philistines and Philistine history in detail. Again, this can only be understood as ignorance, and it disqualifies those guilty as participants in any dialogue. If archaeologists must go it alone as historians of ancient Israel, they will.

Lemche cites with approval Oestigaard 2007, who accuses Dever in particular, but also some Israeli archaeologists, of distorting archaeology to undergird Zionist claims to the land of Palestine—all because they seek to identify *ancient* Israelite ethnicity. Oestigaard likens Dever's approach to that of the infamous Nazi archaeologist Gustaf Kossinna, who attempted to use archaeology to document a super race: it "rests on the same paradigm." Oestigaard's work throughout is a gross caricature of "biblical archaeology" in Israel, based on statements forty years old and other quotations that are distorted but actually advocate the sort of secular, "scientific" archaeology that she envisions. The entire diatribe is based on the notion that archaeology cannot *define* ethnicity, that the attempt to do so is racist. Such fanaticism is difficult to understand, unless it results from the determination to erase "Israel" from history. This echoes Lemche and Whitelam, as well as Thompson (whom she acknowledges as an advisor).[19]

Dever was the first to identify the European protagonists specifically with postmodernism, even though the Seminar volumes had alluded to it as early as 1997 (above). In time, some Seminar members came around to challenging the identification (especially Lemche), but eventually it was conceded that postmodernism had been a factor in revisionism and that extreme postmodernist views would indeed mean an end to history-writing.

Meanwhile, Barr's magisterial state-of-the-art assessment *History and Ideology in the Old Testament: Biblical Studies at the End of a Millennium* (2000) devoted nearly two hundred pages to an analysis of the biblical revisionists as postmodernists. He finds their assertions "unconvincing," "without factual evidence," "ideologically-driven," "incredibly naïve," "dismissive of archaeology," "too absurd to be taken seriously," and "simply wrong."[20]

In 2005 another analysis of trends in Hebrew Bible studies appeared, John Collins's *The Bible after Babel: Historical Criticism in a Postmodern Age*. Here not only was postmodernism acknowledged; it was said to have prevailed. That may be. But postmodernism is best understood as essentially a theory of knowledge according to which there *is* no knowledge. Its full-scale adoption would mean the collapse of history, the end of any history-writing, as a number of scholars have begun to understand.

Already in 1997 distinguished historian Georg Iggers had published his *Historiography in the Twentieth Century: From Scientific Objectivity to the Postmodern Challenge* (German original in 1993). Iggers argued persuasively that, despite some caveats, writing history is not all about ideology, that good historians in practice still assume that an account of actual events is their goal and that it is obtainable within reason. As Iggers puts it:

> This distinction between truth and falsehood remains fundamental to the work of the historian. The concept of truth has become immeasurably more complex in the course of recent critical thought. To be sure the postulate of "an absolute objectivity and scientificity of historical knowledge is no longer accepted without reservation." Nevertheless the concept of truth and with it the duty of the historian to avoid and to uncover falsification has by no means been abandoned. As a trained professional he continues to work critically with the sources that make access to the past reality possible.[21]

In conclusion, it must be pointed out that the more radical forms of postmodernism were passé in many intellectual circles already by the turn of the millennium. There never was a real-life "postmodern condition" (Lyotard 1984), only an "ism"—an isolated movement among a few leftist malcontents, mostly Europeans. For historians, postmodernism was, as the historian Novick suggests, only "symbolic of a circumstance of chaos, confusion, and crisis, in which everyone has a strong suspicion that conventional norms are no longer viable, but no one has a clear sense of what is in the making."[22]

To be fair, however, is there anything to be learned from the postmodernist challenge, which still has some resonance among younger scholars brought up during its onslaught against all the humanistic disciplines in the past generation or so? (It never had any significant impact on the sciences.) And do the biblical revisionists, although naively borrowing its ideology and rhetoric, have a point after all?

The short answer is no. All that postmodernism and biblical revisionism really have to say to historians (and archaeologists) is that all accounts of the past are subjective, all histories partial and provisional. Good scholars have always known that, even if they sometimes failed to see all the implications. Skepticism about the reliability of traditional texts was not invented by postmodernists, nor can it be elevated into a method. As for "incredulity toward metanarratives," postmodernism sought relentlessly to impose *itself* as a metanarrative. Furthermore, both mainstream biblical scholars and Syro-Palestinian, Levantine, or "biblical" archaeologists had outgrown *any* overarching dependence on literal readings of the biblical narrative by the early to mid-1980s—well before postmodernism or biblical revisionism appeared on the scene.

Meanwhile, members of the European Seminar, all revisionists, continue to reject the biblical narratives as genuine historical sources—too late and too tendentious—and to call for writing new histories of Israel. But their "Israel" remains an ideological construct, and their most recent publications are equally ideological. The revisionists often deny that they constitute a school, yet a list of publications of the Copenhagen International Seminar is remarkably consistent and instructive:

- Philip R. Davies, *Rethinking Biblical Scholarship* (2013)
- Niels Peter Lemche, *Biblical Studies and the Failure of History* (2013)
- Thomas L. Thompson, *Biblical Narrative and Palestine's History: Changing Perspectives in Biblical Interpretation* (2014)
- Ingrid Hjelm and Thomas L. Thompson, eds., *Biblical Interpretation beyond Historicity* (2016a)
- Ingrid Hjelm and Thomas L. Thompson, eds., *History, Archaeology and the Bible Forty Years after "Historicity"* (2016b)
- Emanuel Phoh, *Syria-Palestine in the Late Bronze Age: An Anthropology of Politics and Power* (2016)

To these may be added Emanuel Phoh and Keith W. Whitelam, eds., *The Politics of Israel's Past: The Bible, Archaeology and Nation-Building* (2013), and Niels Peter Lemche, *The Old Testament between Theology and History: A Critical Survey* (2008; discussed above).

All the hallmarks of a self-conscious revolutionary movement—a school—are clear here.

1. A new paradigm, an ideology focusing on the Bible and "historicity," promoted tirelessly through escalating rhetoric.
2. The assertion, largely unsubstantiated, that the Hebrew Bible is a "late, Hellenistic construct," an exercise in Jewish self-identification.
3. A conscious identification with "Palestinian" history, ancient and modern.

4. Invoking archaeology, without any credentials or actual use, while demeaning real archaeologists.
5. Claiming the victory.

Lately, even the New Testament narratives and the historicity of Jesus of Nazareth have been called into question by Hjelm, Thompson, and others, again in the Copenhagen International Symposium and other publications.

None of this ongoing campaign is mainstream in biblical studies anywhere, and, despite its cursory appeal to archaeology, it contributes nothing to writing any history of a *real* ancient Israel—but rather denies its reality and even the legitimacy of the effort. Therefore, no critical evaluation of the foregoing literature is relevant to our task here.

In the interlude, the only recent putative history of ancient Israel is an evangelical work, Arnold and Hess's *Ancient Israel's History: An Introduction to Issues and Sources* (2014). This work, however, is a series of programmatic essays. Far from the history envisioned here, it makes scant use of archaeology and therefore will not be considered here. One new possible prolegomenon is the German scholar Reinhard Gregor Kratz's *Historical and Biblical Israel: The History, Tradition, and Archives of Israel and Judah* (2015), largely a literary analysis that is also outside our purview here. The same may be said of Ernst Axel Knauf and Philippe Guillaume's *A History of Biblical Israel: The Fate of the Tribes and Kingdoms from Merenptah to Bar Kochba* (2015). This work is a straightforward analysis of the theme of "biblical Israel," seen as a product of Achaemenid rule of the province of Yehud.

Finally, Hermann Michael Niemann's *History of Ancient Israel, Archaeology and Bible: Collected Essays* (2015) is a series of previous essays, several of them attempting to synthesize certain biblical texts with archaeological sites and data. This is a learned work, and one to be commended for attempting to undertake some dialogue. But it remains logocentric, using archaeological data secondhand and often in an unreliable manner. For instance, Niemann discusses Gezer Strata XI–IX following Finkelstein but citing none of the Gezer excavators or even other mainstream scholars. Thus he claims that Strata X–IX were destroyed by the Egyptians in the last half of the tenth century, "as most accept" (2015, 126). The fact is that only Finkelstein's idiosyncratic low chronology asserts such a late date, and Strata X–IX were not destroyed at all. It is Stratum VIII that was destroyed in the late tenth century, presumably by Shoshenq.[23]

This is only one example, but it underlines the essential fact that even the bestintentioned biblicists may not be qualified to make balanced judgments based on exceedingly complex archaeological data. We need a true dialogue between specialists—not any more monologues. Archaeologists do not make pronouncements about biblical studies, much less offer syntheses. Biblicists should be similarly realistic. What seems lacking is any understanding that modern archaeological data are at least as complex as the biblical texts.

In a long chapter on how archaeology might contribute to new histories of ancient Israel and Judah (2015, 23–61), Niemann cites only the views of Finkelstein (and other biblical revisionists). He completely ignores leading archaeologists such as Ben-Tor, Dever, Faust, Gitin, Killebrew, Mazar, Stager, and others who have written voluminously on the subject since 1990. Finally, he shows no familiarity with the theories, methods, and results of modern archaeology in Israel as it is practiced by the majority, by Israelis or others working in Israel (now almost exclusively Americans).

It is worth noting that all of the above recent literature is by scholars who are biblicists. None are specialists in ancient Near Eastern history or anthropologists or individuals with any training or experience in modern archaeology. It should be obvious that any *archaeological history of Israel and Palestine* (the revisionists' own term) will have to be written by a professional archaeologist. The burgeoning data simply cannot be comprehended by nonspecialist "armchair archaeologists."

Notes

1. Grabbe 1998, 80–100.
2. Grabbe 2001a. The controversy over date had not abated. Somewhat later, Borstad said: "I have not found one single argument in his [Lemche's] article that really can be said to support a dating to Hellenistic times" (2008, 89).
3. Grabbe and Haak 2001.
4. Grabbe 2003c, 311.
5. Uehlinger 2005, 285–86.
6. The edited volume is Grabbe 2007a; the authored is Grabbe 2007b.
7. Grabbe 2008a, 2010. Lemche, however, as late as 2010, was still insisting on answering the question of archaeology and history, "We couldn't see much happening that allowed for a new vista on the subject" (2010b, 150). This is simply

willful ignorance, and it should disqualify one as a participant in the debate. Ben-Tor 1992 and Levy 1995 are never mentioned, nor are Stern 1993 and 2008. Even H. Weippert 1988 is only mentioned twice in passing.

8. See ch. 1 above, with reference to mainstream histories by Soggin (2001), Miller and Hayes (2006), Liverani (2007), as well as a few evangelical works. Useful prolegomena were Day 2004, Williamson 2007, Barstad 2008, and especially Grabbe 2007b. See also a few putative guidebooks (Banks 2006; Moore and Kelle 2011), which, however, demonstrated too little critical use of archaeology to be of much use, unaware of how it had become a primary source for history-writing.

9. Lemche 1997, 130; see also 150–55.

10. Carroll 1997, 100.

11. Postmodernist literature is vast, but for a convenient (and sympathetic) introduction see Lemert 1997, with full references. For trenchant critiques, see Windschuttle 1997; Kimball 2004. For the impact of postmodernism on the Western cultural tradition, see Tarnas 1991; Gress 1998. For examples of critiques from historians and literary critics, see Iggers 1997; Ellis 1989. For critiques from biblicists, see Barton 1996; Barr 2000. The only extensive critique of postmodernism from the perspective of Levantine archaeology is Dever 2001, 6–52, 245–79. Many think the whole discussion passé. Carter and Levy dismiss the whole discussion as "intellectual squabbling." They propose to solve the "maximalist-minimalist" debate simply by adopting anthropological models and communicating better with those of postmodernist persuasion (Levy 2010b, 9–11; Carter and Levy 2010, 207). One wonders if they have ever tried reasoning with postmodernists. Carter's and Levy's "pragmatism" really amounts to *science*, the rejection of which is the essence of postmodernism.

12. See Adam 1995, 18, 19, 27, 31, 69; Barthes 1988, 7; Derrida 1976, 158; Foucault 1980, 154; Lemert 1997, 117 (cf. 95–97); Lévi-Strauss 1963; Ward 2003, 78. For an orientation to New Literary criticism, see Exum and Clines 1993 and essays there. Clines opines "We float on a raft of signifiers under which we signifieds slide playfully like porpoises; but we have to live *as if* the foundations were solid all the way down to bedrock" (Clines 1993, 90). There is no "right" interpretation of a text. Biblical interpreters must devote themselves henceforth to "producing interpretations they can sell" (87), a "goal-oriented hermeneutic" (85). For a critique, see Dever 2001, 10–19. Needless to say *no* history from texts, much less things, can be written on the basis of such relativism. On postmodernism as the impetus, see ch. 1 above.

13. Lemche 2010a, 12. On cultural-memory studies, see Assmann 1997; Davies 2008; Hendel 2010.

14. Barstad 2010, 8.

15. Thompson 1995, 697.

16. See Davies 1995; Provan 1995; Thompson 1995.

17. Dever 1995d, 1995e. These review articles preceded most of the revision-

ist literature, and they were reacting mainly to Thompson 1992 and Davies 1992. They did not introduce the term minimalist.

18. See Dever 2001; Fritz and Davies 1996; Grabbe 1997 (the latter discussed above). In Fritz and Davies, Thompson's chapter was titled "Historiography of Ancient Palestine and Jewish Historiography: W. G. Dever and the Not So New Biblical Archaeology" (1996). The revisionists have objected angrily to polemics: whose?

19. Oestigaard 2007.

20. Barr 2000, 103–78 and passim.

21. Iggers 1997, 12.

22. Novick 1988, 524.

23. Not surprisingly, Niemann has worked closely with Finkelstein at Megiddo, and he has been co-opted to write a chapter in *Megiddo IV*. Elsewhere his fieldwork seems to consist principally of a twelve-day survey of the Zorah-Eshtaol region in 1995 (together with others, principally biblicists; Niemann 2015, 139).

CHAPTER 2

Prelude: The Physical and Cultural Setting at the End of the Bronze Age

Introduction

Archaeology is fundamentally about physicality, about things. An archaeological approach to history-writing begins with the material world as the context within which human change and the meaning of change—the historical process—can be discerned. At the macro level, this means considering the physical environment of the society being studied: geographical features, arable land, other natural resources, climate, seasonal rainfall patterns, trade and communication routes, and neighboring lands and cultures.

This is not to fall into the trap of geographical determinism, as though geography were destiny. Individual initiative and ideology are in the end significant factors, often the most significant factors in shaping culture and influencing historical events. But these phenomena are grounded in the natural environment in which Homo sapiens exists and flourishes. In anthropological terms, *culture*—which is what distinguishes our species—is essentially an extrasomatic adaptation to the constraints of the natural world, that is, patterned ways of manipulating nature to our advantage. Thus *landscape* encompasses both the natural world as well as our human perception of and response to it.[1]

The Primary Data: The Levantine Landscape

The term *Levant* (from the French *lever*, "to rise," as though in the east) has been used in modern times to describe the areas around the eastern

Mediterranean littoral, viewed, of course, from a European perspective: the northern Levant, or modern Lebanon and Syria; and the southern Levant, or Israel, the West Bank, and Jordan. This was, generally speaking, ancient greater Canaan; Anatolia to the north was peripheral, as was the Egyptian Delta to the southwest. The southern Levant is thus the crucial southwestern end of the legendary Fertile Crescent, the cradle of civilization (fig. 2.1).[2]

The northern and southern Levant constitute a unique landmass, one that has had a profound impact on a long succession of cultures from the Neolithic to the present. Its principal geographical features run longitudinally along a narrow north–south corridor between the Mediterranean and the great Syro-Arabian Desert. Thus Canaan and later Israel formed a tiny land bridge linking two massive continents, Africa and Asia, with their territorial ambitions. Bridges are crucial: heavily trafficked, exploited by conquerors, frequently destroyed but always rebuilt.

Ancient Palestine's destiny was to a large extent determined by its precarious location. Across that land bridge came a succession of peoples: Amorites, Canaanites, Phoenicians, Arameans, Philistines, Israelites, Assyrians, Babylonians, Persians, Greeks, Romans, Byzantines, Muslims, Crusaders, Ottomans, and, finally, modern colonialists. Each was distinct and left its mark; all were partially shaped by the same unchanging natural constraints. Ancient Israel, the small southward extension of the southern Levant whose brief floruit we shall consider here, was no exception. It is with these "deeper swells," below the froth and waves of the surface currents, that the Annales historians construct the *longue durée*.[3]

The Physical Setting

The essential longitudinal zones of the southern Levant as distinguished above consist of the following (using some biblical names, even if secondary; see fig. 2.1).

1. The Coastal Plain. From north to south this consists of the Phoenician plain, the narrow plains of Akko and Sharon, and the wider Philistine plain down to the eastern Sinai Desert.

To the north the mountains (below) fall off sharply to the plain, but access to good timber and a few natural harbors favored maritime trade (as with the Phoenicians). Farther south there are rich alluvial soils and good rainfall (25–30 inches annually), but shifting sand dunes and

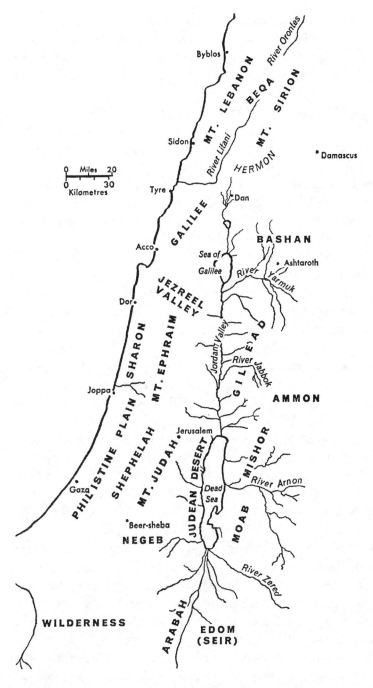

Fig. 2.1. The geographical regions of Israel and Judah (Aharoni 1967, map 2)

marshes limited exploitation in ancient times. Still farther south, the wider Philistine plain facilitated communication, and its rich soils and abundant rainfall (15–25 inches annually) made it the breadbasket of ancient Palestine, effectively dominated by the Philistines through the Iron Age.

Between the coastal plain and the central range (below), there lie low foothills running from the Sharon to the Philistine plain, called the Shephelah (Hebrew: "low-lying"). This was the most significant region in Judah in the Iron Age because of its rich resources and strategic location.

2. The Lebanon Range. The second longitudinal zone lies inland from the coastal plain, designated the Lebanon Range. From north to south it consists of Mount Lebanon; the hills thrusting up from the narrow Mediterranean plain as high as 6,000 feet; the hills of Upper and Lower Galilee, ranging from 3,000 to 2,000 feet, respectively, mountainous but with defensible positions, many open valleys with good soils, and rainfall of 25–40 inches annually; the fertile hill country of Samaria (Mount Ephraim), the heartland of ancient Israel, generally below 3,000 feet and well watered (25–30 inches of rainfall annually); the more marginal hill country of Judah sloping from circa 2,600 feet at Jerusalem down toward the northern Negev Desert, with rainfall diminishing as well, from 5 inches to a marginal 8–10 inches; and the Negev Desert mountains, arid and generally uninhabitable except for isolated forts (fig. 2.2).

3. The Rift Valley. This deep valley formed long ago by tectonic activities extends some 3,700 miles from southern Turkey all the way to the Zambezi River in Mozambique. In the middle portion the Rift Valley is drained by the Orontes River in Syria, in Israel by the Jordan Valley (including the Sea of Galilee and the Dead Sea). At the shores of the Dead Sea, the elevation is some 1,230 feet below sea level.

On both sides of the rift there arise mountain ranges or cliffs as high as 6,500 feet. The western heights in Syria (and in Upper Galilee in Israel) are called the Lebanon Range (above), while those opposite the valley are called the Anti-Lebanon Range (in Syria and Jordan; below). Beyond the latter the vast desert begins. Thus we have a relatively narrow strip of land running through the Rift Valley and its surrounding ravines, linking Africa with Asia. The valley features from north to south the Beqaʻa (Hebrew "to split") in Lebanon and Syria, several hundred feet above sea level and drained by the Orontes River; the Huleh Basin and the sources of

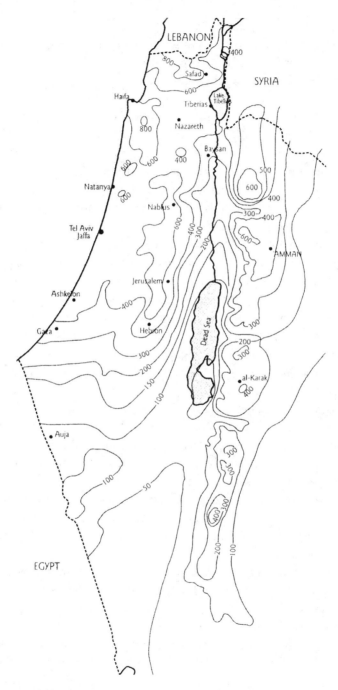

Fig. 2.2. Rainfall map showing isohyets in mm (MacDonald 2000, fig. 9)

the Jordan River; and the Jordan Valley, drained by the Sea of Galilee and the lower Jordan River flowing south into the Dead Sea, falling from some 650 feet below sea level at the Sea of Galilee to nearly 1,300 feet below sea level at the northern end of the Dead Sea.

To the south is the Arabah, a wide, dry trough gradually ascending to sea level where it ends in the Red Sea, much of it uninhabitable except at its southernmost region. To the north, in Syria, the Beqaʿa is a fertile, well-watered region, densely occupied in antiquity and traversed by a major north–south route, the Via Maris, which ran inland here due to marshes farther south along the coast. The Jordan Valley and the Sea of Galilee, despite copious springs and water supplies, posed a challenge for ancient technology, and south of the sea itself there were few permanent sites (Jericho being an exception). The Dead Sea could be exploited only for salt and possibly for bitumen. The Arabah served mostly as an east–west natural border, although obviously porous.

4. The Anti-Lebanon Range. To the east of the deep Rift Valley lies the counterpart of the mountains on the west side, even higher in altitude, up to 5,000 feet above sea level. From north to south we may designate Mount Sirion and its highest peak, Mount Hermon (more than 9,000 feet); the similarly steep hills of Bashan; the hill country of Gilead, up to some 3,000 feet in elevation; the lower hills of Ammon; the rolling hills of Moab, with tableland some 2,000–4,000 feet above sea level; and the largely desert region of Edom, south of the Dead Sea. The whole area south of the Sea of Galilee was heavily forested on the western slopes in the north, more arid to the south. Although reasonably well watered along its western flanks and drained by several perennial streams (the Yarmuk, Jabbok, Arnon, and Zered), the region was only sparsely occupied in most periods, and in the Iron Age its polities consisted mostly of desert kingdoms. The habitable zone tapers off gradually toward the eastern deserts.

5. The Great Desert. Stretching eastward from the Transjordanian plateau some 300 miles to the Euphrates River is the vast Syro-Arabian Desert, inhabited mostly by pastoral nomads and a few oasis dwellers.

6. The Jezreel Valley. The only transverse physical feature of the southern Levant is the Jezreel Valley, which cuts across from the bay around Haifa on the coast today to the Jordan Valley south of the Sea of Galilee. While blessed with deep, rich alluvial soils, the valley lies low—barely above sea level to the west, falling below that level at Beth-Shean—and is poorly drained. It was so marshy in antiquity that virtually all the settlements were in the low hills ringing the valley.

Fractured Topography; Fractured History

It is clear that the southern Levant, the homeland of ancient Israel and her closest neighbors, was in many ways inhospitable. The country west of the Jordan is small—about 250 miles from north to south. At its widest point (near the southern end of the Dead Sea), it is only some 90 miles across. But the southern third of the country comprises the barren Negev Desert, uninhabitable for the most part. The coastal plain north of Tel Aviv is only 25 miles wide, further constricted here and there by marshes to the west and the Samaria hills to the east. The central part of the hill country—Judea, Samaria, and the hills of Galilee—is the heartland, but it is mountainous and broken up by deep ravines that make travel and communication difficult. The only east–west feature in the country, the Jezreel Valley in the north, was too marshy and malarial in antiquity to be occupied. The subtropical Jordan Valley is flanked by steep banks, and the river could not be exploited with primitive technology. The broken topography and starkly differing regional conditions of the country meant that it was scarcely ever really united, with regional factions constantly vying throughout history for scarce resources.

A "Land of Milk and Honey"

All ancient economies were agricultural, so arable lands with good soils and adequate rainfall were essential. But in the southern Levant few regions were ideal. The coastal plain to the south was poorly drained and marshy, the northern portion nearly nonexistent because of the mountains verging almost on the sea. We have noted the inhospitality of the Jezreel and Jordan Valleys. The central mountainous regions had good soils in the intermontane valleys, but the shallow rocky soils of the hillsides were difficult to till and plant without laboriously building terraces. Here and there, however, deep rich *terra rosa* soils did exist, particularly in the Shephelah, or western foothills.

The fractured topography is also reflected in the extremes in elevation. The Dead Sea is almost 1,300 feet below sea level, the Sea of Galilee 650 feet below sea level, the hills of Upper Galilee some 4,000 feet above sea level, and the heights of Mount Hermon more than 9,000 feet above sea level. The hills of Transjordan are similar in height.

Much of the southern Levant was a marginal, arid or semi-arid region suitable only for pastoral nomadism, with annual rainfall of circa 4–8 inches. In Israel and Judah there were no significant rivers or perennial streams (except for the Jordan; above). Most riverbeds were wadis, dry much of the year, then flooded briefly and unusable during the rainy seasons. The annual rains varied greatly, and there was often too little water or too much. In any case, all the rain fell from mid-October to late April, and the long summer months were entirely dry. Temperatures could rise to 130 degrees Fahrenheit in the Negev and the Jordan Valleys, to 100 degrees along the coast, and even to 90–95 degrees in the hill country. In drought years, perhaps one in five, even the winter rains failed (fig. 2.2).

Two Kingdoms

The fundamental structure of this history of "Israel" will be governed by the assumption that from the beginning there were two polities—Israel and Judah—whose differing developments were due in part to differences in their natural environment.[4] Let us, therefore, look at these differences in more detail, especially with respect to the central hill country. (Lower and Upper Galilee were part of the northern kingdom as well, but there the environmental differences are apparent; see above.) Again, some biblical names, although from secondary sources, cannot be avoided. Likewise, the biblical notion of "all Israel" may be difficult to avoid, even though as shall be seen it is a relatively late and tendentious construct of the southern parties that have predominately shaped the biblical tradition.

1. Israel (Mount Ephraim). The hill country here stretches from the southern reaches of the Jezreel Valley some 40–50 miles south to the vicinity of Bethel near Jerusalem, bounded to the west by the foothills above the Sharon plain, and to the east by steppe land falling off toward the deep Jordan Valley, a maximum width of about 30 miles.

The northern portion, from Megiddo to Shechem, consists of relatively low rolling hills (up to circa 3,000 feet), formed mostly by Eocene limestone and broken up by several wide intermontane valleys of chalky Senonian limestone, notably the Shechem and Dothan Valleys. With terracing, the hillsides could produce good quantities of olives, grapes, and other crops, while the deep rich *terra rosa* soils in the valleys were good for the cultivation of grains and cereals. The valleys also carried an extensive system of both north–south and east–west roads, along the Sharon and the great Way of the Sea. At the junctions of these roads there developed major towns such Shechem, Tappuah, Tirzah (Tell el-Far'ah North) at the head of the steep Wadi Far'ah, Dothan, and later Samaria.

All these regions were well watered, with annual rainfall of some 25–30 inches, as well as possessing strong springs. The steppes to the east were considerably drier, but they were nevertheless suitable for extensive dry farming and especially for pastoralism (rainfall diminishing from 12–16 inches annually in the uplands to 8–12 inches down toward the Jordan Valley).

The southern region of Mount Ephraim is somewhat different, with higher and more rugged mountain plateaus rising above 3,000 feet in areas such as Mount Baal Hazor. The Cenomanian limestone resists erosion, producing excellent building stones; however, when it does weather, it produces iron-rich *terra rosa* soils. After deforestation, the area could be fairly densely occupied, but settlement was limited by somewhat unpredictable rainfall (circa 20 inches annually) and the fact that roads had to traverse the mountaintops. This was especially true of the main north–south roads, which followed the watershed along which the main towns developed. To the east and west, difficult roads up into the hills provided security.

In summary, Mount Ephraim (later Samaria) possessed all the natural resources for extensive development as a self-sustaining polity. It was isolated enough to be well protected, yet open to trade and cultural influence from Phoenicia to the northwest and the Aramean city-states to the north and northeast. It was characterized by large urban centers such as Megiddo, Ta'anach, Beth-Shean, Tel Reḥov, Dothan, Tell el-Far'ah, Shechem, Shiloh, Gibeon, and other sites, most of them flourishing already in the Early Bronze Age (third millennium BCE). The northern kingdom of Israel and its development in the Iron Age must therefore be understood in terms of the *longue durée* approach favored by Annales historians (above).

2. Judah. The hill country of Judah lies south of the Jerusalem–Gezer line, extending into the hills of the northern Negev near Beersheba, a distance of only some 45 miles. At its widest at this point it is at most 50 miles. Its geology and topography are generally similar to that of Mount Ephraim but with elevations generally below 3,000 feet. It has less rainfall, up to 25 inches annually around Jerusalem (on the watershed) but only 4–12 inches south of Beersheba, below the limit for dry farming and suitable only for pastoralism. Soils at higher elevations in the north are less *terra rosa* than chalky rendzinate clays, deteriorating the farther south one goes. In particular, the mountains of the rugged central range are not easily traversed from west to east, and they fall off sharply to the east of the watershed. For instance, the Judean Desert begins on the outskirts of Jerusalem and descends nearly 4,000 feet into the Jordan Valley in a distance of less than 15 miles. The entire eastern slopes, as well as the southern portion of the hill country, are suitable mainly for pastoralism. Occupation throughout the region was more scattered and more sparse than in the northern hill country. Major towns developed mostly along the north–south road near the eastern edge of the watershed, such as Jerusalem, Beth-Zur, Hebron, and Beersheba.

Judah is essentially an intermediate zone between the Shephelah and the Jordan Valley, more marginal and more isolated than Mount Ephraim and the Samaria hills. Its economy was mixed, featuring horticulture, viticulture, dry farming, and pastoral nomadism. Trade with its neighbors—Philistia to the west and the peoples of Transjordan to the east—was sporadic, and relations could be hostile from time to time. In all periods throughout the Bronze and Iron Ages, Judah lagged behind the north in virtually every aspect of economic, social, and cultural development. That fact, often overlooked by biblicists, historians, and even archaeologists, will turn out to be significant for our subsequent history of Israel and Judah.

The Secondary Data: Perceptions of the Land by the People of the Bible

The inhabitants of ancient Israel and Judah were acutely aware of their environment, more so than we moderns, because their very lives depended upon practical knowledge of the way nature works. Although they lacked our scientific understanding and terminology, they were sophisticated in their own intuitive and experiential way. Happily, some of their popular worldview finds its way into the Hebrew Bible, despite the elitist outlook of its writers and editors. It is this secondary source that an archaeologically based history of Israel may profitably consider.[5]

The Land Itself

The ancients did not know that their land was unique, since they had no basis for comparison (except perhaps for Egypt). Nevertheless they appreciated it for its own qualities, which they indeed knew well. This good land, this "land of promise," was a gift and therefore precious.

That theme resonates through the Hebrew Bible. Moses pleads with Yahweh: "Let me cross over to see the good land beyond the Jordan" (Deut 3:25).[6] He assumes that Yahweh has promised the land, for he says to the people: "God has brought you into the land that he swore to your ancestors, to Abraham, to Isaac, and to Jacob, to give you—a land with fine, large cities that you did not build" (Deut 6:10). It is a land "flowing with milk and honey" (11:9). Deuteronomy 8:7–10 is worth quoting in full:

> For the LORD your God is bringing you into a good land, a land with flowing streams, with springs and underground waters welling up in valleys and hills, a land of wheat and barley, of vines and fig trees and pomegranates, a land of olive trees and honey, a land where you may eat bread without scarcity, where you will lack nothing, a land whose stones are iron and from whose hills you may mine copper. You shall eat your fill and bless the LORD your God for the good land that he has given you.

Several passages that contain the promised-land theme describe the intended territory of the Israelite people in some detail. Thus Deut 1:6–8:

> The LORD our God spoke to us at Horeb, saying, "You have stayed long enough at this mountain. Resume your journey, and go into the hill country of the Amorites as well as into the neighboring regions—the Arabah, the hill country, the Shephelah, the Negeb, and the seacoast—the land of the Canaanites and the Lebanon, as far as the great river, the river Euphrates. See, I have set the land before you; go in and take possession of the land that I swore to your ancestors, to Abraham, to Isaac, and to Jacob, to give to them and to their descendants after them."

One should also note the summaries in Josh 10:16–17 and 12:8–24 (the latter a list of Canaanite kings and their cities).

The Hebrew Bible is aware of the natural and cultural boundaries of ancient Israel and Judah. Numbers 34 is the classic text, as Yahweh specifies to Moses what their "inheritance" in Canaan will be: it will stretch from Egypt to the borders of Lebanon (Lebo-hamath). Other texts mention several more specific regions of the land, although they cannot conceive of the modern, empirical classification that we have offered. Here are some examples:

Fig. 2.3. Perceptions of geographical regions in the Hebrew Bible

Region	Text
The Mediterranean ("Great Sea")	Josh 9:1
The "land west of the Jordan"	Josh 12:7
The Sharon plain	1 Chr 5:16; 27:29
The "way of the sea"; "King's Highway"	Isa 9:1; Num 20:17
The Shephelah (foothills of Judah)	Josh 11:16; 15:33–42; 1 Kgs 10:27
The hill country	Josh 11:16; 24:33
The Jordan Valley	Josh 12:7
Galilee	Josh 11:2; 19:35–38
The Jezreel Valley	Josh 17:16; Judg 1:27
The Dead Sea	Gen 19:28; Deut 3:17; Josh 3:16
The Arabah (southern Jordan Valley)	Deut 2:8; 3:8
The "land east of the Jordan"	Josh 13:27
The eastern desert	Judg 6:1–3
Bashan	1 Kgs 4:13; Amos 4:1
Gilead	Deut 3:10; 4:43
Moab	2 Kgs 3:4
Ammon	Num 21:24
Edom	Num 21:4; 34:3–4

Natural conditions of the land are also alluded to in many texts. The unique weather pattern is attributed to Yahweh, who "will open for you his rich storehouse, the heavens, to give the rain of your land in its season and to bless all your undertakings" (Deut 28:12). Yahweh "makes the clouds rise at the end of the earth; he makes lightnings for the rain and brings out the wind from his storehouses" (Ps 135:7). Job 38:22 also mentions "storehouses of snow," thus the concept of the weather being a sort of "overflow" of Yahweh's abundance. Further, the phrase "the early rain and the later rain" (Deut 11:13–17; cf. Jer 5:24) is an apt description of what usually happens. In mid-late October, as the wind shifts around to come in from the Mediterranean, there will be a sudden downpour. Then, after a brief clearing, the winter rains set in seriously. Between early December and the beginning of February, 75 percent of the region's total rain will fall.

The typical daily and seasonal extremes of temperature are described in several texts. Jacob complains about the fact that "by day the heat consumed me, and the cold by night" (Gen 31:40). The fierce dust storms—the sirocco (Hebrew *šārāb*)—that sweeps in from the desert is decried: "a hot wind … from … the bare heights in the desert" (Jer 4:11). Thus the land is one that "devours its inhabitants" (Num 13:32).

There were not only storms but frequent droughts. Yahweh "will shut up the heavens, so that there will be no rain and the land will yield no fruit" (Deut 11:17). The wadis (riverbeds) we have noted sometimes "dried up because there was no rain in the land" (1 Kgs 17:7). There are wells (Num 21:16) and cisterns (Isa 36:16), but they may fail.

The eternal cycle of the seasons that we have described in some detail is alluded to, but only to recognize two seasons:

> As long as the earth endures,
> seedtime and harvest, cold and heat,
> summer and winter, day and night
> shall not cease. (Gen 8:22)

In the following chapters we shall pursue further how the natural conditions of ancient Canaan impacted the daily life of most people in ancient Israel, especially the ordinary folk who constituted the bulk of the population. There we will indulge in speculation about how ordinary people, not only those who wrote the Bible, felt about their environment, its danger, and its promise.

Canaan at the End of the Bronze Age

As noted above, cultural factors are even more important than geographical factors in shaping human history. But here, too, the physical data are primary, that is, the *archaeological* data, including, of course, the extrabiblical texts that have been brought to light by either deliberate excavation or chance discovery. In any case, it is evident from our data that early Israel, like its nearest neighbors, emerged in the wake of the collapse of the Bronze Age in Canaan in the thirteenth–twelfth century.

The fact is that our knowledge of the Bronze Age and its collapse is almost entirely dependent on the abundant archaeological data now at hand. The biblical texts on this "prehistory" of Israel—principally the stories of patriarchal migrations in Genesis—are of little historical value. The narratives may contain some genuine historical memories, based perhaps on long oral traditions, but the stories were reduced to writing centuries after the events that they purport to describe (ch. 1). Furthermore, the biblical texts are obviously tendentious, intent upon explaining Israel's origins as due to the intervention of Yahweh in history on behalf of his chosen people.

The biblical writers knew little about the Levant in the mid- to late second millennium, except that peoples called Canaanites (and Amorites) had preceded them in the land. The writers were also aware of specific towns or cities that did exist and that we now date to our Middle or Late Bronze Ages, such as Shechem, Bethel, Hebron, and Gerar (Beersheba dates only to the Iron Age). They knew little or nothing of the Egyptian Empire that had reigned in the Amarna age or of the collapse of Egyptian hegemony beginning in the late thirteenth century. In particular, their portrait of Canaan and the Canaanites is a caricature. We must, therefore, begin our narrative about ancient Israel with a synthesis of what we know of Canaan in the Late Bronze Age based on the primary, archaeological data.[7]

The Principal Sites

The major Late Bronze II fourteenth–thirteenth-century archaeological sites in southern Canaan may be listed as follows (figs. 2.4 and 2.5). Since the Transjordanian sites will be discussed in chapter 3 on the Iron I period, we shall concentrate here on sites in Cisjordan.

In synthesizing the material culture from these sites we shall employ a model pioneered by the New Archaeology in the 1970s but often discredited nowadays because of its somewhat mechanistic application: General Systems Theory (GST). This model of cultural change was adopted from the biological sciences, presuming that its description of the function or dysfunction of several subsystems in governing the equilibrium of a biological organism was directly applicable to cultural systems. If one or more of these interrelated, delicately balanced subsystems begins to fail, they feed off each other to create an increasing downward spiral until the

---

Fig. 2.4. Major Late Bronze Age II sites
in southern Canaan or the southern Levant

Israel

Hazor XIV–XIII	Beth-Shemesh IV
Tell Keisan 13	Tel Batash VII–VI
Megiddo VIII–VIIB	Tel Miqne VIIIB–A
Taʿanach	Ashdod XIV
Beth-Shean IXA–VII	Lachish VII–VII
Shechem XIII–XII	Tell Beit Mirsim C_{1-2}
Aphek X_{13-11}	Tel Ḥalif IXA–VIII
Gezer XVI–XV	Tel Seraʿ XI–X
Tel Mevorakh XIII–XII	Tell el-ʿAjjul IIIB

Jordan

Tall Ziraʿa	Tall as-Saʿidiyeh XII
Tell Abu el-Kharaz IX	Deir ʿAlla (Dayr ʿAlla) E
Irbid	Beqaʿa Valley sites
Tell el-Fukhar	Tell el-ʿUmeiri 14–13
Pella	

---

entire system spins out of control and the death of the organism ensues. The key concepts of GST are health and well-being as *equilibrium* and decline and death as *collapse*.[8]

General System Theory in Practice

The GST model in general has been applied experimentally to the end of the Early Bronze Age, and occasionally one finds it mentioned in passing in other studies in our discipline. In particular, the related notion of the collapse of ancient societies (rather than, for instance, destruction) was in vogue briefly in the past generation. It may be time to resurrect a model that could still be of heuristic value if stripped of the reductionist and antihistorical biases of the New Archaeology, now passé. In this case, the relevant subsystems for the archaeologist hoping to analyze ancient sociocultural systems would be:

1. Site type and distribution, including demographic projections
2. Socioeconomic structure
3. Political organization
4. Technology
5. Culture: ideology, literacy, art, religion, ethnicity ("aesthetics")
6. International relations

In the following discussions of the history of ancient Israel and Judah, the GST model will be deliberately employed—an innovation for both biblical studies and archaeology. Its principal relevance will be in its potential for illuminating change and the explanation of change, the essence of history-writing (ch. 1). Initially this model will help to account for the unique cultural and historical milieu in which early Israel emerged. This was the end of the Bronze Age throughout the eastern Mediterranean and the Levantine world, even though we must focus more narrowly on archaeological sites in Israel and Jordan.[9]

Site Type and Distribution

The Late Bronze Age (1500–1200) generally follows the pattern of urban development in the Middle Bronze Age (2000–1500). It is variously subdivided and dated as follows:

LB IA: 1550–1470
LB IB: 1470–1400
LB IIA: 1400–1300
LB IIB: 1300–1200

Another scheme recognizes a transitional phase at the beginning and again on the Late Bronze/Iron I horizon:

LBI: 1550–1400 (Egyptian Eighteenth Dynasty)
LBII: 1400–1300 (Amarna age)
LBIII: 1300–1150 (Egyptian Nineteenth and early Twentieth Dynasties)

After the massive destructions at the end of the Middle Bronze Age, many sites were abandoned briefly in the Late Bronze I period, regaining their former size and importance only by the Late Bronze II phase (1400–1200), if then. Some sites never recovered entirely, and because of the long decline of other sites, some scholars have mistakenly underestimated the urban character of the Late Bronze Age in southern Canaan.[10]

It must be emphasized that all of the sites listed in figure 2.4 above were sizeable towns, and most would qualify as cities by the criteria applicable to this region of the ancient Near East. For instance, Tell Keisan and Megiddo are about 15 acres each, which would suggest a population of some 1,500 people on the usual model; Lachish is about 30 acres, or 3,000 people; Ashdod is some 70 acres, or 7,000 people; and Hazor is the largest, at about 180 acres, or 18,000 people.

Most Late Bronze II sites were smaller, under 10 acres, and most of the new sites founded near the end of the period were small, rural settlements. The overall changes in site size and demography are best understood by comparison with the preceding Middle Bronze II–III period.[11]

Fig. 2.5. Comparison of Middle and Late Bronze Age sites

Middle Bronze	*Late Bronze II*
330 sites known	100 sites known
54 excavated sites	22 excavated sites
16,500 acres built-up area	510 acres built-up area
150,000 est. population	50,000 est. population

A rank-size analysis, which compares the number of settlements with their size and rank in a multitiered society, is also instructive.[12] In the Middle Bronze Age there were fewer very large sites, suggesting a comparatively well-integrated urban system with relatively few centers and a homogeneous polity. By contrast, in the Late Bronze II era there were more medium-sized and smaller-sized sites, indicating in all likelihood a less-integrated system of local, autonomous city-states. Nevertheless, Middle Bronze hill country sites such as Shechem, Shiloh, Beth-Zur, and Hebron were greatly diminished. Some coastal sites such as Aphek and Tell el-ʿAjjul became small Egyptian forts (as did Beth-Shean). Several port towns are also known, such as Tell Abu Hawam, Shiqmona, Tel Nami, Tel Michal, and Tel Mor. The latter situation is precisely that reflected in the most relevant textual evidence we have: the Amarna letters (see below).

There was also a shift in the location of sites in the Late Bronze Age, not only overall, but in terms of regional differences. Surveys have shown that the coastal plain, the Shephelah, and the upper Jordan Valley were densely occupied, although many settlements were small. In Galilee there are very few Late Bronze settlements, none of them urban in character. In the central hill country, heavily occupied in the Middle Bronze Age, there are fewer sites in the Late Bronze Age, and the population may have been dispersed into rural areas or even partly nomadic. All the above shifts in settlement type and distribution from the Middle Bronze to the Late Bronze Age will have significant implications for the decline and end of the latter by the late thirteenth century.

In Transjordan, previous estimates of sparse Late Bronze Age occupation, based largely on early surveys of Glueck and others, must now be revised. Despite the evidence, however, it must be pointed out that Late Bronze occupation on the Transjordanian plateau was relatively scant, just as it was in the hill country west of the Jordan. That is significant, since these are the areas where some scholars seek the origins of the earliest Israelite peoples (ch. 3).

Despite a certain degree of urban renewal in the Late Bronze Age, the decline in overall population from the Middle Bronze Age—from circa 150,000 to 50,000—is striking. Much of that decline may be explained by the abandonment of some sites, as well as the shrinking size and numbers of sites still occupied in the Late Bronze Age. But where did so many of the survivors of the Middle Bronze Age destructions go? They are not likely to have simply disappeared, much less migrated to the marginal zones or to more distant areas of Canaan.

A few scholars posit a growing pastoral nomadic population in western Palestine from circa 1500 to 1200, particularly in the central hill country. This was supposedly the reservoir from which Israel's earliest population was drawn in Iron I; that is, these are pastoral nomads in process of sedentarization (below). This is Finkelstein's view, but he can offer no empirical data mostly because he ignores the considerable evidence on the invisibility of nomads in the archaeological record. Even the most extensive pedestrian surface surveys are unlikely to document nomads or their movements. Sherd scatters may reflect only a farmstead or a pastoral encampment, but they cannot specify the origins of the settlers.

The only evidence Finkelstein might offer for his nomadic theory derives from his own (and others') estimate of some 12,000 people in the hill country in the Late Bronze Age. Taking into consideration the usual estimate of 10 percent for the pastoral nomadic component, based on ethnographic parallels in the Middle East, we would then have a nomadic population of only some 1,200 in the fourteenth–thirteenth century—hardly a "reservoir" from which to draw the 40,000 or so people that we have in the region by the twelfth century.

Finkelstein's "oscillation" theory to explain the population decline from the Early Bronze I into II–III, and from the Middle Bronze III into Late Bronze I, and from Late Bronze II into Iron I (the Proto-Israelite era) is entirely speculative except for his second phase. In Early Bronze IV we do have massive evidence for the abandonment of the urban centers in favor of extensive one-period pastoral encampments in the hinterland and numerous isolated cemeteries. Despite Finkelstein's insistence, there is not a shred of evidence for any such substantial Late Bronze Age pastoralists. The population does seem to have declined, but we do not know how or why.[13]

It is the decidedly urban character of the Late Bronze Age, despite a smaller population, that we must keep in mind. That is seen in several well-documented aspects of the material culture. (1) We have a proliferation of large-scale architecture, especially a series of elaborate patrician houses, large palaces, and monumental temples that outstrip even those of the impressive Middle Bronze Age at numerous sites. (2) Tombs have produced rich assemblages of luxury goods, including exotic imports from Syria, Cyprus, Greece, Crete, Egypt, and even Mesopotamia. (3) An international network of trade throughout the Mediterranean is evidenced by the above imports, especially pottery, but also by precious metals, sculptures, ivories, jewelry, cylinder seals, and the like. Land routes are known to have been supplemented now by maritime trade (several shipwrecks). (4) Finally, a corpus of inscriptions, although small, includes written evidence in Old Canaanite, Akkadian cuneiform, and Egyptian hieroglyphics (below).[14]

The only anomaly in this picture of cosmopolitan wealth, power, and sophistication is what some have regarded as the near total lack of fortifications. In some cases, the massive Middle Bronze Age fortifications could be reused, as no doubt at Hazor, Shechem, and perhaps Megiddo. In the case of a site such as Gezer, the massive Outer Wall seems to have been constructed in the Late Bronze Age. There are also a few other sites where Late Bronze Age city walls were constructed (Tell Abu Hawam, Jaffa, Tell Beit Mirsim, and Ashkelon; cf. Tell el-'Umeiri in Transjordan).[15] Nevertheless, it is clear that many Late Bronze Age sites, even prominent ones such as Lachish, were largely unfortified. The most likely explanation is that Egyptian military control in the Levant throughout the Late Bronze Age simply precluded such defenses (below).[16]

Socioeconomic Structure

The foregoing presentation of the basic sites already suggests an unprecedented elite class, however small. Palaces, rich tombs, a proliferation of imported goods, a variety of art forms, familiarity with writing—all these document a wealthy, cosmopolitan ruling class. In the case of writing, a thirteenth-century cuneiform tablet found at Taʿanach recounts the dealings of a scribal schoolmaster with the son of a nobleman who has not paid him for his services.

Even more decisive written evidence for a highly stratified society comes from the well-known Amarna archive. This consists of some 350 Akkadian cuneiform tablets found in 1887 at Tell el-Amarna in Middle Egypt, letters written by petty princes in Canaan to their overlords in Egypt, notably Amenhotep III (1390–1352) and Amenhotep IV (1352–1336).[17] Some twenty major "central places" (above) or local cities and city-states are mentioned in southern Canaan, including many of the prominent Late Bronze Age sites discussed above. They would include the locations listed in figure 2.6 (* = excavated; see also fig. 2.7).

Fig. 2.6. Major urban centers mentioned in the Amarna letters

*Hazor (XIV)	Gath-padalla
*Akko	*Shechem (XIII)
Hannathon	*Jaffa
Achshaph	*Gezer (XVI)
Shimon	*Jerusalem
*Megiddo (VIII)	*Gath
*Taʿanach (?)	*Ashkelon (21)
Shunem	*Lachish (VIII)
Gina	Gaza
*Beth-Shean (IXA)	Yurza
*Pella (?)	

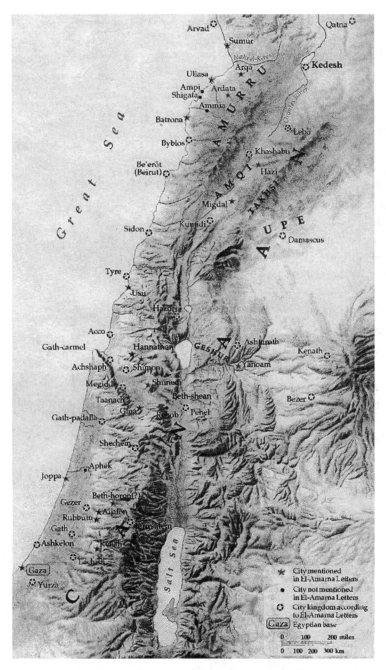

Fig. 2.7. Principal centers in LB Canaan as reflected in the Amarna letters (Rainey and Notley 2006, 79). © Copyright Carta, Jerusalem.

Sometimes the rulers identify themselves as governors but occasionally as kings. Other elites include the resident Egyptian commissioners and envoys. But alongside these officials there also appear other Egyptian officials, such as inspectors of stables or commanders of chariotry, petty officers, archers (including Nubian), scribes, and others. In addition, the palaces and forts would probably have supported a large class of other elites and functionaries.

Prominent among these socioeconomic classes were the Habiru, apparently a motley class of peoples that some have categorized as urban dropouts, landless peasants, nomads, freebooters, highwaymen, and lawless malcontents of all sorts in the countryside.[18] A perusal of the Amarna letters reveals these Habiru (Akkadian *sūtū*) not as an ethnic group, not even as a homogeneous socioeconomic class. They appear variously (1) as inhabitants of the steppes along the eastern borders of the Egyptian Empire in Asia, although not necessarily as pastoralists; (2) they are rebellious, lawless elements, threats to stability; (3) they could be transferred or taken prisoner by Egyptian authorities; (4) they could seize lands, or on occasion they could be ceded land, although they are never portrayed as urbanized; (5) they could be recruited as mercenaries, even serving with infantry and chariots; and (6) they tended to remain at large and sometimes sought refuge in the hill country. Clearly these Habiru were regarded by the Canaanite urban authorities as a serious threat, often blamed for the misfortunes that had to be reported to the Egyptian authorities.

Below (or alongside) these socioeconomic classes were the peasants. In most cases, as in the Middle Bronze Age, a feudal model is not applicable to ancient Canaan, because we have little or no evidence of a landed gentry (although likely). But we do have such a class in the Late Bronze II period, as evidenced by the Amarna correspondence. In the nature of the case, there is little direct evidence of peasants in the archaeological record, because we have scarcely identified or excavated any rural hamlets or farmsteads. Nevertheless, all authorities assume the existence of such a rural element of the population, perhaps even predominant in terms of relative numbers.

Political Organization

The Amarna letters also eloquently document political organization in the Levant in the fourteenth–thirteenth century. The entire area was part of the Egyptian Empire in Asia. The area was not officially annexed, but it was divided into three or four administrative districts, of which the southern one in Palestine was ruled from Kumidi in the north and Gaza in the south. The highest ranking official in these (and other) centers was the *rabisu*, the resident Egyptian high commissioner. Under him were lower Egyptian officials, then the local Canaanite rulers. The Egyptian military contingent kept order but enforced heavy tributes.

It is clear from the Amarna correspondence that Palestine's political landscape was divided into numerous small, competitive city-states, probably as a deliberate Egyptian divide-and-rule policy. The letters reveal in detail the rivalry of the local petty princes, desperately vying with each other for Egyptian favor, all the while undermining their rivals with gossip and intrigue. This situation would have invited widespread corruption and loss of public confidence.

The Amarna letters document, among other mandatory tributes, (1) slaves, numerous "female cupbearers," even wives and sons of the local princes as captives (or hostages); (2) up to 2,000–3,000 silver shekels and payments of gold; (3) jewelry, luxury furnishings, and costly garments; (4) weapons; and (5) grain, foodstuffs, and cattle.

There have been many assessments of Egyptian rule in Canaan, but all stress the dire economic consequences due to the heavy tributes that Egypt demanded. While the Amarna letters belong to the fourteenth century, there can be little doubt that the decline already in evidence there can only have accelerated into the thirteenth century as the Late Bronze Age was tottering to an end.

Larger towns along the coast and in the northern valley were perhaps able to meet their quotas, despite periodic resistance. But the more marginal hill-country regions and the Transjordanian plateau were hard-pressed. The result of Egypt's rapacious economic policies was the continued fragmentation of the local political structure as well as the impoverishment of many areas (below). More than anything else, this contributed to the general decline, which probably began even before the beginning of the Twentieth Dynasty (1295–1186).[19]

Egyptian power was centered in a string of "governors' residencies," essentially forts and garrison towns. These include a number of Late Bronze II excavated sites (see figs. 2.8 and 2.9).

The Aphek residency, for instance, was a massive two-story, multi-roomed structure. Among the finds were Egyptian pottery vessels and

Fig. 2.8. Late Bronze II Egyptian-style residencies

Beth-Shean VI; Palace 1500; commander's residence

Aphek X_{12}; Palace VI/Building 1104

Tel Mor VIII; administrative building

Tell el-Ḥesi City IV (= VIII)

Tel Seraʿ IX; Building 906

Tell Jemmeh J–K

Tell el-Farʿah YR; citadel

Deir el-Balaḥ VII

Tall as-Saʿidiyeh XII; residency, palace

---

written remains in Hittite, Akkadian cuneiform, and Egyptian. The Tel Seraʿ residency (Building 906) produced a group of Egyptian bowls and ostraca inscribed in the Egyptian hieratic script, some recording large quantities of grain paid to the storehouse of the governor. One text refers to "year 20," probably reckoned from the accession year of Ramesses III, thus circa 1165.[20]

A further indication of the extension of Egyptian rule into the beginning of the Iron I period (thus Late Bronze III; above) is the Egyptian residency at Beth-Shean, Level VI, which produced Egyptian inscribed objects as well as a large collection of Egyptian-style pottery produced locally, probably by resident Egyptian potters. This building apparently dates to the reign of Ramesses III (1184–1153). An even later date for the end of Egyptian rule in Canaan is provided by a pedestal of a statue of Ramesses VI (1143–1136) from Megiddo and a cartouche of the same pharaoh found at Lachish.[21]

Higginbotham's study of these residencies is the most thorough. She attempts to characterize the nature of Egyptian rule and interactions with local Canaanite officials in terms of current models such as *core–periphery*, *peer polity*, and *elite emulation*. In any case, Egyptian administration in the fourteenth–thirteenth century seems to have shifted from economic and political domination to more military occupation and direct imperialist rule. The residencies cited above she describes in terms of both "administrative buildings" and "central hall houses" or as a category of "three-room houses" (at Beth-Shean, the Commander's Residence of Level VI).[22]

Bunimovitz has employed the model of Central Place Theory in order to provide a political map of Late Bronze Age Palestine. This model, first

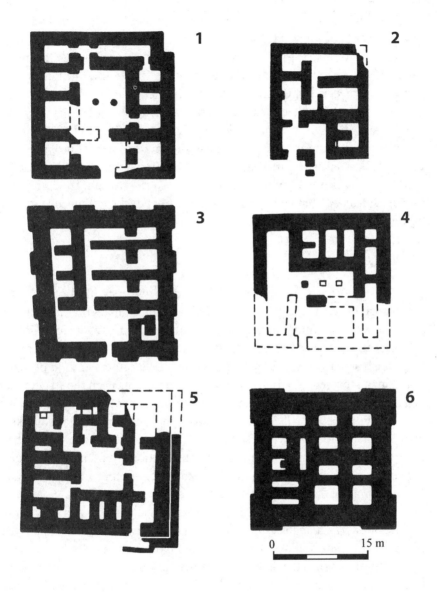

Fig. 2.9. Egyptian-style residencies (after Killebrew 2005, figs. 2.2, 2.4–2.7). 1: Center-Hall House 1500, Beth-Shean VI; 2: Governor's Residence (Palace VI), Aphek X₁₂; 3: Citadel, Tel Mor VIII–VII; 4: Building 906, Tel Seraʿ IX; 5: Building YR, Tell el-Farʿah South; 6: Fortress, Deir el-Balaḥ VII

developed for flat terrain in the Netherlands, attempts to plot the location of a number of dominant sites in an area, region by region. Then drawing Thiessen polygons, these sites are linked together geometrically, presumably showing the territory that each ruled. Rarely used in Levantine archaeology because of the more hilly terrain, Central Place Theory in this case provides a map that corresponds reasonably well with a map of sites drawn on the basis of the Amarna letters (figs. 2.6 and 2.7). In this analysis, we have a cluster of ten to twenty semiautonomous centers approximately 25 miles apart, each dominating an area of 1,000 square miles or less. Here again, the fragmented political landscape of southern Canaan is graphically illustrated.[23] That will be a factor in the final decline of the area when we discuss that further below.

Technology

Archaeology is particularly well suited to deal with one kind of history, the history of technology, which was even more fundamental to culture and survival in antiquity than in modern times. One aspect of technological innovation is architecture. We have already mentioned the elaborate, well-constructed villas, places, and administrative centers of Late Bronze Age Canaan (as well as temples; see below). Surpassing even the structures of the Middle Bronze Age, these required a mastery of large-scale building techniques, especially skill with surveying, masonry, timber works, plaster, and the decorative arts. Many of these structures would not be equaled until the Roman period. Their construction would have been not only costly but would have required the existence of other socioeconomic classes alongside those already documented.

The study of the ubiquitous pottery that archaeologists must deal with depends in part on analyses of ceramic technology. The Late Bronze Age ceramic repertoire follows that of the highly developed Middle Bronze Age. Although some forms are now somewhat degenerate in form and finish, they are still very well wheelmade and are fired in efficient kilns. The homogeneity of the repertoire indicates a standardized industry that was capable of supplying a large commercial market. In addition, several specialized forms are developed and mass-produced, notably the "Canaanite" store jars in which wine and oil were transported all over the eastern Mediterranean world. The imported pottery that is so conspicuous in the Late Bronze period has been discussed above.

Culture: Ideology, Literacy, Art, Religion, Ethnicity

Under the broad category of culture we may consider several other aspects of life in Late Bronze Age Canaan. Throughout this work we will use the ethnic term *Canaanite* to refer generally to the peoples of the geographical entity defined above as Canaan (or the Levant). Some have objected to its use as an ethnic designation, because the textual data are somewhat ambiguous. There is also a tendency in today's postmodern climate to regard ethnic boundaries as fluid and often to deny that ethnicity can be identified in the archeological record (ch. 3). Nevertheless, there is no better term available, and if we can recognize Hittites, Hurrians, Arameans, Egyptians, and other peoples of the region in antiquity, why not Canaanites?[24]

The use of the term *Canaanite* here, however, is principally a geographic designation for the northern and southern Levant. It must not be construed to imply a homogeneous population throughout the region, because we know how diverse the population was. We have clear textual evidence for resident Hittites, Hurrians, and, as we have seen, Egyptians throughout Canaan in the Late Bronze Age. All these ethnic groups are referred to by name in the Amarna letters. Indeed, this correspondence regularly refers to the country as Hurru, the land of the Hurrians. Hurrian names occur frequently in texts of all kinds. Finally, it has been suggested that the Late Bronze I Cypriot-style bichrome ware might have been manufactured by resident Cypriot craftsmen in branch factories along the Levantine coast.[25] Even Greek sailors were likely to have been known now and then.

Clearly we confront an international, multicultural, polyglot society in Late Bronze Age Canaan. For instance, the scribes who wrote the Amarna letters to the Egyptian court spoke Canaanite and used the local alphabetic script, but they wrote in Akkadian cuneiform script, and they were also familiar with Egyptian idioms. There must have been scribal schools, at least in some areas, although literacy would not have been widespread.

Apart from the Amarna correspondence, our largest literary corpus is found in the thousands of cuneiform mythological, legal, and historical texts found at Ugarit on the Syrian coast, dating to the fourteenth–thirteenth century. The language may not be best described as Canaanite, but it reflects the culture that we designate here as Canaanite, although in its most elite urban form. Both this alphabetic cuneiform and the Akkadian cuneiform script are in evidence, certainly in the northern Levant and also to some extent in the south. In addition, we have several inscriptions in the alphabetic Proto-Sinaitic (or Old Canaanite) script.[26]

The prevailing ideology in the region was no doubt derived from the long West Semitic cultural tradition of the region, but the lore of the Eastern Semitic world (Mesopotamia) is also in evidence in literary traditions. Both the Hittites and Hurrians who are well represented were non-Semitic peoples, that is, Indo-Europeans from north Syria and Anatolia. We shall see more of this cosmopolitan ideology when we look at religion and cult.

The art of Canaan in the Late Bronze Age was international, sophisticated, varied, and in wide evidence. At every urban site, and especially in the rich tombs of the period, we have superb works in basalt sculpture, precious and semiprecious metals, glyptic art (seals and cylinder seals), ivory carving, jewelry, and decorated local and imported pottery.

Temples and cultic paraphernalia are more evident in the Late Bronze Age than in any other period in Canaan. Some twenty or more temples of the era have been excavated thus far, several existing contemporaneously at a single site. They incorporate Egyptian elements in some cases, Syrian or Mesopotamian elements in other cases. Some are *migdol* (fortress) temples; others are long-room bipartite or tripartite temples; still others are broad-room or square "maze" temples. Several of these temples are rebuilds of Middle Bronze Age temples, but others were newly established in the Late Bronze Age and then underwent several phases of construction. At some sites, such as Hazor, Beth-Shean, and Lachish, there are three contemporary temples in somewhat limited exposures, suggesting that several more might have existed at each site. Perhaps each deity had his or her own temple (see below).

Cult paraphernalia consists mostly of standing stones, altars, offering tables, basins, and votive offerings. Thus the veneration of the deities apparently involved animal sacrifices, food-drink offerings, and the presentation of votives or costly gifts. Found in both temple and domestic contexts, numerous terra-cotta female figurines suggest that cultic practices were concerned with the notion of fertility or plenty—ensuring human reproduction as well as the fertility of the animals and fields, upon which the entire economy depended.

Here we are unusually fortunate in having a large corpus of contemporary texts, many of which are cultic and mythological in nature.

The Ugaritic texts, noted above, give many details about sacrificial and other cultic rites. More significantly, they provide us with extensive textual portraits of many of the deities of the Canaanite pantheon and their activities. The senior pair was El and his consort Asherah, rivaled by the younger deities Baal and Anat. Another female deity is Astarte. Mot is the god of death, Resheph the god of health, Dagan the grain god. There are other minor deities as well. What we glean from the Ugaritic texts fits quite well with the physical evidence of multiple temples brought to light by archaeology.[27]

The End of the Late Bronze Age (ca. 1250–1150)

The irony of the portrait that we have given of a vibrant, prosperous, cosmopolitan Canaanite society in the Late Bronze Age is that it all came to an end relatively suddenly, and with it the long Bronze Age Levantine cultural sequence that stretched back to circa 3500.[28]

Collapse

What went wrong? There have been many attempts to explain the end of the Bronze Age. There were no doubt many factors. (1) Any investigation of the transition from the Bronze to the Iron Age in the southern Levant circa 1200 must begin with the larger context. It has long been known that there was a general collapse in the entire eastern Mediterranean world and beyond in the late thirteenth century, leading earlier scholars to posit a long "dark age" in the subsequent Iron I period. In Greece and on Crete, the palace civilization came to an end. In western and southern Anatolia, displaced peoples and new invaders swept across the country, devastating many sites and ending the Hittite Empire. On Cyprus, invading Mycenaeans imposed themselves on the Eteo-Cypriote population (along with Sea Peoples; below). In Syria many sites come to an end, and at Ugarit the texts are explicit in describing both land and sea battles, after which the great urban centers sank into obscurity. In Mesopotamia the venerable Old Assyrian and Old Babylonian regimes collapsed.

Finally, the Egyptian Empire in Asia, extending all the way up to the Anatolian plateau, tottered to an end, and Egypt entered a long period of decline in the Third Intermediate period (below). It almost appears as though we have a "domino effect" in which peoples displaced by disturbances in one region migrated to other regions and triggered other disturbances.

The overall phenomena is clear, whatever the explanation, but here we will look mainly at the Levant, especially southern Canaan, where two new ethnic groups will soon appear on this horizon: Sea Peoples and Proto-Israelites (ch. 3). It is the *nature* of these disturbances that has caused a continuing debate, one that we need not pursue in detail here, except with reference to the southern Levant.

In general, causal theories have included natural disaster, climate change, dramatic technological innovation, especially in warfare, large-scale migrations of people, armed invasions, local rivalries and destructions, long-term cyclical oscillations (as with the Annales school), and broader systems-theory notions of collapse that include several of the above factors. It is the latter view of the complexity of the causes for the end of the Bronze Age in the southern Levant that we shall adopt here.

Causes of the Collapse: An Overview

Before looking at individual sites, several general caveats are necessary. (1) The end of the long Bronze Age civilizations was not due to any particular episode but was rather the result of a long period of decline in Canaan from as early as 1250 to 1150. The conventional date of 1200 for the transition from the Late Bronze to the Iron I period is somewhat arbitrary. Late Bronze Canaanite cultural influences (and peoples) continued well past that date (below).

(2) The process of dissolution was exceedingly complex, with many historical, cultural, ideological, and even possibly environmental factors in the degradation. There was no single catalyst that brought about what we shall describe as "systems collapse."

(3) There were many regional differences in the process of decline, due in part to varying socioeconomic and cultural differences, but due also to southern Canaan's diverse topography and environment.

(4) Finally, the end of the Bronze Age and the transition to the Iron Age may well be part of the long-term, cyclical oscillations that the Annales school has sought to define (the *longue durée*). Finkelstein has adopted aspects of this model, in part to explain the end of the Late Bronze

Age, but his characterization of the highlands of Canaan in this period as affected decisively by local socioeconomic and demographic factors ignores a great deal of the conflicting evidence. In particular, his coupling of the Late Bronze–Iron I transition with the Early Bronze I–III/ IV transition—as though both were similar, recurring "cycles"—is quite misleading. It obscures the numerous unique features operative in the thirteenth–twelfth century that we shall address here, both on archaeological and textual grounds.[29]

The Decline of Egypt in the Nineteenth and Twentieth Dynasties

We have already described the Egyptian Empire in Asia in the Amarna age of the Eighteenth Dynasty (ca. 1360–1340). Under subsequent kings, especially the Ramesside Nineteenth Dynasty, Egypt began to lose control of the northern and southern Levant. The post-Amarna age in the late fourteenth–early thirteenth century and the restoration of the Theban dynasty after the heresy of Amenhotep IV (Akhenaten) was a period of anarchy (Horemheb was a usurper), confusion, social upheaval, corruption, and a revolution in religious beliefs. This was significant, in spite of the accomplishments of Seti I (1294–1279), who also campaigned in the southern Levant, albeit with only limited success, to judge from the archaeological record.

Ramesses II (1279–1213) was, to be sure, still a powerful king, but he was often preoccupied with his own colossal and expensive building projects in Egypt. And like his Eighteenth Dynasty predecessors, he seems to have neglected contacts with far-flung Asia (a neglect seen already in the Amarna letters; above).

Ramesses II moved north to Kadesh on the Orontes in Syria in 1275 to confront the Hittite king Muwatalli II in an attempt to recover control of the "land of the Amurru" (the Amorites). He claimed a decisive victory, and upon his return to Egypt he inaugurated an impressive propaganda campaign to glorify his triumph, scenes of which were carved on the walls of all the major temples. But this was a pyrrhic victory: the battle (for which we possess versions of the peace treaty from both parties) ended in a stalemate. Subsequent campaigns reconquered some vassal states, but they all soon reverted to Hittite control, and Egypt was never again able to dominate the northern Levant (Syria and the land of the Amurru).

Ramesses II was succeeded briefly by his son Merenptah (1213–1203), whose famous Victory Stela of circa 1208 claims to have devastated the "land of Hurru" (i.e., Palestine), especially the city-states of Ashkelon, Gezer, and a certain Yenoam (perhaps the upper Jordan Valley or Transjordan; see below). The stela also contains the first mention of "Israel," designated by the determinative sign as a people or ethnic group rather than a state-like entity.

This Israel is said to have been wiped out, yet this is typical Egyptian bombast. Ashkelon, also mentioned, shows no major destruction attributable to Merenptah, nor does Gezer, except for some disturbances. As for any "Israelites" in the central hill country, an analysis of the map reconstructable from the stela shows that the Egyptians probably avoided that area. Their intelligence was no doubt hearsay, and they found it expedient to move around the central hill country, not likely encountering any Israelites, much less utterly destroying them (ch. 3).

Invasions of Sea Peoples: Confronting the Egyptians

It was in the region of Ramesses III (1184–1153 or 1195–1164) that the Egyptian Asiatic empire finally began to fall apart. First, in his fifth year and again in his eighth year, this pharaoh had to fight off further advances of the Libyans. Then in his eighth year (1176) he moved to repel a coalition of peoples migrating from the breakup of the Mycenaean world and spreading throughout the Aegean and eastern Mediterranean. Known to modern scholars collectively as "Sea Peoples," they had already tried to penetrate Egypt from the west during the reign of Merenptah. They had earlier marauded by land and sea across Anatolia, toppling the Hittite Empire. Then they moved down the plains of Cilicia and northern Syria, razing Alalakh and Ugarit.[30]

From cuneiform tablets found at the Ugaritic port of Ras Ibn Hani, we know that Ugarit's king, Ammurapi, wrote desperately to the king of Cyprus, saying that, while his troops were far afield in Hittite country opposing the invaders, the invaders had approached by sea and had done great damage. In an earlier letter, the Hittite king identifies the invaders he has encountered as the "Shikalayu, who live in ships."

The Sea Peoples had invaded Cyprus a generation or so earlier, ultimately using it as a platform from which to launch further sea raids. A series of disturbances, destructions, abandonments, rebuilds, and new foundations on the island of Cyprus seems to extend from the late thirteenth into the twelfth century. At many of these sites, the Late Mycenaean IIIC pottery phase is supplanted by Late Mycenaean IIIC:1 wares (plus Late Cypriot III). In addition, we have new hearths, distinctive cooking jugs, and nonperforated loomweights. Many of these same Mycenaean- and Aegean-style cultural traits appear in Canaan in the twelfth century (below). Virtually all authorities agree that these innovations in material culture document a substantial immigration of new peoples from the Aegean world, amounting to large-scale colonization. Steel summarizes these changes as follows.

> [There is] a dramatic reconfiguration of the social, political and economic organization of the island..... Many of these changes are frequently attributed to the arrival of a new element from the Aegean and can be paralleled by the apparent influx of a new population group in the southern Levant (the Philistines).[31]

The pertinent Cypriot sites would include:

Fig. 2.10. Late thirteenth- and early twelfth-century Cypriot sites with evidence of new cultural elements (= LC IIC–IIIA)

Alassa-Pano *Mandilaris*	Maroni-*Vournes*
Enkomi	Myrtou-*Pigadhes*
Hala Sultan Tekke	Palaepaphos
Kalavasos-*Ayios Dhimitrios*	Pyla-*Kokkinokremnos*
Kition	Salamis
Kourion	Sinda
Maa-*Palaeokastro*	Toumba Tou Skourou

Ramesses III had to repel an invasion of Sea Peoples attempting to invade the Delta in his eighth year (1176 or 1187). The reliefs on the walls of his temple at Medinet Habu show in great detail fleets of Mycenaean-style warships and great battles at sea, as well as large forces of men, women, and children traveling overland in ox-drawn carts with all their impedimenta. The Mycenaean sailors wear short kilts, light armor, and a curious feathered helmet that has Mycenaean and Aegean parallels. An Egyptian text describes several groups: the Shikalayu, the Sherden, the Denyen (Greek Danaoi?); the Tjekker (Teucrians?), Weshesh (unknown), and a people identified in

Egyptian as *peleset*, clearly the biblical *pəlištîm*, or Philistines. Ramesses was well prepared, however, and claims to have turned them back. Then, having moved a large force to Djahy (perhaps on the Phoenician coast, where there may have been Egyptian forts), he claims to have settled them in fortresses. Previous scholars thus regarded the Philistines—the only group well-known archaeologically (see below)—as Egyptian mercenaries, but more recent evidence shows that under Ramesses III the Egyptians at best tried to strengthen their forts and contain the triumphant Sea Peoples there.[32]

We have noted above the existence of a number of Egyptian forts and "governors residencies" at several sites, some presumably established as early as the Amarna age in the fourteenth century. Of particular interest here is the fate of these Egyptian administrative centers at roughly the same time as the appearance of the Sea Peoples in the early twelfth century, especially those along the southern coast of Canaan.[33]

At Deir el-Balaḥ, in the Gaza strip, there is no evidence of a destruction of Stratum VII (no floors were found), but in Strata VI–V, dated probably to the time of Ramesses III in the twelfth century, there are overall changes that might be related to the arrival of newcomers.

Petrie's Building YR at Tell el-Farʿah (South) produced from its final phase of this era an ivory carving with Mycenaean motifs, as well as three scarabs of Ramesses III. Then, in subsequent phases, Philistine pottery appears, but apparently without any preceding destruction layer. The rich tombs of Cemetery 500 belong to this horizon.

At Tell Jemmeh, Petrie's level J–K, with Philistine pottery (and a kiln), is preceded by a large, multiroomed courtyard structure that has been considered an Egyptian residency.

At Tel Seraʿ there is a destruction of the Stratum IX residency (Building 906) that is dated sometime after circa 1164 by an Egyptian ostracon mentioning the "twentieth year" of a pharaoh, presumably Ramesses III. Philistine bichrome pottery then appears for the first time in Stratum VIII.

Petrie's City IV at Tell el-Ḥesi, the residency of which produced a fragment of an Amarna age tablet, has a big destruction layer, but it cannot be closely dated.

The large residency at Tel Mor VIII–VII, dated to the thirteenth century, continues into Strata VI–V, probably of the early twelfth century (Ramesses III?). There does not appear to be a destruction on this horizon.

The impressive Stratum X_{12} Aphek residency (Palace VI/Building 1104) was destroyed in a huge conflagration, followed by early Iron I material in Stratum X_{11}. The excavators speculate only that newcomers may have been responsible for these changes.

The destruction of the residency of Beth-Shean VI, mentioned above (Building 1500), can be dated only approximately. Originating in Stratum VII, dating to the time of Ramesses II in the thirteenth century, the residency was rebuilt in Stratum VI, evidently in the reign of Ramesses III. It was then violently destroyed, the destruction dated to Ramesses III by an inscribed lintel. In the debris there was found a large quantity of Egyptian-style pottery made locally, as well as some twenty sherds of imported Mycenaean IIIC:1 (monochrome) pottery that belong to the early twelfth century. The excavators decline to identify the destroyers, but a Philistine destruction circa 1170 seems unlikely.

In light of both Ramesses III's claim to have repelled the attempted invasion of the Sea Peoples and the archaeological data just adduced concerning the fate of Egyptian administrative centers, what can we say about the relations of these two peoples after circa 1175? While authorities vary on various phases of Philistine occupation and expansion, there is a general consensus. In stage 1, in the early twelfth century, Ramesses III suffered setbacks in the destruction of some administrative centers (Tel Seraʿ and possibly Aphek and Beth-Shean) by invading Sea Peoples, especially the Philistines along the southern coast. Egyptians could not prevail, but evidently they attempted to establish a *cordon sanitaire* to contain the Philistines. This phase is marked by the appearance of small quantities of imported Late Mycenaean IIIC:1 monochrome ware, along with local imitations. There are also native Aegean and Mycenaean cultural traits.

In stage 2, during the reigns of Ramesses IV–VI (1153–1136), the Philistines expanded inland, perhaps becoming partly acculturated (or, as some think, "creolized"). This phase is marked by the development of the classic Philistine bichrome pottery, combining Mycenaean and local late Canaanite features. During this phase Egyptian hegemony declined and eventually collapsed altogether.

The last vestiges of Egyptian presence in southern Canaan are bronze scraps found below the massive destruction layer of Lachish Stratum VI bearing the cartouche of Ramesses III and now also a pedestal of a statue of Ramesses VI found at Megiddo. With that, the magnificent Egyptian New Kingdom in Asia came to an end, not with a bang but with a whimper. Pharaonic Egypt eventually sank into a long decline in the Third Intermediate period (1069–664), never again to venture outside the Nile Valley.[34]

Philistines and Other Sea Peoples

Let us turn now to other early twelfth-century destructions in southern Canaan that can be attributed more specifically to the invasion of various Sea Peoples there, especially the Philistines along the southern coast, as well as the Shikalayu and perhaps other groups (Tjjeker?) farther north.

The appearance of the group known as Philistines in Canaan in the early Iron I period, as well as the Shikalayu and Tjjeker, in all probability, has long been clear from both the Egyptian data already discussed above and the archaeological record. According to both the biblical texts (although much later) and the later Neo-Assyrian records, the heartland of the Philistine settlement consisted of a pentapolis along the southern coast of Canaan: Ashdod, Ashkelon, Ekron, Gaza, and Gath. Each of these city-states was ruled by a *seren* (Hebrew "tyrant"; cf. Greek *tyrannos*). All but one of these five cities has been located and extensively excavated in the last forty years or so.

At Ashdod, Stratum XIV of the late thirteenth century was destroyed and covered at least in some areas by a thick debris layer, as also at the nearby harbor town of Tel Mor VII. In the succeeding resettlement, quantities of Late Mycenaean IIIC:1 monochrome-style pottery were found. In later strata the classic Philistine bichrome pottery appears, locally made. Other Aegean-style cultural traits are in evidence.

At Ashkelon, some 10 miles to the north, we have a possible destruction followed not only by LM IIIC:1 pottery but also by distinctive cylindrical clay loomweights with Cypriot and Mycenaean connections, as well as an abundance of pig bones. At this time a large seaport was established, perhaps 150 acres or more in size.[35]

At Ekron (Tel Miqne) some 12 miles inland from Ashdod, the evidence is even more extensive, resulting from nearly twenty seasons of excavation (1981–1996). The Late Bronze Age ends with the destruction of Stratum VIII, and Stratum VII represents an abrupt new era, with large quantities of locally made Mycenaean IIIC:1 wares and a unique kiln, Aegean-style figurines, Aegean-style ivory-handled knives, an inscribed bovine scapula, a megaron-style cultic structure with hearths, and new fortifications. By Stratum VI of the mid- to late twelfth century, a large urban center is flourishing, at least as late as circa 1140. The Area AA palace was totally destroyed, but it yielded a large and elaborate hoard of carved ivories, on one of which was a cartouche of Ramesses III.[36]

In the Shephelah, Gezer XIV shows some disturbances, perhaps reflecting the campaigns of Merenptah circa 1210, whose Victory Stela names the site after Ashkelon (below). A cartouche of his was found by Macalister.[37] Strata XIII–XI produced Philistine bichrome pottery, but the site continued Canaanite cultural traditions.

Inland in Judah we confront a mixed picture. Beth-Shemesh 7 was perhaps destroyed, but likely in the early twelfth century. Nearby Tel Batash VI, on the other hand, shows no destruction on this horizon, but its population may have become at least partly Philistine (above). Tell Beit Mirsim C_1 was destroyed at the end of the Late Bronze Age, then reoccupied quickly in Iron I. Tel Ḥalif IXA–X yields a similar picture. Neither site, however, has yielded any significant Philistine material.

Philistine Gath has now been located at Tell eṣ-Ṣafi (Tel Zafit), just south of Ekron, where excavations began in 1996 and continue. Stratum 9 ends the Late Bronze Age. Thus far the early twelfth-century levels are not clear, although both Late Mycenaean IIIC:1 and Philistine bichrome wares are in evidence (Strata 8–7). By the eleventh century, a major city flourishes, characterized by a degenerate style of Philistine pottery (Stratum 6).

Ancient Gaza has not been positively identified, but if its remains lie beneath modern Gaza, they are unlikely ever to be excavated.

Other Thirteenth- and Twelfth-Century Destructions

Having attributed much of the collapse at the end of the Late Bronze Age to invading Sea Peoples and inadequate response by the declining Twentieth Dynasty Egyptian forces in Canaan, let us now look at other sites on this horizon, some destroyed, some not.

A few sites in Galilee were destroyed, notably Hazor. Here the entire lower and upper city of Stratum XIII, 180 acres in extent, was violently destroyed in a destruction that left masses of debris everywhere. Fortifications, several monumental temples, the most impressive palace complex known in southern Canaan—all were totally pillaged, the ruins left exposed as the site was abandoned for a generation or more.

The date of this destruction cannot be specified beyond circa the mid-thirteenth century, nor can the invaders be identified. Yadin (and the current excavator, Ben Tor, to some extent) regarded this as dramatic evidence of the Israelite "conquest" of Canaan, but others attribute the catastrophe to natural causes or perhaps to internecine warfare.[38] In any case, no Philistine pottery has been found at the site, and it appears too far inland to have been in the path of the Philistines or any other Sea Peoples.

In the Jezreel Valley, we have already noted the end of the Egyptian fort of Beth-Shean VI (Building 1500), probably toward the end of the reign of Ramesses III, circa 1150 (although Stratum VII had possibly already seen its construction). The agents of this destruction are unknown. A few Late Mycenaean IIIC:1 sherds were found there, but very little Philistine bichrome ware. A Philistine destruction and reoccupation do not seem likely.

At the west end of the Jezreel Valley, the Nineteenth Dynasty Egyptian fortified port of Tell Abu Hawam was destroyed at the end of Stratum VA. But imprecise stratigraphy and scant publication have left the date uncertain beyond the late thirteenth or early twelfth century. Occupation continued into the early Iron Age. Some authorities consider that the early twelfth century is marked by two waves of Sea Peoples settling there, as they did farther south along the coast.

In the heart of the Jezreel Valley lies the great mound of Megiddo, straddling the Via Maris and the scene of numerous battles throughout history (Hebrew *hār-məgiddôn*, from which the Greek "Armageddon" derives). Stratum VIIB was violently destroyed, then rebuilt in phase A and destroyed again. If a statue base of Ramesses VI (from an unclear context) belongs to Stratum VIIA, that would explain the event as a massive destruction at the very end of the Late Bronze Age, followed by a gap in occupation.

The most extensive destruction anywhere in Judah is that of Lachish VI, where the site was totally destroyed and then deserted for at least a century and a half. The date of the destruction must be as late as the time of Ramesses IV, whose cartouche was found on some bronze scraps. There is no Philistine pottery whatsoever at the site. Albright attributed the destruction to invading Israelites, but there is no evidence for that.

In the Jordan Valley, Tall as-Saʿidiyeh XII was completely destroyed and then abandoned for a time. The destruction, however, may have taken place as early as 1300. The excavator's assertions of Sea People influence are debatable.

Deir ʿAlla (Dayr ʿAllā) was also destroyed, and a cartouche of Queen Tausret (ca. 1185) found in the debris yields a *terminus post quem*. A small quantity of Philistine bichrome ware is said to have been found, along with twelve cuneiform tablets written in what appears to be an alphabetic Cypro-Minoan script. Yet it is difficult to believe that ethnic Philistines could have penetrated this far inland (or this early). It is worth noting that in all the Transjordanian plateau, there is only one definite Philistine bichrome sherd.[39]

In the Vacuum: New Peoples in Iron I

Assuming the utility of General Systems Theory, the salient facts for our purposes here are: (1) a widespread series of perturbances in the Mediterranean world system set off a downward spiral that brought the centuries-long Bronze Age equilibrium to an end circa 1250–1150; and (2) in the wake of the collapse of old polities there arose several interrelated new ethnic groups that would in time come to form new states or city-states, among them the Proto-Israelites. Let us look first at the rise of groups other than the latter, which will provide the broader Levantine historical and cultural context within which early Israel arose (ch. 3).

The Philistines

Despite the skepticism now in vogue about identifying ethnicity in material culture remains, there can be little doubt with regard to the immigrants and invaders characterized above either as to (1) the identity of these newcomers along the coast as the Philistines of the Egyptian textual sources or (2) their Aegean/Mycenaean origins and cultural heritage (see above and further ch. 3).

The principal issue is whether these new Philistine elements and presence in twelfth-century Canaan are to be explained simply by the diffusion of Mycenaean cultural influences or rather were introduced by large-scale invasions of new peoples, in this case our Sea Peoples, migrants coming largely from the Aegean world via Cyprus and probably also down the Levantine coast from Anatolia.

The excavators of the principal sites and also mainstream Israeli and American scholars adhere confidently to the invasion hypothesis, among them Dothan, Gitin, Mazar, Ben-Shlomo, Bunimovitz, and particularly Stager.[40] A few other scholars favor the diffusionist approach, notably Sherratt, who denies any invasions. Killebrew acknowledges the presence of newcomers in Canaan, characterized by what she calls Aegean-style material culture, but she sees a smaller cadre of invaders with more Anatolian traits than most other scholars would allow. Finkelstein's publications on the early Philistine settlement have to do mostly with defending his idiosyncratic low chronology and thus lowering the date of Philistine bichrome ware. Yet he also acknowledges the large-scale appearance of newcomers.[41]

Stager posits two waves of immigration. First there was the destruction of sites and their replacement by new urban installations throughout the primary area in the southern Philistine plain in the early to mid-twelfth century, accompanied by both Mycenaean IIIC:1 style and locally produced bichrome wares. Within this area some 30 miles long and 12 miles wide, there may have been a population of 25,000 or more. Stager posits a large-scale displacement of the local Canaanite population, although he thinks that the few remaining Egyptians coexisted somehow with the newcomers.[42]

In stage 2, in the mid-twelfth to early eleventh century, Philistine control expanded inland and northward and overran the remaining Egyptian outposts. All the Egyptians could do was to attempt a containment policy, which ended with the death of Ramesses III in 1153 (or 1164). The Philistine population may have doubled by then due to natural increase, and as they expanded into the hill country, the Philistines came into inevitable conflict with another ethnic group entrenched there, the early Israelites (below).

The obvious Aegean and Mycenaean influences on early Philistine culture were probably diffused by sea via Cyprus—a kind of jumping-off point, as we have said, for various groups of migrants displaced and moving southward toward the Egyptian Delta and the southern Levantine coast after a generation or so. Above we listed the sites that seem to have been settled by Sea Peoples invading Cyprus (see fig. 2.10 above).

Turning now to the biblical evidence, although secondary, it is evident that the pertinent texts, even though they are some centuries later than the appearance of the Philistines in Canaan, do contain some genuine historical memories. The writers know that the "exodus route" avoided the southern Levantine coast because a contemporary people, the Philistines, were entrenched there (Exod 13:17). These people are regarded as uncircumcised (i.e., non-Semitic; Judg 15:18), from the Mediterranean world (Caphtor, or Crete; related to but not Cyprus; Amos 9:7; Jer 47:4), each city being ruled by a *seren* (Hebrew "lord"); finally, on the eve of the founding of the Israelite monarchy, they had expanded sufficiently to pose a severe threat (ch. 4). The information that the writers of the Hebrew Bible had pertaining to the Philistines may have been scant, but in general it was correct, despite the time lag and the expected bias.[43]

The Phoenicians

It is generally accepted that Iron Age Levantine peoples known collectively in later sources as Phoenicians were the cultural heirs of the Late Bronze Age Canaanite civilization after its collapse, especially along the Levantine coast, where they continued as seafarers. Their appearance in the archaeological record is already apparent in the thirteenth century at such coastal sites as Al-Mina, Tell Afis, Tell Sukas, Arwad, Byblos, Tyre and Sidon, and Sarepta in Syria. In modern Israel, coastal sites such as Achzib, Tell Keisan, 'Atlit, and Dor have produced significant Phoenician remains.[44]

The Phoenicians appear as "Fenkhu" already in the time of Thutmose III in the fifteenth century. They are later among such peoples as the Sea Peoples portrayed in the scenes and texts on the walls of Ramesses III's temple at Medinet Habu (above), thus Egypt's foes along the northern Levantine coast in Syria. They do not appear to have been destroyed or even displaced by the latter, and it has been suggested that they may have been allies. In any case, they remained in place well into the twelfth–eleventh century (ch. 3).

The Phoenicians later become well known throughout the Mediterranean, trading widely by sea, planting colonies in Cyprus, in Africa at Carthage, and elsewhere, and mining metals as far west as Sardinia and Spain. In particular they spread the alphabetic script developed earlier in Canaan far afield, seeing it adopted, for instance, in Greece as early as the eleventh century. Phoenician architecture (ashlar masonry) and Phoenician art forms such as ivory-carving and glyptic art found their way throughout Syria and Israel in the Iron Age. Still, despite their expansion and their fame, the earliest history of the Phoenicians is not well-known archaeologically.

Early Iron Age Phoenician sites along the coast of Israel have been only partially excavated, and in most cases they remain unpublished. Discussion will be deferred to chapter 3, where the pertinent sites will be analyzed.

The biblical data, considered here and elsewhere as a secondary source, are not unexpectedly of little help. The writers knew nothing of the origins of the Phoenicians, who came to their attention only when their narratives come to the Solomonic era. Tyre is then regarded as an ally; Sidon, on the other hand, is consistently vilified. The fact that the rise of both Phoenicia and Israel was contemporary and shared a number of features is not part of the biblical writers' view of matters. For them, Phoenicians were "pagans."[45]

The Arameans

The Arameans first appear in the steppes between the Khabur and the Euphrates Rivers in the Middle Assyrian period in the mid-second millennium.[46] Then in the eleventh century, the annals of Tiglath-pileser I and Assur-bel-kala speak of them as the Akhlamu. They were a pastoral nomadic group in the Jebel Bishri Mountains in the eastern Syrian Desert whom the Neo-Assyrians sought to contain and diminish on the frontiers of their westward expansion.

Previous scholarship saw the Arameans as invaders from the Syrian Desert, in accord with the "wave theory" of the time: this was another cyclical intrusion of nomads who periodically overran the settled areas, the supposed eternal conflict between the desert and the sown. By the tenth century, on any view, these intruders had established a series of city-states such as Carchemish, Ḥalab (Aleppo), Hama, Damascus, and others, some of them new foundations. We also have many other archaeological sites whose ancient names are not known. The Arameans thus came to dominate nearly all of the northern Levant (Syria), vying with the indigenous Neo-Hittite peoples there.

The wave theory—the notion of desert parthenogenesis—has long since been discredited. There were never hordes of nomads in the steppes, much less in the great desert. Nor were these pastoralists land-hungry masses pushing into the more fertile zones at any moment of weakness. As Rowton and many others have pointed out, pastoralists, agriculturalists, and townspeople all interacted in a diversified, dimorphic economy and society in the ancient Near East.[47]

Hélenè Sader has done the most to show how the new model better explains the rise of the Arameans, using recent archaeological surveys and excavations. As she puts it:

As a result of the general collapse of the great powers of that time and the collapse of the individual city-states backed by these powers that were economically and socially bankrupt, the Aramean nomads became free from political control and were, at the same time, the only group that had the means to survive. So the emergence of the Arameans is to be understood not as the cause but rather as the result of the collapse of the urban system.[48]

There is very little clear archaeological evidence for ethnic Aramean settlements in modern-day Israel or Jordan before the ninth century BCE, so we will defer discussion in detail until chapter 3.

The Ammonites, Moabites, and Edomites

The peoples of the marginal areas of the Transjordanian plateau were known until recently chiefly from the biblical and the cuneiform sources (from which their modern names derive). Fairly extensive surveys and now several excavations have clarified the history of all the above peoples and have documented that most become visible in the archaeological record only as "tribal kingdoms" beginning in the eighth century at the earliest. That phenomenon is no doubt due to the natural environment, which provides few resources conducive to permanent, large-scale settlement.[49] The broken topography, the widely varying soil types, and the scant rainfall all combined to restrict population in Transjordan and to keep it from attaining state-level organization until quite late in its history. The area typically remained inhabited by indigenous nomadic tribes throughout the Bronze and early Iron Ages, and rarely did supra-tribal polities emerge.

The region stretching from the hills of Bashan and Gilead in the north down to Amman was forested in antiquity and received up to 20–25 inches of rainfall annually. From Amman southward into Moab, low rolling hills give way to a high, relatively dry plateau. Farther south, Edom is mostly desert-like. Immediately to the east of all these regions, however, lies the steppe land, and beyond that the desert.

In Bashan and Gilead, east of the Sea of Galilee, Tell esh-Shihab, Tall Zira'a, and Tell el-Fukhar have excavated Late Bronze Age levels. Other small sites are known from surveys. In the Yarmuk Gorge and southward, Late Bronze sites include Tell Abu el-Kharaz, Irbid, Tell el-Ḥuṣn, Pella, Tell Deir 'Alla (Tall Dayr 'Alla), and Tall as-Sa'idiyeh.

In the Baqʿah Valley and the Ammon area we have Umm ad-Dananir, Ṣafuṭ, Amman, Saḥab, and Tell el-ʿUmeiri (Tall al-ʿUmayri).[50]

Moving south into Moab, there is no evidence thus far for walled Late Bronze Age towns, although surveys have located a few sites. The only well-known town site thus far is Tell el-ʿUmeiri, some 6 miles south of modern-day Amman. There we find in Strata 14–13 a Late Bronze Age town of the late thirteenth century, especially well illustrated in Stratum 12 by a monumental building in Area B. The excavators propose that this building was erected following a severe earthquake destruction circa 1200 and may reflect an early "Israelite" settlement (see ch. 3).[51]

In Edom there are no Late Bronze Age sites, since cultural development there lagged behind the remainder of Transjordan until very late in the Iron Age. Egyptian records, however, attest to a nomadic population.[52]

The Shasu

Nineteenth Dynasty Egyptian texts refer to nomadic and seminomadic people in the region of southern Transjordan (possibly farther north and even in Cisjordan) known collectively as Shasu. The Shasu do not constitute an ethnic group but are portrayed rather as lawless, marauding, hostile nomads whom the Egyptians had to keep in check to guard their remote eastern borders.

The term *Shasu* appears to come from an Egyptian term meaning "to move on foot, wander," by extension "to plunder." It is equivalent to Akkadian *sutû*. The Shasu appear already in the fifteenth century, the time of Egypt's Eighteenth Dynasty, becoming more common in the Nineteenth Dynasty. They seem to have been dispersed along the eastern border of the Egyptian Empire in Asia, from Transjordan, especially in southern Moab and Edom (Mount Seir?), extending up into the Beqaʿa and beyond, and also in the Negev. They were concentrated in the "the land of Khurru," or Canaan, broadly speaking. They appear in the Amarna letters as "lawless," "plotting rebellion"; sometimes, however, they are coopted as mercenaries. They can be portrayed as pastoralists, allowed by the Egyptians to graze their flocks in Goshen, in the eastern Delta. The Egyptians attempted to "transfer" them, that is, sedentarize them, but apparently were unsuccessful. Frequent mention has been made of the phrase "the Shasu of *yah*," presuming that the latter is our earliest reference to the deity Yahweh.[53]

The Beginning of the End

Thus far we have looked at the lives of great men and their public deeds—at a sort of disembodied series of events that one might call the historical process. That is what most histories do. However, history is also shaped by the masses of ordinary folk and the myriad everyday decisions they make on the basis of what they perceive, rightly or wrongly, as "the meaning of things"—and archaeology is eminently suited to the quest for that meaning.

The texts of the "great tradition" are indeed essential for writing ancient intellectual history, but they are fleshed out, brought to life, as it were, only when we pay similar attention to the *lesser* traditions of everyday life. As Eric Wolf puts it in his work *Europe and the People without a History*:

> We cannot now agree to write only the history of the victorious elites. Both social historians and the sociologists of history have shown that the ordinary folk were both an active agent in the historical process, its victim, and a silent witness of it. We need to discover the history of the "people without history," that is to say the diverse active histories of the "primitive" minorities, the peasants, the workers, the colonized and the immigrants.[54]

In short, having asked thus far what happened as the Bronze Age tottered to an end, we must now ask: What was it really like? What did people in Canaan feel when they saw the approaching dusk and watched the light as it failed?

Here we must indulge in a bit of speculation, because the artifacts, although tangible expressions of ideas—of perceptions and intentions—do not speak for themselves. We must give them voice, if possible the authentic voice of those anonymous folk who made and used them. The archaeological remains—a text not edited and reedited in antiquity—can thus become their testament.

Let us now portray in more personal detail the milieu that we have described toward the end of the Bronze Age in Canaan. First, it would have been apparent to almost everyone that the old order, the millennium-old sway of Canaanite culture, was coming to an end. People would have had the sense that for a very long time they had lived in a world that, although uncertain, nevertheless seemed relatively stable.

For as long as anyone could remember, as far back as oral tradition stretched (often centuries), there had been familiar institutions. Sophisticated, prosperous urban city-states dominated the landscape and through trade gave Canaan a significant place on the international stage of Mediterranean geo-politics. The palace economy and patrimonial society guaranteed stability and secured the future. The ubiquitous monumental temple, an established priesthood, a long mythological tradition, and familiar rituals—all these assured that the gods were active and favorable.

To be sure, it was the elites who prospered most, and the masses, some little more than peasants, would have felt disenfranchised. There was a good deal of corruption and petty squabbling among both the resident Egyptian high commissioners and the petty local Canaanite princes, as the Amarna letters testify. But at least the administrators kept order despite competition, adverse conditions, and growing uncertainty.

With the destruction of some administrative sites in the late thirteenth and early twelfth centuries, as well as the gradual collapse of other urban centers, chaos ensued. We can only imagine what happened when the Egyptian forts and residencies described above were attacked and their officials were slaughtered or fled, when the premises were looted and left standing in ruins for all to see. What then? Now who was in charge?

In particular, the departure of the last Egyptian officials, who had been regnant for some three hundred years, must have been unsettling. Even though they might have been widely despised as intruders, Egyptians had represented stability. The mighty Egyptian Empire in Asia, especially during Egypt's zenith under Ramesses II, had seemed eternal. Now its local officials retreated before the advance of the Sea Peoples, whose incursions devastated the southern coastal regions in less than a generation. The harassed Egyptians first attempted a standoff, then sought to establish a *cordon sanitaire*, then decamped in disarray, leaving behind a power vacuum that all would have felt. The result was a sense of chaos, confusion, and mortal fear: the end seemed at hand.

The upper classes, who had been dependent on Egyptian largesse, would now have become pariahs: outcast, discredited, and impoverished. Some might have been hunted down and exterminated. The poor were now poorer still, displaced to the countryside, disaffected, like the Habiru known from the Amarna letters (above). They would have been desperate, easily recruited for even violent social revolution. Few people of any class had anything more to lose.

If the fall of the Egyptian palaces and forts had been seen as a threat to order, one must speculate on what the demise of the numerous Late Bronze Age temples we have noted would have meant. Every one of the two dozen or so temples was destroyed or abandoned on this horizon, and none would be rebuilt in the early Iron Age. In the ancient Near East generally, religion and the elaborate religious establishment had been the glue that cemented together the society and the economy. Religious mythology was a powerful consolidating element, legitimating centuries-old traditions that gave people a sense of identity and communal destiny. But now the *temple*—the "house of the god" (Semitic *bêt*)—had fallen into ruins. Either the gods were dead, or they had repudiated their people. Religion, more perhaps than any other cultural institution, was widely perceived as the light that failed.

Into this melee there now came a wave of intruders, more foreign and unfamiliar than the Egyptian overlords had ever been: the Sea Peoples, especially the Philistines along the southern coast. These "sackers," as Homer called them, were of Mycenaean and Aegean lineage. They were Greek-speaking immigrants from far away, forcibly imposing themselves on the local population in a series of violent destructions that must have seemed horrifying. They brought with them an entirely new and different culture: they were *Europeans*, the heirs of a long, distinct classical tradition unfamiliar to the Semitic world. Arriving by land and sea, they did not simply overrun the local populace; they no doubt slaughtered many of the Canaanite inhabitants and drove thousands of others into the hinterland as refugees in their own country.

Archaeologists and historians speak somewhat cavalierly of destructions, which after all do produce some of our best evidence for culture and cultural change. But it was not just sites that were destroyed by the Philistines; it was people, their lives lost or shattered. Thousands might have been slaughtered, thousands of others made refugees, homeless. The bitter hostility of the writers of the Hebrew Bible, although centuries later, is understandable and probably preserved authentic historical memories. The coming of the Sea Peoples would mark the end of an era throughout the eastern Mediterranean world. They had a foothold in the southern Levant, and they were there to stay (as they did for centuries). Many people must have sensed that this was the beginning of a new age in Canaan, a new polyglot population, language, and culture.

The Sea Peoples, however, were not the only newcomers in the early twelfth century. In the northern Levant, Neo-Hittites, Hurrians, and Arameans were all in movement, many pressing down into southern Canaan, unimpeded by any central authority, sometimes impelled by trying to escape their own misfortunes. The borders were open, the guards gone.

In Syria, Neo-Hittites were survivors of disruptions in Anatolia to the west, perhaps caused by the Dorian invasions remembered in the Homeric epics. Along the southern coast, and even inland, the Sea Peoples were ransacking sites and displacing local peoples, who then migrated into Syria and even farther south. There Syro-Hittite and Aramaean art, architecture, and iconography would survive, conserving older cultural elements, and this would have a significant impact on the Iron Age in both the northern and southern Levant.

Neo-Hittites appear alongside Aramaean tribal peoples who were making inroads into northern Syria, soon to establish their own nascent city-states there. For whatever reasons, the Arameans also pushed farther southward into the southern Levant, gradually ensconcing themselves in Upper Galilee, the areas to the east of the Sea of Galilee, and up onto the Golan Heights. Before long they, too, would encounter early Israelite settlements there, and for several centuries into the Iron Age Arameans and Israelites would be locked in conflict (below, ch. 5).

The Habiru, whom we have already met, were not newcomers in Canaan toward the end of the Bronze Age; they had been around on the fringes of society for perhaps several centuries. The Amarna letters of the fourteenth century portray them dramatically as a potent menace to the settled areas. A survey of these letters from southern Canaan shows them in many roles: (1) outcasts; (2) social dropouts whose group one could join; (3) sometimes recruited as Egyptian mercenaries; (4) associated with some pastoralists, such as the Shasu. As the Egyptian Empire collapsed, these rebellious elements of the volatile sociocultural mix in the southern Levant were unleashed to wreak further havoc. The Habiru were not an ethnic group, however, much less related to the later Hebrews of a similar-sounding name. They were probably alternatively supportive and competitive in relation to these later newcomers. But in any case, the Habiru remained a destabilizing force in the social upheavals of the time, opportunists as always.

In Transjordan, groups closely related to transitional Iron I peoples on the other side of the Jordan were slowly emerging from former tribal allegiances, on their way toward new affiliations in Ammon, Moab, and Edom. Among the other pastoral nomads presumably in movement we have the Shasu, whose presence we have already seen attested in Egyptian documents. There they are portrayed not only as nomads but as rebellious peoples who had never submitted to the central authorities and remained a menace to order.

Collapse and Its Aftermath

Recent literature on the deterioration and final collapse of socioeconomic and cultural systems has stressed several factors. Anthropologist Robert Rappaport has argued that all such known systems are to some extent "maladaptive." They come into being and attain a relative stability through a series of accommodations between opposing forces—core and periphery—that achieve a fragile balance, a "punctuated equilibrium" (or "homeostasis," in General Systems Theory).[55] Robert Netting points out that mechanisms that make for growth, however, can easily become pathologies, especially when the central authorities attempt to manipulate affairs in order to usurp the role of the larger system. The result is a "hypercoherence" that imperils the flexibility of the institutions that deal with stress, thus threatening the stability of the system as a whole. The result is a failure of several subsystems that in turn affects the whole in a domino effect that leads to disaster.

Norman Yoffee summarizes recent thinking on collapse as follows:

> Collapse, in general, ensues when the center is no longer able to secure resources from the periphery, usually having lost the "legitimacy" through which it could "dissemble" goods and services of traditionally organized groups. The process of collapse entails the dissolution of these centralized institutions.... A "maximizing" strategy, in which the political center tends to channel resources and services for its own, rather than for societal ends, in which support and legitimization from the periphery are therefore eroded, can lead to collapse. Economic disaster, political overthrow, and social disintegration are the likely products of the collapse.[56]

Colin Renfrew had already advanced the notion of systemic collapse in 1979 with respect to the prehistory of Aegean cultures. He saw temporary equilibrium as the result of the interaction of two opposing social structures: a positive "anastrophe" force and a negative "catastrophe" force.

Among the factors presumably at work were those we have adduced here: administrative incompetence, the dissolution of an elite class, economic disaster, and radical shifts in settlement patterns and population.[57]

Numerous other authorities have observed that, in fact, all complex societies become unstable as they move inexorably toward a tipping point, after which collapse becomes inevitable. The Aegean and Levantine worlds in the thirteenth–twelfth century were no exception.[58]

These descriptions of collapse and its causes, by both leading cultural anthropologists and Near Eastern scholars, are near-perfect descriptions of the situation in the southern Levant at the end of the Bronze Age in the late thirteenth and early twelfth centuries. It is not only the archaeological data, but also the textual data that confirm this.

The Amarna letters previously discussed document the above social ills eloquently. (1) There are perennial conflicts over land and resources, competition between the petty princes and commoners. (2) The central authorities continually undermine each other in an attempt to manipulate the situation and enrich themselves. (3) When the Egyptian authorities, who had imposed a degree of stability, withdraw after long neglect, the local rulers lose authority and the economic system collapses.

Examples of these ills abound in the Amarna letters, especially what Yoffee calls "meddling." The king of Megiddo writes to complain that Lab'ayu, king of Shechem, is carrying out hostilities against him. Lab'ayu attacks Milkilu, king of Gezer, and denounces him to the pharaoh. Milkilu, in turn, complains that Yanhamu, king of Pella, has defrauded him. The king of Hebron claims that Lab'ayu's successor, Abdi-Heba, has seized his lands. Finally Abdi-Heba, king of Jerusalem, asserts that because of the pharaoh's failure to intervene, "the land of the king is lost in its entirety."

It is noteworthy that in the Amarna letters several of the petty princes rationalize their loss of control and the resultant social chaos by implicating disruptive elements such as the Habiru (above). Others document the heavy tribute that they have been forced to pay, resulting in economic disaster. Still others complain of the laissez-faire policies of their Egyptian overlords, which undermines what little authority they have. Throughout these poignant letters, we get a picture of a system spinning out of control—a case study in systemic collapse.

There is archaeological corroboration for the conspicuous consumption of the petty princes of the Amarna period. Three consecutive rulers of Gezer are known, probably a typical local dynasty of elites: Milkilu, Ba'lu-

Shipti, and Yapa'-Haddi. In excavations in Fields VI and XI at Gezer, two elaborate fourteenth-century palaces have been found, the latter extensively looted but nevertheless yielding a hoard of luxury objects, including Egyptian imports and some gold foil.[59]

Elsewhere, other sites mentioning local rulers have produced impressive palaces, not to mention tombs filled with luxury goods, including imports from Cyprus, Greece, and other international entrepôts. As the rich got richer, the poor got poorer. That, too, is reflected in the Amarna letters: commoners taxed to death; landless peasants; roaming, destitute people in the countryside; unfortunates captured and sent as slaves to Egypt.

Among the other factors that have been invoked as causes for systemic collapse are such natural disasters as drought and consequent famine or earthquakes as known destroyers. As for climate change, an earlier generation of scholars sometimes followed Rhys Carpenter, who in 1966 sought to explain the fall of the Mycenaean palace civilization by a prolonged drought, proposing that a similar natural disaster had taken place in the eastern Mediterranean. But there is little empirical evidence for anything more than the occasional local food shortages that were endemic to the region.[60]

A recent analysis of pollen cores taken from the Sea of Galilee claims that in climatic terms "the driest event throughout the Bronze and Iron Ages occurred 1250–1100 BCE at the end of the Late Bronze Age.... The Late Bronze dry event was followed by dramatic recovery in the Iron I."[61] The authors claim further that both the textual and the archaeological evidence corroborate their wide-ranging reconstruction of conditions in the Levant and even in the Nile Delta. They go on to explain the rise of the Iron I polities in the southern Levant—early Israel, the Aramean city-states, Ammonite and Moabite territorial polities, and even Edomite sites—as due primarily to the exploitation of wetter and warmer conditions after circa 1200. The crux of their argument turns out to be the assertion of Finkelstein (a coauthor) for some time that the earliest Israelites were "sedentarized pastoral nomads," that is, peoples from fringe areas forced by drought to settle down.

There are numerous problems with this highly speculative, draconian solution to the problem of explaining the collapse of the Late Bronze Age eastern Mediterranean civilization.

(1) The authors' prime case study is the settlement crisis in the Early Bronze IV era, circa 2350–2000 (their Intermediate Bronze). Yet all author-

ities agree that vast numbers of people did not "settle down" then; they *became* pastoral nomads, almost entirely abandoning the settled zone.

(2) The authors conclude from their own data that in the above Early Bronze IV period "no major shift in human exploitation of the environment" took place. At best this argument is contradictory; at worst it is simply wrong. The change from the urban Early Bronze III to the Early Bronze IV rural-nomadic society and economy could not have been more radical.

(3) A further contradiction is the authors' insistence that destructions at a number of Late Bronze–Iron I sites (Megiddo, Hazor, Beth-Shean, Aphek, Lachish, etc.) were due in some way to drought. If so, were "invading nomads" the villains? And is that how they proposed to "settle down"? Finally, in a prolonged drought, would the best survival strategy of pastoral nomads be to become sedentary subsistence farmers and traders?

(4) The authors themselves note that their "uprooted peoples" did not necessarily settle down but "retreated from the urban centers." That movement from the lowlands verifies the model of early Israelite origins adopted *here* (ch. 3), not theirs.

(5) Another contradiction is that their overall reconstruction of a prolonged drought places it circa 1250–1100 BCE in one passage, but elsewhere they put the "crisis" in the "tenth and eleventh centuries BCE"— precisely when their "recovery" should have taken place.

(6) Finally, the notion that the ascendant Egyptian Ramesside Nineteenth Dynasty (1295–1186) coincided with an "environmental and settlement crisis" would be news to most Egyptologists.

This recent study, obviously motivated (and funded) by Finkelstein, is an example of "scientism" masquerading as history—full of distortions, oversimplifications, and grandiose reconstructions based more on ideology than documented facts. There is no doubt that prolonged drought was likely *one* factor in the collapse that we have clearly seen. It was not, however, the prime mover, hardly the sole explanation of change. It was rather one among many factors in a broad, systemic collapse of the economy and society.[62]

There is some evidence for earthquakes in the southern Levant circa 1200, not surprising, since the region is well known for tectonic disturbances. At Tell el-ʿUmeiri in Transjordan, a large four-room house of the later thirteenth/early twelfth century (Building B) seems to have collapsed suddenly with all of its contents intact, possibly due to an earthquake. Deir

'Alla (Dayr 'Alla) phase E may have been destroyed by an earthquake, dated circa 1200 by C-14 determinations and a cartouche of Queen Tausret (1188–1186). At Megiddo, a later domestic dwelling, Building 00/K/10 (Stratum VIA), is similarly destroyed, again with all of its contents, including in this case the bodies of seven of its inhabitants. Since earthquakes of this magnitude are not localized, it is likely that such damage was quite widespread, even though archaeologists have not been fortunate enough to detect it.[63]

Already weakened by internal contradictions, and perhaps natural disasters, as well as the cessation of international maritime trade (as witnessed by the end of Cypriot and Mycenaean imports), the end of the system was inevitable. It required only an external destabilizing force, a trigger, to set off the final downward spiral. That trigger was no doubt the massive invasion of the Sea Peoples—Europeans bringing with them an intact foreign culture, one that would quickly dominate and persist for centuries.

Yet even so, local populations did not suddenly disappear. They simply dispersed, as on the occasion of earlier collapses, as at the end of the Early Bronze III period (ca. 2400–2000) or the end of the Middle Bronze Age (ca. 1500–1450). In both these instances, large numbers of town peoples reverted to rural subsistence and pastoral nomadic strategies to survive, leaving the towns and cities underpopulated or even deserted. It is obvious that the countryside in the hinterland—even the semiarid steppes—provided sanctuary and sustenance.

It is these oscillations, rather than periodic nomadic invasions (the reverse of the process), that characterize the *longue durée* in the Levant. Yet there are very few final collapses—and following every cyclical collapse we see what has been called the principle of resiliency, of "near decomposability," an eventual recovery and the reestablishment of a new order. That is what happened in the twelfth–eleventh century in the southern Levant, both east and west of the Jordan Valley.

The result of what we are regarding here as a gradual systemic collapse between circa 1250 and 1150 was predictable: anarchy, the rending of the social fabric that had held society together for centuries. In the ensuing chaos, some groups floundered. But others may have survived by finding a new niche for themselves. Novel and more diversified economic strategies, new social roles, and no doubt new locations beyond the reach of other displaced groups vying with each other over the spoils of the former Egyptian Empire all characterized the beginning of the Iron Age.

It was in the northern and in particular the central hill country that some of the above groups found a new, promising frontier. The population of these marginal areas had never reached the carrying capacity of the region in the Late Bronze Age. Now the rural areas were more open to settlement than ever and would prove attractive to survivors of the urban collapse seeking refuge and a new start. Nature abhors a vacuum; so does history.

In short, the end of the long Bronze Age culture in the southern Levant was an Axial Age, one of those rare occasions when a culture finally arrives at a crossroads where everything changes, and nothing will ever again be the same.[64]

Notes

1. See the papers in Maeir, Dar, and Safrai 2003, including that by Dever (2003c) on the EB IV period.

2. For basic works on geography, see Aharoni 1979 and particularly the extensive and thoroughly documented historical atlas of Rainey and Notley (2006; cited hereafter as Rainey, since it is he who covers the Bronze–Iron Age evidence). However, the atlas must be used with caution, since Rainey sometimes adds "events" in biblical history that did not happen; see further below.

3. For orientation to the Annales school generally, see Bintliff 1991; for its potential use in archaeology, see Dever 1988; Stager 1998; Bunimovitz 1995a; Faust 2007a. For observations by a biblicist, see Barstad 2007 (although overly optimistic).

4. Until recently most histories dealt simply with *an* Israel, with little recognition of how different the context and trajectories of the two kingdoms were. See, however, Miller and Hayes 1986; 2006. Several archaeologists have also stressed the difference—the importance of regionalism—such as Finkelstein 1995b, 357–59; 2002; Faust 2012a, 26–27. When I mean to designate the entire region on occasion, I shall use the term *Israel*, as the Hebrew Bible generally does.

5. One must not carry the notion of an elitist Hebrew Bible to the extreme. For the Bible's value, however limited, in depicting daily life, see King and Stager 2001; Dever 2012. Nevertheless, ordinary folk are scarcely portrayed in the major source used here, the Deuteronomistic History.

6. Except as noted, biblical quotations are from the NRSV.

7. On Israel's prehistory, especially the supposed patriarchal era, see Dever 1977, 2003a; Thompson 1974; Van Seters 1975; McCarter 2011. The only recent history to begin with this supposedly historical era is Provan, Long, and Longman 2003, a work of evangelical scholars. The use of the term *Canaanite* is sometimes regarded as problematic, at least as an ethnic identification. See Lemche 1991;

Na'aman 1994a; Rainey 1996b. Nevertheless, I shall use the generic term here for *general* description of the land and people.

8. On general systems theory more broadly, see Renfrew and Bahn 1991, 321–26; cf. Hole and Heizer 1977, figs. 77–78. For an application to archaeology and the history of Canaan/Israel, see Dever 1989, 1995b. On the notion of "collapse," see Yoffee and Cowgill 1988; Tainter 1988. Renfrew's model of "anastrophe/catastrophe" is obviously related, as is the Annales school's "cyclical" approach; see n. 3 above and the conclusion of this chapter. See further below and nn. 57–62.

9. There is a vast literature on the end of the Levantine and Mediterranean world and the supposed dark age following the collapse. A full review will be found conveniently in Ward and Joukowsky 1992; the chapters by Caubet, Dever, Sader, and Yon are relevant here. See also Cline 2014 and several essays in Backhuber and Roberts 2009, especially Bell 2009; see further below and nn. 57–62.

10. See Gonen 1992; but cf. the rebuttal in Bunimovitz 1995b, 323–29.

11. For the basic survey data, see Finkelstein, Lederman, and Bunimovitz 1997; Bunimovitz 1994; Zertal 1993. See also Broshi and Finkelstein 1992. For convenient résumés, see Finkelstein 1993; Ofer 1993; Zertal 1993.

12. Few archaeologists have undertaken such rank-size analyses; but cf. Bunimovitz 1995b, 323 (LB); Faust 2012a, 197–205 (Iron Age).

13. Finkelstein's views on large numbers of Late Bronze pastoral nomads, in contrast to Bunimovitz 1995b (n. 10 above), will be treated in much more detail in chapter 3.

14. See the summary in Bunimovitz 1995b, with full references; see also A. Mazar 1990, 232–94.

15. See Gonen 1992 for the negation of city walls in the Late Bronze Age, followed by many scholars, such as A. Mazar 1990, 292 (written before Dever 1993b; below). For the Gezer evidence, see Dever 1986, 1993b. A glance at the detailed section in Dever 1993b, 48 (see also the photo, 1993b, 49), will show that the Late Bronze Wall 22002 is clearly earlier than Wall 2200, the latter apparently the one with Macalister's ashlar towers. No one has refuted this evidence. Even if not many city walls were constructed in the Late Bronze Age, the typical massive city walls were not entirely ruined and could have continued in use; cf. Bunimovitz 1995b. Gonen's pessimism may result partly from her mistaken notion of the Late Bronze Age as nonurban (above).

16. On the nature and extent of Egyptian control, see Ahituv 1978; Na'aman 1981; Weinstein 1981; Redford 1992; Singer 1988a; Gonen 1992; Bunimovitz 1995b; Rainey 2006, 77–103; van Dijk 2000.

17. Definitive analyses of the letters are Moran 1992; Rainey 1996a. For overviews, see Redford 1984; Na'aman 1981, 1992, 1997; Bunimovitz 1995b; Killebrew 2005; Rainey and Notley 2006, 77–90. See also the references in n. 16 above.

18. For the following, see Rainey 2006, 77–90 and references there, summarizing earlier studies such as Greenberg and Giveon. The older equivalency ʿ*apiru* = Hebrew should be given up; it has no linguistic or historical basis.

19. See Rainey 2006, 110.

20. For the Egyptian-style residences and other architecture, see Oren 1985; Hasel 1998; Higginbotham 2000; Killebrew 2005, 58–64. They will be treated in more detail in ch. 3. For the northern Sinai, see pertinent sites in Oren 1987. For locally made Egyptian-style pottery, see Killebrew, 2005, 67–80; Martin 2011. Macalister's Maccabean Castle and the modern excavation's Palace 14120 are fragmentary and not closely dated, but they are certainly Late Bronze palatial buildings of the Amarna Age. See Dever 1993b and cf. Bunimovitz 1986–1987; Singer 1986. On the possibility of dates of Ramesses III some eleven years earlier, see n. 30 below.

21. See the convenient summary in Killebrew 2005, 67–80. See also n. 22 below. On dates of Ramesses III, see n. 30.

22. Higginbotham 2000, 263–301. Her characterization of Building 480 as an Egyptian-style residency is far-fetched, given the nature and late date of the site. See further chapter 3 below on these residencies and their destruction. Higginbotham's interpretation of these "residencies" as local ("elite emulation") rather than evidence of Egyptian direct rule flies in the face of the evidence; cf. Killebrew 2005, 54–55.

23. Bunimovitz 1995b, 323–38.

24. Regarding the term *Canaanite*, see references in n. 7 above. On ethnic boundaries, see the detailed discussion in chapter 3.

25. See Epstein 1966; A. Mazar, however, thinks the reverse, that Levantine potters resided in Cyprus, where they manufactured the bichrome wares (1990, 360–61). On maritime trade, see further below.

26. On Ugarit generally, see Sader 1979; Yon, Sznycer, and Bordrevil 1995. On Ugaritic religion and cult, see Tarragon 1980; Dever 1987; M. S. Smith 2001; Pardee 2002; Coogan and Smith 2012. On the Proto-Siniatic inscriptions, see generally McCarter 1996, 67–73.

27. See the references in n. 26 above; only Dever 1987 makes much of the archaeological data.

28. The most convenient summary is found in the various chapters in Ward and Joukowsky 1992. The chapter by Dever (1992d) deals specifically with ancient Palestine; add now Killebrew 2005, 37–42; several of the chapters in Bachhuber and Roberts 2009; Jung 2010. See nn. 3, 8, and 9 above.

29. See nn. 3 and 8 above. Finkelstein's major discussion of "recurring cycles" will be found in 1994b, 1995c. Chapter 3 below explores this issue further with regard to the emergence of early Israel.

30. For orientation to the Sea Peoples and the Philistines, see Dothan 1982, 1998; Stager 1995, 2006; Singer 1998; Dothan and Dothan 1992; Stone 1995; Oren 2000; Gitin 2010; Barako 2000, 2003; Killebrew 2005; Ben-Shlomo 2006; Shai 2006, 2011; Uziel 2007; Yasaf-Landau 2010; Maeir, Hitchcock, and Horwitz 2013. Brug 1985 and Ehrlich 1996 are secondary sources. The latest discussion, with full references, will be found in Killebrew and Lehmann 2013. The full

discussion of the Philistines will be deferred until chapter 3. It should be noted that recent reappraisals of Egyptian New Kingdom chronology would raise the dates for Ramesses III by some eleven years, to circa 1195–1164. See Schneider 2010, 202.

31. Steel 2004, 187. Cyprus as a "jumping-off place" for the migration of Sea Peoples is assumed by most scholars, but the Cypriot evidence is often not specified. See Dothan 1998; Bunimovitz 1995b; Stager 1995; Killebrew 2005, 199–201, 232–34. For views of Cypriot specialists, see Åstrom 1993; Iacovou 1998; Antoniadou 2007; Leriou 2007; Karageorghis 2011; Steel 2014. Several of the sites in our chart here are discussed there. For similarities to the Philistine pottery found at sites in Israel, see Killebrew 2005, 219–30; Ben-Shlomo, Shai, and Maeir 2004; Dothan and Zukerman 2004; Ben-Shlomo 2006; Bunimovitz 2011. See further chapter 3. Sherratt's idiosyncratic view of the Sea Peoples as simply "mercantile entrepreneurs" in Cyprus has been refuted in particular by Dothan and Stager. See nn. 40 and 41 below.

32. Stager 1995, 340–48; Gitin 2010. Note the recent higher date for Ramesses in n. 30 above. For the Medinet Habu reliefs, as well as Papyrus Harris and the Ostracon for Ramesses, see Rainey 2006, 109–10 and references there.

33. See Killebrew 2005, 58–63 and n. 22 above for the details on the following. See further chapter 3.

34. For the Third Intermediate period, see the authoritative work of Kitchen 1986.

35. Stager 1995, 342–46. However, Dan Master, now Field Director, minimizes any destruction.

36. Gitin 1998, 2010.

37. Dever et al. 1986, 59–60; cf. Macalister 1912, 2:331–32.

38. Ben-Tor, Ben-Ami, and Sandhaus 2012, 7–26. See now the alternate view of the Associate Director, Sharon Zuckerman (2007). Strata XII–XI then represents a "squatter occupation."

39. Strange 2000.

40. See Dothan 1998; Gitin 1998, 2010; A. Mazar 1990, 300–307; Bunimovitz 1995b; Barako 2000, 2003; Ben-Shlomo 2006; Killebrew 2005, 197–201, 232–34; Yasur-Landau 2010; Stager 1995; Maeir, Hitchcock, and Horwitz 2013. Yasur-Landau's principal contribution is to trace overland routes across the west and south coast of Anatolia. See n. 31 above.

41. Cf. Sherratt 1998, 2003; Killebrew refers to "urban colonists" with an Aegean-style culture (2005, 233–34). Finkelstein assumes a more gradual process, dating mostly to the eleventh century. On his low chronology, see Finkelstein 1998b and chapter 4 below.

42. Stager 1995, 334–40. For other attempts to distinguish chronological phases, see Finkelstein 1995a; 1998b; Killebrew 2005, 206, 234.

43. On the exodus and "cultural memory," see Halpern 1993; Assmann 1997; Propp 2000; Hendel 2001, 2006, 2010; see also Davies 2008 generally. Hendel

argues that the memory of servitude under the Egyptians refers to bitter experiences in Canaan. But this is very speculative, and it does not explain how the story got transferred to Egypt in later tradition. On the biblical memories, see Machinist 2000; Stager 2006; Gitin 2010. See further the discussion of the exodus in chapter 3, especially n. 2.

44. There and the following sites are treated in much more detail in chapter 3. On the Phoenicians, see generally Lipínski 2010; Aubet 2001; see also chapter 3.

45. See Lipínski 2010.

46. The fundamental works are Sader 1987, 1992; 2010; Dion 1997; Daviau, Wevers, and Weigel 2001; Lipínski 2000, 2010; and now Younger 2016. See further chapter 3.

47. Rowton 1974; cf. 1976.

48. Sader 1992, 16.

49. Bienkowski 1992. On the Ammonites, Moabites, and Edomites generally, see Aufrecht 2010; Dion and Daviau 2010; Lemaire 2010, all with full references. The tenth-century metal-working establishment found recently by Levy and others, although contested, may push the date of Edomite state formation somewhat earlier. See Bienkowski 1992; Bienkowski and van der Steen 2001; Levy et al. 2004; Levy 2009, 2010b. See further chapter 3.

50. For a useful survey, see Herr and Najjar 2008, 322–16. See also the surveys of Mittmann 1970.

51. For summary, see Herr and Clark 2009; London 2011a.

52. See references in n. 49 above.

53. See Rainey 2006, 92–96, 103, 111–12. Cf. Giveon 1971; Redford 1992, 228–29, 269–80; Hasel 1998, 217–39. The role, if any, of the Shasu in the emergence of Israel will be discussed in detail in chapter 3.

54. Wolf 1982, 9–10.

55. Rappaport 1997; cf. also Netting 1977; and especially Yoffee and Cowgill 1988. See also Tainter 1988.

56. Yoffee 1988, 13.

57. Renfrew 1979.

58. See Cline 2014 and references there. Notions of collapse, however, go back to nineteenth-century observers such as Nietzsche and Spengler.

59. Dever et al. 1986, 36–43. See also Singer 1986; Bunimovitz 1986–1987.

60. Carpenter's far-ranging views on a thirteenth-century drought (1966) have not won acceptance; see Killebrew 2005, 35. Rainey and Notley (2006, 112), however, invoke the notion of drought, no doubt as an explanation for the sedentarization of his Shasu pastoralists. The textual evidence from the last days of Ugarit has also been thought to reveal a drought; see Killebrew 2005, 48 and references there. Droughts, however, were perennial in the southern Levant, but there is little geomorphological evidence of a pandemic drought in the mid- to late thirteenth century. A study of rainfall fluctuations in northern Israel over the last six thousand years by geographers has documented some six drier periods and six

wetter periods. These correlate roughly with changes in the number and density of settlements, suggesting for instance that the Iron I–II periods coincide with wetter phases, as we would expect. But the evidence is too imprecise to suggest that the preceding thirteenth century was one of widespread drought. See Netser 1998. See further several essays in Bachhuber and Roberts 2009. See also below and Langgut, Finkelstein, and Litt 2013.

61. Langgut, Finkelstein, and Litt 2013, 149.

62. Langgut, Finkelstein, and Litt 2013.

63. See Herr and Najjar 2008, 313; van der Koij 1993, 339; Gadot and Yassur-Landau 2006. On earthquakes generally in our region, see Cline 2011.

64. The phrase, coined apparently by Karl Jaspers, has been popularized by Israeli sociologist Shmuel Eisenstadt. See Arnason, Eisenstadt, and Wittrock 2005 for a full discussion.

CHAPTER 3

The Emergence of Israel in the Light of History

Introduction

A generation or so ago many histories of ancient Israel began with the patriarchal narratives in Genesis, attempting to give this "prehistory" some historical foundations. A classic case was Bright's *History of Israel* (2000; orig. 1950). Later histories, however, such as those of Soggin (1985) and Miller and Hayes (1986), were more skeptical and began essentially with the origins of Israel in Canaan circa 1200. That skepticism has only increased recently, and the lack of definitive archaeological evidence in support of such a prehistory—again, the primary source—has been a decisive factor.

The complexity of the literary traditions enshrined in Genesis, part of the J, E, and P sources of the Pentateuch, has been examined intensely by biblical scholars and need not detain us here. For the archaeologist as a historian, it matters little who wrote these stories, when, or for what purposes. Whether they are theologically useful or morally edifying is equally irrelevant for the moment. What matters at this point is whether these stories contain any useful historical information that may help to elucidate the origins of the peoples known as Israelites in Canaan in the Iron Age. The answer must be largely negative.

The archaeological data adduced by Albright, Bright, Speiser, de Vaux, and other earlier scholars have been successfully challenged by Thompson, Van Seters, Dever, and others. Meanwhile, the literary traditions have been reworked by Van Seters and many other biblical scholars. The result has been to conclude that there is little history of events to be gleaned from the pentateuchal narratives. The stories are relatively late, compiled at least four hundred years after our first historical evidence for any Israel. Furthermore, their tendentious agenda—attempting to validate Israel's claim to the land—makes them largely useless for historical reconstruction.

The most that can be said is that there may have been some authentic memories, or oral traditions, that were available to the authors and redactors of Genesis, perhaps some literary sources as well. Thus traditions of the migrations of the ancestors of Israel from Mesopotamia to the land of Canaan and their sedentarization there are understandable today in the light of well-documented movements of the Amorites in the late third–second millennium. Stories of their later descent into the Egyptian Delta and subsequent enslavement there accord well with what we know of the penetration of the Amu or West Semitic peoples from Asia, especially during the Hyksos era in Dynasties Fifteen–Seventeen and the aftermath.

All this means is that some of the events narrated in Genesis may have some historical basis, but there is no direct archaeological corroboration. Indeed, the patriarchal stories as they now stand combine so many diverse elements from so many periods that the narratives cannot be dated or placed in any one archaeological phase or historical era. There the matter must rest. Renewed archaeological quests, further speculation, or more minute analysis of the biblical texts are not likely to be productive for the historian. These stories are part of a late literary construct, an attempt to create a prehistory and an identity during the monarchy, one that is beyond our reach. The story is more cultural memory than history.[1]

Exodus and Wilderness Wanderings: The Sinai

When we come to the extensive accounts of the exodus of the Hebrews from Egypt in the book of Exodus, or the migrations through the Sinai and Transjordan in Numbers, we might seem to be on firmer historical ground. Since these narratives are directly connected to those in Joshua–Judges, which must be considered in looking at the settlement horizon, closer attention is required here.

Once again it is the archaeological data that we shall consider primary—especially since the biblical narratives at this point, also part of the pentateuchal traditions, suffer from the same drawbacks noted above. Here the extrabiblical data are minimal or nonexistent. There is no reference whatsoever in Egyptian texts to any of the events described in the biblical texts. Needless to say, neither is there any rationalization or archaeological evidence to account for the miraculous happenings in the stories.

Of the dozens of sites listed for the Sinai wanderings in Numbers, only one or two can be positively identified or have been excavated. Tell el-Borg, in the Delta on the Pelusiac branch of the Nile, may well be biblical Migdol, to judge from recent excavations. At the other end of the journey, biblical Kadesh-barnea is no doubt to be located at the oasis of ʿAin el-Qudeirat, in the eastern Sinai, where the nearby site of ʿAin Qudeis still preserves the name. Israeli excavations there revealed a fortress of the tenth–seventh century, when the place may have become a pilgrim site. Recent reexamination of the unpublished pottery, however, shows that there is some Iron I pottery (ca. twelfth–eleventh century) but no thirteenth-century material.[2]

The Sojourn in Transjordan

A perusal of the Israelite itinerary in the Sinai and Transjordan in the books of Exodus and Numbers does not inspire much confidence in the historian. Here we have an epic tale of thousands and thousands of closely organized tribal peoples traveling en masse through the land with all their tribal and clan paraphernalia. They set up elaborate tent camps along the way, where a portable shrine and elaborate priestly and cultic activities are carried out. Passing through Transjordan, this tribal confederation is said to have seized more than thirty Canaanite towns as well as large territories such as those of the Amorites, Amalekites, Edomites, Gileadites, and others (see figs. 3.1 and 3.2 below for the following; see also fig. 4.3).

Such details are hardly likely to have been preserved in oral tradition for five hundred years or more. Several of the sites or "encampments" in Transjordan can perhaps be identified. Among them are biblical Dibon (Arabic Dhiban), the capital of Moab; and Heshbon (Arabic Ḥesban). Both have been excavated by conservative biblical scholars motivated to confirm the biblical accounts of Israelite destructions (Num 21:21–32). But neither site was occupied in the requisite mid- to late thirteenth century. There are a few twelfth- and eleventh-century sherds, but there is no architecture. These sites became towns only in the ninth century at the earliest.[3]

More recently, biblical Iye-abarim has been identified with Khirbat al-Mudayna al-ʿAliya. Excavations, however, reveal a fortified town beginning only in the eleventh century.[4] Otherwise, most of the thirty or more sites mentioned in Numbers are unknown. In any case, extensive excavations in central and southern Jordan in the last twenty to thirty years

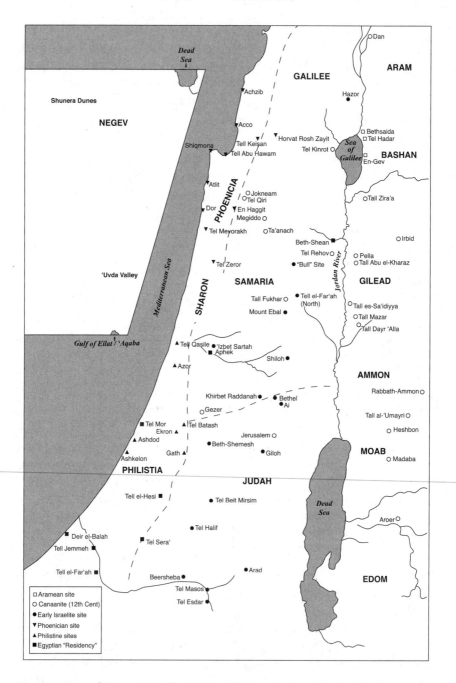

Fig. 3.1. Map of Canaanite, Phoenician, Philistine, Aramean, and early Israelite sites, twelfth–eleventh century. Map by Giselle Hasel.

Fig. 3.2. Major Canaanite and non-Canaanite transitional Late Bronze–Iron I sites (excluding continuing Canaanite sites and Egyptian residencies; see also fig. 4.3)

	Late Bronze II	Iron IA	Iron IB	Iron IIA
	1200	1100	1000	
Transjordan				
Tall Ziraʿa ——→	rebuild ———	——→ ?		
Pella ——→	VII			
Tall Abu Kharaz VIII–V—→?				
Tall Irbid 2 ——→	I			
Tall Fukhar ——————→				
Tall Saʿidiyya XII ——→	XIB gap	XIA ———	→X	
Dayr ʿAllā E ——→	A–D →|	E ——→J	K–L	
Beqʿah Valley ——→				
Tall al-ʿUmayri 14–13→	12 hiatus	11	10?	
Phoenicia				
Achzib ——→?				
Akko Fortress A ——→				
Tel Abu Hawam VA–B (= 5–4)	C?	IVA (= 3–1)	IVB?–III	
Shiqmonah	settlement———	——→?	A	
Tell Keisan 13	12 11	10 9c–a	8c–a	
ʿEn Haggit B1/14	B1/13 B1/12	B1/11–10 B1/9→?	IIB–A fort	
Rosh Zayit		?	IIB–A fort	
Dor ——→?	G/10 G/9	G/8 G/7 G/6	A/10	
Tell Mevorakh	——	VIII	VII	
Tel Zeror village	pits	casemate	storehouses	
Tel Michal XV	——	——	XIV–XIII	
Philistia	Stage 1: Ramesses III	Stage 2: Ramesses VI–XI		
Tel Qasile	XII XI	X	IX (VIII?)	
Tell Batash VI ——→	Vc ←	—Vb Va	IV	
Ekron VIIIA ——→	VIIA–B VIA–B	VA–C IVA–B	gap	
Gath 9 ——→	8 7	6	5	
Ashdod XIV ——→	? XIIIA–B	XIIB–A XI	X	
Tel Mor VIII–VII	VI V	IV III		
Ashkelon 21	20 19	18 17	——	
	Tell Jemneh J K			
Tell el-Farʿah South ←	—Cem. 500, 900			

have shown that there were few fortified towns before the eighth century, when the first tribal states emerged. One of the exceptions to date is Tell el-ʿUmeiri (cf. also Khirbat al-Mudayna al-ʿAliya and Lehun).

Several archaeologists have attempted to connect early Iron I sites in Transjordan with an Israelite destruction and/or occupation in the early twelfth century. These will be treated, however, when we come to the excavated sites. Few, if any, give evidence of anything other than a continuous, local Late Bronze/Iron I transition (see below). To be sure, Egyptian topographic lists from the time of Thutmose III in the fifteenth century to the reign of Ramesses II list several sites in Transjordan that are also mentioned in the Hebrew Bible. Among them are Ashtaroth, Edrei, and Tob (in addition to Jordan Valley sites such as Abila, ʿIyyon, and Pella). But these toponyms likely define regions rather than specific sites.[5]

The biblical portrait of Sinai and Transjordan at the time of any exodus (now clearly thirteenth century) is unrealistic. Apart from a few possible memories in oral tradition, the writers are obviously viewing the region from their point of view in the seventh century or later. Again, the biblical texts are a secondary source; archaeology, the primary source, is largely silent. To be sure, recent studies by archaeologists (as well as most biblical scholars) have suggested that behind these stories there may be authentic memories of a small "exodus group," essentially the two southern tribes of Judah and Benjamin. Sometimes designated significantly "the house of Joseph," these groups were the principal authors of the traditions as we now have them. Not surprisingly, they included in their story of self-identity *all* Israel. But as far as we know archaeologically, the ancestors of most Israelites and Judeans had never been in Egypt. The biblical narrative of the exodus is best understood, therefore, as metaphorically true: a story in cultural memory of Yahweh's superiority to the pharaoh and the gods of Egypt, a story of liberation and manifest destiny.[6]

Late Bronze II/Iron I Sites (Late Thirteenth–Twelfth Century)

True to our intent to take the archaeological data as our primary source, we will begin not with the biblical account of the Israelite settlement of Canaan in the books of Joshua–Judges but rather with the presentation of the relevant archaeological evidence. Nothing is more fundamental to recognizing historical and cultural development than an analysis of changes in settlement patterns. At the transition from the Bronze to the Iron Age, circa 1250–1150, which we have already characterized in chapter 2, these changes are profound and revealing. We shall look first at non-Israelite sites for purposes of comparison.

As noted in chapter 2, several Late Bronze Age sites in Cisjordan were not destroyed toward the end of the thirteenth century and did not come to an end until the mid- to late eleventh century. In addition, a few less well known sites in Transjordan may span this horizon. Since the latter are more peripheral to our inquiry here regarding early Israel, we shall look at them first (see figs. 3.1 and 3.2 for the following).

Transjordan

The Late Bronze II–early Iron I horizon in Transjordan is not well understood: excavations are recent and often published only in preliminary form.[7] In general, a few sites do show a destruction somewhere in the late thirteenth or early to mid-twelfth century, among them Tall Ziraʿa, Irbid, and Pella, with, however, subsequent reoccupation (see figs. 3.1 and 3.2 for these and the following). At Tall as-Saʿidiyeh, the Late Bronze Strata XII–XIB Egyptian residency (below) is destroyed circa 1150, followed by a long gap. The vast cemetery, the tombs of which show wide contacts, spans this era. Stratum XIA represents a poor rebuild in the mid-eleventh to early tenth century. Like Deir ʿAlla (Dayr ʿAlla), Tall as-Saʿidiyeh (Zaphon?) appears to be a Canaanite trading center with far-flung contacts.

At Deir ʿAlla (Penuel? Succoth?) the Late Bronze temple level (Phase E) was destroyed circa 1200, to judge from a scarab of Queen Tausret (1888–1186) found in this level. There follow twelfth-century Strata A–C, with some pseudo-Philistine sherds and twelve tablets in an undeciphered script (Cypro-Minoan?), apparently destroyed by an earthquake circa 1150 (C-14). Stratum D represents a rebuild in the twelfth–eleventh century, extending perhaps to Stratum L, with a C-14 date of circa 990. Deir ʿAlla appears to have been a Canaanite Late Bronze and Iron I trading center with wide contacts. There is nothing to suggest an Israelite destruction or settlement in the twelfth century (below).

Tell el-ʿUmeiri, a prominent site on the Ammon–Moab border, is one of the best excavated and published sites thus far. Stratum 14, belonging to Late Bronze II, exhibits a defense wall, temple, and monumental architecture—rare for Late Bronze Age Transjordan. A period of decline (Stratum

13) then ends circa 1200 in what appears to be an earthquake. Stratum 12, of the early to mid-twelfth century, is characterized by two large pillar-courtyard houses (Buildings A and B) enclosed by a casemate-like wall. The pottery has some affinities with the early Iron I pottery of Cisjordan. Stratum 12 ends violently, followed by a hiatus circa 1150–1100, then a poor rebuild in Stratum 11, circa 1100–1050. Because of the transitional nature of the Tell el-ʿUmeiri material, we will return to it shortly.[8]

Several other Transjordanian sites show few if any late Late Bronze destructions, including Tall Ziraʿa, Tell Abu el-Kharaz VIII, Tell el-Fukhar, and the Beqaʿa Valley sites near Amman. Farther south, in Moab and Edom, the Iron I period is rather poorly attested. If the extensive copper-smelting operations in the Wadi Fidan do prove to begin as early as the eleventh century, that would be significant.[9]

Before leaving Transjordan, we should note that none of the archaeological evidence for either continuity or discontinuity on the thirteenth–twelfth century horizon necessarily has anything to do with supposed Israelite incursions. Where there are destructions, the agents are not known. The emerging early Iron Age polities there are best understood as new foundations following the gradual collapse of the local Late Bronze Age Canaanite civilization and descended from it. The area, although peripheral because of its natural resources, had been and remained closely related to Cisjordan. If any ethnic identity were to be postulated this early, these peoples could be described as Proto-Ammonites and Proto-Moabites—comparable to but not identical with their Proto-Israelite neighbors (below).

A few other Iron I sites east of the Jordan River may be identified as Aramean (fig. 3.1). The most significant is Tel Hadar, a small mound on the northeast shore of the Sea of Galilee, excavated by Kochavi beginning in 1987. Stratum VI is a walled Late Bronze village. Stratum V then represents an early Iron I occupation marked by silos. Stratum IV, of the eleventh century, features a large tripartite building and other monumental structures adjoining the old Late Bronze city wall. A Euboean Protogeometric krater is among the earliest Greek imports in the Iron I Levant, supported by C-14 dates in the late eleventh century. Tel Hadar was probably the capital of the kingdom of Geshur.

ʿEin-Gev, a low mound 6 miles down the shore, is another Aramean site. Stratum 5 has a tenth-century solid wall, followed by a casemate wall in Stratum 4 of the late tenth century. The site may be biblical Aphek.

At the confluence of the upper Jordan River and the Sea of Galilee is Bethsaida (et-Tell, a 20-acre mound). Stratum 6 seems to represent the tenth century, but only Stratum 5 of the ninth–eighth century is well known.

Cisjordan

Of Canaanite sites west of the Jordan that continued into Iron I, Megiddo VIIB, destroyed about 1200, then quickly rebuilt, yields the most coherent picture (see figs. 3.1 and 4.3 for the following). In Stratum VIIA the royal palace near the gate, a large *migdôl* (tower) temple, and domestic houses all followed Late Bronze Age norms and suggest a large, prosperous town. Of particular importance is a large hoard of carved Syrian-style ivories found in a basement annex of the temple, an indication of the wealth and sophistication still prevailing in this final phase of Canaanite civilization. The site was completely destroyed at the end of Stratum VIIA, circa 1150, to judge from a cartouche of Ramesses III (or possibly later, if a pedestal bearing the cartouche of Ramesses VI [1143–1136] belongs to this stratum). The following Stratum VIIB is built on an entirely different plan.[10]

Tel Kinrot (Chinnereth, Tell el-ʿOreimeh) is a small tell atop a prominent hillock overlooking the northwest shore of the Sea of Galilee. Stratum VI represents a refounding of the larger Bronze Age town (ca. 12 acres), now only a village of some 2.5 aces in the twelfth century. Stratum V of the eleventh century features a large stone town wall 35 feet wide that may have reused an earlier wall, contiguous with a large block of rectangular Canaanite-style courtyard houses arranged in an orthogonal plan. The pottery continues earlier Iron I traditions. Stratum V is destroyed at the end of the eleventh century, followed by a poorer occupation in Stratum IV (tenth century). An Iron I village of perhaps two hundred people, Tel Kinrot is a good example of Late Bronze–Iron I continuity, but its large defensive wall is exceptional.

Shechem (Tell Balaṭah), 30 miles north of Jerusalem in a major pass leading down into the Jordan Valley, had been a major Middle–Late Bronze Age city-state. Stratum XII was not, however, destroyed circa 1200 but continued into early Iron I Stratum XI without major disturbances until its destruction circa 1100. After that, the site was virtually unpopulated until the Iron IIA period.

The same continuity of culture is seen at Gezer and Lachish. At Lachish the Stratum VI Fosse Temples went out of use, but they were replaced by the Acropolis Temple. This was an elaborate Egyptian-style structure that produced many items, such as Egyptian faience and ivory objects, in particular a gold-foil plaque depicting a nude goddess astride a war horse. In addition, there were Mycenaean and Minoan imports. Two bowls inscribed in Egyptian hieratic mention the fourth and the tenth–nineteenth years of a pharaoh, probably Ramesses III. Around 1140 the site was destroyed, then abandoned until the late tenth century. There is no Philistine pottery in the destruction debris, so the perpetrators are unknown. An Israelite destruction seems unlikely.[11]

The Phoenician Coast

In Cisjordan, the northern coastal plain (now in Israel and Lebanon) witnesses a general continuity of Canaanite Late Bronze Age culture into the Iron I period, when peoples eventually known as Phoenicians (the Greek term) gradually supplant the local population. However, these sites, especially those in Lebanon, are not extensively excavated and published (see figs. 3.1 and 3.2 for the following).

Along the modern Israel coast there are several Phoenician sites. At Akko, on the Bay of Haifa, there is another good anchorage. There the Late Bronze Age Egyptian fortress came to an end in the thirteenth century. It was replaced, probably in the twelfth century, by a new settlement with industrial installations. Levels dated to the eleventh century have produced Phoenician and Cypro-Phoenician pottery. There is some Philistine bichrome ware, but it does not provide an ethnic identification (see below and fig. 3.8).

At Achzib, Iron II Phoenician remains are abundant. There is also some evidence of earlier occupation, probably due to its excellent location and magnificent natural harbor. Most of the rich tombs with Phoenician and Cypriot connections belong, however, to the tenth–seventh century.[12]

Tell Keisan, on the Plain of Akko and originally closer to the sea, is the best known. There Stratum 13, with Late Mycenaean IIIC wares, is said to have been destroyed by fire circa 1200. The subsequent Stratum 12 features an extensive buildup of domestic areas, accompanied by Philistine bichrome and Cypriot or imitation wares. By Stratum 9c–a, perhaps of the eleventh century, there is evidence of a city plan with massive, well-built structures, characterized by Phoenician bichrome pottery. That city seems to replace the smaller settlement and was destroyed circa 980. The overall evidence suggests a cultural Late Bronze/Iron I mix that seems to characterize early coastal Phoenician sites.[13]

Another important site is Tell Abu Hawam. Unfortunately, several excavation projects over the years have failed to clarify the stratigraphy and chronology of the Late Bronze–Iron I horizon. Apparently Hamilton's Stratum VB (more recently Phases 5–4), with Late Cypriot and Late Mycenaean wares, was destroyed by fire sometime in the early to mid-twelfth century. There follows a phase (C, 3?) characterized by a city wall, a citadel, and Philistine bichrome pottery. The most recent excavators suggest that this marks the arrival of new population elements related to, but not identical with, the Sea Peoples of Egyptian records (below). The natural harbor on the Bay of Akko was probably in use this early and would have favored maritime trade.[14]

Dor may well have been the most important coastal Phoenician town on this horizon. The Late Bronze Age, however, is poorly known, and the transition to the early Iron I period (Phase G/10) is thus far scarcely attested. Phases B1/12, D/13, G/9 are destroyed circa 1100–1050. Phases B1/10, D2/11–10, and G/8–7 then represent a new foundation of a walled town in the late eleventh century with a bastion and massive architecture, extending over some 20 acres. After a destruction, Phases B1/9 and D2/9 continue the same building traditions into the late eleventh/early tenth century. A B1/8, D2/8, G/6 hoard of nearly 19 pounds of silver fragments, circa tenth century, was packed into seventeen bags and sealed with bullae, giving some idea of the city's wealth. The site-wide destruction circa 1100–1050 would be the level associated with the eleventh-century Egyptian Tale of Wen-Amon, which describes Dor as "a town of the *škls*" (Shikalayu; but circa 1000 on the low chronology). These peoples, however, cannot simply be equated with one particular group of the Sea Peoples. Furthermore, the rarity of Philistine pottery in the twelfth-century levels and the prevalence of Egyptian store jars, Cypriot and local imitation wares, and local Phoenician bichrome and red polished pottery suggests rather a cosmopolitan Phoenician culture by the tenth century.[15]

Inland from the Bay of Haifa up into the low-lying foothills of western Lower Galilee, surveys have found some forty Iron I Phoenician villages, with a total built up area of some 1,350 acres, but chronological precision is impossible.

In today's Syria and Lebanon, the known Phoenician sites are, from north to south, as follows.[16]

Fig. 3.3. Phoenician sites in the northern Levant

Al-Mina	Tell ʿArqa
Ras al-Bassit	Byblos
Tell Afis	Beirut
Tell Sukas	Sidon
Arwad	Sarepta
ʿAmrit	Tyre
Tell al-Kazel	

All in all, it appears on the basis of our limited evidence at present that the Phoenicians expanded south along the Levantine coast in Israel only as far as Dor in the twelfth–eleventh century. They did not extend their territory very far inland until the tenth century.[17] Nevertheless, beyond the southern Levant we have good evidence for extensive Phoenician mercantile activity as early as the eleventh century. Phoenicians apparently quickly took advantage of the collapse of Canaanite civilization in the Levant and began to expand westward by sea. Tiglath-pileser I (1114–1076) refers to "receiving tribute" from Phoenicians at Byblos, Sidon, and Arwad, speaking of ships at the latter region. The Wen-Amon story, circa 1075, mentions ships anchored at Byblos and Sidon, probably Phoenician vessels. More than thirty Iron I–II shipwrecks are now known in the Mediterranean, some of which are no doubt those of Phoenician traders. Several eleventh-century sites in Cyprus witness their presence, some documented a bit later by inscriptions such as the Nora inscription. There they are already colonists. At Carthage in North Africa, on Sardinia, and even in Spain, Phoenicians are present in some numbers by the tenth century at the latest. It is ironic that in their homeland, the Levantine coast, they are less well known.

Before leaving the Phoenicians behind and turning to the contemporary Philistines, it may be helpful to summarize the significance of the scant textual evidence (nonbiblical) for these ethnic designations, in addition to Ramesses III's enumeration of several groups of Sea Peoples (above). A text of a letter sent to the last ruler of Ugarit before its destruction circa 1200 (and thus earlier than Ramesses IIII) mentions the Shikalayu, undoubtedly perceived as a threat. The Onomasticon of Amenope, circa 1125, lists after Ashkelon and Ashdod Sherden, Shikalayu, and Philistines. That list has been presumed to be in geographical order, from north to south, leading some scholars to locate the Sherden somewhere south from Ugarit to

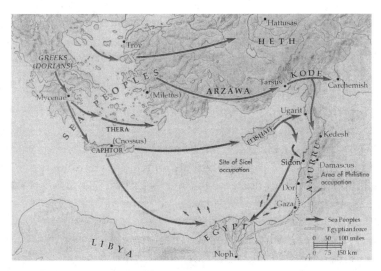

Fig 3.4. Movements of Sea Peoples circa 1180 (or slightly earlier) (Rainey 2006, 108). © Copyright Carta, Jerusalem.

Akko, the Shikalayu at Dor (as in the Tale of Wen-Amon), and the Philistines along the southern Levantine coast somewhere south of Tel Aviv. But the conventional order of Egyptian topographical lists is confused here, and in some cases (Dor) the identification is unsupported by any archaeological evidence. The above scenario also assumes that the invading Sea Peoples advanced from the northern to the southern Levantine coast by land, whereas the best evidence we have suggests several, probably successive, waves of settlement, by both land and sea (fig. 3.4). The only thing clear is that one group—the Philistines of both the Ramesses III and the biblical texts—were entrenched along the southern Levantine coast by the early to mid-twelfth century.[18]

Egyptian "Residencies" in the Twelfth Century

We have already noted in chapter 2 (fig. 2.9) several Egyptian residencies and forts at Canaanite sites that survived the onslaught of the Sea Peoples and persevered until the mid-twelfth century or so (figs. 3.1 and 3.2). Among them are Beth-Shean VI, Tel Aphek X$_{12}$, Tel Mor VIII–VII, Tell el-Ḥesi IV, Tell Jemmeh J–K, Tell el-Farʿah (South) Building YR, Tel Seraʿ IX, and Deir el-Balaḥ VII. Despite this "twilight" of Egyptian presence in the southern Levant, the Asiatic empire had been lost, in large part due to the invasions of the Sea Peoples whom Ramesses III claims to have defeated. Before we discuss the end of all these Egyptian residencies circa 1175–1140, we need to look closely at contemporary peoples who may have been a factor.

Sea Peoples Sites in the Twelfth–Eleventh Century

We have already noted in chapter 2 the destructions along the southern Levantine coast, some of which are attributable to invading Sea Peoples circa 1180 known from the texts and reliefs of Ramesses III (figs. 3.1, 3.2, and 3.5). Following that we see the establishment of the first new Iron I settlements, characterized initially by Late Mycenaean IIIC:1 monochrome pottery and other Mycenaean, Aegean, and Cypriot cultural traits. The most impressive of these new foundations are those of the "Philistine Pentapolis": Ashdod XIIIBA; Ashkelon 20, 19; Ekron VII–VI (Tel Miqne); and Gath 8–7 (Tel Zafit; Gaza is unidentified and unexcavated). Here again we shall take a regional perspective.[19]

    1. The Southern Coastal Region. First we shall look at several southern coastal sites that characterize Stager's Stage 1, dating to roughly the time of Ramesses III (1184–1153) and characterized by Late Mycenaean III:C1 style wares. These were sites where the first wave of Sea Peoples established a beachhead. From south to north they include the following (see figs. 3.1, 3.2, and 4.3).[20]

    The Egyptian Late Bronze Age fortress and residency at Deir el-Balaḥ (Stratum VII) in the Gaza strip was rebuilt in Stratum VI, then continued in use into Strata V–IV in the late twelfth to mid-eleventh century. Domestic structures and installations now indicate some change in function. Cemetery 300 with its anthropoid coffins (fifty of them found) had originated in Stratum VII, but it still continued in use in Strata VI–IV, and kilns for firing the lids were found in situ. Philistine bichrome pottery is questionable. The Egyptian-style anthropoid coffins may have been used by Sea People settlers, but they are now known not to be an ethnic marker. All in all, Philistine newcomers may have overrun this Egyptian outpost and perhaps settled there in small numbers.[21]

    Tell el-Farʿah (South) Building YR and Tell Jemmeh J–K, coastal sites north of Deir el-Balaḥ with Egyptian residencies, could be included here. After they ended (not necessarily in a destruction), they exhibit Philistine pottery and burials, so they may be considered peripheral Philistine sites.[22]

Fig. 3.5. Sea Peoples wagons and chariots (T. Dothan 1982, figs. 5–6)

Stratum 21 at Ashkelon, belonging to the late thirteenth/early twelfth century, seems to have suffered some destruction or at least a major disturbance. Stratum 20 is then characterized by a new architectural plan, locally made Late Mycenaean IIIC:1 monochrome wares dated to the reign of Ramesses III (Stager's Stage 1), nonperforated cylindrical clay loomweights of Aegean style, carved ivories, Cypro-Minoan signs, and a high percentage of pig bones. The newly founded seaport extended for as much as 125 acres, fortified by a mudbrick rampart. Subsequent Phase 19 has a new plan, a mixture of monochrome and bichrome wares, hearths, chalk tubs, and foundation deposits. Phase 18 of the eleventh century has only bichrome pottery, and Phase 17 has degenerate bichrome wares, with the beginnings of red-slipped Ashdod wares (LPDW: Late Philistine

Decorated Ware). Ashkelon is remembered by the biblical writers as part of the "Philistine pentapolis" (above), as indeed it was.[23]

Ashdod XIII, a well-planned but unfortified town of some 20 acres in the early to mid-twelfth century, follows a heavy destruction layer. It produced quantities of imported plus locally made Late Mycenaean IIIC:1 monochrome pottery, alongside Canaanite ceramic styles. "Ashdoda" figurines represent a seated Aegean-style terra cotta goddess. Stratum XII is the major, fortified town, when Philistine bichrome ware dominates. A seal has an apparent Cypro-Minoan inscription. Stratum XI shows continuity into the early tenth century, but a massive city wall and three-entryway gate are added, and the upper and lower cities now grow to some 100 acres. Stratum X belongs to the early to mid-tenth century, and the preponderance of late degenerate wares (LPDW) marks the last distinctly Philistine material culture.[24]

At nearby Tel Mor, the Egyptian fortress and residency of Strata VIII–VII was destroyed, perhaps by an early wave of Sea Peoples. A new settlement in Stratum VI, however, has a smaller fort that seems to mark a hiatus. Then Strata IV–III, with Philistine pottery, follow.[25]

2. The Yarkon Basin. North of the cluster of Philistine sites along the southern coast, there is another group of Stage 1 sites in the Yarkon Basin.

Right at the mouth of the Yarkon River in the confines of modern Tel Aviv, at a convenient anchorage, lies Tell Qasile (fig. 3.6). Unlike most other Philistine sites, it is founded de novo in the early twelfth century. Two architectural phases in Stratum XII exhibit a well laid out block of domestic houses, some of courtyard type. An offset-entrance temple (Temple 369) yielded an ivory knife handle of Cypriot type. Here, as at Ekron, there were Aegean-style hearths. In Stratum XI, a fortified town of the late twelfth–eleventh century, Temple 200 replaces the earlier structure. In a small holy of holies and a nearby favissa were found numerous cult objects, including fenestrated offering stands, an anthropomorphic mask, an ivory bird-shaped cosmetic bowl, terra cotta figurines, votive vessels, and other objects. The first degenerate Philistine pottery, featuring a red slip with black paint decoration (Ashdod ware; LPDW) now appears. In Stratum X an even larger temple was built, again with many cultic items, preserved in a fiery destruction layer of the early tenth century.[26]

Throughout these two centuries in Iron I, Tell Qasile was a well-planned, orthogonally laid out urban site with a variety of well-constructed public and domestic buildings. Some were pillar-courtyard houses (below). At 4

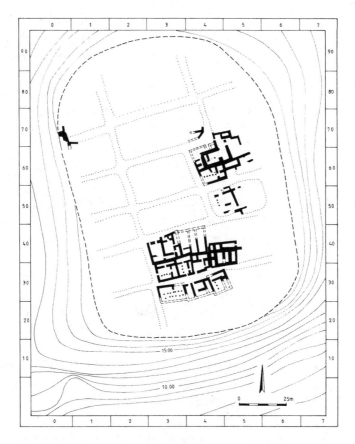

Fig. 3.6. Plan of Tell Qasile, Stratum X (Herzog 1992, fig. 7)

acres, the town could well have had a population of 400 or more. Even more than several other Philistine towns, it reflects newcomers who arrived with a fully developed urban culture associated with Cypriot, Mycenaean, and Aegean traits, including a rectangular grid plan.

In old Joppa were found in Level III a few Philistine remains from salvage operations, notably the well-preserved skull of a lioness in a temple, reminiscent of the Philistine lion rython found in the Tell Qasile temple.[27]

At Aphek, at the headwaters of the Yarkon River, the Late Bronze residency (Building 1104) is replaced in Stratum X_{11} by a large residential quarter accompanied by Philistine pottery. In Stratum X_{10} were found Ashdoda figurines and a clay tablet with an inscription in an undeciphered script.[28]

A large cemetery was excavated among modern houses at Azor on the southern outskirts of Tel Aviv that yielded shallow burials with quantities of Philistine bichrome pottery, along with an Egyptian Nineteenth Dynasty scarab.[29]

North of Tel Aviv, at Jerishe (Tel Gerisa), there are three architectural phases with Philistine bichrome pottery, terra cotta figurines, and several pillar-courtyard houses (below). The site is a village no doubt associated with nearby Tell Qasile.[30]

3. Inland Sites. A group of inland sites in the Shephelah represent an early Stage 1 or possibly Stage 2 Philistine expansion from the coastal beachheads. We shall look at these again from south to north.

At Tel Haror (Tell Abu-Hureireh; Gerar), Stratum 7 is succeeded by Strata 6–5 sometime in the twelfth century, then by Stratum 4–3 in the early eleventh century with quantities of Philistine bichrome pottery.

Nearby Tel Seraʿ (Ziklag?) is one of the southern sites with an Egyptian residency (Building 906 of Stratum IX). In the destruction debris were found several bowls and ostraca inscribed in Egyptian hieratic script and recording large quantities of grain. One refers to "year 20," perhaps of Ramesses III (1184–1153). Stratum VII produced typical Philistine bichrome pottery as well as pillar-courtyard houses. Again, the material culture seems to reflect a peripheral site on the border with Judah.

Farther north in the Shephelah are the two remaining sites of the biblical Philistine pentapolis. The first is Philistine Gath, now finally identified with Tel Zafit (Tell eṣ-Ṣafi) roughly 13 miles southeast of Ashdod. Current excavations (1996–) have achieved only limited exposure of Philistine levels thus far. Temporary Stratum 8 follows a destruction level in the early twelfth century. It is characterized by Late Mycenaean III:C1 pottery. Philistine bichrome then is typical of Stratum 6, and Stratum 5 seems to have degenerate Philistine motifs (as do other sites, related to red-slipped and painted Ashdod ware; LPDW). An iron knife handle resembles bimetal Aegean-style knives found at Tel Miqne and elsewhere. Stratum 5 ends in the late eleventh century; Stratum 4 belongs to the tenth century, including Phoenician wares.[31]

Ekron (Tel Miqne), following a major destruction, exhibits in Stratum VIIA–B large quantities of locally made Late Mycenaean III:C1 monochrome ware (Philistine 1), along with Canaanite ceramic forms and pottery kilns. The new town on the 10-acre acropolis was laid out on a north–south grid plan, with a mudbrick fortification wall and distinct domestic and industrial quarters. The lower city adds 40 acres. Pebbled hearths are reminiscent of the Aegean world. By Stratum VIA–B, of the late twelfth–early eleventh century, Late Mycenaean III:C1 monochrome pottery continues, but in diminishing quantities. The first Philistine bichrome wares (Philistine 2) are seen and now dominate the repertoire. Stratum V, belonging to the early to mid-eleventh century, produced a cult room (Temple 351), pebbled hearths, unperforated loomweights, an inscribed scapula, a bimetallic ivory-handled knife, bronze brazier wheels, and a terra cotta bathtub (fig. 3.7). Many of these features reflected Cypriot and Mycenaean culture. The following Stratum IV ends in the early tenth century, after which the lower city industrial area is abandoned, and only the 10-acre acropolis continues to be occupied.[32]

Tel Zippor II (Tell Sipori), 7 miles southwest of Gath, represents a small Stage 1 or 2 settlement, one of the few rural Philistine sites known. It features Philistine pottery and several pillar-courtyard houses.

4. Peripheral Stage 2 Sites. The following are sometimes classified as Philistine sites, but they are border sites with a mixed population, and they were probably not ethnically Philistine. The lone peripheral Stage 2 site in the far south is Tell el-Farʿah (above). The Philistine enclave apparently did not extend farther south because of the Egyptian border.

Several sites farther north and inland in the Shephelah characterize Stage 2 of the Philistine settlement. They document the expansion of settlement right up to what will become the natural border of Judah later in the monarchy. They all lack Late Mycenaean IIIC:1 monochrome pottery, as well as the more Aegean-style material culture of the coastal and some Yarkon Basin sites.

Tell Beit Mirsim, Beth-Shemesh, Tel Batash, and Gezer form a south–north border of sorts, a buffer-zone, between the Philistine Shephelah and the western flanks of the central hills, where an Israelite enclave sooner or later emerges (below).

Tell Beit Mirsim C ends in a destruction at the end of the Late Bronze Age. Subsequent Stratum B_{1-3} was flimsy, characterized mainly by numerous grain pits (like many Philistine sites). In Phase 1 there seems to have been little or no Philistine pottery; in Phase 2 bichrome wares appear, followed in Phase 3 by "post-Philistine" pottery (LPDW).

Beth-Shemesh is an unfortified town with three Iron I levels (Levels 6–4). Large buildings ("patrician houses") of the first level of the mid-twelfth century were destroyed by fire. The pottery is similar to early Iron

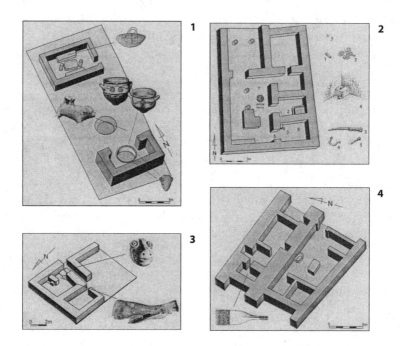

Fig. 3.7. Early Philistine structures and contents (eleventh century). 1: Ekron VIIB; 2: Ekron V; 3: Ekron V; 4: Ashdod XII (Dothan 2003, 194, 195, 203, 209)

Age pottery at nearby such as like Tel Batash and Gezer. There are only small quantities of Philistine bichrome ware, and Late Bronze Canaanite styles are still prevalent. Pig bones, however, were entirely absent. Stratum 5, of short duration, shows a squatter occupation above the patrician houses. Stratum 4, the last of the Iron I levels, perhaps in the late eleventh century, produced the first clear pillar-courtyard house, as well as an alley flanked by an industrial installation. Stratum 3 (old III) then represents the first monumental structures at the site, in the tenth century (below). The current excavator suggests that there may have been a Philistine presence at the site but no Philistine control; further, the mixed cultural traditions suggest a more Phoenician character and a period of ethnic conflict and perhaps acculturation in the eleventh–tenth century that fits the picture at Gezer quite well.[33]

Tel Batash (biblical Timnah), 15 miles inland from Ashdod, seems to represent (with Tel Zafit/Gath) the eastward extension of Philistine settlement in the late twelfth century. Stratum V is characterized by

abundant Philistine bichrome pottery, several phases of domestic structures, and a podium structure that may be part of a defense system. Tel
Batash appears to be a sort of daughter city of Ekron. Stratum V ends not
with a destruction but with a period of abandonment. In later periods,
Batash will become part of the border with Israel and will take on Israelite characteristics.

Gezer, a 33-acre site just north of Tel Batash and approximately 14
miles inland from the coast, lies along the Via Maris at the juncture of
the southern coastal plain, the Sharon plain, the inner Shephelah, and
the flanks of the central hills. Stratum XIV of the Late Bronze II horizon
ends without a site-wide destruction but rather with a disturbance and an
interval of widespread pitting and filling operations in Field VI. This era
may well be attributed to Pharaoh Merenptah, whose Victory Stela of circa
1208 mentions Gezer and whose inscribed pectoral was found at the site
by Macalister.

Stratum XIII is then marked by a large, multiroomed granary (Granary 2400) with a few sherds that recall but are not identical to Late
Mycenaean III:C1 wares. There is not, in fact, a single clear sherd of monochrome ware. This stratum ends with a major destruction. Stratum XII, of
the early twelfth century, sees two large courtyard houses (the Northwest
and Northeast Houses in Field VI), built over the ruins of the granary,
accompanied by the first Philistine bichrome ware. These houses, too,
end in a fiery destruction. Rebuilt in Stratum XI of the early to mid-eleventh century, they are destroyed again. From the debris comes not only
Philistine bichrome ware but also ceramic swan heads from *kernoi* (trick-
vessels) similar to those found at Tell Qasile and a terra cotta circumcised
penis. In the following phase, Stratum X, red-washed and a few degenerate Philistine styles of pottery (LPDW) are seen (late eleventh–early
tenth century). The series of destructions in the twelfth–eleventh century
at Gezer—unmatched anywhere else in Philistia and its immediate environs—demonstrates the stormy nature of the Philistine expansion as it
reached the limits of its natural borders.[34]

While at least the early Philistine coastal sites (Stage 1) are urban in
character, the more mature Philistine phases encompass not only inland
towns like the above but also a number of rural hinterland sites known
from surveys, sites necessary to supply a growing population with agricultural products.[35]

One inland Shephelah site that is conspicuously lacking in Philistine remains is Lachish. The Stratum VI city was violently destroyed circa 1140, then lay abandoned until circa 900. Not a sherd of Philistine pottery was found in extensive excavations of two long-running projects. Proponents of the idiosyncratic low chronology use this gap in occupation to posit that Lachish (and other sites) were reoccupied only after the Philistine monochrome and bichrome wares were extinct, thus lowering the date of Philistine occupation and Iron I by anywhere from half to a full century (ch. 4). Such a drastic chronological revision is unwarranted. Simply put, the Philistines did not push that far inland in Stages 1 or 2, or indeed for that matter anywhere else that early, so the absence of their distinctive pottery means absolutely nothing (see further ch. 4).

Summary of Philistine Culture

The presentation of the above data scarcely does justice to the rich documentation made available by recent excavations. Much more is now known about the early Philistines than about the early Israelites. Nevertheless, a summary is adequate to place the Philistines in the picture of new Iron Age peoples emerging in the wake of the collapse of Canaanite civilization that is documented here and in chapter 2. Several features must be highlighted, even if there is some overlap.

The distinctive material culture of the Philistines and the other Sea Peoples now known is what may be called broadly an Aegean or Levanto-Aegean style. That term designates an amalgam of cultural traits from the Minoan and Mycenaean world, mediated to the Levant via Cypriot and Anatolian adaptations—in effect, a widespread koine culture emerging at the end of the Bronze Age in the eastern Mediterranean world and in the Levant. The elements of this common late thirteenth–early twelfth century culture vary from place to place, but one thing is clear: it diffused widely, relatively suddenly, both by sea and by land. It is equally clear that, when this culture arrived along the Levantine coast after a generation or so, it was a foreign element but still vibrant. Yet cultures do not arrive, people do, and in this case they migrated in sufficiently large numbers that they helped overwhelm a local cultural tradition that was already in a steep decline.

Invasion theories, in contrast to diffusion models, have been in disrepute for some time in anthropology and archaeology, but largely because a former generation of scholars invoked them too often and also overworked them. A few archaeologists still resist the notion of large-scale Philistine invasions along the Levantine coast. Robert Drews, a classicist, claims that *Philistine* is only another name for local Canaanites: "the 'national migrations' posited for the second millennium BCE are figments of the ancient and modern imagination." Susan Sherratt, closer to the field, accepts diffusion rather than invasion models. She falls back on the notion that the Sea Peoples' cultural traits were carried to the Levant by traders from Cyprus.[36] But how did those Sea Peoples, clearly foreign to the island, to judge from a mass of evidence (above), *get* to Cyprus if not by sea?

In Cyprus, as we have seen in chapter 2, new peoples arriving toward the end of the Late Mycenaean/Late Cypriot III period established colonies along the coast but did not penetrate very far inland. Lacking a foothold, these seafarers would likely have turned to the southern Levantine coast, only some 80 miles distant. The several shipwrecks that we have, as well as the depiction of ocean-going Sea Peoples sailing ships on the Medinet Habu reliefs of Ramesses III, show that such voyages were quite feasible. Large numbers of Sea Peoples in Cyprus had both the motivation and the means to invade and settle the Levantine coast, and they brought with them centuries-old, strong cultural and ethnic traditions from the Bronze Age in the Mediterranean world. No other model will account for the many destructions that we have along the Levantine coast in the early twelfth century or the relatively sudden appearance of an entirely new Aegean-style material culture.[37]

Several shared elements of this new material culture are evident in the archaeological record of the Philistine sites discussed above.

- pottery in Late Mycenaean III:C1 monochrome style imported and local (Stage 1)
- bichrome pottery (Stage 2).
- orthogonal urban planning
- temples reflecting *megara* hearths
- large-scale grain production and numerous storage pits
- wine production
- distinctive cooking jugs of Anatolian type
- conspicuous pork consumption (and perhaps dogs)
- evidence of ritual feasting
- textiles

- ◆ Bimetallic, ivory-handled knives
- ◆ inscribed bovine scapulae
- ◆ clay tablets and seals in a Cypro-Minoan (?) script

All of these distinctive material cultural traits—ethnic markers, for most scholars, even some skeptics—are well documented in recent publications on Philistines in the Aegean and the southern Levant. We need only highlight the distinctive pottery, always our most sensitive medium for perceiving cultural characteristics and documenting cultural change (see fig. 3.8 for the following).

The fundamentally Aegean character of this pottery has been recognized almost from the outset. Today, however, we can be much more precise. Three phases of development are clear. (1) A monochrome phase is closely related to Late Mycenaean IIIC:1 styles widespread on the mainland and throughout the Aegean, especially in Cyprus. Designated Phase 1, a few sherds of these vessels appear as imports at some Iron I sites such as Beth-Shean (surprisingly rare elsewhere). This phase is confined to the original Philistine settlements in the twelfth century, extending perhaps to the end of that century, with more Aegean influence.

Phase 2 is defined by the emergence of a unique, exclusively *local* style of bichrome ware, featuring both Mycenaean-style geometric and zoomorphic motifs (such as birds and fishes). This ceramic style overlaps with that of Phase 1 but is more Cypriot, then extends well into the eleventh century, prevalent at all Philistine and even a few peripheral sites. It represents the full floruit of Philistine settlement.[38]

Phase 3 is a late, degenerate style featuring black geometric design painted over a thin red wash or slip. Originally called Ashdod ware, from the site where it was first recognized, it is now often designated Late Philistine Decorated Ware (LPDW). It overlaps with eleventh-century bichrome ware, then continues in use into the mid- to late tenth century, where it overlaps with early red-slipped and hand-burnished wares. Its "degenerate" character fits well with Philistine settlements where the population is gradually becoming acculturated, combining both original foreign elements and local Canaanite (and Judahite) cultural influences.[39]

Recent excavations in Turkey have provided further evidence that some Sea Peoples had not only an Aegean origin but had also emigrated to the Levantine coast overland through Anatolia. Several sites, such as Troy and Miletus on the west coast, as well as sites in Cilicia, reveal an intrusive early Iron Age, post-Hittite culture. This suggest an Aegean origin in items such as fine ware (Gray Ware), certain cooking vessels, clay loom-weights (spools), and figurines, all much like those found at Philistine sites in Israel.

Particularly intriguing are two inscriptions. One found at Çineköy in Cilicia is a bilingual inscription, in Phoenician and Luwian, in which King Warika (Urikki in the Neo-Assyrian sources) introduces himself as "King of *dnnym*," evidently to be associated with the *dnnym* of Ramesses III's Sea Peoples. His Luwian title is "king of Hiyawa," probably a short form of the well-known Late Bronze Age country of Ahhiyawa, the Aegean *koine* (Homer's Achaioi). The second inscription was found in deep soundings in the Aleppo Citadel, where a hieroglyphic Luwian inscription names the king who rebuilt the temple with the magnificent basalt orthostats as Taita, specifically the king of "Palistin." This place name also occurs at several sites in the Orontes Valley, as well as the coast south of Iskenderun.

Of particular importance is Tell Ta'yinat, Neo-Assyrian Kullania, probably the capital of the kingdom of Palistin. Excavated early Iron Age levels reveal Aegean-style pottery, including Late Mycenaean III:C1 wares, cylindrical loomweights, and clay figurines. The Aegean-style pottery is locally made, then gives way to red-slipped burnished ware. Fragments of a hieroglyphic Luwian inscription found around Building XIV refer to a king who may have been Taita's successor, ruling at a site named Palis-tin (there spelled Walistin). This Palistin may have eclipsed Aleppo as the dominant city in northern Syria. Intriguing as this is, there are problems with a chronology that can only be broadly specified as early Iron I.[40]

One can extrapolate from the artifactual evidence something not only of Philistine culture itself but of ethnic identity. The Philistine set-tlers brought certain elements of the palace civilization of the Minoans and Mycenaeans. There is a well-defined concept of urbanism, as reflected in town layout, domestic construction, use of space, and development of industry. There is a sort of aristocratic aspect of this culture from the beginning. This sense of ethnic identity is only intensified as the Philistine culture comes into contact with the local culture, but then it is gradually modified. The result is a hybrid culture by the Iron II period, perhaps best termed Neo-Philistine. Many scholars have commented on this gradual cultural interaction, a phenomena sometimes called hybridization, cul-tural diffusion, creolization, or synoecism, evident in both Cyprus and the southern Levant.[41]

Fig. 3.8 (left). A selection of Philistine pottery. Numbers 1–7: Late Mycenaean IIIC:1 monochrome wares; 8–20: Philistine bichrome wares; 21–27: Late Philistine Decorated Ware (LPDW)

Late Mycenaean IIIC:1 (Philistine) Monochrome: 1: Krater, Ekron VII (Mountjoy 2013a, fig. 3:22); 2: krater, Ekron VII (Mountjoy 2013a, fig. 8:50); 3: krater, Ekron VII ((Mountjoy 2013a, fig. 6:40); 4: krater, Beth-Shean N3 = Level VI? (Sherratt and Mazar 2013, fig. 9:28); 5: krater, Troy LHIIIA2 (Mountjoy 2013b, fig. 16:1); 6: krater, Ialysos, Aegean (Benzi 2013, fig. 1:2); 7: krater, Sarafand, Syria (Lehmann 2013, fig. 1:5)

Philistine Bichrome: 8: krater, Gezer, unknown provenience (Amiran 1970, pl. 90:2); 9: pyxis, Gezer; unknown provenience (Amiran 1970, pl. 90:6); 10: krater, Gath 7 (Maeir 2013, fig. 10:5); 11: krater, Ekron (Mazow 2005, 195); 12: jug, Tell el-Farʿah South, Tomb 552 (Amiran 1970, pl. 90:9); 13: jug, Tell el-Farʿah South, Tomb 542 (Laemmel 2013, fig. 6:39); 14: jug, Tell el-Farʿah South, Tomb 601 (Amiran 1970, pl. 90:5); 15: krater (Third Semitic) (Macalister 1912, 3:pl. CLXIII:1); 16: krater, Tell el-Farʿah South, Tomb 542 (Laemmel 2013, fig. 6:24); 17: flagon, Tell Qasile XI–X (A. Mazar 1985, fig. 32:9); 18: flask, Gezer; unknown provenience (Amiran 1970, pl. 90:13); 19: spouted jug , Tell Qasile XI (A. Mazar 1985, fig. 12:1); 20: stirrup-jar, Gezer; unknown provenience (Amiran 1970, pl. 90:10)

Late Philistine Decorated Ware: 21: store jar, Ashdod X (Dothan and Ben-Shlomo, 2005, fig. 2:1); 22: pyxis, Khirbet Qeiyafa (Garfinkel and Ganor 2009, fig. 6:22.3); 23: jug, Gath 4 (Maeir 2013, fig. 21:4); 24: jug, Gath 4 (Maeir 2013, fig. 21:7); 25: krater, Gezer 3 (Dever et al. 1986, pl. 47:3); 26: jug, Tell Jemmeh (Ben-Shlomo and van Beek 2014, fig. 12:8b); 27: krater, Tell Qasile X (A. Mazar 1985, fig. 29:13)

None of the above cultural traits is found in Late Bronze Age Canaan or, for that matter, in Iron I Israelite villages (below). They are, however, well attested on Crete, on the Greek mainland, along the Anatolian coast, and particularly in Cyprus.

Along the southern Levantine coast this distinctive Aegean-style assemblage first appears in the early twelfth century. The date is fixed circa 1180 (or a bit earlier) by the inscriptions of Ramesses III in his eighth year. Furthermore, the invasions are dramatically illustrated by the pictorial reliefs found on the walls of Ramesses's temple at Medinet Habu (above). The Sea Peoples are quite different in appearance from the Egyptian defenders. Their sailors come on distinctive high-prowed sailing vessels, whereas the Nile boats are rowed. They are accompanied overland by soldiers as well as hordes of women, children, and baggage transported on large ox-drawn carts. This evidence, taken together with a string of destructions all the way from Tarsus in Anatolia down the coast to Ugarit in Syria, and witnessed in particular by the series of destructions along the southern Levantine coast that is documented in chapter 2, would seem to be decisive. These are new-comers—not Semitic peoples, but Greek-speaking Europeans.

Not only does this distinctive Aegean-style culture appear full-blown and largely established by force, but it is sufficiently energetic to expand quite far inland within a generation or two. Stager estimates that in his Stage 1 the territory controlled by Philistines enclosed a coastal region some 30 miles long and 12 miles wide, or an area of 360 square miles. Based on the size of the pentapolis cities alone, there would have been an urban population of some 25,000. By Stage 2, natural growth might well have doubled that number. By any estimate, at the end of the elev-enth century the Philistines (and other Sea Peoples) would have effected permanent changes on the landscape and cultural identity of the local inhabitants, even if somewhat acculturated themselves (above).[42]

Some have argued that the Philistine culture, while of Aegean origins via Anatolia and Cyprus, was not urban at all and, furthermore, that it developed only gradually. It was not a violent imposition or defensive. It did not perpetuate mercantile, sea-going trade, but it was based rather on a land economy and sought interrelations with the local Canaan-ite population. This is an effort at balance, but as an overall model it is unpersuasive.[43]

Size alone qualifies several Philistine sites as urban: Ashkelon at 125 acres, Ekron at 50 acres, and Gath at 125 acres. In addition, most sites boast monumental architecture as well as evidence of urban planning. Even Tell Qasile—a small town established de novo—shows a clear orthogonal (Hippodamian) town plan (fig. 3.6).

Philistine material culture persisted until the end of the Iron Age sev-eral centuries later, when the coastal region was finally overrun by the Babylonians and many sites were destroyed in 604. Perhaps best designated Neo-Philistine, these later peoples may have been partially acculturated, but they were never fully assimilated.[44] The Iron II pottery shows a mix-ture of Judean and distinctive coastal forms. Phoenician script, very close to the Hebrew script, was now adopted, and former Greek speakers now presumably communicated in a West Semitic dialect. The Old Canaan-ite (and Israelite) goddess Asherah was venerated in local shrines. Yet the Philistine terra cotta female figurines are easily distinguished from the typical Judean pillar-base figurines (below; ch. 4). The Philistine border with Judah can be established by the distribution of the above and other cultural traits, although it was always somewhat porous and shifted from time to time. Thus, as we have seen, sites such as Beth-Shemesh and Tel Batash are somewhat difficult to define ethnically.

Skeptics who do not control the archaeological data sometimes assert that we cannot define ethnicity on the basis of material culture remains alone. Yet no specialist doubts the applicability of the ethnic label *Philistine* in this case. The archaeological assemblage alone documents such recognizable cultural traits as site distribution and type, social structure, lifestyle, house form, food ways, religious rituals, and even language (although thus far undeciphered). In addition, we have the textual witness that is presumed to be essential: the Ramesses III and other Egyptian descriptions, Neo-Assyrian annals, Babylonian chronicles, and the biblical accounts, all specifically naming the Philistines and other Sea Peoples.

Stager, the major proponent of the invasion scenario adopted here, concludes:

> The Philistines brought with them templates of city planning and concepts of urban organization that Canaan had not experienced before. In addition, the Philistines brought with them a whole range of human resources and institutions to realize such organization. Behind the archaeological residues of the Pentapolis one can detect, however faintly, the activities of a diverse community of warriors, farmers, sailors, merchants, rulers, shamans, priests, artisans and architects.[45]

The Philistines persisted so long in ancient Palestine and had such powerful influence that, ironically, it was they, rather than the Israelites, who gave the land a name still used today. Greek sailors, venturing along the coast in the fifth century, learned from the local inhabitants the name *Philistine* and applied it to the southern Levantine coast. By Roman times it became Palaestina, designating the Roman province of Judah. The Byzantines perpetuated the name for what was later the "Holy Land." Arabs knew the land then and now as Filistin.

The arrival of Philistine material culture, dated conclusively no later than circa 1175, was so intrusive and so powerful that we must think further about its likely impact. How would the Philistines have encountered the only surviving local Late Bronze Age polities, the few twelfth-century "New Canaanite" sites we have seen, particularly the several early- to mid-twelfth-century Egyptian residencies discussed above?

The few surviving late Canaanite sites, such as Megiddo VIIA and Gezer XIV, ended sometime in the twelfth century, but the archaeological evidence is ambiguous. A bronze statue base of Ramesses VI, attributable to Stratum VIIA or VIIB at Megiddo, would date its violent destruction by fire as late as circa 1140. The agents are unknown, but the rarity of Philistine Phase 1 pottery in subsequent Stratum VIB precludes Philistine occupation, which fits what we know of their limited penetration (if any) this far north and inland, even after forty to fifty years.[46]

The date of the end of Gezer XIV, which shows only limited disturbances, can only be reckoned from the *terminus post quem* provided roughly by Macalister's unstratified cartouche of Merenptah (1213–1203). Philistine bichrome pottery first appearing in Stratum XIII suggests some Philistine presence, but only in Stage 2 and only peripherally. There is no reason to posit a Philistine destruction or any substantial Philistine population.

It is the several Egyptian residencies that are at issue here, because they represent the last foothold of the Egyptian domination of Canaan as it tottered to an end in the twelfth century (fig. 2.9). Were the Philistine intruders a factor in the collapse and disappearance of the Egyptian Empire in Asia? The only Egyptian residency in the north or very far inland is Building 1500 of Beth-Shean VI lower. A lintel, a statue base, and cartouches of Ramesses III provide a *terminus post quem* of circa 1175. In subsequent Stratum VI upper there were a few Late Mycenaean IIIC:1 sherds, but this by no means indicates a Philistine (or Sea Peoples) occupation. Again, Beth-Shean is far removed from the sphere of Philistine influence.[47]

It is noteworthy that the other Egyptian residencies are located in Philistia proper. The end of Building 1104 at Aphek (Stratum X_{12}) cannot be dated beyond the early to mid-twelfth century; the same is true of Petrie's Tell el-Ḥesi City IV or Tell Jemmeh J–K. Tell el-Farʿah (South), however, can at least be dated post–Ramesses II by inscriptional evidence, which would coincide roughly with the well-documented presence of Philistines in the area. Hieratic Ostraca from Tel Seraʿ IX, referring to year 20 of a pharaoh, probably Ramesses III, would date the end of building 906 there to circa 1165.

While it cannot be proven, it is reasonable to suggest that the appearance of the Philistines in force around 1175 would have brought them inevitably into conflict with waning Egyptian forces along the southern coast, where they likely prevailed over an already-diminished Egyptian presence. If the Egyptian forces sought a compromise by attempting to establish a *cordon sanitaire*, they failed. The last Egyptian forces disappear by the time of Ramesses VI (1143–1136), just when the Philistine Stage 2, or bichrome, phase is coming to its peak. These can scarcely be unrelated developments.

Other Iron I Sites in Cisjordan Representing New Patterns (Twelfth–Eleventh Century)

It is now known beyond doubt that the Israelite settlement in Canaan can no longer be seen in accordance with the biblical account of an "exodus and conquest" in the fifteenth century. The events in question must be placed on the Late Bronze/Iron I horizon circa 1250–1150 discussed above. In the vacuum created by the collapse of the long Bronze Age Canaanite civilization, the various new peoples and polities already introduced were joined by yet another group, whom many scholars long considered ethnic Israelites. In the interest of honest inquiry, however, we shall postpone that issue. In keeping with our intent to take the archaeological data as a primary source for history-writing, a survey of putative Israelite archaeological sites of the twelfth–eleventh century is necessary, that is, the facts on the ground. Here a regional approach will be helpful. Much of our data comes from extensive Israeli surveys in Israel and the West Bank since the early 1900s, which have mapped some 250 relevant sites. The fundamental work is Finkelstein's 1988 *The Archaeology of the Israelite Settlement*. Here again, a General Systems Theory approach will be utilized, beginning with settlement type and distribution.

Surveys (see figs. 3.1, 3.5, and 3.9 for the following; see also fig. 4.3)

1. Lower and Upper Galilee. In Lower Galilee, extending northward from the Jezreel Valley, there are five known Late Bronze Age sites. By the Iron I period that number had grown to as many as twenty-five, with an estimated population of some 2,500 by the eleventh century. In the more remote and rugged Upper Galilee, there are eight Late Bronze Age sites, growing to as many as forty by the eleventh century with a population of up to 40,000.[48]

2. Central Hills. The majority of known sites are located in the biblical tribal districts of Manasseh and Ephraim, more than two hundred. A comparison with the preceding Late Bronze Age is particularly instructive. In the former period there are fewer than thirty known sites, but by the

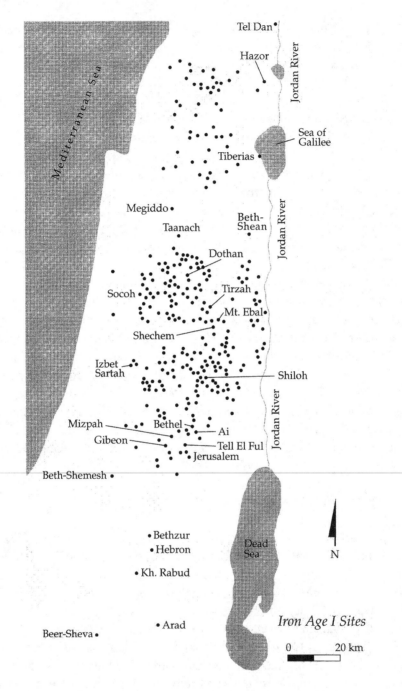

Fig. 3.9. Excavated and surveyed putative Israelite sites (Shanks 1992, 11)

eleventh century there are 218 sites, a nearly sevenfold increase. While surface-survey data must be used cautiously, certainly not yielding absolute numbers, the relative percentages can be quite reliable. The estimated population of these survey sites is even more impressive. Assuming the usual coefficient of population to built up area, we may have an eleventh-century population of some 20,000 in the central hill country alone—up from about 3,000 in the fourteenth–thirteenth century. Such a demographic explosion cannot possibly be explained by natural population increase; there must have been a substantial in-migration (below). Finkelstein invokes a supposed reservoir of nomadic pastoralists in the hill country, from which earliest Israel drew. In the only full-scale demographic study that we have, drawing upon widely accepted studies in population dynamics, Sharon rejects these as "phantom pastoralists." Of these and their presumed invasion in Iron I, he concludes: "The glaring defect in both these hypotheses is the lack of a pool of manpower to supply an invasion, much less a situation of demographic pressure to motivate one."[49]

All of these more than two hundred sites are located either in the hill country rising above the coastal plain and the Shephelah to the west or toward the hilly flanks and the steppe lands beyond that to the east. They range from Jerusalem on the watershed to the south, up to the Jezreel Valley some 50 miles to the north. They can all be dated to the late thirteenth–twelfth century on the basis of pottery. The density of these sites in such a small confine, and especially their relatively sudden appearance, is striking. The settlement pattern in itself is noteworthy and marks a substantial change from the Late Bronze Age that must by explained.

Settlement type is also diagnostic. While few of the survey sites have been excavated, their main features are clear. (1) They are all small unwalled, virtually one-period villages. (2) Most of them are under 3 acres in size, suggesting a maximum population of 200–300, and in many cases they are smaller. (3) They are established not on the ruins of earlier Canaanite towns but de novo, on virgin soil. (4) Most are located on naturally defensible hilltops, near springs, open valleys, and hillsides suitable for terrace agriculture. The typical house types are commensurate with what appears to be a local agrarian society, not the result of conquest by outsiders. (5) The small, widely dispersed settlements themselves are in stark contrast to those of the concentrated, highly urbanized Canaanite Late Bronze Age society. We shall regard the central hill-country sites as the most clearly Israelite (figs. 3.1 and 4.3).

3. The Judean Hill Country. The hill country of Judah, from Jerusalem down to the northern Negev, was much less densely settled in Iron I than the hills to the north, due in part to a more marginal environment (above). Surveys have shown that there were fifteen Late Bronze Age sites in the region. That number had risen by Iron I to circa sixty sites, with an estimated population growing to some 5,000 to 6,000 by the eleventh century. The sites here are similar to those described above, except for being generally smaller and more ephemeral. Farther south, in the Beersheba Valley, there were almost none. The few sites that have been excavated will be discussed below.

The Shephelah is sometimes seen as a separate zone, extending from the Judean hills proper across rolling, lowland foothills as far as the Philistine plain. The region was extensively occupied in the Late Bronze Age, but in the Iron I period settlement was sparse, no doubt because of Philistine expansion. Excluding Philistine sites, there may have been a total population in the twelfth–eleventh century of no more than 1,500–2,000, based on the few excavated sites. Surveys have produced almost no other settlements. As Faust has shown, this region remained a Canaanite enclave in Iron I, like areas in the north.[50]

4. The Yarkon and Sharon Plains. Here there were few clear Iron I sites in the Late Bronze Age and only some ten in Iron I, with a population of perhaps 2,500 by the eleventh century. The sparse occupation in most periods is explained by the marshy conditions. The Via Maris (Way of the Sea), along which sites were more likely to be located, ran somewhat inland, hugging the low foothills despite its name. In any case, before the tenth century these sites are more likely Phoenician or possibly Philistine rather than ethnically Israelite.[51]

5. The Jordan Valley and Transjordan. The Jordan Valley itself had very few sites in any period, due to its subtropical nature. There was abundant water in the river itself, but already in prehistoric times the river had cut such a deep channel that its waters could not be exploited with the primitive technology available. Along the hilly flanks to the west at higher altitudes, there are a few Iron I sites, but they are marginal (see below for an assessment). In the valley itself there are none. Jericho, one of the few sites in any period, was abandoned at the end of the Late Bronze Age and the beginning of Iron I.

On the Transjordanian plateau, the few Iron I known sites have been discussed above. The only putative Israelite site in Transjordan in the twelfth century is Tell el-ʿUmeiri, which will be brought into the picture shortly.

The all-important survey data presented here can now be summarized.

Based largely on Finkelstein's *The Archaeology of the Israelite Settlement* (1988) and the essays in Finkelstein and Na'aman, *From Nomadism to Monarchy: Archaeological and Historical Aspects of Early Israel* (1994), we can tabulate the survey results as follows:

Fig. 3.10. Comparison of Late Bronze and twelfth- and eleventh-century sites by region

Region	Number of Late Bronze Age and Iron I Sites		Estimated Population by Eleventh Century
Upper Galilee	8	23/40	2,300–4,000
Lower Galilee	5	25	2,500
Jezreel Valley	many	?	?
Sharon plain north coastal plain	?	10	2,500
	—	—	—
Shephelah (foothills)	?	2	500
Manasseh	22	96	1,000–2,900
Ephraim	5/6	122	9,650
Jerusalem area	8?	12–30	2,200–4,500
(Benjamin)	—	—	2,200
west Jordan Valley	?	20	2,200
Judean hills	7	18	1,250
Judean Desert	?	few	100
Beersheba Valley Negev Desert	?	2–3	150–200
	—	—	—
TOTALS	58	331–366	40,650–55,000

We must stress that the total number of survey sites grew from fifty-eight in the Late Bronze Age to more than three hundred in the Iron I period. Using these data, and looking only at the hill country north and south of Jerusalem, one could arrive at a population estimate of 10,000 by the twelfth century, perhaps up to 20,000 by the eleventh century.

Other estimates for the Iron I population differ in absolute numbers, but they are comparable, relatively speaking. Stager estimates the total built-up area of Canaan in the Late Bronze Age as 500 acres (36 sites), with a population of perhaps 50,000. The total built-up area in the Iron I period could then have been 1,500 acres (687 sites), with an estimated population of 150,000 (perhaps too high). For the central hill country alone, which we tabulated above, Stager gives population estimates that are higher than Finkelstein: 36 Late Bronze Age sites, but 319 Iron I sites. More than 90 percent of the latter are new foundations. Again, the figures suggest a four- to tenfold increase in the number of sites from the thirteenth into the eleventh century, with a corresponding increase in population.[52]

Most of the Iron I sites found in these surface surveys were, not surprisingly, small villages and hamlets, not large tells. All these Iron I sites cannot automatically be assumed to be "Israelite," even in the central hill country, where excavations reveal that many sites can be so distinguished. Nevertheless, the general picture of a radical shift in settlement type and distribution, as well as in the size of the population, is confirmed.

As Stager concludes:

> This extraordinary increase in population in Iron I cannot be explained only by natural population growth of the few Late Bronze Age city-states in the region: there must have been a major influx of people into the highlands in the twelfth and eleventh centuries BCE.... That many of these villages belonged to premonarchic Israel ... is beyond doubt.[53]

Excavated Iron I Sites (see fig. 4.3 for the following)

1. Lower and Upper Galilee. Few early Iron I sites have been excavated in Lower Galilee, although surveys indicate a considerable increase over the Late Bronze Age. Three excavated sites deserve attention, although their ethnic affiliation is uncertain. Tell el-Wawiyat, a 1-acre village in the Beth-Neṭofa Valley, was excavated in 1986 and 1987 by Dessel, Nakhai, and Wistoff. Stratum IV belongs to the mid-thirteenth-century; Stratum III, spanning the late thirteenth–early twelfth century, represents the poor resettlement of an earlier town that was on a trade route. Stratum III appears to be a small agricultural settlement with two rather large farmhouses, together with spacious open areas. The pottery is still strongly in the Late Bronze tradition. The site seems more Canaanite than Israelite.[54]

Tel ʿEn-Zippori, just north of Nazareth, was excavated in 1993–2000 by Dessel and others. A small village of circa 4 acres, it was occupied in the Late Bronze Age (Stratum V), then in Stratum IV of the twelfth century a large building continued in use. In Stratum III, in the eleventh century, a large multiroomed public building was constructed. The evidence suggests a relatively sophisticated small Canaanite town that continued well into the twelfth and the eleventh century[55]

Karmiel is a small (2/3-acre) one-period site a few miles east of Akko in the low foothills. It was excavated in 1997 and 2003 and revealed several small, well-built rambling houses, some with courtyards. The scant pottery has its closest parallels in Tell Keisan 9c, of the mid-eleventh century. Cooking pots constitute 51 percent of the repertoire; locally made large pithoi, not of the collar-rim type but "Galilean," constitute 15 percent; other store jars constitute 16 percent. There are no imports. This is the expected picture for Iron I rural sites. Like the above Lower Galilee sites, Karmiel appears to represent a continuing rural Canaanite (or early Phoenician) population in the region.[56]

The more rugged and remote Upper Galilee was first extensively surveyed by Aharoni in the 1950s, where he found a number of small settlements in the Mount Hermon region that he attributed to incoming Israelites. He excavated one site, Tel Harashim, near Peqi'in. Although not published in any detail, it appears to be a hilltop site circa 1.5 acres in extent with a casemate wall, below which are terraces. Stratum III represents a very small village, of which only one structure is clear, interpreted as a dwelling used in part as a foundry (a sort of furnace and two ladles). The scant pottery includes distinctive northern types that have affiliations with Phoenician sites in Lebanon, especially the large banded pithoi or store jars. Aharoni dated his Upper Galilean (i.e., Israelite) sites to the late or even the mid-thirteenth century, although at the time there were few parallels. Nevertheless, their ethnic affiliation remains unclear.[57]

A few other sites in Upper Galilee include Sasa, where three Iron I levels were discerned (Strata III–I), a small village dated to the eleventh century by collar-rim store jars. An unusual find was a *kernos* (trick vessel) similar to Philistine *kernoi* at Tell Qasile.

Har Adir is situated at more than 3,000 feet above sea level and is quite isolated. Salvage work in 1975 revealed a casemate (doubled-walled) fortress, first constructed apparently in the late eleventh century. A significant find was a large carbonized steel pick from Stratum III, the earliest such iron implement known for the Iron Age. It cannot be determined, however, that the site is Israelite.[58]

The above village sites in Upper Galilee (and a few others) are located where there was no Late Bronze Age occupation. As Aharoni put it:

They are small settlements, the biggest among them comprising an area
no greater than about one acre. Some of them are built on hill-tops and
some are situated on the slopes or in the valleys; the distances between
them average no more than one to two miles and sometimes less. The
deciding factor in the choice of a location for the settlement was a convenient approach to the small and scattered plots of land under difficult
mountain conditions. Most of them were certainly unwalled settlements. This is a typical picture of families and clans at the beginning of
the settling process. They inhabit small, adjacent settlements in rugged,
forested, mountain regions.[59]

The pottery of the above sites reflects both continuing Late Bronze Age
types, especially in the large "Galilean" pithoi or store jars, some of which
have affinities to those of Tyre and the Phoenician coast (above). At two
other excavated sites, however, an early Iron I occupation succeeded that
of major Late Bronze Age city-states.

In summary, in Galilee there are some forty new Iron I sites, mostly
1–4 acres in extent. Founded in the late thirteenth/twelfth century, they
combine Late Bronze, Iron I, and Phoenician characteristics. Their identification as Israelite sites is dubious.

One of the principal surveyors of Galilee, Frankel, summarizes it
this way:

> The transition from the Late Bronze Age to the Iron Age in the coun-
> try in general, and in Upper Galilee in particular, combined change and
> continuity. Change is manifested in the destruction of the large cities in
> the lowlands, and in the emergence of a new settlement pattern of small
> sites in the mountains. Continuity is expressed in the ceramic assem-
> blages and in the geopolitical division of the country. In the main, the
> changes are part of a momentous process that occurred in the whole of
> the Eastern Mediterranean.[60]

2. The Upper Jordan Valley and Central Hill Country. Excavated Iron
I sites in the upper Jordan valley and the central hill country north of Jerusalem (Mount Ephraim) consist of (1) a number of large cities or town sites
that may continue from the Late Bronze Age but represent new foundations;
and (2) small villages, most of which are founded de novo. Our survey will
take each category from north to south, beginning with the larger sites.

Tel Reḥov (Tell eṣ-Ṣarem) is a prominent 25-acre mound overlooking
the Jordan Valley 3 miles south of Beth-Shean. It was excavated by Amihai

Mazar from 1997 to 2012. The Late Bronze Age town was not destroyed and continued into the Iron IA period (although not well attested). Stratum VII then belongs to the eleventh–early tenth century, well constructed but destroyed, then rebuilt and destroyed again. Stratum VI, with an entirely different plan, belongs to the Iron IIA period, or the tenth century (ch. 4). There are no Iron I fortifications. The Iron I houses are all rectangular, laid out in an orthogonal plan, many with adjacent pits. The pottery is local, including red slip; there are only a few Philistine bichrome sherds. A series of C-14 dates from the twelfth into the early ninth century supports a picture of continuous cultural development. If the Iron I occupation had spread over the entire mound, Reḥov (biblical Rehob) would have been a prosperous Canaanite city of some 2,000, representing a regional Jezreel/ Jordan Valley culture.[61]

Dan (Tell el-Qadi), at the headwaters of the springs feeding the upper Jordan River, was excavated from 1966 onward for many years by Avraham Biran. Although its significance is diminished by imprecise stratigraphy and scant publication, there is evidence of an early Iron I village. The impressive city of Stratum VI comes to an end, perhaps sometime in the early twelfth century, in a manner that is unclear. It is followed by a gap in the mid-twelfth century. Stratum VB–A then is represented mainly by pits and silos, as at Hazor. The pottery consisted mostly of domestic vessels, especially cooking pots and Galilean store jars (above). Stratum V exhibits pillar-courtyard houses, as well as pottery similar to that of Stratum VI. A few crucibles and fragments of clay bellows were found. Stratum VA ends in a destruction dated by the excavator to circa 1050. Continuing Canaanite traditions suggest that Dan is not an Israelite site.[62]

Hazor, excavated by Yadin and others in 1955–1958, was easily the most impressive Late Bronze Age city in northern Palestine, the 180-acre lower city the equal of the largest contemporary sites in Syria. Its violent destruction (Stratum XIII) has been discussed above. Following a gap, succeeding Strata XII–XI represent a squatter occupation characterized mostly by numerous rubbish pits of the eleventh century. A small shrine of this horizon features a small hoard of bronzes, including a well-preserved figure of a seated Canaanite El, typical of Late Bronze Age exemplars. But this is undoubtedly a leftover found in the ruins of the Canaanite city, and its significance for the early Israelite cult is debatable (below). Only in Stratum X of the tenth century does the settlement revive, now only on the much smaller acropolis, but with no clear structures and nothing clearly

Israelite.[63] Stratum X belongs to the tenth century and is usually dated to the united monarchy (below).

Dothan is an imposing 15-acre mound overlooking a fertile valley in the heartland of Samaria. It was excavated in the 1950s and 1960s by amateur archaeologists, but only a small portion of the material has been published, and its Israelite character is uncertain. A large tomb (Tomb I) spans the thirteenth–eleventh centuries, with more than one hundred bodies and at least a thousand vessels. It seems to indicate continuity into Iron I, but that is all one can say. The scant evidence for domestic occupation precludes any ethnic identification.[64]

Tell el-Far'ah (North), probably biblical Tirzah, was excavated by Pére Roland de Vaux in 1946–1960 but has only partially been published by others. Stratum VIb of the Late Bronze Age continues without interruption into Stratum VIIa of the twelfth–eleventh century. There are, however, new domestic areas, including a few pillar-courtyard houses that are quite large. The site, however, continues Canaanite traditions well into the early Iron I period, like Dan, Beth-Shean, Megiddo, and other northern sites.

Ta'anach, 7 miles north of Dothan, has been interpreted as an early Israelite site, but Stratum IA–B, extending until a destruction sometime in the mid-eleventh century, does not yield any clear evidence. Shechem exhibits a continuous occupation into the twelfth century (Strata XII–XI), then a gap in the eleventh century. That would support the biblical portrait of a treaty relationship with early Israelite sites (below).[65]

Tell el-Ful (biblical Gibeah) is a small, prominent hilltop site on the northern outskirts of modern Jerusalem, with a magnificent view in all directions. It was excavated by Albright in 1922–1923 and 1933, then again by Lapp in 1964. The principal structure is a casemate and corner-tower fort, dated to the eleventh–tenth century (Fortress I–II). A few Iron I sherds (Period I) on bedrock below the monumental fortress, as well as an ephemeral floor, may suggest a brief early Israelite occupation. After a gap, Period II may represent Albright's "Saul's rude fortress."

In addition to these Iron I town sites in the central hills, we have a number of excavated village sites. In the northwestern hills, bordering the Jezreel Valley, are three small Late Bronze Canaanite villages that continue into Iron I. (1) Tel Qashish is a mound 2–3 acres in size. Stratum V was violently destroyed circa 1200, succeeded by a smaller settlement in Stratum IV. (2) Yoqne'am XVIIIA–B follows a gap in the Late Bronze Age. It is a small twelfth-century unfortified village, the pottery of which combines earlier Canaanite form, Phoenician, and even a few possible Philistine types. The houses are undistinguished except for a large olive-processing installation. Stratum XVII ends in the eleventh century.

Nearby Tel Qiri IX–VIII is another twelfth-eleventh century unforti-fied village. Several consecutive phases of well-constructed houses indicate a stable, prosperous community dependent upon agriculture and cottage industries. The pottery combines collar-rim store jars and Phoenician types. Some vessels probably had a cultic function.[66]

Shiloh (Khirbet Seilun), an 8-acre site some 20 miles north of Jeru-salem, is situated at the head of a small, fertile valley. It was excavated early on by Danes, but Finkelstein carried out major excavations in 1981–1984. Finkelstein's new excavations confirmed the fact that after a long abandonment in the Late Bronze Age Shiloh was resettled in the twelfth century (Stratum V). Along the inside perimeter of the old abandoned Middle Bronze Age city wall (seventeenth–sixteenth century), which now served as a sort of terrace wall, there was built an adjoining row of pillar-courtyard houses of early type, surrounded by many stone-lined silos. The abundant pottery consisted of early twelfth-century types, including sev-eral of the large collar-rim store jars discussed above. Of the biblical cultic center Finkelstein found no trace, although he speculated that an earlier Canaanite shrine might have been reused for such an installation. Shiloh was then destroyed in a huge fire around 1050, which left up to 6 feet of debris overlying the ruins. It was never again an important town, probably since urbanization during the early monarchy caused the center of popula-tion to shift elsewhere (below).

Tell en-Naṣbeh (biblical Mizpah?) is located on the main road from Jerusalem about 8 miles to the north. It was excavated in 1926 by Badé, Wampler, and McCown, who published a final report in 1947. The site was occupied in the Late Chalcolithic/Early Bronze I, then abandoned and resettled circa 1200–1150 (Stratum 4). Little architecture was found, but collar-rim store jars and some Philistine bichrome wares, plus numer-ous cisterns, attest to scant Iron I occupation. The collar-rim store jars are typical of early Israelite settlements elsewhere, but not exclusively, so the ethnic identification of Tell en-Naṣbeh remains uncertain.[67]

There are two possible Iron I cultic sites in the region of "Mount Ephraim." The first is the Bull Site, a small, isolated hilltop site a few miles east of Dothan (fig. 3.11). It was excavated briefly in 1978–1979 by Mazar, following the discovery of a fine bronze zebu-bull figurine on the surface,

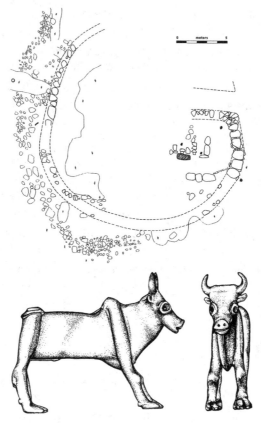

Fig. 3.11. The Bull Site, twelfth century (Mazar 1982, figs. 2, 5)

similar to those known from Late Bronze Age Hazor and Ugarit. A low stone circular wall enclosed an area that featured a stone altar, a *maṣṣēbâ* (standing stone), a few bits of bronze, a fragment of a cult stand, and scant early Iron I sherds. This is clearly an isolated, open Iron I cult site, probably like the biblical Israelite *bāmôt*, or "high places."

The other possible Iron I cult site is controversial. An isolated hilltop installation atop Mount Ebal, overlooking the Shechem pass, was excavated in 1982–1989 by Zertal. A large subrectangular boundary wall enclosed an area of about 1 acre, in which the only structure was a large stone podium surrounded by a low enclosure wall, approached by a sort of ramp, and featuring two adjacent courtyards. In the courtyards were several large store jars dug in the ground (or in fills) that contained the burnt bones of sheep, goat, small cattle, and fallow deer. Small finds included two scarabs, one dated to the reign of Ramesses II (1279–1213). These dated one or both of the two building phases.

The excavator claimed that this was the very altar built by Joshua near Shechem (Josh 8:30–32). Most other scholars, however, interpret the Mount Ebal installation as an isolated farmstead or perhaps a watchtower. The bones of fallow deer are not ritually correct in the Hebrew Bible; furthermore, the bones seem to predate the stone podium (phase 2). Nevertheless, some cultic functions may be surmised.[68]

'Izbet Ṣarṭah, excavated in 1976–1978 by Finkelstein and well published, may be the site that illuminates early Israel best. It is a small site located on the lowest foothills of the central ridge, overlooking the coastal plain. Stratum III consists of a few tattered rectangular houses on bedrock, presumably arranged in an oval plan (only six were cleared), with a few silos. The pottery, still strongly reminiscent of local Canaanite Late Bronze Age forms, would date Stratum III to the late thirteenth century. Stratum II follows after a gap and sees a doubling of the site to some 10 acres. Now there are substantial pillar-courtyard houses, some with adjoining rooms (fig. 3.12). One well-built house is about 1,700 square feet and is surrounded by more than forty silos. One silo produced a four-line ostracon in Old Canaanite script, an abecedary or schoolboy's practice text. The pottery is clearly Iron I and dates to the eleventh century. By now, 'Izbet Ṣarṭah was a well-established village of about 100 or so.

Baruch Rosen, the paleobotanist on the staff, showed that in Stratum III cattle bones constituted 43 percent of the total, down to 23 percent by Stratum II. Furthermore, from the beginning the site was able to produce a surplus of food. As he puts it: "In sum, the economic system of 'Izbet Sartah is typical of a sedentary settlement based on agriculture and animal breeding." Taken together, the data from 'Izbet Ṣarṭah argue against, not for, Finkelstein's theory of nomads in process of becoming sedentarized. These look like experienced farmers, familiar with local conditions, moving up into the hill county.[69]

Nearer to Jerusalem there are several Iron I sites that may be Israelite. Bethel (Beitin), 10 miles to the northeast, was excavated by Kelso and Albright in 1927, 1934, and again in 1954, 1957, and 1960. The results have been published, but the stratigraphy is unreliable, and Kelso's interpretations were clearly influenced by a fundamentalist agenda. There are no stratum numbers. There appears to be no major destruction at the end of a somewhat insubstantial Late Bronze Age occupation, but a "patrician

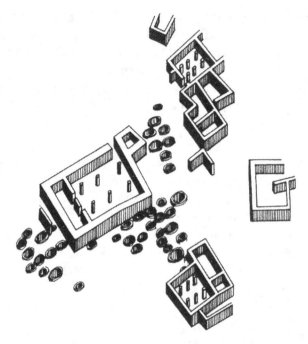

Fig. 3.12. Pillar-courtyard houses and silos, ʿIzbet Ṣarṭah II (Finkelstein and Silberman 2001, fig. 12)

house" and a supposed temple went out of use. The Iron I settlement is said to be characterized by ramshackle huts. The published pottery consists mostly of large collar-rim store jars and cooking pots. The latter are closely paralleled by cooking pots at Shiloh, Ai, Giloh, and other Israelite sites of the twelfth century.[70]

Ai (Khirbet et-Tell) is a 2-acre site some five miles north of Jerusalem, magnificently situated at the head of a deep wadi (ravine) descending into the Jordan Valley. Its name in both Hebrew and Arabic means "ruin heap." That accurately describes the steep mound, which was abandoned toward the end of the Early Bronze Age and lay in imposing ruins until circa 1200. The site was excavated in 1933–1935 by a French excavation led by Judith Marquet-Krause (published by her husband, Yves Marquet, after her early death).

Renewed excavations carried out in 1964–1970 by Callaway, an excellent stratigrapher trained by Kenyon, clarified many details. On the deserted acropolis there was established an early Iron I unfortified village characterized by several well-preserved houses, as well as some occupation among the ruins of the monumental Early Bronze temple on the acropolis (Strata X–IX). Every house had its own cistern, dug with some skill into Senonian chalk layers that become impermeable when wet. Some houses were as large as 800 square feet and could have accommodated up to eight people. Agriculture was evidenced by extensive terraces on the hillsides below the site, by an iron-plow point, and by quantities of utilitarian stone tools. The ceramic repertoire featured mostly collar-rim store jars and flanged-rim cooking pots. There were no imports or Philistine wares. Two phases of occupation were discerned, suggesting that Ai continued into the eleventh century, after which it was abandoned.[71]

Nearby Khirbet Radanna (possibly biblical Beeroth) is a small 2-acre hilltop site on the western outskirts of Ramallah, founded de novo. Salvage excavations were carried out by Callaway and Cooley in 1969 and 1970–1974, but the results are published only in preliminary reports. In several fields there came to light clusters of pillar-courtyard (or four-room) houses, usually two flanking a shared courtyard (fig. 3.13). Most had *tabûns* (ovens) in the house or courtyard, and several had deep cisterns cut into the exposed bedrock. Attached to these houses were outlying sheds, workshops, and animal enclosures. An inscribed jar handle reads ʾahil[ud], a name known from the Hebrew Bible. There was also evidence of metalworking, such as crucibles and tuyères, as well as bronze objects. The latter included axes/adzes, daggers, a spear, and a plow point. The surrounding hillsides all the way down to the spring in the valley below were extensively terraced. The site probably comes to an end sometime in the mid-eleventh century at the same time as Ai.[72]

Khirbet ed-Dawwara (identification unknown) was excavated in the 1990s by Finkelstein. It is a small hilltop village near Ai, dating to the late eleventh–tenth century. It was built on an oval-shaped plan, with several well-developed pillar-courtyard houses constructed against and bonded into a peripheral wall some 6 feet wide. Thus far it is perhaps the only town wall we have from the twelfth–eleventh century. The site continued into the tenth century. Khirbet ed-Dawwara may well have been ethnically Israelite in the early phase, but it is not typical of other hill-country sites.[73]

Giloh (biblical Baal-perazim?) is a small hilltop site on the southern outskirts of Jerusalem. In 1978–1979 Mazar did a salvage campaign. The site is sometimes thought to be identified with the Giloh mentioned in Josh 15:51, but that is unlikely. Mazar's prompt report and discussion of Giloh is still one of the best balanced and most helpful treatments of the issues

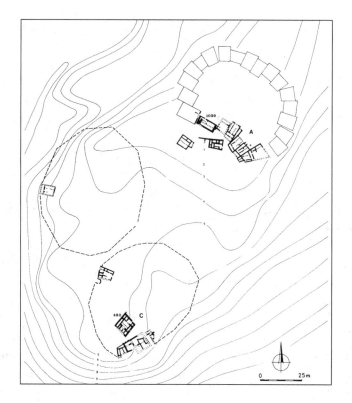

Fig. 3.13. A group of houses at Tel Masos, Stratum II (Herzog 1992, fig. 6)

to be found anywhere. The settlement produced only the fragmentary remains of a house or two, but significantly these are of the pillar-court-yard or of four-room style often associated with early Israelite villages. If the entire site had been built up (and preserved), Giloh might have had up to ten of those houses, by Mazar's estimate, which would yield a total population of 100 or so. There is some evidence of a perimeter wall, but this may be later, since there is an Iron II defensive tower at the north end of the site.[74]

Pottery from one of the buildings at Giloh has turned out to be particularly significant, because it is a small but representative corpus that was analyzed expertly by Mazar. He drew numerous parallels from discoveries at other sites to show (1) that the Giloh pottery, typical of other early Israelite sites in the hill country, is late thirteenth–early twelfth century in date; and (2) that it is in the Late Bronze Age Canaanite tradition. One may note especially the transitional cooking-pot rims and the large store jars with a reinforcing band around the neck—the so-called collar-rim jars that have been thought by many archaeologists to be characteristic of early Israelite sites (below).

3. The Judean Hill Country. South of Jerusalem the hill country gradually tapers off to Beersheba and the Negev Desert beyond. The soils are lighter clay (rendzinate) and are progressively less well watered. Nevertheless, there are several excavated Iron I sites.

In the hill country proper, Beth-Zur, Tekoa, Carmel, and Ma'on have sometimes been considered early Israelite sites. Beth-Zur (Khirbet eṭ-Ṭubeiqah), on the main north–south road, rises some 1,000 feet above sea level and commands an excellent vista. It was excavated in 1931 and again in 1957 by Sellers. The site was not occupied in the Late Bronze Age, but it was resettled after a long gap sometime perhaps in the late twelfth century. Several pillar-courtyard houses of Stratum III belong to this horizon, as well as possibly the terraces on the hillsides below the mound. A fire destroyed the village sometime in the eleventh century, after which it was largely abandoned in Iron II. It may have been an early Israelite site.

It is only in the steppe lands east of Beersheba that we have numerous excavated Iron I sites, some of them of great significance. Beersheba (Tell es-Seba') is a small mound on the eastern outskirts of modern Beersheba. Excavated in 1967–1976 by Aharoni and Herzog, Strata IX–VI were initially dated to Iron I, but the chronology is disputed. The Iron I village has been reconstructed as an oval-shaped settlement, like Tel Esdar and Tel Masos (below). But only pits and a few floors were found in Stratum IX. The first houses in Stratum VIII are prototypes of the later, fully developed pillar-courtyard houses of Stratum VII, a planned village of perhaps the late eleventh century. Cattle bones are said to be common. Stratum VI then represents a change to a more "urban" character, with smaller houses more densely built up, perhaps coming to an end by the early to mid-tenth century.[75] Stratum V may end circa 925 BCE.

Tel Esdar is a 5-acre site halfway between Beersheba and Dimona. A small loessal hill in a region of marginal rainfall, it was excavated in 1963 and 1964 by Kochavi. Stratum IV represents a late fourth-millennium village. Stratum III, following a gap of some 1,500 years, belongs to the eleventh century. It features a dozen or so pillar-courtyard houses arranged continuously in an oval plan, all the entrances facing inward. The scant pottery included collar-rim store jars and flanged-rim cooking pots. The excavator dated the poorly preserved remains to the eleventh century, ended by a destruction. Stratum II then belongs to the tenth century but seems to be only a small farmstead.

Tel Malḥata is a very visible mound of circa 3.5 acres some 13 miles northeast of Tel Esdar, on the loessal steppes. It was excavated in the 1960s and 1970 by Kochavi and Beit-Arieh. There are Late Chalcolithic through Middle Bronze remains, then a gap. The early Iron I site (early period C) grew to circa 3.7 acres. The Middle Bronze town wall seems to have been reused later, in Iron II. But only scant remains could be attributed to Iron I. Phase C ends circa 925 BCE.

Tel Masos (possibly biblical Hormah), 8 miles east of Beersheba, is one of the most important excavated Iron I villages that we have. Joint Israeli–German excavations in 1972–1975 were directed by Aharoni, Kempinski, and Fritz. As in some other northern Negev sites, there was Chalcolithic and Middle Bronze occupation. Then after a gap of some three hundred years, a large Iron I village (15 acres) was established, the largest yet known. Stratum IIIB represents a slightly constricted area of settlement, possibly by seminomadic pastoralists in the late thirteenth century. Stratum IIIA then reveals a complex of contiguous pillar-court-yard and some broad-room houses, arranged in an oval, as at Tel Esdar (above; see also fig. 3.13). There was also a large "fortress-like" structure in Area C, adjacent to the southern part of the ring of houses. A destruction ends Stratum IIIA, perhaps in the late twelfth century, followed by a more substantial rebuild in Stratum II. That village continued into the tenth century or so, then was destroyed circa 975 BCE by unknown agents. A date for Stratum III is provided by an Egyptian Nineteenth Dynasty scarab, perhaps of Ramesses II.[76]

There has been considerable discussion of Tel Masos, made possible in part by the substantial data provided for consideration by the final report (1983). One of the directors, Fritz, developed a theory that Stratum IIIA broad-room houses evolved from a bedouin-style tent, with its division of an open area in front for outdoor activities (the forerunner of the court-yard) and an inner shelter and sleeping section. In fact, only one structure seems to be a broad-room house, and even that looks more like a corridor and a side room attached to a typical pillar-courtyard house. In Stratum II there are no such buildings. Finkelstein then adopted the notion of a tent prototype in support of his nomadic-origins hypothesis. Few other scholars have accepted the tent analogy, mostly because the supposed ethnographic parallels are dubious (below).

Tel Masos III–II does differ from many other early Iron I villages thought of as Israelite. For one thing, it is larger than most, perhaps as large as 10–15 acres. At the usual ratio of 100 persons per acre, that would yield a population of up to 800, rather too large for a village. Yet only a small portion of the site was excavated, with only about eight houses revealed. The uses of the remainder of the site—at least 75 percent—are unknown, since the entire central area remains unexcavated and was possibly used for outdoor activities, storage, stabling of animals, and the like. One reconstruction of the outer ring would build on the seven or so excavated houses so as to yield a total of about twenty-five pillar-courtyard houses. Based on an average size of about 1,000 square feet and the usual estimate of one person for 100 square feet, these twenty-five houses would yield a total population of up to 250, quite reasonable for a larger village.

Several other features distinguish Tel Masos III–II. The ceramic repertoire includes a few more sophisticated coastal bichrome vessels that may have Cypro-Phoenician connections. There are a few Midianite sherds and even several Philistine sherds. Furthermore, careful sieving and analysis of animal bones (often neglected) showed that, while 60 percent were of sheep and goat, 23 percent were cattle. Stock breeding requires considerable experience and skill, especially in marginal regions such as the northern Negev. Several clay crucibles and unrefined copper ores were found, as well as several bronze implements (including a lugged axe), indicating local metalworking. Finally, the fortress (?) suggests at least some urban traditions. The above features militate against Fritz's and Finkelstein's nomadic-origins theory. In early reports, Kempinski and Fritz had commented on the fact that the new settlers at Masos were "well integrated into the culture of their Canaanite neighbors." Some scholars have attempted to portray Tel Masos as the center of a desert "tribal confederation or kingdom," even a state, the nucleus of the northern Negev settlements we have descried, sustained partly by trade. The assumption is that Building 1039 is an Egyptian-style residency. The evidence, however, does not support such a grandiose interpretation.[77]

In the Judean or southern hill country, there were few Late Bronze sites but eighteen Iron I sites. The principal surveyor, Ofer, summarizes matters as follows:

> Groups of diverse origins settled in the Judean Hills, having diverse relations among themselves and with families throughout the entire south

and center of the country, on both sides of the Jordan. In some cases the settling families had closer ties with the inhabitants of regions out-side of the Judean Hills than with their neighbors.... The settlement of these groups in nearby regions intensified their common characteristics and created economic and social ties. The impetus for their unification in an all-encompassing framework was provided by the appearance of common enemies.... But in this process the extended family, especially the separate paternal house within it, continued to retain their former importance. The concept of a "tribe" for Judah lacks any concrete con-tent, and seems to be a late, artificial application to the history of the families which settled in the land of Judah.[78]

In summary, the excavated Iron I sites in the central hill country, taken together with survey sites, indicate a precipitous growth from thirty to forty sites in the Late Bronze Age to at least two hundred in Iron I. Most are small villages established de novo, 1–3 acres in extent. That could sug-gest a population of 100–200 each, or a total of 30,000 or more. The sites are close to each other but distant from the few continuing Canaanite cities (Megiddo, Beth-Shean). That denotes an agro-pastoral lifestyle, a redis-tributive economy, and a tightly knit social structure. We shall argue here that these people of the central hill country were Merenptah's "Israelites."

4. Transjordan. We have already surveyed several Late Bronze–Iron I sites on the Transjordanian plateau (fig. 3.2). Only a few sites may be pertinent here, such as Tell el-ʿUmeiri, on the outskirts of modern Amman on the Ammonite–Moabite border. The site has been excavated since 1984 by Clark, Geraty, and Herr. Here there are some of the few known Late Bronze Age monumental structures in Transjordan, including a reused city wall and a large palace. The Strata 14–13 site was destroyed circa 1200, perhaps by a massive earthquake. The succeeding Stratum 12 town was entirely different, constructed over the ruins using a new rampart to enclose an area of domestic dwellings. Two houses (Buildings A and B) are pillar-courtyard houses similar to but not identical with Iron I houses in Cisjordan. As already noted, one house seems to have had cultic elements. The Iron I village (or town) dates to the early to mid-twelfth century, then was destroyed apparently in a military attack, the houses left with nearly all their furnishings intact. A secondary destruction may have been caused by an earthquake. The succeeding levels suggest a decline.

The pottery from the early Iron I Buildings A and B at Tell el-ʿUmeiri has been inventoried but only published provisionally. A corpus from a slightly later Iron I structure in Field H, however, has been fully published. The excavator says that this latter pottery differs significantly from that of the pillar-courtyard houses above and is later. The latter assemblage, Herr asserts, is nearly identical to that of the Iron I hill-country Israelite settlements and that it demonstrates that the biblical tribe of Reuben had indeed moved to the east into Moab by the early twelfth century.

The Stratum 11 Field H published pottery, dated by Herr to the late eleventh century, is not, however, at all typical of eleventh-century pottery in Cisjordan. There are few of the diagnostic Iron I collar-rim store jars. As the excavator admits, the cooking pots—even more diagnostic—are so far unique except in the Moab region. If the early Iron I assemblage looks "Israelite," that at a later stage in the eleventh century clearly does not.[79]

A few other Late Bronze Age Transjordanian sites show continuity into the early Iron I period. These include Tall as-Saʿidiyeh and Tell Deir ʿAlla (Dayr ʿAlla) in the Jordan Valley, already discussed, which represent a continuing Canaanite/Egyptian presence. On the Ammonite/Ṣafuṭ plateau the Biqah Valley, Umm ad-Dananir, Amman, Saḥab, and a few other sites toward the Moabite border show the same continuity (above). Farther south there are a few Iron I fortified sites, but the hinterland is almost entirely pastoral. None of these sites, however, with the possible exception of Tell el-ʿUmeiri (above), exhibits any of the ethnic markers that we will adduce presently in identifying our Israelites. The local population could best be identified as Proto-Ammonites, Proto Moabites, Proto-Edomites, and so on. Apart from the biblical narrative—already shown to be fanciful—there would be no reason for scholars to suggest anything but indigenous changes.[80]

Summary of the Material Culture of the Iron I Village Complex

In summarizing the material culture of the foregoing Iron I sites of the twelfth–eleventh century, a General Systems Theory model will again be employed.

Settlement Type and Distribution

The first subsystem to be considered—settlement type and distribution, together with demography—has been covered above in detail in describing the sites. The point to be emphasized here is that nearly all of these sites are located in regions that were not densely occupied in the preceding Late Bronze Age Canaanite period or were not occupied at all, especially in the central hill country and in Judah. In these areas the highland frontier was open to colonization. Only a handful of Canaanite cities are attested, and they were mostly in the process of decline by the mid-twelfth century or so, just as the ones we take to be Israelite villages were in the ascendance, and these older centers themselves would yield to new patterns of settlement. In addition, the Egyptian administrative centers still in existence nearby were tottering to an end, as we have seen.

Socioeconomic Structures

The new Iron I sites that now emerge, mostly in the hill country, are all small villages ranging from less than 1 to 3–4 acres, with a population anywhere from a few dozen to a few hundred. None has any urban character whatsoever. Apart from one or two larger structures (at Tel Masos), there is nothing approaching monumental architecture. There are none of the large palaces or temples of the preceding Late Bronze Age. None of the sites has a city wall, with the possible exception of Khirbet ed-Dawwara, whose date is more likely eleventh–tenth century (above).

The typical pillar-courtyard house is best seen as a farmhouse providing a large nuclear or extended family with all its needs. Such a family has been called the *bêt 'āb*, the "house of the father" (as in the Hebrew Bible). The common cluster of such houses, sharing some walls and a courtyard, would then be the residence of an extended or multigenerational family (the biblical *mišpāḥâ*) (below).

These houses are often referred to in the literature as four-room (or "three-room") houses, because the plan is that of a u-shaped structure with two or three rooms (or banks of rooms) surrounding a central courtyard. One or more of the side rooms are set off from the courtyard by pillars that are either monoliths or made of stacked stones. Often these side rooms, especially to the right or left, are cobbled and would have been used as stables. The back room usually has an earthen surface. There is good evidence that the pillars supported an upper story. The typical village house has some 800–1200 square feet, twice that if the upper story is included. They are better termed pillar-courtyard houses, since they may have three, four, or more rooms (see figs. 3.12 and 3.13 above; see also ch. 4).

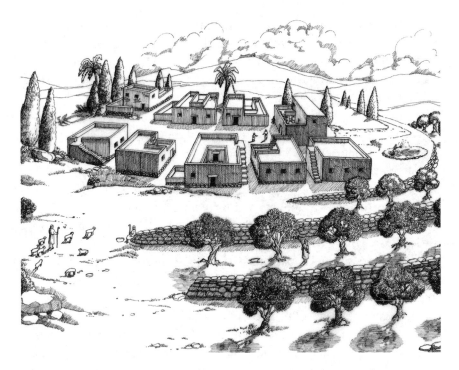

Fig. 3.14. Plan of a typical early Israelite village (Giselle Hasel)

These pillar-courtyard houses would have made ideal farmhouses, easily sheltering anywhere from five individuals (the usual estimate for a nuclear family) to ten or more (an extended family). A cluster of several such pillar-courtyard houses, with a population of several dozen, would make up the typical village that we have seen in the Iron I settlements already described (fig. 3.14). The courtyard, whether roofed or not, often had a *tabûn* (oven) that would have been used for food preparation, the supplies close at land in the back room. The side rooms could have been stables, easily mucked out, the dung used as fuel. The rising heat would have helped to warm the rooms on the upper floor, where the family probably shared meals and other communal activities, as well as sleeping. The roof would have been used in good weather for drying foodstuffs.

The small villages we have seen characterized by these tightly spaced pillar-courtyard houses are all far removed from the few remaining urban centers, yet within reach of each other. The Beersheba sites discussed above are all located with a 10-mile radius. Most of the sites known from surveys in the central hill country are even closer to each other. There is no concept of defense. The ring plan of many sites, often situated on a natural rise, would have provided all the protection needed, that is, from animals or marauders. In any case, the isolated location and the likelihood of village solidarity would have made any further defense unnecessary. These are not the houses of conquerors or of any intruders at all.

These villages are devoid of any outside influences. There are none of the Mycenaean, Cypriot, or other ceramic imports that are typical of Late Bronze Age sites, nor are there Philistine wares. Apart from Transjordanian sites such as Tell el-ʿUmeiri, there are no Egyptian objects. The local pottery is very much the same from site to site, given the regional differences that we should expect. Most villages would have been largely self-sufficient but capable of producing a surplus to be used in bartering with nearby villages. At ʿIzbet Ṣarṭah (above), the first settlers in Stratum III already produced a substantial surplus, as staff specialists in paleobotany have shown. Some villages were probably specialized, as suggested by evidence for metalworking (below).[81]

The ceramic repertoire is utilitarian; large store jars, cooking pots, bowls, and jugs are predominant forms (below). At Iron I Shiloh, Stratum V collar-rim and other store jars made up 55 percent of the repertoire, cooking pots 10 percent, jugs 17 percent, bowls and multihandled kraters (large bowls) 13 percent. At Giloh, store jars and cooking pots were 76 percent of the total.[82] The twelfth-century "Israelite" pottery shows clear continuities with thirteenth-century Canaanite forms (figs. 3.15 and 3.16).

Other objects typically found in the pillar-courtyard houses were also utilitarian. Grinding stones of basalt, limestone mortars and pestles, and flint sickle blades are common. Bronze axes, adzes, points, awls, and needles are typical. The few iron implements consist of plow points, knives, goads, and sometimes a steel pick (Har Adir). There are no real weapons.

All the above are utilitarian items that would have been suitable for village farmers and herdsmen. They do not reflect urban life, which is dependent on production and trade, but rather an agro-pastoral, village-based society and economy. This is what the distinguished anthropologist Marshal Sahlins aptly described in his *Stone Age Economics* as "the tribal community in miniature … politically underwriting the conditions of society—society without a Sovereign." Sahlins described this further as the "domestic mode of production," in contrast to the "Asiatic" or "despotic" model.[83]

The term *egalitarian* has been used indiscriminately by some scholars for this society, but no truly egalitarian society has ever been found.

Recently the term communitarian has been suggested as an alternative by Gottwald, whose *Tribes of Yahweh: A Sociology of the Religion of Liberated Israel, 1250–1050 BCE* seemed to have given the term *tribe* almost canonical status.[84]

Beyond the villages and their typical farmhouses, there are other features that point to an agrarian lifestyle, but these will be treated below under technology.

Political Organization

It is clear from the foregoing discussion that the Iron I villages presented here do not form anything like city-states, much less states. It is not, as some suppose, that the village complex here is too small. In cross-cultural analyses of what are called "state-formation processes," it has been shown that polities as small as 25,000 or so can legitimately be regarded as true states, such as the Maya lowland states. By comparison, the total population of the Iron I villages discussed here has been estimated as 40,000–50,000 by the eleventh century—easily large enough to have formed before long the "early inchoate state" of cultural anthropologists.[85]

It would appear that there is either a reluctance to enter into larger-scale political organization or simply no need for it. An Israelite state will not emerge for at least another century or more. On the other hand, it is doubtful that what we see in these newly established Iron I villages represents what some have called a tribal structure, in this case, a pastoral nomadic or tribal society in process of becoming sedentarized. Below it will be argued that such a model is not in keeping with ethnographic analogies. It would have no warrant were it not for the pervasive notion of the "nomadic ideal" that is supposed by some biblical scholars. There is simply no evidence for a nomadic or pastoral background for most of these early Iron I villagers. They are experienced farmers and stockbreeders (below). Their social coherence need not be explained by recourse to tribal origins. The communitarian ethos discussed above is adequate; no further centralized political theory or organization was required.

Technology

The new socioeconomic and political structure of our Iron I villages is reflected in, and partly brought about by, new or modified technologies.

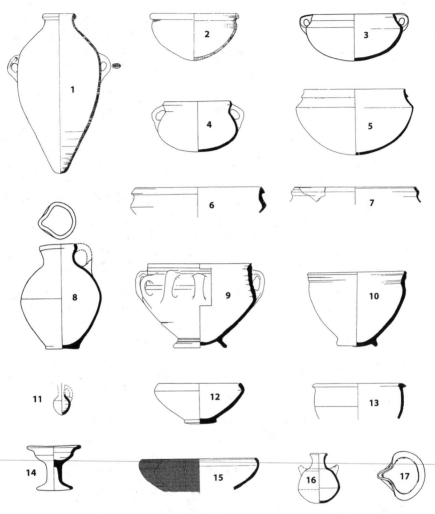

Fig. 3.15. Israelite pottery, twelfth–eleventh century. 1: store jar, Giloh (Mazar 1981, fig. 8:1); 2: cooking pot, Giloh (Mazar 1981, fig. 7:1); 3: cooking pot, Tell Esdar III (Kochavi 1969, fig. 14:2); 4: cooking pot, Shiloh V (Finkelstein 1993, fig. 6.50:3); 5: cooking pot, Hazor XII–XI (Ben-Tor, Ben-Ami, and Sandhaus 2012, fig. 1.2:13); 6: cooking pot, Shiloh V (Finkelstein 1993, fig. 6.50:2); 7: cooking pot, Tel Masos III (Fritz and Kempinski 1983, fig. 131:14); 8: jug, Tel Esdar III (Kochavi 1969, fig. 14:5); 9: krater, Shiloh V (Finkelstein 1993, fig. 6.46:7); 10: krater, Shiloh V (Finkelstein 1993, fig. 6.46:3); 11: juglet, Tell Masos III (Fritz and Kempinski 1983, fig. 131:15); 12: bowl, Shiloh V (Finkelstein 1993, fig. 6.40:1); 13: krater, Shiloh V (Finkelstein 1993, fig. 6.57:2); 14: chalice, Tel Esdar III (Kochavi 1969, fig. 14:7); 15: bowl, Tel Masos III (Fritz and Kempinski 1983, fig. 131:11); 16: pyxis, Tel Masos III (Fritz and Kempinski 1983, fig. 133.7); 17: lamp, Tel Esdar III (Kochavi 1969, fig. 14:10)

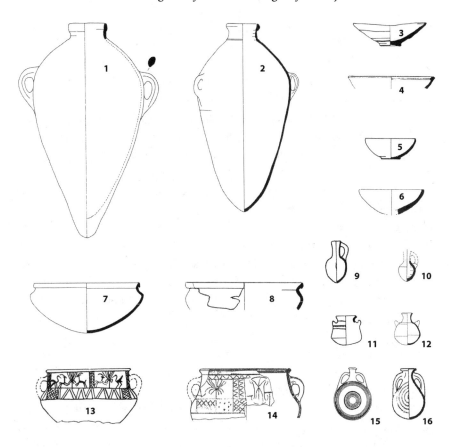

Fig. 3.16. A comparison of typical Late Bronze Canaanite and early Iron I Israelite ceramic forms. 1: Gezer XV; 2: 'Izbet Ṣarṭah III; 3: Gezer XV; 4: 'Izbet Ṣarṭah III; 5: Gezer XV; 6: Shiloh V; 7: Gezer XV; 8: 'Izbet Ṣarṭah III; 9: Megiddo VIII; 10: Tel Masos III; 11: Lachish, T. 4011; 12: Tel Masos III; 13: Lachish, Fosse Temple III; 14: 'Izbet Ṣarṭah III; 15: Lachish, Fosse Temple III; 16: Izbet Ṣarṭah III

The construction seen in the large, efficient farmhouses is not ad hoc vernacular architecture. It required considerable building skills, especially in planning, laying out, and constructing villages and houses in the rugged hill country, where there were few precedents. Pastoral nomads would not likely have had the experience or the requisite skills for such building projects. While the particular farmhouse module is innovative, there are a few buildings that suggest a prototype.[86]

The construction of extensive terrace systems is perhaps even more arduous, certainly more labor-intensive and a reflection of extensive long-range planning. Terracing the hillsides for a distance of half a mile or more around the hilltop sites would have required immense foresight, effort, and teamwork. Tons of rocks and small stones were dug up and used in constructing long rows of parallel terraces, high enough and strong enough to withstand the pressure of the soil behind them. The soil itself had to be sifted through, moved into place, and consolidated for plowing. Such terraces had to be continually rebuilt and strengthened in order to withstand erosion on the steep hillsides. If one terrace breaks upslope, all the terraces below will quickly be breached, and the topsoil will soon gully down into the valley.[87]

Similar centuries-old terrace systems can still be seen in the West Bank, even more so in the mountains of southern Lebanon. But where terraces are abandoned, they soon fall into disrepair. Terraces surrounding our Iron I sites are common, although not at all sites (such as those in the Beersheba region). Nor are they necessarily an innovation, since we do have some evidence for terraces in earlier periods. It is the *intensification* of the terrace system, and its deployment for sustained agricultural economy that is dependent on it, that is new in Iron I. Dating terrace systems is admittedly difficult, but the clue here is that sites like Ai, Radanna, and others in the central hill country are one-period sites, where the adjacent terraces—so integral to the function of the site—can scarcely be dated to any period other than Iron I.

Technology also created another feature of our Iron I villages: plastered cisterns.[88] Rainfall in the hill country is adequate for agriculture, but the rains cease entirely from late April through early October. There are few perennial springs in most areas and no running streams or rivers, only wadis (seasonal streambeds). Storing water during the long summer season was a necessity. The lack of appropriate technology may be one reason for the relatively sparse hill-country occupation before the Iron Age. We do have occasional earlier cisterns dug into the bedrock, but they are not usually plastered, so they would not have held water very well. It seems that the use of slaked-lime plaster made more efficient cisterns widely available now. The pillar-courtyard houses at Khirbet Radanna have several cisterns, some quite deep. They have an enormous capacity, no doubt sufficient to sustain a small or even a large family, together with animals that needed to be watered. Such cisterns are still seen in use in West Bank villages today.

A related technology was that of digging stone-lined silos to store grain for long periods. An Iron I pillar-courtyard house at ʿIzbet Ṣarṭah has more than forty such silos surrounding it (see fig. 3.12). Stone-lined silos are vastly superior to pits in the ground, which characterize many earlier sites. In the latter rot and rodents would likely have destroyed more than half of the stored grain. Again, these stone-lined silos are not necessarily an innovation, but their extended, systematic use is new.[89]

Metallurgy was not as common in the early Iron Age as might be expected. Stone, flint, and bronze implements continued in use. Iron is relatively rare for several reasons. Sources of iron are rare in the region, a few mines being known only in Transjordan. Iron implements are difficult to forge, they are brittle and often break, and, in any case, they rust easily. Iron was introduced in the Iron I period, as we know from some of our sites (and others), but it did not produce a technological revolution, at least not immediately.[90]

It is in ceramic production that we see technological changes most readily, but in combination with some conservative tendencies. Iron I pottery looks much like Late Bronze Age pottery in form, but analyses by ceramic technologists have shown that it is often handmade rather than thrown on a wheel (figs. 3.15 and 3.16). There is little paint. In addition, there are few if any Mycenaean, Cypriot, or Philistine imports. The one form that is distinctive is the so-called collar-rim store jar, previously used as a diagnostic ethnic trait. Now, however, these store jars are attested in Transjordan, and there they can extend into Iron II. Nevertheless, they are common at well-defined early Israelite sites, whereas they are rare at Iron I Canaanite sites.[91]

Ideology

Under the heading of ideology one may include various aspects of material culture where we can more readily discern individual and collective ideas at work, that is, less purely technological motivation and more aesthetic, artistic, and even religious factors, however nebulous.

The early Iron I cult places at the Bull Site, and possibly in the Mount Ebal installation, have already been discussed. It must be pointed out that these are the only definite public cult places that we have. There were probably household shrines here and there, as at Tell el-ʿUmeiri in Transjordan (above). But we have almost no evidence of the cultic objects that we might expect, such as altars, standing stones, offering stands, votive vessels, or figurines. These objects first appear, at least in numbers, only in the time of the monarchy (ch. 4). Certainly we have none of the temples that had proliferated in Late Bronze Age Canaan.

What does the artifactual evidence say about religious belief and cultural practice in our Iron I villages? Taking the Bull Site as authentic, and presuming that it is representative, one would conclude that the old Canaanite belief system still prevailed. The bronze zebu bull is almost identical to one found at Late Bronze Age Hazor, even in the smallest details. In addition, as well known from contemporary Ugaritic mythological texts, the epithet of El, the head of the Canaanite pantheon was "Bull El." The bull was widely seen as the symbol of vitality and fertility, some of the principal concerns of ancient religions in the Mediterranean world. At the Bull Site, fragments of ceramic offering stands would have come from cultic vessels that we actually have found elsewhere, used for the food and drink offerings through which one returned to the gods a token of what they had provided. Other sherds, as well as bronze fragments, attest to votive offerings. Even in its ruined state, the shrine yields a picture of religious beliefs and practices in the hill-country villages near where it was found (the site is only 5 miles east of Dothan).[92]

Apart from the bull found at the above site, we have little evidence of art in any form (and this could be an heirloom). There are a few Egyptian-style scarabs and a handful of simple "stick-figure" stamp seals (fig. 3.17). However, we have none of the sophisticated Canaanite art forms widely attested in the previous era, such as ivory carving, glyptic art, jewelry, stone work, and the like.

Taken together with the complete lack of monumental architecture and the absence of imported luxury wares in pottery, this paucity of artistic expression of any kind gives us the picture of a village culture that was isolated, aesthetically impoverished, and lacking an elite class that could have or would have desired and used luxury items. We are dealing rather with subsistence farmers and herders who made all the everyday objects that they needed.

One aspect of material culture that embodies ideas par excellence is writing. An inscribed sherd is an artifact that represents (re-presents) an idea. We have few such ostraca from the Iron I period. The Old Canaanite alphabet had already been in existence, along with Akkadian cuneiform, for centuries, and we have many Late Bronze Age examples of both scripts. But Hebrew ostraca begin in the tenth century (e.g., the Gezer Calendar). One exception is the ʿIzbet Ṣarṭah ostracon from the

Fig. 3.17. Early Iron Age seals. 1: Ashdod (Keel 1997, 667:12); 2: Radanna (Lederman 1999, 4); 3: Tell el-Farʿah North (Keel and Uehlinger 1998, no. 177a); 4: Beth-Shean (178a); 5: Revadim; reads *l'ab* (160); 6: Beth-Shemesh (180a)

eleventh century (above), which is a very primitive abecedary, undoubtedly a schoolboy's practice exercise: on one line the letters are written backward, their proper order is confused in places, and the other lines are gibberish. It is almost certainly evidence that the vast majority of the rural Iron population was illiterate. The other ostracon is from Khirbet Qeiyafa, presently undeciphered.[93]

External Relations

A final subsystem to be considered is external contacts or foreign relations typical of more developed societies. Here we have already noted the isolation of the Iron I villages, witnessed in many aspects of material culture. There were a few authorities in the remaining urban centers, but there is no evidence that the villagers had any contact with them. Indeed, in what will be described below as a deliberate withdrawal to colonize the highland frontier, our villagers had literally gone out of their way to avoid all external authority. As Sahlins put it, "a society without a Sovereign" (see above).

Having surveyed virtually all of the sites of the twelfth–eleventh century on both sides of the Jordan that could possibly be considered Israelite on strictly archaeological grounds, what historical information can we glean? Before moving on to textual data and the problems of ethnic identification, a summary of what we know thus far may be helpful.

1. The more than two hundred known Iron I sites represent a dramatic shift in settlement type and distribution, dated precisely to the Late Bronze–Iron I transition circa 1250–1150.

2. None of these sites is established on the ruins of a destroyed Canaanite city or town. They are founded either on long-deserted Bronze Age sites or de novo, mostly in the hill country or in areas such as the Beersheba valley that previously had only been sparsely inhabited.

3. Demographic projections show an increase in population in the principal settlement area, the central hill country, from roughly 10,000 in the thirteenth century up to 40,000 by the eleventh century. There must have been considerable in-migration.

4. All these sites are small, isolated villages, unfortified, devoid of monumental architecture, relatively poor in material culture. The social, economic, and political structure reflects a rural, agrarian, communitarian society. This is in sharp contrast to the urban culture of the Late Bronze Age.

5. There are general continuities with Late Bronze Age Canaanite culture, seen particularly in ceramics and probably in cultic traditions. In particular, the Iron I Israelite pottery is strongly in the Late Bronze tradition (fig. 3.16). On the other hand, there are some clear discontinuities in the aspects noted above, particularly in house form and technologies related to agriculture and the domestic mode of production.

6. The archaeological evidence, taken together, suggests major but gradual socioeconomic and political changes among the indigenous population of Canaan on the Late Bronze–Iron I horizon.

If history-writing is about change and the explanation of change, the above are the phenomena that the archaeologist and the historian must confront, based initially on the archaeological data.

The Hebrew Bible and Archaeology: Theories

Having surveyed the archaeological data independently as our primary source, then having looked at reasonable interpretations on their own terms, we can now turn to our other source: texts. Some of the pertinent extrabiblical texts have been incorporated into the discussion all along, since they, too, are artifacts, practically speaking. Even the biblical texts could be considered what archaeologists call curated artifacts, but their veracity can be and must be questioned. As we saw in chapter 2, a cooking pot cannot lie; it is just what it appears to be, and its indisputable original "meaning" lies in the intent of its maker and the uses of its owners. But texts can and do lie or mislead. Even at best, they may be ambiguous.

Biblical Texts

In selecting biblical texts upon which to comment, we need to note first the appropriate chronological context. For instance, traditional analyses of chronological notes in the biblical texts came up with a date of 1446 for the exodus; then subtracting thirty-eight years for the wilderness wandering, we arrive at a date of circa 1409 for the initial phase of the "conquest." Today all scholars, even most evangelicals, have abandoned that date. The few holdouts, neither mainstream biblicists nor archaeologists, can safely be ignored. The only feasible date for the early Israelite settlement in Canaan is circa 1250–1150.[94]

1. The Sinai Wilderness. The difficulty posed by a late (or even early) date for the events in question is that the biblical texts to be adduced here are much later. The archaeological data by definition are contemporary. By consensus, the narratives in the Hebrew Bible consist of stories told by the writers much later, and for reasons that are more didactic than historical, at least in our modern sense of disinterested, factual history.

The pertinent texts in the books of Exodus, Numbers, Deuteronomy, Joshua, Judges, and Samuel are all parts of relatively late, composite accounts attributed to sources known as J, E, and P, plus the Deuteronomistic History (Dtr). None of these sources can have been compiled in its present form much before the exile. Even if these sources do draw on older oral or written traditions, there remains a problem for the historian and the archaeologist: How much reliable historical information can we derive from these sources? Here an answer will depend largely on whether there are what may be called convergences between the two sources. If the archaeological data presented above—our primary source—contradict the biblical texts, we have no choice but to regard the latter as extraneous and proceed. Only if the two sources are in substantial agreement do we have grounds for reading the texts as prima facie evidence. Even then one should ask: Is the account true, that is, historically reliable beyond a reasonable doubt?[95]

The biblical texts that narrate an exodus from Egypt are well known and require little discussion here. The most comprehensive discussion of their background is that of Hoffmeier's *Ancient Israel in Sinai: The Evidence for the Authenticity of the Wilderness Tradition* (2005). Hoffmeier is an evangelical scholar but also a well-trained Egyptologist and the director of a significant excavation project in the Egyptian Delta. After an exhaustive survey of Egyptian literature and culture, as well as the topography of the Delta and Sinai, he is able to document only a few sites that might be identified with the biblical account of the sojourn of the Hebrews in Egypt and their itinerary after they supposedly escaped from slavery.

The Rameses of the biblical texts (Exod 1:11) has long been located at Pi-Ramesses, which flourished circa 1270–1120. Pithom (Exod 1:11) is almost certainly Tell el-Maskhuta, excavated several times and known to have been occupied in New Kingdom times. Biblical Succoth (Exod 12:37; Num 33:3–5) was probably in the Wadi Tumilat, where there are several possibilities for the site's location. Biblical Etham (Exod 13:20), on the edge of the wilderness, might be located in the Lake Timsah region, near Qantara. Hoffmeier's own contribution is to be acknowledged. He has shown that his site of Tell el-Borg, on the Pelusiac branch of the Nile, is probably the biblical fortress of Migdol (Exod 14:20).[96]

Beyond that, Hoffmeier has a long excursus on the Red ("Reed") Sea crossing and the years of wandering in the wilderness of Sinai. Yet in the end he has no archaeological evidence, any more than Israeli archaeologists had in their determined search in the 1970s. He can only conclude that the events narrated in Exodus and Numbers as historical might have happened. As he puts it: "It seems to me that it is easier to believe that the Bible accurately preserves an authentic picture of the travels and life in the Sinai wilderness than to suppose that authors six to seven centuries later … got so much certifiably correct."[97] History-writing, however, is not about belief or wishful thinking; it is about evidence that we can show to be factual beyond a reasonable doubt.

Several scholars, such as Egyptologist Donald Redford, have suggested that the knowledge of the biblical tradition demonstrated by the writers regarding Egypt probably stems from the Saite period in the seventh–sixth century.[98] This is precisely when most biblical scholars would date the penultimate formation of the Pentateuch (above), and it would explain several specific Egyptian place names in the texts. But no matter when or where these texts were written, they do not provide us with much useful information on the distant Egyptian origins of any Israelites in the highlands of Canaan or their journey to that land. There the archaeological data are our only source of contemporary, first-hand, demonstrably reliable data (although, of course, these data, too, are subject to interpretation).

2. Itineraries in Transjordan. The biblical texts dealing with the itinerary of the Israelites beyond the Sinai, in the Negev and Transjordan, are closer to home. We have already surveyed most of the archaeological sites of the thirteenth–twelfth century there, noting that the principal Israelite victories claimed at Dibon and Heshbon have no archaeological support whatsoever, the sites having been mostly uninhabited in the thirteenth century. Further, if Arad is biblical Hormah, it has no Late Bronze occupation or destruction.

Almost none of the other sites named in Numbers, Deuteronomy, Joshua, and Judges have been positively identified and excavated. Two possible exceptions would be Deir ʿAlla (possibly biblical Succoth; not the same as the Succoth in Egypt) and Tall as-Saʿidiyeh (possibly Zaphon). At Deir ʿAlla we have a destruction of Stratum E circa 1200, followed by a sort of squatter occupation, which could be seen as evidence of an Israelite conquest (above). Succoth is said to have been given to the tribe of Reuben, but no conquest is mentioned (Josh 13:27). At Tall as-Saʿidiyeh, the Late Bronze occupation in Stratum XII ends with a destruction circa 1150, followed by a gap in occupation. Zaphon is also assigned to the tribe of Reuben (Josh 13:27). Tell el-ʿUmeiri has already been discussed, but it cannot be identified with any biblical site.

All this does not mean, of course, that archaeology has proven the biblical description of the route through Transjordan to be entirely fictitious. But it does mean that the historian has no empirical evidence, only the testimony of the biblical writers. Most scholars would agree, however, that the witness of the biblical texts is compromised by their writers' transparent theological agenda. Theirs is a literary construct—the history of the history—not the real history of the Israelite peoples in the Iron Age.

3. The Conquest of the Land West of the Jordan. It is the conquest narratives in Joshua, and to a lesser degree in Judges, that are most relevant, since they deal with the region west of the Jordan. These, too, have been exhaustively analyzed by biblical scholars and need not detain us here. The issue is simply whether the primary data—the archaeological evidence—lend these stories any credence.

A close reading of the pertinent texts yields the following picture. In the book of Joshua, and to some extent in Judges, some thirty-seven sites in Canaan west of the Jordan are said to have been taken, that is, seized and presumably destroyed. The data can be summarized as follows.

Fig. 3.18. Canaanite sites in Joshua and Judges said to have been taken by the incoming Israelites (circa 1200)

Site	Reference	Identification; Status
Achshaph	Josh 12:20	Khirbet el-Harbaj; LB, Iron I pottery
Adullam	Josh 12:15	Khirbet ʿAdullam; unexcavated
Ai	Josh 7:2–8; 12:9	abandoned 2300–1200
Aphek	Josh 12:18	LB destruction; then Philistine
Arad	Josh 12:14	no LB occupation; no Iron I
Beeroth	Josh 18:25	unidentified
Bethel	Josh 8:17; 12:16	LB destruction; Iron I sherds
Bezek	Judg 1:4	Khirbet Ibziq; unexcavated
Debir	Josh 10:38; 12:13	Khirbet Rabud; no LB destruction
Dor	Josh 12:23	Phoenician in twelfth century
Eglon	Josh 10:34–35; 12:12	Tell ʿEton; LB unclear
Gaza	Judg 1:18	unexcavated
Geder	Josh 12:13	unidentified
Gezer	Josh 12:12	no LB destruction; then Canaanite
Gibeon	Josh 10:1	little LB occupation
Goiim	Josh 12:23	unidentified
Hazor	Josh 11:10; 12:19; Judg 4:2	LB Stratum XIII destruction; agents unknown
Hebron	Josh 10:36; 12:10	little excavation; little evidence
Hepher	Josh 12:17	Tel el-Ifshar?

Hormah	Josh 12:14	identification uncertain (Tel Masos?)
Jarmuth	Josh 12:11	Khirbet el-Yarmuk; no LB occupation
Jericho	Josh 12:9; 24:11	no thirteenth- or twelfth-century occupation
Jerusalem	Josh 12:10; Judg 1:8	no LB destruction
Jokneam	Josh 12:22	Yoqneʿam; LB Stratum XIV destroyed; then gap
Kedesh	Josh 12:22	Tel Qades; no LB occupation
Kiriath-jearim	Josh 18:14	unexcavated
Lachish	Josh 10:31; 12:11	LB Stratum I destroyed; then long gap
Lasharon	Josh 12:18	———
Libnah	Josh 10:29; 12:15	unidentified
Madon	Josh 11:1; 12:19	unidentified
Makkedah	Josh 10:28; 12:16	Khirbet el-Qom; no LB occupation
Megiddo	Josh 12:21	Stratum VIIA destroyed mid-twelfth century
Shimron-meron	Josh 12:20	unidentified
Taʿanach	Josh 12:21	Iron village; destroyed late twelfth century
Tappuah	Josh 17:8	———
Tirzah	Josh 12:24	Tell el-Farʿah (North); no LB destruction
Zephath	Judg 1:17	Khirbet Sitt Leila; unexcavated

Of these sites in Cisjordan said to have been taken, that is, destroyed, thirty-four of them are listed in the book of Joshua but only three in Judges: Bezek, Jerusalem, and Hazor. Of the thirty-four sites in Joshua, only Hazor, Zephath, Gaza, and perhaps Bethel could possibly have been overcome or even threatened by incoming Israelite peoples, much less by local lowland refugees or nomads. There may have been some regional conflicts between the local population and the new settlers who are by now well documented. But in the light of the overwhelming archaeological evidence, there was no large-scale warfare on the thirteenth- and twelfth-century horizon, except that initiated by the Philistines along the coast. The book of Joshua gets it entirely right only once; it omits Shechem in Josh 12, which turns out to be correct, since the site was not destroyed (above). The inevitable conclusion is that the book of Joshua is nearly all fictitious, of little or no value to the historian. It is largely a legend celebrating the supposed exploits of a local folk hero.[99]

It is well known that in the first chapter of Judges, by contrast, we have a list of more than a dozen sites *not* conquered—in some cases sites (e.g., Hazor) that the book of Joshua claims had been destroyed. The two accounts can easily be compared by contrasting figures 3.18, 3.19, and 3.20 here. They certainly cannot be reconciled, however, even though the final redactors of the Hebrew Bible put them back to back. Evidently even they could not sort out the confusion. The following chart summarizes the pertinent data.

Fig. 3.19. Sites said in the book of Judges not to have been taken by the incoming Israelites

Site	Stratum; Status
Achzib	not destroyed; Phoenician (?)
Ahlab	unidentified
Aijalon	Yalo?; unexcavated
Akko	LB occupation; not destroyed
Aphek	Stratum X_{12}; Canaanite into twelfth century
Arad	not occupied until tenth century
Beth-anath	Safed el-Battih?; unexcavated
Beth-Shean	Stratum VI; Canaanite into twelfth century
Beth-Shemesh	Stratum 7; destroyed, then Philistine
Dan	Stratum VI; Canaanite into twelfth century
Dor	Philistine
Ekron	Stratum VII; Philistine
Gaza	unexcavated; Philistine
Gezer	Stratum XIV; not destroyed, continues
Gibeon	uncertain
Hazor	Stratum XIII; destroyed by unknown agents

Jokneam	Yoqneʿam; Stratum XIX; destroyed by unknown agents
Kitron	unidentified
Lachish	Stratum VI; destroyed circa 1150
Megiddo	Stratum VIIB; Canaanite into twelfth century
Nahaloi	unidentified
Rehob	unidentified; several possibilities
Shaalabbin	unidentified
Shechem	Stratum XII; not destroyed, continues

True to our intent to use the archaeology data as a litmus test in evaluating of the Hebrew Bible as a source for history-writing, let us turn now to a comparison of the books of Joshua and Judges.

Fig. 3.20. Comparison of themes in the books of Joshua and Judges

Joshua	**Judges**
1. Swift, total conquest	1. Symbiosis with Canaanites
2. Philistine population vanquished; Midianites and others, as well	2. Amalekites continue
3. Huge territory; immediate conquest	3. Small, decentralized entity
4. Centralized reorganization; rapid change	4. Long socioeconomic process of evolution
5. "Tribal" solidarity under rule of Joshua	5. "Communitarian" society; "domestic mode of production"
6. Covenant with Yahweh	6. Family religion; polytheism
7. Little interest in ordinary folk, daily life	7. Numerous detailed sketches of village life
8. Little or no accord with archaeological data	8. Accords in some detail with the archaeological data

The conclusion in the light of archaeology is inevitable. The book of Joshua looks like a late, Deuteronomistic construct preoccupied with theological concerns, such as the Sinai covenant, centralization, and the temple, that were paramount particularly in the exilic and postexilic era.

Its authors were scarcely familiar or concerned with life in the early Iron Age settlements. The book of Judges, by contrast, has the ring of truth about it. The core of the narrative consists of stories about everyday life in the formative, prestate era, when "there was no king in Israel [and] all the people did what was right in their own eyes" (Judg 21:25). The portrait of as much as two hundred years of struggles under charismatic leaders with other peoples in the land—of a long drawn-out process of socioeconomic, political, and cultural change—is more realistic than that of the book of Joshua, which is really the celebration of a legendary hero.

In particular, several of the stories of everyday life in Judges are full of details with which any archaeologist is familiar. These would include Ehud's upper chamber (Judg 4); the palm tree where Deborah sat (Judg 4–5); Gideon's household (house of the father), with its oxen, threshing floor, winepress, household shrine, and village kinsmen and collaborators (Judg 6–7); Jephthah and the elders of Israel (Judg 11); dialectical variations and the shibboleth incident (Judg 12); the Nazarites and nostalgia for simpler times (Judg 13); Samson and the Philistines (Judg 14–16); Micah's household shrine (Judg 17; 19); and the annual agricultural feast and betrayals of the daughters of Shiloh (Judg 21).

Stager's classic 1985 article on the archaeology of the family was a breakthrough in the hoped-for dialogue between archaeology and biblical studies. In slightly modified form, the biblical socioeconomic and societal terms can be correlated with the archaeological data as follows.[100]

**Fig. 3.21. Socioeconomic terms from the Hebrew Bible
with suggested archaeological correlates**

Hebrew Term	Meaning	Archaeological Evidence
geber	individual in a nuclear family	individual household
bêt-ʾāb	the "house of the father"; a multigenerational family or lineage	family compound of several pillar-courtyard houses
mišpāḥâ	the extended family, or clan, several lineages	the cluster of several compounds, the whole village
šēbeṭ	the tribe	regional groups of villages
bᵊnê yiśrʾēl	all the tribes, or the "sons of Israel"	the entire network of hill-country settlements

---

Here a selective reading of passages in Judges, plus Samuel, does accord well with the archaeological data. In Transjordan, as noted above, only two of the more than thirty sites listed in the Hebrew Bible have been positively identified and excavated: Dibon (Dhiban) and Heshbon (Ḥesban). Both lack any but ephemeral Late Bronze Age remains, and they did not become towns until well into the Iron Age.

Biblical apologists (e.g., some evangelical scholars) tend to ignore the archaeological data because it is challenging. For them, if one must choose one's facts, the biblical facts trump all others. In some cases, conservative scholars argue that the Bible never claims that the Israelites *destroyed* all the sites listed in Josh 12. Only three are said to have been "destroyed by fire": Jericho (Josh 6:24), Ai (8:19), and Hazor (11:11). That is true. But how do these scholars suppose the Israelites took all the other cities listed as conquered? The Hebrew verb in Josh 12:7 is *nkh*, "to smite." Is it feasible to think that a large force of Israelite warriors surrounded a given city, that the terrified inhabitants then simply surrendered (or conveniently disappeared), and thus the city came into Israelite hands, peacefully, as it were? The argument that the biblical writers really did not *mean* to say that these sites were destroyed is disingenuous.

There is no way out of archaeology's argument from silence, which is deafening when taken seriously. There was no statistically significant destruction of Canaan or mass slaughter of its inhabitants at the end of the Late Bronze Age, even with Philistine invasions. That disposes of the first model to be discussed, the traditional conquest model.

Mendenhall said as much as the above in 1962, in defending the second model: peaceful infiltration. In *The Tenth Generation: The Origins of the Biblical Tradition*, he put it succinctly:

> There was chaos, conflict, war, but of one thing we can be absolutely certain. Ancient Israel did not win because of superior military weapons or superior military organization. It did not drive out or murder en masse whole populations. The gift of the land meant merely that the old political regimes and their claim to ownership of all land was transferred to God Himself.

In Mendenhall's opinion, then,

> There was no real conquest of Palestine in the sense that has usually been understood; what happened instead may be termed, from the point of

view of the secular historian interested only in socio-political processes, a peasant's revolt against the network of interlocking Canaanite city states.[101]

Mendenhall's peaceful infiltration model, the next to be discussed here, was borrowed largely from the theories of Alt's and Noth's school of territorial history, pioneered in the 1920s and following decades and taken up finally by Weippert in the 1970s. In this view, the first Israelite settlers were pastoral nomads from Transjordan who initially crossed the Jordan seasonally in search of water and pastures, then in the course of their migrations eventually became sedentarized there.[102] It must be noted that at the time there was little or no evidence for this (or any other) model, and the ethnographic data discussed below will show how tenuous such a notion of sedentarized nomads is.

The American scholar Norman Gottwald carried the notion of indigenous origins even further, invoking an explicitly theological motive for nomadic tribal people settling down. The title of his 1979 book says it all: *The Tribes of Yahweh: A Sociology of the Religion of Liberated Israel, 1250–1050 BCE*. This was a magisterial work, highly original, exhaustively documented—a breath of fresh air in the stale world of conventional biblical studies. But the Marxist notion of class warfare was transparent (giving Gottwald's model, the third, the name *peasants' revolt* theory), and there is no archaeological evidence for sedentarized tribes then or now, as will be shown presently. Nor can religion be seen necessarily as the prime mover in cultural change.

Gottwald's *Tribes of Yahweh* drew much attention and generated fierce controversies at the time, but today it represents little more than a chapter in the history of scholarship. The term *tribe* is too vague to be useful any longer; there is now little evidence for Yahwistic monotheism until late in the monarchy; *liberated Israel* carries with it notions of class warfare that are modern constructs; and the *sociology* is that of the biblical writers and their world, not that of early Israel (although there were social factors). Only Gottwald's stress on indigenous origins is relevant for archaeological discussions today.[103]

Numerous other Israeli, European, and American biblical scholars have weighed in on the discussion of the best ways to interpret the biblical evidence, such as it is. None of these discussions, however, has gained universal acceptance, and they are mostly obsolete in the light of newer data.[104] First, however, before moving on, the one nonbiblical text we happen to have must be introduced, the well-known Victory Stela of Pharaoh Merenptah, securely dated to 1208 plus or minus a year or so.

Nonbiblical Texts: The Merenptah Stela

Ramesses's son Merenptah (also spelled Merneptah; 1213–1203) confronted an invasion of the Delta by Libyans and Sea Peoples in his fifth year. Celebrating his victory, he erected a Victory Stela found at Thebes. The poem reads:

> The princes are prostrate, saying "Mercy!"
> Not one raises his head among the Nine Bows.
> Desolation is for Tehenu; Hatti is pacified;
> Plundered is the Canaan with every evil;
> Carried off is Ashkelon; seized upon is Gezer;
> Yanoam [Yenoam] is made as that which does not exist;
> Israel is laid waste; his seed is not;
> Hurru is become a widow for Egypt!
> All lands together, they are pacified.[105]

The pertinent references are to sites and peoples in Hatti, the standard designation for the land of Canaan. Three specific towns are listed. Ashkelon and Gezer are both well known. Following that is Yenoam, a site whose location is uncertain (see below). All three of these entities are marked by the standard Egyptian determinate sign for "country" or "state," in this case city-states. The fourth reference is to a group, "Israel," marked instead by the sign for "people." And since the designation is a plural gentilic, this reference is to the Israelite peoples, that is, a socioeconomic group who are not centrally organized. The text then declares of this group that it is "laid waste; his seed is not."

Merenptah's Victory Stela has been much discussed since its discovery, in particular since this is the earliest reference to Israel that we have, several centuries earlier than any biblical text, and precisely dated. The reference to Israel's seed has been variously interpreted as Israel's grain supply or as Israel's progeny. But in either case, a total Egyptian victory over the Israelite people is claimed. That was obviously not the case, so the matter need not concern us further here.[106]

A few skeptical scholars at one time claimed that the Egyptian word *ya-śi-r-ʾ-l* (*yaśir-ʾel*) should be read "Jezreel," as a place name, in this case the Jezreel Valley in northern Israel. But this idea has long been refuted by Egyptologists. Several of the biblical minimalists have gone further. Thus Thompson has declared:

> The reference to an "Israel" as the spouse of Canaan in an early Egyptian inscription is hardly the same as evidence for the historical existence of the Israel of the Bible. This text renders only the earliest known usage of a name. It does not refer to the "Israel" we know from the Assyrian period and which is mentioned in both Assyrian and Palestinian texts.[107]

Thompson's whole point is that Merenptah's "Israel" is mythological, not historical. Since the pharaoh did not actually destroy this Israel, that may be the case. Nevertheless, the stela mentions the "Israelite peoples," and thus it proves their existence somewhere in Canaan well before circa 1208. The alternative to this explanation of the term in the text is to suggest that the Egyptian scribe made up the name and by accident it is identical to the biblical name. Whitelam declares more modestly that the Merenptah inscription "offers very little unambiguous evidence about the nature and location of ancient Israel."[108]

The fact is that the Merenptah inscription tells us a great deal about early Israel—and from an independent point of view that cannot be faulted for biblical bias. At minimum, we learn that:

1. There existed in Canaan by 1210 at latest a cultural and probably a political entity that called itself "Israel" and was known to the Egyptians by that name.
2. This Israel was well enough established by that time among the other peoples of Canaan to have been perceived by Egyptian intelligence as a possible challenge to Egyptian hegemony.
3. This Israel did not constitute an organized state like others in Canaan but consisted rather of loosely affiliated peoples, that is, an ethnic group.
4. This Israel was not located in the lowlands, under Egyptian domination, but in the more remote central hill country, on the frontier.

At Ashkelon and Gezer we have already noted the archaeological evidence pro and con for a Merenptah destruction. For Ashkelon we even have an

Egyptian relief depicting the siege of the walled city. Yet in both cases the Egyptian pharaoh seems to be boasting (as usual). That is certainly the case with Israel, which the Egyptians, despite their claim of total destruction, seem to have avoided entirely (below).

The one problem we have lies in locating Yenoam and identifying it with any known site. Most scholars, assuming that the Egyptian toponyms are in a recognizable geographical sequence, have looked farther north than Ashkelon and Gezer. Aharoni had identified Yenoam with Arabic Tell el-ʿAbeidiyeh, at the southern end of the Sea of Galilee. Somewhat later Naʾaman proposed the site of Tell esh-Shihab, in southern Transjordan, which Aharoni had identified instead with biblical Kiriath-anab, farther east. There is no archaeological evidence for either site.[109] In any case, the reference to Israel does follow the mention of Yenoam, so that must be considered.

There are several bits of textual evidence for locating Yenoam. (1) In the Amarna letters a ruler of Ashtaroth confronts his rival at Yenoam, presumably nearby. Ashtaroth is probably to be located at Tell Ashtara. The coupling of the site with Edrei in the Hebrew Bible (= Derʿa), some 12 miles to the south, would perhaps confirm this location. (2) A stela describing a campaign of Seti I (1294), found at Beth-Shean, lists Yenoam after Beth-Shean, but then it lists Akko and other coastal sites farther north, as well as Hazor in Upper Galilee. Here the geographical order does not necessarily place Yenoam in Bashan. (3) The Karnak Stela of Seti I (above) depicts Yenoam near an unidentified fortified city surrounded by shrubs and trees, but the location is unclear. (4) The reliefs of Merenptah, whose Victory Stela we have discussed and which mentions Yenoam, show the pharaoh attacking a city on foot. It cannot be identified, but Rainey thinks that the terrain, differing from that of the pharaoh's chariot at Ashkelon and Gezer, suggests another location (below). Yet he admits that the relief also shows the pharaoh attacking Akko on foot. This is the sum total of our evidence for locating Yenoam (see excursus 3.1).

The pictorial reliefs at Karnak in question were long attributed to Ramesses II, but Yurco's brilliant reanalysis showed that they were probably commissioned by his son and successor Merenptah. The reliefs depict an Egyptian battle somewhere in Canaan, with horses and chariots trampling victims from three cities, the only name preserved being Ashkelon. Yurco identified some of the prostrate victims (his scene 4) wearing skull caps as Israelites. Rainey, however, argues that, while the scenes do depict

Israelites in Canaan, they are really Shasu settled there. He also thinks that, in addition to Ashkelon, the names of Gezer and Yenoam can be restored (as named in Merenptah's Victory Stela).[110]

The Revival of Pastoral Nomadic and Peaceful Infiltration Models

We have already given a critique of the principal models for understanding the origins of Israel in earlier scholarship: (1) conquest; (2) peaceful infiltration; (3) and peasant revolt. Yet since the second approach seems to have experienced something of a revival, not only in the work of Rainey discussed above but in other forms, we must look at it more closely. Here both the archaeological and the ethnographic data will come into play.

Israel Finkelstein is a pivotal figure in the discussion of Israelite origins. He was a prime mover in Israeli surveys in the 1970s–1980s in the West Bank, published with others in 1993, 1994, and 1997. He directed excavations at two key sites: ʿIzbet Ṣarṭah (1976–1978) and Shiloh (1981–1984), both well published (Finkelstein 1986; Finkelstein, Bunimovitz, and Lederman 1993). Finkelstein's early analysis of the survey data in *The Archaeology of the Israelite Settlement* in 1988 was the first comprehensive synthesis. Up to the early 1990s, Finkelstein had simply assumed the Israelite ethnicity of the Iron I village sites, and he had not offered much of a theory of his own, beyond some dissatisfaction with the current models (above). In a series of publications beginning in 1991, however, he gradually developed a model that was essentially a revival of the old Alt–Noth "territorial history" approach, coupled now with an adaptation of the theories of the Annales school of Braudel and others, emphasizing the *longue durée*.[111]

Finkelstein's views on the Iron I settlements in question can be summarized as follows.

1. The long-term, cyclical changes in settlement type and patterns reflect a phenomenon best regarded as "oscillation." A predictable factor in cultural change, it involves shifts back and forth between sedentism and nomadism.

2. In this case, the early Iron Age settlements following the Late Bronze collapse circa 1200 reflect the resedentarization of local pastoral nomads. They had originated in the central hill country as displaced persons following the earlier collapse of the Middle

Bronze Age city-states circa 1550–1450. Although invisible, this nomadic population explains the apparent decrease we see in Late Bronze Age population estimates.

3. The surge in population in the twelfth century reflects the large-scale movements of these pastoralists from the steppe regions down toward the Jordan Valley and up into the hill country, where they established new villages.

4. The pottery of the Iron I villages shows discontinuity with the largely urban Late Bronze Age settlements, reflecting the nomadic background of the settlers.

5. Iron I technologies such as constructing terraces, digging cisterns, and building silos are not innovations but reflect older Bronze Age traditions. Thus these settlers were not newcomers.

6. Since we cannot determine ethnicity on the basis of material culture remains, it is illegitimate to call the settlers "Israelites." In any case, the Iron I culture is too diverse to define narrowly. It represents simply another cycle, driven largely by natural conditions.

Several of Finkelstein's points are well taken, and they are in accord with the views of other archaeologists such as Bunimovitz, Dever, Faust, Mazar, Stager, and others. Taking the perspective of the *longue durée* is indeed important in assessing cultural change, and indigenous models do now prevail in all circles. Finally, there surely were former pastoral nomads in the ethnic mix of the early Iron I population. Nevertheless, much of Finkelstein's argument is purely speculative and must be rejected. Let us take the above assertions point by point.

(1) The earliest sedentary wave of oscillation Finkelstein puts at the end of the Early Bronze I period, circa 3100. After that he sees a decline in Early Bronze II–III, which in his model would result in a major dislocation of population. However, nothing of the sort occurred. The ensuing Early Bronze II–III period sees a continuing, expanding *urban* culture. Finkelstein's second wave follows the major collapse at the end of Early Bronze III, circa 2500. Yet in the following nonurban Early Bronze IV period, circa 2500–2000, all authorities agree that the survivors of this collapse fled *from* the settled areas and *became* pastoral nomads in the hinterland—the opposite of Finkelstein's presumed nomadic process of inevitable sedentarization.[112]

As for the third oscillation wave, after the collapse of the Middle Bronze Age urban culture, there is simply no evidence for a large nomadic population in the countryside following that. Here the Late Bronze Age Amarna letters document a highly urbanized city-state system, the only rural elements being the Habiru, hardly pastoral nomads. This "nomadic" notion has been refuted effectively by Bunimovitz:

> Though it is true that many of the large urban centers which formed the backbone of settlement in Middle Bronze Age Canaan dramatically diminished in size, it should be emphasized that they remained urban in character.... The moderate Late Bronze Age cities controlled a much diminished rural sector. Indeed during most of this period hardly any rural settlements existed in the highlands and in few other regions of the country.[113]

Finkelstein's nomads are indeed invisible, as they often are in the archaeological record. He largely ignores the ethnographic literature.

(2) Finkelstein's demographic projections belie his own arguments. He acknowledges, with other authorities, that the nomadic element of the population (as in Rowton's dimorphic societies) typically makes up no more than 10–15 percent of the total population. Using his own estimate of 10,000–12,000 for the central hill country in the Late Bronze Age, we arrive at a reservoir of potential settlers consisting of no more than 1,200 on the eve of the population shift well documented circa 1200. There is simply no way to account for rapid growth—from perhaps 20,000 by the twelfth century, much less the estimated 30,000–40,000 by the eleventh century—on the basis of natural increase alone. As noted above, there must have been a substantial in-migration from somewhere else in Canaan, even if the entire nomadic population had become sedentarized. The only question is: *Where* within Canaan?[114]

(3) As for the presumed movement into the hill country from the steppe lands to the east, again Finkelstein's numbers are questionable. He states that in his southern Samaria (Ephraim) surveys "most of the early Iron Age I sites (75%–90%)" were located in the eastern part of the region, that is, "on the desert fringe and the eastern flank of the central range." The later phase of settlement, however, he locates in the "intermontane valleys of the central range, and flat areas, such as the Bethel plateau."[115]

Finkelstein's original site-distribution maps and demographic projects do not separate these two phases. In subsequent discussions, his Iron

I data turn out to be almost exclusively eleventh century, although he dates the first wave of settlement to the twelfth century. But if this is the case, then where is the twelfth-century evidence? Only in one map does Finkelstein distinguish the two phases. But how then does he know that the pottery of his eastern sites is earlier? Zertal made a similar west-to-east argument, and he even published some cooking-pot rims that can be assigned broadly to one century or another. But his statistics, too, can easily be refuted (see excursus 3.2).[116]

Let us turn now to Finkelstein's second Iron I village-pastoral "nomadic" connection: the typical pillar-courtyard house as a sort of domestic adaptation of a bedouin tent. This idea was first developed in the 1970s by Fritz, codirector of the Tel Masos excavations discussed above. Fritz took special note of the open central or side courtyard, flanked by a number of small rooms; he called these dwellings broad-room houses. It seemed to him that such a plan perpetuated the arrangement of bedouin tents, the outdoor sitting area in front of bedouin tents being the forerunner of the courtyards. His interpretation is problematic, though, for these two living spaces have entirely different functions. The area directly outside a tent is usually a meeting place where men congregate, talk, and offer hospitality. In any case, the only broad-room house in Stratum III consists of Building 34. This is a rather typical pillar-courtyard house, the entrance of which is not clear. An adjacent room with two *tabûns*, or ovens, is not in front but to one side.

One of Finkelstein's major arguments in favor of the early Israelites as sedentarized nomads rests on typical round or oval village plans that he sees as reflecting bedouin-like tents drawn up in a circle, like Conestoga wagons in a defensive position. Using old photographs, he illustrates one sort of triangular tent arrangement of bedouin tents, partially enclosing a small area.[117] This, however, is misleading: these tent formations are clearly the rare exception.

More detailed, critical ethnographic studies have shown that only when threatened by armed conflict are bedouin tents drawn up in this formation. Ordinarily they are laid out in a longitudinal line, spaced apart, all facing the same direction, preferably to the east when topography permits.

An ethnographic study of bedouin tents by Saidel has thoroughly refuted the tent–house–village plan scenario of Finkelstein (and also of Fritz and Herzog). Saidel, with many other ethnographers, shows that analogies drawn from the *modern* sedentarization of pastoral nomads are misleading. In almost every case, they have been forcibly settled, and the ad hoc layout of closely spaced concrete-block houses reflects little or nothing of traditional pastoral nomadic lifestyle and values. Until very recently, the tent layout described above prevailed, as it probably had done throughout antiquity.

Saidel describes the bedouins documented by nineteenth- and twentieth-century ethnographers as "living fossils." He goes on to observe that "disparities in the size and shape of contemporary Bedouin tent camps, as recorded by ethno-archaeologists, with those from the 19th–20th centuries CE, demonstrate that Bedouin encampments in the southern Levant and northern Arabia have changed significantly over the past 100 years." Thus "the parallels drawn … between the four-room house of Iron Age I Palestine and Transjordan and the Bedouin tent are baseless."[118]

Rainey's model of early Israel as sedentarized nomads from Transjordan, discussed above, was buttressed, as he acknowledged, by recent ethnographic work by Eveline van der Steen that was published after Fritz, Kempinski, and Herzog had advanced a similar model. Van der Steen, however, based her research on the sedentarization of *modern* pastoral nomads in Transjordan in the nineteenth and twentieth centuries CE. Among the reasons for the abandonment of a nomadic lifestyle (what Barth termed "falling out") were: (1) the accumulation of too much wealth and thus the need for better markets; (2) the depletion of herds and the need to diversify, as in trading; (3) population pressure; and, most of all, (4) the successful attempts of state authorities to settle nomadic populations.[119]

Van der Steen then attempts to apply these modern analogies directly to the changes in settlement patterns and demography on the Late Bronze–Iron I horizon in both Transjordan and Cisjordan. In the wake of the systemic collapse that we have documented, "it is to be expected that the same traumatic events would have motivated ancient pastoralists in the same way that they did sedentary peoples." She concludes, "The reorganization of society at the beginning of the Iron Age must have caused a complete redivision and reorganization of the available soil."[120] In van der Steen's reconstruction, Transjordanian pastoral nomads constituted an influx of new peoples in Cisjordan—whom we label Proto-Israelites— who were so suddenly and completely sedentarized that they became "a militant group," so powerful that it confronted Merenptah's troops circa 1210.[121]

There are numerous objections to van der Steen's reconstruction of early Israel. It is based not only on speculation, with little documentation of the copious archaeological data, but it also depends almost entirely on modern analogies, the applicability of which she is unable to show. Above all, she simply assumes that her reasons for the sedentarization of pastoral nomads were operative in the Late Bronze Age, circa 1250–1200.

The fact is that on that horizon all four of her factors were, to the best of our knowledge, nonoperative. We know little about fluctuations in wealth and poverty. There could hardly have been a sufficient population surplus in Transjordan that pastoralists were forced to overrun western Canaan, settling there. In particular, the competition for soil would have affected local subsistence farmers, not pastoralists, who need pasture lands and do not till the soil except occasionally in the course of their migrations. Finally, the Egyptian authorities had never succeeded in pacifying the Shasu, the only nomadic pastoralists our texts identify in Transjordan, no doubt because of their *reluctance* to settle.

Few other scholars have been persuaded by the "tent prototype." Stager's detailed and sophisticated analysis puts it best:

> The pillared house takes its form not from some desert nostalgia monumentalized in stone and mudbrick, but from a living tradition. It was first and foremost a successful adaptation to farm life: the ground floor had space allocated for food processing, small craft production, stabling and storage; the second floor was suitable for dining, sleeping, and other activities.... Its longevity attests to its continuing suitability not only to the environment, especially where timber was available, but also for the socioeconomic unit housed in it—for the most part, rural families who farmed and raised livestock.[122]

Robert Coote adds:

> There is no reason to wonder where the new settlers got their new housing ideas any more than their new building skills. Both lay quite within the capabilities of the lowland farming class, tribal and otherwise, of the thirteenth century and earlier.[123]

The disinterested observer may get the impression that Finkelstein's overriding theory of the pastoral-nomadic origin of the earliest Israelites has influenced his interpretation of the archaeological evidence, as well as leading him into unwarranted speculation.

Theories on the Sedentarization of Pastoral Nomads

In the light of the revival of models of nomadic sedentarization, a short discursus is in order. We need to look anew at some of the extensive literature in ancient Near Eastern studies, ethnography, and anthropology.[124] There is a general consensus on several points regarding southwestern Asia. (1) Pastoralists and settled populations live in a delicately balanced, constantly shifting symbiosis dictated in part by natural conditions. (2) The nomads, however, deliberately favor their lifestyle, and they tend to resist sedentarization rather than seeking it. (3) They become sedentarized mostly by force exerted on them by the central authorities. Otherwise, they may settle either in times of prosperity, when they need to market surplus animals, or in periods of extreme stress such as a drought or famine.

The essential dynamics of this process have remained unchanged over millennia, due to the unique natural conditions of the region. Only very recently—perhaps in the past half-century or so—have modern states been able to effect major changes. In the ancient Near East the complex interaction of the rulers of the Mesopotamian city-states and the peoples of the steppe is vividly portrayed in the Mari cuneiform correspondence of the eighteenth century BCE, where the Amorites (the Amurru, "westerners") resisted forcible sedentarization but were eventually restricted in their movements. Nevertheless, later texts show that they continued their migrations and did not become entirely settled in Mesopotamia and Canaan until many centuries later. Even today in Israel and Jordan, the authorities have not been able to settle large numbers of bedouin, who traditionally regard themselves as the true "Arabs of the Desert" and despise the *fellahin*, the farmers and townspeople. *Ideology*, not just the natural environment, drives the lifestyle of pastoralists.

A fundamental work is a 1980 collection of essays entitled *When Nomads Settle: Processes of Sedentarization as Adaptation and Response*. In the introduction editor Philip Salzman describes sedentarization as one particular aspect of sociocultural change, driven by both environmental conditions (functionalism) and by ideology. The goal for pastoral nomads in this process is to maximize and, in a sense, to institutionalize the means of livelihood in changing circumstances. One of Salzman's observations is particularly relevant here:

Among the Bedouin of the southern Sinai (Marx 1977) are found two mechanisms for institutionalizing alternatives, "operational generalization" and "asserted ideology"—in response to alternating conditions of political security/insecurity and economic activity/lack of opportunity—which have characterized this area of international turmoil decade after decade.[125]

After clearly defining the terms *nomadism* and *sedentism* (as too rarely done), Salzman delineates three models of the process from one state to the other, even though they may be overly generalized: (1) "drought and decline," in which case pastoralists are forced by unfavorable climatic conditions and the loss of herds to gravitate toward agriculture and village life, even if only temporarily; (2) "defeat and degradation," in which case pastoralists are forcibly settled either by tribal conflicts or more often by military conquest or state control; and (3) "failure and fall-away," in which case pastoral strategies alone are inadequate; thus herds may become too large and require access to market towns, or a shortage of animals will necessitate the abandonment ("dropping out") of a nomadic lifestyle.[126]

Salzman notes that these processes are not universal and timeless, nor are they inevitable or irreversible. There are obviously discernible cycles of nomadism–sedentism, as has been shown by many studies of ancient Mesopotamia, for instance. Sedentary peoples can become nomadic, and settled nomads can be "renomadized." Nevertheless, there seems to be one constant among the variables: the nomadic ideal.

Biblical scholars, even the few who are acquainted with the literature on pastoral nomadism, have long exercised themselves over which model might help to explain the rise of early Israel. Thus we find long discussions of tribes, acephalous social organization, or segmented lineages, and the like. The fact is that none of these models is applicable or needed if, as we shall show, the earliest Israelites were mostly various local peoples displaced by the upheavals at the end of the Late Bronze Age, not primarily pastoral nomads. The "twelve tribes of Israel" is a fictional construct of the biblical writers centuries later. Like Noth's amphictyony, or tribal confederation, the notion should be abandoned. Had it not been for the biblical metanarrative, no one would ever have thought of it.[127]

Rainey finds the ancestors of his early Israel, which he thinks must originate in Transjordan, among the Shasu, whom we have already discussed. These widely dispersed people do appear to be mostly pastoralists.

Some of them live on the fringes not only of southern Transjordan (Edom) but also in the mountains of the "land of Amurru" (Canaan generally). But Rainey produces absolutely no *motivation* for their moving en masse into the central hills or for their becoming rapidly sedentarized in the late thirteenth–early twelfth century. There were no urban authorities to coerce them, no market towns for their products, no natural conditions such as systemic drought that we know of that would have compelled a major change in lifestyle. The Egyptians, who had dealt with the Shasu for centuries, never succeeded in settling them except in small numbers.[128]

Even if some of the Shasu had settled west of the Jordan in the vacuum that we have documented, their numbers would have been far too small to account for the population explosion that we see in only a generation or two. Both Rainey's and Finkelstein's nomadic sedentarization theories fail for the same reason: there is no evidence whatsoever for them, archaeological or textual. Furthermore, the theory flies in the fact of what we know about the sedentarization of pastoral nomads in the region over a period of nearly four thousand years. The sedentarization of large numbers of pastoral nomads, Shasu or others, in the late thirteenth century could be satisfactorily explained *only* if there were (1) urban authorities capable of forcibly settling them and strongly motivated to do it, (2) widespread drought that necessitated a retreat from the hinterland, or (3) new market towns that were required to dispose of excess animals.

Needless to say, neither Rainey nor any of the other proponents of the sedentarized nomads hypothesis for the origins of the Israelite highland villages can offer any such evidence. The supposed urban authorities and market towns, for instance, are conspicuously absent on the Late Bronze–Iron I horizon, as we have shown in detail.

Climate change has been invoked as a factor in shifting settlement patterns in the ancient Near East since the pioneer works of Elsworth Huntington early in the twentieth century. More recent studies have brought some scientific clarification, but any exact correlation between drought and settlement changes is still impossible. For instance, a recent study by Israeli climatologists utilizes cores taken from the Sea of Galilee and the Dead Sea, along with measurements of the shifting sand dunes along the coastal plain. Six wetter and six drier epochs seem to correlate generally with changes in settlement patterns and demography during the Bronze and Iron Ages.[129]

Nevertheless, there are some striking irregularities. For instance, the period from circa 2200 is described as a near-peak period of warmer and drier conditions, yet this corresponds precisely with the Early Bronze IV (or Intermediate Bronze) phase, when virtually all urban sites were abandoned and the majority of the population became seminomadic—the opposite trend of what Finkelstein projected. In addition, Avner has shown that it was in the Early Bronze Age, during a period of increasing desiccation, that the Negev Desert reached its maximum population.[130]

In conclusion, the data do seem to show a period of *relative* warmer and drier condition circa 1400–1200, but it would be rash to posit a major systemic drought precisely in the late thirteenth century that *in itself* triggered the forced, large-scale sedentarization of nomadic groups such as the Shasu of Transjordan, much less Finkelstein's "invisible nomads" of the central hill country. In any case, a prolonged drought would have made farming no more attractive than herding—quite the opposite. Why would large number of people have *become* subsistence farmers precisely in a period of severe drought?[131]

This ideal of pastoral nomadism can be traced back as far as the great fourteenth-century Arab historiographer Ibn Khaldun, who drew the distinction noted above between the true Arab of the desert (*badawi*, i.e., bedouin) and the lesser farmers and townspeople (*fellahin*). Whether this has always held true may be debatable, but it is clear that Middle Eastern pastoralists, ancient and modern, have always *preferred* the nomadic or seminomadic life, and they have resisted sedentarization wherever possible.

The old notion of perpetual conflict between "the desert and the sown"—the idea of hordes of land-hungry nomads always ready to press into the settled zone—is an outmoded, romantic, and Eurocentric concept left over from the infancy of ethnography. It should be abandoned. More recent studies of the classic Rwala bedouin of Syria, for instance, have shown how ill-suited they are for sedentary life—and how resistant they are. William Lancaster's *The Rwala Bedouin Today* documents in particular their reluctance to accept wages for day labor, especially government jobs. They "despise the behavior of peasants," even if the latter may have skills they themselves do not possess.[132] Whatever their ambivalence, the bedouin value their freedom, their tribal independence, above all else. Even under forced sedentarization, the dilemma is still not resolved today.

Another model for the origins of early Israel also allows for a substantial number of pastoral nomads from Transjordan in the Iron I ethnic mix, although it is more nuanced. Faust's 2006 work, *Israel's Ethnogen-*

esis: Settlement, Interaction, Expansion and Resistance, is one of the few full-scale discussions of Israelite origins to take into account archaeology, anthropology, ethnography, and critical biblical studies. Faust is quite positive about identifying Israelite ethnicity (ethnogenesis) in the material culture remains, although he does take into consideration the caveats of Barth, Emberley, Jones and others (as well as Finkelstein). Central, however, to all nomadic sedentarization models is the question of what *motivated* such movements.

Faust argues that there are great similarities between the Iron I assemblage on both sides of the Jordan. Thus he proposes (as Rainey does) that some of the earliest Israelites originated in Transjordan, perhaps among the Shasu and other seminomadic pastoralists. He cites the Hebrew Bible as demonstrating an Israelite presence there, appealing for support to very conservative (i.e., evangelical) scholars such as Douglas R. Clark, Larry G. Herr, Chang-ho C. Ji, and Randall W. Younker. Nevertheless, he points out that the presence of Iron I Israelite four-room houses in Jordan has been misunderstood and greatly exaggerated (there is, in fact, only Building B at Tell el-ʿUmeiri). Faust, however, does not actually discuss the Transjordan sites. In the end, he opts for an ethnic mix in early Israel, as nearly all authorities do. It is only the relative proportion of these groups that he debates, as most authorities do.[133]

Faust's sedentarizing nomads model fails to address the problem that Rainey has: there are not enough nomads to account for the population explosion that we can easily document in Iron I. He also overlooks the significance of a point that he himself makes, that ethnicity is most likely to become a concern when a group is in competition with others, in this case, the Iron I Philistines. Yet there are no Philistines in Transjordan in the Iron I period nor in the central country, where Merenptah's Israelites must have been recognized as an ethnic group by circa 1230 at the latest—some fifty to sixty years before our Philistines appear. In questioning Dever's Cisjordanian lowland model, Faust asserts that this model cannot explain *how* Israelite ethnicity develops; obviously, he cannot either. Faust appears to be skeptical about the agrarian reform model advanced here (below), but he makes little attempt to refute it. In the end, his model, too, envisions an ethnic mix in which there were undoubtedly some lowlanders as well as former nomads.

Like Rainey's notion of pastoral nomads tribally organized, most models for understanding early Israel that have been advanced by biblical scholars for some years now have assumed that we are dealing with a tribally organized society. That appears to stem from the so-called nomadic ideal of the Hebrew Bible. To be sure, the Pentateuch and the Deuteronomistic History are set within the framework of the "twelve tribes of Israel." The old ideal of tribal structure persists and fuels fundamentalist and nativist movements like that of the Nazarites, the antistatist group that emerged when the idea of a monarchy was first broached. Then when things go bad—as the prophet Samuel warned they would—the rallying cry of dissident groups was "To your tents, O Israel!" But this is all myth: most of the ancestors of Israel had never lived in tents, certainly not in the Iron Age. The nomadic ideal of the Hebrew Bible rests on a utopian dream that has little to do with reality. It is no more historical than many of the other theological constructs of the Hebrew Bible. The "cultural memory" has been invented, not remembered, just as with the exodus story.

As for the use of the term *tribe* in the Hebrew Bible and in much of biblical scholarship, the concept itself is so vague that most anthropologists and ethnographers have abandoned it as useless for comparative studies. If the view of the model of Israelite origins advanced here is taken seriously, the tribe has no explanatory power.[134]

A few archaeologists have unwittingly bought into the notion of tribal origins, especially Finkelstein with his sweeping theory of sedentarizing pastoral nomads. Similarly, the argument of Fritz and Kempinski, that the typical pillar-courtyard Iron I house is an adaptation of the bedouin tent, presupposes a nomadic background for the settlers. It is Rainey, of course (though not an archaeologist), who takes this notion the furthest, seeing nearly all the Iron I villagers as settled Shasu pastoralists. As we have noted, however, neither the demographic nor the ethnographic data lend any support to the nomadic ideal. Most pastoral nomadic groups known throughout history have indeed been tribally organized, as many studies have shown. But that fact in itself does not mean that the earliest Israelites had descended from such tribal groups.[135]

It is noteworthy that Rainey, while clinging to the notion of Israelite tribes, does little or nothing with the infamous tribal boundary list in Josh 15, which bristles with dozens of sites that many scholars have tried to identify. Nor does Rainey deal at length with the list of sites not conquered, as we do here. Furthermore, he virtually passes over the Joshua list, obviously because most of the sites noted there cannot be identified.

He notes, however, that the list of Solomonic districts is similar, and we will discuss it in the light of archaeology in chapter 4.[136]

A variation of Rainey's theory deriving the early Iron I hill-country settlers from Transjordan is Herr's Reubenite hypothesis (on which, in fact, Rainey based his own ideas). Here the principal excavator of Tell el-ʿUmeiri recognizes several phases of early Iron I occupation. The prior Stratum 13 represents the last of the Late Bronze Age occupation, which has some urban features and presumably ends circa 1200 in an earthquake. Stratum 12 reuses some of the earlier ramparts. The pottery shows strong continuity with that of Strata 14–13, but it now includes collar-rim store jars. Stratum 12 is dated circa 1200 by the excavators and was probably destroyed circa 1150. It brought to light Buildings A and B—pillar-courtyard houses of a sort—that produced a large repertoire of twelfth-century pottery and other objects in situ. The remarkable state of preservation is probably due to a sudden military attack that drove off the inhabitants. Stratum 11 follows, and then there is little occupation until the tenth century.

Herr argues (1) that the Stratum 12 houses and their material remains are almost identical to the Iron I assemblage in the hill-country villages in Cisjordan; (2) that Stratum 12 is earlier ("more advanced") and therefore in effect the prototype of the latter; and (3) that Tell el-ʿUmeiri is a Reubenite site, in keeping with traditions describing tribal Israel in the Hebrew Bible. He doubts, however, that the destruction of Stratum 13 is due to an Israelite invasion (either earthquake or tribal squabbles).[137]

There are difficulties in accepting these claims. Herr himself is cautious about reading the biblical accounts as history. Furthermore, he relates his Reubenites not to Stratum 12, with its presumed similarities to the Israelite culture on the other side of the Jordan, but rather to Stratum 13, which is a prosperous walled town with a developed complex society by about 1200 BCE. That would make the Stratum 12 complex that Herr uses for Israelite comparisons later. In that case, it cannot be used as a "prototype" for the central hill-country settlements in Cisjordan. The latter cannot be anything other than Merenptah's Israelite peoples, who must have been present there long enough to have developed both a clear ethnic identity and a force sufficient to be taken seriously by Egyptian intelligence—well before 1208.

The chronological argument alone would undermine Herr's Transjordanian prototype, just as it does Rainey's. Herr himself may sense that, because he concludes finally:

When we move to the plateau of Transjordan, we can no longer assume an "Israelite" identification.... There would be no national groups called "Israel" and "Ammon" in early Iron I. Instead there were tribes and tribal alliances like those reflected in the earliest biblical literature, such as the song of Deborah.[138]

That picture complements the model of Proto-Israelites advanced here for the other side of the Jordan (below). The early Transjordanian people were contemporary Proto-Ammonites and Proto-Moabites—not the progenitors of either archaeological or biblical Israel in the early Iron I period.

Even if one were to take the biblical narratives at face value as history, there are problems. The Reubenites are said to have settled in the vicinity of Heshbon after claims that it had been destroyed. The archaeological data are overwhelming: there was no such destruction, no town there to have been destroyed. Furthermore, the tribe of Reuben is closely connected with the Judean tribes of Benjamin and Judah, and in the text it appears to have migrated there in part. Rainey regards its presence in Transjordan as due to a "later migration"; if so, which way were they going? It is noteworthy that, while Reuben appears in the various conquest narratives in Numbers, it is conspicuously absent from the later tribal boundary lists in Joshua and Judges. All in all, biblical "Reuben" is a weak reed on which to erect any hypothesis about Israelite origins, and invoking biblical scholars as authorities, when all our evidence is archaeological, is no argument.

Finkelstein's claim that the Iron I ceramic repertoire represents new "nomadic" elements, distinct from those of the Late Bronze Age repertoire, is similar. As he puts it: "Although it is possible to point to a certain degree of continuity in a few types, the ceramic assemblage of the Israelite Settlement types, taken as a whole, stands in sharp contrast to the repertoire of the Canaanite centers."[139] This ceramic argument is basic, because as leading anthropologists put it, "Pottery is our most sensitive medium for perceiving shared aesthetic traditions, in the sense that they define ethnic groups, for recognizing culture contact and culture change, and for following migration and trade patterns."[140]

We described above how pottery helps to fix the chronology of our Iron I hill-country sites. Let us look now at how the pottery of the Iron I settlers in Cisjordan may help us to determine their origins and their cultural distinctiveness. Several facts are pertinent.

(1) First, studies by ceramic specialists have demonstrated that, despite similarities in the basic forms of Late Bronze Age and Iron I pottery, the potting techniques were often different. In particular, Iron I pottery generally reveals fewer wheel-forming techniques, except in its finishing. The shift to hand-made vessels would seem to indicate a change from large-scale industrial production to cottage industry (above). Each family, or perhaps a village potter or two, would have made locally all the pottery that was required—a fairly simple repertoire, as we shall see.[141]

(2) The ceramic repertoire of our Iron I villages shows many overall continuities with that of the Late Bronze Age II, but it contains far fewer individual forms. Shiloh is perhaps the best published site thus far. The large collection of Stratum V pottery consists of only the following types.[142]

Fig. 3.22. Ceramic percentages of Shiloh Stratum V

Type	Number	Percentage
collar-rim store jars	24	40
store jars	9	15
jugs	10	17
juglets	1	2
kraters (large bowls)	5	8
bowls	3	5
cooking pots	6	10
other	2	3

The percentages at Shiloh may be skewed somewhat by the fact that much of the complete or restorable pottery came from what appear to have been storage areas, as Finkelstein notes. At other Iron I villages, however, store jars and cooking pots also predominate. At Giloh, for instance, store jars and cooking pots made up 76 percent of the repertoire. The ceramic data, therefore, strongly suggest a utilitarian ceramic repertoire that is more characteristic of rural than of urban sites and one that is also better adapted to an agricultural economy based on domestic production. The only significant differences, contra Finkelstein, are seen in relative *percentages*, not in the basic ceramic forms that are always more diagnostic. The comparisons in figure 3.16 above easily demonstrate the continuity.

Finkelstein turns to other material culture traits, cisterns and silos, saying that these are not relevant since they are not really new. That may be, as most scholars acknowledge, but it is the *combination* and the deliberate and *extensive adaptation* to an agrarian lifestyle and socioeconomic structure that are new in Iron I. This complex technological strategy has no precedents, and it cannot be adequately explained by simply invoking notions of sedentarized pastoral nomads. It reflects a long acquaintance with local Canaanite traditions of subsistence farmers, agro-pastoralists, and villagers. Again, these newcomers originated among the indigenous Late Bronze Age population, but they adapted familiar cultural traditions to the requirements of the marginal zones they colonized in Iron I (below).

Some of the best evidence that the highland settlers were not mostly pastoral nomads but were experienced subsistence farmers and villagers comes from Finkelstein's own site of ʿIzbet Ṣarṭah. There staff member Baruch Rosen demonstrated that from the beginning the settlers produced a substantial agricultural surplus. Already in Stratum III cattle bones constituted 43 percent of the total, further evidence of successful farming and stockbreeding. As Rosen put it, "To sum up, the economic system of ʿIzbet-Sartah is typical of a sedentary settlement based on agriculture and animal breeding."[143]

Later studies of ʿIzbet Ṣarṭah and Ai provide even more statistics on the production capacity of the Iron I villages, comparing it to twentieth-century Arab villages nearby. The conclusion was that the mixed economy was quite similar. These Iron I settlements are not nomadic encampments; they are agro-pastoral, settled villages.[144]

The other aspect of technological change, equally important, is house construction, which is substantially new for the early Iron Age. Above we examined the construction and use of the typical pillar-courtyard domestic dwelling. These houses, like other technological innovations, do have a few precedents in structures at Late Bronze Age sites such Tel Batash, in transitional Late Bronze–Iron I Canaanite sites, in some Philistine sites, and in a few sites in Transjordan. But the examples are very few, and they are all from town sites. Again, the point is that the full development of this house form and its ubiquitous adaptation in rural villages *is* new—and it reflects a shift from urban to rural lifestyles. Here, as with ceramic developments, both the elements of continuity and discontinuity must be considered and well balanced—and seen within the context of local Canaanite, not foreign or imported, cultural traditions.

Finally, Finkelstein's overall conclusion that we cannot define any Israelite ethnicity on the basis of the Iron I village material culture assemblage must be taken seriously. That leads to our next topic.

Archaeology and Ethnicity

The issue of ethnicity has a long history in both anthropology and archaeology. During the heyday of the Culture History school, regional archaeological assemblages were compared and confidently labeled, such as the Mississippi Woodlands peoples. The artifacts themselves often supplied ethnic labels, although more generic, such as the Folsum point culture in the American southwest or the Bell Beaker culture of eastern Europe. Such ethnic labels were the only ones available, since there were no texts from these prehistoric societies.

Newer Theories

With the demise of the Culture History school and the brief floruit of the New or Processual Archaeology in the 1970s, concerns about specific ethnicities were neglected in favor of general covering laws. Postprocessual and cognitive processual archaeology paradigms have dominated since the early 1990s, as the reductionist New Archaeology approach was rather quickly discredited. But the newer, more current emphases on ideology and the meaning of things, while welcome, have not led to a renewal of more positive emphasis on recognizing ethnicity in the archaeological record.[145]

Meanwhile, postmodernist assertions that "all claims to knowledge are only social constructs" began to erode confidence in identifying ethnicity as anything but a social construct. It became almost mandatory to assert that "ethnic boundaries are fluid," in many cases interpreted to mean that they do not really exist. The biblical revisionists took up this theme uncritically. Whitelam opined that "it is no longer possible to distinguish an 'Israelite' material culture from an indigenous material culture in terms of the archaeological data." Lemche claimed that the "Canaanites did not know themselves that they were Canaanites."[146]

Thompson, always the most extreme, declares that the very notion of "ethnicity" is illusory: "The concept of [Israelite] ethnicity, however, is a fiction, created by writers. It is a product of literature, of history-writing." Or again:

> Ethnicity, however, is an interpretative historiographical fiction: a concept construing human relationships, before it is a term (however conducive to descriptions based on material remains …). Ethnicity is hardly a common aspect of human existence at this very early period.[147]

If Thompson's nihilism were accepted, none of the social sciences would be possible, since none would have any empirical foundations.

For a time biblical, Syro-Palestinian, and other archaeologists sought a more positivist approach to the problem of material culture and ethnicity. Some depended on Fredrik Barth, whose reformulation of the issue has had widespread influence (below). It is seen in its extreme, very politically correct version, in the work of Sian Jones's *The Archaeology of Ethnicity: Constructing Identities in the Past and Present* (1997). The term *constructing* in the title is revealing: here there is virtually no such thing as ethnicity. It is only what people imagine about themselves; it is too fluid even to pin down.

A Dead-End?

A recent overview by Faust suggests that the study of ethnicity among American and Israeli archaeologists has come to something of a dead-end,[148] yet his own work has charted a more promising course, particularly his *Israel's Ethnogenesis: Settlement, Interaction, Expansion, and Resistance* (2006). Here he takes up Barth's notion that ethnicity is best defined and sharpened by a group's interaction with "the other," or, as Barth puts it, "self-ascription and ascription by others." The latter definition implies that there *are* what archaeologists call material correlates of behavior. If not, archaeology would prove an impossible quest.

Other studies by Bloch-Smith, Dever, Faust, Finkelstein (early), Finkelstein and Na'aman, Mazar, Stager, Nakhai, and others made modest claims to be able to distinguish an archaeologically based "Israelite ethnicity." Yet skeptical voices were heard early on, especially from Finkelstein, who had a change of mind following critiques of his 1988 *Archaeology of the Israelite Settlement*. By the early 1990s he was arguing that, since Iron I cultural traits such as pottery and house forms have antecedents in the Late Bronze Age Canaanite culture, they cannot be seen as Israelite. Only the absence of pig bones might possibly be an ethnic marker. It is not until the monarchy and the Iron II period that we can identify a real Israel.[149]

It is the question of presumed "ethnic markers" or cultural traits that has become fundamental. A turning point came with the 1969 publication of *Ethnic Groups and Boundaries: The Social Organization of Cultural Difference*, edited by the eminent ethnographer Fredrik Barth. Barth rejected conventional notions of ethnic traits as monolithic and unchanging, mainly physical manifestations. These boundaries are cultural—societal, flexible, dynamic, in effect, fluid. As Barth put it in his introduction to the volume, "we can assume no simple one-to-one relationship between ethnic units and cultural similarities and differences." Identifying ethnicity is not simple, of course, or confined to genetic traits. It also depends on culture—on "assigned" meanings—and those can and do change over time. Yet it must be kept in mind that Barth's fluidity does *not* mean that ethnicity cannot be recognized in the archaeological record, in material culture remains, as so many skeptics have mistakenly claimed.

Like many other scholars, Dever utilized Barth's definition of an ethnic group as a population or people who: (1) are largely biologically self-perpetuating; (2) share a fundamental, recognizable, relatively uniform set of cultural values, including language, realized in cultural forms; (3) constitute a partly independent "interaction sphere"; (4) have a membership that defines itself, as well as being defined by others, as a category distinct from other categories of the same order; and (5) perpetuate their self-identity both by developing rules for maintaining ethnic boundaries as well as for participating in inter-ethnic social encounters.[150]

It is obvious that some of these ethnic traits are genetic, that others are cultural, and that a few are both. Such defining characteristics as an individual's place of birth, skin color, body type, native language, and early acculturation are clearly not fluid. They cannot be changed at all, even if one wished to do so. Other aspects of ethnicity may change, as either an individual or a culture matures. Thus in time we can become the "other" in some cases, at least in the modern globalized world. Yet it must be kept in mind that in the ancient world, such modifications in behavior and cultural adaptation were scarcely possible.

Ethnic boundaries may indeed be somewhat flexible, but only in terms of gradual acculturation as ethnic groups interact over time. Nevertheless, Israelites remained Israelites by and large throughout the Iron Age, and Philistines remained Philistines until the end. Thus ethnicity *can* be recognized and can be described, at least in general terms.

The widespread notion that material culture in itself cannot reflect ethnicity is absurd, a product of postmodernist dogma. Ethnicity is a reflection of thought and behavior, that is, of *culture*, and if archaeology and the analysis of material culture remains do not reflect culture itself, they are impotent. It is no accident that the skeptics here are either biblical revisionists who have belatedly bought into postmodernism or a few archaeological minimalists like the current Finkelstein.

One way to understand Israelite ethnicity better is to highlight elements of continuity and discontinuity, as outlined below in chart form.

Fig. 3.23. Comparison of material cultural traits and their implications for ethnicity on the Late Bronze–Iron I horizon

Trait	Late Bronze–Iron I Continuity	If New, Indicates What?
1. Settlement type and distribution	Discontinuous	Rural dispersion
2. Demography	Discontinuous	Population explosion in the hill country (?)
3. Technology (pottery, etc.)	Continuous	Local origins but now "degenerate"; few new elements indicate agriculture
4. House form	Discontinuous	Extended family, clan
5. Economy	Discontinuous	Agrarian; "domestic mode of production"
6. Social structure	Discontinuous	Communitarian
7. Political organization	Discontinuous	Tribal; prestate
8. Art; ideology; religion; language	(below)	(below)

Where to Go from Here?

A modification of Barth's trait list was employed by Dever in an attempt to contrast the material culture of several Iron I Canaanite and Philistine assemblages with that of the hill-country complex, thus to define a different and distinctly Israelite culture. It was argued that, if we can define those ethnic groups archaeologically, why not early Israel? Erring on the side of caution, however, Dever suggested the term *Proto-Israelite* for the Iron I period. Although there is a marked continuity from Iron I and all the way through into Iron II and the monarchy, these early settlers were not yet Israelites in the sense of being citizens of a nation-state. Nevertheless, they were their authentic progenitors. It is this *continuity of material culture* that is decisive.[151] Yet if a textual witness is required, we have it in the clear reference to the "Israelite peoples" in the Merenptah inscription (above).

Dever's positivist attempt met with a sharp response from Finkelstein as well as Kletter. Both claimed that he had misunderstood Barth's critique of the trait-list approach.[152] But Barth did not deny the possibility of such a trait list (nor did he refer to archaeological data at all). He simply cautioned that such a list was not sufficient in itself to define ethnicity. That may well be true. As Stager notes, "Without clear indications from texts, I seriously doubt whether any archaeologist can determine the ethnic identification of Iron I villagers though material culture remains alone."[153]

Nevertheless, it would seem clear that such obvious cultural characteristics as language, settlement type and house form, concepts of communal life, and even cult would leave some trace in the archaeological record. Indeed, such notions are now in vogue in the most recent theoretical formulations in archaeology. The notion of *habitus* in the work of Pierre Bourdieu's *Outline of a Theory of Practice* (1977) is almost a mandatory reference. Bourdieu argued that human practices cannot be deduced only from their underlying social conditions but must be discerned in relation to the objective structures that define those conditions. Thus *habitus* is "naturalized history," that is, context, and the context of practice is precisely what archaeology can offer—in some cases, better than texts.[154]

A sociologist often cited by younger archaeologists, even in our field, is Anthony Giddens. His *The Constitution of Society* (1984) advances the notion of "structuration," which holds essentially that social practices are ordered across space and time, that social actions are not brought into being simply by social actors but that those actors reproduce the conditions that make their activities possible. That sort of "materialism" was already highlighted by Marx, and in less dogmatic form it has always been found congenial by most archaeologists.[155]

As the above theories are sometimes developed, there results a new paradigm, in Kuhn's sense in his *The Structure of Scientific Revolutions* (1962). A clear alternative to older processual models is a *historical*-processual archaeology that recognizes that history and ethnicity are made by "how people embodied their traditions, how they acted and represented themselves."[156] However banal, that is what ethnicity is all about—and discerning it is what archaeology does, and may do even better than texts, which are often very idealistic.

The related theory of agency (how things are used to effect change) in contemporary archaeological theory has been applied specifically to defining ethnicity by New World archaeologists such as Charles Orser. He shows, for instance, that material culture remains help to show how the Chinese of California and the Irish of New York distinguished themselves from native American groups—even though superficially they may have appeared to be in process of assimilation.[157]

Continuity, Discontinuity, and Israelite Ethnicity in Iron I and II

While there are elements of discontinuity with the Late Bronze Age (as with ethnic traits; see above), there is a direct, unbroken continuity from the Iron I period into and through the Iron II period—a total timespan of more than six hundred years. That continuity is easily demonstrated in some of the most fundamental aspects of culture and cultural change. (1) The four-room or pillar-courtyard house not only continues in use for centuries but becomes the predominant Iron II type, even in urban settings. Furthermore, recent studies have shown that this unique house form embodies several aspects of a traditional ethos, or "Israelite mentality," especially in its reflection of egalitarianism and family solidarity. Some would reject this as undue positivism, but it is in keeping with the best of current archaeological theory in the larger discipline. Several archaeologists have invoked the study of Geoff Emberling (1997), which takes as diagnostic traits for distinguishing ethnicity things such as house form (along with cuisine and burial customs).[158]

(2) It is in the pottery—always diagnostic—that we see even more

continuity from Iron I all the way through Iron II (see fig. 3.16 above). That fact is so obvious that all specialists take it for granted. All the basic ceramic types can be traced through a long evolution. The gradual changes are almost predictable and have to do mainly with statistical proportions. The only foreign elements in the repertoire are Cypriot, Phoenician, or later Assyrian ceramic forms that are imports and easily recognized and explained.

(3) The "domestic mode of production" described above in Iron I continues to characterize Iron II socioeconomic and cultural organization. Israelite society remains essentially family-oriented, even during the monarchy and through various attempts at centralization. The state remained in some ways an arbitrary and unstable form of political organization.

(4) In Iron I the evidence of cult that we have is scant, but it is reminiscent of the old Canaanite cult in such features as veneration of El and other deities, animal and food sacrifices, ritual feasting, and other rites. We now know that Israelite folk or family religion (and even organized religion) were characterized by many of the same older Canaanite features from start to finish. Even the old Canaanite mother goddess Asherah was widely venerated, and this was not syncretism but rather native Israelite in character. Only in the exile did the Yahweh-alone movement prevail, when Book religion finally triumphed over nature cults.

(5) Writing is so rare that we have only a handful of Iron I ostraca, but the old Canaanite script in evidence there is adopted directly and expanded into a national script and language in Iron II, one that is beyond doubt Israelite, that is, Hebrew.

(6) Among the other major ethnic traits that Emberling and other anthropologists recognize as legitimate denominators are cuisine and mortuary customs. The most significant aspects of foodways in our Iron I Israelite villages is the striking lack of pig bones—especially in contrast to their abundance at contemporary Philistine sites. The percentage at presumably Israelite sites approaches zero. These data must be used with caution, however, since the avoidance of pork consumption could be due to regional environmental differences or other factors. But it may also reflect the antiquity of some of the later ethnic boundaries detailed in the Hebrew Bible.

More recent data, however, require a reassessment of the whole problem. It now appears that pig bones are also rare in Iron I in (1) many lowland, continuing Canaanite sites and (2) nonurban Philistine sites. It also seems that by Iron II, pigs were consumed at Israelite sites in the north, compared to the south. Thus it may be that the biblical ban on pork consumption is relatively late. It probably represents an "orthodox" Judean perspective that developed in the eighth–seventh century, as Deuteronomistic reforms shaped the tradition, eventually reduced to writing. Thus this ethnic marker is not as useful as once thought. The statistics can be tabulated as follows.[159]

Fig. 3.24. Percentage of pig bones at representative Late Bronze–Iron I sites

Sites	Late Bronze	Iron I
Philistine		
Ashdod	?	10.5
Ashkelon	?	2.3
Ekron	8	18
Gath	?	13.5
Tel Batash	5	8
Israelite		
Shiloh	6	0.17
Ai	—	0
Arad		
Beersheba		
Beth-Shemesh	1.6	0
Dan	?	0
Lachish	6–7	—
Tel Masos	?	0
Khirbet Radanna	—	0

(7) For reasons not readily explainable, we have almost no burials for the Iron I period. Tomb 1 at Dothan spans the thirteenth- and twelfth-century horizon, but the site is not demonstrably Israelite. Elsewhere there are almost no rock-cut tombs. This curious phenomenon has been addressed by several scholars,[160] but all we can say is that most of the ordinary folk who would have made up the population in our Iron I villages were probably buried with little ceremony in simple pit-graves, where the remains would have left little or no trace. Later Israelite burials in Iron II do yield evidence of distinctive cultural traits (ch. 4).

The only reasonable explanations for these and other cultural expressions that evolve throughout the entire Iron Age and are evident in material remains is that we are dealing with a population that is largely homogenous and indigenous. By contrast, the contemporary Iron I–II Philistine culture evolves in a significantly different way despite some evidence of acculturation (above). The implications seem clear.

If the peoples of the southern Levant west of the Jordan in the Iron II period in the era of the monarchy were mostly Israelites—which no authority would dispute—then ipso facto the peoples of Iron I, their immediate predecessors, were as well. That is why the term *Proto-Israelite* (above) may be useful. The Iron I villagers may not have been citizens of a fully developed Israelite state and culture, which came into being only a century or two later, but they were their authentic progenitors.

Locating Merenptah's "Israelites"

It is admittedly difficult to affix an ethnic label on the basis of material culture alone. After all, the terms *Canaanite, Egyptian, Philistine, Phoenician, Aramean*, and so on are documented in texts that we have. So is *Israelite*. The Merenptah inscription (above), exactly contemporary with our Iron I settlements and devoid of any later theological biases, refers to these people by name. Furthermore, a map of Merenptah's itinerary, whether mythological or not, has an obvious lacuna in the central hill country—precisely where the majority of the Iron I settlements are located. If this is not Merenptah's Israel, where is it? And if the settlers were not his Israelite peoples, who were they? Skeptics have no answer to these questions.

Recognizing that there is, however, some variety among the Iron I settlements cited here—presumably all ethnic Israelite—some scholars have sought to distinguish both regional variants and basic settlement types.

Broad Regional Differences

The vast majority of our Iron I sites are in the hill country: (1) the central hills (Mount Ephraim and Manasseh); (2) the hill country of Judah, extending down to the Beersheba Valley; and (3) the hills of Lower and Upper Galilee. The sites in (1) and (2) show considerable similarity in house form, pottery, and technology. The Galilee sites (3), however, more remote, show several distinctive features, especially in the large pithoi (store jars), which have Tyrian or Phoenician connections. There the question of Israelite ethnicity must perhaps be left open. Some scholars would associate these with other ethnic groups known from the Hebrew Bible or other texts, such as Hittites (or Neo-Hittites), Hivites, Perizzites, or Amalekites. None of these designations, however, has any archaeological warrant. The cultural memory of these (and other) peoples by the writers of the later Hebrew Bible is vague, and it is always polemical. Early Israel is correctly portrayed, however, as a "mixed multitude," especially in the book of Judges. That accords well with the archaeological data (below).

Regionalism and Chronology

The diversity of settlement types apparently reflects the above reality, as several scholars have noted. Finkelstein coupled settlement type with both regional differentiation and chronology. His early phase would be marked by the elliptical settlement plans of some settlements; the second phase would have been the development of a more fully integrated plan, with a row of contiguous pillar-courtyard houses forming a perimeter of sorts. But it is difficult to see much difference in these phases. Furthermore, Finkelstein's notion of the circular plan deriving from a tent-circle prototype has no foundation whatsoever in ethnography (above).

Herzog rejects the central village plan as Israelite, considering sites so characterized as Canaanite. His Israelite sites are those that have an irregular plan, such as Ai and Radanna. Fritz regards the ring-shaped villages as early Israelite settlements. He thinks that in time there developed agglomerated villages like Herzog's sites. Fritz also distinguishes farmsteads, of which Giloh would be an example. London has also sought to recognize rural work stations, and perhaps also cult places, in early Iron I.[161]

At the present state of our knowledge, none of these classifications wins universal support. The fact is that all of our Iron I sites share sufficient material and cultural similarities that enable us to characterize them as belonging to a society that is overwhelmingly nonurban and represents a significant innovation in much of Iron I Canaan. Yet inner phasing is difficult over this two-century period.

The village sites in the hill country north and south of Jerusalem, from the Jezreel Valley to the Beersheba basin, are much more homogeneous and reflect more of the distinctly Israelite traits that are taken here to be diagnostic. The far fewer Iron I sites in Lower and Upper Galilee are peripheral to the central and southern village complex and in some ways are more Phoenician in terms of their material culture (although the pottery is related to the other hill-country sites). Some of the scant early Iron I sites in Transjordan have been regarded as Israelite, even as evidence for the presence there of the biblical tribe of Reuben. But the evidence consists of one house or two at one site at Tell el-ʿUmeiri, plus doubtful presuppositions regarding both comparative ceramics and chronology (see above).

The dating and phasing of the Iron I sites discussed here is complicated by a lack of definitive evidence. Absolute chronology depends on a few Egyptian Nineteenth Dynasty seals, rather than the cartouches of Ramesses III–VI that we have at several non-Israelite sites. We have a scarab of Seti II (1200–1194) at Tel Masos in Stratum III. The Mount Ebal site yielded a Nineteenth Dynasty seal. Deir ʿAlla and Khirbet Radanna each produced a Twentieth Dynasty scarab (1186–1069). At Deir ʿAlla and Akko we have cartouches of Queen Tausert (1188–1186); these are not, however, early Israelite sites.

There are a few C-14 dates from Late Bronze/Iron I destructions. At Deir ʿAlla, Stratum D/C may end circa 1140. At Tall Ziraʿa near the Yarmuk Gorge, two C-14 dates for the end of the Late Bronze Age are 1220–970, but neither is precise enough to be of much help. Tell Abu el-Kharaz IX may end circa 1200–1150, according to C-14 dates.

Few scholars seem to have noted that earthquakes at several sites circa 1150 may reflect actual events. At Deir ʿAlla, the destruction circa 1140 noted above would support an earthquake hypothesis, as would the Tell Abu el-Kharaz date. The destruction preceding Buildings A and B at Tell el-ʿUmeiri was attributed by the excavators to an earthquake circa 1200, but a slightly earlier destruction would fit very well. Finally, a large house of Megiddo VIA was destroyed by a violent earthquake that left clear evidence circa 1000.[162]

These dates in the early twelfth–eleventh century are at sites unlikely to be Israelite, and they are too late for the Merenptah inscription, which can be dated closely to 1208 and speaks of an Israel already in place, considered well enough established by Egyptian intelligence to be a threat (above). Beyond that, we can only say that the transitional Late Bronze II/early Iron I pottery falls roughly into this time frame. But the date of 1200 is obviously somewhat arbitrary.

Most of the few excavated sites (and all of the hundreds of survey sites) lack sufficient stratigraphic precision to say much about phasing within the twelfth–eleventh century. The few well-established, multistrata Israelite sites include 'Izbet Ṣarṭah III–I and Tel Masos III–II. Both appear to have been established in the very late thirteenth century, then continued into a twelfth-century phase of more stability and were finally abandoned sometime before circa 1000. Giloh and Ai are also phase 1 sites, but their end is unclear.

A few newly established eleventh-century sites probably represent a fully developed phase 2 Iron I culture (Iron IB), such as Beth-Zur III, Beersheba IX–VIII, and Tel Esdar III. This may represent a phase of more fully sedentarized village culture, as well as a degree of territorial consolidation and expansion.

As for Transjordanian sites, the date of circa 1100 for the Tell el-'Umeiri A and B houses is too imprecise to put them securely into any except the most general archaeological phase and cultural sequence. These houses and their ceramic repertoire cannot be regarded as the "prototype" of the early Iron I complex on the other side of the Jordan (as Rainey does; above). There are similarities between the two archaeological assemblages, although they are by no means identical. Both the similarities and the dissimilarities are best explained by arguing that the few Transjordanian and the many Cisjordanian early Iron I villages (and small towns?) are all part of the same phenomenon. The marked changes in settlement pattern and type, as well as in socioeconomic and cultural developments, are part and parcel of the koine Iron I polities that emerged in the southern Levant in the wake of the widespread collapse at the end of the Late Bronze Age circa 1200, but a more precise date is impossible. These local polities were obviously related and undoubtedly in contact with each other, as the archaeological data demonstrate, but they were to some degree ethnically diverse.

They included Iron I Levantine peoples such as Arameans, Phoenicians, Israelites, and, in addition, peoples in Transjordan who in time would come to be known as Ammonites, Moabites, and Edomites. The former developed into city-states or state-like polities by the tenth century, while the latter remained organized into tribal states. At present, the Israelites are by far the best known archaeologically. There is no reason, however, to force their history (much less that of the biblical construct) upon the other contemporary peoples of the southern Levant. The fact is that, apart from the biblical portrait of an Israelite conquest in Transjordan, few scholars would ever have thought of this region as part of Iron Age Israel.

A New Model for Understanding Early Israel: Agrarian Reform[163]

There is now overwhelming support in favor of a new model for early Israel. The traditional conquest, peaceful infiltration, and peasant revolt models have all been overturned in the light of the archaeological data presented here. There is now a universal consensus among not only archaeologists but also biblical scholars that a new ethnic group called "Israelites" came from among the indigenous peoples of the region (even Transjordan is part of Canaan). The only question is: Where within Canaan? In spite of its consensus status, the emerging indigenous origins model does not have a specific name. It is sometimes called a "disso-lution" model (or better "collapse," as above), a "sedentarized nomads" model (Finkelstein, Rainey, and others), or a "mixed multitude" (Killebrew and Dever).

One way to specify this model further is to flesh out out the por-trait of a newly established village complex and rural society in the hill country by coupling older data with more recent anthropological theory. Thus we can return to further evidence drawn from the Amarna letters already discussed.

The Amarna Letters

These detailed eye-witness accounts of conditions in the southern Levant toward the end of the Late Bronze Age, surveyed in chapter 2, are con-sistent in painting a portrait of disputes and class struggles over land. The result was the creation of a large underclass of dispossessed, restless people. In addition to the Habiru, who are described in detail, we must suppose that there were other groups equally disenfranchised. Further, by the mid- to late thirteenth century, in addition to these displaced peoples, there were other even more desperate groups. Scholars speak somewhat cavalierly of the destruction wrought by invading Sea Peoples on this horizon, but these destructions must have resulted in the displacement of thousands of people who would have fled inland and become refugees.

The tottering economy, the administrative chaos as Egyptian rule began to collapse, and the domino effect of peoples in movement would have made the absorption of a large number of refugees difficult, if not impossible. In an agricultural economy, as this was, access to land was a matter of life or death. To be sure, some of these disruptions may have reached their peak only in the early twelfth century, after Merenptah's Israel came into being. But the entire mid-thirteenth to mid-twelfth century was an age of vast upheavals.

It is these local land-hungry peasants and outcasts—not imaginary pastoralists—who formed the reservoir from which the hill-country colonists were derived. Only they had the motivation to uproot themselves so drastically and in such large numbers. Previous models have floundered on the neglect of this fact. Mendenhall's and Gottwald's social revolt model did embrace the notion of change (displacement), but they did not invoke appropriate sociological models, nor did they have the archaeological data that we now have.

The Frontier

Neither Mendenhall nor Gottwald, both of whom mined the Amarna letters for information, could have consulted the 1978 work of Gerhard Lenski and Jean Lenski. In their book *Human Societies: An Introduction to Macrosociology*, they observe that frontiers:

> provide a unique opportunity for departures from the sociocultural patterns so deeply entrenched in agrarian societies. Those who respond to the challenge of the frontier, to its dangers and its opportunities, are primarily men with little to lose, with little at stake in the established order. Thus they are likely to possess a willingness to take great physical risks and a proclivity for independence and innovation. As a result, new ways of life commonly develop in frontier areas, innovations are readily accepted, and older rigidities give way.[164]

We do not imply, of course, a national frontier or border in the modern sense. The whole of what is today Israel, the West Bank, Jordan, and southern Lebanon and Syria was at the time all part of Greater Canaan, which the Egyptians usually designated "the land of the Hurru," that is, of the Hurrians. The real borders within this larger entity were ecological, and they were constantly shifting with changing environmental conditions.

Much of the area was marginal land, not only geographically but perceptually as well. Even in good times, these were considered remote and hostile areas, even though they were not that distant physically.

Rowton has characterized the landscape and society of these regions of the Middle East as "dimorphic," or characterized as having two basic configurations. What is unique is that here, in contrast to the Great Desert of Arabia, arid and semiarid zones are interspersed with arable lands in a sort of jigsaw pattern. Thus pastoralists roaming the steppes were frequently in contact with townspeople, as they still are today. In fact, bedouin cannot prosper or even survive without trading their surplus animals and animal products to more sedentary peoples. (Finkelstein's theory of supposedly isolated nomads in the hill country in the Late Bronze Age ignores this well-known phenomenon.) Thus both the geographical and the psychological boundaries are always in flux. What all of the foregoing implies is that tribal peoples could settle from time to time, and settlers could easily become retribalized. Urban folk could gravitate to small villages in the hinterland; villagers might flock to the big city.

Withdrawal

Flight has often been invoked as the motive of peoples relocating in large numbers, which is the phenomenon that we must explain in Canaan on the Late Bronze–Iron I horizon. Ethnographers sometimes picture this phenomenon of cyclical migration in terms of not sedentarization but rather its exact opposite: retribalization. In extreme conditions, once-nomadic peoples who have long been settled have been known to revert to pastoral nomadism, throwing off government control for looser tribal affiliations. Sometimes this is called *withdrawal*; in fact, this is the very term used by Mendenhall and Gottwald. Like other urban dropouts, such as the Habiru, the early Israelites in this view were those who chose to withdraw from society, in this case migrating to the more remote and sparsely populated hill country.

It is time to take up the notion of withdrawal again, but now with much more new supporting archaeological evidence and with different ideas about its motives. It was not only flight from intolerable conditions, or a supposed revolutionary Yahwistic fervor, that propelled people toward the frontier; it was more a quest for a new society and a new lifestyle. People wanted to start over—and in the end, that *was* revolutionary.

In order to elaborate the thesis of withdrawal, however, we must first show that the Iron I hill-country settlers had formerly been sedentarized, and in the lowlands of Canaan at that, whether in the urban centers or in the countryside. The reasons for seeing these areas as the population pool (rather than the hinterland in the central hills or the eastern slopes) are the following.

(1) Anyone hoping to meet the challenges of colonizing the rural areas of the hill-country frontier, and expecting to succeed as agriculturalists, must have had prior experience as subsistence farmers somewhere else in Canaan, as we have already suggested. It is inconceivable that nomads settling down could have managed to do much more than survive. Some probably did settle as conditions allowed, but nomads alone cannot have created the extensive, highly integrated, successful agricultural society and economy that we have in the hill country in early Iron I.

Hopkins had analyzed these formidable difficulties in his *The Highlands of Canaan: Agricultural Life in the Early Iron Age* (1985). In particular, he enumerates the preconditions that had to be met: (1) a close-knit social fabric; (2) the ability to mobilize labor on a large scale; (3) knowledge of environmental variations; (4) the technology necessary to clear forests, hew cisterns, and construct extensive terrace systems; (5) strategies for risk management and reduction; (6) the capacity to produce and store surpluses; and (7) provisions for long-term land tenure and conservation.[165] Hopkins does not regard all these preconditions as necessarily preexisting among the hill-country settlers (the art of terrace building, for example, which they would not have known beforehand). But he does show that these conditions must have been conceivable and that they developed successfully very soon. The earliest American colonists at Plymouth and Jamestown perished in large numbers, some the first year. The hill-country settlers also would have perished, had most of them not already been preadapted.

(2) Apart from agricultural experience and basic competence, there is, of course, the question of motive. Why would peasants, any more than pastoral nomads, want to uproot themselves and migrate to the inhospitable hill-country frontier? The answer may be rather simple, if one accepts the picture above of the miserable conditions in the heartland of Canaan toward the end of the thirteenth century. Canaan was on the verge of total collapse. Many villagers and peasant farmers, as well as the landless Habiru, were already impoverished and socially marginalized. They had

little to lose. Withdrawing was prudent, if not necessary. It may even be that more than a century of rebellion and repression had given these various groups of dissidents some sense of social solidarity. There may have existed an ideology that made revolution seem possible, even inevitable. This theory is speculative, of course, and like Mendenhall's and Gottwald's peasant revolt it has little direct archaeological evidence to support it. Nevertheless, our current knowledge of the general archaeological context of Canaan toward the end of the Late Bronze Age makes this scenario quite realistic. The description of the frontier by Lenski and Lenski above is certainly apt.

A Motley Crew

We have already stressed the heterogeneous nature of the people of Late Bronze Age Canaan, their longtime adaptation to the shifting frontier, and their growing restiveness by the end of the period. It should, therefore, be no surprise that we will now advocate an explicit model for the Iron I hill-country colonists—Proto-Israelites—that accounts for a variety of groups, all of them dissidents of one sort or another. Among them would be included the following: (1) urban dropouts—people seeking to escape from economic exploitation, bureaucratic inefficiency and corruption, taxation, and conscription; (2) Habiru and other social bandits (Hobsbawm's term), rebels already in the countryside, some of them highwaymen, brigands, former soldiers and mercenaries, or entrepreneurs of various sorts—freebooters, in other words; (3) refugees of many kinds, including those fleeing Egyptian injustice, displaced villagers, impoverished farmers, and perhaps those simply hoping to escape the disaster that they saw coming as their society fell into decline; (4) local pastoral nomads, including some from the eastern steppes or Transjordan (Shasu), even perhaps an "exodus group" that had been in Egypt among Asiatic slaves in the Delta. All of these peoples were dissidents, disgruntled opportunists ready for a change. For all these groups, despite the obstacles to be overcome, the highland frontier would have held great attraction: a new beginning.

The idea of early Israel as a motley crew is not all that revolutionary. The biblical tradition, although much later, remembers such diverse origins. It speaks not only of Amorites and Canaanites in close contact with Israelites but also Jebusites, Perizzites, Hivites (the latter probably

Neo-Hittites), and others. All could have been part of the Israelite confederation at times. The Gibeonites and Shechemites, for instance, are said to have been taken into the Israelite confederation by treaty. Some were born Israelites; others became Israelites by choice. The confederation's solidarity, so essential, was ideological, rather than biological—"ethnicity."[166]

A few others have suggested a mix of long-time settlers in Canaan, including, of course, some pastoral nomads. Even Fritz, whose tent prototype for our pillar-courtyard houses we have dismissed above, adopts a model in keeping with ours here. As he put it:

> It is much more likely that there was an intensive cultural contact that can only have come about through a long period of co-existence. Before the establishment of the settlement in the twelfth century, the settlers presumably lived for some generations in the vicinity of the Canaanite cities without entirely giving up their nomadic lifestyle. This means, however, that the founders of the settlement did not come directly from the steppes but had already penetrated the settled region in the thirteenth century or possibly even earlier and had entered into a form of symbiosis with the Canaanites.... The "settlement" of the land therefore does not represent a seizure of the land from the outside. Instead, it is a development in the transition from the Late Bronze Age to the Iron Age.[167]

Wolf's conditions for the social revolution noted above are amply met in the Amarna correspondence. The Late Bronze/early Iron I population of Canaan was certainly mobile, as made clear both by texts describing the elusive Habiru already dispersed in the countryside and by archaeological evidence documenting a major population shift to the hill country.

As for leadership, or external sources of power, it is noteworthy that the Amarna letters mention chiefs of the Habiru. The Hebrew Bible, of course, attributes the role of leadership first to Joshua and then to his successors, the judges. These early folk heroes were essentially successive charismatic military leaders who are portrayed in Judges precisely as men (and one woman) of unusual talents who were able to rally the tribes against the Canaanites. Direct archaeological evidence for any of these specific persons is lacking, of course, since the archaeological record without texts is anonymous (although not mute). But the Iron I hill-country villages do exhibit a remarkable homogeneity of material culture and evidence for family and clan social solidarity. Such cohesiveness—a fact on the ground—had to have come from somewhere. As Lenski and Lenski have observed (above), the challenges and hardships of the frontier would have tended to strengthen whatever sense of solidarity already existed.

As for defensible mountain redoubts where the rebels could take refuge from the urban authorities, the central hill country of Palestine, now extensively colonized, fits the description perfectly: it is a (relatively) distant frontier.

The highly polarized society of Late Bronze Age Canaan, clearly evident in both the textual and the archaeological records, is an excellent example of Wolf's cleavages that often serve as the catalyst for social revolutions.

Agrarianism and Land Reform

At this point we may introduce the other element of the agrarian frontier reform model: the term *agrarian*. It refers essentially to land and landholding, originating with the agrarian laws (Latin *agrarius*, from *ager*, "field, open country") of ancient Rome, which were intended to distribute conquered and other public lands equally among all citizens. In practice, however, most agrarian reforms either were never really instituted or the reform movements failed. As we have seen, ancient Canaan did not acknowledge even the theoretical principle of agrarianism. All public lands belonged to the sovereign—the pharaoh or his surrogates, local Canaanite kinglets who were even more rapacious.

The new mode of production saw the sovereign displaced and the family unit—the patrimonial society—substituted for the state apparatus. The later biblical writers downplay the sociology of Israel's beginning, but it is nevertheless evident in the theology that they preserved. While some may see their work simply as a later rationalization, we may regard it more realistically as part of an authentic folk memory (i.e., cultural memory).[168]

Despite its apparent explanatory power in the case of early Israel, the notion of agrarianism has seldom been employed among biblical scholars and almost never by archaeologists. Neither Gottwald, Hopkins, or even Faust mention agrarianism. Yet land reform *must* have been the driving force behind, and the ultimate goal of, the early Israelite movement. No other scenario really makes sense of what we now know from all sources. Chaney ends his provocative 1983 study with these prescient words.

While it remains a working hypothesis, a model of peasant and frontier revolt has been found to accommodate and illuminate the data provided by the Amarna archive, Syro-Palestinian archaeology, and the biblical tradition, and to do ... so within parameters defined by the comparative study of agrarian societies by social scientists.... The writer will consider this paper a success if it served to enlist new results in that ongoing process.[169]

If early Israel indeed constituted an agrarian movement with strong reformist tendencies driven by a new social ideal, it would not be unique. Agrarianism is about more than land; it is utopian. There have been countless such rural revolutionary movements in history, many of them originally as small, isolated, and insignificant as that of early Israel seemed to be. One need look no further than an American history textbook: the Oneida community of the 1800s in New York was founded as a perfectionist society based on biblical principles of absolute equality. Unfortunately, their utopian views on marriage and family life went too far, and the movement was bitterly criticized. Another experiment in rural communal living was carried out in the early 1800s at New Harmony in southwestern Indiana, founded by strict religionists of German extraction. Better known, of course, is the eighteenth-century Shaker movement. It was characterized by a deep religious spirit, commitment to absolute equality, temperance, and simplicity in all things. Unfortunately, the Shakers also practiced chastity and celibacy, so over time they became nearly extinct. The Amish in Pennsylvania constitute a far more successful rural communitarian movement—an excellent example of the phenomenon of withdrawal based on religious notions. All these and many other reformist movements in history are essentially agrarian, based on principles of land reform and shared agricultural production.

Advocating an agrarian reform model for understanding the emergence of early Israel within Canaan does not mean necessarily embracing the peasant revolt model of Mendenhall and Gottwald in toto. The rural population of Canaan in the Late Bronze and Iron Ages were peasants only in a simplistic sense, because we do not seem to have the fully developed medieval feudal system that would entail. But we clearly do have a large, landless, disenfranchised lower class, both townspeople and farmers. What was prescient in Mendenhall's and Gottwald's model was a sense that a socioeconomic revolution was taking place and the recognition that the prime movers were part of the indigenous population of Canaan.

Our assessment here of the historicity of the conquest and settlement narratives in the Hebrew Bible may seem rather negative, but if the agrarian reform model has any merit, it would explain why the "promised land" theme of the later writers of the Bible was so tenacious, why the hope for the redemption of the land survived even into postexilic times (and perhaps why it resonates so powerfully still today). That focus on possession of land, on the rural life as the good life, runs throughout the Pentateuch, the Deuteronomistic History, and the prophets. The perennial hope will be fulfilled when "they shall all sit under their own vines and under their own fig trees, and no one shall make them afraid" (Mic 4:4). Here the biblical memory is genuine; it goes back to earliest Israel's experience as a people without a land.

A comparison of the two sources of data for the twelfth- and eleventh-century settlement horizon—the archaeological and the textual—can be summarized in a somewhat simplified chart form.

Fig. 3.25. Comparisons of the data from archaeology and the Hebrew Bible

Convergence; proven	Possible but uncertain; evidence ambiguous	Divergence; disproven
		Large-scale exodus from Egypt
Canaanite origins	Elements from Transjordan and nomads	Sinai wandering
Symbiosis with Canaanites, Philistines; "mixed multitude"	Percentages in the ethnic mix	Sudden, pan-military conquest of Canaan; population vanquished
Setting of Judges		Setting of Joshua
Agro-pastoral villages; communitarian socioeconomic organization	Relations with continuing Canaanite sites	Unified twelve-tribe league under Joshua
"Poly-Yahwism"; folk/family religion	Origins of Yahwism	Exclusive Yahwism; Sinai covenant central

No state-level polity; period of judges	Reasons for prestate level; differences of Philistines	Israel unique

Conclusion

The archaeological evidence for the Late Bronze Age–Iron I transition circa 1250–1150 in Canaan illuminates a period of destruction, social upheaval, and population movements. Following the collapse, there emerge several small polities in the region, both in Cisjordan and in Transjordan. All reflect an increase in population in the rural and hinterland areas, particularly in the central hill country west of the Jordan, where the frontier was open.

There an ethnic group that is known in contemporary textual sources as the Israelite peoples can be seen in the archaeological record. Particularly striking are both elements of continuity and discontinuity with the preceding and contemporary Canaanite culture. The settlers are neither invaders bent on conquest nor predominantly land-hungry pastoral nomads. They are mostly indigenous peoples who are *displaced*, both geographically and ideologically. They find a redoubt in areas previously underpopulated, well suited to an agrarian economy and lifestyle. In time, these people will evolve into the full-fledged states of Israel and Judah known from the Hebrew Bible (ch. 4), but for the prestate era, archaeology remains our best witness.

By *social revolt* we mean here primarily socioeconomic and cultural *changes* that are often driven partly by ideological factors, even if subconsciously, and in that sense constitute a revolution. By the term *reform* that we apply to describe the changes that manifestly did take place in the early Iron I period, we intend simply to embrace those ideologies that were partly responsible. That does not imply a homogeneous, well-organized, programmatic social protest movement—quite the contrary. The phenomenon that we confront is not a top-down movement but very much a bottom-up revolution. That does not deny the importance of environmental conditions, nor does it contradict functionalist arguments. It does, however, consider that it is ultimately new *ideas* that mark new epochs in history.

Archaeologists and biblical historians dealing with early Israel might have consulted works such as Eric Wolf's *Peasants* (1966) and *Peasant Wars of the Twentieth Century* (1969). The only scholar in our fields to make any extended use of Wolf's studies of modern peasants in class-structured societies is Chaney, whose 1983 publication presented various models for early Israel. Chaney observed this of Wolf's work, even before the current archaeological evidence became available:

> While such comparative studies cannot prove that ancient Israel emerged from a Palestinian peasant's [*sic*] revolt, they can allow us to determine whether there existed in Late Bronze and early Iron I Palestine a concatenation of conditions which in other agrarian societies have proved conducive to broader peasant revolts.[170]

Chaney goes on to summarize Wolf's argument that among the requisite conditions for revolt are: (1) a "tactically mobile" segment of the population, mobile both physically and ideologically, and (2) a group that is thus "able to rely on some external power to challenge the power that challenges them," without which revolutions are never successful. In addition, (3) the areas where dissident elements have their effectiveness strengthened still further will be those that "contain defensible mountain redoubts." Finally, (4) the possibilities for success will be enhanced if there are "reinforcing cleavages," or painful sources of social conflict, such as national, ethnic, or religious divisions. Chaney correctly notes that Wolf's conditions for social revolt are amply reflected in the Amarna letters. He is one of very few scholars to have made such a connection, although it seems obvious. Even archaeologists who have advanced models of their own on Israelite origins have neglected these data.

Whatever model we adopt in attempting to explain the origins of early Israel in Canaan, two caveats are in order. (1) Models are constructs: they do not equal Truth but are imposed on facts as interpretive tools in order to draw appropriate inferences. They *may* have explanatory value, but much depends on which model we choose and how well it actually fits the facts. (2) What all current models used to explain the phenomenon of early Israel have in common is that they focus on *indigenous* origins somewhere within Greater Canaan, and they portray an ethnic group that somehow embraces many elements of the local population. The remaining debate among specialists largely concerns the percentages of such groups as local refugees, displaced subsistence farmers, various dissidents and dropouts, former pastoral nomads, and perhaps even a small exodus group, whether or not they had actually even been in Egypt. The old conquest model is gone forever.

The agrarian reform model advanced here fits all the facts currently available in the archaeological evidence, and it offers a cogent explanation for the process by which a people called Israel gradually emerged in the light of history in Canaan in the Late Bronze–Iron Age transition circa 1250–1100. While this model challenges traditional and simplistic readings of the biblical narrative, it can comprehend old oral traditions that may be reflected in stories in the books of Judges, Samuel, and other biblical memories.

Notes

1. On the biblical "patriarchs," see n. 7 in ch. 2. The "Amorite hypothesis" is treated in the references there. The clearest evidence of Amorites (i.e., Canaanite peoples) penetrating the Delta is now Manfred Bietak's excavations at Tell ed-Dabʿa (Avaris); see conveniently Bietak 1981.

2. For orientation to the problem of the historicity of the biblical exodus from Egypt, see n. 43 in ch. 2; for the scant archaeological data, see Dever 1997c; Weinstein 1997; Redmount 1998. On the Hebrew Bible's "cultural memory" (or "mneomemory"), see Assmann 1997; Hendel 2001; 2010; Davies 2008; and cf. the summary and critique in Barstad 2010. Hendel (2001) and Naʾaman (2011) have built on the notion of "cultural memory" to argue that the biblical exodus tradition is misplaced: the "Egyptian oppression" was really in Canaan under local overlords. See also an entire symposium on the exodus in cultural memory (Levy, Schneider, and Propp 2015). Yet the fact is that the biblical narrative, fiction or not, is clearly set in Egypt, not Canaan. The whole history is of the people whom "Yahweh brought out of Egypt." In any case, neither can explain *why* the story is told as it is. A Canaanite real-life setting does, however, fit the newer archeological data. In practice, cultural memory amounts to little more than *tradition*. For conservative and evangelical reactions, see Bimson 1981; Millard 2004; and especially Hoffmeier 1997, 2005. On the possible Sinai routes and sites, see Hoffmeier 2005; Oren 1987; Hoffmeier and Makhsoud 2003; Hoffmeier and Moshier 2006. On Kadesh-Barnea, see Cohen and Bernick-Greenberg 2007.

3. On Dhiban generally, see Tushingham 1993 and references there; add now Routledge 2004. On Ḥesban, see the résumé in Geraty 1983. A useful summary of possible biblical sites in Transjordan is B. MacDonald 2000. On the pertinent archaeological sites, see Bienkowski 1992; Herr and Najjar 2008; Fischer and

Bürge 2013; Kefafi and van der Kooj 2013; Porter 2013; Herr 2014; Routledge 2004. Porter and Routledge offer the most extended analyses.

4. See B. MacDonald 2000, 72, with references.

5. See Kitchen 1992; cf. Rainey 2006, 67, 72–73. The work of Boling 1988 may be dismissed as bibliocentric.

6. See, for instance, the reconstruction in Dever 2003d, 229–34. On cultural memory, see n. 2 above.

7. See references in n. 3 above and nn. 8–9 below on Ammonite, Moabite, and Edomite inscriptions; add Aufrecht 2010; Dion and Daviau 2010; Lemaire 2010.

8. For Tell el-ʿUmeiri, see Herr 1999; Herr and Clark 2009 and references there. For their "Reubenite" hypothesis connecting Tell el-ʿUmeiri with Israelite incursions in Transjordan in early Iron I, see further below; cf. the similar refutation by Finkelstein 2011d. Porter (2013) and Routledge (2004), both authorities on the Transjordan, emphasize the unique local features there.

9. See references in n. 3 above; for northern Transjordan, add the surveys of Mittmann 1970. On the recent Wadi Fidan excavations, see further below and chapter.

10. See Ussishkin 1985.

11. Further on Gezer, see below.

12. See Briend and Humbert 1980; cf. Artzy 2003; Raban 1998; Gilboa 2001, 2005.

13. Lehmann 2001.

14. There have been a number of excavation projects at Tell Abu Hawam over the last several decades, none fully published. The stratigraphy is much debated; the summary here attempts to reconcile the differing interpretations. See conveniently Balensi, Harrera, and Artzy 1993. South of Tell Abu Hawam is another Phoenician port, ʿAtlit, but the harbor there cannot be dated earlier than about the eighth century; see further chapter 5.

15. The Dor stratigraphy and chronology are much debated. For the best summary by the current excavators, see Gilboa and Sharon 2008, 2013 (from a low-chronology perspective, however). See also ch. 4 and n. 47. In the stratigraphy referenced above, the first element identifies the area of the excavation, the second the phase. Thus B1/12 = Phase 12 of Area B1, D/13 = Phase 13 of Area D, and so on. For the notion that Dor was originally a Philistine site but later became Phoenician, see Stern 2000, 201. On the Tale of Wen-Amon, see Rainey 2006, 132; add Gilboa 2005, 2008 with reference to Dor and the Shikalayu as Phoenicians, not Philistines. Gilboa also considers Phoenician the northern coastal sites discussed here such as Tell Abu Hawam, Tell Keisan, and Akko. El-Ahwat, inland from Dor, has twelfth-century pottery, but Zertal's (2012) view that it is a "Sherden site" is doubtful. On early Phoenician culture, especially trade, see Markoe 2000; Sagona 2008. See also n. 16 below.

16. For Syria and Lebanon, see Akkermans and Schwartz 2003, 360–88;

Luciani 2014; Heinz and Kulemann-Ossen 2014. See also general discussions in Aubet 2001; Lipinski 2010; and further discussion in chapter 4. On Phoenician colonies and seagoing trade—possibly in collaboration with their Philistine southern coastal neighbors—see Beitzel 2010; Faust 2013a, 183–86. Bauer (1998) has argued that the Philistines deliberately entered into "decentralized maritime trade" related to (and perhaps partially integrated with) the parallel emergence of Phoenician and Israelite trade networks in the eleventh–tenth century. Lipinski, however, regards the "Israelite connection" in the Hebrew Bible as mythical (2010, 272). See generally Gilboa and Sharon 2008.

17. See references in nn. 15 and 16 above and further discussion in chapter 4. Stern (2013) has argued that coastal sites from Dor all the way up to Acco, and even inland sites such as Yokneʿam and Tel Qiri, were "Philistine" rather than Phoenician. His arguments, however, are unpersuasive. See further n. 36 below.

18. See Rainey 2006, 110.

19. The summary of the following Philistine sites draws upon the best syntheses now available, including one by the director of the site of Ekron, which provides us with the most extensive excavations and publications. See Gitin 2003, especially 2010; and cf. Stager 1995. References would also include the site entries in Stern 1993, 2008; and see the syntheses in Dothan 2003; Gitin 2003; Killebrew and Lehmann 2013; Mazow 2014; Faust 2015. Gitin's monochrome wares = Philistine 1 or Stager's 1; bichrome wares = Philistine 2 or Stager's Stage 2: and the so-called Late Philistine Decorated Ware (LPDW) = Philistine 3. On the LPDW pottery—red-slipped with black-painted lines—as well as its antecedents, see now the definitive work of Ben-Shlomo 2006. The terminology of Gitin and Stager has not been universally adopted; for traditional views, see Faust 2015, 170.

20. For the distinction between Stages 1 and 2, see Stager 1995; he includes, however, several northern sites that are taken here to be Phoenician (below).

21. See now Dothan and Ben-Shlomo 2005.

22. The stratigraphy and chronology of these two sites, dug long ago by Petrie, are very imprecise.

23. See now Stager, Schloen, and Master 2008, 2011; cf. Stager 1995.

24. See Dothan and Ben-Shlomo 2005; Ben-Shlomo 2003, 2006; Ben-Shlomo, Shai, and Maier 2004.

25. See Barako 2007, 25–30.

26. For further analysis of house plans, see now A. Mazar 2009; cf. Faust 2015 on some of Tell Qasile's other somewhat usual features.

27. Renewed excavations beginning in 2009 have begun to synthesize older salvage excavations by Kaplan and others and promise to provide new data. See provisionally Peilstöcker and Burke 2011.

28. To earlier reports add now Gadot and Yadin 2009. Other Yarkon Basin Iron I sites have some Philistine pottery but are probably not ethnically Philistine; see Faust 2015, 176.

29. See Ben-Shlomo 2012. There is one unique cremation burial.

30. See Herzog 1993.

31. Add to earlier reports Maeir 2012; and see Maeir, Hitchcock, and Horwitz 2013.

32. The best summary is Gitin 2010.

33. See Bunimovitz and Faust 2001; Bunimovitz and Lederman 2006, 2008.

34. Stager (1995, 342) regards Gezer as a peripheral Philistine outpost. A few others think it the capital of a small Philistine province (Gadot 2008). These views, however, go well beyond the evidence. The two large houses in Field VI produced some Philistine bichrome pottery and fragments of two *kernoi* like those at Tell Qasile. The overall culture of Stratum XII–XI, however, remains in the Canaanite tradition, with possibly some Philistine elements, as at Beth-shemesh and Tel Batash. See further below. On the Philistines as uncircumcised, see Faust 2015, 185 (who does not, however, cite the Gezer phallus).

35. On the Philistine rural hinterland, see Gadot 2008.

36. Drew 1998, 39; see further Drews 1993; Sherratt 1998. Barako effectively refutes the latter; see 2000, 513–30. On Cyprus as a jumping-off point for the invasion of the southern Levantine coast, see chapter 2. On whether it was the Philistines, rather than the Phoenicians, who pursued maritime trade in Iron I, see Gilboa 2005, who opts for Phoenician merchants dominating. On seafarers and ships in this period, see Bauer 1998; Wachsmann 1998; Ballard et al. 2002; Artzy 2003; Beitzel 2010; Cline 1994. For a review of the old "diffusion or invasion" theories, arguing that invasion is back in style, see Chapman 1997; Bell 2006.

37. The most comprehensive and best balanced view of both land and sea routes is Yasur-Landau 2010.

38. On the Medinet Habu reliefs, see Dothan 1982, 5–13; Stager 1995, 338. On the migrations through Anatolia and Syria, see n. 40 below. On the Aegean cultural traits, see Stager 1995, 344–48; Dothan 2003; Killebrew 2005, 197–245; Ben-Shlomo, Shai, and Maier 2004; Ben-Shlomo 2006, 2008, 2010, 2011; Shamir 2007; Ben-Sholmo, Shai, and Zuckerman 2008; Ben-Shlomo and Press 2009; Gitin 2010, 320–49; Yasur-Landau 2010, 216–81; Bunimovitz 2011; Maeir, Hitchcock, and Horwitz 2013 (with full bibliography). See also below on ethnicity.

39. On Philistine pottery, see the general works cited in n. 19 above. Add specifically, with full references, Ben-Shlomo 2006; French 2013; Killebrew 2013; Lehmann 2013; Mountjoy 2013; Sherratt 2013; and Sherratt and Mazar 2013. To Ben-Shlomo 2006, add now Faust 2015, who relates the LPDW to acculturation. He thinks these "degenerate" wares are not directly deriviative from Philistine bichrome but were more influenced by Phoenician (and perhaps Cypro-Phoenician) wares—even proposing that by Iron II coastal Philistines may have become "Phoenicianized."

40. See the discussion in Harrison 2009. Yasur-Landau 2010 is the most outspoken proponent of a route through Anatolia and down the Syrian coast.

41. Most authorities argue that the Philistines were never truly assimilated

but were in time "acculturated"; see Stager 1995, 348; Stone 1995; Barako 2000, 2003; Killebrew 2005, 233; Ben-Shlomo, Shai, and Zukerman 2008; Gitin 2010, 325; Yasur-Landau 2010, 288–94; Faust 2015, 184–89. Uziel 2007 opposes acculturation in favor of "cultural fusion" as a reaction; cf. Faust and Lev-Tov 2011; Maeir, Hitchcock, and Horwitz 2013.

For Cyprus, see Iacovou 1998, 335; Steel 2011 190; Harrison 2009; cf. n. 31 in chapter 2. See below on ethnicity. Stager (1995) is the most outspoken of the sudden invasion and urban imposition model; cf. Gitin 2010, 324–25. Killebrew (2005) sees a more gradual process of colonization, as do Maier, Hitchcock, and Horwitz (2013). See also below on ethnicity.

42. Finkelstein's "few thousand" in the early Philistine period is a minimal estimate (Finkelstein 1995a, 236). Yasur-Landau gives an estimate of circa 20,000 for the twelfth–eleventh century, with some 12,500 in the pentapolis cities, growing to some 30,000 by the tenth century (Yasur-Landau 2010, 295).

43. Argued most forcefully by Yasur-Landau, 2010, 282–309. Maeir, Hitchcock, and Horwitz 2013 argue for a more complex and gradual process of ethnogenesis, embodying a degree of cultural interaction with the local population from the beginning. Most authorities still characterize the appearance of the Sea Peoples along the southern Levantine coast as a relatively sudden, forcible invasion of "urban colonizers," as Killebrew puts it; see 2005, 209–16; cf. Stager 1995, 245–48; Gitin 2010, 324–25. See nn. 40–41 above on origins; see below on ethnicity.

44. Stager 1995, 345–48; see n. 41 above. On the development and persistence of Philistine identity, see Gitin 2010, 302–49; Maeir, Hitchcock, and Horwitz 2013.

45. Stager 1995, 345. See nn. 40–41 above. For a negative view of Philistine ethnicity, see Bunimovitz 1990. Faust (2015, 173), however, summarizes the positivist view that material culture—especially pottery, in this case—does reflect ethnicity.

46. Ussishkin 1985.

47. Add now A. Mazar 2006; Mazar and Mullins 2007; Panitz-Cohen and Mazar 2009.

48. For the basic survey data used in the following, see Finkelstein 1988; Broshi and Finkelstein 1992; Finkelstein and Magen 1993; Finkelstein, Lederman, and Bunimovitz 1997; Finkelstein and Na'aman 1994; Finkelstein, Lederman, and Bunimovitz 1997; Lehmann 2001; Gadot 2003; Zertal 2004, 2007. See summaries in Bloch-Smith and Nakhai 1999; Stager 1995; Dever 2003d, 97–100; Killebrew 2005, 149–96; Faust 2006b, 111–34; Nakhai 2010. Zwingenberger 2001 draws detailed site maps for the central hillcountry (156 sites), but she does not even cite the basic surveys. Miller 2005 is of no independent value; it employs outdated models and social-science jargon.

49. Sharon 1994, 127. See further below.

50. For Judah and the Shephelah, see Ofer 1994, 2001; Faust 2013b, 206–9. On the importance of rural sites, see Faust 2006b, 116–20.

51. See Gadot 2003, 2008; Gilboa 2005.

52. See Stager 1998, 134–35; Sharon 1994.

53. Stager 1998, 134–35.

54. Bloch-Smith and Nakhai 1999, 82; Nakhai 2003.

55. Bloch-Smith and Nakhai 1999, 82; Nakhai 2003.

56. Gal, Shalem, and Hartal 2007.

57. Aharoni 1957, 142–50; cf. Gal 1992a; Frankel 1994; Ben-Ami 2004.

58. On Sasa, see Golani and Yogev 1996; and Stepanski, Segal, and Carmi 1996. On Har Adir, see Aharoni 1957, 131–50; Davis 1985.

59. Aharoni 1979, 177.

60. Frankel 1994, 34.

61. For preliminary reports, see Mazar 2005, 2007, 2008a, 2008b. On the unique character of the site continuing into Iron II, see chapters 4 and 5.

62. The Iron Age levels at Dan remain largely unpublished, but see the 1999 dissertation of David Ilan (2011). See also Arie 2008.

63. To preliminary reports, add now Ben-Tor, Ben-Ami, and Sandhaus 2012. Yadin's Strata XII–XI is now better understood as a single, brief horizon, mostly eleventh century, still possibly "Israelite," but with no conclusive evidence.

64. See Master et al. 2005 for the only field report there is; the stratigraphic work of Free in the 1950s–1960s and his staff was primitive. On Tomb I, see Cooley and Pratico 1994.

65. In addition to earlier reports, see Rast 1978. The well-stratified and well-published Iron I pottery, although not essentially Israelite, is diagnostic for this period and into Iron IIA.

66. On Yoqneʿam , add to preliminary reports Ben-Tor, Zarzecki, and Cohen-Anidjar 2005. On Tel Qiri, add Ben-Tor and Portugali 1987.

67. See the reworking of the material by Zorn 1997, 1999; Brody 2011.

68. Zertal 1986–1987, 1991. A much fuller report is now available in the work of Hawkins 2012, a staff member. His views are skewed, however, by his evangelical presupposition of an "Israelite conquest." For minimalist interpretations, see Fritz and Kempinski 1983; Naʾaman 1994b. Mazar (1990, 348–50), however, allows for some cultic significance.

69. See Finkelstein 1986, 151. The site would fit the biblical location of Ebenezer, on the inner border with Philistia. On food production, see B. Rosen 1986; cf. Sasson 1968 and see further below.

70. Bethel was so badly excavated and poorly published that little can be said. There was a destruction sometime at the end of the Late Bronze Age, followed by a sort of squatter occupation with pottery similar to Ai and Giloh. See reviews by Dever 1971 and Finkelstein and Singer-Avitz 2009.

71. Iron Age Ai remains unpublished except for Callaway's preliminary reports.

72. The full material is available only in Lederman's unpublished dissertation (1999).

73. See Finkelstein 1990b. Na'aman (2012b) regards the site as Philistine, but the absence of any of the well-known Philistine cultural traits makes such an identification improbable. In any case, it is unlikely that the Philistines ever penetrated that far inland. For another late eleventh/early tenth-century town wall, see Khirbet Qeiyafa (ch. 4).

74. See A. Mazar 1981. Mazar's tower at the site is almost certainly later; see chapter 5 below. The perimeter wall may also be later.

75. For a reworking of the site, see Herzog 1994, 134–36. Herzog also covers the whole Beersheba Valley with its other sites.

76. Fritz and Kempinski 1983.

77. Kempinski and Fritz 1977, 144. The opinion of the ethnographer van der Steen that Tel Masos was the center of a vast Negev tribal polity—a "tribal state" based on widespread trade—is a fantasy. See van der Steen 2010, 2013. Cf. Holladay 1995, 383–85, who interprets Pillared Building 1039 as a large stable, presumably evidence for some sort of centralized administration. That goes well beyond the facts.

78. Ofer 1994, 112.

79. For Tell el-ʿUmeiri, see Herr and Najjar 2001, 2008; Herr 2006, 2007, 2009; Herr and Clark 2001; London 2011a. For a few vessels from House A, see Herr 2006, figs. 1–21, dated by Herr to the transitional Late Bronze/Iron I horizon (the pottery from House B is said to be virtually identical). Yet it is worth noting that only a few of the collar-rim store jars (figs. 7–8) are close to the twelfth-century highland Israelite sites. Most are closer to Iron I Galilean sites. Some cooking pots do resemble thirteenth/twelfth-century forms west of the Jordan, but others do not. Some kraters are also different, as are many bowls. One has the impression that this pottery is similar to that in Cisjordan. But it is not identical, much less the "prototype" of the central hill-country repertoire, as Rainey maintained. See further below. As Herr himself says, "the best parallels come from Tell el-ʿUmeiri itself" (2006, 71). On the eleventh-century pottery, see Herr 2007. Finkelstein's typical attempt to rework the stratigraphy and chronology carries little weight (Finkelstein 2011d, 2013), but he does refute the Reubenite hypothesis, as I do here. See n. 80.

80. Herr agrees, despite supporting the "Reubenite" hypothesis. See Herr and Najjar 2008, 324–25.

81. B. Rosen 1986. A more detailed analysis of the economy of the Iron I hill-country sites was undertaken by A. Sasson (2008), using case studies and basing his calculations on detailed examination of land use and caloric requirements. His conclusions strongly support those of Rosen. Animal husbandry was important, but grain exploitation was much more significant, since surpluses contributed to the inhabitants' economic security.

82. Most authorities agree on ceramic continuity from the Late Bronze Age

into the early Iron I period. For documentation, see Dever 1995a, 1997b; see also the summary in 2003d, 118–25. Finkelstein (1996b, 1997) argues, however, that the pottery of the Iron I "Israelite" sites is quite different. He ignores the fact that the differences are only statistical; the repertoire is very much the same, but for obvious reasons the pottery of the rural settlements is much more utilitarian and therefore limited to a few types. See further below.

83. Sahlins 1972, 95.

84. Gottwald 1993. Further on egalitarianism and early Israel, see Faust 2006b, 70, 79, 95–117. In practice, Faust's egalitarianism really comes down to the more tractable issue of equality, which he sees evident in a distinctive Israelite ethos reflected in such material-culture categories as pottery and house form. See also above on the so-called pillar-courtyard house at Tell el-'Umeiri, certainly not an Israelite house.

85. See above and chapter 4; see also Dever 1997b.

86. See conveniently the discussion of Faust 2006b, 71–78 with references—especially the distribution map in fig. 9.2. Faust, however, underlines the salient fact: these houses predominate, and are consistent over a long period of time, only in ancient Israel. It is, therefore, legitimate to regard them as "ethnic markers," although obviously not exclusively so.

87. On the technology and difficult dating of terraces, see the fundamental work of Stager 1982; 1985a, 5–9. Dever has repeatedly dealt with the significance of terraces in the Iron I highland economy. See Dever 1992c, 1995a, summarized in 2003d, 113–15. Hopkins had argued (1985, 167–83) that terracing was unnecessary, since the highlands were not densely settled and farmers could move easily to new land. Borowski, however, a careful student of ancient Israelite life-ways, easily refuted this notion (1988, 10–11). Gibson's attempt at rebuttal (2001), arguing that terracing predates the Iron I period, ignores the point that only in the latter period does this technology become widespread and clearly linked with a new economy and lifestyle. Finkelstein's similar skepticism (1996b, 1997) can be dismissed, since it evidently stems from his presupposition that the Iron I highland settlers were pastoral nomads, not experienced subsistence farmers (below). Many of the photographs of Finkelstein's own Iron I sites in the central hills show elaborate terrace systems.

88. Like terraces, plastered cisterns predate the Iron Age. They are found, for instance, already well developed in clear Middle and Late Bronze contexts at Gezer. Again, however, it is the coupling of widespread cistern technology to a new *agricultural* society and economy in Iron I that is innovative. See Stager 1982; 1985a, 9–11.

89. For a summary of sites with silos, see Hasel 1998, 213–15. Cf. Dever 2003d, 105–7.

90. On iron and iron technology, see ch. 4 n. 54. There is some evidence of twelfth-century iron working at Radanna among our Israelite sites, as well as at Dan and Deir 'Alla.

91. On Iron Age ceramic production and socioeconomics generally, see Wood 1990. On the specific significance for Israelite origins in Iron I, see Franken and London 1995, stressing the shift to cottage industry and more handmade production. On the overall continuity of Late Bronze–Iron I ceramics, see above and n. 82. On ceramics and Israelite ethnicity specially, see Dever 1995a, but cf. the negative assessment of Finkelstein 1997. A summary of the distribution of collar-rim store jars will be found in Killebrew 2005, 177–81.

92. On the Bull Site, see the original publication of Mazar (1982a) and add discussions in Zwickel 1994, 212–15; Keel and Uehlinger 1998, 198; Zevit 2001, 178–79, 250–51; Dever 2005a, 135– 36; Hess 2007, 246, 248; Albertz and Schmidt 2012, 235.

93. On the Gezer Calendar, the ʿIzbet Ṣarṭah ostracon, the Tel Zayit abecedary, and the Khirbet Qeiyafa ostracon, see Ahituv 2008, 17–18, 249–57; add now Tappy and McCarter 2008; Garfinkel and Ganor 2009, 243–57. Whether the scripts are styled Old Canaanite or Paleo-Hebrew, the language is certainly Hebrew.

94. On the problematic nature of the biblical texts as historical sources, see ch. 1 n. 4. Note that Hoffmeier, a prominent evangelical scholar, has moved down to the late thirteenth-century date, and he chides his fellow-conservative scholars for not following suit (see 2007).

95. On how a model of two, independent but "converging" sources might work out, see the extensive treatment in Dever 2001. Revisionists have dismissed this approach as "undue harmonizing," but it is simply sound historical method. Here, as elsewhere, I am employing the jurisprudence model outlined in chapter 1.

96. See Hoffmeier and el-Maksoud 2003; Hoffmeier and Moshier 2006, references to earlier literature.

97. Hoffmeier 2005, 249.

98. See Redford 1992, 275–80.

99. No doubt some of the "cultural memory" now invoked by biblicists is at work. But the biblical story is more invented than recalled. On the cultural memory of the Hebrew Bible, see n. 2 above.

100. Stager 1985; cf. the slight modifications in Schloen 2001. Both studies advance the model of a "patrimonial" society; see further below.

101. Mendenhall 1973, 225; 1962, 73.

102. Weippert 1971, summarizing the earlier views of Alt and Noth.

103. Finkelstein has accused Dever of being a "Gottwaldian" (1992, 63), yet Dever has consistently rejected Gottwald's "Yahwism" as the major engine driving the Late Bronze/Iron I changes.

104. See the convenient résumé of models in Nakhai 2008, 124–25.

105. The translation here is that of John A. Wilson in *ANET*, 378. The idiosyncratic readings of Ahlström and Edelman (Ahlström and Edelman 1985; Edelman 1996) may be dismissed. See further below.

106. The literature on the Merenptah inscriptions and reliefs is vast, but see Kitchen 1998, 2003; Stager 1985b; Yurco 1986; 1997; Redford 1986; Singer 1988a; Hasel 1994; 2004; Rainey 2001, 2003; Dever 2014. See also summaries in Faust 2006b, 163–66, 185–86. For minimalist, or even nihilist, interpretations, see nn. 107–8 below.

107. T. Thompson 1999, 79.

108. Whitelam 1996, 210; see also Edelman 1996, 25–26, who denies the reading "Israel."

109. Aharoni 1967, 385; Naʾaman 1997. Possibly a better site now known is Tall Ziraʿa; see Vieweger and Häser 2007.

110. See references in n. 106 above.

111. For these views, see Finkelstein 1995b, 354–55. On the surveys—on which Finkelstein's views largely depend—see references in n. 48 above.

112. On the EB IV cycle, see Dever 1995d and full references there.

113. Bunimovitz 1995b, 324.

114. On the dynamics of population growth, which militate against the sedentarized-nomads hypothesis, see Stager, cited in n. 43 above.

115. Finkelstein 1988, 191; 1992, 64.

116. Finkelstein 1988, 186–89. Cf. Zertal 1991, 1994. For a refutation of Zertal's supposed statistics, see Dever 1995a, 1998a, 1998b.

117. On the nomadic ideal, see below and nn. 118, 127, 134, 136.

118. Saidel 2008, 476. See also Saidel 1997, 2009. Saidel's discussion of bedouin tents arranged in line is amply documented in Saidel 2009, figs. 5:6, 5:7. The latter and other essays are included in Szuchman 2009, which contains many other valuable discussions of nomads, tribes, and the state in the ancient and modern Middle East.

119. Van der Steen 2004, 91–101; see also 2013.

120. Van der Steen 2004, 107; see also 2013.

121. Van der Steen 2004, 221; see also 2013.

122. Stager 1985a, 17.

123. Coote 1990, 133; see also Lederman 1992.

124. The literature is vast. For general orientation and references, see Johnson 1969; Barth 1969; Rowton 1976, 1977; Dever 1977; essays in Bar-Yosef and Khazanov 1992: van der Steen 2004, 2013; Saidel and van der Steen 2007; and essays in Szuchman 2009. On the resistance to sedentarization, see particularly Lees and Bates 1974; Salzman 1980; Khazanov 1994; Barfield 1993. On the Mari pastoralists, see Luke 1965; Matthews 1978. On the Israeli, Negev, and Sinai bedouin, see Amiran and Arieh 1963; Marx 1967; Bailey 1980. On the archaeology of nomads, see S. Rosen 1988; Banning 1986; Rosen and Avni 1993 (on "invisibility"); add Cribb 1991. For early literature on pastoral nomadism and theories of Israelite origins, see Hauser 1978; Thompson 1992 (largely made redundant now by the new archaeological evidence). See further the discussion and notes below.

125. Salzman 1980, 7.

126. Salzman 1980, 10–11.

127. For independent refutations of the widespread presumption of a "nomadic ideal" in the Hebrew Bible, see Dever 1998b; Hiebert 2009. Hiebert concludes that "the entire sweep of Israel's origin traditions in the Pentateuch, from the creation of the world to the promulgation of law at Mt. Sinai, describe Israel's beginnings in terms of sedentary agriculture rather than nomadic pastoralism" (2009, 204). The antistatist battle cry "To your tents, O Israel!" is a nostalgia for a past that never was. As Hiebert shows, the biblical "good life" is not that of the lawless hinterland but rather that of an ordered, settled life. See nn. 117 and 134 here.

128. See n. 53 in chapter 2. For earlier studies, see Kitchen 1998; Giveon 1971; Redford 1992, 215–80; Ward and Joukowsky 1992; Hasel 1998, 217–39. Faust (2006b, 183–87) sees some Shasu among the early Israelites but cannot specify their numbers, nor can he give any motivation for their becoming sedentary. In the end, he regards early Israel as a "mixed multitude," as Dever, Killebrew, Stager, and others do (below; see further excurus 3.1).

129. On *tribe*, see older notions in Sahlins 1968, where an evolution from "tribe to band to chiefdom to state" was presumed, a notion now largely abandoned. For critical updates, with relation to biblical studies, archaeology, and early Israel, see Hauser 1978; Bienkowski 2009b; van der Steen 2004, 2013. For the general abandonment of the term *tribe* as nebulous and even pejorative, see Bienkowski 2009b, 16–17. Szuchman, in introducing a volume entitled *Nomads, Tribes, and the State in the Ancient Near East: Cross-Disciplinary Perspectives*, argues that "the term 'tribe,' itself, and many of the attributes associated with it, notions that have troubled anthropologists for some time, seem even more fluid and amorphous according to recent literature" (Szuchman 2009, 1). It is now more appropriate to speak of *peoples, socioeconomic units*, or *ethnic groups*, or perhaps *heterachical* or *communal* societies. See also Ofer in n. 50 above. Bienkowski points out criticism of "segmentary societies" by Shryock 1997 and Layne 1994.

See Netser 1998 in an important collection of essays entitled *Water, Environment and Society in Times of Climatic Change* (Issar and Brown 1998), with full bibliography. See also Langgut, Finkelstein and Litt 2013. Several essays on possible climate change at the end of the Aegean and southern Levantine Late Bronze Age will be found in Bachhuber and Roberts 2009. For Rainey's appeal to drought, see 2006, 103. See also n. 130 below.

130. See Netser 1998, fig. 1.1; and Avner 1998, 187. Drought has long been invoked as a factor in the general collapse of the Bronze Age civilizations around the eastern Mediterranean world. However, the textual evidence that we happen to have is ambiguous. There were, as always, short-term droughts and periodic grain shortages, but there is little precise evidence of a prolonged, systemic drought serious enough to have caused the collapse. For a recent synthesis and full bibliography, see essays in Bachhuber and Roberts 2009. Stiebing's view of drought as triggering the emergence of the earliest Israelites, like Rainey's similar

notion, lacks any support and in any case makes little sense; see Stiebing 1989, 167–87; Rainey 2006, 112 (citing Stiebing 1989). Cline (2014) has recently argued that drought was the major factor in the widespread collapse at the end of the Late Bronze Age, a view that is oversimplistic.

131. On whether or not pastoral nomads are visible in the archaeological records, see Banning 1986; S. Rosen 1988; Rosen and Avni 1993. The answer seems to be yes and no. Nomads are clearly visible in the EB IV period, but in the Middle and Late Bronze Ages they are not. Finkelstein's claim to have isolated "pastoral nomadic" settlements and cemeteries (1995b, 355–56) is without any foundation. It is worth noting that Bunimovitz's definitive study of the Late Bronze Age concludes that there was a diminished rural sector and that indeed during most of this period hardly any rural settlements existed in the highlands (1995b, 324). Any nomads would thus have been invisible. Elsewhere (1994, 200) Bunimovitz does speak of the withdrawal of several nomadic groups from the lowlands (as argued here) to become sedentarized in the highlands.

The salient point is that there undoubtedly were some former pastoral nomads in the early Israelite mix, but they were not predominant, nor were they exclusively from the central hills (Finkelstein) or from Transjordan (Rainey's Shasu).

A large cemetery of tombs without any grave goods at the copper smelter at Khirbet en-Naḥas in the Wadi Feinan (ancient Punan) has been attributed to Shasu (Levy 2009; Levy, Najjar, and Ben-Yosef 2014). But it seems unlikely that pastoral nomads would have voluntarily worked in the inhuman conditions in the copper smeltery there. See further chapter 4.

132. Lancaster 1981, 106.

133. See Faust 2006b, 17–19, 168–85.

134. See nn. 117 and 127 above. Dever has offered a critique of the notion of the biblical "nomadic ideal" and its adoption by a past generation of biblicists; see Dever 1998b, with full references. Ofer, who directed the Iron I survey of the Judean hill country, observes that "the concept of a 'tribe' for Judah lacks any concrete content, and seems to be a late, artificial application to the history of the families which settled in the land of Judah" (1994, 117).

135. Even Fritz, who had adopted some version of a tribal nomadic origin, finally concluded that any such nomads had long lived in continuity, in a "symbiosis" with settled lowland peoples, as seminomads (Fritz 1981a, 69–71; see Fritz 1981b, 1987; Fritz and Kempinski 1983). On the flawed tent analogy, see above. On the Shasu, see n. 128 above and n. 54 in chapter 2.

136. Rainey 2006. See 2007 for elaboration of the argument, even asserting that Moabite is the "prototype" of Hebrew. Although elsewhere Rainey ridicules anthropological theory, here he naively borrows van der Steen's (2004) ethnographic and anthropological model—based not on ancient pastoral nomads but on nineteenth- and twentieth-century bedouin in southern Transjordan. See nn. 124 and 127 above.

137. Herr and Clark 2001; see Herr 2006 for contemporary House A and its

pottery (not available to Rainey when he wrote in 2006 and 2007). Herr himself gives few Iron I ceramic parallels west of the Jordan, an indication that Rainey's comparisons are invented.

138. Herr and Najjar 2008, 324–25

139. Finkelstein 1988, 274–75.

140. Ehrich 1965, vii–viii.

141. Cf. London 1989; Wood 1990.

142. See Finkelstein, Bunimovitz, and Lederman 1993 for this pottery.

143. B. Rosen 1986, 151.

144. The calculations are presented by A. Sasson (1998), who was Finkelstein's student. He concludes that "pastoral societies have been attributed with too great an influence: various models have connected pastoralism with every socioeconomic process that has taken place in Eretz-Israel." He disavows theories that see the nomads as "the catalyst that brought about the collapse of urban systems" (1998, 3). Sasson's detailed reconstruction of the economy of typical agricultural villages, ancient and modern, is the best evidence yet that the model of large-scale "nomadic sedentarization" is a figment of the imagination of modern scholars.

Further support for the agricultural background of the Iron I settlers comes from Tel Masos, where cattle bones were 23 percent of the total. Pastoral nomads in the southern Levant rarely herd cattle, which require extensive pasture lands, water, and skill in breeding. See Fritz and Kempinski 1983, 215.

145. For the latest surveys on archaeological theory and method in our field, see the essays in Levy 2010a, with full references. The *new pragmatism* in the title, however (and in Levy's chapter), is rather simplistic. See particularly the chapters by Dever and Joffe. For the broader picture, see the chapters in Preucel and Mrozowski 2010.

146. See Whitelam 1996, 228; Lemche 1991, 152.

147. Thompson 1999, 234; 1997, 175; Whitelam 1996, 228. Cf. Jones 1997, 2010 on ethnicity. References to "fluid" ethnic boundaries in the biblical and archaeological literature are too numerous to cite, but see, for example, Skjeggestad 1992; Finkelstein 1996b, 1997; Edelman 1996; Kletter 2006; Herzog and Bar-Yosef 2002. The latter declares that "ethnicity, in most cases, is ideology imposed by political powers to dominate and control subordinate groups" (Herzog and Bar-Yosef 2002, 169). The ideology here is clearly that of postmodernism. Equally absurd is Lemche's claim that "the notion of Philistine ethnicity stands and falls with the notion of an Israelite ethnicity because our main source for Philistine ethnicity is the Old Testament" (2012, 27). This forecloses the discussion by simply excluding archaeology as a possible source, scarcely a defensible argument.

148. See Faust 2010b, with reference to the literature and an extensive, well-balanced critique. See also nn. 147 and 149–50.

149. See Finkelstein 1991; 1992; 1996b; especially 1997. On the significance of pigs, see below and nn. 150 and 159. See Barth 1969, 10–11; cf. Dever 1995a; 2003, 192–95. Kletter (2006) argued that Dever had misunderstood Barth, who

supposedly rejected these very "trait lists," but Barth's point was that these traits are not in themselves sufficient to define ethnicity, which can be more complex. Barth, of course, said nothing about ethnicity in the archaeological record. The "minimalism" now in vogue comes mostly from biblical minimalists such as Edelman (1996), Lemche (2012), and Skjeggestad (1992) or from postmodern theorists such as Jones (1997), who has no first-hand acquaintance with our archaeological data.

For an extensive critique of postmodernism and its negative implications for archaeology, see Dever 2001. Israeli archaeologists have been slow to respond, but see now Bunimovitz 2011; Faust 2006b, 235–36; 2012a, 8; Maeir 2010. For general orientation to the problem of defining ethnicity in material culture remains, see Killebrew 2005, 8–10; Faust 2006b, 15–19; and references in both. Sparks 1998 deals only with biblical concepts.

150. For the preceding quote, see Barth 1969, 14; for the definition, 10–11; cf. Dever 2003d, 192–93. In anthropological terms, the former or genetic approach is "primordial" or "essentialist," the latter "instrumental" or "functional." See Jones 1997, 65–112. It seems obvious that both approaches have merit. See further Knapp 2001; he credits postmodernism with the prevailing skepticism, yet points out that "ethnicity" is really culture, i.e., nationhood. That can certainly be recognized in archaeological remains, even though archaeologists should be more cautious and more deliberate. See nn. 147, 149, and 159.

151. See Dever 1991a; 1992b, 206; 1993a for the term *Proto-Israelite*. On cultural continuity, see Dever 1992c; 1994b; 1995c; 2007b, 58–60; Finkelstein 1996; 1997, 223; R. Miller 2005, 63.

152. Finkelstein 1997; Kletter 2006.

153. Stager 1985c, 86. However, Stager himself later on was fully confident about identifying Israelite ethnicity, mainly on the basis of material culture (1998, 134–35).

154. Bourdieu 1990. For the application of Bourdieu's *habitus* to the Israelite house—identifying it ethnically—see Yasur-Landau 2010, with reference to previous studies. See also Faust 2006b, 152, 153 See further below on houses.

155. Giddens 1979.

156. Pauketat 2001, 86.

157. Orser 1984.

158. See above and especially chapter 4 on house form and ethnicity.

159. See the data and discussions in Hesse 1986; 1990; Hesse and Wapnish 1997; Hellwing and Adjeman 1986; Tamar et al. 2013. Various interpretations are summarized in Killebrew 2005, 219; Faust 2006b, 35–40. The growing consensus is that the near complete absence of pig bones in early Israelite sites *may* be a significant ethnic marker. But the data must be used cautiously, since there may be other variables that are unknown or cannot be quantified. For the revised appraisal here, see Meiri et al. 2013 and literature there. The assertion that European wild

boars were brought by the Philistines to the Levant has been questioned, due to what may be flawed samples and statistics.

160. The absence of Iron I burials may be explained simply by the accidents of discovery and excavation or, on the other hand, by cultural differences or even by geographical constraints. For the phenomenon and skeptical interpretations, see Bloch-Smith 1992, 2004. Kletter (2002a) believes that the absence of rock-cut tombs may indicate an impoverished society, too poor to provide for elaborate burial. Faust (2004a) is more optimistic, but he also suggests an "egalitarian society" with no need for ostentatious burials. See further chapter 5 for the Iron II evidence.

161. London 1989.

162. Details will be found in the discussion of the individual sites above. On Tall Zira'a, see Vieweger and Häser 2007; on Tell Abu el-Kharaz, see Fischer and Bürge 2013. On the pros and cons of earthquake dating, see Bunimovitz and Lederman 2011; Cline 2011.

163. The following is freely adapted from Dever 2003d, 167–89, which see for additional details.

164. Lenski and Lenski 1978, 229.

165. Hopkins 1985, 265–75.

166. This latter statement has been misconstrued to mean that it supports Gottwald's theory of "Yahwism" as a driving force. Yet Dever has supported only Gottwald's notion of indigenous origins (Dever 2003d, 110), leaving theology as an important factor, but one difficult to illustrate archaeologically. For another misunderstanding, see the view of Moore and Kelle 2011, 126.

167. Fritz 1981a, 69–70.

168. On recent emphasis on "cultural memory," see n. 2 above. None of these studies, however, relates this hermeneutical model to the archaeological data, which of course in this case are not "remembered" but are frozen at one moment in time.

169. Chaney 1983, 72.

170. Chaney 1983, 61; Cf. Wolf 1966; 1982. Faust does cite Wolf's 1982 work (2006b, 87).

EXCURSUS 3.1

Rainey's Transjordanian Shasu as "Earliest Israel"

Based on his identification of Yenoam with a site in northern Transjordan, Rainey proceeds to locate Merenptah's "Israel," listed next, in that region. Thus the origins of the Israelite peoples lie in Transjordan. He connects these people with the well-known Shasu of that region discussed above.[1]

Because Rainey's nomadic-origins model has been uncritically embraced in one way or another by other scholars, we must give it considerable attention here. The best way to analyze arguments regarding an archaeological assemblage, especially those advanced by nonspecialists, is to ask: What would be required to *confirm* such arguments, based strictly on the archaeological data?

To confirm Rainey's theory of Shasu nomads in Transjordan as the real Proto-Israelites in the thirteenth century, one would have to demonstrate the following at minimum.

1. Merenptah's inscription is correctly ordered topographically; it reflects an Egyptian itinerary and deals with real events. Thus, it is a reliable source for writing history.
2. Yenoam is in northern Transjordan, and since Israel is listed next, it must be located there as well.
3. The closest parallels to the early Iron I hill-country ceramic assemblage in Cisjordan are found in the Late Bronze pottery of Transjordan, the prototype. Thus, the Israelite settlers must have come from the local population there.
4. The Shasu pastoral nomads known from Egyptian New Kingdom texts constitute the reservoir from which this ethnic movement must be drawn. It was they who brought the Transjordanian

ceramic and cultural traditions to Cisjordan, in the course of becoming sedentarized there.

5. The resultant Iron I material culture reflects the prior nomadic lifestyle of the Shasu.

6. Finally, the narratives in the book of Numbers are reliable, and they confirm the fact that the earliest Israelites were pastoral nomads already in the process of being sedentarized in Transjordan before entry into the land of Canaan.

Let us examine the archaeological evidence that might support these claims.

(1) The Merenptah inscription does not contain the usual Egyptian itineraries in Canaan. The listing of Ashkelon and Gezer, however, is realistic, so the location of Yenoam, although not precisely identified, should be farther north. But other, far more reliable Egyptian itineraries, such as those of Thutmose III and Seti I, list Megiddo and/or Beth-Shean as the major objectives to the north. The Merenptah inscription's two identifiable sites, plus one not easily identified, followed by a summary that mentions an "Israelite people" not specified geographically, is hardly an itinerary usable for historical purpose. Furthermore, the archaeological evidence shows that the stela is propaganda: Ashkelon and Gezer were not destroyed circa 1208, and neither were Merenptah's Israelites. A straightforward reading of the Victory Stela would suggest not only that it is fiction but that the Egyptians never actually encountered the "Israelite peoples." They should be sought where the Egyptians did not claim to have gone, in Cisjordan, precisely where the dozens of early Iron I archaeological settlements that we have are found. Whatever its fictional character and its lack of geographical precision, the Merenptah inscription does attest to the existence of some Israel somewhere in Canaan but not in Transjordan.

(2) The pottery cited by Rainey all comes from urban sites in northern and central Transjordan, as noted. But the Egyptian texts portray the Shasu as pastoral nomads, not sedentarized even by Egyptian force, and located mostly in southern Transjordan (Edom). How can one suppose that they were the carriers of the ceramic and cultural conditions in question? Pots do not move of themselves; people do. Rainey concludes that Yenoam "has to be in Bashan or the Hauran" (northern Transjordan or the Golan Heights). As he explains, "One must look for a logical place for the Egyptian army to continue to from Yano'am for their encounter with 'Yasir'il. It comes to mind that somewhere in Transjordan would

make geographical sense."[2] Rainey makes several unwarranted assumptions in this argument, as well as in his subsequent attempt to derive the Israelites from Transjordan. These assumptions must be analyzed in some detail. Whoever reconstructs a pattern of ethnic movements and cultural transmission must explain a source, a route, and a motive. Simply positing "pastoral nomads in process of sedentarization," Shasu or otherwise, is not evidence.

As for Rainey's notion that the early Iron I sedentary villages in Cisjordan reflect such changes as those above, the archaeological data totally contradict that as an explanation. The material culture there attests a people long familiar with the local environment, pottery, building techniques, and general cultural traditions. Even Rainey (elsewhere) agrees that "the continuation of the Canaanites can be seen in pottery tradition, small artifacts and settlement planning and location."[3]

Rainey's conclusion from his treatment of the Transjordanian data is that this is where the immediate ancestors of the early Israelites had dwelt. And without explaining the connection, he argues that the inhabitants in question must be the well-known Shasu of Egyptian Nineteenth Dynasty texts. We have summarized the data in chapter 2. The Shasu are consistently portrayed as pastoral nomads living in tents and herding flocks, located mainly in "Shasu land" in "Mount Seir," almost certainly Edom. They are marauders threatening the trade routes, scarcely controlled in their movements but sometimes penetrating the Delta and allowed to pass. It is significant here that the Shasu show no sign of being inhabitants of Cisjordan, and there is no evidence that the Egyptians attempted to settle them there or anywhere else, for that matter.

In a thorough review of all the Egyptian evidence, Hasel has shown that the Shasu of Ramesses II and Merenptah stand in sharp contrast. (1) The names are distinct and do not overlap. (2) They occupy different regions, the Israelites in the land of Hurru and the Shasu in Mount Seir/ Edom. (3) The subsistence and economy of the two peoples differs, one pastoral nomadic, the other a settled people.[4]

Finally, Rainey thinks that the book of Numbers confirms the picture of the earliest Israelites as sedentarized nomads in Transjordan. As evidence for these people having been sedentarized pastoralists in Transjordan in the Late Bronze Age, Rainey cites passages such as Gen 46:34; 47:3–4; Num 20:19; 32:1, 37–38; and Judg 11:2. It is worth looking at several of these passages.

Gen 46:34: The patriarchs are to tell the pharaoh that they are shepherds in the land of Goshen, specifically to confound the settled Egyptians.

Gen 47:3–4: They do as they are instructed.

Num 20:19: The children of Israel during the later exodus pass Edom to water their cattle but promise to journey on.

Num 32:1, 37–38: The tribe of Reuben had cattle and asked Moses to allow them to remain in Gilead because there was good pasture land there. Moses objected but later gave in.

These are all the biblical passages Rainey cites in defense of his pastoral nomadic origins. The first two deal with the patriarchal era centuries earlier (our Middle Bronze Age?) and have nothing to do with the Late Bronze Age backgrounds of the settlement horizon in the thirteenth–twelfth century. Furthermore, this is obvious rationalization: in the larger picture in Genesis, the patriarchs are slaves, not free herdsmen.

The passages in Numbers portray the Israelite tribes as resisting sedentarization or occasionally trying to rationalize it, against Moses's objections: this is not the ideal. Everywhere else in Numbers, the Israelites are consistently described as transients on the way to their real objective: the conquest of the land west of the Jordan. Again and again on their journeys through Transjordan, the Israelites are said to have "camped," "pitched their tents," and then moved on (Num 4–6). The verb here is *nûaḥ*, which means essentially to "rest, lie down," that is, to pause. Other terms, such as *yāšab*, "to dwell" (or *gēr*, "resident alien"), are rarely used to describe the Israelites in the dozens of references. The overall portrait of the Israelites in Numbers is not that of a settled people or even of pastoral nomads at any stage but rather of transients moving through a hostile land. (The local Shasu pastoralist will be treated below.)

Finally, Rainey's reading of the biblical texts, even if it were warranted, begs the question of historicity, of the reliability of the sources here. We have already shown that of the many Transjordanian sites said in Numbers to have been taken by the Israelites, only Dibon and Heshbon have been positively identified and excavated—and at both sites that "destruction" is proven by the archaeological evidence to be fictitious. To be sure, these are only two sites, but it is still 100 percent. If the book of Numbers is unreliable in this case, the burden of proof is on anyone who takes it to be trustworthy in other instances.

Rainey's preoccupation with Transjordanian pastoral nomads as Proto-Israelites recalls the peaceful infiltration model of Alt and Noth in the 1930s, whose territorial history approach not coincidentally inspired Rainey's later historical geography approach. These scholars take exactly the opposite approach of the one followed here. They start with the biblical text, then look for a geographical setting that might make it plausible. Our approach, to the contrary, is to start with the archaeological data—much closer to the events in question in time and context—and only then to look at the text to see what anthropologists call "the goodness of fit."

In Rainey's adaptation of the geographical model, if it *could have* happened, it *did*. For example, he argues that the biblical accounts of the conquest of Jericho and Ai reveal such an intimate, "amazing" knowledge of the topography that these stories must have originated in the twelfth century. He even draws a detailed map of these "events," showing the Israelite advance from Gilgal to Bethel as though its occurrence were beyond doubt. Yet he never mentions the well-known archaeological evidence that destructions at Jericho and Ai cannot possibly have taken place circa 1200: both sites had long been abandoned and were unoccupied at the time.[5]

Likewise, Rainey maps the Israelite route through Dibon and Heshbon, despite the fact that these sites, too, were uninhabited in the thirteenth century (as we now know), when the Hebrew Bible claims that Israelite conquests had taken place (Num 21:25–26, 30; 32:3; Deut 2:26–37; 3:6; Josh 13:26–27). Again, Rainey makes no mention of the negative archaeological data, well known. All this goes to show how even a good scholar can be led astray by an *idée fixe*.

Notes

1. See Rainey 2007, 2008a, 2008b. See the rebuttal in Dever 2011. See n. 2 below.

2. Rainey 2006, 99.

3. Rainey 2006, 125.

4. Hasel 1998, 217–39. See also chapter 2 and n. 53. Redford had also posited that early Israel originated from Shasu migrations, but he wrote before the emergence of the mass of evidence we now have (1992, 275–80).

5. Finkelstein 1988, 191; 1992, 64.

EXCURSUS 3.2

Finkelstein's "Sedentarized Pastoralists"

In 1988 Finkelstein had listed only fourteen sites in his desert fringe out of a total of 115. That amounts to only 12 percent, not "75–90 percent." The pottery of these fourteen survey sites consists of worn sherds, mostly diagnostic (as he himself says elsewhere). Four of the fourteen sites have one clear twelfth-century cooking pot each of a type familiar at Shiloh and Giloh (above). The remainder of the pottery consists largely of store-jar rims, which Finkelstein acknowledges cannot be separated into twelfth- and eleventh-century phases. His "two waves of pastoral nomads, from west to east," rests on four sherds at four sites.

A final point on the locations of some of the individual desert-fringe sites. Two photographs of Khirbet Yanun—one of the four sites where there is evidence of some twelfth-century occupation—show clearly that this is a hilltop site, that it has terrace systems all around, and that it overlooks a fertile valley. It hardly seems accurate to describe it as "desert fringe." Only Khirbet er-Raḥaya and esh-Sheikh Mazar appear to be situated at the head of a deep decline leading down to the steppe zone. One of Finkelstein's general Iron I sites, Khirbet el-Marjameh, was partially excavated in the 1970s by Mazar. Marjameh is situated on a hilltop some 18 miles north of Jerusalem, just east of the main road to Shechem (above). To call Marjameh a "desert fringe" site is misleading. It is rather typical of many central-ridge sites, with heavily terraced hillsides, located near a major spring, and adjacent to a fertile valley. Furthermore, this 10-acre site, heavily fortified, was dated to the monarchy by Mazar (ca. tenth century on), and he reports no Iron I remains at all.[1]

Finkelstein's other argument for south Samaria rests on the contentions (1) that the oval or circular plan of several early settlements reflects the socioeconomic and cultural background of bedouin tents drawn up in a circle and (2) that the individual pillar-courtyard or four-room house derives from the typical bedouin-like tent of pastoral nomads. Here the arguments are not only speculative; they are without any foundation.[2]

First, the oval or circular plan results not from a town wall girdling the site but rather from houses built side by side so as to form a sort of enclosed perimeter. Typical examples that Finkelstein cites are Beersheba and ʿIzbet Ṣarṭah III (plus, it seems, some of the hilltop villages found in the Israeli surveys). However, the Beersheba that Finkelstein cites is the village of Stratum VII, which dates to the late eleventh or early tenth century. The late twelfth-century–early eleventh-century level at Beersheba, the earliest occupation, would be Stratum IX, of which only storage pits and cisterns were found, and no plan could be discerned.

As for Finkelstein's own site of ʿIzbet Ṣarṭah, which is indeed of crucial importance, we have already noted several objections to his interpretation. The plan published of Stratum III is largely conjectural and consists of only parts of some half-dozen adjacent structures (out of a projected twenty-four or so), of which some walls curve slightly. Finkelstein claimed that 40 percent of the "peripheral wall" was uncovered. One can easily see by looking at Finkelstein's plan that that is not so. The other reason why it is doubtful that ʿIzbet Ṣarṭah was a pastoral encampment is staff member Baruch Rosen's calculation from the zoological and botanical remains that the site produced a substantial agricultural surplus—unlikely for pastoral nomads. In fact, in the earliest stratum, Stratum III, cattle bones constituted 43 percent of the total, and the number *decreased* by Stratum II to 23 percent. Neither of these pieces of evidence looks like "nomads settling down." As Rosen concluded of the economy: "To sum up, the economic system of ʿIzbet-Sartah is typical of a *sedentary* settlement based on agriculture and animal breeding." One must add the paper by one of Finkelstein's own field supervisors, Zvi Lederman, entitled "Nomads They Never Were."[3]

The third site that Finkelstein adduces to support his nomad theory is Tel Esdar, a site in the Negev 12 miles southeast of Beersheba, discussed above. Kochavi excavated it in 1963–1964. The plan of Stratum III does show part of what seems to be an oval-shaped settlement, but Esdar III is best dated to the late eleventh or even the early tenth century. Finkelstein considered it an Israelite site in 1988, describing it as being less than an acre in size, thus fitting his criterion of small. However, Moshe Kochavi, the excavator, says that Tel Esdar was a 5-acre site.[4]

Notes

1. See Finkelstein, Lederman, and Bunimovitz 1997, 330–31, 782. See the discussion of Dever 2003d, 158–61.

2. Finkelstein 1988, 254–59.

3. B. Rosen 1986, 151, emphasis added. See also Lederman 1992.

4. Finkelstein 1988, 58; Kochavi 1969, 2.

CHAPTER 4

The Rise of Territorial States: The Tenth Century

Introduction

The tenth century, traditionally the Iron IIA period, saw sweeping changes in southern Canaan, on both sides of the Jordan. In Transjordan, more marginal tribal states were slow in developing and did not really flourish before the eighth or even the seventh century. In Cisjordan, however, a trajectory toward more centralized forms of social and political organization had already begun in the Iron I period (twelfth–eleventh century). By the early to mid-tenth century, the movement had gathered momentum, at least in the south, in Judah. In the following we will trace this development, distinguishing north from south, and once again taking the archaeological evidence rather than the biblical texts as the primary data.

Two problems in recent scholarly discussion will detain us briefly. First, the discussion of the rise of territorial states in both the north and the south has been hindered by the failure of most scholars to develop criteria for *defining* what we mean by the term *state*. What constitutes a state in the wider literature, particularly in anthropological and ethnographic theories, in what is called state formation processes? Second, the issue of *chronology* has become paramount. Chronology is the backbone of history: if we cannot date events with some precision, we cannot document change, and therefore we cannot write history. For the Iron II period, the advent of the so-called low chronology in the 1990s has posed a severe challenge for both archaeologists and biblical historians. To put the issue succinctly, are the conventional archaeological hallmarks of the Solomonic era—the biblical united monarchy—still to be dated to the tenth century, or are they to be down-dated to the ninth century, the age of

Ahab? If the latter date can be proven, there is no more "age of Solomon." Let us therefore turn to the issue of the chronology of the tenth century, the Iron IIA era of most archaeologists.

The Tenth Century: Chronology and Terminology

Until the mid-1990s, the chronology of the Iron I–IIA horizon was subject to some differences of opinion, although none very radical. The American or Albright–Wright scheme was as follows:

Iron IA: 1200–1150
Iron IB: 1150–1000
Iron IC: 1000–918/900
Iron IIA–B: 900–700

Israeli archaeologists differed principally in their date for the beginning of Iron IIA, seeing it as earlier and marking the rise of the Israelite monarchy:

Iron IA: 1220–1150
Iron IB: 1150–1000
Iron IIA: 1000–925
Iron IIB: 925–720
Iron IIC: 720–586

The latter is the scheme adopted here, not because it is more "biblical" but because it suits the current archaeological data and phasing better.

By the 1990s, there was more dissent. The most radical revision put forward was the so-called low chronology of Finkelstein (there is no "high") and a few of his colleagues and students. The principal result was to move the Iron I–IIA transition down almost one hundred years and incidentally (?) to rob the biblical united monarchy of all its archaeological correlates. The reasons for the differences between the traditional scheme and that of Finkelstein and others are complex, but the contrasts can be presented in simplified form as follows.[1]

Fig. 4.1. Alternative schemes for Iron I–II chronology and terminology

	Iron IA	Iron IB	Iron IIA	Iron IIB
	1100	1000	Shoshenq 925/900	Arameans 800
Model				
conventional	Iron I		IIA	IIB
modified conventional	Iron I		Iron IIA	Iron IIB
A. Mazar		980	830	
Herzog/Singer-Avitz	Iron I		Iron IIA	Iron IIB
Finkelstein		950	800	
Sharon et al.	Iron I		Iron IIA	Iron IIB
Bunimovitz/ Lederman	Iron I		Iron IIA	Iron IIB

We need not get bogged down in the details of this controversy, which has become heated. But before proceeding to write any history of the eleventh–tenth century, we do need to justify the chronology and terminology to be used here. That entails deconstructing the low chronology, after which we shall cite it only occasionally, and only for balance. It will be dismissed mostly as simply a contrarian argument (see further excursus 4.1).

Finkelstein's idiosyncratic low chronology rests on several assertions, all of which have little or no basis in fact. There are several arguments, some of them developed sequentially since the mid-1990s.

(1) The initial argument was one from silence: the absence of Late Mycenaean IIIC:1 monochrome pottery from Lachish V after its destruction in the late thirteenth century. Therefore, it was argued, such Philistine wares must have appeared only later.

(2) When Finkelstein's colleague Ussishkin began excavating Jezreel in 1996, it appeared that the Iron Age ninth-century pottery was very similar to that of Megiddo VA/IVB, formerly dated to the tenth century (i.e., Solomonic). And since Jezreel was known from the biblical narratives to have been a winter retreat for Ahab (1 Kgs 18:45), the date of Megiddo VA/IV should be moved down into the ninth century, almost a century lower.

(3) Finkelstein and his student Norma Franklin then argued that the ashlar masonry of Megiddo VA/IVB was similar to that of Building Period

I at Samaria, using the same Egyptian short cubit. Since Samaria was established only in the ninth century by Ahab (another biblical datum), both masonry styles must be dated only then.

(4) As the discussion continued, Finkelstein came to rely more and more on C-14 dating, which he argued supported only his low chronology.[2]

Finkelstein then proceeded systematically to rework the stratigraphy of site after site (even in Transjordan) to fit his low chronology. Since the widespread notion of an Israelite united monarchy in the tenth century (the age of Solomon) was now threatened, the debate spread to biblical scholarship. It even made headlines in Europe and America.

Finkelstein's idiosyncratic low chronology has had a considerable effect, despite the fact that it has recruited few adherents among mainstream archaeologists. Revisionist biblical scholars (and a few other doctrinaire skeptics) adopted it readily for obvious reasons, even though it was not nearly radical enough for them (ch. 1).

Yet upon closer scrutiny, there is almost no empirical evidence in support of Finkelstein's drastic reduction of Iron Age dates, as critics have pointed out again and again. Finkelstein, however, has largely ignored critics (except for his bête noire Mazar) and has pursued his agenda with remarkable persistence, turning out a seemingly endless stream of publications. The result has been a fierce, prolonged controversy among archaeologists and confusion among nonspecialists. Here, however, we shall summarize the reasons why the low chronology is unacceptable and then move on.[3]

Finkelstein's argument regarding Lachish VI is obviously one from silence, and like all such arguments it can be dismissed. Philistine monochrome ware does not appear there, early or late, simply because the Philistines did not penetrate that far inland. As many critics pointed out, we are dealing not with chronological separation but with cultural separation. For instance, Tel Miqne VII (Ekron) has produced vast quantities of Philistine monochrome pottery, while contemporary Stratum XIII at Gezer—7 miles away as the crow flies—has not produced a single sherd in twenty seasons of excavations.[4]

As for Finkelstein's assertion that sites contemporary with the Egyptian Twentieth Dynasty (1186–1069) have not produced Philistine monochrome ware, that is simply not true. Several Philistine sites exhibit this pottery in the early years of the reign of Ramesses III (1184–1153 or 1195–1164; ch. 3). Among them are Ashdod XIII, Ashkelon 20, and Ekron VII.

Critics of Finkelstein's use of Jezreel as a ninth-century peg on which to hang his low chronology have noted that, having become an outspoken opponent of "biblical archaeology," Finkelstein does not hesitate to appeal to biblical sites such as Jezreel and Samaria. More seriously, it has long since been shown that the pottery of the mid- to late tenth century at well-stratified sites is so similar to that of the early to mid-ninth century that fine-grained chronological distinctions cannot be convincingly made.[5]

That fact is especially important when comparing the northern ceramic sequence with that of Judah to the south, where cultural evolution is relatively slower. But even there, the excavations at Lachish, directed by Finkelstein's colleague Ussishkin, have demonstrated the tenth–ninth-century ceramic continuity. As for similarities in ashlar masonry at Jezreel and Samaria, that means little or nothing. Such ashlar masonry can be found earlier and certainly at much later sites.[6]

The debate over C-14 dates continues, with hundreds of articles and several international symposia devoted to the subject. Some dates appear to support Finkelstein's low chronology at Megiddo; others support Mazar's conventional (or better, modified) chronology at nearby Tel Reḥov. A joint project of archaeologists and scientists at the Weitzman Institute in Rehovot is analyzing hundreds of samples from dozens of sites, but so far the results are provisional. Meanwhile, the differences on the crucial Iron I–IIA transition have narrowed a bit, down to forty to fifty years.[7]

All authorities agree that future C-14 dates are not likely to resolve the issue completely, due to factors of uncertainty built into the method itself. It is noteworthy that the conventional or modified chronology is and always has been mainstream, despite the distractions. It is the chronology that will be adopted here, with no further defense. At best the low chronology is possible; it is not probable by any criteria, and it is certainly not proven. History cannot be written on the basis of possibilities.[8]

The Archaeological Setting for the Iron I–IIA Transition

No matter which chronology and terminology is adopted, the period from the late eleventh into the early ninth century marks a major transition, like that of the thirteenth–twelfth century. Once again, the archaeological evidence reflects the movements of several ethnic groups and concomitant changes in material culture.

The End of the Canaanite Culture

By the late eleventh century and the transition to the Iron IIA period, the last of the Canaanite city-states in the north were coming to an end. Megiddo VIA, an impressive city, ends in an enormous conflagration circa 1000 BCE. The destruction has traditionally been attributed to King David, but the low chronology (above) would place it later, attributing it to the raid of Shoshenq circa 920. Still, an earthquake cannot be ruled out.[9]

At Beth-Shean, another Jezreel Valley site where Canaanite culture persisted well into the Iron Age, Stratum VI of the Iron IB period ends. By the tenth century, Stratum V upper (= current S1) represents an Israelite town that lasts, according to the excavator, until the Shoshenq destruction (below). However, the "Israelite" character is not altogether clear.

At Tel Reḥov, near Beth-Shean, Stratum VI and the Canaanite city end circa 980, followed in the tenth century by Stratum V. Here again, however, the material culture of Reḥov in the tenth century is not typical in many ways of the more decidedly Israelite sites elsewhere.

The Expansion of Philistine Territory

The Philistine settlements along the Levantine coast in Iron I have already been noted in chapter 2. By the Iron IB period, in the eleventh century, the Philistines had consolidated their foothold, and by the early to mid-tenth century (Iron IIA here) they had expanded into the Shephelah and were approaching the natural border of Judah in the Shephelah, or low foothills. By now, border towns such as Gezer, Tel Batash, Beth-Shemesh, Tel Zayit, and even Tell Beit Mirsim had been influenced by Philistine culture, as Philistine bichrome pottery shows. The approximate border is shown in figure 4.2, although, to be sure, the ethnic boundary was in flux.

In spite of assumed Philistine expansion in the tenth century, a number of Philistine sites show evidence of prior destructions sometime in the late eleventh century. Among them would be Ashdod XI, Ekron IVB, and Tell Qasile X. Phoenician sites as well had undergone disturbances in the late eleventh century, among them Tell Keisan 9 and Tell Abu-Hawam IVB. The causes of these destructions are not clear, although earlier scholars had attributed some of them to the campaigns of Saul or David (below).

Fig. 4.2. Map of tenth-century sites, distinguishing ethnic groups (map by Giselle Hasel)

Fig. 4.3. Canaanite, peripheral Philistine, and putative early Israel sites, Iron I–IIA (° = continuing Canaanite site; ▪ = Egyptian residency)

LBII	Iron IA	Iron IB	Iron IIA	Iron IIB
1200	(1150)	1100	1000	925–900
	Twentieth Dynasty	Twenty-First Dynasty ——————————————→		
VI——→	gap Dan VB°	VA° IVB°	IVA° ————————→	III
XIII——→	gap	Hazor XII–XI°	X IX————→	VIII–V
		Tel Ḥarashim III	II?	——
——	Tel Kinrot VI°	V°	IV————————→	III
VI lower▪→	Beth-Shean VI°▪ lower (= S3)	VI upper° (= S2)	V lower (= S1)	V upper?
		Tel Reḥov VII	VI V——→	IV
VIIB————→	Megiddo° VIIA VIB	VIA° ————————→	→VIB VA/IVB→	IVA
			Tel ʿAmal IV–III	II
VI_b——	→Tell el-Farʿah° VII_a ————	————————————→	VII_b ————————→	VII_{c-d}
gap	Yoqneʿam XVIII°A–B	XVII°	XVI XV XIV	XIII–XII
	Tel Qiri IX°	VIII°	VIIA ————————→	VIIB–C
	IA Taʿanach IB ————	———→ gap	IIA–B————————→	III–IV
XII ————→	Shechem XI	gap X	Samaria PPI–II	III
——————	Aphek X_{12}°▪	X_{11} X_{10}	X_9 X_8	
			Tel el-Hammah L	
XIV	Gezer XIIII°–XII°	XI°	X IX VIII	VII
←———	ʿIzbet Ṣarṭah III	II	I ——	
gap	Shiloh V	gap	town (?)	
	Bethel —————————	——→ ?		
	Ai —————————————	——→ ?		
	Khirbet Raddana ————	——→ ?		

LBII	Iron IA	Iron IB	Iron IIA	Iron IIB
1200	(1150)	1100	1000	925–900
	Twentieth Dynasty	Twenty-First Dynasty		
	Giloh ——————→ ? ←——————— Khirbet ed-Dawwara			
		←———— Tell el-Ful I II —→ gap		
		Khirbet Qeiyafa IV ————————→		
VII■	Tel Mor VI■ V	IV		
		15	Jerusalem 14	13
7?	Beth-Shemesh 6	5 ——————————→ 4 3 —→		
VI	Tel Batash V	gap?	IVA–B	III
Lachish VI ——→ gap		gap	gap V ——→IVA	
←——— Tell el-Ḥesi "IV"		?	?	VIId
C	Tell Beit Mirsim B_1	B_2	B_3	A_1
IX■ ——→Tel Seraʿ VIII ■ ——			——→ VI–VII	VI
7	6, 5 Tel Haror	4 3 2		
	VIIIA VIIIB	Tel Ḥalif VIIA	VID	VIC–B
Citadel■	Tell Jemmeh J–K	G–H	E–F	C–D
	IX	Beersheba VIII	VII VI V	IV
Citadel YR■	Tel el-Farʿah (South)	(Cemetery 500) X—→	Tel Malḥata C	
IIIB←	—Tel Masos IIIA	II	I?	
	?←——— Tell Esdar III		gap? II	
Deir al-Balaḥ VII° VI V IV			Arad XII ————————→	XI
			Negev forts ———————→	
			Tell el-Kheleifeh I?	3
			Kadesh-barnea 4	3

In any case, the general turbulence of the mid- to late eleventh century is clear, both along the coast and even to some degree inland. The question is whether these disturbances were part of the process of acculturation, the early phases of which we discussed in chapter 3. One possible clue may lie in the degenerate Philistine monochrome ware (Ashdod, or better, Late Philistine Decorated Ware) that characterizes most of the Philistine levels noted here (below).

By the tenth century, sites along the coast can be listed as follows.[10]

Fig. 4.4. Coastal sites of the tenth century

Phoenician sites in the north

Achzib	Shiqmona A
Akko	Dor A/10, G/6
Tell Keisan 8 c–a	Tel Mevorakh VII
Tell Abu Hawam IIIB–A	Tel Mikhmoret (?)
Rosh Zayit IIB–A	Tel Zeror (?)

Yarkon/Sharon plain: Phoenician/Philistine (?)

Makmish	Gerisa 4
Tel Poleg	Aphek X_8
Tel Michal XIV–XIII	Azor

Philistine sites in the south

Tell Qasile IX–VIII	Gath 5
Villages along the Sharon plain	Tel Seraʿ VII
Ashdod XI–IX	Tell Jemmeh E–F
Ekron III	Tell el-Farʿah South A, Cemetery 200

There are further disruptions in the early tenth century, but only two sites appear to have been destroyed at that time: Ashdod X and Ekron IVA. The agents are unknown in both cases, but some authorities hold that by the tenth century the Philistines were weakened and in danger of being overwhelmed by their neighbors: Phoenicia to the north and Judah to the east. Some have attributed these destructions to David (below).

Sites such as Akko, Tell Keisan 8c–a, Tell Abu Hawam IVA, and perhaps Shiqmona to the north and Dor G/6, which had reflected a mixture of Phoenician and Philistine cultural traits, have become entirely Phoenician by the tenth century. Some scholars, however, think that Dor may have become Israelite by the end of that century.[11]

Despite setbacks, the distinctive Philistine culture to the south is still evident, although there are changes that suggest a degree of acculturation. The classic bichrome pottery gives way to a degenerate hybrid repertoire, which is characterized by black painted geometric designs over a thin red wash (Ashdod ware, or LPDW). Gradually an Iron II "coastal repertoire" emerges, combining red-washed/slipped wares and adaptations of inland Judahite styles. In time, the Iron II Philistines will come to adopt the Phoenician script as well as aspects of the Canaanite-Israelite cult (ch. 5).

Even if they were beginning to be acculturated (not assimilated), the Philistines probably posed a considerable threat to Judah. The population of Ekron may have been as large as 5,000, of Ashkelon 5,000, of Ashdod 10,000. Estimates of the total population of the pentapolis alone run as high as 25,000 in the twelfth–eleventh century and perhaps 50,000 by the early tenth century.[12]

By contrast, Judah had a population probably much smaller, perhaps only 25,000. Furthermore, Judah's population and resources were stretched thin, and it had no political organization. The Philistine enclave, while relatively smaller, was concentrated and rich in resources, and it was organized like a palace economy around a few large city-states. In head-on confrontations, the Philistines would appear to have had the advantage (below).

The Aramean Border

We have already noted in chapter 3 the growth of Aramean sites in the formative Iron I period, alongside early Phoenician and Israelite sites, as all their territorial claims grew.

Tel Hadar, a site of 2–3 acres on the northeastern shore of the Sea of Galilee, was excavated by Kochavi in 1987. Stratum IV may have ended in an earthquake circa 1000. Stratum II features a double concentric defensive system of the tenth century, inside of which is a type of triple-colonnaded building found later at Israelite sites and thought to be a storage facility, in this case for grain. Stratum II was completely destroyed, apparently sometime in the tenth century, then abandoned for several centuries. It may have been related to a district Aramean center at 'Ein-Gev, 4 miles to the north.[13]

At the northern end of the Sea of Galilee, Bethsaida (et-Tell) is a 20-acre mound near the shore of the Jordan River where it enters the sea. Stratum 6a–b represents the founding of the city in the tenth century, which boasts heavy city walls, a monumental gate, a *bit hilani*–style palace, and granaries. It seems to have been the capital of the kingdom of Geshur in Transjordan, destroyed violently in the ninth century.[14]

'Ein-Gev is a small, low mound right on the eastern shore of the Sea of Galilee, excavated off and on in 1963–1968. Stratum 5 is the earliest settlement, probably founded in the early tenth century, followed by a casemate-walled town in Stratum 4. Few domestic dwellings could be planned. 'Ein-Gev was presumably related to Bethsaida, Tel Hadar, and other Aramean towns farther north.[15]

The Abandonment of Hill-Country Sites in the Eleventh Century

A number of twelfth- and eleventh-century sites surveyed above have been regarded as early Israelite settlements. Those most readily identified as ethnically Israelite are in the central hill country stretching from the Jezreel Valley in the north to the Beersheba Valley in the south. This is the area that later will become the heartland of the Israelite and Judahite states.

A look at figure 4.3 above will show that nearly all of these villages came to an end between circa 1100 and 1000, many showing a gap or abandonment thereafter. That includes Ta'anach IB, Shiloh V, Bethel, 'Izbet Ṣarṭah II, Khirbet Radanna, Tel el-Ful I, Giloh, Tel Masos II, Tel Malḥata C (?), and Tel Esdar III. Of these sites, only Bethel, Shiloh, and perhaps Tel Masos were reoccupied circa 1000–900, in all cases after a gap of a half-century or so, when urbanization first occurs.

In the General Systems Theory approach taken here, such a major shift in settlement type and distribution cannot fail to have significance, especially since there is no clear evidence of major ethnic movements. What happened was clearly a wholesale shift of population away from the rural areas, where many smaller settlements were simply abandoned. In no case do we see any signs of destructions or even disturbances due to other causes.

The phenomenon of the abandonment of so many rural settlements has been analyzed in detail by only a few archaeologists, notably Faust. He shows that such a widespread phenomenon can best be understood in the light of two factors: the relatively rapid urbanization that characterized the late eleventh–tenth century, especially in the hill country; and the rise of the Israelite/Judahite monarchy that is surely related, not an incidental development.[16]

Faust's view of state-formation processes will be discussed presently, along with other theories. The point here, however, is that such a major change in population, as well as in settlement type, political, socioeconomic, and cultural organization, cannot be ignored. Nor can the change be explained away by using the low chronology to manipulate stratigraphy.

Israelite Urban Sites

The general shift from rural to urban sites during the course of the tenth century is obvious. To document how sweeping that change was, we need to look at a number of sites in detail, first some major sites where urbanization was dramatic (in geographical order). Population estimates assume that not all the area was built up.

Fig. 4.5. Tier 1–6 Israelite sites, tenth century (Iron IIA here)

Site, Stratum	Acres	Population (est.)
Tier 1: Capitals		
Jerusalem 14	5–10?	1,000
Tier 2: Administrative Centers		
Hazor XBA–IX	8–15	1,000
Megiddo VA/IVB	15	1,000
Gezer IX–VIII	33	2,500
Beth-Shemesh IIA (= 4)	10	800
Tier 3: Cities (10 acres and up)		
Dan IVA	10–20?	1,000
Ta'anach IIA–B	11	300
Beth-Shean V lower–upper	10	800
Tell el-Far'ah VIIb	15	1,000
Samaria PI–II	?	?
Shechem X	15	1,000

Tier 4: Towns (3–10 acres)

Yoqne'am XVI–XIV	10	800
Bethel	4	200
Gibeon	5	300
Tel Ḥamid	10?	300
Tel Batash IV	7	400
Tel Ḥarashim II	10?	400
Tel Zayit III	7.5	400
Beth-zur	4	200
Lachish V	8–10?	300
Tell el-Ḥesi VIId	3	200
Tell Beit Mirsim B₃	7.5	400
Tel Ḥalif VIB	3	200
Tel Sera' VII	4	200
Beersheba VI–V	3	200
Arad XII	?	100
Tel 'Ira VIII	6	300
Malḥata C	4	200

Tier 5: Villages (1–3 acres)

Tel Qiri VIIA	2–3
Tel 'Amal IV–III	1
Tell el-Hammah	1

Tier 6: Forts

Tell el-Ful II	50
Khirbet ed-Dawwara	100
Khirbet Qeiyafa IV	100?
Negev forts	100?
Kadesh-barnea 4	100?

Population estimates will be lower than for the ninth–eighth century (ch. 5), since it is presumed that the initial occupation was relatively small-scale. Tier 5 villages are too poorly known to list. Many of these sites were Canaanite in the twelfth–eleventh century but became Israelite by the tenth century (Philistine, Phoenician, and Aramean sites are not included here; see below). In this and following syntheses we shall employ a multitier settlement hierarchy, based largely on size and type (refer back to fig. 4.5).

Excavated Israelite/Judahite Sites in Geographical Order

Dan. A large tell on the Syrian border, Dan remained a Canaanite site in terms of material culture until the tenth century. Stratum IVB was destroyed around 1000 in what may have been an earthquake. Stratum IVA then represents a more intensive settlement, suggesting a more industrialized city, with a substantial iron production and a managed economy that included trade. The town was now apparently defended by a city wall. One of the excavators attributes these developments to the consolidation of Dan as a "new territorial state." Tel Dan may have become "a town in which the nuclear family became the most common household unit," reflecting, however, a more dense urban environment.[17]

Beth-Shean. Stratum VI lower and upper (S3–2) represent an Iron I Canaanite city under Egyptian rule in the twelfth century, destroyed in the late twelfth century, then again circa 1000 (earthquake?). Stratum V lower (= S1b) appears to be an Israelite town of some 10 acres with several monumental buildings, possibly evidence of a tenth-century Israelite district center. This town comes to an end circa 920, probably in the Shoshenq destruction.

Hazor. Stratum XB–A represents a new, heavily fortified upper city of the mid-tenth century established after a long gap during most of the twelfth–eleventh century, when a sort of squatter occupation was evident. The city now boasts a casemate city wall and a monumental four-entryway gate featuring ashlar masonry (fig. 4.6). Hazor's position is so commanding that it earns its reputation as "the head of all those kingdoms." Stratum IX is then destroyed in the late tenth century, probably by Shoshenq (below).[18]

Megiddo. Stratum VA/IVB is a composite stratum designating the work of both the Chicago and the Israeli excavators, founded in the early to mid-tenth century. This stratum succeeds the massive destruction of the Stratum VIA city and ephemeral Stratum B and is characterized by an altogether new, planned city. In this city we have a monumental four-entryway city gate and casemate wall, multiroomed Palaces 1723 and 6000, several administrative buildings and houses constructed of ashlar masonry, a number of Proto-Aeolic capitals, and cult-corners (fig. 4.7).

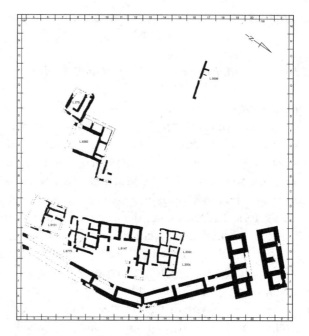

Fig. 4.6. Plan of Hazor, Stratum Xa (Ben-Tor, Ben-Ami, and Sandhaus 2012, plan 2-8)

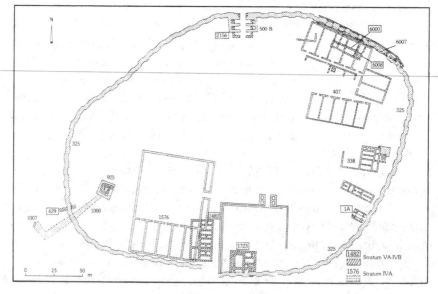

Fig. 4.7. Plan of Megiddo, Stratum VA/IVB (Stern 1993, 1016)

The city covers about 15 acres, but much of the area within the city walls was probably taken up by public buildings. Thus the population may have been only a few hundred, most of them elites and civil servants and their families. By any criteria, Megiddo VA/IVB is a royal city (although the so-called Solomonic stables are later; see ch. 5). Its superb location astride the Via Maris where it debouches onto the Jezreel Valley gives it the best strategic control of any site in the north of the country.

Taʿanach. Stratum IIA–B belongs to the tenth century. It is an 11-acre city, like Megiddo 6 miles to the northwest, overlooking the Jezreel Valley. Neither the German nor the American excavations of Lapp (1963–1968) have been fully published, but Taʿanach IIA–B seems to represent the growth of a small eleventh-century town into a regional center by the tenth century. Of particular interest is an extensive cultic installation that gives us perhaps our best evidence of religious practices early in the monarchy (below).

Tell el-Farʿah North. The town of Tell el-Farʿah North, biblical Tirzah, the capital of the northern kingdom for a time, was rebuilt in Stratum VIIb in the late tenth century along the lines of its predecessor. It was characterized now by pillar-courtyard (or four-room) houses that we have already seen in many Iron I Israelite villages, but they are more developed and are often somewhat better constructed. A *naos* or temple model, often associated with the goddess Asherah (or Hathor), with parallels in Cyprus and Transjordan, was found in one of the houses. A compact group of these houses is located adjacent to an inset-offset city wall and a two-entryway gate, leaving access along the inside of the city wall (fig. 4.8). Only a small portion of the mound was excavated, but if the dozen or so houses in that area are any indication, Tell el-Farʿah could have had a population of 1,000 or more. This site, like Megiddo, was a planned Israelite urban site. It was destroyed sometime in the late tenth century, then lay abandoned for a time. While not an administrative center like Megiddo, it, too, was strategically located, at the head of the steep Wadi Farʿah leading down into the Jordan Valley, and it was well watered by the springs nearby.

Tell el-Ful. Tell el-Ful is a small prominent hilltop site some 3 miles north of Jerusalem. Both the excavations of Albright in the 1920s and of Lapp in the 1960s have identified the site with Saul's "rude fortress" of the late eleventh century at Gibeah. Stratum II represents two phases of a square building with thick walls and protruding corner tower, dated circa 1025–950. No contents were found in either dig, both salvage campaigns.

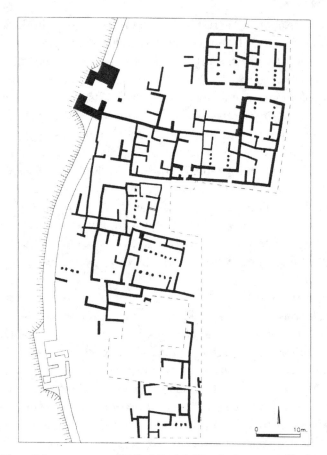

Fig. 4.8. Plan of the gate area of Tell el-Farʿah North, Stratum Vllb (Herzog 1997, fig. 9; showing the gate unblocked, contra Herzog)

But the isolated structure, so prominently situated, can hardly be other than an early fort (here tier 6).

Jerusalem. Jerusalem deserves separate attention because of its pivotal role as the capital of a putative Israelite state, but also because the archaeological evidence is so controversial that we must sort through it critically before proceeding to any discussion of state-formation processes and capitals.

There have been dozens and dozens of excavations in Jerusalem in the past 150 years, but few were modern archaeological projects, and fewer still have conducted excavations over large areas. Jerusalem is a living city, neither a museum nor simply an archaeological site.[19] Skeptics such as the biblical revisionists are fond of declaring that there is no archaeological evidence for Jerusalem as the capital of an early state. This ignores the fact that the requisite excavations on the Temple Mount have never taken place, nor will they. It also begs the question of competence: if it is the external evidence that will be decisive, as is obvious in this case, then experienced archaeologists will have to make a judgment. Where an archeological consensus is reached, historians, biblicists, and others have their work to do. That is the assumption of the discussion here.

The reasons for extraordinary controversies over the archaeology of Jerusalem are apparent. Jerusalem is unique, and it arouses unique passions. The issues are not only archaeological and historical; they are also theological, nationalistic, and, unfortunately, involve the egos of archaeologists. Nevertheless, despite the fierce differences of opinion that grab headlines, there is an identifiable consensus of opinion among archaeologists once we sideline the few extremists.

The principal archaeological evidence comes from excavations in the areas adjacent to the Dome of the Rock and the Al-Aqsa Mosque, the only areas accessible on the Temple Mount. The large-scale clearance to the south and west, conducted by Avigad and Mazar after the 1967 war, have to do mostly with the later Second Temple period. It is the excavations of Kenyon before the war and the major projects of Yigal Shiloh and other Israelis since in the City of David that concern us here.[20]

A monumental construction that has been investigated for more than a century is the "stepped stone structure" on the eastern slopes of the Ophel south of the Temple Mount. This is a massive, sloping stone rampart above the Gihon Spring in the valley. Probes have shown that it consists of a series of interlocking compartments, each with two layers of fills, capped by a rubble core and a compact stepped mantle of small stones (fig. 4.9).

This rampart was constructed, in all likelihood, to consolidate the steep slopes leading down to the Kidron Valley and to provide a platform on which to construct major buildings near the Temple Mount. In the Iron II period, a series of fine pillar-courtyard houses was built on it, the roof of each lower one providing a terrace for the next house above. The stepped stone structure continued in use as an element of Jerusalem's fortification until the Maccabean period. The question here is when it was constructed and what its original function was.

Kenyon was able to show that it was pre-Hellenistic, but in finishing her uncompleted work Shiloh's excavations in his Area G demonstrated

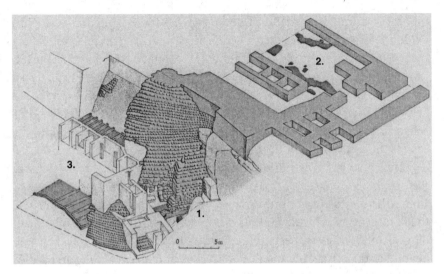

Fig. 4.9. Isometric plan. 1: stepped stone structure; 2: Citadel of David; 3: domestic houses (E. Mazar 2009, fig. 2)

that the stepped stone structure ran under the Iron II houses and was therefore earlier. Since no datable remains could be associated with the rampart's original construction or living surfaces, the date must be determined from the materials in the underlying fills. In archaeological method such materials provide a *terminus post quem*, that is, a date after which the installation in question must have been constructed. But the "after" may consist of only a brief construction phase.[21]

Proponents of the low chronology such as Finkelstein have been predisposed to declare that there was no Judahite state before the late eighth century, when we do have evidence of monumental architecture. Thus Finkelstein, Ussishkin, and Herzog have argued that the stepped stone structure, as well as Eilat Mazar's Citadel of David connected with it (below), belong to the late Iron II period or even the Persian era or later. That, however, is simply an assertion, one dictated by the low chronology's a priori views.[22]

The ceramic material is neither as extensive nor as precise as we might like. It does, however, yield evidence for several conclusions beyond a reasonable doubt. Jane Cahill, an original staff member of Shiloh's City of David project before Shiloh's untimely death, has continued to publish the Area G material. Of significance here is the pottery sealed below the stone mantel. From a corpus of several hundred sherds, Cahill has recently published a representative selection. The bulk of the material dates to the Late Bronze Age, when the Amarna letters demonstrate that Jerusalem was a major city-state. But there are clear examples of pottery, especially flanged-rim cooking pots, that have close parallels to sites elsewhere dated to the tenth century. Cahill's conclusion—the only one based on a detailed analysis of the pottery—is worth quoting.

> Analysis of the ceramic evidence in light of data currently available from other excavations demonstrates that the latest possible date for the ceramic assemblage recovered from the rampart's underlying fills is the early Iron Age I, approximately the twelfth century B.C.E. Moreover, probes cut through the stepped mantle demonstrate both that it capped and sealed the rubble core, and that the rubble core was, in at least the area probed, bonded to stone fill retained by a substructural spine wall. Consequently, the stepped mantle, the rubble core, and the interlocking substructural terraces must have been contemporary and should be identified as component parts of a single structure.[23]

Cahill concludes that the stepped stone structure was constructed in the Iron I period but was reused in the period of the biblical united monarchy, perhaps as early as the Davidic era.

Finkelstein's convoluted arguments for a ninth- to eighth-century date for the stepped stone structure are obviously arguments from silence; there is no stratified pottery from that horizon. It is possible, of course, that builders a century or two after the Iron IIA period would have left no trace whatsoever of the pottery of their era, but it is extremely unlikely, given the magnitude of the project. It is worth noting in passing not only that Finkelstein's presuppositions are drawn from his low chronology but also the fact that several of the authorities he quotes for support are biblicists whose opinions on the interpretation of complex archaeological data such as comparative ceramic analysis carry no weight.[24]

The most reasonable conclusion is that the stepped stone structure represents the "Jebusite" city of the Hebrew Bible. Although that is based on secondary sources, it does satisfy the archaeological evidence. In that case, the Millo, or "filling," credited to David, Solomon, and other kings would be a reference to an earlier monumental terraced structure visible and well known to later biblical writers (below). Such a cautious conclusion cannot be dismissed simply as old-fashioned biblical archaeology. It is in accord with an interpretation of the data that is neither minimalist nor maximalist.

More controversial is a monumental building adjoining the stepped stone structure at its northern end, excavated in 2005–2007 and interpreted by excavator Eilat Mazar as the biblical Citadel of David, which she dated to the tenth century (see fig. 4.9). This excavation continuing Benyamin Mazar's work has aroused opposition, even accusations of improper funding and motivations, yet several facts are clear. (1) This is indeed a monumental structure, just south of where a later Iron II gate complex leading to the Temple Mount has been found, including some inscriptional evidence. (2) Furthermore, the pottery known to date includes several forms that have traditionally been dated to early Iron IIA, or the tenth century. Skeptics argue that these sherds date to the ninth century. They may, in view of what we now know of ceramic continuity in the tenth–ninth century, but they are not *necessarily* later than the tenth century. Unfortunately, later robbing of this structure, and the fact that it rests largely on bedrock, preclude us from having the corpus of restorable pottery that might prove more definitive. Meanwhile, it is worth remembering that the absence of evidence is not evidence of absence. Neither is skepticism a method.[25]

Pottery dated to the tenth century has also been found elsewhere in excavations in Jerusalem, both in Avidad's and Shiloh's exposures in areas of domestic occupation. Although these sherds were found in fills and cannot be used to date specific buildings, they do attest to relatively widespread occupation beyond the Temple Mount. The best-preserved and well-stratified private dwellings were those excavated by Shiloh in Area G. These houses were finally destroyed in the Babylonian campaigns of 586. They clearly have a long history, but it is not unreasonable to suppose that some of them may go back to the tenth century. Again the lack of direct evidence is not surprising, since extensive excavations beyond the Temple Mount area and the recently restored Jewish Quarter have rarely been undertaken.

Farther north, Warren's discovery on the northeastern Ophel has been reinvestigated by Kenyon and B. and E. Mazar. The latter interprets this area as a gate complex to the acropolis, incorporating a Solomonic city wall. Again, the published pottery includes clear tenth-century forms, although not in situ. The datable material, including store jars with Hebrew inscriptions, is eighth century, representing perhaps a continual rebuild of this monumental structure.[26]

In summary, Jerusalem by the tenth century shows substantial growth in size and population, with at least some evidence of monumental structures. It was not, however, a magnificent capital city ruling over a vast empire (no reasonable scholar today thinks so).

The archaeology of Jerusalem is complex, and it will likely remain controversial due to our limited data base, as well as the implications that various interpretations may have for biblical and even theological studies. Nevertheless, a reasonable and balanced approach to the *archaeological* evidence that we now have yields the following summary.

(1) Some scholars have asserted that Jerusalem in the tenth century was simply "too small" to have served as the capital of any Judahite kingdom or state. The few archaeologists who support the low chronology also naturally argue that Jerusalem was too small. Ussishkin asserts that it was smaller and poorer compared with Lachish IV, but without telling readers that Lachish IV is dated to the ninth century by all authorities. Finkelstein maintains that in Jerusalem a king may have ruled over a "small village," "a highland stronghold which did not include much more than a modest palace and a shrine, over ... ruling a sparsely settled territory with a few sedentary villages and a large pastoral population."[27]

Such statements ignore the evidence of several investigations and surveys showing that tenth-century Jerusalem was probably at least 10 acres in size, with an estimated population of some 1,000, or even up to 25 acres and a population of as many as 2,000–3,000. And in the surrounding countryside of Judah, surveys by Ofer have mapped at least 270 tenth-century sites, with a built-up area of some 5,000 acres and a population of up to 50,000.[28]

The facts, inconvenient for minimalists, have led leading archaeologists to more balanced and sophisticated judgments. Steiner, who was on Kenyon's staff, concludes that, while Jerusalem was not the capital of a large state, it was "not poorer or more backwards than the famous sites of Megiddo and Hazor." It was "a new settlement that established itself firmly on a mostly barren hilltop as the center of an emerging state, competing with the northern cities in power and beauty."[29]

Mazar, whose authoritative summations are the best balanced, concludes: "The city at the time of David emerges as a city that was small in size but included a stronghold unique to the period, and it could have functioned as a power base of a political entity." He likens Jerusalem to a medieval *Burg*, "a stronghold centered in a rather small town that may nevertheless have been a center for leaders who established their own small state."[30]

Stager notes the survey data of Ofer cited above, concluding that, while Jerusalem in the tenth century may not have been a large urban center, it served as "the symbolic center, the capital of the cosmion," "the embodiment of the sacred in society—a city upon a hill." (The notion of a cosmion, the "subuniverse" of James, is borrowed from Ernst Voegelin.)[31]

The distinguished historian Nadav Na'aman, himself no maximalist, has argued on the basis of the Amarna-age city that Jerusalem by the tenth century was no "cow-town," opposing the views of Finkelstein and Ussishkin (and also the early Steiner). Na'aman goes on to say that the biblical texts are important sources, some early, and they should and can be used in conjunction with archaeological data. He concludes:

> Thanks to extensive archaeological research we can establish that over the course of the tenth–ninth centuries BCE, Judah developed from a rural, sparsely inhabited hill country polity to a state with a set of borders, fortified cities and a medium-sized centre.[32]

Cahill, a member of Shiloh's excavation team, has done the most to clarify Jerusalem's size and status. Based on rare first-hand experience and the only detailed examination of the pottery, she has effectively debunked the assertions of minimalists. She concludes:

> The archaeological evidence demonstrates that during the time of Israel's divided monarchy, Jerusalem was fortified, served by two water-supply systems, and populated by a socially stratified society that constructed at least two new residential quarters.[33]

Finally, it should be noted that by the empirical criterion developed here, tenth-century Jerusalem *was* a "city," even at the minimal estimate of its population at 1,000 (above).

(2) It has been claimed by skeptics that in tenth-century Jerusalem there has been found "no monumental architecture," indeed no archaeological evidence at all.[34] Several observations are in order. First, such statements disregard or misrepresent the archaeological data that we now have. Second, these statements depend *totally* on the adoption of the low chronology, which, as we have shown, collapses upon closer scrutiny. The supposed late date of monarchial Jerusalem (often eighth century; see below) is not a conclusion; it is a presupposition.

(3) The argument that those who hold out for Jerusalem as a tenth-century state capital are motivated by a desire to save the biblical notion of a great united monarchy are simply raising a red herring. No mainstream archaeologist or biblical scholar today holds such a maximalist view, not even very conservative or evangelical scholars.

(4) The only judicious, documentable position is the middle-of-the road course articulated by a growing number of archaeologists, notably Mazar in several recent publications. Jerusalem in the tenth century was the modest capital of an early state. All this means is that the extreme views of Finkelstein, Herzog, and Ussishkin (all low-chronology proponents) should be treated with suspicion in the future.[35]

Needless to say, the pronouncements of other minimalists, like those of the biblical revisionists, can be dismissed altogether. Even the best-informed biblical scholars lack the first-hand acquaintance with the data and the competence to make authoritative judgments on exceedingly complex matters of stratigraphy and comparative ceramic typology. The archaeological data really *are* primary now.

Gezer. Gezer is another strategically located site, a 33-acre mound on the last of the central hills as they slope down to the Shephelah, at a major crossroad on the Via Maris where a branch route leads off across the Aijalon Valley and up to Jerusalem. After a phase of degenerate Philistine red-washed pottery (LPDW) in the late Iron I period (Strata X–IX), the city of Stratum VIII is founded in the mid-tenth century. The casemate city wall and four-entryway gate of ashlar masonry are almost identical to the defenses of Hazor X. Palace 10,000 adjoins the gate to the west. A series of ashlar towers set into Macalister's Outer Wall appears to belong to this stratum, which would constitute a defensive wall over a mile in length around the whole site. Few private houses have been excavated, but several pillar-courtyard houses of later Iron II probably originated in Stratum VIII. The site shows a heavy late tenth-century destruction, especially in the gate area, probably in the Shoshenq raid circa 920 (below).

Beth-Shemesh. Beth-Shemesh lies in the Shephelah circa 8 miles southeast of Gezer, commanding a view across the Sorek Valley leading up to Jerusalem. Phase 4 of the recent excavations (= older Stratum IIa) belongs to the mid-eleventh to early tenth century and is the last of the Iron I levels. It already exhibits pillar-courtyard houses (some pillars are monoliths), but there is no monumental architecture. There seems to be little destruction. Succeeding Phase 3 (= older Stratum IIb–c) belongs to traditional Iron IIA, beginning in the mid-tenth and continuing into the eighth century.

Beth-Shemesh is now transformed into what is clearly a major administrative center. It features a massive city wall built of cyclopean boulders, still preserved over 6 feet high in places, partially casemated. A large public structure in Area B is some 2,500 square feet in area. A massive underground cruciform water system was dug deep into bedrock, reached by a round shaft with steps. A tripartite storage building and other constructions flank a large plastered plaza. Several private houses were of the pillar-courtyard type, very well constructed with monolithic pillars. Red-slipped and hand-burnished pottery is now common.

Among the ceramic finds was a complete wine set. A double-sided game board is inscribed with the owner's name in Hebrew, *hnn* (Hanan; the same name appears at neighboring Tel Batash/Timnah). Beth-Shemesh seems not to have been destroyed in the late tenth century, like most of the other Israelite sites. The excavators interpret Beth-Shemesh 3 as a crucial border fortress of the early monarchy, fronting both Philistine Ekron and Gath, each just 7 miles to the west.[36]

In addition to the urban sites discussed here, we have a number of smaller tier 4 villages.

Tel Ḥarashim. Among the small tenth-century sites is Tel Ḥarashim in Upper Galilee. It was excavated by Aharoni in the 1950s and described as an early Iron I site with perhaps Phoenician connections. Aharoni neglected, however, to describe a rebuild in the tenth century, when a casemate wall is in evidence (Phase II).[37]

Tel Qiri. Stratum VIIA is a small unfortified village of 2–3 acres in the northwestern Samaria hills bordering the Jezreel Valley, excavated by Ben-Tor in 1975–1977. Throughout Strata IX–V of the Iron I–II period it exhibits little change. The houses are of a straggling ad hoc sort, not of pillar-courtyard type. The remains all reflect a simple agro-pastoral domestic lifestyle typical of small villages. There are many silos and olive presses. The animal bones were mostly sheep and goats (80 percent) with some cattle bones (15 percent). Opinions are divided over whether Tel Qiri was ethnically "Israelite"; the lack of pillar-courtyard houses does not decide the matter. It may have been simply a village with ad hoc architecture.

Yoqneʿam (Jokneam). Yoqneʿam XVI–XIV is a walled town up to 10 acres in size, following an unfortified settlement of Iron I (Stratum XVII, perhaps destroyed by an earthquake). Its prominent position guarding a major pass from the Samaria hills into the Jezreel Valley would have made it an important regional center.[38]

Tel ʿAmal. Tel ʿAmal is a small, low mound of less than an acre some 3 miles west of Beth-Shean. Strata IV–III belong broadly to the tenth century and reveal an unwalled village with several ad hoc houses. Domestic industries such as weaving and dyeing are well represented. A cult room yielded several altars and offering stands. A store jar bore the Hebrew name *ḥmš*. The pottery included both Cypro-Phoenician and local red-slipped vessels. Both Strata IV and III ended in destructions. The site would appear to be Israelite in the tenth century.

Tell el-Hammah. Tell el-Hammah is a small, steep 1.25-acre mound in the Jordan Valley, overlooking the river. The Iron I levels were destroyed, then followed by a tenth-century stratum of domestic occupation quite rich in pottery and artifacts (L terrace), including cult items. It represents a small Israelite village apparently destroyed by Shoshenq circa 920.[39]

Khirbet ed-Dawwara. This is a small, one-period village some 6 miles northeast of Jerusalem on the border of the desert. It had a solid defense wall, up to 10 feet wide, with a series of closely spaced pillar-courtyard houses adjoining the wall. It is one of the earliest walled villages of the monarchy, dating to the late eleventh or early tenth century. It is the only such walled village known in the central hill country.[40] Here it is considered a tier 6 fort (fig. 4.10).

In addition, several small tier 4 towns and tier 5 villages of the tenth century may be listed, although not discussed here: Tell Beit Mirsim B_3; Tel Ḥalif VID; and Tel Malḥata C. Tell Zayit III (Libnah?) is a walled town of about 7 acres, but excavations in progress have not been published.

Smaller Tenth-Century Sites

Khirbet Qeiyafa. Only 5 miles south of Beth-Shemesh in the Sorek Valley is Khirbet Qeiyafa. It guards another pass, probably the major pass from the Shephelah up to Jerusalem and beyond, the Vale of Elah. Qeiyafa is essentially a one-period site (only an ephemeral Persian–Hellenistic building and an Islamic farm are later), perched high atop the ridge on the north side of the valley. It has a magnificent view to the west, overlooking Azekah only a mile or so distant, with a view even farther west toward Gath, some 7 miles distant. The 6-acre site was not taken to be important until excavations by Garfinkel commenced in 2008.

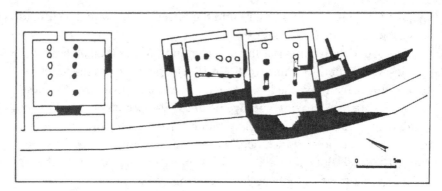

Fig. 4.10. Plan of pillar-courtyard houses and town wall at Khirbet ed-Dawwarra (Finkelstein 1990b, fig. 22)

The hilltop settlement (Stratum IV) is founded de novo on bedrock. A city wall constructed of large boulders runs some 600 yards around the site. The wall is unique in having two three-entryway gates: one facing west and one looking south over the Vale of Elah. Qeiyafa is clearly a Judahite-planned site, laid out all at once, the small courtyard houses built side by side and integrated into the casemate city wall—exactly as at ninth–eighth-century Beersheba, Tell Beit Mirsim, and other Judahite administrative centers (and unique to them). In addition to the circular row of houses, there is a tripartite storage building and a small cult room in the center of the site (fig. 4.11). Two imported miniature Cypriot barrel juglets in Cypro-Geometric Bichrome ware are very rare and are among the earliest known examples, testifying to links with coastal Phoenician trade. A five-line ostracon found near the gate is written in what appears to be a Proto-Canaanite script (fig. 4.12). It cannot be read entirely, but it seems to contain words such as *mlk* (king), *špṭ* (judge), and perhaps the names of deities (El, Baal). Two other inscriptions are known in the same script.

There can be little doubt that Qeiyafa is a barracks town, considered here a tier 6 fort. It was constructed and provisioned by some central authority as a buffer against the Philistine border towns to the west. It cannot be simply a vernacular village, not with its difficult access and monumental construction. The pottery of Stratum IV is crucial. It is clearly early, by consensus late eleventh- or early tenth-century at the latest. The repertoire contains no Philistine bichrome ware, but it does feature the degenerate Philistine Ashdod ware (LPDW) well known from the eleventh–tenth century, pottery that is not, however, confined to sites with

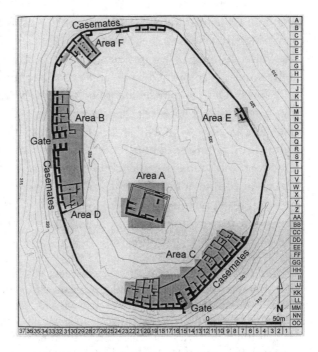

Fig. 4.11. Plan of Khirbet Qeiyafa, Stratum IV (Garfinkel, Ganor, and Hasel 2014, fig. 2.1)

Fig. 4.12. Khirbet Qeiyafa ostracon (Garfinkel and Ganor 2009, fig. 14.3)

an ethnic Philistine population. It occurs, for instance, in Judah at Gezer, Beth-Shemesh, and Beersheba in late Iron I and even in the north. A large repertoire of store jars features identical stamp impressions. The early date of the pottery is confirmed by several C-14 determinations.

Khirbet Qeiyafa may be identified tentatively with biblical Shaaraim, "two gates." A few references connect that site with the vicinity of the Vale of Elah, as well as with Philistines. In any case, the existence of a well-planned and provisioned border fortress of the late eleventh or early tenth century is indisputable evidence of some sort of centralized authority capable of commanding men and material, keeping written records, and even importing rare luxury goods via Phoenician traders.

On the recently published Ishbaal inscription from Qeiyafa, Rollston, a leading epigrapher, has observed:

> This inscription constitutes further evidence for the presence of trained scribal professionals in the southern Levant during the late eleventh and early tenth centuries BCE. Those who wish to argue that there were no trained scribal professionals in ancient Israel and Judah during the tenth and ninth centuries continue to find themselves defending a position that is flying in the face of the epigraphic evidence for the entire southern Levant.[41]

Arad. Arad (Tel Arad) is some 18 miles east of Beersheba, in the same general natural environment but situated on a prominent hill. Stratum XII represents a small village established in the late eleventh or tenth century on a promontory overlooking the long-abandoned Early Bronze city below. Stratum XII is characterized only by fragmentary remains (including perhaps a *bāmâ*, or altar). In Stratum XI, however, the first phase of the citadel that will continue with alterations until the end of the monarchy is established.

The earliest phase of the citadel is obscured by later construction, but it seems to have consisted of a square enclosure with protruding towers and a narrow gate. Faulty stratigraphy and the lack of final excavation reports preclude us from saying much more. The temple, the only full-fledged Israelite temple ever found, clearly belongs to a much later phase (below). Nevertheless, we do seem to have evidence for an early tenth-century fort at this Judahite border site. That would go very well with the evidence presented (below) for the network of dozens of smaller forts scattered across the Negev to the south. Arad, in fact, may well have been the coordinating site for the entire region. Stratum XII seems to have been destroyed along with these forts in the Shoshenq raid circa 920.[42]

Lachish. Lachish V represents a resettlement of this strategic site after a long gap in the late twelfth–eleventh century, although it was not now fortified. The remains are scant, except for the Solar Shrine found by Aharoni. The town was destroyed by fire, which the excavators attribute to the campaign of Shoshenq circa 920. If this chronology is accepted, Lachish V represents a new foundation of the monarchy, but one that does not yet see its establishment as a regional administrative center.[43]

Beersheba. The mound of Beersheba (Tell es-Saba‘) is a small tell (3 acres) east of the modern city, near springs along the Beersheba Valley. It lies at the southern end of the Judean foothills, where they slope down to the northern Negev. It is therefore a marginal site, although the loessal soils are suitable for dry farming and the location provides a defensible position. It forms the natural southern border of Judah.

Stratum IX, belonging to the eleventh century, represents one of the first Iron Age settlements in the Beersheba Valley, which had been deserted for at least 1,500 years. There are only pits and a few hovels, indicating the early Israelite village discussed above. Stratum VIII then sees a more permanent settlement at the end of Iron I, with forerunners of the typical Israelite pillar-courtyard houses.

Stratum VII, following a brief gap, was founded in the early tenth century and reflects a major change. We now see a planned city, with pillar-courtyard houses side by side forming an oval-shaped settlement that could easily be defended. The rich ceramic assemblage is typical of the late eleventh- to tenth-century horizon. Large quantities of cattle bones, along with sheep and goat bones, indicate a mixed agro-pastoral economy. This phase ends not in a destruction but rather in the more concentrated settlement pattern of Stratum VI. The site seems to reflect a gradual transitional phase as towns develop in the hinterland, previously utilized largely by nomadic pastoralists.[44]

The Negev Forts. More than fifty small, one-period forts are scattered over the remote central Negev highlands south of Beersheba, all the way down to the Maktesh Ramon krater (fig. 4.13). They are mostly located on hilltops, close to water sources, some distance from each other. Most are round or elliptical in shape, with casemate walls enclosing an open central area. In some cases, there are adjoining pillar-courtyard houses. There are also some unfortified hamlets nearby. The pottery includes crude Negebite wares, which have a long time span. The rest is typical of tenth-century sites to the north.

Some scholars have dated the Negev forts to the eleventh century, supposing them to be defenses against the Amalekites or others. Most authorities, however, date them to the tenth century, especially since the Shoshenq list of sites destroyed circa 920 mentions the Negev several times. In that case, the extensive network of forts guarding the southern borders of Judah and the trade routes through Kadesh-barnea toward the Red Sea is further evidence of centralized administration in the tenth century. The oval fort at Kadesh-barnea 4 belongs to this horizon, although there are some earlier sherds.[45]

Other Sites That May Have Become Israelite. A few Canaanite, Philistine, and Phoenician sites appear to have become more aligned with the burgeoning Israelite culture in the hill country in the course of the mid- to late tenth century. This assumes, of course, that the above sites had also become, or already were, Israelite (see fig. 4.3).

Tell Qasile is one example. Stratum XI represents the next-to-last Philistine settlement, characterized by red-washed and black-painted Ashdod wares (LPDW) of the mid- to late eleventh century. Stratum X, however, sees major changes. The Stratum XI temple (Building 131) was enlarged and reused, many of its ritual vessels found in the destruction that ended this stratum. Stratum IX, with two subphases, belongs to the mid-tenth century and may reflect a degree of acculturation between Philistines and Israelites. The red-washed and slipped pottery now in obvious use is virtually identical to the pottery of inland Israelite sites such as Gezer IX–VIII and Beth-Shemesh 4–3. Stratum VIII ends circa 920, apparently in the Shoshenq raid, after which there is a gap.[46]

Dor is an Iron I Phoenician site destroyed sometime around 1100–1050. Phase G/6 then sees some monumental construction, but in general it continues with the preceding stratum. The domestic architecture and pottery show continuity into the Iron IIA era, but the site does not likely become Israelite and is more likely Phoenician. Phoenician red-slipped and Cypro-Phoenician or Black-on-Red (= Cypro-Geometric III) wares from Cyprus dominate the Stratum A/10 repertoire; local wares thought to be Iron IIA Israelite pottery do not appear until later. On balance, Dor looks more Phoenician than Israelite in the early to mid-tenth century.[47]

Tel Seraʿ, another Philistine site, is comparable in some ways. Stratum VIII is the last of the Philistine phases. Stratum VII succeeds it with no

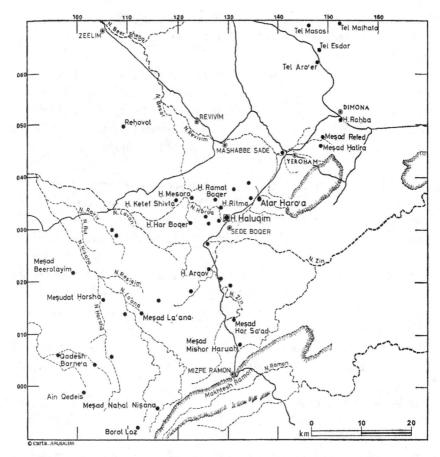

Fig. 4.13. Map of Iron II sites and fortresses of the central Negev (Cohen 1976, fig. 1)

signs of a destruction. The excavator regarded this sequence as evidence of a tenth-century Israelite settlement that developed organically from the Philistine habitation. Stratum VII was a well-planned city, with fine examples of pillar-courtyard houses, some preserved up to the second story and showing signs of stairwells. Stratum VII was long-lived and extended into the ninth century. It is a good example of a small town of the early Israelite monarchy, although the population may have remained in some sense Philistine at this border site (as Tel Batash and Beth-Shemesh; below).

Tel Kinrot (Chinnereth) is a Canaanite town in Stratum V, destroyed possibly by an earthquake circa 1050. Stratum IV following in the tenth century is attested only by ephemeral remains but was destroyed again circa 900. The Early–Middle Bronze extent was circa 10 acres, but the Isra-elite town was probably smaller. There is a city wall, but it seems to have reused the Stratum VI city defenses.

Tel Batash IV (Timnah) is a border town like nearby Beth-Shemesh. Stratum V follows a destruction and features a well-laid town with closely spaced houses and a city gate with towers. The population was probably mixed. Red-slipped and hand-burnished pottery is similar to that of typi-cally Israelite sites. Stratum IV ends with the Shoshenq raid circa 920, after which there was a gap.

Tel Rehov appears to be another example of a former Canaanite city that came under Israelite influence in the tenth century. Strata VII–VI are the last of a continuous development of Canaanite culture since the twelfth century Stratum V, however, belongs to the tenth century and marks a change. The town is now well laid out in insulae, with exception-ally well-constructed mudbrick houses rich in domestic finds. The houses are not of the pillar-courtyard type but continue local building traditions. In a later phase a mud-brick city wall was constructed, with a tower in one area. A number of cult objects were found, including figurines, a horned ceramic altar, and numerous chalices. There is some evidence of damage by earthquakes and fires, but Stratum V may not be destroyed until some-time circa 900; a C-14 date of circa 920 suggests a slightly earlier date (i.e., Shoshenq). The ceramic repertoire includes both red-washed and red-slipped wares as ay Gezer IX–VIII, Tell Qasile X–IX, Beth-Shemesh 4–3, and Tel Batash IV.[48]

Tel Rehov, like Megiddo and Beth-Shean (and possibly Dan), gives some evidence that the end of the Bronze Age Canaanite cultural tra-ditions was prolonged until as late as the eleventh–tenth century. That has suggested to some that the northern part of the country did not come under Israelite (i.e., Judahite) rule in the tenth century, that a state emerged there only in the ninth century. The implication of that notion will be discussed when we come to the issue of state-formation processes in due course.[49]

Surveys

In the past twenty-five years or so archeologists have paid much more attention to surveys, especially since excavation has become so expensive and many sites, such as those in the West Bank, are off-limits. As a result, we now have many more unexcavated than excavated sites for almost all periods. There are obvious limitations of surveys, which can only retrieve surface remains, and at best those that happen to have survived. Nevertheless, surveys, when thorough and systematic, can yield relative percentages that are reliable enough for comparative purposes.[50] The principal data are ceramics.

What has been called Iron IIA pottery can be distinguished generally from Iron I pottery, but a collection of surface finds cannot really determine much more than the fact that a particular site was occupied in one or more of several periods. The size of each settlement is also uncertain, since only a part of it may have been occupied at a given time.

In the central hill country north of Jerusalem, we do have statistics that suggest a marked increase in the number and density of settlements by the tenth century. There may be twice the number of sites compared with Judah (below). This represents a peak, since the number of settlements (at least rural settlements) then declines in Iron II.

Surveys in the Jezreel and in Lower and Upper Galilee have produced results that are more difficult to quantify.[51] Israeli surveys in Judah and the Shephelah, however, show a significant increase in the number of settlements and in population growth from the Iron I into the early Iron II period. The comparison can be seen in the following table taken from Lehmann's analysis.[52]

Fig. 4.14. Population growth from Iron I to Iron IIA, according to Lehmann

Iron I, twelfth–eleventh century	Iron IIA, tenth century
Judah	
Built-up area: 10.5 acres	Built-up area: 21 acres
Population: 5,000–8,000 (10,000?)	Population: 8,000–
Shephelah	
Built-up area: 100 acres	Built-up area: 240 acres
Population: 6,000–12,000 (28,000?)	Population: ?

Lehmann claims to be basing his work on data in Ofer's unpublished Hebrew dissertation. Ofer, however, had already published an English summary of his survey in Judah (not including the Shephelah).[53] It is interesting to compare the two estimates.

Fig. 4.15. Population growth from Iron I to Iron IIA, according to Ofer

Iron I	Iron IIA
Built-up area: 42 acres	Built-up area: 62 acres
Population: 4,200	Population: 6,200

Despite the differences in absolute numbers, both Lehmann's and Ofer's estimates show a growth of at least 25 percent in the population from Iron I to the tenth century. The population estimates here can be viewed in different ways. Some Israeli archaeologists differ on whether Iron IIA denotes the tenth century or the ninth century (above). Their population estimates may thus differ from the ones here, which are based on a typical coefficient of 100 persons per built-up area. Finally, the Shephelah numbers here combine Judahite and Philistine sites in a somewhat arbitrary manner. All things considered, however, the population in Judah did increase substantially from the Iron I to the early Iron II period. The same general phenomenon is seen in the Shephelah.

That striking growth must be explained in some way, and the most likely explanation is that both the number of sites and the size of individual sites grew. Consequently both the rural population and the population of recently established urban centers had grown substantially by the tenth century.

This phenomenon has been taken as a refutation of Faust's notion of a shift in settlement patterns due to urbanization in the tenth century, but that need not be the case. Faust's main point is that many of the *excavated* sites of Iron I are abandoned at the beginning of the tenth century and the growth of cities. That is indisputable if one looks at figure 4.3 above. The only Iron I Israelite sites that do continue from the eleventh into the tenth century are Tel Masos I and perhaps Tel Esdar II. Even so, both are permanently abandoned by the mid- to late tenth century. Faust's point is that most of these early Israelite rural sites do not develop into the urban sites of the Iron II period. Rather, new sites were founded in the tenth century, mostly rural, and it is these plus the few urban sites that will show continuity and expansion throughout Iron II. His argument is based on stratigraphic sequences that are clear.

A few others at excavated Shephelah sites are supported by extensive survey data. In Faust's view, the gradual resettlement of the Shephelah in the tenth century, after a long gap in Iron I, was made possible by the decline of Philistine influence in the region. As a result, people from the highlands moved westward, establishing a network of rural settlements under the aegis of a fledgling Judahite state. The hub, however, remained in the highlands, as indicated by the growth observed at excavated sites such as Beth-Shemesh, Lachish, Tell Beit Mirsim, and particularly Khirbet Qeiyafa.[54]

The only other early Israelite sites that could have developed into urban sites of Iron II are Dan, Hazor, Shechem, and Tell en-Naṣbeh, and an Iron I "early Israelite" occupation at all four is dubious. These sites show only some pits, a few ephemeral structures, and some Iron I pottery. They are not typical in any way of the growth of the early Israelite villages discussed above.

The shift from a rural to an urban population by the tenth century is evident in both the north and the south, and it has considerable significance for any theory regarding the rise of the state. Because there are regional variations in settlement patterns, however, the discussion beyond this point will distinguish north from south, that is, Israel from Judah.

That being said, a certain ambiguity cannot be avoided. While *Israel* will usually be the term for the northern kingdom and *Judah* for the southern kingdom, occasionally *Israel* will designate the Iron II people as a whole (as in the Hebrew Bible). In that case, the context should make the use of the term clear. Henceforth it should also be noted that the terms *Iron IIA* and *tenth century* may be used interchangeably, on the basis of the conventional chronology and terminology fully discussed above and adopted hereafter.

A Summary of the Tenth-Century Israelite Sites

In summing up the changes that distinguish Iron IIA from Iron IB—the late eleventh to the tenth century in the framework used here—we shall employ a General Systems Theory approach, just as we did for Iron I. That will facilitate the contrast.

Settlement Type and Distribution; Demography

It is clear that the tenth century saw a major shift from a predominately rural settlement pattern to one in which major urban centers developed. This change did not take place overnight, of course, and the rural population continued to grow along with the population of newly established sites. Within a generation or so, however, many of the original Israelite villages had been abandoned, and in their place there developed growing towns and cities.

In the eleventh century, only a few sites west of the Jordan would likely have qualified as cities by criteria that would be useful. To be sure, there is no universal agreement on what constitutes a city. The assumption that cities must have city walls has proven invalid, nor is absolute size a useful criterion.

One way of looking at urbanization has suggested that a population aggregate develops into a more deliberate form of social and economic organization when it outstrips its ability to feed and supply its needs and must become capable of dominating the surrounding countryside. That model has been applied, for instance, to early Mesopotamia. There the flat terrain and well-irrigated fields, as well as multiple growing seasons, enabled a relatively large population to feed itself. Therefore, the threshold for a true city to emerge may be as high in size as up to 100 acres and a population of some 10,000. There are several cities that large in Mesopotamia.[55]

Such a model does not work for ancient Palestine or the southern Levant. There the terrain is difficult, especially in the hill country; water is scarce and irrigation largely impossible; and the growing seasons are short and unpredictable. The terrain and scarce water sources alone mean that village farmers could scarcely have commuted more than a mile or two beyond their domiciles. If they were to carry tools to the fields and carry the harvest back, even that small a catchment area would have been difficult. Within such an area, it has been estimated that a village of several hundred would have reached the urban threshold.[56]

Comparative studies of cities worldwide supports such a model. Kolb's seminal work proposes that a site of 25 acres but with a population of only 1,500 qualifies as a city. Other scholars would put the threshold at anywhere from 1,000 to 3,000. Childe's famous list of ten criteria for defining a city has been supplemented by many recent studies. They differ, of course, but there is a consensus on a few basics. Above all, the modern city is not a good comparison. The major factors in defining an ancient city are not size, fortifications, or writing. What counts are: (1) a permanent location and a certain density of population; (2) planning, with diverse facilities, including public space; (3) a core of monumental architecture; (4) evidence of social stratification and specialized craftsmanship; (5) expressions of a common, identifying ideology; and (6) above all, control of the hinterland. The last point agrees particularly well with our model here.[57]

By the above criteria, only a few eleventh-century sites might qualify as cities, among them perhaps Beth-Shean, Megiddo, and Gezer. As we have seen, none of these seems yet to be ethnically Israelite. By the end of the tenth century, however, a century later, the number of cities had grown to some dozen or so, based principally on their size and estimated population. The basis for estimating population is that of Naroll, whose work on ethnography has been generally adopted by Levantine archaeologists.[58]

Fig. 4.16. Tenth-century Israelite cities and their estimated populations, using Naroll's coefficient of 100 persons per acre but assuming that not all the area of a site was built up

Site and Stratum	Size in Acres	Population
Dan IVA	10–20	1,000
Hazor XB–A	8–15	1,000
Megiddo VA/IVB	15	1,000
Beth-Shean V lower	10	800
Ta'anach IIA–B	11	800
Yoqne'am XVI–XIV	10	800
Tell el-Far'ah North VIIb	15	1,000
Jerusalem 14	5–10	1,000?
Shechem X	15	1,000
Gezer VIII	33	2,500
Beth-Shemesh 3 (= IIb/c)	10?	800

Several studies have suggested that the population of Israel west of the Jordan in the twelfth century was circa 25,000, in the eleventh century circa 50,000, and by the tenth century up to 100,000. These estimates may be of limited use, however, since we cannot assume that a 10-acre site, for instance, was entirely built up in the initial phase of the Iron II period.

Where the data come mostly from surveys, as is often the case, it is scarcely possible to divide the sherd material into clear-cut phases or to estimate the built-up area.

The fact of increased urbanization is clear, but explanations of its causes differ. Finkelstein argued that cities developed of necessity not on the basis of any ideology but because of population expansion and changed socioeconomic realities, especially the intensification of agriculture and the need to manage surpluses. Some hold that the traditional familial social organization could not sustain itself in the face of Philistine competition. These arguments have much in common with the General Systems Theory approach here—on the conflicting forces of what is called fusion and fission. But in no case can ideology be ruled out as a mere epiphenomenon, as the New Archaeology's functionalist explanations supposed.

Socioeconomic Structure

The small, rural Iron I Israelite villages, all very similar, with homogeneous features such as pillar-courtyard houses, have sometimes been described as egalitarian. It is true that there is little or no evidence of an elite class in these agro-pastoral settlements. But the term *egalitarian* suggests modern class distinctions (and ideals) that are not really applicable. The term *communitarian* seems more neutral and better suited.[59]

The tenth century, when increasing urbanization is evident, was no doubt characterized by more social stratification and economic diversification, since a city cannot function otherwise. There would now have been builders, shopkeepers, purveyors of goods and services of many kinds, artisans, metalsmiths, owners of farms in rural areas, potters, petty administrative officials, and in all likelihood those engaged in specialized activities such as scribes or cult personnel. While most people still lived at a subsistence level, a few entrepreneurs could have prospered and might have accumulated enough wealth to have created what we would now call capital. It is true that most of the now common pillar-courtyard houses are very similar, but there are a few tenth-century buildings that appear to be elite structures, such as the Hazor Area B citadel, Palaces 1723 and 6000 at Megiddo, and Palace 10,000 at Gezer.

As for economic activity, it is obvious that many if not most people in the Iron IIA Israelite towns and cities were no longer farmers or herders: they were townspeople, even managers. The rural population was still significant, of course, and essential. But absentee landowners were more common now, as we know from the slightly later Samaria ostraca (ch. 5). Where the exchange of goods in the earlier villages had been ad hoc, mostly by informal barter of surpluses, now more managed, redistributive (or "down-the-line") trade became common. It would have been mandatory in an urban environment, where agrarian self-sufficiency became more and more difficult.

Several scholars have suggested an economy that was more deliberately state-sponsored. Knauf has argued that the economic recession at the end of the Late Bronze Age had reversed itself by the tenth century, fueled by reviving Mediterranean trade, as well as by copper production in the Arabah. The latter is now more likely in view of Levy's discovery of extensive mining activities in the Wadi Fidan as early as the eleventh century. Holladay believes that overland trade with south Arabia was already in operation and that intensified agriculture had created substantial wealth. The patrimonial model of Stager, Masters, and Schloen would also suggest the accumulation of wealth by an emerging elite class.[60]

There is other evidence of long-distance trade by the tenth century. The distinctive Cypro-Phoenician, or better, Cypriot Black-on-Red I–II and Cypro-Geometric I–III pottery has been found in good contexts at a number of tenth-century sites such as Megiddo VA/IVB, Hazor X, Kinrot IV, Taʿanach IIB, Beth-Shean V upper, Tel Reḥov V, Tell el-Farʿah VIIb, Tel ʿAmal III, Tell el-Hammah L, Tell Beit Mirsim B₃, and elsewhere. The early Phase I wares have now been shown mostly to have originated in Cyprus, then brought by Phoenician maritime trade to the southern Levantine coast, where some were imitated. The Iron I village culture could not have fostered such international trade, which appears suddenly in the early to mid-tenth century. Even if the tenth-century Israelite towns participated only through Phoenician intermediaries, we have here another aspect of a state-managed economy.[61]

Political Organization

We have characterized early Israel above as a "society without a sovereign," following Sahlins's model of a domestic as opposed to a despotic mode of production. By the tenth century, all that was changing. The growth of cities, as well as the increasing social stratification and specialization of the population, required some degree of centralized management, simply in order for urban sites to function. This means that a political structure developed beyond that of the village, where a few revered elders adjudicated differences and helped to maintain order. Towns and cities soon saw the emergence of various officials, still probably charismatic rather than elected, but now vested with some degree of authority. In Iron II, we will see definite evidence of such officials in the form of impressive governors' residences, often near the city gate (ch. 5).

Possible evidence of regional administrative centers and professional administrators—even kings—will be discussed when we come to view Iron IIA Israel as a state and we assess the biblical evidence. But the existence of a class of governing officials must be inferred already in the earliest phases of the tenth-century period, on the basis of the archaeological evidence alone. Here the question of the famous Solomonic district lists (1 Kgs 4:7–19) comes into focus. Many biblical scholars and historical geographers have wrestled with the issue of the historicity of the biblical narratives here and elsewhere in the Hebrew Bible. Few archaeologists, however, have sought possible archaeological correlates. If the biblical accounts, although much later, did happen to preserve authentic historical memories, the following might be suggested as administrative centers, on the basis of the archaeological evidence that we now have.[62]

Fig. 4.17. Solomon's administrative districts, with possible centers

District	Place (or Tribe)	Possible Capital
1	Ephraim	Shechem; Tell el-Farʿah
2	Dan (?)	Gezer; Beth-Shemesh
3	Socoh; land of Hepher	Socoh; Aphek
4	Dor	Dor
5	Jezreel	Megiddo
6	Gilead	Ramoth-gilead? (Rumeith)
7	(west Jordan Valley)	Beth-Shean; Megiddo
8	Naphtali	Hazor
9	Asher/Zebulun	Jokneam
10	Issachar	Tall Zerʿin (?)
11	Benjamin	Gibeon
12	Judah	Jerusalem

It is impossible to authenticate an administrative district on the basis of the biblical texts alone, not only because these texts are much later but also because there are obviously omissions and contradictions in the various accounts. For instance, Dan and Reuben are sometimes located in different regions. Some districts are not named after any tribe, even though they were presumably based on the old "twelve-tribe league." They are given only geographical coordinates in 1 Kgs 4:7–19, and that is the case for all the districts, only individuals and town names being given. Elsewhere only four tribes are named: Asher, Benjamin, Issachar, and Naphtali. Even Judah is omitted. Thus the list in figure 4.17 is somewhat arbitrary.

The point here is that, if administrative districts had existed in the tenth century, most of the cities listed here as possible centers would qualify. Shechem, Gezer, Dor, Megiddo, Beth-Shean, Hazor, and Jerusalem—seven of twelve—are all major urban sites strategically located. Jokneam is a lesser possibility; Socoh is unidentified (Khirbet Shuweiket er Ras?). The list seems to derive, however, from northern circles. It does not correspond exactly to the old tribal boundaries in Judges; the territories are sometimes vague and perhaps partial (even Jerusalem is omitted); and many sites cannot be identified. It is of interest, however, that a north–south division already appears to be recognized. The names of the governors are unknown to us except from other biblical texts, but it is significant that all are typical Israelite-Judahite names. Further, of the twelve, seven resemble old tribal names compounded with ʾāḥî-, "my brother," or bēn, "son of."

Of the district capitals suggested here (including the names not supplied in 1 Kgs 4), all but three have been excavated and exhibit features such as location and major architecture that would qualify them as district centers. Tell el-Farʿah VIIb, Gezer VIII, Megiddo VA/IVB, and Hazor X are especially distinguished. Of the others, Hepher or Socoh and Mahanaim are either only provisionally identified or remain sparsely excavated. Tall Ziraʿa is an exceptionally impressive mound just east of the southern Sea of Galilee along the Yarkon Gorge, now being excavated, with Iron Age remains. To be sure, the possibility of such administrative centers does not mean that their existence is proven. However, the archaeological data do supply a context, suggesting that the biblical narratives need not be judged as fantastic. They may incorporate older oral traditions.

Ramoth-gilead is presumably to be identified with Tell er-Rumeith in northern Transjordan. A small structure of the tenth century excavated there

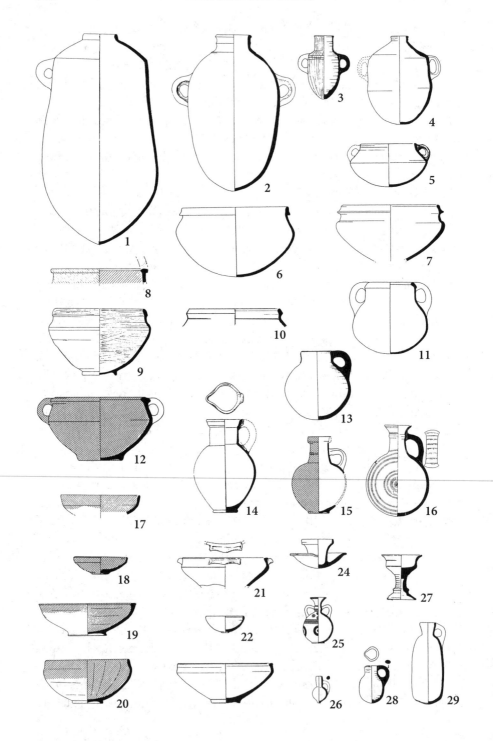

Fig. 4.18 (left). Typical northern and southern Israelite ceramic forms of the Iron IIA era, tenth century. 1: store jar, Megiddo VA/IVB (Finkelstein, Ussishkin, and Halpern 2000, fig. 11.35:3); 2: store jar, Hazor XBb (Ben-Tor, Ben-Ami, and Sandhaus 2012, fig. 2.29:9); 3: amphora, Taʿanach IIA–B (Rast 1978, fig. 36:3); 4: store jar, Megiddo VA/IVB (Finkelstein, Ussishkin, and Halpern 2000, fig. 15.5:9); 5: cooking pot, Khirbet Qeiyafa IV (Garfinkel and Ganor 2009, fig. 6.6:5); 6: cooking pot, Megiddo VA/IVB (Finkelstein, Ussishkin, and Halpern 2000, fig. 11.38:4); 7: cooking pot, Megiddo VA/IVB (Finkelstein, Ussishkin, and Halpern 2000, fig. 15.3:12); 8: krater, Khirbet Qeiyafa IV (Garfinkel and Ganor 2009, fig. 6.6:5); 9: krater, Taʿanach IIA–B (Rast 1978, fig. 42:2); 10: cooking pot, Jerusalem 14 (De Groot and Bernick-Greenberg 2012, fig. 5.3:3); 11: cooking pot, Megiddo VA/IVB (Finkelstein, Ussishkin, and Halpern 2000, fig. 11.38:1); 12: krater, Gezer VIII (Dever et al. 1974, pl. 31:22); 13: cooking jug, Taʿanach IIA–B (Rast 1978, 50:2); 14: jug, Khirbet Qeiyafa IV (Garfinkel and Ganor 2009, fig. 6.17:7); 15: jug, Gezer VIII (Dever et al. 1974, pl. 31:3); 16: flask, Tell el-Farʿah VIIb (Chambon 1984, pl. 50:5); 17: bowl, Jerusalem 14 (De Groot and Bernick-Greenberg 2012, fig. 5.1:14); 18: bowl, Gezer VIII (Dever 1986, pl. 47:6); 19: bowl, Megiddo VA/IVB (Finkelstein, Ussishkin, and Halpern 2000, fig. 11.36:11); 20: bowl, Megiddo VA/IVB (Finkelstein, Ussishkin, and Halpern 2000, fig. 11.36:9); 21: bowl, Khirbet Qeiyafa IV (Garfinkel and Ganor 2009, fig. 6.3:27); 22: bowl, Gezer VIII (Dever 1986, pl. 47:4); 23: bowl, Khirbet Qeiyafa IV (Garfinkel and Ganor 2009, fig. 6.3:26); 24: gravy boat, Megiddo VA/IVB (Finkelstein, Ussishkin, and Halpern 2000, fig. 11.38); 25: juglet (Cypro-Phoenician Black-on-Red II), Megiddo VA/IVB (Finkelstein, Ussishkin, and Halpern 2000, fig. 11.3:28); 26: juglet (black burnished), Megiddo VA/IVB (Finkelstein, Ussishkin, and Halpern 2009, fig. 15.6:18); 27: chalice, Khirbet Qeiyafa IV (Garfinkel and Ganor 2009, fig. 6.8:1); 28: juglet, Taʿanach IIA–B (Rast 1978, fig. 4:11); 29: juglet, Megiddo VA/IVB (Finkelstein, Ussishkin, and Halpern 2000, fig. 11.40:6)

in Stratum VIII was destroyed toward the end of that century. Nevertheless, it is not clear that it was a fort, as claimed. The extension of Solomon's rule into Gilead, Ammon, and Moab is problematic, however, in view of what we now know of the archaeology of Jordan in the Iron Age (above).

While it is doubtful that sites on the Transjordanian plateau in Gilead, Ammon, and Moab were ever under Israelite control in the tenth century, a few sites in the Jordan Valley present a different set of issues. Pella, Tall as-Saʿidiyya, Tell el-Mazar, and Tell Deir ʿAlla (Succoth?) are all close to the Jordan River, in what would have been biblical Gilead. All were occupied in the Iron Age, but phasing and dates are unclear, and we do not have an adequate view of the material culture in any one period.

Pella is not mentioned by name in the Hebrew Bible, and the Iron Age material suggests a continuation of Canaanite culture. At Tall as-Saʿidiyya (perhaps biblical Zarethan) Stratum XII is probably tenth century and does have pillar-courtyard houses. It could have been destroyed in the Shoshenq raid, but it is not listed in the itinerary. Phase E at Tell Deir ʿAlla is dated circa 1000 by a C-14 sample, but there is nothing specifically Israelite in the material culture. Given the uncertainty of the site identification and the nature of the excavated material, little more can be said.

Technology

Many aspects of technological innovation are evident in Iron IIA. One of the most obvious aspects is town planning and building techniques that are a concomitant of urbanization. Several of the new cities reflect a well thought out concept of what a city should look like—especially administrative centers such as Hazor, Megiddo, and Gezer. There and elsewhere we see massive fortifications, city gates, palaces, industrial and storage facilities, and an agglutinative arrangement of domestic houses. Someone is orchestrating all this, and with a sure knowledge of surveying and construction techniques, as well as an understanding of the constraints of natural local conditions. The new urban sites are often superbly adapted to their environment and especially well equipped for defense requirements. That can hardly be fortuitous.

Another aspect of new technology is seen in ceramic production. Heretofore potting had been largely a cottage industry. Now, however, there is evidence of a more centralized, industrial-like production. Many of the typical Iron I forms continue, but now they are increasingly wheelmade, and the repertoire is more varied yet more standardized. In particular, many Iron I red-washed vessels now become red-slipped and hand-burnished. Several scholars have seen the latter—long taken as diagnostic for Iron IIA—as reflecting the emergence of an ethnic identity, indeed of the manipulation of material culture to enhance such an identity (an ethnic marker comparable to the distinctive Philistine bichrome ware). Other industries may have become more centralized as well, but the evidence is not as clear.

Of particular importance for the tenth century is the balance of ceramic continuity and change now and the implications for defining an emergent state. Iron I ceramic traditions, in both continuing Canaanite sites and in early Israelite sites, are seen in the similarity of forms such as typical large ovoid store jars; kraters, cooking pots, hemispherical bowls, juglets, and even rarer forms such as chalices and cup-and-saucer vessels (cf. fig. 3.12 with fig. 4.18). Many of these ceramic traditions go all the way back to the Late Bronze Age.

On the other hand, there are several significant innovations that characterize the tenth-century (or Iron IIA) transition, and most will continue to define the remainder of the Iron II period. It is that *ceramic continuity* throughout the Israelite monarchy—a period of some four centuries—that is our best evidence for the existence of an Israelite state. (There are, of course, many other elements of material culture that also demonstrate continuity, such as house form, burial customs, cult practices, and the like.)

Among the changes that are most diagnostic for the tenth-century transition is the emergence of north–south distinctions in forms such as cooking pots, which reveal not only regional differences but also a slower rate of typological evolution in the south. There we see "archaizing" features such as a preference in the south for elongated, flat rims rather than the more developed concave rims in the north. That difference is ignored by proponents of the low chronology, who see the concave cooking-pot rims in the north as necessarily *later*, as they are in the south. Thus Hazor X and Megiddo VA/IVA are moved down from the tenth to the ninth century, to "match" the ninth-century Omride capital at Samaria.

Yet a glance at figure 4.19 here will show that concave flanged-rim cooking pots in the north are precocious, as it were, and emerged not only in the ninth century (as in the south) but as early as the eleventh and even the twelfth century. That datum, rarely noted, means that the date of concave flanged-rim cooking pots can just as easily be *raised* as lowered. With that observation, the supposed ceramic evidence for the low chronology collapses.

Other tenth-century ceramic innovations include the widespread use of hand burnishing over a darker red slip, in contrast to the Iron I light, unburnished red wash. This distinctive technique, long recognized as diagnostic for the tenth century, or Iron IIA, occurs in both the north and the south (fig. 4.20). Hand burnish is thus one more unifying feature of an Israelite state with at least some cultural influence that extended to the north, even as far as Hazor. Again, this phenomenon is often ignored or minimized by revisionists.

Finally, Cypriot imports now resume, after ceasing with the end of the Late Bronze Age except for a few eleventh-century examples at coastal

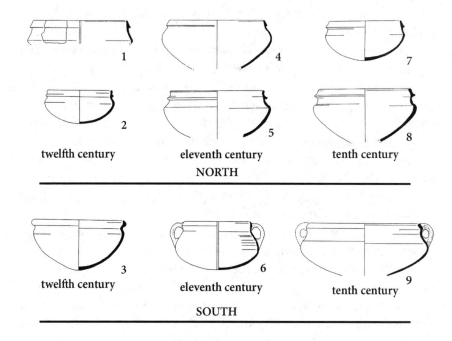

twelfth century   eleventh century   tenth century

NORTH

twelfth century   eleventh century   tenth century

SOUTH

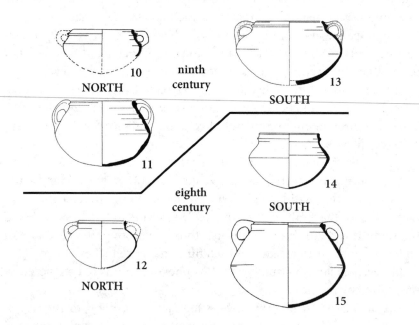

NORTH   ninth century   SOUTH

eighth century   SOUTH

NORTH

Fig. 4.19 (left). The development of cooking pots from the twelfth to the eighth century, showing general continuity. 1: Megiddo VIB (Finkelstein, Ussishkin, and Halpern 2006, fig. 13.51:9); 2: Megiddo VII–VI (Loud 1948, pl. 85:14); 3: Giloh (A. Mazar 1981, fig. 7:1); 4: Megiddo VIA (Finkelstein, Ussishkin, and Halpern 2006, fig. 13.53:8); 5: Hazor XII–XI (Ben-Tor, Ben Ami, and Sandhaus 2012, fig. 1.7:9); 6: Shiloh V (Finkelstein, Bunimovitz, and Lederman 1993, fig. 6.50:4); 7: Tel el-Far'ah North VIIb (Chambon 1984, pl. 52:3); 8: Megiddo VA/IVB (Finkelstein, Ussishkin, and Halpern 2006, fig. 15.3:12); 9: Tel Masos II (Fritz and Kempinski 1983, pl. 150:4); 10: Hazor (Yadin et al. 1958, pl. LVII:15); 11: Megiddo IVA (Finkelstein, Ussishkin, and Halpern 2006, fig. 15.8:3); 12: Tell el-Far'ah VIId (Chambon 1984, pl. 53:5); 13: Arad XI (Singer-Avitz 2002, fig. 8:7); 14: Gezer VIA (Gitin 1990, pl. 22:4); 15: Arad X (Singer-Avitz 2002, fig. 25:6)

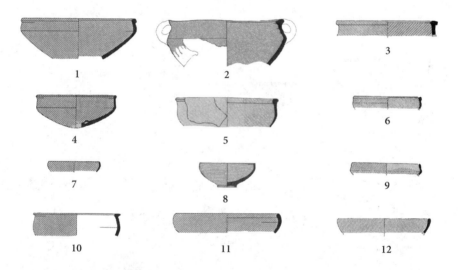

Fig. 4.20 (above). Red-washed pottery of the early to mid-tenth century from southern sites, representing a stage before the general introduction of red slip and hand burnishing. 1: krater, Gezer IX (Dever et al. 1974, pl. 30:11); 2: krater, Tell Qasile X (A. Mazar 1985, fig. 46:12); 3: krater, Khirbet Qeiyafa IV (Garfinkel and Ganor 2009, fig. 6.6:6); 4: bowl, Gezer IX (Dever 1986, pl. 43:11); 5: krater, Tell Qasile IX (A. Mazar 1985, fig. 53:5); 6: bowl, Khirbet Qeiyafa IV (Garfinkel and Ganor 2009, fig. 6.1:9); 7: bowl, Gezer IX (Dever 1986, pl. 43:13); 8: bowl, Tell Qasile X (A. Mazar 1985, fig. 46:1); 9: bowl, Khirbet Qeiyafa IV (Garfinkiel and Ganor 2009, fig. 6.3:16); 10: krater, Gezer IX (Dever et al. 1974, pl. 30:2); 11: bowl, Gezer IX (Dever et al. 1974, pl. 30:13); 12: bowl, Khirbet Qeiyafa IV (Garfinkel and Ganor 2009, fig. 6. 1:19)

Phoenician sites such as Dor (sometimes called Cypro-Phoenician wares). Phoenician bichrome and Cypriot Black-on-Red I and II juglets and bowls now appear in both the north and the south (fig. 4.21). These imports to Israelite sites, like the local wares discussed above, continue into at least the ninth century, and they document not only cultural conformity and continuity but also a flourishing maritime trade that could only have been sustained by a state.[63]

Iron gradually becomes more common in the Iron IIA period. Iron

Fig. 4.21 (left). Phoenician bichrome (nos. 1–9), Cypriot Black-on-Red I–II (10–14), and Phoenician red-polished (15–20) wares. 1: jug, Hazor Xa (Ben-Tor, Ben-Ami, and Sandhaus 2012, fig. 5.10:4); 2: jug, Dor (Gilboa 2001, fig. 11:5); 3: jug, Tomb Z I, Achzib (E. Mazar 2003, fig. 5.10:1); 4: flask, Hazor IXb (Ben-Tor, Ben-Ami, and Sandhaus 2012, fig. 5.10:2); 5: bowl, Abu Hawam IV (Hamilton 1935, 29 no. 153); 6: beer jug, Megiddo VIA (Loud 1948, pl. 75:22); 7: beer jug, Dor (Gilboa 2001, fig. 12:3); 8: jug, Dor (Gilboa 2001, fig. 11:8); 9: jug, Dor (Gilboa 2001, fig. 10:10); 10: krater, Megiddo VA (Loud 1948, pl. 90:3); 11: barrel juglet, Tomb 79, Azor (Dothan 1961, pl. 34:5); 12: bowl, Dor B9a (Gilboa 1999, fig. 5.1); 13: jug, Megiddo V (Lamon and Shipton 1939, pl. 8:16); 14: bowl, Megiddo V (Lamon and Shipton 1939, 30:140); 15: juglet, Megiddo V (Lamon and Shipton 1939, pl. 17:87); 16: jug, Achzib tomb (Amiran 1969, pl. 92:7); 17: jug. Achzib tomb (Amiran 1970, pl. 92:1); 18: jug, Samaria, Trench E207 (Crowfoot, Crowfoot, and Kenyon 1957, fig. 22:7); 19: flask, Tell Qasile X (Mazar 1985, fig. 35:10); 20: bowl, Hazor V (Yadin et al. 1958, pl. LIV:6); 21: bowl, Hazor X–IX (Yadin et al. 1958, pl. XLV:15); 22: juglet, Achzib tomb (Amiran 1970, pl. 92:10)

may be better than bronze for heavy tools, but it is brittle and rusts away in most cases. By the tenth century, however, the number of iron implements has at least doubled compared to Iron I, as detailed at a number of sites. Tools and weapons predominate, but there is also some jewelry.[64]

Ideology, Art, and Cult

These subsystems—categories of thought, of aesthetics—are more difficult to discern in material culture remains alone, but we do have some evidence of change by the tenth century. The development of urbanism discussed above is clearly the manifestation of an idea, the physical embodiment of a certain culture or lifestyle. That ideology is evident in the large Iron I urban Philistine centers, and it is seen in some degree in tenth-century Israelite towns and cities as well. Where it comes from is less clear. But it is certainly a step beyond the typical mentality of the village.

Artistic expression of any kind is rare in the tenth century. Most tools and other objects are strictly utilitarian. Farmers and herders had neither the time nor the skill to pursue art for art's sake. There are few terra-cotta figurines, no ivory carvings, no fine bronzes, no sculpture. We have only a few simple stick-figure stamp seals in the Iron I style (ch. 3). Despite the advent of urbanism early in the Iron II period, the arts did not flourish until a more advanced civilization produced a class of specialists who had the leisure, the skills, the means, and the inspiration to pursue art.

Religious beliefs and practices are an obvious reflection of ideology. By the tenth century we do see a development from the cult of Iron I. There we saw only one or two isolated open-air cult places, with very little cult paraphernalia. By the tenth century, however, we see a tendency to centralize the cult in a particular location in a town or city. At Megiddo, Tell el-Farʿah, Tel Reḥov, and Khirbet Qeiyafa we have tenth-century village or house shrines, complete with altars, temple models, female figurines, terra-cotta incense stands, incense burners, and various cultic vessels. The iconography is not fully understood, but it often involves sacred trees, lions, and perhaps representations of male/female deities. Some of these motifs are associated with the old Canaanite mother goddess Asherah.[65]

At Lachish, we have a more public cult installation in Cult Room 49. Here there are benches, fenestrated offering stands with detachable bowls, chalices and other vessels, and four-horned limestone altars. This small shrine probably served an extended family or a small neighborhood.

At Taʿanach we have another tenth-century public shrine that features the following: a large stone olive press, an altar, a hearth and an oven, a cistern, iron knives, a bowlful of astragali (knuckle-bones) for divination, votive vessels, a nude female figure, a mold for making female figurines that are usually associated with Asherah, and two spectacular offering stands featuring lions, sacred trees, a winged sun disc, and quadrupeds (fig. 4.22).

At Tell el-Farʿah North there is an even more public cultic installation: a gate shrine. It features a large standing stone (the biblical maṣṣēbâ) and a basin or olive press. In a private house nearby were found female figurines and a naos, a temple model, again associated with the cult of Asherah.

In summary, the cult by the tenth century was much more centralized and formalized, and the deities, while still in the Canaanite tradition, were more specific. These features will soon reflect a national cult. Whether there was as yet an institutionalized priesthood is unclear, but there must have been local shamans or soothsayers. Finally, if there had been a national shrine or temple in Jerusalem (below), that would be definitive proof of a national religion.

Another aspect of ideology is writing, the embodiment of cultural ideas in a form that can easily be disseminated and handed down. In the tenth century we can supplement the eleventh-century abecedary from ʿIzbet

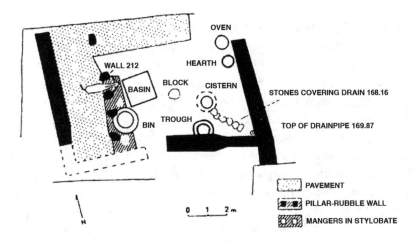

Fig. 4.22. Taʿanach shrine (see Lapp 1964, fig. 12)

Ṣarṭah with a few other examples of growing literacy. A well-dated tenth-century abecedary comes from Tel Zayit III in the Shephelah, engraved on a large visible stone, perhaps as a display inscription of sorts. The script is probably Proto-Canaanite. To the same general category belongs the Khirbet Qeiyafa inscription.[66] In the same script is the Gezer Calendar, found by Macalister in an indeterminate context but dated paleographically to the tenth century. Significantly, it is a mnemonic device, a poem defining the seasons of the year, probably a schoolboy's practice text. Thus we are a step closer to literacy.

It will be at least another century or two, however, before Hebrew inscriptions of any significant kind begin to appear. Several scholars have suggested that writing and the control of written materials was a function of a centralized authority, a tool for creating a national identity. If so, we have at least a forerunner of the Hebrew language and the shaping of Israelite self-consciousness.[67] The above are scant texts, to be sure, but they are all related to learning an old Canaanite script and adapting it to new cultural realities.

A final aspect of ideology, ethnicity, will be discussed under foreign relations below, since ethnicity is an aspect of ideology—fundamentally a question of who we think we are—but also a construct that is shaped in part by external relations.

Foreign Relations

The Iron I Israelite villages that we surveyed earlier were isolated from the outside world. Their pottery continues local Canaanite traditions, but there are no Cypriot or Mycenaean imports, and even local Philistine sherds are rare. Most sites are clustered in enclaves, rather distant from the remaining Canaanite urban centers, on the hill-country frontier or in the long-deserted Beersheba Valley.

Aramean towns were developing to the east and northeast, as were Phoenician towns in Lower Galilee and along the northern coastline. Among the tenth-century sites in the north that appear to be ethnically Aramean are Bethsaida 6a–b, Tel Hadar II, 'Ein-Gev 5–4, and (to some extent) Tel Reḥov VI–IV and Tel Kinrot IV. The area around the Sea of Galilee and up and down the adjacent Jordan Valley thus remained an Aramean enclave, continuing from Iron I well into Iron II. It was probably the southernmost extension of the Aramean city-state of Damascus, known as the kingdom of Geshur. It did not become involved with the kingdoms of Israel and Judah until the Aramean incursions of the ninth century (ch. 5).

Bethsaida, a 20-acre site on the north shore of the Sea of Galilee at the confluence of the upper Jordan River, was no doubt the capital of the kingdom of Geshur. Stratum 6a–b of the tenth century represents a prosperous city, well defined by a wall and a massive triple-entryway gate. A large *bit hilani* building seems to have been reused as a palace. The city continued to thrive until a widespread destruction in the mid-ninth century.

Tel Hadar II, farther south on the shore, is a small tenth-century site (2.5 acres) but fortified with a double concentric wall. A triple-colonnaded building (the earliest of this type) was probably a granary. Among the ceramic forms were Phoenician bichrome vessels. Stratum II ends in a conflagration.

'Ein-Gev is a small village, also on the east shore of the sea, founded in the tenth century. Strata 5–4 feature a perimeter wall that became a casemate wall, but the domestic structures inside were poorly preserved. In the ceramic repertoire there were some Phoenician bichrome vessels. The site was destroyed toward the end of the tenth century.

Tel Kinrot IV, on the opposite shore of the Sea of Galilee, and Tel Reḥov VI–V, some 20 miles down the Jordan Valley, have both been described above, because by the tenth century they both seem to have come under Israelite control. Nevertheless, the distinctive material culture suggests a mixed population, with continuing Aramean elements, even in the cult. The pottery of Reḥov reflects very wide contacts, with Phoenician bichrome (Red-on-Black III) and even imported Greek wares.[68]

Taken together, these Aramean sites in the north indicate that in the earliest days of the Israelite monarchy there was little armed conflict. There were a few destructions circa 1000 that some have attributed to an Israelite conquest, but that is going beyond the evidence. Tel Reḥov in particular exhibits the cultural continuity of this region. It was not until the Shoshenq raid circa 920 (below) that these sites show major destructions. Then in the ninth century, the Aramean incursions from farther north provoked regional clashes with the kingdom of Israel and even with Judah (ch. 5).

On the other side of the Jordan, we see the contemporary early stages of state-formation processes, best known at present in Moab. Before considering the biblical narratives regarding the early Israelite monarchy's relations with Moab (or Edom), we need to attempt a synthesis of the archaeological data on putative tenth-century polities there. Unfortunately, that analysis can only be provisional, given the state of recent excavations and publications. The best site summaries show that there are a number of tenth-century regional settlements, especially south of Amman, as well as tombs here and there. The principal sites, from north to south (excepting Amman) may be characterized as follows.[69]

Tell el-'Umeiri Integrated Phase 10, in the southern suburbs of modern Amman, represents the tenth-century remains, above the two early Iron I houses A and B of the twelfth century (IP 13–12) and a large room in Field H of the eleventh century. Unfortunately, only a single storeroom in Field H was found, other remains being above IP 12–11.

Nearby Tell Jawa, a very large mound, has a destruction at the end of Iron I (Stratum X), followed by Iron Age remains dating mostly to the ninth century (Stratum IX). A bit farther south, the situation at the large tell of Jalul is unclear, but there are Iron II remains.

Madeba, a very large site, presents a picture in which the fortified town began in the Late Bronze/Iron I period (Field Phase 10) with fortifications. Subsequent Field Phase 9 produced fragments of monumental buildings, dating perhaps to the eleventh–tenth century. A pillar building of succeeding Field Phase 8 was dated provisionally to Iron IB (ninth century?).

Three sites bear variants of the name Mudeina (Mudayna): (1) al-'Aliya, a walled town, seems to be limited to the eleventh century; (2)

el-Mu'arraja, with a casemate wall and towers, dates to the same horizon; (3) eth-Thamad has remains from the ninth–eighth century.

Lehun is a cluster of occupied areas, one featuring a fortress of the ninth century, possibly with casemates. An Iron II fortress follows.

At Balu' most of the surface remains, obscured by massive boulders, belong apparently to the late Iron II period (eighth–seventh century?).

Archaeologists most familiar with the excavations and surveys on the Moabite plateau interpret them as representing an early stage of the coalescence of "tribal states," not well developed before the eighth century As Bienkowski puts it:

> Prior to the Iron Age, in the second millennium BCE, large parts of Jordan were occupied by pastoralists who lived in tents and herded sheep, called *shasu* by the Egyptians.... It is these groups who eventually settled in what became the kingdoms of Moab and Edom.[70]

The highly varied types of settlements and architecture, says Bienkowski, "points to a heterarchical system rather than a strong, centralized administration" in Ammon, Moab, and Edom in the Iron I period.[71] In Moab we do not see any centripetal tendencies until the ninth century, in Edom only much later. Aramean cultural influence is evident farther north, in Bashan and Gilead. The Assyrian destructions in the late eighth century bring the florescent Iron II period to an end (ch. 5).

Notwithstanding this cumulative evidence, Finkelstein and Lipschits have tried to reconstruct a unified "Moabite territorial polity" as early as the late eleventh/early tenth century. Its hub, they think, was at Balu', protected by a "chain of fortresses." The economy was fueled by trade in copper produced in the Wadi Fidan. This state-like entity ended only with the raid of Shoshenq circa 920. Only by radically redating most of the sites and indulging in unwarranted speculation (especially about copper trade) can such a scenario be justified.[72]

Routledge, in a major study of Iron Age Moabite polities, adopted a middle-of-the-road alternative, acknowledging "regional centers" with "attached communities." His theory, based partly on the ninth-century Moabite stela, was that of segmentary tribal lineages evolving into a deliberate, centralized hegemony manipulated by elites.[73]

In sum, Moab in the tenth century was developing toward eventual statehood in its own slow, distinctive way. What is striking is that the Iron I era appears to be the most formative, with Iron IIA (the tenth century) a period of setback following several notable disturbances and destructions circa 1000. Some have been tempted to attribute these to David's supposed campaigns in Transjordan, but that is going far beyond the evidence (below). We are probably correct in seeing local rivalries that had characterized the region for centuries, where any form of centralized administration was what Bienkowski calls a thin veneer.

We can deal with Edom rather quickly, since, as we have seen, a state (or better, tribal state) emerges there not earlier than the eighth century. The only town sites known are Buṣeirah (Bozrah), Tawilan, and Umm el-Biyara (Sela?), all now dated not before the eighth century.[74]

Levy's recent discovery of enormous mining and smelting installations at Khirbet en-Naḥas and elsewhere in the Wadi Feinan in the Jordan Valley, with a cemetery of hundreds of cist tombs, is C-14 dated as early as the late eleventh–tenth century. This challenges the low dates of Bienkowski and the majority of scholars regarding any centralized authority in Edom this early. Yet such industrial-scale operations presuppose some such authority. That authority is not likely to have been Egypt, whose Asiatic empire had collapsed at least a century earlier. Levy proposes either an early Edomite administration able to coerce the local Shasu pastoral nomads into what would have amounted to slave labor or possibly an early Judahite kingdom.[75]

Turning back now to Cisjordan, where the burgeoning Israelite state in the tenth century had closer neighbors, we need to look at the Phoenicians, whose territory along the northern coast was an extension of the homeland in the northern Levant. We have already listed the principal sites above, with the exception of Rosh Zayit located along the coast.[76]

Without going into details about individual sites, several features in common may be summarized.

- There may be evidence of newcomers in the Iron I period, the population continuing into Iron II.
- Cist tombs and cremation burials are distinctive.
- Maritime trade is in evidence, with some harbors constructed (Dor; Akko?).
- The towns are well planned, with fine three-room pillar and courtyard houses.
- There is strong craft specialization, that is, metallurgy, fine arts, and seals.

- ◆ New cult practices appear, such as those at a solar shrine.
- ◆ Above all, the ceramic repertoire includes local Phoenician red-slipped and polished and bichrome wares and imported Cypriot Black-on-Red I–II and Cypro-Geometric I–III wares. In addition, there are locally made hybrid forms combining these wares with local Canaanite and inland wares.

Inland, the impressive fortress of Rosh Zayit IIB–A (biblical Cabul?) marks the eastern border with Israelite Lower Galilee. Gal has surveyed this area and has shown that by the tenth century (conventional Iron IIA) several significant changes become evident. Most Iron I sites were abandoned, but rural sites increase in number. As many as fifteen new towns were established, some fortified. Finally, the border now shifts eastward to accommodate these changes in settlement type and pattern. These inland sites prospered into the mid-ninth century, when the Aramean incursions brought them to an end.[77]

Much of Gal's data comes from surveys, so we cannot really characterize these Lower Galilee sites, except to say that they do appear to reflect a sort of détente between northern Israel and southern Phoenicia in the tenth century—just as in the accommodation we have seen with Arameans in the north.

A significant clue is found, as often, in the pottery. The northern Phoenician sites are characterized not only by imported Cypriot Black-on-Red I–II and Cypriot White Painted I wares but also by local Phoenician bichrome and red-polished wares. The latter wares consist mostly of elegant pitchers with long necks and trefoil or flared mouths. There are also heavy-based carinated bowls and flasks with painted rims. These distinctive vessels are entirely covered with a thick, dark red slip, beautifully burnished (fig. 4.21). Evidence of the sort of reciprocal tenth-century relations described above is seen in the occurrence of this Phoenician pottery not only at the coastal sites discussed above but also in deposits and tombs at tenth-century Israelite sites in the north such as Hazor X and Megiddo VA/IVB.[78]

The expanding Philistine settlements along the southern coast were Israel's closest neighbors, and, as we have seen, there was some degree of interaction, especially at the height of Philistine expansion in the late eleventh–tenth century (below). This could have been perceived as a threat, but a positive effect seems to have been that the process of creating an Israelite national self-identity was hastened.

The excavators of Beth-Shemesh, a site right on the border with Philistia (only 7 or 8 miles east of Ekron and Gath), have argued that that was indeed the case. There is some Philistine bichrome pottery in Strata 6–4 (as at nearby Gezer XII–XI), so there may have been a few resident Philistines. Yet the absence of the pig bones that characterizes many Philistine sites is striking. The avoidance of pork by the local inhabitants may have been deliberate. If so, it could be taken as a form of resistance to the threat of Philistine dominance, an issue of "us against them," which often intensifies ethnic solidarity. In the view of Bunimovitz and Lederman:

> Further inquiry reveals a twofold change in the settlement pattern of the region between Lachish and Tell eṣ-Ṣafi-Gath: on the one hand, an almost complete abandonment of the countryside, and on the other, great expansion of urban life. In sheer contrast, settlement in the northern Shephelah, from the Sorek Valley to the region of Gezer, continued almost unchanged.... Since it is hard to believe that the entire Canaanite population of the southern Shephelah was completely annihilated by the Philistines, a reasonable alternative is a purposeful policy of *synoecism*—urban nucleation—evident in the LH IIIC post-palatial Aegean and adopted by the newcomers.... According to this suggestion, the Canaanite rural population within the Philistine heartland, as well as the inhabitants of neighboring sites such as Lachish, Tel Zayit, and others, was displaced from its own towns and territory and relocated in the main Philistine centers.[79]

Defining Statehood: The Case of Judah

The issue of the origins of the state in both Israel and Judah has been the subject of raging controversy in recent years. The fire was started in the 1990s, on the one hand, by the biblical revisionists and their rejection of the biblical united monarchy of the tenth century, and, on the other hand, by Finkelstein's low chronology that would down-date all the supporting archaeological data to the ninth century.

Recent Literature on the State

Here the biblical revisionists can safely be ignored, because for most of them the Hebrew Bible is a Persian or Roman period literary construct with little or no historical value. The biblical united monarchy is thus obviously fictitious. Further, despite occasional appeals to archaeology, they exhibit neither patience nor competence. As Thompson put it:

> In the history of Palestine that we have presented, there is no room for a historical United Monarchy, or for such Kings as those presented in the biblical stories of Saul, David or Solomon. The early period in which the traditions have set their narratives is an imaginary world of long ago that never existed as such. In the real world of that time, for instance, only a few dozen villagers lived as farmers in all the Judean highlands.... There could not have been a Kingdom for any Saul or David to be King of, simply because there were not enough people.[80]

Liverani, a scholar with far more breadth of learning, takes much the same view in his *Israel's History and the History of Israel* (2007). The former is a Hellenistic literary construct; most chapters in this portion of his book begin with "The Invention of...." In the contrasting part of the book, some real history of an earlier Israel is envisioned, but it is minimal, and the archaeological data are inadequately adduced.[81]

In the early revisionist literature, the very notion of any early Israelite state was dismissed without, however, giving any definition of the term *state*, much less any use of the relevant archaeological data. Not until 1995 and 1996 did Schäfer-Lichtenberger offer any definitions of a state based on the anthropological literature. Lemche could only opine that in the transition from the Amarna age to the supposed Israelite state there was involved only a shift from one "patronage society" to another. That is neither a definition of a state nor an explanation of change.[82]

Until recently, archaeologists fared little better in their neglect of anthropological theory with regard to state-formation processes in the wider literature. Finkelstein, for instance, has offered no explicit definition of a state in any of his numerous publications since 1995. We encounter several terms used indiscriminately: chiefdom, dimorphic chiefdom, full-blown state, client state, national state, regional or territorial state, multiethnic state, polity, entity, city-state, and Saulide confederacy or polity.[83] It is noteworthy that, in spite of a failure to specify just what a state consists of and the declaration that one cannot have arisen in the tenth century in the south or north, Finkelstein nevertheless declared early on:

The genuine exceptional event in the highlands of the southern Levant in the late-second to early-first millennium BCE was not the "Israelite Settlement," but the emergence of the United Monarchy—the unification of the entire region and most of the lowlands under one rule.[84]

How that is to be reconciled with Finkelstein's other conclusions is unclear. The contradictions and inconsistencies do not seem to bother him. Beginning already in 1995, Finkelstein had begun to develop his own alternative to the biblical united monarchy, or, for that matter, any tenth-century kingdom under David. Instead, he eventually came up with a "Saulide territorial polity" with its head not in Jerusalem but at Gibeon 6 miles to the northwest. Although Gibeon is mentioned in the Shoshenq list circa 920, there is no clear archaeological evidence of occupation in the tenth century, much less monumental architecture. Yet out of nothing Finkelstein reconstructs a state-like polity that claims to have ruled as far north as the Jezreel Valley. If Saul, then why not his successor David, for whom we do have extrabiblical textual evidence? This is a counsel of despair.

Dever reviewed some of the voluminous literature on state-formation processes in several papers in 1994–1997, as did Masters in 2001. In 2004 Kletter published a tour de force not only offering a thorough critical discussion of the literature on statehood but in the process giving a devastating critique of Finkelstein's low chronology and his unsatisfactory views on Israelite statehood (above). Finkelstein's only model—from band to tribe to chiefdom to state—has long been discredited.[85]

Developing a Trait List

In much of the literature on statehood, particularly in its relation to ethnicity (the national state), trait lists are criticized as inadequate or rejected completely. Yet few seem to hesitate to employ such lists when linking material culture to the notion of peoplehood in some cases. Thus Philistines are confidently identified on the basis of pottery, settlement type, house form, foodways, everyday implements, cult, burial customs, and the like. Trait lists may not be entirely satisfactory, but we cannot proceed to contrast and clarify entities without some such criteria—in this case artifacts, widely regarded as the material correlates of behavior. And culture *is* behavior.[86]

Many anthropologists have attempted to develop models, or criteria, for defining statehood. The literature is too exhaustive to summarize here, but a few guiding principles may be gleaned.[87]

1. Modern concepts of nation-states cannot be projected back into antiquity.
2. Older neo-evolutionary, typological models of a progression from band to tribe to chiefdom to state are no longer viable.
3. There is no necessary trajectory toward statehood; the question should be reframed not about how but why states develop at all.
4. States can coalesce rapidly, but they may collapse just as rapidly.
5. All societies exhibit hereditary social inequality; describing it explains very little.
6. No single model can comprehend social diversity, complexity, and change, which is what statehood is all about.
7. A behavioral approach may be best, focusing on the state as the arena in which power plays out.
8. It is more important to recognize diversity and change than to ask whether they constitute a state level of organization.
9. In the end, it is neither size nor complexity that defines statehood but centralization and the power to coerce.

These caveats notwithstanding, several scholars have developed trait lists, among them Claessen and Skalnik, although they themselves are cautious. They define the characteristics of their early state—a step beyond the inchoate early state—as follows:

1. A certain population (exact minimum unknown, perhaps 25,000).
2. A definite, distinct territory, although the outer borders are often loosely marked.
3. A political organization and central government, with one center but usually without codified law, professional judges, and police corps.
4. Being independent; the ruler has supreme military command and a bodyguard and can use the population for military service; the ruler keeps the territory from breaking into smaller regions.
5. A minimal two-tier social stratification, that is, rulers and ruled.
6. A regular surplus of goods that sustains state organization, generally not through regular taxes.

7. A state ideology that gives legitimacy to the ruler, which is supported by a priesthood.[88]

Holladay's "archaeologically discernible characteristics of a state" (1995) are obviously based on Claessen and Skalnik (although without citation). To their list Holladay would add a few other characteristics: a population over 20,000; urbanization; frontier defenses; palaces distinguishable from temples; and a writing system.[89] Holladay concludes confidently that Israel in the tenth century gives clear evidence of all these attributes (thus the biblical united monarchy).

Dever had already adopted a version of Claessen and Skalnik's earlier stage, the inchoate early state, as a working model for understanding the emergence of the Israelite and Judahite state in the 1970s. He broadened the discussion later to include an argument that urbanization is not a necessary precondition for the rise of state-level political organization. The Han dynasty in China is recognized as an early "pristine" state, yet the empire was never really urbanized. But size does count, even though we cannot usually quantify it as an absolute threshold. Several lowland Mayan polities are recognized as states, but some have a population no larger than 25,000. It is centralization, not size, that counts. Dever argued that Israel's population by the tenth century could have reached 100,000—certainly large enough—but that the fundamental evidence comes rather from the archaeological data that provide clear evidence for centralization.[90]

It is the ability of authorities to coerce goods and services, to dissemble them from the countryside, that distinguishes a state. If a particular model were preferred, it would be Claessen and Skalnik's inchoate early state or the *peripheral* model of others. The trigger for such developments (as in a General Systems Theory approach) is not clear on archaeological grounds alone. The biblical writers invoke the Philistine threat to account for (and rationalize) the rise of the monarchy, but that assertion must be measured against the archaeological evidence before it can be taken as credible (below).

Stager and his students Masters and Schloen have developed the notion of a dominant "patrimonial society" in both ancient Canaan and Israel, following up insights from Max Weber. Masters reviews many of the tenth-century sites discussed here, regarding them as evidence not only of growth and urbanization but also of statehood. He also adopts Claesson and Skalnik's model of the early inchoate state because it enables one to embrace the notion of "continued dominance of family relations in the political field." Masters insists that we must ask a different question: How was Israel able to *appropriate* a form of patrimonial society? He speaks of examining a trajectory but he does not pursue any strategy for doing so.[91]

The Iron IIA Period and State-Formation Processes

Despite the inadequacy of any single model for comprehending state formation, there are a few criteria that seem obvious and would find general assent. Simplifying the above, we can say that defining a state level of organization would require, at minimum, evidence of: (1) a degree of social stratification that would facilitate the emergence of a class of leaders; (2) centralized institutions of governance that could wield power and manage goods and services; and (3) the development of a national identity that consolidates wide support. Without these characteristics, no state, even of the most primitive form, would emerge or survive for long. None of these developments is inevitable, of course, but where they are evident they help to define a state.

If we take these criteria one by one, we can see from the archaeological evidence already presented at length that by the tenth century Judah, and probably Israel, had indeed reached a state level of organization. The earliest Israelite–Judahite polity has often been described by biblical scholars as conforming to a "segmentary tribal" model or simply as acephalous. The first model can be disregarded because we have shown that the notion of a tribal confederation is a late biblical construct. The second model overlooks the fact that even the simplest forms of social organization are not truly egalitarian. The earliest Israelite villages in the hill country must have had some form of charismatic leadership, validated by a sodality or voluntary association among equals, based on common interests.

What we see by the tenth century is the evolution of a much more stratified society. The urban centers now in evidence would have required the development of specialists of many kinds (above), but also the rise of elites capable of managing a much more complex form of economic activity. We have already listed many of these middle- and upper-class folk, far removed from the farmers and herders of the earlier villages.

Centralization is also in evidence. Planned cities, monumental architecture, palaces, administrative buildings, storage facilities, defensive installations, and patrician houses all came into being as a result of some sort of authority exercising power sufficient to coordinate resources and individuals—and, if necessary, to coerce support. The evidence of such concentrated political power is clearly seen in individual cities that have now developed. That, however, might reflect simply a loose confederation of city-states, perhaps in competition with each other (as in the Amarna age). Thus we must pursue the topic further.

Some of the best archaeological evidence for centralization comes from sites such as Hazor, Megiddo, and Gezer, where very similar tenth-century monumental city walls, four-entryway gates, and palaces are seen. This is not vernacular architecture; it reflects a highly centralized authority, as well as a consensus on what an Israelite city should look like. These cities are new foundations—royal establishments by any criteria. The low chronology, however, would rob us of all this evidence by moving it (along with Iron IIA) down a century or so. But we have shown why such a drastic reduction of chronology is unacceptable, and most archaeologists agree.

The controversy may now be laid to rest by recent excavations at Khirbet Qeiyafa in the Judahite Shephelah. This site has been described above, but the implications of Qeiyafa must be emphasized here. (1) This is essentially a short-lived, one-period site whose late eleventh–early tenth-century date is secured by a ceramic repertoire that even low chronology advocates agree is very early. (2) This is a strategically located fortress right on the border with Philistia that was deliberately planned, constructed, and provisioned, despite logistical difficulties. (3) This can only be understood as a government-backed barracks town, the houses incorporated into the casemate wall, just as they are at later Judahite district centers such as Beersheba, Tell Beit Mirsim, and Tell en-Naṣbeh. The notion that Khirbet Qeiyafa is simply a rural village or a Philistine site is absurd. Qeiyafa provides iron-clad evidence of the sort of defense planning that only a centralized government was capable of achieving—in short, a nascent Judahite monarchy or, if one wishes, a kingdom.[92]

Khirbet Qeiyafa alone, with its date more than a century earlier than the low chronology and the Iron I/IIA transition, settles the question of when a Judahite monarchy emerged, however limited. That date for such a state is not in the eighth or even the ninth century, as proposed by Finkelstein somewhat later. It is in the early tenth century *at the latest*. The discussion of Judahite statehood must now proceed with that new datum in mind.

If further evidence of a tenth-century centralized state were needed, it would come from the network of more than fifty forts strung across the northern Negev highland and the fort at Kadesh-barnea (4) in the Sinai (above). Even low-chronology advocates agree that these forts must belong to the tenth century on the basis of the ceramic evidence, as well as the fact that the Shoshenq raid securely dated to circa 920 lists them several times as being destroyed (below). These forts cannot possibly have been built and manned by highland villages such as those of the Iron I period. They are evidence of a centralized Judahite government in the tenth century.

Primary States

Primary states are considered to be the few known to have arisen on the basis of *internal* developments. Most states are classed as secondary states, those that develop in response to external factors, usually threats posed by competing forces. Many scholars have argued that it is in such competitive situations that ethnic identity is most likely to be crystallized (above). The notion of solidarity—of peoplehood—will already have been present in nascent form, as with any social group. But the possibility of extinction may force a group to coalesce and to define itself more deliberately. That does not necessarily mean the creation of a national identity, as with modern nation-states. But it does imply a clear distinction between *us* and *them*, which is necessary to motivate a people to unite as efficiently as possible to defend themselves.

We have already characterized Judahite border sites such as Tel Batash (Timnah), Beth-Shemesh, and especially Khirbet Qeiyafa as outposts where some degree of acculturation and, of course, competition with Philistines was already taking place by the late eleventh or early tenth century. By the mid-tenth century, however, Philistine pressure increased. The result would have been an identity crisis for the local population, which might still have been "Canaanite" but would soon become "Israelite" by means of resistance.

Thus an Israelite ethnic consciousness would have been sharpened by the tenth century, first developing in Iron IIA along the shatter-zone but inevitably moving inland as the Philistine threat intensified. A centralized government in Judah would have sought to respond by efforts at forging a deliberate and self-conscious ethnic identity—just as the competing Philistines had long since done. Only in that way could a fledgling state hope to survive.

This may seem speculative (even biblically biased), but the presumed Philistine expansion in the late eleventh–early tenth century can be documented on strictly archaeological grounds. The threat to Judah was real, and evidence of a response to the challenge is seen in tenth-century border fortresses such as Khirbet Qeiyafa and even in the Negev forts, although they confronted other borders.

Despite the insistence of the biblical writers that the rise of the monarchy was caused by the Philistine threat, the archaeological evidence of possible Israelite–Philistine military clashes in the late eleventh–early tenth century has scarcely been investigated. Faust, to his credit, has dealt with this issue. In 2006 he constructed an elaborate scenario that attempted to credit Philistine expansion with all of the following: (1) the abandonment of almost all of the rural settlements surveyed in the hill country in the eleventh century; (2) the destruction of the excavated sites of Shiloh, Bethel, Ai, Radanna, Khirbet ed-Dawwara, and probably Tell el-Ful in the mid-eleventh century; (3) the subsequent destruction of ʿIzbet Ṣarṭah, Tel Ḥarashim, and Tel Masos by the late eleventh century; (4) the forced concentration of the population in a few urban centers such as Tell el-Farʿah, Bethel, and Tell en-Naṣbeh; and (5) the events (above) that triggered state-formation processes in Judah.

That is a dramatic portrait of what might have happened, but it is unpersuasive. Faust gives no stratum numbers, indeed little documentation or details for the Israelite sites he enumerates. What is more telling, he does not look at the stratigraphy of the Philistine sites—the supposed perpetrators—either before or after the events of the mid- to late eleventh century. One need only to look at figures 4.2 and 3.1 and the site reports to analyze Faust's scenario; the situation—the facts on the ground—is far more complicated. In particular, the complex stratigraphy of the Philistine sites—which must have been impacted by whatever was going on in the mid- to late eleventh century—cannot be overlooked. Further, one must explain why the Philistines would have attacked the numerous late eleventh-century villages, which they could easily have by-passed. It is clear that there is little evidence to support Faust's early elaborate reconstruction of an overpowering Philistine threat. What threat there may have been appears to have been thrown back by Judahite forces, thus achieving a détente.[93]

If one looks at the sites along the Judean border with Philistia, where any encounters might have occurred, a significant picture emerges. The presumed opposing sides would have lined up approximately as follows.

Fig. 4.23. Philistine and Judahite border sites circa 1000 (cf. figs. 4.1 and 4.2)

Philistine sites	Israelite sites
Tell Qasile X	Gezer X
Tel Batash V	Beth-Shemesh 5 (= III)
Ekron IVA	Khirbet Qeiyafa IV
Gath 6	Tell Beit Mirsim B_2
Ashdod XI	Beersheba VIII
Ashkelon 17	

The question (ignoring the biblical texts for the moment) is whether any of these sites show archaeological evidence of destructions on this horizon. If so, how do they appear to differ in the aftermath? In short, *was there any real Philistine threat?*

The first fact to be considered is that all of the late eleventh-century Philistine sites listed above were disrupted, even partially destroyed, circa 1000 and weakened thereafter. The Israelite (in this case Judahite) sites, on the other hand, do not seem to have suffered any significant destructions—with the exception of Gezer, which may have been raided somewhat later by the Twenty-First Dynasty Pharaoh Siamun (978–959).[94]

What is even more interesting is the fate of sites on both sides (as it were) following the supposed crisis, that is, in the early to mid-tenth century. Somewhat surprisingly, the Philistine sites give clear evidence of some sort of decline. Tell Qasile, on the coast, is badly destroyed at the end of Stratum X and has a gap in occupation following that. Tel Batash (Timnah), right on the border, also has a sort of hiatus after Stratum IV during which simply built houses appear. Two towers may have been erected now, but there does not seem to be a functioning city wall until Stratum II. Coastal Ashdod produced no building remains immediately following the destruction of Stratum XI. Ekron, again on the border, has a long gap following the end of Stratum IVA until the late eighth century.

Ashkelon, to the south, yields a picture of only scant building remains and some pits and silos after the destruction of Stratum 17 (Stratum 16). Gath (Tel Zafit) is being excavated, but provisional Phase 5 seems to end with a disturbance, followed by a less clear occupation in Phase 4.

By contrast, the Judahite sites along the border that might have been affected by Philistine expansion show no evidence of destruction circa 1000. Moreover, they flourish in the following period. Gezer and Beth-Shemesh, both on the border, now develop into impressive, well-fortified urban sites, probably district administrative centers—their initial Judahite build-up. Khirbet Qeiyafa is founded on the border precisely at this time, no doubt intended to forestall any Philistine advance in this strategic region. The site did end, but there are indications that the Israelite border to be defended now moved to nearby Socoh (or Azekah?), both equally advantageously situated. The borderland Shephelah is especially noteworthy; this nearly abandoned region now underwent dramatic growth in settlement and population.[95]

Judahite sites farther south and inland, less strategic defensively, were not directly affected. Tell Beit Mirsim B$_2$ is succeeded by Stratum B$_3$ with no evidence of disturbance. Beersheba changes from a small settlement in Stratum VIII to a well-planned walled town in Stratum VII, perhaps as a response to a Philistine threat, although more imagined than real. Arad XII is founded in the early to mid-tenth century, but the unwalled settlement does not suggest any need for defense this far inland. Still father south and more remote, Tel Esdar II remains unaffected. Tel Masos I continues from Stratum II with several changes and some indication of decline, then ends toward the late tenth century. Finally, it is worth noting that the dozens of Negev forts were constructed precisely in the tenth century, although more related to defending trade routes than a defense against Philistine advances this far distant. Kadesh-barnea 4 (the earliest fort) may also belong to this horizon.

Two other Judahite sites are significant on this horizon. 'Izbet Ṣarṭah, a small village hovering on a small hillock overlooking the Philistine plain only 2 miles from Aphek, comes to an end with Stratum 1 circa 1000 and is deserted thereafter. That is probably due to the fact that it was the westernmost of the Iron I Judahite villages and was exposed from the beginning and easily overrun. Shiloh V ends circa 1100 and is followed by a gap in occupation, then is reduced to a small village thereafter. It is unlikely, however, that the Philistines ever advanced this far inland.

There is compelling evidence that Philistia never extended farther north than Dor on the coast or farther inland to the northeast than the Judean border at the Gezer–Bethel line. There, however, a number of other destructions may also be detected circa 1000. Continuing Canaanite sites such as Yoqneam XVII, Beth-Shean VI upper (= S2), and Megiddo VIA were destroyed (Megiddo devastatingly so). Some earlier scholars were inclined to see these destructions as evidence of Saul's or David's reputed wars against the Philistine, but that does not accord with what we now know of the Iron Age Philistines.[96]

The possibility of Judahite advances this far north must be considered as an alternative. On the conventional chronology adopted here, the above destructions can be dated circa 1000. Whatever the reasons, one thing is clear. The impressive buildup of Yoqneam XV–XIV, Megiddo VA/IVB, and Beth-Shean V lower (and possibly also Dan IVA and Kinrot IV) represents a transition from walled Canaanite towns to new urban centers that may certainly be considered Israelite (in the biblical terminology) in terms of a change in material culture. That is seen particularly in new urban planning and in the ceramic repertoire,[97] where Philistine pottery is absent but typical Israelite tenth-century pottery now appears.[98]

Along the northern coast, Phoenician sites such as Dor, Tell Abu Hawam IVA, and Tell Keisan 9 were destroyed circa 1000. These, however, are not Philistine destructions, nor are they likely evidence of Israelite (Judahite) incursions this far afield. Some scholars have attributed the transition from Dor Phase 9 to Phase 8 as reflecting an Israelite takeover, but that is a later biblical construct without clear archaeological evidence to support it.

Finally, to the northeast, in what appears to be an Aramean enclave, Tel Hadar, on the eastern shore of the Sea of Galilee, was destroyed in a tremendous conflagration that ended Stratum IV, after which the site was abandoned for several centuries.[99] Tel Reḥov, on the other side of the Jordan, witnesses a total change in material culture in tenth-century Stratum V, after a period of construction, deconstruction, and rebuilds in Strata VII–VI. The result, whatever the cause of the disturbance, is what appears to be a distinct regional variant of Israelite/Judahite culture in the north.[100]

In sum, the archaeological evidence, assessed entirely independent of any presumed biblical data, suggests that armed conflicts between the nascent Judahite monarchy in the late eleventh/early to mid-tenth century and its potential enemies did occur, at least in the south. Furthermore, these campaigns were successful enough that in the north several sites came under Judahite control, while along the southern coast the Philistines were effectively repelled and contained within acceptable borders for the duration of the Iron Age.

Further evidence for the latter development is seen in the fact that it is precisely on this horizon that a distinctive degenerate Philistine pottery called Ashdod ware (LPDW) appears at both Philistine and Judahite sites. This is essentially a hybrid ware, an aspect of the general development of a southern "coastal" repertoire that reflects a mixed Philistine, Phoenician, and Judahite ceramic tradition that extends from the tenth to the late seventh century. Finally, it is during this period—the tenth century and its aftermath—that virtually all of the unique material culture Philistine traits noted above gradually disappear.[101]

The excavator of Ekron observed that

> While cultic practices and much of the material culture from the Philistines' initial period of settlement in the 12th century exhibit Aegean influences, over the next two centuries, they gradually adopted into their own religious practice elements of Semitic and Canaanite beliefs and of the culture of their neighbors. Thus, by the 10th c. BCE, Philistine culture markers had all but disappeared.[102]

All in all, the archaeological evidence is consistent in portraying a Judean/Israelite kingdom that, although relatively undeveloped and constrained by natural borders, was able to establish and maintain both a territorial integrity and a distinctive material culture by the tenth century. Both suggest the emergence of a national Israelite self-identity, one that will persist for several centuries.

It was not only the Philistines who posed a threat to the fledgling state, but before long it would be the Egyptians to the south, quiescent since the collapse of the Egyptian Empire in Asia in the twelfth century. Although it could not have been sensed, Pharaoh Shoshenq of the Twenty-First Dynasty would carry out a devastating campaign throughout Judah and Israel circa 920 BCE. Such a campaign could scarcely have been aimed at a coalition of villages in the central hill country. The Shoshenq raid presupposes a well-organized polity in former Canaan, and there is good evidence that its action was directed against heavily fortified sites of the late tenth century and was successful (below).

The development of an Israelite state and ethnicity is seen in other aspects of the tenth century material culture, although they are less visible in the archaeological record. Thus we have noted the development of a certain style in town planning and architecture, innovations in industries such as ceramic production, the consolidation of the cult, and perhaps the beginning of a national language, script, and a rudimentary literary tradition.

These and the above cultural developments as ethnic markers may be dismissed by skeptics, especially those who do not control the archaeological evidence. But there can be no reasonable doubt about the existence of such an ideology—an ethos—not simply as an arbitrary social construct but as a reality that was embodied in a wide variety of material culture remains. After all, the Iron II material culture is clearly in continuity with that of Iron I and reflects its full flowering. On the basis of the correlation of that culture with the Merenptah Victory Stela, if we can recognize Israelites in Iron I, then their successors in Iron II were also Israelites. The people of a state now knew themselves to be, and were known by others, as Israelites.[103] In other words, the Proto-Israelite peoples have now become the inhabitants of a kingdom or state named Israel. Very shortly, by the ninth century, Aramean, Moabite, and Assyrian inscriptions will identify matter-of-factly such an Israel, and even a dynasty of kings (below).

The State in the North: Back to Chronology

The case for the emergence of a state in Judah by the tenth century, even if an early inchoate state, is persuasive to all but a few proponents of the low chronology. Their argument is not based as much on state formation processes as it is on chronology. They disregard the evidence adduced here and hold that no state such as we have described could have emerged in Judah before the eighth century (the date now increasingly conceded to be as early as the ninth century).[104]

That these are doctrinaire pronouncements is perhaps best seen in the fact that Finkelstein almost never mentions one datum that would seem to be definitive. The Tel Dan stela (fig. 4.29 below) refers not only to David by name but defines a dynasty (bêt) of his, as well as a state called "Israel," even naming two well-known kings (below). If David is to be dated before his son Solomon, he must have ruled over Israel not later than circa 950.

That means that there was such a state in Israel or Judah (or both) by the mid-tenth century

The corollary of the low chronology is that a Judahite state, or united monarchy in the artificial construct of the biblical writers, could not possibly have ruled in the north in the tenth century. There the emergence of a distinctive Israelite state took place independently, and only in the ninth century.

Given the continuing controversy, we must address the chronological issues without being biased by the biblical notion of a *united monarchy*. The term itself never occurs in the Hebrew Bible (although the presupposition is there); it is a distraction and is best avoided. Here the archaeological data are primary. But what are the issues, and how do the various arguments address them?

The Low Chronology and a Northern or Israelite State

Finkelstein, the originator and principal advocate of the low chronology, has published numerous studies in which he argues for a ninth-century date for the founding of an Israelite state (in contradistinction to a Judahite state in the south, which is even later).[105] The argument, however rigorously and single-mindedly pursued, rests on several presuppositions, all of them dubious.

First is the assumption that the so-called united monarchy of the Hebrew Bible is fictitious: the sources are too late and too tendentious to be reliable. Critics have pointed out how simplistic that is. Second, it is asserted that there is no extrabiblical witness to a state of Israel before the ninth century, when the Neo-Assyrian annals, for instance, mention "Ahab, king of Israel" at the battle of Qarqar in 853. That argument ignores the fact that the Assyrians could not have recognized an Israel before their ninth-century push westward into the Levant and their first encounter. This is an argument from silence. More important, the late-state argument completely disregards the Tel Dan inscription, which identifies beyond doubt a state of "Israel," as well as a dynasty of one "David" (above). In addition, the name David may be reconstructed on the ninth-century Moabite stela.[106]

In short, Israel's neighbors knew of its existence and took that fact seriously by the mid-ninth century at the latest. Such a state cannot have sprung into existence overnight. Further, if the dynasty is that of the biblical David (even if only in the south), the date would have to be earlier than that of his son and successor Solomon. Now the death of Solomon can be fixed at 923 plus or minus a few years by the synchronism of Solomon with the raid of Shoshenq circa 920 (perhaps 918), said in 1 Kgs 14:25–28 and 2 Chr 12:1–12 to have taken place in the fifth year after Solomon's death (below).[107] Allowing a minimum rule for this king, short of the "forty years" round number in the Hebrew Bible, we arrive at a date well fixed in the mid-tenth century for the existence of a state of Israel. That does involve giving some credence to the biblical narrative, but the *essential* data come from extrabiblical sources that tend to confirm this source in this particular instance.

The question of whether David and Solomon's rule, or a Judahite state, extended to northern Israel as early as the tenth century, however, is not thereby resolved. That issue takes us back to chronology, the backbone of history-writing. The question is not whether an Israelite or northern state could have emerged as early as the tenth century (or even the question of why), but rather whether we can conclude that it *did* so, on the basis of well-documented stratigraphy and sound chronology.

The Shoshenq Campaign, Circa 920

It has long been recognized by archaeologists and historians that the most reliable fixed date for the Iron I and IIA period in the southern Levant is provided by the topographic list of Pharaoh Shoshenq of the Egyptian Twenty-Second Dynasty, carved on the southwest wall of the Karnak temple in Luxor. A raid is depicted there on both the list of more than one hundred cartouches bearing place names and also in the accompanying pictorial reliefs that portray the pharaoh holding his conquered foes on leashes. Shoshenq's Asiatic campaign must be dated before his death in 924 (or, on a lower chronology, in 918), and thus a date circa 920 at latest is established (see fig. 4.24).[108]

The Shoshenq list is broken in places, but some lacunae can be filled by observing that in general the battle itinerary is in geographical order (although apparently arranged in boustrophedon fashion). The two registers contain a number of places identifiable with known southern Levantine towns, but they are mostly in the north—a datum that turns out to be significant. Jerusalem and the Judean highlands are conspicuously absent, although the Negev is mentioned several times.

There have been numerous discussions of the Shoshenq list, but the

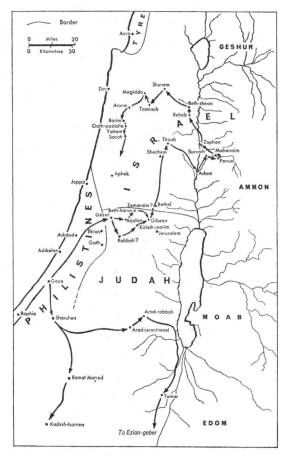

Fig. 4.24. Route of the Shoshenq campaign, circa 920 (Aharoni 1967, 284)

most authoritative are those of Kitchen, an eminent authority on the Egyptian Third Intermediate and earlier periods, and of Anson Rainey, a philologist and our foremost historical geographer. To make a long discussion short, the following chart is offered showing (1) place names that can be identified with excavated sites; (2) other identifiable place names; and (3) the strata attributed to a Shoshenq destruction circa 920 by mainstream archaeologists, in comparison with the low chronology. This chart epitomizes the chronological problem and, it will be argued, points to its solution. The order is south to north (fig. 4.25).[109]

Fig. 4.25. Excavated sites with destruction levels, both listed and
unlisted on the Shoshenq inscription, with corresponding
stratum, chronology, and numbers, circa 920

Site Number	Egyptian Term	Levantine Excavated Site, Stratum Number	Low Chronology
84, 90, 92	P-Na-g-bu	the Negev (of)	——
23	Gabbaʿôna	Gibeon (Stratum ?)	——
12	[G] a-[d] a-rú	Gezer VIII	IX
59	Ta-rú-sa-ā	Tirzah/Tell el Farʿah VIIb	VIIb
14	Ta-ʿn-k-ā	Taʿanach IB	IIB
17	Rú-h̭-bá-ā	Reḥov V	VI
16	Bí-ta-ša-lā	Beth-Shean V lower	VI upper
27	Ma-k-d-ô	Megiddo VA/IVB	VIA
Not Listed		Arad XII	XII
		Beersheba V	VI
		Tel Ḥalif VIB	VII
		Tell Beit Mirsim B_3	B_2
		Tell el-Hammah?	L
		Tel Batash IV	V
		Tel el-Ful II	I
		(Dor 9)	10?
		Tel Qiri VIIA	VIII
		Yoqneʿam XIV	XV
		Tel Kinrot IV	V
		Hazor X	XI
		Dan IVA	IVB

Several facts are established by the Shoshenq data. First, the pharaoh's extensive campaign in the southern Levant—to more than one hundred places, none in Judah—makes no sense if it had been directed merely at the Iron II highland villages, hardly a threat or of interest to Egypt. The objective must have been a well-established polity in southern Canaan, with no alternative but a tenth-century state, in this case Judah. (Even Finkelstein concedes the date; see below.) In the north, that is, Israel, it is no coincidence that virtually every excavated site has brought to light a major destruction attributable to this and no other horizon.

Both the stratigraphy and the ceramic typology attest to the correlation of the excavated levels and the Shoshenq date, although admittedly without the external data we might not be quite so precise. The burden of proof would seem to be on any scholar arguing for a different correlation. Only Finkelstein does, so how do his arguments fare in the light of the evidence cited here?

For a very long time Finkelstein ignored the Shoshenq data, declaring in fact that there were no fixed chronological dates between Merenptah circa 1200 and the Neo-Assyrian campaigns and the texts of the late eighth century. Only in 2002 did he finally address the issues posed by the Shoshenq evidence.[110]

Here he takes the Shoshenq list seriously and even explains why: "there can be no doubt" about the biblical reference to it in 1 Kgs 14:25 (although elsewhere, of course, the biblical narrative is not trustworthy). Then he proceeds arbitrarily to redo the stratigraphy of all the relevant sites, both north and south, to suit his low chronology. He moves the supposed destruction at virtually every site in figure 4.25 down from circa 920 into the ninth century. That means that he would move the *earlier* strata into the right-hand column instead of to 920.

It cannot be stated too strongly: there is no other reason for such a drastic lowering of the Iron Age dates than Finkelstein's a priori adoption of a chronology that is lower by almost a century. There is not a shred of empirical evidence for such a revision. That can be seen by looking at the twenty-one sites for which we have evidence relevant to a destruction, giving the levels that Finkelstein would attribute to the Shoshenq raid circa 920.

Fig. 4.26. Finkelstein's presumed 920 destructions
(* = site named on the Shoshenq list)

Site	Archaeological Evidence
*the Negev forts	destroyed, then abandoned
*Gibeon	no evidence
*Gezer IX	destruction; probably Siamun, 970
*Tell el-Far'ah VII$_a$	Iron I; no destruction
*Ta'anach IIB	slight occupation; no destruction

*Reḥov VII	late Iron I; no destruction
*Beth-Shean VI upper	destroyed, date uncertain
*Megiddo VIA	big destruction
Arad XII	small settlement; no destruction
Beersheba VI	no destruction
Tel Ḥalif VII	no destruction
Tell Beit Mirsim B$_2$	no destruction
Tell el-Hammah	no destruction
Tel Batash V	meager Iron I; no destruction
Tel el-Ful I	no destruction; then gap
Dor 10	early Iron I; no destruction
Tel Qiri VIII	no destruction; marked continuity
Yoqneʿam XV	no destruction
Tel Kinrot V	no data
Hazor XI	no structures
Dan IVB	no destruction

In addition to these sites in Cisjordan, four sites in Transjordan are listed: Penuel (no. 53); Hadashta (no. 54); Socoh (no. 55); and Adamah (no. 56). Only the latter, however, can be firmly identified (Tell Dami-yah). The most prominent excavated sites in Transjordan with material dated to the mid- to late tenth century are Tall as-Saʿidiyeh, Tell el-Mazar, and Tell Deir ʿAlla, and none shows any clear destruction on this hori-zon. Levy's "Shoshenq destruction" in the Wadi Fidan (above) is entirely speculative.

It will be seen at a glance that, of Finkelstein's twenty-one supposed destructions circa 920, only two or three are even remotely possible. One of these virtually all authorities agree on, as does Finkelstein himself: the Negev forts. Another, Megiddo VIA, does yield evidence of a massive destruction (above), but the agents are unknown. If Stratum VIA repre-sents the Shoshenq destruction, the destruction of subsequent Stratum VA/IVB is left without any explanation. The only possible later candidate would be the Aramean incursions of the late ninth century (below). That supposition, however, would compress Stratum IVA into an impossibly short time span, since Stratum III is clearly the post-Assyrian destruction phase, circa 732 and later.

As for Gezer, there the archaeological evidence is totally against Finkelstein's hypothetical reconstruction. Stratum IX ends with a major destruction of the last of two phases marked by degenerate Philistine pottery (LPDW), which cannot be dated any later than the early tenth century. The most likely candidate is Pharaoh Siamun (978–959) of the ill-fated Twenty-First Dynasty. This would accord with 1 Kgs 9:15–17, which says that an Egyptian pharaoh had taken Gezer and burned it with fire before ceding it to Solomon. Despite Finkelstein's charge that the Gezer chronology is based on the biblical narrative, it is based rather on stratigraphy and comparative ceramic typology.

The ceramic evidence is decisive. The Field III gate and adjacent Palace 10,000 are characterized by a unique and relatively short-lived repertoire of pottery that is treated with a thin, streaky light red or reddish-brown ("drab") *wash*, never burnished. These wares occur everywhere at the very end of Philistine levels but before the widespread appearance of *slipped* and burnished pottery beginning in the early to mid-tenth century. The appearance of these at other sites, wares on which the Gezer dates depend, can be charted here (cf. fig. 4.20 above).[111]

Fig. 4.27. General phases in the development of red wash, slip, and burnish (some overlap)

---

1. Light red wash, no burnish: mid-eleventh–mid-tenth century (all southern sites)

Tell Qasile XI–X	Tel Batash V
('Izbet Ṣarṭah II)	(Khirbet Qeiyafa IV)
Gezer X–IX	Tel Masos II
Beth-Shemesh 4	

---

2. Red wash plus darker red slip, hand burnish: early tenth–mid-ninth century

Hazor X–IX	Lachish V–IV
Taʿanach IIB	Tell Beit Mirsim B_3
Tell Qasile IX (?)	Tel Ḥalif VIIA
Gezer VIII	Arad XII–XI
Tel Batash IV	Beersheba VI–V
Beth-Shemesh 3	Tel Masos I

3. Dark red slip, wheel burnish begins and dominates:
ninth century

Beth-Shemesh 3	Lachish IV
Tel Batash III	Tel Ḥalif VID–C
Gezer VII	Arad XI
Tel ʿEton II–I	Beersheba IV

Finkelstein's denial (with Ussishkin and Herzog) of a united monarchy—of *any* Israelite or Judahite-sponsored state in the north before the ninth century—is obviously totally dependent upon the validity of his idiosyncratic low chronology, and upon closer scrutiny, that chronology turns out to have no basis whatsoever in fact, as we have shown. Thus his redating of the Hazor, Megiddo, and Gezer monumental gates and city walls to the reign of Ahab in the ninth century must be rejected on strictly archaeological, not biblical grounds.

It has frequently been noted that Jerusalem and Judah are conspicuously missing on the Shoshenq list—this despite the biblical writers' claim that the pharaoh laid siege against Jerusalem (1 Kgs 14:25–28). Rainey explains this lacuna by asserting that the northern kingdom was part of the Judahite state, and the southern kingdom posed the greater threat (and, of course, the Negev forts were attacked). Finkelstein proposes that Shoshenq attacked a coalition centered around Gibeon, thus explaining the lack of any mention of Jerusalem. There is a reference to Gibeon (no. 23), but the archaeological evidence does not suggest any important occupation of this horizon. It may be that the badly damaged lower register contains southern sites in addition to the Negev forts.[112]

The only remaining question is whether the well-documented tenth-century Israelite state in the north was an extension of contemporary Judahite rule in the south or whether such a state arose independently. The biblical presumption of the former scenario will not be taken here as prima facie evidence (see below). It is rather the archaeological evidence that is primary. What does a disinterested examination of that evidence show? It is possible, after all, that two contemporary parallel states arose, whether simultaneously or sequentially, each to be explained by different causes. The Philistine threat in the south would then be invoked, as well as the final collapse of Canaanite culture in the north, both witnessed in the archaeological record.

The archaeological evidence is admittedly inconclusive, especially as we cannot be sure of the actual events or processes that set in motion the trajectory toward statehood in the north. In the south the Philistine expansion, well documented and precisely in the late eleventh/early to mid-tenth century (above), seems an adequate, if proximate, cause. In the north, however, the equally well-documented and contemporary final collapse of Canaanite culture is not an adequate explanation in itself for the rise of an Israelite state in its place. Such a stage of revolutionary social change was not inevitable, even if it did happen. Where does that leave us?

The lingering Canaanite influence in the north is clear at such sites as Megiddo VIA, Beth-Shean VI upper, and Reḥov VII. In particular, these sites do not exhibit the typical Israelite pillar-courtyard houses (although Tel Kinrot IV and Tell el-Farʿah VIIb do). If Megiddo were a barracks town, perhaps such houses would not be expected. The fact that the cult in the north is somewhat exotic and reflects older Canaanite traditions is irrelevant, now that we know how syncretistic Israelite and Judahite religions really were. The strongly urban character of these few early tenth-century sites in the north is not surprising, since contemporary southern sites such as Gezer VIII and Beth-Shemesh 4–3 are almost equally impressive.

The best evidence for the extension of Judahite rule into the north in the tenth century (the biblical notion of a united monarchy) is probably the four-entryway gates and casemate city walls at Hazor and Megiddo, which all agree are nearly identical to the same constructions in Gezer VIII. Here the controversy over the date of these defenses has raged for years, prompted, of course, by the low chronology—not by the efforts of some to prove the Bible, as charged. Dates derived from C-14 analyses at Hazor and Gezer are not yet available, and despite Finkelstein's confident assertions about the date of the Stratum VA/IVB gate at Megiddo, it has not been touched since the Chicago excavators left it half-excavated in 1939 (see excursus 4.1 for details).[113]

The current C-14 dates for Megiddo Stratum VA/IVB are capable of differing interpretations, but Finkelstein himself acknowledges that the pottery of Stratum VA/IVB and Stratum IVA is virtually identical, a fact that is now widely accepted. Meanwhile, the pottery of nearby Tel Reḥov V and IV is also nearly identical, and C-14 dates suggest the tenth century for the former, the ninth century for the latter. That means that the Megiddo gate *could* be ninth-century in date, but a tenth-century date is equally plausible. The same would obviously hold for the Hazor and Gezer gates (and thus for a united monarchy after all).

Finkelstein has recently backed off from his low chronology by some twenty to thirty years (and by a century and a half for a Judahite state), and he himself presents two possible scenarios: his scenario one presents a high chronology (but a straw man, *too* high), with Megiddo VI possibly destroyed by an earthquake; and scenario two, which would support the low chronology. Now he leaves it to the reader to choose. Here we would have chosen scenario two, except that it attributes the destruction of Megiddo VB, Ta'anach I, and their contemporaries to the raid of Shoshenq circa 920. Megiddo VB, however, shows no evidence of any destruction. If it ends, it must be early in the tenth century, so here Finkelstein's chronology is too high. Ta'anach IIA (not I) ends in a destruction that virtually all other authorities would date to circa 960–920, supporting the conventional chronology.[114]

If all this seems confusing, it is. That is partly because a perusal of Finkelstein's numerous publications in defense of his low chronology reveals how convoluted, how contradictory, and even how cavalier his assertions are. If we reject his logic, let us take him at his own word. In 2002 Finkelstein had concluded:

> The key site for identifying the Shoshenq horizon in the south, and, in fact, the entire country, is Tell 'Arād.... The only possible candidate for Shoshenq's raid is the small, poor village of Stratum XII.[115]

What is striking here is (1) the fact that the destruction of Arad XII is dated by virtually all archaeologists to the raid of Shoshenq, including Finkelstein; and (2) if Arad XII is thus dated to the late tenth century and it is the "key" to everything else, then all the other sites in figure 4.25 here must also be dated to that event. So Finkelstein's paradigm collapses under its own weight.

The extensive discursus here may seem tedious, even polemical. But a thorough critique of Finkelstein and his low chronology is necessary. Without the clarification offered here, many readers will continue to be misled, in particular nonspecialists, and we could not proceed with any history of the tenth–ninth century.

Raz Kletter, one of Israel's most incisive archaeological thinkers, and hardly a conservative or a defender of biblicism (to the contrary), has deconstructed Finkelstein and the low chronology in a fashion that is difficult to refute. As Kletter puts it:

> The LC [low chronology] is not based on sound methodology, but largely on negative evidence and on an outdated model of social evolution. It does not include methodological contributions but rather suffers from some several methodological errors. Hence, the LC is not a new paradigm…. Much like a book of fiction, a theory presented to the academic world must be explored and evaluated by scholars other than those who wrote it. If it has to be constantly nourished and kept alive by frequent changes and revisions from its author, it does not deserve a place of its own. Scholars can mention in a note which chronology they use, and follow it consistently. But it is time to move towards more fruitful avenues of research, away from a debate about 50 years, which is fueled by ego and by such a doubtful theoretical basis. There is a whole world to study, as our own limited chronology tickles away.[116]

If Finkelstein's low chronology collapses, so does his "late state" in the north—just as his eighth-century state in Judah does.

The Biblical Narrative and the Origins of the State

True to our principle of assessing the biblical narratives separately and secondarily, we now turn to the relevant texts. As we have already seen, Finkelstein, as well as the biblical revisionists, typically accuse those who disagree with their views of being old-fashioned "biblical archaeologists." That has been the case especially with the excavation of the Gezer gate. That charge is simply not true; here we have treated the archaeological evidence for the origins of the Israelite state(s) dispassionately, as though the Hebrew Bible had never been written. We have posited a state (or two states) in the tenth century and therefore a king of necessity. But we have not needed names.

The biblical narratives that deal with the evolution of a supposed tribal confederation into a full-blown state—from charismatic judges to an anointed (and divinely ordained) king—are contained in portions of Samuel and 1 Kings. A close reading of the relevant passages here will be unencumbered by problems of literary composition, date, and theological relevance, for these are extraneous (ch. 1). Our inquiry deals only with the possible value of the texts, as they now stand, as a source for *history-writ-*

ing, and that judgment is made on the basis of archaeology as the primary source and thus a reliable critique. What we are looking for is what anthropologists call the "goodness of fit."

The results of this inquiry can be presented in a much-simplified form in figure 4.28 here. By "proven," we mean proof not in a scientific sense, but in a more modest, jurisprudence model of "the preponderance of the evidence," and "beyond a reasonable doubt." "Disproven" then means that there is a contradiction between our two sources, and the archaeological data are considered definitive. "Unproven" does not mean proven wrong, only that there is insufficient evidence, or that the evidence from one or both sources is ambiguous. In that case, the historian is best advised to leave the question open. Further speculation is not likely to be productive. The conclusions drawn here on the kings of a possible united monarchy can be shown in chart form, according to our continuum, from "proven" to "disproven."

Fig. 4.28. Biblical narratives analyzed in the light of the archaeological data for the late eleventh–tenth century

Proven	Unproven but Possible	Disproven
Saul		
◆ fortress at Gibeah	◆ defeat of Ammonites, Moabites, Edomites, and Arameans	◆ defeat of Philistines
◆ fortress at Khirbet Qeiyafa		◆ border to Euphrates
◆ battle at Vale of Elah		◆ death at Gilboa
David		
◆ collaboration with Philistines	◆ "David's Citadel"	◆ border to Euphrates
◆ charismatic leader	◆ defeat of Philistines	
◆ dynastic murders	◆ war with Arameans	
◆ dynasty founder	◆ defeat of Ammonites, Moabites, and Edomites	
◆ building up Jerusalem		
◆ Philistines as threat		

Solomon

◆ Phoenician connection	◆ rule in north	◆ vast empire
◆ Hazor, Megiddo, Gezer	◆ administrative districts	◆ grandiose capital
◆ Jerusalem as capital	◆ corvée system	
	◆ Jerusalem temple	◆ Ezion-geber, sea trade
	◆ *millo*	
	◆ chariot cities	
	◆ war with Moab	
	◆ death near Shoshenq's time	

Saul, the Bible's first king, is said to have subdued and enslaved Moab; campaigned in Ammon, Edom, and Gilead and taken tribute there; defeated the Arameans in Syria; and even extended his power to Tyre. The archaeological evidence for the reign of Saul, however, is minimal. The destruction levels that might coincide with his brief reign (ca. 1020–1000 on the basis of biblical reckoning) would include Beth-Shean VI upper, Reḥov VI, Megiddo VIA, ʿIzbet Ṣarṭah I (?), and Tel Batash V.

The Megiddo Stratum VIA destruction is massive (above), too much so for a ruler who looks more like a petty chief than a king. The Chicago excavators had suggested that an earthquake might have been possible, and the renewed excavations have produced some dramatic additional evidence.[117]

ʿIzbet Ṣarṭah is unique among these five sites in that it is one of the few Israelite villages that extend into the Iron IIA period. We have seen that all the others except Tel Esdar were abandoned sometime in the eleventh century, so these two probably came to an end in the same way a bit later. No destruction of Stratum I is evident, however.

Timnah (Tel Batash) is a Philistine site that continues into the tenth century and is not destroyed (above). Stratum IV, belonging to the mid- to late tenth century, has been interpreted by the excavators as under Israelite control by now, but it is undoubtedly of mixed ethnic identities as a border town between Philistia and Judah. Stratum III was probably destroyed in 701, then Stratum II extends until the Babylonian destructions in 605.

In summary, the biblical description of Saul's wars with the Philistines and his destruction of several of their sites finds little support in the archaeological record, although the Philistines may have been held at bay (above). Even more doubtful are claims that Saul fought against the Amalekites, Ammonites, Moabites, Edomites, and even Arameans in Syria. That is possible but unlikely. The Mesha stela in Moab may mention the "house of David," but the reading is uncertain, and the stela dates to the reign of Ahab.[118]

One intriguing bit of evidence, however, comes from the excavations at Khirbet Qeiyafa, summarized above. The very early date of the pottery at this border fortress—late eleventh–early tenth century—is accepted by all authorities (even Finkelstein). In addition, there is the fact that the site clearly reflects a centralized government. That leaves only one candidate for a king if the biblical account of the rise of kingship were to be accepted: Saul. Solomon's dates, reasonably well established, are at least fifty years too late.

Here one may turn to 1 Sam 17:1–3, which describes a battle of Saul with the Philistines in the Vale of Elah, "between Socoh and Azekah." Both sites are well known, but they have only been scarcely investigated. Across the valley from Socoh, and within sight of both Socoh and Azekah to the west, is Khirbet Qeiyafa, commanding the heights. Qeiyafa is now tentatively identified with biblical Shaaraim ("two gates"). In Josh 15:33–36 Shaaraim is listed after Azekah, only about a mile west of the site, which tends to confirm the identification. The point is that in this one case there is a striking convergence between the archaeological evidence and the biblical text. That earns the epithet *proven* or *likely* here.

The only other possible positive correlation of text and artifact is the notice in 1 Sam 15:34 that Saul apparently had a residence, perhaps a stronghold, at Gibeah before he became a full-fledged regent. Gibeah is usually identified with Tell el-Ful, a magnificently located site (not a tell) just north of Jerusalem. Excavations by Albright, generally confirmed by Lapp, reveal a fortress with thick walls and square towers in Phase II, dated to the late eleventh century. Otherwise, the absence of archaeological evidence for the brief reign of Saul is not surprising, all things considered.

In summary, stories of the legendary exploits of Saul no doubt reflect the realities of a much later era, probably the eighth century or so, when the biblical writers had more reliable sources concerning their neighbors.

It must be borne in mind that anyone aspiring to leadership in Israel in the hill country in the late eleventh century would have been coming out of what was essentially a village culture and would therefore have been a rustic. Indeed, that is precisely how the stories in Samuel describe Saul. A farm boy, he was selected arbitrarily, largely for his impressive appearance. The idea that this boy could soon have mustered and led an army of fellow-villagers against well-established Aramean city-states as much as 100 miles to the north strains one's credulity.

Now we turn to Saul's successor, David. David is said in the Hebrew Bible to have reigned forty years, as did Solomon. If the latter's death can be fixed five years before the raid of Shoshenq circa 920 (above), that would place David's reign circa 1000–960. The biblical regnal years, however, are obviously round numbers. David is thus more likely to have reigned around 980–950.

David begins his rise to power as an outlaw, a brigand attacking a Philistine militia at Hebron. Hebron has been partially excavated and published. There is Iron I and II occupation, but little more can be said. David is credited with a number of other victories in 1–2 Samuel. These involved (1) successful wars against the Philistines from Gezer to Gath, taking "Gath and its villages" (1 Chr 18:1); (2) wars against the Arameans under Hadadezer in southern Syria; (3) the pacification of Ammon; (4) the conquest of Gilead and Moab; and (5) the restoration of Israel's borders all the way to the Euphrates.

According to 2 Sam 10:6–19, David campaigned against Ammon, which had conspired with the Arameans. The towns mentioned in David's battles are Rabbah, Beth-rehob, Maacah, Ish-tob, Rehob, and Helam (in addition to Zobah, in northern Syria). Rabbah (often Rabbath-ammon) is clearly Ammon, modern Amman. If Beth-rehob is Tel Reḥov, in the upper Jordan Valley near Beth-Shean, it is irrelevant; if not, it is unknown. Maacah may be the name of a district east of Dan, that is, biblical Bashan. Ish-tob and Helam are unidentified.

The only relevant tenth-century archaeological data might come from Amman. There, however, we have only a possible tomb and a few ill-defined sherds. A tomb at nearby Saḥab may belong to this horizon. However, since Amman has scarcely been excavated, the lack of evidence means very little.[119]

The reference to Zobah, a well-known Aramean kingdom north of Damascus, is interesting, but it means only that the biblical writers knew of its existence in their own day, much later. The reference need not be taken as evidence of ancient sources, much less of the authenticity of the story.

Apart from the later biblical texts, we have only the tenth-century Shoshenq list, which mentions a few possible sites in Transjordan, all near Deir ʿAlla in the Jordan Valley: Mahanaim (no. 22); Penuel (no. 53); and Adam (no. 56). These sites may not be mentioned in stories of David's wars because they are assumed to be in Israelite hands. In any case, even if identified, these sites have not been excavated.[120]

There are also accounts of Davidic victories at Gob, a site that is unknown, and at Gath. Philistine Gath is now certainly identified with Tel Zafit (Tell eṣ-Ṣafi). Phase 6 there ends sometime toward the late eleventh century but with no trace of a destruction thus far.

Finally, the death of Saul, David's predecessor, fighting the Philistines atop Mount Gilboa makes little sense topographically or militarily, nor is there any evidence that the Philistines ever penetrated that far inland. At nearby Beth-Shean there are only a handful of Philistine sherds, indicating nothing more than sporadic trade at a site that remains mostly Canaanite, not Philistine (above).

In sum, there is no archaeological evidence to support David's alleged wars with Ammon. The archaeologists most familiar with the area and with the archaeology of Jordan in general only suggest possible Israelite presence, along with Arameans, on the plateau of Irbid and Ajlun and perhaps in Moab. Otherwise, we appear to be dealing with local Ammonites, Moabites, and Edomites. Herr concludes of the archaeology of Jordan:

> The early centuries of Iron II are presently very difficult to document in Jordan. Specifically, the tenth century assemblage of pottery is not easy to isolate, making many of the attributions here uncertain. Some could be placed slightly earlier in Iron I. Roughly half of the material attributed to this period comes from tombs, many of which contain mixed ceramic assemblages. Because of these uncertainties and the lack of any significant, large excavations, we cannot make generalizations regarding settlement patterns or zones of material culture. In spite of this dearth of materials, it is possible that already by this time, we can suggest incipient national groups that controlled parts of the plateau.[121]

The victories claimed over the city-states of Syria and virtually all the tribal kingdoms of Transjordan are not credible, nor is there any archaeological support for them. The archaeology of Jordan is now so far advanced that the tribal kingdoms there are known to have their own local history. There is simply no room for any sizeable Israelite presence there anywhere in the early Iron II period. Israelite sovereignty over the Aramean city-states as far north as Damascus (and even Aleppo) is even less credible. As for the border of Israel extending at any time to the Euphrates, that must be dismissed as fantastic. The fact that standard Bible atlases confidently map such events does not mean that they actually happened.[122]

The only incident for which the biblical writers seem to have had reliable information is their reference to David going up against one Hadadezer, an Aramean king who was the son of Rehob. This is none other than Hadadezer, king of the major Aramean polity at Zobah, north of Damascus. The account of such a battle is fantastic, but the biblical reference to Hadadezer is credible. He is known to have ruled at Zobah, and although his dates are unknown, he may have been a contemporary of David.[123]

Local wars against the Philistines seem also plausible, as we saw above, as does their eventual containment. Yet there are problems. For instance, David is said to have overrun the Philistines from "Geba to Gezer" (2 Sam 5:25). Geba is not clearly identified, but it may be located south of Ai, some 12 miles north of Jerusalem. That is hardly Philistine territory. As for Gezer, also not really Philistine, there are conflicting stories. In Samuel, David is said to have taken Gezer, but 1 Kgs 9:16 famously says that Gezer remained non-Israelite until an Egyptian pharaoh destroyed the city by fire, then ceded it to Solomon. The excavators of Gezer have tentatively attributed that city, Stratum IX, to Siamun of the Egyptian Twenty-First Dynasty (ca. 978–959). Stratum VIII then exhibits the four-entryway gate, casemate city wall, and palace that are taken here to represent the first Israelite establishment. Both accounts cannot be true.[124]

The claim to have subdued "Gath and its villages" is also open to suspicion. Gath was close to the Judean border, but the destruction (if any) of Stratum 6 is dated in the late eleventh century, too early by many years. In addition, Stratum 5, spanning the so-called Davidic era, is not destroyed at all in the tenth century As for the rest of Philistia, figure 3.1 above shows that most sites continued well past David's time, and the causes of their end circa 900 are unknown.

The biblical writers may well be correct in remembering that Philistine expansion in the late eleventh–tenth century constituted a threat to the nascent kingdom of David. But the notion that David totally subdued

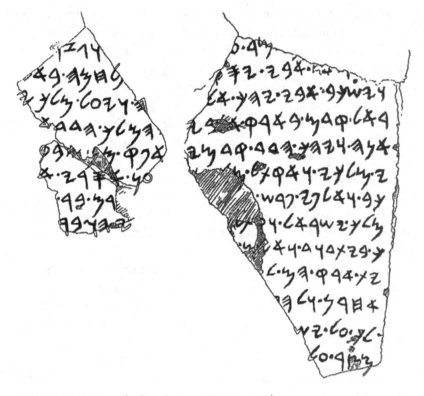

Fig. 4.29. Dan stela (McCarter 1996, no. 70)

the Philistines is unrealistic. At best, he may have kept them temporarily in check, a fact that does seem to be supported by the archaeological data (above).

Nevertheless, archaeology has produced some surprising evidence that a King David did exist, that he ruled over an Israel, and that he founded a dynasty that was remembered later. The Tel Dan stela, an Aramaic inscription found in 1993–1995 in the outer gate plaza, refers specifically to the "dynasty of David" (*bêt-dāwîd*) and to an "Israel," even naming two kings known in the Hebrew Bible: Jehoram of Israel, Ahab's son; and Amaziah of Judah.

The stela was found as a broken stone incorporated into an outer gate wall that was destroyed in the Assyrian destruction in 732. But the paleography, as well as the apparent reference to Hazael of Damascus, dates the original very close to 741, when the alleged Aramean victory took place. Skeptics have tried to read anything but *bêt* (clearly "dynasty") or "David" (variously *dôd*, "uncle," or *bêt-dāwîd* as a place name, like Beth-lehem; see fig. 4.29).

The revisionists have apparently never abandoned in print their absurd insistence that the inscription is a modern forgery. An unforced reading can only conclude that the inscription—hardly to be accused of biblical biases—means just what it says. There *was* a historical David, and he was the founder of a *dynasty* well known to his neighbors. It should also be noted that there has been a suggestion that the name David also appears on the ninth-century Mesha inscription from Dibon (Dhiban) in Moab. The point here is that, if the biblical David was an attested historical person, it is not fantastic to suppose that his son Solomon also was.[125]

In David's favor, it should be observed that a number of aspects of his career as outlined in the Hebrew Bible do fit the known archaeological situation in the mid-tenth century. That would include David's collaboration with the Philistines, his later opposition to the threat they posed, his rise to power not through dynastic succession but by charismatic gifts and intrigue (serial murders), and his efforts to shape Jerusalem, a former Canaanite (Jebusite) enclave, into a new national center. None of these supposed activities can be proven, of course, certainly not on the basis of direct archaeological evidence. But they are plausible, and they suggest that the later biblical writers and final redactors had oral and perhaps even written sources that may go back as far as the early Iron II period.

It is Solomon, however, who is portrayed in the Hebrew Bible as the hero of a golden age. During his forty years he rules an empire that stretches from the Mediterranean to the Euphrates; he establishes a grandiose capital in Jerusalem, where everything seems gold-plated; he takes a yearly tribute of gold that amounts to more than 400 pounds; he can field an army of 12,000 charioteers and 1,400 chariots; he employs 150,000 workers to build a fabulous temple and other structures unlike anything anyone has ever seen; he imports horses from Anatolia and chariots from Egypt; he fosters maritime trade with the east coast of Africa via his seaport at Ezion-geber; his fame spreads to Arabia and Egypt; and he has 700 wives and 300 concubines, including the daughter of the Egyptian pharaoh.

Most of this is obviously the stuff of legend. When it comes to any possible supporting evidence from archaeology, there is none. Finkelstein has charged that archaeologists like Dever at Gezer and others have been trying to legitimate the Hebrew Bible's portrait of a golden age. This is simply not true, as a perusal of the literature will show.

The archaeological evidence is mixed. There are few destruction layers to be investigated, since Solomon evidently came to the throne in a period where a détente with the Philistines had already been achieved (above). Thus he was free to devote himself to consolidating his realm and perhaps also to cultivating the arts.

One of Solomon's accomplishments is said to have been a rapprochement with the neighboring Phoenician peoples along the coast and in Upper Galilee, even establishing a cordial relationship with Hiram of Tyre. The Jerusalem temple was in fact said to have been built with major assistance from Phoenician architects, artisans, and masons. This Hiram is evidently Hiram I, known also as Ahiram, who ascended the throne in circa 970–930, whose sarcophagus is now in the Louvre.

Of Solomon's famous temple in Jerusalem, it is often asserted that there is no actual evidence that such a fantastic structure as that described in 1 Kgs 6–9 ever existed. But then no one has ever been able to excavate on the Temple Mount, where it would have been located. In many cases, skepticism about the trustworthiness of the biblical narratives is warranted, since the ancient events and things they describe centuries later would long since have disappeared and been forgotten.

It is unlikely, however, that the detailed descriptions of a Jerusalem temple erected early in the monarchy would have been totally fabricated. However early the actual date of such a temple might be, it is likely that the structure would still have stood until the Babylonian destruction in 586. That means that the biblical writers in the seventh century (the Deuteronomistic Historians) are describing a real structure, one that existed in their day and was well known to them, even if in a modified form. The fact that some of the Hebrew terms in 1 Kgs 6–9 are difficult or rare is easily explained if the writers were unfamiliar with the technical vocabulary that would have been used to describe a unique structure of an earlier day, along with its complex furnishings.

It is true that we have no direct archaeological evidence for the temple described in the Hebrew Bible, but we do have an abundance of parallel examples from Iron Age contexts throughout the southern Levant. They illustrate in detail what a monumental temple built in Jerusalem in the tenth century would have looked like, quite apart from any biblical-inspired presuppositions (fig. 4.30).

The distinctive tripartite plan—three rooms arranged sequentially in a long-room plan—is known from dozens of examples in the Levant, going

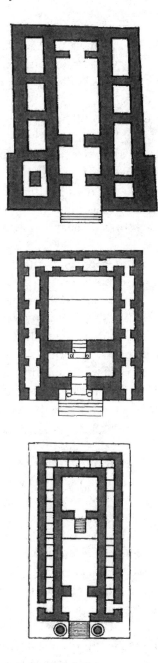

Fig. 4.30. Comparison of tripartite temples. 1: temple at Tell Afis, Syria, ninth–eighth-century (Mazzoni 2014, 44); 2: the ʿAin Daraʿ temple, ninth–eighth century (Monson 2005, 933); 3: reconstruction of the Solomonic temple (*IDB* 4:537)

all the way back to the early second millennium. It is a plan especially common in Syria and in Bronze and Iron Age Canaan. The closest parallels come from a ninth-century Aramean temple excavated at Tell Taʿyinat in Turkey, and especially from the contemporary temple at ʿAin Daraʿ in northern Syria (see fig. 4.30).

The latter exhibits numerous archaeological and iconographic features that are almost exactly like those of the biblical temple, including: (1) a tripartite plan very close in size; (2) twin columns at the entrance; (3) a cella or inner sanctum where the cult image, real or imagined, would have been displayed; (4) cherubs guarding the entrance outside or inside; (6) an ambulatory around the sides and rear; (6) triple-recessed windows; and (7) decorations consisting of chain designs, lilies, pomegranates, lions, and bulls.

Elsewhere in the Levant there are many other features of a "Solomonic temple" that now make sense, however inscrutable the biblical text in its present form may seem. The ashlar masonry and the stones prefitted at the quarry, then assembled onsite, are easily explained by reference to tenth–ninth-century ashlars found at Megiddo, Gezer, and Samaria, some bearing identical masons' marks. Likewise, the description of Solomon's masons and craftsmen imported from Hiram, king of Tyre, makes perfect sense when we see the Phoenician-style ashlar masonry at these sites. The enigmatic courses of stone alternating with wooden beams (earthquake protection) are well known from Syria, where they occur with ashlar masonry, as well as in the construction of the lower city wall at ninth-century Samaria. The square, spoke-wheeled bronze braziers for heat and light with round tops, decorated in a cast bronze network pattern featuring cherubs and lions, are paralleled almost exactly by braziers from Salamis in Cyprus, dated to the twelfth century.[126]

None of this parallel evidence proves the existence of a tenth-century temple in Jerusalem, but it does mean that it is no longer possible to declare the biblical description fantastic. Further, a royal temple would be expected of a Solomon. Other rulers of the petty kingdoms of Syria and Anatolia built for themselves the very same complex that the biblical writers attribute to Solomon. For example, the ninth-century Aramean acropolis at Tell Ḥalaf and at Zincirli (Samʾal) feature a palace, administrative buildings, and a temple, all closely connected and surrounded by their own enclosure wall.

The most controversial archaeological data with a possible relation to

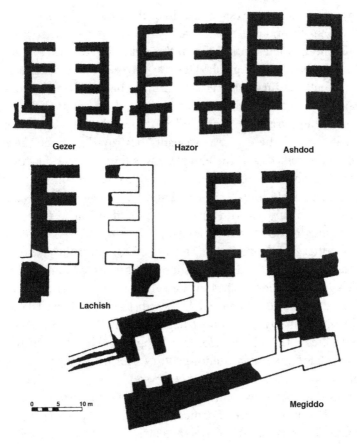

Fig. 4.31. City gates of the tenth century (adapted from Herzog 1992, 266)

Solomon is undoubtedly that concerning the Field III city gate and case-mate wall of Gezer VIII.[127] These monumental constructions were dated by the excavators to the mid-tenth century on the basis of the fundamental tools of archaeology: meticulous stratigraphy and comparative ceramic typology—not, as charged, on a literalistic reading of 1 Kgs 9:15–17 (see fig. 4.31).

That well-known text describes how Solomon took over a city ransacked by the Egyptian pharaoh, then "built" it (Heb. *bānâ*, "to build, rebuild") along with Jerusalem, Megiddo, and Hazor. Nearly identical gates and walls were found at Megiddo VA/IVB and Hazor X, and Yadin had famously related all three to Solomon's centralized administration in Jerusalem, attributed to a sort of bureau of civil engineers. The Gezer exca-

vations set out neither to defend Yadin or the Hebrew Bible, much less the
conventional chronology, which was not yet an issue in the 1960s.

The fine-grained stratigraphy in the Field III gate, with section drawings of every baulk, distinguished fourteen street levels in the gate, ranging
from the tenth century to the Hasmonean era in the second century. What
is clear is that, after the third street, there was a great conflagration that
left burned and cracked stones still visible in the masonry of the west
outer-gate tower. The gate was so badly destroyed that the tower walls
had to be buttressed, and the entryway was then reduced to three flanking piers. Excavations in the outer two-entry gate downslope, a mirror
image of the Megiddo gate, revealed similar damage. There were found
displaced ashlar blocks with mason's marks identical to those at tenth-
century Megiddo and Samaria (above).

The pottery on the floor of Palace 10,000 adjoining the gate to the west
was of a distinctive red-washed, unslipped or burnished ware that has close
parallels in other Judean sites of the early mid-tenth century, especially
Tell Qasile X and Beth-Shemesh 4. Such distinctive pottery characterizes
a short phase after the floruit of degenerate Philistine red-washed and
painted wares (LDPW) but before red-slipped and hand-burnished wares
come to predominate at late tenth-century sites, continuing into the ninth
century as we now know (see fig. 4.20 above).

The Shoshenq list evidently includes Gezer. The cartouche (no. 12) is
damaged, but the sequence of names and the topography suggest restoring
the name Gezer, right after Gaza (no. 11). Next come the sites of Beth-
Horon and Aijalon, close by.[128] The destruction of the Field III gate after a
period of use may be dated to the Shoshenq raid circa 920. That would fall
right at the time of Solomon's death. This is the only reasonable date for what
was a major destruction, not to be equaled until the late eighth-century
Neo-Assyrian destructions, when the gate was once again destroyed. The
low chronology simply has no candidate for any ninth-century destruction.
The Aramean incursions to be treated in chapter 5 rarely penetrated far
into this region, according to the scant archaeological evidence. It is worth
noting that a series of other sites also have late tenth-century destructions,
among them Hazor X and Megiddo VA/IVB, which exhibit almost identical four-entryway city gates. These sites, as well as the others mentioned on
the Shoshenq list, can be dated to the tenth century without invoking the
name of Solomon or vindicating the biblical writers. It is archaeology that
corroborates the text in this case, not the other way around.

One further aspect of the biblical account to be investigated in the light of the archaeological data is the list of Solomon's administrative districts and their centers in 1 Kgs 4:7–19 (above). These lists have been exhaustively analyzed by biblical scholars and topographers. According to the biblical tradition, Solomon established twelve administrative districts, ostensibly so that each could supply his government in Jerusalem for one month, but also capitalizing on memories of the old twelve-tribe league. What the archaeological evidence suggests, when considered independently, is that the Solomonic district lists rest, at least partly, on older traditions. These may preserve some historical memories, even though in their present form they are part of the Deuteronomistic Historians' intent to aggrandize Solomon's rule. Thus they can be listed in the "unproven but possible" category in figure 4.28 above.

One recent datum must be added to possible archaeological evidence relevant to Solomon's exploits in Transjordan. Levy, Adams, and others have been excavating in the Wadi Feinan (Punon; biblical Edom) in the lower Jordan Valley, known from antiquity for its copper mines. At the 25-acre site of Khirbet en-Naḥas ("ruin of copper") these archaeologists have brought to light a long-lived, intensive copper mining and smelting industry. There is a large, rectangular fortress with a three-entryway gate; numerous adjacent residences, including four-room or pillar-courtyard houses; huge scattered slag heaps; and a cemetery of as many as one thousand shallow pit graves that apparently contain the bodies of workers.

Of interest here is a series of calibrated C-14 dates that cluster around two principal use phases of these facilities: (1) an initial phase in Iron I, twelfth–eleventh century; and (2) a peak in "Iron IIA/B," tenth–ninth century. In addition, there are collar-rim store jars, early Midianite pottery known from early Iron Age Qurayyah, Cypriot Black-on-Red II wares closely dated to the tenth–ninth century, and black dipper juglets with high neck and button-base that find their best parallels in tenth-century sites in Cisjordan. In addition, two scarabs have twelfth–tenth-century parallels. These dates have been questioned by advocates of the low chronology (predictably), but they withstand close critical scrutiny. Therefore, the conventional notion that Edom approached a state-level of political organization only in the eighth century may need to be reevaluated.

The question is whether the existence of an apparently state-sponsored metal-working industry in the tenth century in Transjordan could have something to do with state-formation processes on the other side of the Jordan, that is, in Judah. It may be related; at least it is contemporary and in relatively close proximity. Nevertheless, Khirbet en-Naḥas is clearly an Edomite site, by no reasonable criteria an Israelite/Judahite site. At best, there may have been a trade relationship for mutual benefit, as both Israel and Edom moved toward a level of organization, even if Edom lagged behind.[129]

A related issue concerns Solomon's reputed copper mines at Eziongeber, identified with Tell el-Kheleifeh, in the southern Arabah, just north of the Gulf of ʿAqaba/Eilat. The site was excavated in 1938–1940 by Nelson Glueck, who popularized it as King Solomon's copper mines. However, he never published a final report. The workup of the material by Pratico much later has shown that the evidence of copper smelting was imaginative and (2) that the fortress at Tell el-Kheleifeh does not antedate the eighth century.

New evidence may revive the old, long-discredited notion of King Solomon's copper mines. Ben-Yosef and colleagues have recently reexamined Rothenberg's old sites at Timnah in the lower Arabah. New excavations produced a series of C-14 dates with far-ranging conclusions. The old view relating the extensive copper-working installations to Egyptian interests in the Late Bronze Age must be abandoned. Ben-Yosef and his colleagues conclude that (1) Timnah 30 and other mining sites began only in the eleventh century; (2) they peaked in the tenth century, were disrupted in the Shoshenq raid circa 920, then revived somewhat only to end by the late ninth century; and (3) although sophisticated in some ways, these operations were initiated by "a local, semi-nomadic tribal society," but possibly aided by foreign (i.e., Edomite) agents, perhaps even a Judahite monarchy.[130]

Finkelstein, who (oddly enough) had been moving his dates for the Khirbet en-Naḥas copper-working site up somewhat (although he still thinks the fort eighth century in date) seized upon the tenth–ninth-century evidence and proceeded to construct a vast "settlement network" of sedentarized nomads in the Negev highlands. The catalyst for this movement was the highly specialized Wadi Feinan and Arabah copper industry, which resulted in a "complex, chiefdom-based local society."

The possibility of Edomite sponsorship was considered, but it was dismissed because there is general agreement that a state level or even tribal society did not arise in southern Transjordan before the eighth century at

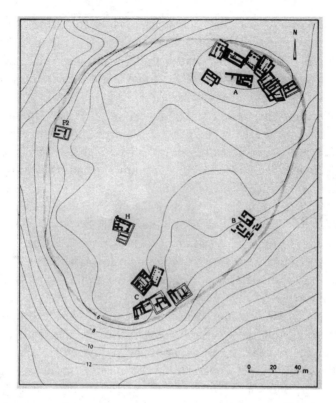

Fig. 4.32. Plan of Tel Masos, Stratum II (Kempinski 1993, 987)

the earliest. Instead, Finkelstein and his colleague Martin fall back on the old "Tel Masos desert chiefdom" model that Finkelstein, van der Steen, and a few others had previously espoused.[131]

They acknowledge some problems, but they are not deterred. Yet these problems are severe. (1) Tel Masos is a relatively large size (ca. 15 acres), but only about one-tenth of the site was excavated (fig. 4.32). Around the perimeter were found a number of typical Iron Age pillar-courtyard houses of Stratum II, their outer walls forming a sort of defensive barrier (although not a city wall).

(2) The only possible Stratum II administrative complex is Building 80 in Area C, a center-hall building described as a "fort," with an adjoining pillared building. Building 1039 in Area A may be a storeroom. These buildings are indeed more monumental than those typical of other Negev Iron I–II sites, but they hardly qualify Tel Masos as the "hub" of an extended Negev chiefdom.[132]

(3) Some trade with the Phoenician coast is implied in the pottery, but there is no evidence that trans-shipping of pottery or any other commodities was involved. Only a metalsmith's workshop and a few copper fragments were found, as with several other early Israelite sites (Khirbet Radanna).

(4) By consensus, the relevant Stratum II at Tel Masos dates to the late eleventh century and ends circa 1000 or shortly thereafter, too early to relate to even a nascent Judahite polity, kingdom, or state that would have been able to organize a widespread copper-mining and smelting operation on an industrial scale.[133]

(5) Finkelstein's positing a wholesale voluntary settlement of pastoral nomads willing to work in inhuman conditions defies everything we know about the sedentarization of such nomads.[134] They *had* to have been enslaved, and the notion that the small site of Tel Masos II—even if contemporary with the Arabah-Negev copper working—could have mustered such force begs one's credulity.

(6) Finally, Finkelstein's scenario cannot provide the sine qua non for a massive copper-producing industry: markets. The small site of Tel Masos cannot possibly have managed the necessary trading network, much of which certainly depended on the maritime trade we know was engaged in by Phoenicians in the tenth century or even earlier. Phoenician influence is seen, for instance, in ceramic imports from Cyprus, as well as the spread of its own coastal wares, well documented at many sites both north and south. Only a Judahite state, however small, could have fostered such trade, but the local copper was more likely for local consumption.

In summary, Finkelstein's and van der Steen's Masos chiefdom is a figment of their imaginations. If there is any tenth-century central administration, it is not at Tel Masos, nor can it be Egyptian or Edomite.[135] Finkelstein short-circuits the complex discussion of Judahite statehood by continuing to deny the existence of a Solomonic kingdom. But then he constructs an entirely fanciful Saulide polity with its center not at Jerusalem but at Gibeon, "the hub of an emerging territorio-political formation, which endangered the Egyptian interest in Palestine," thus becoming a target of Shoshenq. In his view, this "kingdom" extended its sway all the way up to the Jezreel Valley. Thus it, rather than Jerusalem, ruled the Wadi Arabah/Negev complex.[136]

The Wadi Feinan and Wadi Arabah copper industry of the tenth–ninth century, however, makes sense only as an enterprise of a Judahite kingdom or state. It would then have been aligned with the contemporary network of dozens of Negev fortresses and the clusters of houses found near them, which would have provided regional administrative centers, defense, and probably a source of workers (perhaps with some partly sedentarized pastoral nomads; see above).

This entire complex was no doubt part of the rationale for the Shoshenq campaign circa 920, which claims specifically to have destroyed "the Negev," along with Arad (XII). All authorities agree on the date of these destructions, even Finkelstein. However, his low chronology requires him to date the end of Tel Masos II down to the Shoshenq raid, rather than circa 1000 with virtually everyone else.[137]

If one looks at the larger picture of copper production, maritime trade, and Cypro-Levantine relations from circa 1200 to 1000, a tentative scenario can be envisioned as follows. Many copper-producing or shipping centers along the coast in Cyprus were disrupted, some destroyed at the end of Late Cypriot IIIA, in what appear to be incursions of "Aegeanized" Sea Peoples. Among them are presumed to be the Philistines of Ramesses III's inscriptions and reliefs, characterized by Mycenaean III:C1 monochrome pottery.

By 1180 at latest, these Sea Peoples (and perhaps others) appear along the southern Levantine coast, where imported and local (?) monochrome pottery (Phase 1) is soon displaced by Philistine bichrome pottery (Phase 2). The Philistines may have continued maritime trade with Cyprus independently from the twelfth into the eleventh century, either through ports at Ashkelon and Ashdod (i.e., Tel Mor), or in collaboration with Phoenician traders farther north along the coast. However, twelfth-century contacts with Cyprus are not attested at any early Iron I sites in Canaan. Neither Cypriot pottery nor (apparently) copper imports are well attested until late Iron IB, circa 1050. By that time, the first Cypriot pottery appears at both coastal Phoenician sites such as Achzib, Akko, Tell Keisan, Tell Abu Hawam, and Dor (White Painted I; Cypro-Geometric I) as well as at inland sites such as Megiddo (VIA: Cypro-Geometric I ware and a White Painted I krater) and Tell el-Farʿah North (White Painted I–II vessels), and such wares also appear at the Judahite site of Khirbet Qeiyafa (Cypro-Geometric II?).[138]

Phoenician bichrome pottery also appears now for the first time, circa 1050, and it is likely that as Phoenicia and its seaports expand in the eleventh century, the Phoenicians became the principal intermediaries in Cypro-Levantine trade. The imported Cypriot wares are the best clue, but clear Cypriot copper imports are lacking, while a local industry is in evidence. The disruptions in Cyprus did not end copper production in Iron I, but they may have affected exports adversely.

The beginning of a local Levantine copper industry in the Wadi Feinan, Wadi Arabah, and the southern Negev in the eleventh century may be explained by the dearth of imports from Cyprus after the eleventh century, as well as the disappearance of Egyptian hegemony already by the late twelfth century. The peak of southern Levantine copper production in the tenth–ninth century then coincides with the rise of a Judahite polity or kingdom/state. In that case, the copper was not for export, although contacts with Phoenicia and Cyprus are well manifested by then (Phoenician Red Polished and Cypriot Black-on-Red I wares). Rather, increasing supplies of copper were needed for local markets—one more witness to early state-formation processes, at least in Judah in the south. If so, it is not fantastic to suppose that the biblical memories of King Solomon's copper mines rest on some historical events, however exaggerated.[139]

As for Solomon's supposed sea trade with the east coast of Africa, that rests on nothing more than vague biblical allusions, even if Ophir could be located. Could Solomon have had something to do with the exploitation of copper ores in the Jordan Valley and transported them abroad? Perhaps, but that cannot be proven; at best it is possible.[140]

Three final aspects of Solomon's reign as depicted in the Hebrew Bible remain to be considered. The corvée system, or forced conscription of labor, is described in 1 Kgs 5:13 and is said to have mustered 30,000 men. Such a labor force would help to explain the monumental structures we have seen at several sites, all evidence of central planning. But the figure is much too high (like the 150,000 workers for the temple). The total population of Israel and Judah by the tenth century is estimated to be little more than 100,000.

There are several biblical references in the Hebrew Bible to a Millo, or "filling," that was built or rebuilt in Jerusalem by David, Solomon, and others. This was evidently a major construction, because it is listed as part of Solomon's buildings that were erected on the acropolis by corvée labors, such as his palace, the temple, and the city walls (1 Kgs 9:15). There is good reason to see this filling, or terrace system, as the massive stepped stone structure described above.

Jerusalem is notoriously short of an adequate water supply. From very ancient times, at least from the Middle Bronze Age, the Gihon Spring below the eastern slopes of the hill of Ophel (the city of David) has been exploited as efficiently as possible. The most famous water system is the so-called Hezekiah's Tunnel of the late eighth century. An earlier vertical shaft cut from the level of Iron Age surfaces inside the city upslope reaches all the way down through bedrock to the spring. Called Warren's Shaft after the nineteenth-century discoverer Sir Charles Warren, this shaft was thoroughly reinvestigated by Shiloh in the 1980s. It cannot be dated independently, because like such water systems elsewhere it may contain pottery from many different periods. Following Shiloh and other scholars, many have regarded Warren's Shaft as a tenth-century construction intended to give access to the spring from midslope. It might then be David's ṣinnôr, or secret tunnel (2 Sam 5:8). That suggestion cannot be proven of course, but it is plausible. In any case, such an impressive engineering feat could only have been undertaken by some central authority, perhaps in David's time but more likely during the long and better-established rule of Solomon.[141]

Summary

This chapter has sought to chart the rise of small territorial states in the southern Levant in the early Iron II period, circa 1000–900, among them principally Israel and Judah (the biblical "all Israel"). The archaeological evidence has been surveyed as our primary source, then compared to the narratives in the Hebrew Bible in order to form a composite picture where the two sources may be compatible. A brief summary is now in order.[142]

First, there is a major shift from a peripheral and isolated agro-pastoral village culture in the twelfth–eleventh century to a highly centralized urban culture by the tenth century, one that was capable of unifying and governing large areas of both Judah and Israel. In particular, we see a three-tier hierarchy of sites that is a clear reflection of social stratification and diversified economic strategies, as well as the concentration of political power.

Tier 1. There are several large cities with a population of more than 1,000 and monumental architecture, including fortifications. They are strategically located and well equipped to serve as regional administrative centers. They would include:

Dan IVA
Hazor X
Tell el-Farʿah VIIb
Beth-Shean V lower
Megiddo VA/IVB
Yoqneʿam XV–XIV
Taʿanach IIA–B
Shechem X
Gezer VIII
Beth-Shemesh 3
Jerusalem 14
Tell Beit Mirsim B$_3$

Tier 2. There are a number of smaller towns with a population of circa 300–1,000 that also exhibit densely built up areas, some fortified as well. These would include:

Kinrot IV
Hamath (Tell el-Hammah)
Gibeon
Timnah IV (Tel Batash)
Tel Ḥalif VIB

Tier 3. A number of tenth-century villages of up to about 300 people are known, generally unwalled and located in the hinterland. They would include:

Tel Qiri VIIA
Tel Qashish III

In addition, there are the several dozen small forts in the Negev, as well as more central forts that are not typical settlement sites. One would be Gibeah (Tell el-Ful II), on the outskirts of Jerusalem. Another would be Khirbet ed-Dawwara, a small walled settlement on the desert fringe northeast of Gibeah. "Solomon's seaport" at Ezion-geber must be reevaluated. A reworking of Glueck's excavations at Khirbet Kheleifeh by Pratico had shown that most pottery of Fortress I is probably not earlier than the eighth century, but some sherds may be earlier. Farther afield, the earliest fortress at 'Ain el-Qudeirat in the eastern Sinai, near the spring, biblical Kadesh-barnea, had been dated to the tenth century, but again there now seems to be earlier material. If the Kheleifeh I fort and Kadesh-barnea 4b (the oval fortress) were flourishing in the tenth century under Judahite administration, they might have been involved with copper working and trade with the Timnah and Wadi Feinan industries, possibly in conjunction with the Negev forts.[143]

Finally, dozens of small tenth-century villages, hamlets, and farmsteads are known, none of them properly excavated, however.

The shift in settlement type and pattern alone would justify defining the tenth century, or the Iron IIA period, as the era of statehood by widely adopted criteria. The newly established states of Israel and Judah (unless they were unified) were not, of course, fully formed. It is for that reason that the designation "early inchoate state" is preferable.

These states came into existence relatively suddenly sometime in the early tenth century by a process involving several primary factors. The first was probably natural growth and complexity as Israelite society evolved. From the eleventh to the tenth century the population grew from about 60,000 to as much as 100,000. Villages gave way to towns, and towns grew into cities. The larger of these cities soon saw a concentration of wealth and power that enabled them, indeed, required them, to become regional centers. Despite some evidence of a growing sense of Israelite ethnic identity, however, there would have been continuing rivalries for power. Ironically, the geo-political map of the tenth century may have resembled that of the Amarna age four centuries earlier. Then it was Egyptian domination that held things together, and when that collapsed, so did society soon thereafter, as we saw in chapter 2.

There was no inevitable trajectory in all this, as earlier evolutionary schemes had presupposed (from tribe to chiefdom to state). The state is not necessarily the highest level of progress and social organization, a sort of manifest destiny of all peoples. That is a modern Western construct, one that has not yet played itself out convincingly. Nevertheless, at a certain stage of development most early societies did reach a threshold, a certain challenge that had to be met by some form of change, even radical change.

One such change was an experiment in the kind of greater cohesion that only a centralized form of government could provide. In the General Systems Theory approach employed here, that would entail the integration of a number of subsystems into a functioning whole, one that created a new even if fragile equilibrium. Thus the organism could function and maintain its momentum, at least for some time.

Such cycles of growth and decay—of centripetal and centrifugal forces—are easily observable in the biological sphere. So are they in societies, although not in the same functionalist manner? Ideology does play a significant role in social evolution, but it is difficult to imagine which ideology might have prevailed in Israelite society by the Axial Age in the tenth century, had the notion of statehood not occurred to at least a few. What would have been the alternatives?

It is noteworthy that the situation that archaeology constructs provides a milieu in which the narratives in Samuel make good sense. Here the stories that reflect ambiguity about kingship—the conflict of tradition and social progressivism—are realistic. This is a sort of subplot, since the Philistine threat is taken as the most pressing concern, and it did exist. But it may be a rationalization advanced by some parties to justify their ambitions for statehood. Here the portrait of the judge-prophet Samuel, caught in the middle, reflects what must have been the anxiety of countless thousands in Israel on the threshold of a radical experiment in social organization. In short, here the biblical writers seem to be dealing with a real situation in an earlier period in Israel's history, not the ideal history of the later Deuteronomistic Historians, who took kingship as divinely preordained. That brings us to the second factor.

Running through the narratives in the book of Samuel, and extending well into Kings, is a leitmotif: the shadow of Philistine expansion and the very real possibility that Israel might be annihilated. The struggle of two peoples for control of a small and marginal land had been going on for two centuries. When Israel was ensconced in the foothills and intent only upon survival, while the Philistines were gaining a foothold along the coast, contacts may have been rare and uneventful. We have seen that along the border at sites such as Gezer, Beth-Shemesh, and Timnah, there was a mixed population in Iron I. But as Philistia grew in size and power, as the archaeological evidence shows, armed conflict seemed inevitable. One of the results was undoubtedly an intensification of Israelite ethnic identity, forged in a conflict, as ethnicity often is. Even the skeptic must admit that by now, in the tenth century, we can identify ethnic Israelites, even without texts like those of the Hebrew Bible.

In the literature on state-formation processes that we surveyed above, an overall distinction is made between primary and secondary states, whatever specific model one adopts. Primary states develop on the basis of internal factors, while secondary states are brought into existence largely as the result of external factors, usually conquest. That is precisely what the Israelite confederation in the hill country faced in the late eleventh–early tenth century.

Here the biblical writers have gotten it right: the threat was real. We do not have to accept their theological frame of reference to appreciate their candor in facing facts. However, it is still the archaeological data that are definitive. We would have known about the Philistine threat without ever having heard of a Samuel.

The chronology of these developments is fixed first by the stratigraphy of more than two dozen tenth-century sites, where the conventional chronology shows a remarkable convergence, one summarized here. No other scenario—certainly not the low chronology—can account for the uniformity of the evidence. The exact dates of Saul, David, and Solomon are largely irrelevant, and it is not the biblical scheme that dictates our dates or our terminology, as some critics claim. Our phasing here is archaeological.

The end of this century-long period of state formation is fixed by the Shoshenq raid discussed above. It can be placed near the end of Solomon's reign, not on the biblical synchronism with Solomon's death but on astronomically fixed Egyptian chronology. Shoshenq, the biblical Shishak, reigned 945–924 on a higher chronology or 939–918 on a lower chronology. A date toward the end of his reign is usually preferred, thus circa 920 here for his campaign in the Levant. Raising the date by ten to twenty years would not affect our phasing here, which distinguishes Iron I from Iron IIA on strictly archaeological rather than on biblical grounds (above).

It should also be stressed that lowering the date of that transition to circa 980, as with Mazar's "modified conventional chronology," would also make little or no difference. After all, the historian wants to know whether a given event happened in the late eleventh century or the early tenth century, not what term archaeologists choose to call that time span. That is why, having discussed in detail the differences among archaeologists, we have proceeded to deal with absolute chronology wherever possible.[144] This is a history of Israel and Judah, not of archaeological terminology.

The resultant history of Israel and Judah in the tenth century is admittedly not the full, narrative history of events (*Geschichte*) that we might desire, certainly not the metanarrative (*Heilsgeschichte*) of the Hebrew Bible. Our history is often lacking in individual names without reference to the biblical stories (with the notable exception of David). Furthermore, many of the details in the stories in the Hebrew Bible cannot be accounted for in the archaeological record. They must, therefore, be left in the realm of possibility, unless they appear so fantastic that they lack any credibility.

Ours is a partial and provisional history, but it deals with realia where we have sufficient evidence. The problems of interpretation in both sources are addressed, and an attempt is made to give the Hebrew Bible the benefit of the doubt. The historian can do no better.

Finally, we should keep in mind that the book of Kings is, not surprisingly, all about kings. It does not claim to encompass much more in its narrative than a few of their deeds and the judgment that they wished to pronounce. This is the story of "great men and their public deeds"—history written from the top down. Even if archaeology could confirm the many details of the lives of Saul, David, and Solomon as they are portrayed in the Deuteronomistic History, it would add little or nothing to the broader, more realistic history that we have outlined here—history from the bottom up.

Notes

1. The literature is vast. For Mazar's scheme, see 2005, 2008a, 2011; cf. Mazar and Bronk Ramsey 2008, 2010; A. Mazar et al. 2005. For Finkelstein, see 1999a, 1999b, 2002, 2003a, 2003b, 2005d; 2010a; 2011a; Finkelstein and Piasetzkey 2003a, 2003b, 2006a, 2006b, 2011a, 2011b. For Bunimovitz and Lederman, see 2006; cf. Bunimovitz and Faust 2001. For Herzog and Singer-Avitz, see 2004, 2006. For Sharon et al., see Sharon et al. 2005. For rebuttals of Finkelstein, see Kletter 2004; Frese and Levy 2010; Levy 2010b; see also Gal 1992a; 2003; Ben-Tor 2000; Ben-Tor and Ben-Ami 1998. For general orientation to chronology and the rise of the monarchy, see Dever 1997a, 1997b, 2004, 2005b and references there; Kletter 2004; and see especially the essays in Levy and Higham 2005. On Khirbet Qeiyafa and chronology, see below. For the most part I will abandon the confusing Iron IIA term, referring simply to the tenth or early ninth century in the following. See also excursus 4.1.

2. The most convenient summaries and detailed critiques of Finkelstein's changing views are Kletter 2004 and Frese and Levy 2010, both with full references. See also n. 1 above, n. 4 below, and excursus 4.1 below.

3. See n. 1 above and references there; see also excursus 4.1 below.

4. Finkelstein first elaborated the ceramic argument in a 1993 symposium, supported by Ussishkin (see Ussishkin 2000), even claiming that Philistine monochrome pottery appears at Gezer (it does not). On the general issue of monochrome pottery—the Late Mycenaean IIIC:1b wares—see most recently Killebrew 2000; Dothan and Zuckerman 2004; Yasur-Landau 2010; Ben-Shlomo 2006, especially 81–87. On the notion of chronological versus cultural separation, see Bunimovitz and Faust 2001.

5. On the supposed Jezreel connection, see Finkelstein 2005b, 36–37; Ussishkin 2000. Note, however, the numerous objections to the use of Jezreel, conveniently cited in Frese and Levy 2010, 189–90. On tenth–ninth century ceramic continuity, see Zimhoni 1997b; Ben-Tor and Ben-Ami 1998; Mazar and Carmi 2001; A. Mazar 2005; Dever 2005b; A. Mazar 2007.

6. See Zimhoni 2004, 1643–1788. For a rebuttal of Franklin's argument on ashlar masonry, see the discussion in Frese and Levy 2010, 191–93.

7. That is clear if one compares the latest statements of A. Mazar 2011; Mazar and Bronk Ramsey 2010; and Finkelstein and Piasetzkey 2011a, 2011b. It is worth noting that Finkelstein actually moves up to Mazar's dates for the end of Reḥov V at circa 920 and Stratum IV at circa 840; see Finkelstein and Piasetzky 2011a, 52. Many of the references deal with C-14 dates, especially Levy and Higham 2005. For the Weitzman project, see Sharon et al. 2005.

8. Kletter exposes the critical weaknesses of the low chronology, then concludes: "Before it is proven, no far-fetched historical conclusions should be based on it" (2004, 44). See further below on state formation and excursus 4.1.

9. See Cline 2011; cf. the opposing view of Bunimovitz and Lederman 2011, 44–45. For the low-chronology perspective, see Finkelstein 2002.

10. It is too cumbersome to document each site individually, but see in general the entries in Stern 1993, 2008, with full bibliography. For overviews, see Gilboa 2001; Gitin 1998; Shai 2011; Killebrew and Lehmann 2013.

11. So Stern 1990; 2013, 201. See, however, Gilboa 2001, 453–55; also on the Philistine-Phoenician "symbiosis," see Gilboa 2001. See also fig. 3.1 above. For the Phoenician-style Black-on-Red (or Cypriot) pottery, see below.

12. On the degree of Philistine acculturation, see chapter 3 and references in n. 27. For population estimates, see Stager 1995, 342–44. On the Philistine threat to Judah, see below.

13. On the Arameans generally, see chapter 2 and n. 46. A C-14 date for the Stratum IV destruction is 1043–979; see A. Mazar 2011, 108.

14. See further Arav and Freund 1995, 1999, 2004, 2009.

15. See nn. 13 and 14 above.

16. Faust 2000; 2003a; 2006b, 113–34. Cf. Finkelstein 2005c; Lehmann 2003;

Herzog 2007, whose attempts at rebuttal are obviously due to the denial of any monarchy in the tenth century. See Faust's defense in 2012a, 256–57; cf. the critique of Grabbe 2007b (although as a historian, not an archaeologist). See further below on whether the Philistines caused this shift.

17. Ilan 1999, 146–47.

18. Here I follow Ben-Tor's renewed excavations and extensive reworking of Yadin's Strata X–IV (Ben-Tor and Ben-Ami 1998; Ben-Ami 2001). Na'aman (1997) and Finkelstein (1998b) have tried to lower the dates of the destruction of Stratum XA from Shoshenq circa 920 to the days of Hazael and the Aramean incursions circa 840. Their key argument, however, is based largely on comparing the Megiddo pottery with that of Jezreel, dated, ironically, by biblical correlations. But the site was badly destroyed, and the stratigraphy is unreliable. Second, Finkelstein's argument that the pottery of late tenth and early to mid-ninth century in the north is very similar has long been known and acknowledged by all authorities (the southern sequence, rarely adduced, is different; see below). That, however, is irrelevant; similarity does not prove identity. Ben-Tor's reply to Finkelstein (2000) addresses these points, as well as the sort of "historical dead-reckoning" involved. For these arguments, see Ben-Tor and Ben-Ami 1998.

19. The bibliography is extensive, but for orientation and references the standard works see the chapters in Vaughn and Killebrew 2003. See especially the references in Killebrew 2003, 330–31. The basic data are conveniently presented in the entries in Stern 1993, 2008. See also nn. 21–24 below. The best summaries are Mazar 2008a, 2010a, with extensive references.

20. For a summary of Kenyon's work, see Steiner 2003; Cahill 2003, 35–40. For Shiloh's excavations, see Cahill 2003. For Avigad's excavations, see Geva 2003. See also entries in Stern 1993, 2008.

21. Most discussions of chronology overlook this obvious fact. See further n. 25.

22. On the stepped stone structure, see Mazar 2006; Finkelstein 2001, 2011b; Herzog and Singer-Avitz 2004; Cahill 2003; Lehmann 2003; Finkelstein et al. 2007; Ussishkin et al. 2007; Faust 2010c; E. Mazar 2006; 2009; 2011; A. Mazar 2008a, 2010a, 2010b. Cahill's detailed discussion—the only one to present the pottery—confirms the Iron I date (twelfth–eleventh century) supported also by Faust. See Cahill 2003, 34–66; Faust 2010c. Finkelstein's, Ussishkin's, Herzog's, and Singer-Avitz's postulation of an eighth-century date, or even a Hellenistic date, is entirely without foundation. The *latest* possible date for the sealed pottery is the tenth century. See, for instance, Cahill 2003, fig. 1.9a:14 for a typical eleventh–tenth century cooking pot rim. See also tenth-century wares from overlying Strata 14–13 structures in Area G; Cahill 2003, figs. 1.13a, 1.14a. In particular, the red-slipped and hand-burnished wares are diagnostic. Finkelstein's claim that eighth-century sherds were found within the structure has been decisively refuted by Mazar; cf. Grabbe 2008b, 225. Mazar's 2008a analysis is the best balanced. It is worth noting that Na'aman (2014, 61)—a resolutely critical biblical historian—

concludes that the "large stone structure" makes good sense as David's palace and that the biblical accounts do preserve very early traditions. He also regards the "stepped stone structure as the biblical *millo*. The supposed late date of this monumental architecture is what partly drives the notion of the eighth century as the earliest possible date for the emergence of the Judahite state. See Finkelstein 1999b, 2001b, 2003b, 2010a; Ussishkin 2003; Herzog and Singer-Avitz 2004. More recently Finkelstein has gradually moved up to a ninth-century date (2011c) for a "formative state." Before that, in the tenth century, Finkelstein acknowledges only a "dimorphic chiefdom." The model of chiefdoms has, however, long been discredited; see Yoffee 2005 and references there. See further below on state formation processes. See nn. 23–25 below.

23. Cahill 2003, 53.

24. This is especially evident in Finkelstein 2002 (Ahström, Edelman; Herrman; Niemann; Rost; van der Toorn). But note that eventually Finkelstein envisioned a "Saulide confederacy" with its hub at Gibeon, stretching all the way up to the Jezreel Valley. See below and n. 84.

25. See E. Mazar 2007, 2009, 2011; E. Mazar and B. Mazar 1989. E. Mazar's several publications (2007, 2009, 2011) fueled the controversy. One issue was whether the so called David's Palace was part of the stepped stone structure to the south (above) or a separate construction. Finkelstein, Herzog, and Singer-Avitz and Ussishkin (Finkelstein et al. 2007) argued that the former (the "large stone structure," as it came to be called) was not even a building with integrity and that all or many (the latter Finkelstein) of the walls were Hellenistic in date. Amihai Mazar (2005; cf. 2007, 2010a) agreed that the two structures belonged together. He argued, however, that they were probably constructed originally in Iron I (the "Jebusite fortress"?) but were reused in the tenth century. Faust (2010c) thought that both might be one construction in function, but he raised doubts. He agreed that the large stone structure originated in Iron I and was only reused in the tenth century, that is, not built by David as a palace. Finkelstein (2011c) tried to refute Faust, A. Mazar, and E. Mazar. There the matter rests.

Here we shall follow principles adumbrated above, separating the biblical and archaeological evidence. For the latter source, pottery is crucial. The fundamental rule in ceramic typology is that it is the *latest* pottery that is diagnostic: it provides a *terminus post quem*. The date of the material can be earlier, but it must be *this* late. If the absence of later material can be explained, in practice an assemblage (not a few scattered sherds), comparable to well-dated assemblages at other sites, and preferably anchored by independent textual-historical sources, yields the best picture.

The pottery sealed (in archaeological terms) below the mantle of the stepped stone structure was first published by Cahill in 2003, carefully described and dated to the tenth century by reference to other sites, such as Arad XII, which all authorities would date similarly. Then in 2011 E. Mazar published some of the large stone structure pottery, scant but also sealed. A close examination of the cooking pots of both sites—generally acknowledged to be one of the most diagnostic forms—shows that they are all typical tenth-century forms, with a characteristic long, flat flange at the rim. There is not one of the concave flanged rims that begin in the ninth century in the south (earlier in the north, even eleventh century). See Cahill 2005, figs. 1.9a, 1.13a; E. Mazar 2011, 108, 131. The pottery from Jerusalem Stratum 14 was not published until 2012, but it also has only the elongated, flat cooking pot rims. See De Groot and Bernick-Greenberg 2012, fig. 3. Again, the parallels are with southern Israelite sites such as Arad XII, Beersheba VI–V, and the like.

When Faust and A. Mazar wrote in 2006, they did not discuss the above pottery, but it confirms their dates for the construction and reuse of the large stone structure. If both structures are linked, then both date to the Iron I–IIA horizon. Even if they are separate structures, however, the same date is indicated. That is a rational argument entirely separate from biblical considerations.

26. See E. Mazar and B. Mazar 1989; E. Mazar 2011, 145–47.

27. Finkelstein 2003a, 79; see also Ussishkin 2003, 109.

28. See Ofer 1994; 2001, 91; H. Geva 2003, 203–8; Stager 2003, 66; A. Mazar 2006, 267; Lehmann 2003, 130–36.

29. Steiner 2003, 363. Cf. Cahill 2003, 40–54, 70–71 and references there.

30. Mazar 2005, 268.

31. Stager 2003, 66–69.

32. Na'aman 1996b, 1997. Add now Na'aman 2013, especially 2013, 248.

33. Cahill 2003, 72.

34. Ussishkin 2003.

35. For the above and the best balanced summaries of tenth-century Jerusalem elsewhere, see Na'aman 1996a, 1997; Killebrew 2003; Lehmann 2003; Steiner 2003; A. Mazar 2003, 2007; Stager 2006; Na'aman 2013. For minimalist views, see Finkelstein 2005b, 2010a; Ussishkin 2003. All these have references to extensive earlier literature. For state-formation process, as well as the "Solomonic temple," see below.

36. See Bunimovitz and Lederman 2006.

37. Whether the tenth-century fort can be "Israelite" is uncertain, since it is unpublished. See Ben-Ami 2004.

38. See Ben-Tor, Bonfil, and Zuckerman 2003; Ben-Tor, Zarzeki-Peleg, and Cohen-Amidjar 2005.

39. Cahill 2006.

40. Finkelstein 1990b. Faust (2006b, 129–33) thinks that Dawwara lasted well into the late tenth century and was destroyed by the Philistines. On the other hand. Na'aman (2012b) argues that it was a "Philistine stronghold." Fritz (1995, 235) denies that the site was walled. In any case, the Philistines never penetrated this far inland, as we have seen. Khirbet ed-Dawwara was no doubt a defense against presumed Philistine incursions, as Finkelstein thought.

41. See Rollston 2015. On Khirbet Qeiyafa Stratum IV, see Garfinkel and

Ganor 2009; Garfinkel and Kang 2011; Garfinkel, Ganor, and Hasel 2014. For attempts to redate and redefine the chronology, see Finkelstein and Piasetzkey 2010b; cf. Finkelstein and Fantalkin 2012; Singer-Avitz 2010. Finkelstein's view of the site with the content of a "Saulide confederation at Gibeon" (Finkelstein and Fantalkin 2012) is entirely speculative, clearly an attempt to avoid the implications of a tenth-century state or kingdom with its capital at Jerusalem. The notion of Na'aman (2008) and Lemaire (2011, 104) that Qeiyafa is "Philistine" flies in the face of all the evidence. Levin (2012) suggests that the site is not Sha'arayim but Ma'gal ("encampment," 1 Sam 17:20). For a judicious summary of the site and its proper interpretation, see now Faust 2013b, 213–14, with full bibliography. On the Cypriot vessels, add Gilboa 2012, who is cautious but would allow for a date as early as "Davidic times" (2012, 145). Cf. Gilboa and Waiman-Barak 2014, where two Cypro-Geometric Bichrome juglets—both exceedingly rare—are dated as early as the mid-tenth century. The same date or even earlier suits the black-burnished juglets. The latest C-14 dates for the end of Stratum IV are 1012–967 (68.2 percent); see Garfinkel and Streit 2014. A second inscription, inscribed before firing on a small jar, contains the name "'Ish-Ba'al," probably an official. See Garfinkel, Golub, Misgav, and Ganor 2015. Cf. Saul's son with the same name. Could Qeiyafa have been destroyed by Saul's rival David (the dates are roughly equivalent) or, less likely, by Philistines in David's wars with them? A lower C-14 date (1024–920, 95.4 percent) could allow for a Shoshenq destruction, but the range is too broad, and the pottery can scarcely date that late.

42. For the definitive reworking of Arad, see Herzog 2001; Herzog et al. 1984. Finkelstein dates the end of Stratum XII to the raid of Shoshenq, circa 920, in line with his low chronology, which would leave the Stratum XI fort in the ninth century (2001, 113).

43. On the dating of Stratum V and Palace A and the gate to the late tenth century, see Dever 1986, 26–28; Mazar 1990, 401. This agrees with Ussishkin's date. On the Solar Shrine, see Aharoni 1975.

44. See the reworking of the stratigraphy in Herzog, Rainey, and Moshkovitz 1977. On the pottery, see Singer-Avitz 2002.

45. On the Negev forts, see Cohen 1976, 1979; Herzog 1983; Finkelstein 1984, 2002; Na'aman 1992; Haiman 1994; Faust 2006c. There is a virtual agreement now on a tenth-century date (even Finkelstein), the sites being destroyed in the Shoshenq raid circa 920. For the C-14 dates, see Bruins and van der Plicht 2005. See further below. Kadesh-Barnea Stratum 4, the westernmost fort, is the most prominent and best published; see now Cohen and Bernick-Greenberg 2007. For the remarkably high date of the destruction of Stratum 4—not later than the second half of the tenth century—based on the first good C-14 samples from the Negev forts, see Gilboa et al. 2009; see also references in n. 140 below. Despite Gilboa's support of the low chronology, these dates support the conventional chronology and a destruction by Shoshenq, with all other authorities. Further publications now suggest a more refined stratigraphy and chronology for Kadesh-barnea, as

follows: Stratum 4CB (the oval fort) = eleventh–tenth century Stratua 3–2 (the rectangular fort, several phases) = eighth century A few C-14 dates are as early as the twelfth century. See now Singer-Avitz 2008; Finkelstein 2010a.

46. On the question of red wash and slip as a chronological indicator, see A. Mazar 1998. Mazar does not, however, make the critical distinction between a thin, light red streaky *wash* and a thicker and darker red unburnished *slip*. For the former, closely dated stratigraphically to the late eleventh–early tenth century, see B. Mazar 1950–1951, 132–36, A. Mazar 1998, 373 (Qasile IX–X); cf. Dever, Lance, and Wright 1970, 61; 1974, 58 (Gezer X–IX). On the red-washed as well as red-slipped wares, see A. Mazar 2008b, 2017. See further below, fig. 26, n. 111.

47. See Gilboa and Sharon 2008; Sharon and Gilboa 2013. They are reexcavating the site, so their "phase" designations are temporary; further, despite openly favoring the low chronology, they do not publish C-14 dates and hesitate to adopt any absolute chronology. They see only one site-wide "Iron IA/B" destruction, of their Phase B1/9, G/7, D2/9. They date that circa 1000 on the low chronology, but conventional chronology would place it circa 1100–1050. Some have tried to see this destruction as attributable to the biblical accounts of David's conquests, since Dor is claimed as one of Solomon's district capitals (1 Kgs 4:11). Ironically, that destruction could be dated to David's reign only on the low chronology, which traditionalists would not accept. In any case, the following "Iron IIA" culture is not typical of sites that are best considered Israelite. See further excursus 4.1.

48. For the dates of the end of Strata V and IV, see the latest positions of A. Mazar 2011 and Finkelstein and Piasetzkey 2011a, with references there. The former dates the end of Stratum V to Shoshenq circa 920, the end of Stratum IV to the Aramean incursions circa 840, which the C-14 dates support. Earlier Finkelstein lowered these dates by as much as nearly a century, but now he seems to agree more (although not specifically stated) with Mazar; see Finkelstein 2011b, fig. 2. The best orientation to the problems of C-14 dating, with chapters by Finkelstein and A. Mazar (among others) is Levy and Higham 2005. See also n. 114 below.

49. On the notion that some "Canaanite" sites persisted well into the eleventh and even the tenth century, see Finkelstein 2003a, 2006. He uses that assertion to support his contention that no "Israelite" state emerged in the north until the ninth century. This ignores the fact that ethnic boundaries can and do overlap. See further below on ethnicity. Megiddo VIA and Beth-shean V upper may be compared with Reḥov VI in this respect.

50. For the basic surveys, see Finkelstein 1988; Broshi and Finkelstein 1992; Zertal 1993, 1998, 2001; Ofer 1994, 2001; Finkelstein and Na'aman 1994; Finkelstein, Lederman, and Bunimovitz 1997; Lehmann 2001. For convenient summaries, see Finkelstein 1993; Gal 1992a; Ofer 1993; Zertal 1993. For reservations on survey results, see Finkelstein 2002; Faust 2005; 2012a, 199, 256. See also nn. 51–52 below.

51. Zertal 1998, 2001.

52. See Gal 1992a; Zertal 1993; Finkelstein and Naʿaman 1994; Frankel 1994. See also Lehmann 2003, 133.

53. Ofer 2001; see also 1994.

54. For Faust's model on rural settlements, see 2006b, 114–31; 2007a; 2013b. For critiques, see Finkelstein 2005a; Grabbe 2007b. For Faust's detailed data on the expansion of both urban and rural sites in Judah and the Shephelah in Iron IIA, undergirding the other evidence now accumulating for an early Judahite state, see below and 2013b—superseding earlier views (2006b). See nn. 93 and 100 below. Among the tenth-century Shephelah sites Faust lists, however, only Beth-shemesh and Lachish are discussed here. Tel Ḥarasim, Azekah, Tel Zayit, Tel Burna, Tel ʿErani, Tel ʿEton, and Tell Beit Mirsim all have tenth-century remains, but details are unclear or unpublished due to ongoing excavations. See Faust 2013b, 206–11.

55. See Falconer and Savage 1995 for the development of this model.

56. Few attempts have been made to do quantitative analyses of the carrying capacity of typical regions, in order to quantify the limits of food production. But see Hopkins 1985; B. Rosen 1986; A. Sasson 1998.

57. Childe 1950; Kolb 1984. See Holladay's use of a trait list similar to Childe's (without citation; 1995, 373). See now Faust 2012a, 258–61. Faust (2012, 39–41) simply distinguishes rural and urban sites, i.e., villages and towns/cities. He does not specify size but follows scholars such as Efrat and Herzog. See further the three-tier hierarchy in chapter 5.

58. For Naroll's fundamental study, see 1962. For demographic applications, see Shiloh 1970; Broshi and Gophna 1984, 1986; Frick 1985; Stager 1985a; Broshi and Finkelstein 1992; Zorn 1994; Holladay 1995; Finkelstein and Na'aman 1994; Master 2001; Schloen 2001; Hardin 2010; Faust 2012a; Dever 2012. In addition, the surveys referenced in n. 50 above use this model.

59. Gottwald (1993) coined this term to replace *egalitarian* in his magisterial 1979 *Tribes of Yahweh*. Later he opted for the term *communitarian* (1993). Further on an egalitarian society, see Faust 2012a, 9, 24, 221. On socioeconomic structure, see now the fundamental work of Faust 2012a, passim. Faust believes that the nuclear family—rural or urban—was the basic unit but that there was also a state level of organization.

60. See Stager 1985a, 2003; Holladay 1995; Master 2001; Schloen 2001; Knauf 2008; Levy 2010b (Wadi Feinan, with references). Add now Ben-Yosef et al. 2012, with further evidence of a well-developed copper smelting industry in the Jordan Valley that peaked in the tenth century See further below on the Wadi Arabah and southern Negev copper industry.

61. See the definitive study of Schreiber 2003, with full references to the literature and citations of find-spots. The Phase I and II division is hers. Black-on-Red pottery also occurs at Phoenician sites such as Tell Keisan 8, Tell Abu-Hawam III, Achzib, Dor, and the Rosh Zayit fortress.

62. The fundamental study is Na'aman 2006, with reference to earlier literature. Nevertheless, this distinguished historian, while appealing to "context,"

never mentions the possible archaeological data such as those adduced here. See, however, the thorough treatment of Rainey 2006, 174–78, based on the realities of geopolitics. Rainey believes that the list "has long been recognized as an accurate picture of the internal organization and social/ethnic distribution of the population" (2006, 174). See also Stager 2003, 67, who points out that at least six of the twelve sites proposed here as centers, namely, Taʿanach IIB, Megiddo VA/IVB, Beth-Shean V lower, Dor, Beth-Shemesh 3, and Yoqneam XIV. To this list add Gezer VIII; the reading is broken but may be restored on the basis of the order of place names. See Rainey 2003, 186; Naʾaman 1992, 79–80. Nevertheless, as Naʾaman points out, the list in its present form cannot antedate the eighth century at the earliest. Here the question of "cultural memory" comes into play: How much is remembered? How much is forgotten? How much is invented? On cultural memory, see Davies 2008; Wyatt 2008; and especially Kofoed 2011 and references.

63. See London 1989; Barkay 1992, 325–27; Wood 1990; McGovern 1986; C. Meyers 2001; Faust 2002b. The former deal more with ceramic technology and its material/cultural implications, the latter with red slip and burnish as an ethnic indicator, i.e., a clue to the predominance now of a male-dominated industry that reflects a sort of "national style." Nevertheless, Faust gives reasons for caution in using pottery to delineate socioeconomic features in general (2012a, 31).

64. See Coughenour 1976; Waldbaum 1980; Stech-Wheeler et al. 1981; Pigott, McGovern, and Notis 1982; Liebowitz and Folk 1984; and especially McNutt 1990, who gives a list of excavated tenth-century implements, including tools and weapons of many kinds. They are most common at Bethel (11); Megiddo (9); Taʿanach (8); and Tel Beit Mirsim (6). The best source for iron ores seems to have been in Transjordan. In Israel, the earliest steel implement (carbonized iron) is the pick from Har Adir in Upper Galilee, dated to the eleventh century, discussed above. There seems to have been little progress in metallurgy until the ninth century; see chapter 5 below on the Beth-shemesh smithy.

65. See the discussion of the following sites in Dever 2005a, 113–17; on Khirbet Qeiyafa, add now Garfinkel and Ganor 2009; Garfinkel and Streit 2014; Garfinkel, Ganer, and Hasel 2014. On the goddess Asherah, see Dever 1984a; Olyan 1988; Hadley 2000; Zevit 2001; Dever 2005a. For extended discussion and references to the archaeological evidence, see Holladay 1987; Nakhai 2001; Zevit 2001; Yasur-Landau, Ebeling, and Mazow 2011; Albertz and Schmitt 2012; Albertz et al. 2014. For conservative views of ancient Israelite and Judean religion, see Hess 2007 and the literature cited there. See further chapter 5.

66. See chapter 3 above for Iron I. For the Tel Zayit abecedary, see Tappy and McCarter 2008, with essays in addition on earlier inscriptions and on literacy in general, especially Sanders 2008. See also Millard 2005 and references there; Naveh 1987; Niditch 1996; Naʾaman 2000, 2001. For the inscriptions, see most conveniently the corpus of Ahituv 2008. See n. 67 below. For an attempt to down-date local Level III to the ninth century, see Finkelstein, Sass, and Singer-Avitz

2008; cf. the sharp reply of Tappy 2009. According to the latter, Tel Zayit combines both inland Judahite and Philistine coastal elements (as does Tel Batash). On the Khirbet Qeiyafa inscriptions, see above and n. 41.

67. See Ahituv 2008, 252–57; McCarter 2008, 48–54; Sanders 2008, 103–4. The latter suggests that the Gezer Calendar reveals "another way to think about how Israel may have become a state and how it came to be remembered as a state" (2008, 104).

68. On the so-called Cypro-Phoenician wares (= Cypro-Geometric and Black-on-Red I–II), see above and n. 61. On the earliest appearance of imported Greek Protogeometric wares in the late eleventh/early to mid-tenth at sites such as Tell Keisan 9c–a, Megiddo VIA, Tel Kinrot V, Tel Hadar V, Tell Qasile X, and Tel Zafit (Gath 5?), see Maier, Fantalkin, and Zuckerman 2009 and references there. These Greek wares were probably imported via Cyprus, most likely by Phoenician traders. See further Beitzel 2010; cf. Bell 2006. For a C-14 date for the destruction that ends Tel Hadar IV circa 1000, see A. Mazar 2011, 108.

69. For summaries on the following Jordanian sites, see MacDonald, Adams, and Bienkowski 2001; Herr and Najjar 2001, 323–45; 2008, 311–20; Herr et al. 2000, 2002; Harrison 2009; Herr 2014. On Tell Jawa, add Daviau 2003. See also nn. 70–75 below. Na'aman (1992) deals almost exclusively with the biblical narratives concerning the "great kingdom" established by David. On the likelihood of Israelite campaigns in Moab and Edom, see further below.

70. Bienkowski 2009b, 20. See also the sharp critique of Porter and Routledge in 2009b, 10–22. See n. 73 below.

71. Bienkowski 2009b, 20.

72. Here one sees Finkelstein's all-too-typical elaborate reconstruction based on manipulation of the data, as well as inconsistencies with his own earlier views. Ironically, here he casually agrees with Levy's high chronology for the Wadi Feinan metal-working installation (eleventh–tenth century), whereas up to 2005 he had confidently dated it to the ninth century; see Finkelstein and Piasetzkey 2003a; Finkelstein 2005b; Finkelstein and Lipschits 2011. See further below and nn. 75, 129–30, 135, 139.

73. Routledge (2004) presents his anthropological model elegantly, but often the style outstrips the substance.

74. See Bienkowski 1992, 2009a; Bienkowski and Bennett 2002.

75. See Levy et al. 2004; Levy 2009, 2010b and references to other publications; cf. above and n. 72 for the opposing view of Finkelstein, who thinks that Khirbet en-Naḥas is not Edomite. Levy views the Khirbet en-Naḥas installation as triggering the emergence of an integrated Edomite ethnicity already in the eleventh–tenth century, which seems unlikely in the light of the overall data. In addition, his identification of the vast cemetery as "Shasu burials" lacks any supporting evidence, indeed flies in the face of what we know about the sedentarization of pastoral nomads, including the Shasu (ch. 3). One might suggest that the nascent tenth-century Judahite state subsidized metal working and copper

trade in the Jordan Valley (and perhaps also in the lower Wadi Arabah). On the eleventh–tenth-century mining and smelting industry in the Wadi Feinan and the southern Negev, add now Ben-Yosef et al. 2012; Levy, Najjr, and Ben-Yosef 2014. Here Levy proposes another possibility: Egyptian sponsorship of the metal-working operations in the Wadi Feinan. He proposes an "Egyptian presence" in the eleventh–tenth century, even a Shoshenq invasion circa 920. Yet his only evidence consists of a few Egyptian scarabs and amulets, one of Shoshenq. In support of this view, Levy quotes Kitchen's far-fetched notion of Shoshenq's "flying column" raid into Edom. Now he says that the alternate scenario of Judahite sponsorship is beyond the purview of current research. See Levy, Najjar, and Ben-Yosef 2014, 748–60, 978–92. Despite an impressive data-base, fundamental questions remain unanswered. See also below and n. 130.

76. See above. On Rosh Zayit and the Lower Galilee, see Gal 1988–1989, 1992b, 2003.

77. See references in n. 76 above.

78. Cf. Bikai 1987; Schreiber 2003, the latter with charts of find-spots and full bibliography. See also above and n. 61.

79. Bunimovitz and Faust 2001.

80. Thompson 1999, 206.

81. Liverani 2007.

82. See Schäfer-Lichtenberger 1996; Lemche 1998b. See Schloen 2001 for the development of the patrimonial model.

83. These terms are excerpted from Kletter 2004, adding "Saulide confederacy"; see n. 84 below.

84. Finkelstein 1995b, 362. It is just such inconsistency that often vitiates Finkelstein's work. His output is so voluminous that he may simply have forgotten what he wrote earlier. Now he opts not only for a Davidic but a Saulide confederacy. See Finkelstein 2013, 37–61, with references going back as early as 2006.

85. See Dever 1994b, 1997b, 1997f, 2001; Holladay 1995; Master 2001; Kletter 2004. Other positive views are found in Fritz 1995; Knauf 2000, 2008; Master 2001; Joffe 2002; Faust 2003a; Stager 2003; Steiner 2003; A. Mazar 2007, 2008a; Faust 2012a, 190–207. For revisionist, negative views, see essays in Fritz and Davies 1996; Thompson 1996, 1999; Lemche 1998b; Davies 2007; Pfoh 2008. For the archaeological "minimalists," see Finkelstein 1995b, 1999b, 2003a, 2010a; Herzog and Singer-Avitz 2004. Early on the biblical revisionists (and Finkelstein as well) cited the work of Jamieson-Drake 1991 in support of their minimalist positions. He, however, was no authority. He was a biblical scholar with no experience or competence in archaeology. Shortly after publishing this work, Jamieson-Drake left the academic field. His work was never critically reviewed and today is only a curiosity in the history of scholarship. See the incisive critique of Faust 2012a, 29–30. Nevertheless, Lemche, Thompson, and even Finkelstein continually cite him as an authority. For the abandonment of the chiefdom model, see Yoffee 2005

and references there, all the way back to 1993. On Finkelstein's Saulide polity, see above and n. 72 and n. 135 below.

86. On the thorny issue of material culture and ethnicity, the literature is too extensive to cite in detail. See, however, ch. 3 n. 150. Needless to say, all the biblical revisionists deny that any clear "Israelite" identity can be distinguished.

87. The basic anthropological studies are Kohl 1987; Cohen and Service 1978; Claessen and Skalnik 1978; 1981; Khoury and Kostiner 1990; Earle 1991; Rothman 1994; and now the definitive work of Yoffee 2005. An early survey of theories on the state by a biblicist is Frick 1985. Studies by archaeologists are included in n. 85 above. Kletter 2004 is a convenient and authoritative orientation to the use of archaeological trait lists in defining states. Add now Faust 2012a, 190–207. See further below and nn. 88–93 below. The essays in Fritz and Davies 1996 are mostly by biblical minimalists, ideological manifestoes that reflect little or no acquaintance with the archaeological data.

88. Claessen and Skalnik 1978.

89. Holladay 1995, 371–79.

90. Dever 1997b, 1997f.

91. Master 2001; cf. Stager 1985a; Schloen 2001.

92. See n. 44 above. Kletter prefers "kingdom" to "state" (2004, 28), yet he accepts Israel as a state in the tenth century.

93. See Faust 2006b, 112–34 for the above. He does cite some bibliography and summaries in the chart of fig. 12:1, but there is not enough firm data to sustain his argument (he notes controversies over dates). It is hard to escape the impression that Faust is overly confident in the accuracy of the biblical view of a Philistine threat (although he does not actually mount a defense of the biblical narrative). For Faust's more recent view, see n. 54 above and n. 100 below.

94. For the suggestion that Siamun was responsible for the mid-tenth-century destruction of Phase 7A in Field II (Stratum IX), see n. 124 below.

95. Socoh has Iron II material on the surface. Azekah is being excavated, but the Iron Age levels are not yet clear. See Dagan 2011.

96. The Megiddo VIA destruction, dramatically evident in every field excavated, has been convincingly related to an earthquake. See Cline 2011 and references there. Finkelstein's low chronology would, of course, down-date the end of VIA to the raid of Shoshenq, circa 920.

97. Philistine pottery was never common at these sites, especially not Ashdod ware (LPDW), but now it disappears altogether. See n. 101 below.

98. Faust seems to agree (2006b, 117) that the Philistines did not likely venture this far afield. Stern held that Dor became an Israelite site in the early tenth century, after a destruction by David (see 2000, 201). Gilboa, however (2005), sees continuity with coastal Phoenician culture.

99. A C-14 date of 1043–979 (1 sigma deviation) works well for the end of Tel Hadar IV. Cf. A. Mazar 2011, 108.

100. For the end of Stratum V at Tel Reḥov, anchored well by C-14 dates circa

920 (i.e., Sheshonq), see A. Mazar 2011, with reference to earlier literature. Finkelstein's dates for the end of Reḥov V and Megiddo VIA (circa 920) are almost certainly too low, based on revised C-14 dates. He himself now seems to favor circa 980, only some forty years lower than the conventional chronology; see 2011a. See further excursus 4.1.

101. See Gitin 1998, 2010; Shai 2011. Faust (2013b, 2015) sees the LPDW as an aspect of acculturation: "borrowing" from Phoenician and Judahite material culture traits, symbolizing less-hostile relations by the tenth century. Faust also documents the decline of Philistia, but he does not relate this to Judahite power (2015, 186–89).

102. Gitin 2010, 325.

103. The argument from continuity is one of the strongest in linking the "Proto-Israelites" of the Merenptah inscription with the peoples of the tenth century and seeing the latter as full-fledged ethnic Israelites. That argument is developed most explicitly in Dever 2003d, 192–200, although questioned by Finkelstein 1996b and Kletter 2006. The Dan stela clearly identifies a state or kingdom of "Israel" in connection with a dynasty of David that cannot be later than the mid-tenth century.

104. On advocates of the low date, see nn. 1, 4, 7, 16, 18, and 35 above. Supporters of a tenth-century date are also referenced there. See further n. 114.

105. See Finkelstein 2010b, 2011b; Finkelstein and Piasetzkey 2011a, both with references to earlier works. Here he still holds to an eighth-century date for a state in Judah and a ninth-century date in Israel. Note, however, his apparent shift later to earlier dates; see n. 100 above and nn. 106 and 114 below (further on C-14 dates).

106. The literature on the Dan inscription now amounts to hundreds of publications; major publications include Biran and Naveh 1993, 1995; Schniedewind 1996; Lemaire 1998; Na'aman 2000; Ahituv 2008, 466–83; Rainey 2006, 212–13. The revisionists have never retracted in print their charge that the Dan inscription is a "forgery," an indication that it is ideology at work here, not scholarship. Cf. Lemche and Thompson 1994. For the name David on the ninth-century Mesha or Moabite stela, see Lemaire 1994.

It is significant that in recent publications where Finkelstein continues to deny the existence of a Judahite or Israelite state before the ninth century (n. 105 above), he often ignores the clear evidence of the Dan inscription for a tenth-century dynasty of David. Thus he never mentions the inscription in 2003a. In 2011c (193) he does mention it but disingenuously as a datum for the ninth century. Similarly, Herzog and Singer-Avitz 2004 ignore the Dan stela because it is inconvenient for their Judahite state only in the eighth century.

107. This correlation is usually taken as a bedrock chronological datum. Recently, however, Finkelstein has questioned the synchronism, even attributing it to Egyptologists who were supposedly lured by biblical scholars into "a vicious circle" (2002, 110).

108. There is a vast literature on the Shoshenq campaign, but the most relevant publications are Kitchen 2001; Finkelstein 2002; Fantalkin and Finkelstein 2006; Rainey 2006, 186–89; Dever 2014. The idiosyncratic views of Ash 1999; Clancy 1999; and R. Chapman 2009 can safely be ignored.

109. The rendering of Egyptian and Hebrew names here follows Rainey 2006, 185–89. For Transjordan, add Petit 2012.

110. See Finkelstein 2002 for the following.

111. On red slip and burnish, see generally A. Mazar 1998. He does not, however, properly distinguish the early thin, red *wash*. Cf. n. 46 above. Here we have omitted Philistine sites (Tel Batash IV–III may be considered Israelite), although sites such as Ashdod and Ekron do exhibit similar developments. In the north, the sequence is different, but cf. Megiddo and Beth-Shean.

The detailed analysis suggests that the best indicator of a tenth-century date is not the *presence* of hand burnish (which is typical) but rather the *absence* of wheel burnish—especially since the dividing line turns out to be the well-dated Shoshenq raid circa 920.

112. See n. 45 above. Some (e.g., Finkelstein and Herzog) do not see this network of forts as an expression of centralized authority. Yet what else could account for it or the Egyptian raid against these forts?

113. The literature on Hazor, Megiddo, and Gezer in this regard is too voluminous to cite. See, however, the overview, with references, in Knoppers 1997. Add the essays in Handy 1997; Dever 1997b, 1997d. See Finkelstein 2002 for his unsubstantiated charge that Dever's date of the Field III city gate at Gezer to the tenth century was motivated by his attempt to "prove the Bible." An examination of the Gezer reports will reveal the lack of any factual basis. On reading ("excavating") the biblical texts regarding Solomon's exploits, see Fritz 1996; Na'aman 1997; Hendel 2006, 2010; M. S. Smith 2006; Zevit 2008; Friedman 2010; Schniedewind 2010. However interesting, these textual analyses are considered secondary sources in the approach taken here. They have more to do with cultural memory than a history of events. See ch. 3 n. 2.

114. Finkelstein and Piasetzkey 2006a, 2006b; 2011b. Cf. A. Mazar 2011.

115. Finkelstein 2002, 113.

116. Kletter 2004, 44–45.

117. See the review of the issue in Cline 2011 and references there; for the rejection of the earthquake theory, see Bunimovitz and Lederman 2011. The low chronology, of course, would move the end of Stratum VIA down from circa 1000 to circa 925.

118. Lemaire 1994. See also Ahituv 2008, 389–401, in agreement with Lemaire (as also Rainey 2006, 212). For the biblical texts, see 2 Sam 8:2–18; 11:1; 12:26–31; 17:27; 24:5.

119. See the convenient overview in Herr 1997, 168–72.

120. See Rainey 2006, 106.

121. Herr 1997, 132.

122. Rainey frequently "maps" purported events, even though as a critical scholar he knows that they are likely to be fictional. Thus Rainey and Notley 2006, 160–61, depicting David's wars in Transjordan, without any reference to the archaeological data that we now have.

123. See Rainey 2006, 161; Pitard 1987, 89–97.

124. On Siamun, see Dever, Lance, and Wright 1970, 5, 61; Dever et al. 1986, 124. Lance 1976, however, raises some doubts on the name of the Pharaoh. See, however, the positive view of Kitchen 2003, 55. In any case, subsequent Stratum VIII belongs to the mid- to late tenth century. The latest evidence is found in Dever 1984b, 1985a, 1986.

125. On the Dan inscription, see n. 106 above; on the Mesha stela, see Dearman 1989; for recent treatments, see Routledge 2000; Harrison and Barlow 2005. Kitchen (2003, 93) has also tried to read the name "David" on the Shoshenq list, but few will be persuaded.

126. On archaeology and the Solomonic temple, see Dever 2001, 144–57; 2005a, 96–98, 212–14, 275–79 and references there. See also C. Meyers 1992; Bloch-Smith 2002; Monson 2005. Monson (2000) has demonstrated that the ninth-century ʿAin Daraʿ tripartite temple has numerous close parallels to the temple described in Kings.

127. See Dever 1984b, 1985a, 1986, 1993b; Holladay 1990; and references. Finkelstein's critiques have never addressed the data presented in these and other publications, indulging himself only in rhetoric. It is hoped that the renewed excavations of Ortiz and Wolff will produce C-14 samples. See further excursus 4.1 on the chronology.

128. See the discussion above and n. 108.

129. For preliminary reports, see Levy et al. 2004; Levy 2009; 2010a; add now the final report, Levy, Najjar, and Ben-Yosef 2014. See also n. 140.

130. Ben-Yosef et al. 2012. See also above and nn. 72, 75, 129. These authors (and Levy) do not make explicit connections to the Negev forts, but that would seem essential. Did they serve to protect the mining interests?

131. See Martin and Finkelstein 2013. The "Masos chiefdom model" goes far back; see Finkelstein 1995b, 2002, 2005c; Herzog and Singer-Avitz 2004; cf. van der Steen 2010. For Levy's dates, including the fort and an argument for an Edomite lowland polity as early as the tenth century, see Levy, Najjar, and Ben-Yosef 2014; Levy and Smith 2007 (with previous bibliography). For Levy's own model of local Transjordan sedentarized pastoral nomads (the Shasu), see the above work and add Levy 2008, 2009. See also n. 140 below.

132. Fritz and Kempinski 1983, 42. Holladay interpreted Building 1039 as a stable, a rather far-fetched notion (1995, 385).

133. Finkelstein (2002, 114) and Herzog and Singer-Avitz (2004, 227), of course, down-date the end of Stratum II to circa 925, an attempt to make it relevant for their "desert chiefdom." That correlation collapses, with so many others, with the collapse of their low chronology, well documented here.

134. See the discussion in ch. 3 nn. 124–26 and excursus 4.1. For one of Finkelstein's few explicit discussions, see 1995a.

135. See also references in n. 131 above, of which Finkelstein 2002 is the most explicit. The whole "Gibeonite confederacy" is illusory. (1) Pritchard's stratigraphy was so faulty that there are not even any stratum numbers. (2) Virtually nothing can be reconstructed of any tenth-century levels; Finkelstein's "evidence" consists of a couple of walls reconstructed by a student. (3) As for Saul ruling from there, the biblical narratives have him visiting there once—seeing it as a non-Israelite site. (4) Finkelstein's "capital" at Gibeon is clearly his substitute for Jerusalem, a red herring. (5) Finally, if his Saulide polity really extended all the way up to the Jezreel Valley, it is tantamount to the Hebrew Bible's united monarchy. If Saul is a king, why not his successor David, for whom we do have extrabiblical textual sources?

136. See references in nn. 131 and 133 above.

137. For works on which the following synthesis depends, see Mazar 1994; Gilboa and Sharon 2003, 2008; Schreiber 2003; Bell 2009; essays in Sagona 2008; essays in Bachuber and Roberts 2009; Beitzel 2010; and essays in Killebrew and Lehmann 2013 (especially Artzy, Sharon, and Gilboa), Iacovou 2013; Kassianidou 2013.

138. The one exception thus far consists of sherds of two mid-twelfth-century Cypriot vessels (LC IIIA) found in Stratum 20B at Ashkelon. See Master, Mountjoy, and Mommsen 2015.

139. Levy has hinted at the Solomonic connection in popular reports, but this is a bit premature and certainly does not reflect a critical use of the biblical narrative. See the conclusions of Na'aman—hardly a maximalist—who shows that behind the Deuteronomistic History of the seventh century or so there undoubtedly lie older oral and written traditions that may go back to a tenth-century monarchy (2012a).

140. For the suggestion that Ophir may be located somewhere in the Mediterranean, see Beitzel 2010. Like many others, Beitzel discusses another Mediterranean port of trade, Solomon's "Tarshish," probably to be identified as Tartessos in Spain. See 1 Kgs 9:26–28; 10:11–12, 22; 2 Chr 8:17–18; 9:10–11, 21.

141. See Shukron 2004 and references. For earlier bibliography, see Holm-Nielsen 1993.

142. The most up-to-date, authoritative summaries of the archaeological data and their biblical/historical implications are A. Mazar 2008a, 2010a.

143. Recent reassessments of Kadesh-barnea, based on the final report in Cohen and Bernick-Greenberg 2007 and new C-14 dates, have yielded the following picture:
Strata 3–2: the square fortress; eighth–sixth century
Stratum 4b: the so-called oval fortress, with several phases; tenth–eighth century; the Judahite monarchy
Stratum 4c: twelfth–eleventh century; Egyptian-sponsored copper trade, per-

haps related to Tell el-Kheleifeh, Wadi Feinan, and an early phase of the Negev forts

144. See above and excursus 4.1.

EXCURSUS 4.1

C-14 Dates of Megiddo and Tel Reḥov

The controversy about C-14 dates for the key sites in the north—Megiddo VA/IVB and Tel Reḥov V–IV—has raged since 1996. Finkelstein and Mazar and their coauthors alone have published some twenty-five articles since then, not to mention dozens of spin-off articles by other archaeologists (and a few intrepid biblicists), with implications for Cypriot and even Greek Iron I–IIA chronology.[1]

We have already sketched the early developments and have given a general critique. Two more recent developments are noteworthy. (1) Mazar has conceded some ground to Finkelstein and has thus moved the end of Iron IIA from circa 920 (Shoshenq) to circa 830, proposing a "modified conventional chronology" (MCC). (2) Meanwhile, Finkelstein has come up from his "century later" date for the Iron I/IIA transition by a few years, but only to circa 800. That would seem to narrow the gap, but the appearance is deceptive The "compromise" has to do mostly with relative chronology, that is, with *terminology*: When does our Iron IIA end? The absolute chronology of the key sites, however, is not affected that much.[2]

Up until 2005, Mazar had supported the conventional chronology, which ended the Iron IIA period circa 920, with the Shoshenq destructions at a number of sites (above), including Reḥov V, for which a series of C-14 dates from several laboratories clustered around 925–900. Reḥov IV then would have ended circa 840–830, with the well-known Aramean invasions, again in agreement with the C-14 dates for the site.

By 2005, however, Mazar's MCC was willing to date the Iron IIA/Iron IIB transition down from circa 920 to 830. Note, however, that this downdates only the *terminology*. Reḥov V is still said to end circa 920 and Reḥov IV circa 840, and Mazar still strongly upholds the conventional absolute chronology for Reḥov and all the other comparable sites.

Meanwhile, Finkelstein's low date for the violent destruction of Megiddo VIA circa 920 had to be given up, when newer C-14 determinations came out circa 1050–930 (even on the calculation of Finkelstein and his physicist Piasetzky: 1043–996). While Finkelstein apparently concedes a higher date for this admittedly key date, he did not move to adjust his *other* dates upward. (He did finally concede that the Judahite state's origin could be ninth century rather than eighth century, as previously maintained.) However, he now tends to date the end of Reḥov V circa 900 (although with some ambiguity), and Iron IIA may begin circa 920, but the transition from Iron I could have lasted "several decades." Where does that leave us?[3]

The following chart, reproduced from Mazar, may offer some clarification, based still, however, on his MCC scheme. A close comparison with a chart of Finkelstein, published only a few months earlier, is instructive.[4]

	Mazar 2011	Finkelstein and Piasetzky 2011a
Megiddo VIA	980	960
Megiddo VB	950	920
Megiddo VA/IVB	920	860
Reḥov V	920	900
Reḥov IV	830	860 (!)
Hazor X	920	900
Hazor VIII	830	860 (!)

Finkelstein's position here is more nuanced than usual, and it seems almost conciliatory, but that may be misleading. He does declare the heated debates over chronology "have now narrowed to a few decades—a gap that is beyond the resolution of radiocarbon results."[5] Furthermore, his chart contains some surprises, introduced without a word in the text. Not only does his date for the end of Tel Reḥov V now agree substantially with Mazar's date (ca. 900), but his date for the end of Stratum IV is even higher than Mazar's (ca. 860 versus 830). For Hazor, again his date for the end of Stratum X is about the same as Mazar's (ca. 900), and for Stratum VIII it is again thirty years higher than Mazar's (ca. 860 versus 830). On the other hand, for Megiddo VIA Finkelstein now moves up somewhat, from circa 925 to 960, but not to the date of 1000 preferred by the conventional chronology.

In summary, Finkelstein does seem tacitly willing to close the older century-or-so gap to about forty years, even giving in on Tel Reḥov—but without clarifying other dates and in particular without ever admitting that he was wrong about a key site such as Tel Reḥov. Is that the end of the matter, as Finkelstein seems to imply?[6]

Finkelstein has vacillated on C-14 dates over several years. He has claimed repeatedly that there are "dozens" of C-14 dates that confirm his low chronology. Presumably many of these come from his own excavations over many years at Megiddo, a key site—especially in Finkelstein's controversies with Mazar at nearby Tel Reḥov. What are the facts?

The renewed project has published three sumptuous volumes in collaboration with leading scientists. The entire list of published C-14 dates for the relevant Iron I/IIA strata, however, is minimal.

The end of Stratum VIA had been dated by Finkelstein to the Shoshenq destruction circa 920, rather than the conventional date of circa 1000, as we have seen. The one relevant C-14 date in *Megiddo III* for Stratum K-4/VIA is 1062–1006 BCE, with a 90 percent certainty that supports the conventional date almost precisely, not Finkelstein's date almost a century later. The report leaves the crucial date of subsequent Iron IIA Stratum VA/IVB at circa 920, with the Shoshenq destruction.[7]

C-14 dates for the latter, which has usually been taken to define Iron IIA, are published only in *Megiddo IV* and *V*. They run as follows for the level (H-B) equivalent to Megiddo VA/IVB.

		number of dates
RT3948	980–950	2
RT3949	1040–900	2
RT3228	1000–830	2
	1130–790	2

The first two dates fit very well with the conventional chronology for the end of Stratum VA/IVB circa 920. The third date is useless for either chronology, even with the 2 deviation (1 is not as reliable). The Megiddo authors can only say that these dates are "much too high," that they "do not represent a very coherent picture."[8] Actually, they are just right for the conventional chronology, and the two that are reliable are very coherent. It is worth noting that these are the *only* relevant C-14 dates published thus far in Finkelstein's final Megiddo reports. Where are the "dozens"?

Virtually all authorities agree that Megiddo VA/IVB (= new H-5) is contemporary with Tel Reḥov V. Both strata have traditionally been dated to the mid- to late tenth century and thought to end with the Shoshenq raid circa 920, as we have seen.[9] Finkelstein has relied not only on the presumed Megiddo C-14 dates in support of his low chronology—lower by nearly a century in early discussions—but also on C-14 dates from Dor as they became available. The Dor excavators, Ilan Sharon and Ayelet Gilboa, are the principal investigators of a large and well-funded Israel Science Foundation project that is analyzing hundreds of C-14 samples from many sites.[10]

Sharon and Gilboa have been outspoken advocates of Finkelstein's low chronology, implying that an extensive analysis of hundreds of new C-14 dates from dozens of sites will prove definitive. Yet their own published dates from Dor are anything but definitive. They can only suggest that the Iron I–IIA transition dates circa 920–850. However, their Iron I–IIA terminology only follows Mazar's notion of a *modified* terminology. It must be borne in mind that these are only *our* contrived labels; they do not necessarily correspond to specific strata at Dor or elsewhere or to any actual historical eras. At best these labels simply reflect what all authorities now recognize: the continuity from the tenth well into the ninth century, especially in ceramics.

The question of the *absolute* dates of the pertinent Dor strata has not been resolved by Sharon or Gilboa here or elsewhere. In fact, there are no overall stratum numbers for Dor thus far, only a series of chronological "boundaries." As for Mazar's late Iron IIA (ca. 950–830), it is admitted that "no dates are available." In one of the latest discussions, Sharon and Gilboa note "serious discrepancies" between various chronologies, so "we shall not offer the ^{14}C-derived dates as a binding framework here." In fact, no specific C-14 dates are given for Dor strata, only for boundaries for the late Iron I or early Iron IIA periods, here the late eleventh to the late tenth century. Even these "dates" are only peaks shown on several graphic charts, not calendrical dates.[11]

In sum, the Dor dates *as published* thus far could fit either the conventional or the low chronology. Moreover, until the Dor strata *together with* their respective ceramic assemblages can be compared with sites such as Megiddo, Tel Reḥov, and other relevant Iron I–IIA sites, these dates are "floating."[12] They provide at best a relative rather than an absolute chronology. Even then, there is the well-known ± factor in C-14 dating of some forty years as well as systematic differences between laboratories. Finally, Dor is a coastal *Phoenician* site, and its stratification and chronological sequences cannot automatically be taken as typical of inland sites, either Israelite or Judahite.[13]

The above caveats tend to be overlooked even in the most sophisticated discussions, and that oversight has caused enormous confusion among biblical and other historians.[14] The few (indeed almost the only) relevant dates for key strata conventionally dated to the tenth century (Iron IIA here) can be charted as follows.[15]

Dan	Megiddo	Tel Reḥov	Negev forts
IVA	VA/IVB (H-5)	V	H. Haluqim
1046–914	(1) RT3948	(1) 924–902	1052–971
66.7% (1σ)	855–805 (1σ)	68.2% (1σ)	45.7% (1σ)
	980–950 (2σ)		
	(2) RT3948	(2) 945–887	
	1040–900 (2σ)	95.4% (1σ)	
	(3) RT3228		
	1000–830 (1σ)		
	1130–790 (2σ)		

A summary conclusion of the data, based on a model drawn from jurisprudence, would be (1) that some data could be seen as equivocal, (2) that no data conclusively support the low chronology, and (3) that the preponderance of the data still supports the conventional chronology. Thus the scheme advocated here is reliable beyond a reasonable doubt. Further, if we retain the conventional Iron IIA terminology, it fits well with the strata above (and many comparable strata at other sites), belongs in absolute chronology broadly to the tenth century, and may end at a number of sites with the Shoshenq raid circa 920.

Further data might change this picture, but meanwhile prudence would suggest retaining the conventional scheme adopted here. It is consistent, and it best accounts for both the stratigraphical and the historical evidence now at hand.[16]

Notes

1. For the discussion up to about 2003 or 2004, see Levy and Higham 2005 and the many chapters there. More recently, see Mazar 2011; Mazar and Bronk Ramsey 2008, 2010; Mazar et al. 2005; Bruins, van der Plicht, and Mazar 2003; Finkelstein 2005b, 2010b; Finkelstein and Piasetzky 2003a, 2003b, 2003c, 2006a; 2006b; 2008; 2010b; 2011a; Finkelstein and Fantalkin 2012; Fantalkin and Finkelstein 2006. On Greek correlations, see Gilboa and Sharon 2008; Maier, Hitchcock, and Horwitz 2013. See also the extensive discussion in Frese and Levy 2010.

2. On A. Mazar's modified conventional chronology, see 2005, 2011; Mazar et al. 2005.

3. See Finkelstein and Piasetzky 2011a, 2011b; A. Mazar 2010a. Finkelstein seems to agree with Mazar's conventional date for the end of Tel Reḥov V circa 920; see the chart in Finkelstein and Piasetzky 2011b, 108–9; cf. Mazar 2011, 111. In *Megiddo III*, however, C-14 dates for Stratum VIA had already been give as 1026–1006 (90 percent; Finkelstein, Ussishkin, and Halpern 2000, 503)—an even higher date. In any case, the conventional date of circa 1000 for the end of Stratum VIA must now be entirely confirmed—not Finkelstein's date almost a century lower.

4. See references in n. 3 above. Note that here some of Finkelstein's dates are inexplicably higher than Mazar's dates—another indication of how facile he can be.

5. Finkelstein and Piasetzky 2011a, 52.

6. See references in n. 3 above. As noted, Finkelstein has conceded, adopting a higher date for the end of Megiddo VIA, but he did not pursue the implications. For instance, he did not move up Strata VA/IVB accordingly, thus (1) leaving the ephemeral Stratum VB covering one hundred years, and (2) having no candidate for the well-attested Shoshenq destruction circa 920, since this stratum betrays no such destruction.

7. See Finkelstein, Ussishkin, and Halpern 2006, 553–54; Finkelstein, Ussishkin, and Cline 2013, 1120–23. Note that Finkelstein later raised the date for the end of Megiddo VIA to circa 960 and also raised the end of Megiddo VA/IVB to 860 (above).

8. See references in n. 7 above.

9. Instead of dealing with the Tel Reḥov V–IV C-14 dates when they were published—confirming Mazar's dates with almost uncanny precision—Finkelstein avoided the issue by trying arbitrarily to lower the date of Stratum V to compare it with Megiddo IVA, against all authorities (2005b). Then, however, he has no place for Stratum VI nor an explanation for either the end of Strata V or IV. All would agree that the pottery of Strata V and IV are similar, but that is no excuse for confusing or conflating the two. Then, in a further desperate move, he conceded the early date of the end of Tel Reḥov V (above) without ever acknowledging the contradiction. There is no method here; if strata at various sites *can* be

shuffled around to suit lower dates, they *must* be. But these arbitrary, inconsistent, and even contradictory moves vitiate Finkelstein's *originally* productive challenge. See further Kletter 2004.

10. For the project and the publication of the Dor dates, see initially Gilboa and Sharon 2001, 2003 (which all now agree were systematically too low for any chronology). Supplement by further dates in Sharon et al. 2005; Sharon and Gilboa 2013 and references there. The Israel Science Foundation "Early Iron Age Dating Project" began in 1996, the same year that Finkelstein began to promote his low chronology. Cf. Finkelstein 1996a; see further Finkelstein and Piasetzky 2003c, an attack on the Tel Reḥov C-14 dates early on, using the Dor dates.

11. See Sharon et al. 2005, 70, 75–81, 90; Gilboa and Sharon 2008, 152; Sharon and Gilboa 2013, 402–3, 435–37, 453. Some further information on Dor C-14 dates may be found in Sharon et al. 2005. Gilboa and Sharon note in passing, despite some four hundred measurements of more than twenty-one sites in Israel, only four dates relevant for the Iron I/II transition (their dates 920–900) but only one from Dor, Phase D2/8c. Yet they do not give that date in C-14 determinations. They then note that there are nineteen samples for early Iron IIA (their dates 900–800), but again they provide no absolute dates. All we glean from this is (1) a relative sequence of Dor strata and (2) a few very approximate "peaks" for Iron Age *terminology* (in defense of theirs, of course). Cf. Sharon et al. 2005, 66–71, 80; Sharon and Gilboa 2013, 66–71. Nevertheless, they claim unabashedly that the Dor C-14 dates "unequivocally support the 'low chronology'" (2005, 80). As for a chronologically based history—surely a desideratum—they say simply, "We also try to eschew any historical, much less cultural or ethnic correlations in our period designations" (2013, 436, referring only to Gilboa and Sharon 2003, the dates in which they now acknowledge to be too low; see Sharon and Gilboa 2013, 65).

12. It is worth noting that in publications on C-14 dates, Gilboa and Sharon at Dor, as well as Finkelstein at Megiddo, nowhere present the detailed *comparative context* of their samples: ceramic assemblages. Thus contrast Finkelstein in Levy and Higham 2005 and Mazar in the same volume. Finkelstein's two papers present no pottery (and, of course, no ceramic comparison); two uncalibrated dates from Megiddo VA/IVB (which would support either chronology); and only seventeen pages, mostly unsupported assertions. By comparison, Mazar's sixty-one-page paper presents nine pages of pottery from three strata; numerous architectural plans and sections; and sixty-eight detailed C-14 dates and sixteen graphic charts. On the basis of "weight" alone, the unbiased reader of the conflicting arguments would come down on the side of Mazar. Cf. also the detailed discussion of the Tel Reḥov C-14 dates in Bruins and van der Plicht 2005; Bruins et al. 2005b.

13. A. Mazar (2005), together with physicists such as van der Plicht and Bruins, has frequently pointed out that Finkelstein and Piasetzky's Weitzman Institute C-14 dates run *systematically* as much as a century lower than dates from similar (or the same) stratum and context done at the Groningen, Oxford, and

Tucson laboratories. Finkelstein, Gilboa, and Sharon simply wave this away as "much smaller," i.e., not a significant factor (Sharon et al. 2005, 78; Finkelstein 2005b, 302).

14. Thus some European biblical revisionists are fond of mentioning the low chronology, declaring its validity and wide acceptance proven, "as Finkelstein has shown." He has "shown" nothing, only asserted it, as documented here and elsewhere.

15. For Dan, see Bruins et al. 2005; for Tel Reḥov, see Bruins et al. 2005, 271 (cf. Mazar 2005, 29–36); for Megiddo, see n. 7 above; for the Negev forts, see Bruins and van der Plicht 2005, 352. The Megiddo dates require some comment. The first in its 2σ range is good for Strata VA/IVB generally, if not its end. The second is dead on. The third is much too broad to be of any use, even in its 2σ range.

There are other C-14 dates available for more peripheral sites such as Hazor and Tel Yoqneam, for Aramean sites such as Tel Hadar, for Philistine sites such as Tell Qasile, for Phoenician sites such as Keisan, or for more remote desert sites such as the Negev forts and Kadesh-barnea. For a listing of some sixty C-14 dates (BP only), see Mazar 2010b. The eleventh–ninth-century C-14 dates for sites in the Wadi Feinan in Edom are roughly contemporary but difficult to compare with sites in Cisjordan. But even where a few such C-14 dates are published, the necessary comparative assemblages (especially pottery) are not available.

16. Finkelstein, his confidence unabated (?), has recently claimed that Dever's "Solomonic frenzy" has been discredited and that he and other dissidents are rapidly "deserting" to the low chronology (Finkelstein 2005d, 38–39; 2005b, 308). His claim that Dever is willing to accept a lower chronology (2005, 297) is disingenuous. What Dever clearly said in the statement referred to was: "If evidence should mount…," but he argued that it had not (Dever 2005c, 420).

CHAPTER 5

The Consolidation of the State:
The Iron II B Period (Ninth–Eighth Century)

Introduction

It has been argued here that a Judahite state arose in the south of the country in the tenth century with its capital at Jerusalem. Nevertheless that polity, while a true kingdom or state by cross-cultural comparisons, was what anthropologists might call an early inchoate state (ch. 4). The territory it governed was relatively small, its extent northward (Israel) presumed but not clearly determined on the basis of current evidence. The population was evidently small, perhaps 100,000 or so, mostly rural. A few urban sites had developed, none very large, but some were already regional administrative centers, to judge from the monumental architecture that we have.

We are now a long way beyond the village-pastoral culture of the Iron I period in the twelfth–eleventh century (ch. 3). The subsequent ninth–eighth century, by consensus designated the Iron IIB period, will see the growth and consolidation of the state, indeed both a northern state (Israel) and a southern state (Judah). They share many characteristics typical of small Levantine nation-states of the Iron Age, but their paths increasingly diverge. The northern state persists scarcely two hundred years, the southern state another century or so (ch. 6).

Here again the organizing principle of our synthesis of the archaeological data as our primary source material will be General Systems Theory, as it was for the portrait of the tenth century. The approach, even though necessarily topical, will still be diachronic wherever possible—historical in the sense of charting and explaining change rather than being merely descriptive.

The most conspicuous characteristic of the Israelite and Judahite states in Iron IIB is the further growth of the incipient urbanism evident already in the tenth century. But what do we mean by *urbanism*? Oddly enough, few biblical historians or archaeologists define the term beyond some vague notion that a city consists of a large population agglomerate at a site that is usually presumed to have monumental architecture and is fortified. However, unless we can devise some means of quantification, an understanding of historical development will elude us. Therefore, let us approach the problem more analytically.

Establishing a Site Hierarchy and Data Base

Few archaeologists or biblical historians have attempted to develop a hierarchy of Iron II sites in Israel and Judah, beyond using simple terms *city*, *town*, or *village*.[1] Here (as in ch. 4) we will develop a more comprehensive, multitiered hierarchy of sites, which even if necessarily somewhat arbitrary can be of heuristic value. The results may be summarized in chart form (figs. 5.1–5.3).

Fig. 5.1. Tier 1–6 sites in Iron IIB (ninth–eighth century)

Site, Stratum	Acres	Population (est.)
Tier 1: Capitals		
Samaria BP I–VI	upper: 34 lower: 15	500?
Jerusalem 13, 12	15–150 (by late eighth century)	8,000–30,000
Tier 2: Administrative Centers		
Israel		
Dan III, II	50	3,000
Hazor VIII–VA	8–15	500–1,000
Megiddo IVA	15	500
Gezer VII–VI	33	3,000
Tell en-Naṣbeh 3C–A	8 (later ca. 14)	500–1,000

Judah

Beth-Shemesh 3, 2	7	500
Lachish IV–III	31	800
Beersheba IV–III	3	300

Tier 3: Cities (10 acres and up; population 1,000 and up)

Israel

Taʿanach III–IV	11	1,000
Beth-Shean IV	10	900
Reḥov IV–III	24	2,000
Dothan 3–2	15	1,200
Tell el-Farʿah VII$_{c-e}$	15	1,200
Shechem IX–VII	15	1,200

Judah

Hebron	10?	500?
Khirbet Rabud B-III–II	15	1,200
Tel ʿEton II–I	15	1,200
Tel Haror D, E	10 (upper)	800?

Tier 4: Towns (3–10 acres)

Israel

Yoqneʿam XIII–XII	10	800
Tell el-Hammah	7	600
Khirbet Marjama	10	800
Bethel	4	300
Gibeon	5?	400?

Judah

Tel Batash III	7	500
Tel Ḥamid VII–VI	10	800
Beth-Zur	4	300
Tel Zayit		7.5
Tell Beit Mirsim A$_2$	7.5	700
Tel Ḥalif VID–B	3	300
Tell el-Ḥesi VIId	3	200

| Tel Seraʿ VII–VI | 5 | 400 |
| Tel ʿIra VIII–VII | 6 | 500 |

Tier 5: Villages (1–3 acres; population 50–300)

Israel

Kedesh	?
Tel Kinrot III–II	2.5
Tel ʿEn-Zippori	3?
Tel Qiri VII B–C	2.5
Tel Qashish III C–A	2.5
Khirbet Jemein	2.5
Beit Aryeh	1
Khirbet Kla	1.5
Naḥal Rephaim	?

Tier 6: Forts (size not relevant)

Israel	**Judah**
Tel Soreg	Deir Baghl
Khirbet el-Maḥruq	Khirbet Tabaneh
Tell Qudadi	Giloh
	Ramat Raḥel Phase 1 (=VB; late eighth century)
	Khirbet Abu Tuwein
	Buqeiʿa
	Qumran
	El-Khirbe
	Tel Malḥata A
	Arad XI–VIII
	Ḥorvat Radum
	Mezad Ḥazeva V
	Tell el-Kheleifeh (II)
	Kadesh-barnea 3
	Kuntillet ʿAjrud
	Khirbet Abu Tuwein

Tier 1: Capitals. The upper tier of sites would obviously be capital cities, now that Israel and Judah were beyond any doubt well-developed states. Even without the biblical texts, the archaeological and extrabiblical data converge to demonstrate that Samaria was the capital of the northern state, Jerusalem the capital of the southern state. Neither of these cities, however, would have reached our threshold that defines a city within the early Iron II period, that is, a population of more than 1,000 (below). Here, however, size is not necessarily the criterion, since capital cities may be relatively small. Moreover, because so much space is taken up by public and administrative buildings along with open spaces, the civilian population may remain relatively small, only a few hundred or so. Nevertheless, a capital city wields power and influence far out of proportion to its size because of strategic location, concentration of resources, and centralized political power.

Samaria, even with a civilian population of perhaps only 500 or so, was certainly a city. Jerusalem, with probably less than 2,000 population until the late eighth century (below), qualifies equally well as a city. Thus tier 1 here consists of these two capital cities.

Tier 2: Administrative Centers. Just below the uppermost echelon of Iron II sites, and integrally related, would be district or regional administrative centers. Here, too, absolute size is of less significance than strategic location and the ability to dominate a region through the concentration of political and economic power. These are what geographers often call "central places." In the Iron II period we have a number of such places: five in Israel, three in Judah (fig. 5.3). They can be larger or smaller than tier 3 cities (below), but all are characterized by strong fortifications, impressive palaces, complex administrative buildings and storehouses, large open spaces, and well-engineered water systems.

Tier 3 Cities (> 1,000). One approach to the process of urbanization has been to look at what are universally regarded as the first true cities, those that developed in ancient Mesopotamia in the fourth and third millennia. The Sumerian and Akkadian sites usually considered true cities range from 20,000 to 40,000 in population. Recent studies have sought to be more precise by developing a more systematic model based on the *carrying capacity* of a given region, that is, the limits of its ability to support a human population.

The fundamental hypothesis is that a village or town must develop into something we can call a city when the growth of its population outstrips

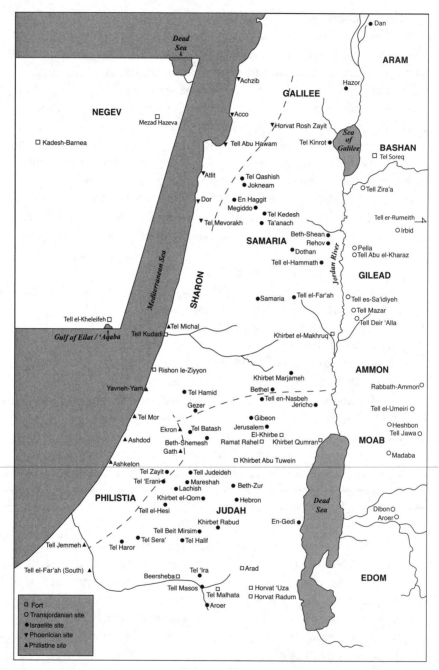

Fig. 5.2. Sites in Israel, Judah, and their neighbors, eighth–seventh century (map by Giselle Hasel)

the means of production. That is, a *city* develops that must now organize the countryside—the outlying agricultural areas, villages, and towns—in order to feed itself. A concomitant is that a central authority must develop, one that must necessarily coerce a population, in effect disembodying goods and services on a larger scale than was previously possible or necessary. The city thus becomes a commercial, political, and eventually a cultural center—a complex, specialized, highly stratified market town, often developing into a regional administrative center.

The flat, rich alluvial plains of ancient Mesopotamia were efficiently irrigated from early times and were capable of producing two crops a year. Studies have shown that the threshold of a population's self-sufficiency may have been a population of around 20,000, after which a larger and more complex city must have developed. As attractive as the above model may be, it will not work for much of the southern Levant, in this case ancient Syria–Palestine, mostly because of scalar differences. Ancient Mesopotamia was the "heartland of cities" (to use Robert MacAdam's felicitous term), but our more marginal region is better understood as "the heartland of villages."

The carrying capacity of almost all the inhabited areas of ancient Israel and Judah was much smaller than that of Mesopotamia or even greater Canaan. That was due largely to the limitations of the natural habitat, as well as the lack of appropriate technology in most cases. Arid or semiarid conditions, with scant and seasonal rainfall, typically posed a severe challenge to agriculture, and pastoralism was sometimes the only option. The hilly terrain made runoff or gravity irrigation impossible, even where wadis and springs supplied some water. Hillsides had to be terraced to conserve rainfall. But the terraces were narrow and required constant maintenance. The soils were still thin and rocky. Intermontane valleys could sometimes be exploited for dry farming, but they were small and often distant (ch. 2).

These natural conditions of the southern Levant meant that agriculture—more typically agro-pastoralism—was always small-scale. Expansion for typical rural villages or small towns where farmers may have resided was confined by geography. In all preindustrial societies, agricultural production was constrained by the fact that people in settled areas, even where conditions were reasonably good, could scarcely commute more than a few miles from their domiciles to the surrounding fields. The practical difficulties of transporting tools and supplies to the fields by hand or on donkey back, of protecting the ripe crops, and of carrying the harvest home made venturing farther than about 2 miles into the hinterland impractical or impossible.

These factors meant that a small town could effectively control an area of no more than about 15 square miles. That may sound like a lot of territory, but estimates are that it could support an agricultural population of only about 1,000 or so.[2] For that reason, we will define a city here as a settlement whose population reaches or exceeds that size, although size is not, of course, the only criterion. For example, Samaria and Jerusalem as capital cities wielded power beyond that indicated by their size, and they were certainly cities by any definition (above). Above about 1,000 in population, size does not seem to matter much. There were, however, natural limits to growth, as always, and the largest Iron II Israelite and Judahite cities (e.g., Dan and Gezer) never exceeded a population of some 3,000. A city such as Hazor, which could have had a population of as much as 15,000 in the Bronze Age, now shrank to no more than a few hundred.

On the basis of our criteria here, only a handful of Iron II cities are well enough known archaeologically to characterize them as such: six in Israel and four in Judah (fig. 5.2).

Tier 4: Towns (300–1,000). Using the criteria adopted here, defining a city is relatively straightforward, positing a threshold of some 1,000 population and up. Distinguishing a town (tier 4 site) from a city, however, is more arbitrary. While the upper limit might be around 1,000 population, the lower limit is difficult to set, although here for purposes of classification it is put at 300 (below which are tier 5 villages).

In addition to absolute size, there are other variables, of course, but most are difficult to discern, more difficult still to quantify. For instance, the presence or absence of a defensive wall is not a reliable criterion; even small villages may be walled in the Iron II period. Nor is town planning particularly significant, since even the smaller towns may now give evidence of deliberate design and function for many structures, as well as for general layout.

Based on our hierarchy of sites here, we have relatively few well-known towns in the ninth–eighth century, most of which were not administrative or commercial centers but were nevertheless provincial towns that could be defended by a town wall. As many as twenty-five such towns are known archaeologically in the ninth–eighth century, with a total estimated population of up to 15,000. That would contrast with an estimated population of some 12,000 for the ten urban sites discussed below. There are no doubt many unknown or unexcavated towns in both Israel and Judah that would change the demographic picture that we now have—not to mention the hundreds of small villages and farmsteads (tier 5) that are known presently almost exclusively from surveys.

Tier 5: Villages (< 300). It has been known for some time that ancient Israel and Judah were predominantly rural societies, the bulk of the population living in small towns or more often in villages and farmsteads. Here we shall assume that a population of some 300 defines the upper limit of a village, again a somewhat arbitrary cutoff point. Only about a dozen or so such villages have been excavated sufficiently to be analyzed here, but extensive surface surveys done in the past generation by Israeli archaeologists have mapped some two hundred similar Iron II villages, most no more than 3 acres (and thus with an estimated population of some 300). At some 3 acres each, that would add as many as 60,000 to the population.[3]

Tier 6: Forts. A final site type can be designated as a fort because it exhibits only military construction and functions, and it obviously lacks a civilian population. Here again size is not the major consideration, although most forts are relatively small, but rather strategic location, usually guarding a crucial border. More than a dozen such sites of the ninth–eighth century have been excavated, mostly one-period. They are located on the borders with Phoenicia and the Aramean enclaves in the north, with the Philistine plain, and with Ammon, Moab, and Edom in Transjordan (population figures are too uncertain to estimate, based on size.)

The Data Base

The multitier site hierarchy that we have introduced has been set forth in figure 5.1 in chart form as well as in the map in figure 2 (see also fig. 5.3). These will serve as our data base. Employing again the General Systems Theory approach outlined in chapter 1, we shall summarize Iron II Tier 1–6 sites in Israel and Judah according to several sub-systems. As in Chapters III and IV, we shall look especially at change over time, attempting to set such change into a larger historical and cultural framework.

Fig. 5.3. **Stratigraphy of major Iron II Israelite and Judahite sites**

Iron IIA	Iron IIB	Iron IIC	("Iron III")
	900	700 600	
IV	Dan III–II		
IX–VII	Hazor VII–VA	IV–III	
IV	Tel Kinrot III–II	I	
V upper	Beth-Shean IV	——	
V (= V5)	IV(=B4) Tel Reḥov III	II	
VA–IVB	Megiddo IVA	III–II	
III	Tel ʿAmal II–I	I	
VIIb	Tell el-Farʿah VIIc–e	VIIe1	
XIV	Yoqneʿam XIII–XII	XI	
VIIA	Tel Qiri VIIB–C	VI V	
	Tel Qashish IIIC–A		
IIA–B	Taʿanach III–IV	V	
XA–B	Shechem IX–VII	VIA–B	V
I–II	Samaria BP I–VI	VII	VII
IV–VIII	Gezer VII–VI	V	IV
4	Tell en-Naṣbeh 3C–A ——→	2	
14	Jerusalem 13–12 ——→	11 10B	10A
	Ramat Raḥel VB (= Ph. 1)	VA (= Ph. 2)	IVB
IIa (=4)	Beth-Shemesh IIb (= 3–2)	IIc (= 1)	——
IVA–B	Tel Batash III	II	I
		Beth-Zur II	I
V	Lachish IV–III	II	I
B3	Tell Beit Mirsim A2	A1	——
	Khirbet Rabud B-III–II	B-I; AII	A-I
	Tel Seraʿ VII–VI	gap? V–IV	
		ʿEin-Gedi V	IV
VII	Tel Ḥalif VID–B	VIA	——
	Tel Zayit	——	
EF	Tell Jemmeh CD	AB	
	Tell el-Ḥesi VIId	VI	
V	Beersheba IV–III	II	
		ʿAroʿer IV–III	II
XII	Arad XI–VIII	VII VI	
4b	Kadesh-barnea 3	2 (1)	——
I (?)	Tell el-Khefeifeh II	III IV	——

Tier 1: Capitals

Samaria. Samaria was without question the capital of Israel, the northern kingdom, during the ninth–eighth century. It is a large mound of some 50 acres, prominently situated in the western hill country of the region to which it has given its name, overlooking the Sharon plain to the west. Its situation is magnificent: in the late afternoon one can catch sight of the setting sun glinting off the water of the Mediterranean, some 30 miles to the west. The site, whose Hebrew name means something like "watchtower," was chosen as the capital in the ninth century because of its strategic location, as well as the fact that it had no significant prior history and was thus neutral ground.

The American excavations in 1908–1910 and the joint British/Jewish Palestine excavations in 1930–1935 were confined almost exclusively to the 4-acre royal acropolis, where the monumental buildings stood. Little is thus known of the pre-Roman lower city, where the civilian population of perhaps several hundred would have lived, except for a stretch of ashlar wall and a tower.

Six phases were distinguished by Crowfoot and Kenyon, designated as both "building" and "pottery" periods, presumed to be contemporary. Upon the publication of the final report in 1957, however, authorities such as Albright, Wright, Aharoni, Amiran, and Avigad (the latter a staff member in the 1930s) began to question the stratigraphy, several arguing that the pottery periods *preceded* the building periods. One consequence was that a pre-Omride era, or tenth-century phase (Pottery Periods 1, 2, or Building Period O), is now recognized. (That would be the Shemer estate of the biblical writers; see below.) For our purposes, this reworking of Samaria's stratigraphy allows us to distinguish two mid-ninth-century periods, here seen as Kenyon's Building Periods I–II.[4]

Phase I (= Pottery Period 3) represents the earliest construction of the monumental buildings on the acropolis (i.e., by Omri, in the biblical view). In this initial stage a solid wall 5 feet wide was constructed upon deep constructional fills and revetments, enclosing an area of some 17,000 square feet. In the southwest corner a palatial building covering 7,500 square feet was constructed, consisting of many rooms surrounding a central courtyard, with a much larger courtyard featuring a plastered floor adjoining the building to the north. The construction of the palace featured irregular bossed masonry in the below-ground courses but finely dressed and dry-fitted ashlar blocks in the upper courses. The latter, the finest pre-Roman masonry ever found in the country, is of Phoenician style (below; see fig. 5.4). Six Proto-Aeolic (or palmette) capitals probably came from the palace.

In Phase II (Pottery Period 3 late; Building Period II) the plan was augmented by enlarging the acropolis, now enclosed on the north and west by a casemate wall 16 feet wide, extending for at least 360 yards (at least one hundred casemates are in evidence). In the area added to the west there was constructed a large multiroomed building of some 5,000 square feet. The symmetrical plan of the building, plus its long offset entrance corridor, suggests that it may have been an archival building (see the ostraca below). At this stage or perhaps later, a large colonnaded building was erected just outside the casemate wall on the west, perhaps another administrative structure. It was probably also in Phase II (or III) that a complex of small rooms was added in the center of the enclosed compound, dubbed the Ivory House because it was said to have produced a hoard of fine ivory inlays of Phoenician type (below). In the northwest corner of the enclosure was a large cistern for storing water. Another structure seems to be a second palace. The Ostraca House inside the casemate wall may also originate here (below). In the biblical view, this would be in the reign of Ahab.

The later phases of the acropolis in the eighth century (Building Periods III–VI, Pottery Periods 4–6) are not clear. But to judge from the ruins of 721 (below), they seem to have preserved and reused all the essential elements of the initial plan and construction as a royal citadel. There is no doubt from the grandiose layout, the dominant public areas, the fine ashlar masonry, the luxurious Phoenician-style ivories, and the administrative documents (ostraca) that Samaria was a capital city worthy of a king. The supporting civilian population, however, would have been relatively small. Concentrated in the largely unexcavated lower city, the population may have been only a few hundred.

Jerusalem. Jerusalem can be said to have emerged already as the capital of the fledging kingdom of Judah by the tenth century (ch. 4). The monumental archaeological features of the city become much clearer, however, in the Iron IIB period, the ninth–eighth century.

Precise inner phasing is difficult because the exposures in the Old City have necessarily been limited, despite many excavations over the past century and a half. If such monumental structures as the biblical Solomonic

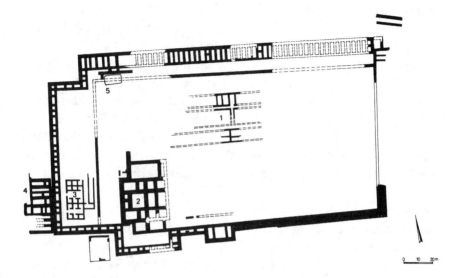

Fig. 5.4. Major structures on the Israelite acropolis of Samaria, Building Period II. 1: residence; 2: first palace; 3: ostraca house; 4: later palace; 5: reservoir (Herzog 1997, fig. 5:22)

temple, the stepped stone structure on the spur of the Ophel hill, and Elilat Mazar's "David's citadel" are correctly dated to the tenth century (above), they would certainly have still been in use in the ninth–eighth century, perhaps even expanded.

Sometime in this era (Strata 13–12) a major defense wall was built to enclose the Temple Mount and the area now called the City of David on the slopes to the south, above the Gihon Spring in the Kidron Valley below. A stretch of solid wall of varying width, some 4,000 yards in length, was exposed by Shiloh's excavation. It ran roughly parallel to the Middle Bronze city wall downslope and apparently reused some of its masonry. This wall provided not only protection but also served as the foundation for several terraces above it, on which were constructed domestic dwellings (the tenth-century stepped stone structure; ch. 4).

In Kenyon's excavations and in Area G of Shiloh's excavations there were brought to light several private houses founded directly on the upper portions of the old stepped stone structure, now partly out of use but still providing an ideal foundation (fig. 5.5). These houses on the slope were designed so that the roofs of the lower ones served as the front terraces of the ones built upslope. Some of the houses were comparatively elaborate, even equipped with built-in toilets. The names of some of the families, probably elites attached to the royal court and temple, are known from epigraphic evidence, such as that from the house of one "Ahiel."

The population grew so much that it now expanded beyond the city wall, down the slope below. These houses were destroyed in 586, as indicated by their pottery and objects, including a group of early sixth-century bullae (below). But it is highly likely that they had been constructed much earlier, even in the tenth century, and had been continually rebuilt and reused. We know that this happened at many other Judahite sites in the ninth–eighth century, due to the lack of major destructions throughout the period.

Remains of other houses were found In Avigad's excavations in the Jewish Quarter of the Old City, as well as considerable quantities of sherds from the ninth–eighth century. The extent of Jerusalem toward the Western Hill (the present Armenian Quarter and Mount Zion) is not well known before the late eighth century or so. But by then the size of the city may have increased from about 15 acres in the tenth century to some 150 acres by the late eighth century.[5]

Apparently constructed in the ninth century and continuing in use into the eighth century (Stratum 12), a massive citadel was located between the Temple Mount's southern edge and the residential quarter of the City of David. The combined plan of Warren's Tower and Eilat Mazar's Ophel excavations reveals a heavily fortified triple-entryway gate with adjoining large storerooms (fig. 5.6). One of the eighth century store jars recovered from the magazines bears the Hebrew name of an official.[6]

The city's growth in population is indicated by the discovery of many Iron Age tombs, located all around the perimeter of the city, extending west as far as Mamilla Road in today's West Jerusalem. Some were found near the Damascus Gate, one particularly fine example a bench tomb long known from the grounds of the École Biblique. Numerous others were discovered cut into the rocky slopes south of the Jaffa Gate, extending south and eastward along the steep cliffs of the Hinnom Valley. The most impressive Iron II tombs are those still visible in the bedrock below the village of Siloam, opposite the Temple Mount. These tombs will be discussed in detail presently, but they give evidence of a considerable domestic occupation, including noble families.[7]

Some of the above remains probably belong to Stratum 13 of the ninth century, but Stratum 12 of the eighth century is better attested. Two

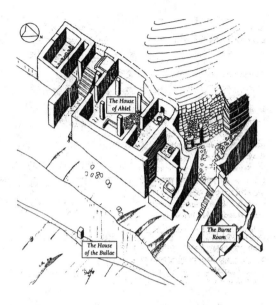

Fig. 5.5. Iron II houses on the stepped stone structure in Jerusalem (Barkay 1992, fig. 9.44)

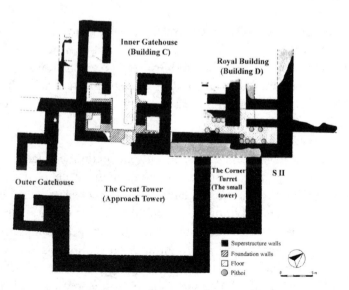

Fig. 5.6. Major elements of the upper City of David on the Ophel in the ninth–eighth century (E. Mazar 2009, fig. 2)

monumental structures clearly belong to the late eighth century: the great
water system and a massive city wall expanding the city far to the west.
Both may have been prompted by the Assyrian threat after the fall of the
northern kingdom in 721 (below).

The water system now combined several major features, including
the old Warren's Shaft, the Siloam channel, and Hezekiah's Tunnel. The
latter was by far the most complex water system in the country. It surely
reflects an ambitious engineering project that could only have been commissioned and funded by royal decree, a fact confirmed by the dedicatory
inscription found carved into stone at the southern end of the main
tunnel. We shall return to this project shortly in discussing political organization and technology.[8]

Further evidence for state-level administration comes from a hoard
of some 150 bullae (seal impressions) found recently in a structure near
the Gihon Spring in the Kidron Valley. They are all anepigraphic, and they
date to the late ninth century, a period previously thought to be without
significant evidence for literacy. They would have sealed papyrus records
of an administrative nature in a sort of counting-house.[9]

Tier 2: Administrative Centers

Dan. Tenth-century Dan (Stratum IVA) has already been discussed. It
represents one of the early Israelite fortified cities, when a defense wall
may have enclosed most of the old Bronze Age precinct of some 50 acres.
Its size, second only to Hazor, and its strategic location at the headwaters
of the Jordan on the natural border with Syria made Dan one of the key
sites of the northern kingdom

Biran's extensive excavations (1966–) were carried out with inadequate
methods and have been published only in preliminary fashion, leaving
the stratigraphy of the tenth–eighth century much debated. Stratum III
belongs broadly to the ninth century. The principal remains are a new
defense system and additions to the cult installation of the acropolis. Now
the city wall is of cyclopean stones, some 12 feet wide, still preserved to a
considerable height. The Area A entrance on the south side features two
gates, the upper one a massive three-entryway gate with an offset entrance.
It is connected on the inner side to a well-preserved cobbled street that
leads up at a steep angle to the upper city (fig. 5.7). In the inner plaza of the
lower gate, formed by the offset entrance, there stood just to the right of

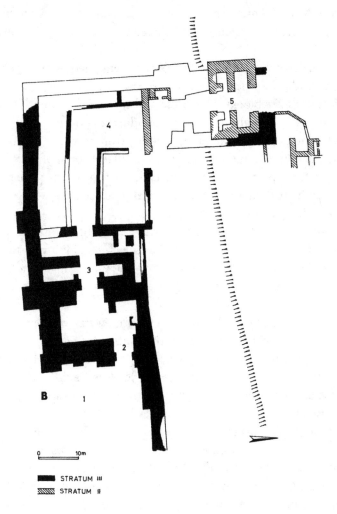

Fig. 5.7. The lower and upper city gates at Dan, Strata III–II. 1: outer plaza; 2: gate-way; 3: lower three-entrance gate; 4: cobbled street; 5: upper three-entryway gate (Herzog 1997, fig. 5:19B)

the gate a platform circa 3.5 by 10 feet, constructed of ashlar masonry with small ornamental column bases at the front corners. This appears to be a throne-like seat with a canopy where the governor of the city could meet visiting dignitaries. Nearby was a low stone altar with five small *maṣṣēbôt* or standing stones. Beyond the postern gate of this small courtyard lay a large paved outer plaza with its own walls and small gateway, the stone pivots (pintels) of which were still in place. Incorporated into the eastern wall were several fragments of an Aramean victory stela in secondary use (below).

The earlier *bāmâ* (high place) was now enlarged by the construction of a stone podium some 60 feet square, constructed of marginally drafted and dressed ashlar blocks. It is preserved up to 5 feet high but probably once stood twice as high (fig. 5.8). This podium has been considered either a free-standing open-air *bāmâ* or, to judge from its inner compartments, possibly the foundation for a temple. Some 40 feet south of the podium, in a large plastered plaza, there was an ashlar-paved platform that probably featured an altar (below). A casemate wall enclosed the whole cult complex, comprising at least 20,000 square feet.

In Stratum II of the eighth century, extending until the Assyrian destruction in 732, the city was rebuilt. The chief addition to the defense system was the addition of an inner two-entryway gate at the top of the cobble-paved street, perhaps a largely ceremonial entrance to a public or citadel area.

The final elements added to the cult area were a monumental stairway some 25 feet wide leading up to the south edge of the podium. In the plaza in front of the podium (above), a large horned altar of ashlar blocks was constructed (of which only one corner was found), surrounded by steps and an enclosure wall. There was also found a small four-horned altar about 11 by 13 inches and 12 inches high. A small three-room complex with a low stone altar and two iron incense shovels nearby, flanking the west wall of the podium, may belong here or perhaps to Stratum III.[10]

Hazor. More than any other Israelite city of the ninth–eighth century, Hazor illustrates the changes in settlement type that define the Iron II period. Stratum IXA, of the late tenth/ninth century, shows little change from Stratum X of the mid-tenth century. It reused the only elements well known: the four-entryway city gate and a short stretch of casemate wall at the eastern end of the upper tell (Area A). Stratum VIII, however, of the early to mid-ninth century, represents an entirely new foundation, one that reflects a new concept of urban planning that will prevail until the fall of Hazor in 732 (fig. 5.9).

The entire 16-acre upper city was now built up, and the fortifications underwent a complete change. The old casemate wall on the south (Area B) was filled up and replaced with a more substantial one. To the east and northeast (Areas A and M), the monumental city gate and casemate wall

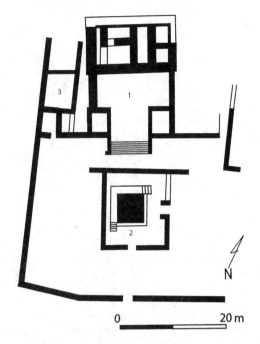

Fig. 5.8. The Dan high place. 1: the *bāmâ*; 2: the large altar; 3: the *liškâ*, or tripartite building (Sharon and Zarzecki-Peleg 2006, fig. 10)

went out of use, supplanted by a solid wall with a postern gate protected by two towers, the solid wall continuing to the west toward the acropolis.

On the western summit (Area B), the defense system incorporated a massive multiroom citadel some 70 by 80 feet, comprising 5,600 square feet of space (fig. 5.10). It was constructed partly of ashlar masonry and possibly used the several Proto-Aeolic capitals found in secondary context (Stratum VII) nearby. The citadel was flanked by a complex of several small rooms interpreted by Yadin as "scribes' chambers." This administrative complex was built into the solid wall on the east and the casemate wall to the west, forming a heavily fortified acropolis.

One of the structures in the center of the upper city was a large tripartite pillared building of the type usually interpreted elsewhere as storehouses. Additional storage was supplied by an adjacent building with two long halls. Renewed excavations by Ben-Tor from 1992 on brought to light in Area A two large stone-lined silos that could have contained 60–70 tons of grain, as well as another tripartite pillared storehouse to the west of the old city gate (fig. 5.9).

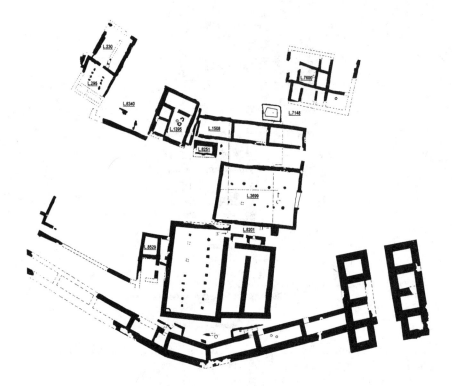

Fig. 5.9. Plan of Hazor VIIIb (Ben-Tor, Ben-Ami, and Sandhaus 2012, fig. 3.1)

A major installation of Stratum VIII was the water system in Area L, constructed inside the casemate wall along the southwest. A rectangular shaft some 80 feet square was dug through existing Strata X–IX structures, with wide steps descending 65 feet through bedrock. An arched tunnel with steps then sloped for some 120 feet to reach the water table, about 120 feet below Stratum VIII living surfaces. This was a monumental feat of engineering that would have required a knowledge of local geology, sophisticated planning, and the oversight of hundreds of workers over many years. The rationale was undoubtedly the need to assure the city of a water supply in case of siege, now that the Neo-Assyrian threat was first becoming evident.

By the mid-ninth century Hazor was twice its tenth-century size. The heavily fortified acropolis now featured a monumental citadel and administrative building, ancillary structures, large-scale storage facilities, and an impressive water system. The relative scarcity of private houses

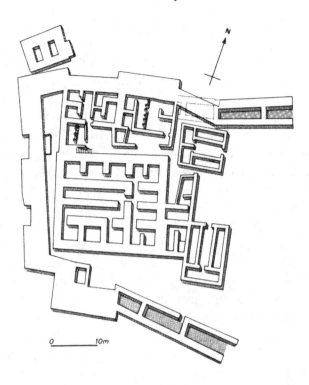

Fig. 5.10. Citadel and elite houses nearby at Hazor, Strata VIII–VII (de Geus 2003, fig. 17)

of the usual four-room type in Israelite cities suggests that in Stratum VIII Hazor was primarily an administrative center dominated by public buildings. The size of its population is unknown, but a figure of circa 1,500 based on the built-up area (above) would probably be much too high, since most of the available space on the acropolis was taken up by public buildings. In any case, Stratum VIII represents a major change over Strata X–IX, no doubt reflecting, as other sites do, the consolidation of the northern state of Israel by the mid-ninth century, or early Iron IIB.

Stratum VII belongs to the late ninth to mid-eighth century, but it represents mostly reuse along similar lines. A large tripartite pillared storehouse is now constructed inside the old casemate city wall and gate in Area A. Stratum VII ends with a fiery destruction in parts of the city, due to unknown causes. Stratum VI sees the construction of houses and workshops over some of the storehouses, as the public areas declined and the private sector expanded. Yadin thought that Stratum VI came to a violent end in the well-known earthquake of 760 (Amos; see ch. 1 above), but Ben-Tor's excavations have not confirmed that. In any case, the trend toward privatization accelerates by Stratum VB–A of the mid- to late eighth century, when several significant changes occur.

The Area B citadel and surrounding buildings are partly built over by a massive, solid offsets-insets city wall and tower, as well as by a colonnaded building and a large four-room house. In the center of the acropolis a large building with long halls was constructed. Now, however, Area A and M contain mostly densely grouped domestic dwellings, courtyards, and industrial installations along meandering streets and lanes. Some of these houses are, however, 500 or more square feet.

Hazor of the eighth century (Strata VII–VA) has been studied in detail by Shulamit Geva, based on Yadin's extensive excavations in 1955–1958. Together with Lily Singer-Avitz's recent study of archaeology and household activities at Beersheba (2011) and several other studies discussed below on domestic architecture and socioeconomic structure, Geva's is one of the most comprehensive analyses yet of the domestic areas of any Iron II urban site. Geva's conclusions can be summarized as follows:

1. The majority of the eighth-century houses at Hazor do not slavishly follow the supposedly Israelite four-room (or pillar-courtyard) house plan, as some have thought. Rather, they are somewhat ad hoc, sharing some features, such as a courtyard (or atrium) and several closed-off inner rooms, but adapted freely to meet the differing needs of individual families.

2. The houses in the inner city, as opposed to a few patrician houses near the administrative centers, are relatively small and cramped, ranging from 800 to 1,000 square feet in living space.

3. These houses are closely grouped and may occasionally share common sidewalls, but each is self-contained, never open to adjoining houses. Privacy is a major concern.

4. Even after disturbances or destructions, the houses are not usually abandoned. They are continually rebuilt and adapted to changes, in this case over nearly two centuries of time.

5. The town plan (if any) is not orthogonal. The houses are clustered along narrow, winding lines, with limited access and poor distant visibility. There are few open spaces for any social or public activities.

6. These rather poor hovels are confined to certain areas, and they contrast sharply with larger, more luxuriant, long-lived patrician houses near the public and administrative buildings.

7. The contents of the houses, often removed during disturbances or looted, consist mostly of utilitarian objects such as domestic pottery and stone or metal tools. There are very few luxury items.

Geva concludes:

> Each dwelling was built or designed to suit the requirements and the convenience of the family living there, with almost total disregard—both socially and aesthetically—of the environment in which it was situated—the neighbors, or the general plan of the quarter.[11]

In summary, there is a notable continuity at Hazor from Stratum X through Stratum VA, a period of nearly three hundred years. However, several phases of urbanization, and presumably of a developing "Israelite" ethos, can be distinguished. (1) Strata X–IX represent a small but impressive fort, one that resembles other contemporary walled regional centers (Megiddo VA/IVB, Gezer VIII) and clearly reflects some degree of state-like centralization (the biblical united monarchy). (2) Stratum VIII represents the full-blown appearance of sophisticated urban planning and the construction of a fortified administrative center that marks the zenith of Iron Age Hazor in the ninth century. This consolidation of urban features is one aspect of a mature nation-state (the biblical divided monarchy, or northern kingdom). (3) Strata VII–V, spanning mostly the eighth century, see a decline in administrative functions but an expansion of the private sector. This phase undoubtedly reflects a growth in population and in socioeconomic diversity as well but also a period of disintegration and a lack of social cohesion as the Assyrian crisis deepened.

Faust has expanded on Geva's observation of the growth of the private sector at Hazor in the eighth century (Stratum VI). He places this phenomenon, which he sees at some other northern sites, in the larger sphere of "core-periphery" models (although on a small scale), where both changing land use and cognitive aspects operate. In his view, as Hazor expanded over time and social stratification occurred, the upper classes moved to new and better residential quarters toward the periphery, while poorer elements came to inhabit the deteriorating core or inner city. This is certainly a phenomenon now easily visible in contemporary cities worldwide, and it reflects the inevitable crisis that occurs as cities expand beyond sustainable resources or the ability of urban planning to cope. The socioeconomic implications of this phenomenon will be brought into the picture below.[12]

Megiddo. Stratum IVA spans almost the entire ninth–eighth century, from the destruction of Stratum VA/IVB by Shoshenq circa 920 (as argued here) to the final destruction by the Assyrians in 732. While the lack of any discernible inner phasing over such a long time period is a disadvantage for defining the later growth of urbanism, the change from Stratum VA/IVB to IVA is instructive regarding its early development.

Stratum VA/IVB, dated here as conventionally to the tenth century, comprises the major features of a heavily fortified, regional administrative center. Some 70 percent of this level of the 15-acre mound was cleared by the University of Chicago expedition, but almost no private dwellings were found, and few of the presumed Israelite four-room or pillar-courtyard type. A few domestic structures in Areas A and C were attributed to Stratum V, but without further precise stratigraphic context (perhaps VA). Only one is of the four-room pillared type (L. IA). Others reveal a sort of agglutinative plan, with many ad hoc small rooms.

Stratum IVA sees several changes, while preserving the basic character of the city. The four-entryway city gate is reduced to a three-way entrance (L. 500). It is now connected to a solid insets-offsets city wall (L. 325) some 12 feet wide, running more than 700 yards all the way around the oval site. The shallow recesses, every 20 feet or so, were probably designed not to serve as towers but rather for stabilizing the wall (fig. 5.11).

Palace 1723 to the south was apparently reused, with the addition of a large enclosure wall and its own gate. Palace 6000, near the gate, goes out of use. But the major change in architecture was the construction of two very large complexes of pillared buildings: one conglomerate near Palace 1723 with a large walled courtyard (L. 1576), the other consisting of smaller pillared buildings near the gate to the north (L. 364, 407; cf. L. 403, 404). These elaborate structures feature a long central hall and what appear to be regular side chambers, the pillars sometimes incorporating stone mangers and tether holes. They were originally attributed to Stratum VA/IVB of the tenth century and thought to be Solomon's stables for his fabled chariotry.

These enigmatic buildings are now known to have been constructed only in Stratum IV of the ninth century, but whether they are evidence of

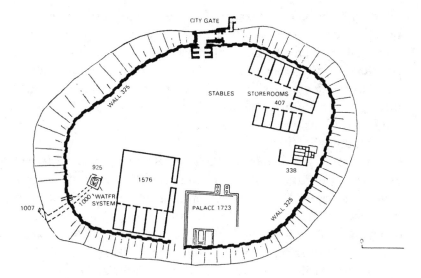

Fig. 5.11. Megiddo, Stratum IVA (Barkay 1992; fig. 9.8; see also fig. 4.7)

Ahab's better known chariot cities is unclear. Despite the best efforts of the team of experts assembled by the reexcavation directed by Finkelstein and Ussishkin more recently, it is uncertain whether these are stables or simply storehouses (as they appear to be when found at several other sites).[13] Nevertheless, for our purposes here, these beautifully designed and constructed buildings provide indisputable evidence for urban planning on a massive scale by the early ninth century. Further evidence of advances in urban development is seen in a large administrative building near the northern complex of pillared buildings (L. 338), probably the governor's residence; five Proto-Aeolic capitals found nearby in secondary use probably originated here.

Even more impressive is the construction of an elaborate water system (L. 925), replacing Gallery 629 of the previous stratum, which simply tunneled under the city wall along the west edge of the mound to reach a spring. Now a shaft some 120 feet deep was dug into bedrock, connected by winding steps down to a tunnel circa 165 feet long that led under the city wall to the spring outside (now concealed). The entire entrance was surrounded by an enclosed wall. Like the contemporary water tunnel at Hazor, the water system at Megiddo was a magnificent feat of engineering. It could only have been carried out by a central authority able to command formidable resources of men and material.

It has been calculated that, if the excavated areas of the mound are considered representative of the total inhabited area, during the ninth–eighth century more than 80 percent of the city was allocated to administrative functions. Again, as in Stratum VA/IVB, relatively few private houses were found. Renewed excavations by Finkelstein and Ussishkin report that domestic dwellings do exist in their Phases H-4–H-3, improving somewhat in quality by the late ninth century. However, these houses are not yet published.[14]

In summary, Megiddo in the ninth–eighth century yields a picture of continuous urban development and centralized administration nearly identical to Hazor VIII–VA. Each of these two large administrative centers, some 35 miles apart and dominating very different landscapes, no doubt controlled a hinterland of many smaller towns, villages, and farmsteads. That pattern of site type and distribution, where a small population is concentrated in a few large centers but the bulk of the population is dispersed in smaller, dependent rural areas, is typical of nearly all urban societies that have been carefully analyzed. (We will return to the rural population below.)

Gezer. This prominent 33-acre mound is strategically located at the junction of the northern Shephelah and the foothills, on the ascent to Jerusalem via the Aijalon Valley where a trunk road branches off from the Via Maris to the west. It has been extensively excavated by British (1902–1909) and American archaeologists (1964–1975, 1984, 1990, 2008–).

Of the twenty-six strata discerned, Strata VII–VI span the ninth–eighth century. Stratum VIII of the tenth century, with its prominent four-entryway gate, a section of casemate wall, and a long stretch of solid wall and numerous towers, has been discussed above, reflecting the establishment of an important administrative center—by far the largest known in the early Iron Age (tenth century).

By contrast, Stratum VII of the ninth century is poorly attested, mostly because the monumental structures in the area were removed down to Stratum VIII by Macalister (below). It is clear, however, that following the Shoshenq destruction circa 920 the city gate was so severely damaged that its western tower had to be heavily buttressed, in effect reducing the gate to a three-entryway style (as at Megiddo).

In Stratum VII the large Palace 10,000 adjacent to the gate on the west was replaced (or, more likely, in Stratum VI) by Palace 8,000. This structure, with its central courtyard surrounded by small rooms, was probably

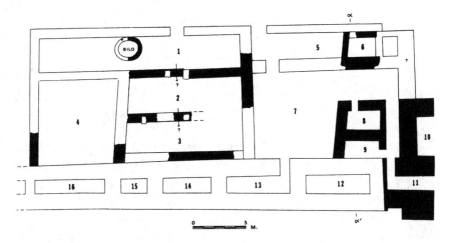

Fig. 5.12. Palace 8,000 adjoining gate at Gezer, Strata VII–VI (Dever 1984b, fig. 4)

a combination palace/administrative building, but its scant material is not helpful (fig. 5.12).

Macalister had cleared most of the mound all the way to bedrock (ca. two-thirds), but primitive methods and schematic (although prompt) publication leave most of his eight strata incomprehensible. His Fourth Semitic period contains dozens of enigmatic house walls that are probably Iron II, but scarcely one of them makes architectural sense.

In Field VII west of the Field III city gate, the American excavators brought to light several exceptionally well-constructed pillar-courtyard houses, compactly grouped. Very well preserved, they were partially destroyed in the 732 destruction (below). These houses may, however, go back originally to the ninth or even the tenth century.

In the renewed excavation of Ortiz and Wolff in the undisturbed area between Fields III and VII (Areas A, B, C) the plan of eighth-century Palace 8,000 was completed, showing it to be a symmetrical structure circa 50 by 50 feet (2,500 square feet), featuring an open center court surrounded by several small rooms (similar to Aramean or Assyrian *bit hilani* structures). This is flanked to the west by two nearly identical structures, Buildings B and C. All three structures are bonded into the rebuilt casemate wall and are almost certainly administrative buildings. Due to Macalister's deep probes, the remains were scant, but a small amount of pottery dates them to the eighth century, destroyed no doubt in 732 (below). North of Building C there was brought to light a relatively well-preserved pillar-courtyard house that would connect with the Field VII houses discussed above, also of the ninth century (temporary Phases 7–6 = earlier VIB–A). It is one of the largest such houses known thus far.

Despite limited exposure with adequate methods, it is apparent that Gezer in the ninth–eighth century continued to be an important district administrative center, albeit with a relatively large civilian population, perhaps up to 3,000.[15]

Macalister's water tunnel cannot now be dated with any certainty, since he cleared it out almost completely. Furthermore, he did not specify the level from which it was cut, the only way that it could have been dated. Some have thought it Middle Bronze, but then it would have been too close to the monumental city gate. On analogy with the water tunnels of the ninth–eighth century elsewhere (Hazor, Megiddo, Gibeon, Jerusalem, Beersheba), the Gezer tunnel might well be assigned to Iron II generally.

Tell en-Naṣbeh. Some 40 miles south of Megiddo, Tell en-Naṣbeh (probably biblical Mizpeh) is right on the northern border of Judah, only about 8 miles from Jerusalem. Almost the entire site was cleared by the American excavations in 1926–1935, which, although methodologically indefensible, has given us a rare, nearly complete Iron Age city plan. However, excavation methods were primitive, and publication was inadequate. Furthermore, the fact that the town suffered no destructions from the tenth to the late eighth century meant that clear stratigraphic separation of inner phases was difficult.[16]

Nearly half of the architecture (70 percent of the mound) brought to light belongs to Stratum 3, with three phases (C–A) that span the ninth century (fig. 5.13). Particularly significant is the fact that Tell en-Naṣbeh was now transformed from an obscure town of the tenth century (Stratum 4) into a major administrative center, one that persisted even into the Babylonian period some three centuries later. The early town had a city wall of sorts (the inner wall) but no gate. In Stratum 3C a massive solid offset-inset city wall was built, extending all the way around the site for some 750 yards. The new city wall ran some 30–100 feet outside the previous wall, raising the enclosed area from 7–8 acres to nearly 14 acres The population could thus have been as much as 1,000, using the usual coefficients. The wall was 13 feet in width and was preserved above bedrock up to 45 feet high. The lower courses were plastered inside and out, and in some places fine ashlar masonry was used. Here and there was an external dry moat.

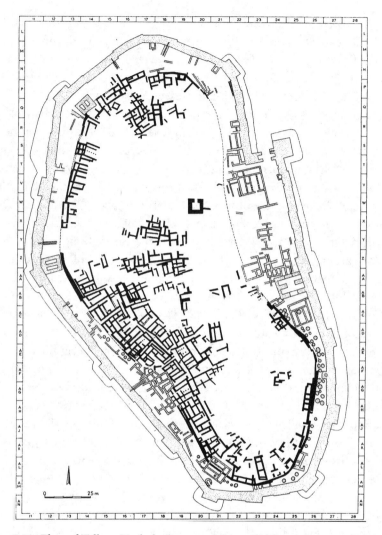

Fig. 5.13. Plan of Tell en-Naṣbeh, Stratum 3C in solid lines; Stratum 3B–A additions in lighter lines (Herzog 1997, fig. 5:26)

There were eleven circular bastions or towers, in addition to two towers flanking the gate to the northwest.

A sort of three-way gate appears inside the east wall, but it may have been left unfinished. The proper city gate lay farther north, but its phasing is unclear. There are, in fact, two gates in this complex. An outer two-entryway gate features an offset entrance, fortified on the outside by a massive tower and circular bastion. There are traces of an inner gate with an adjacent plaza (earlier, Stratum 3C?). The width of the entrance of the outer, main gate was about 14 feet, exceptionally wide for an Iron Age city gate. The Stratum 3 city wall and gate was so well planned and constructed that it remained virtually unchanged throughout the ninth–eighth century, some elements even surviving the Assyrian destructions.

The Stratum 3 plan reveals several distinct elements of urban planning: (1) the elaborate defense system; (2) several large elite buildings near the gate that are almost certainly administrative structures; (3) a well laid out cluster of several dozen houses incorporated into the old (casemate?) city wall and now abutting an open space or ring road running along the inner face of the new wall (some of the four-room type); (4) a few distinct buildings in the more open central space that may have been industrial or commercial installations; (5) large, wider open areas that might have been used for gardens and the like; (6) a unique system of runoff areas, drains, and cisterns that provided a water supply; and (7) dozens of stone-lined cisterns in the open spaces between the two city walls.

No other Iron Age city plan known at present shows such deliberate exploitation of a site's features, needs, and functions. Again, it is the successive phases of urbanization and administration that are significant. But here, unlike Hazor and Megiddo, the civilian sector is more in evidence, not only in numerous private houses, but also in other indications of growing population and planning to meet their needs. We have an extensive (though poorly published) repertoire of domestic and industrial installations, utilitarian pottery and other implements, and grave goods. (We will return to this repertoire in discussing socioeconomic structure.)

Earlier scholars paid little attention to this evidence for town planning, but a reexamination by Faust suggests that here a key feature is the deliberate and consistent way in which an open space is left between the two city walls. Faust finds this feature at a number of other sites both in Israel and Judah, but more typical of the south. In his view, this free access to the city wall from the inside was a basic element in meeting the needs of defense, as well as serving peacetime needs.[17]

Beth-Shemesh. Tell er-Rumeileh is one of the most impressive and strategically located mounds in the Judean Shephelah, although only 7 acres in size. It was excavated by British archaeologists in 1911 and 1912 and by American archaeologists in 1928–1933. Israeli excavations have been ongoing since 1990, and, although only brief preliminary reports have been published, an overview of the site's Iron Age history is possible.[18]

Levels 7–4 (old Stratum III) belong to Iron I, or the twelfth–eleventh century, when a dynamic relation existed between Philistines and ethnic Israelites at this border site. Level 3 (old Stratum IIb) is dated by the current excavators to their Iron IIA phase—not the tenth century, as here, but circa 950–840 in their phasing. That would equate with our early Iron IIB, principally the ninth century. The major features are now massive fortifications of boulders, fieldstones, and mud-brick, still standing over 6 feet high. There is an astonishing underground water system cut into bedrock and reached by steps, fed by extensive runoff channels, with a capacity of some 22,000 cubic feet. Large public buildings and storage facilities produced evidence of commercial activities, including scale pans and grain scoops. A unique iron-working installation is the earliest yet discovered in the Middle East. It represents a secondary smithing installation, as opposed to iron smelting or primary (bloom) smithing.

The current excavators date the first phase of these installations to the mid- to late tenth century and see in them clear indications of state-formation processes in Judah that early. These installations continued in use throughout the ninth century, until a violent destruction brought the site to an end. The cause is not clear, but it is possible that Stratum 3 was destroyed circa 790, when Jehoash, king of Israel, is reported to have encountered Amaziah of Judah in a fierce battle. In any case, Beth-Shemesh in the ninth century was an important border town and district administrative center.

Subsequent Level 2 (old late Stratum II$_b$) belongs to the eighth century and ends with the Sennacherib destructions in 701. This final, more modest Iron Age settlement consists mostly of private dwellings, although olive-oil and domestic production indicate continued prosperity. The site appears to be unwalled now, since the border was no longer in dispute. The olive-oil production, although substantial, was a sort of cottage industry, nowhere near the specialized industrial production of nearby Philistine Ekron in the seventh century. A bowl inscribed *qdš* (holy) hints at priestly functions. A few ephemeral remains suggest a failed attempt to resettle the site in the seventh century.

Lachish. The large, steep mound of Lachish in southern Judah is the most extensively excavated and lavishly published site in the country.[19] We have already discussed the long gap in occupation in Iron I following the complete devastation of the site at the end of the Late Bronze Age. There is neither Philistine nor Israelite occupation in the twelfth–eleventh century.

The date of the refoundation of the city as an Israelite site in Stratum V
is debated, but it may have occurred in the late tenth century (i.e., under
Rehoboam, ca. 928–911). The red-slipped and hand-burnished pottery
could be either late tenth or early ninth century, as we now know.

In any case, Level V represents the first Israelite establishment, spanning the ninth century and continuing into Level III of the eighth century,
during which time Lachish became the largest and most important administrative center and military outpost in Judah. Level II, an unwalled town
of the seventh century, is poorly represented except for a few houses.

Level IV of the ninth century is a 30-acre fortress, planned and constructed on a grand scale (fig. 5.14). A solid masonry wall 20 feet wide
and still standing up to 15 feet encircles the entire roughly square mound,
both faces plastered. Halfway down the steep slope there runs a well-constructed, outer revetment wall, up to 13 feet thick, still visible today to some
height, connected to a glacis, or earthen embankment. The monumental
four-entryway gate on the southwest side is even larger than the somewhat
earlier city gates of this type in the tenth century (Hazor, Megiddo, and
Gezer as argued here). At the bottom of a long sloping ramp is an outer bastion protecting the main gate. There is a deep drain through the roadway
to carry runoff water away so as to strengthen its foundations (as at Gezer).

The most imposing feature of Level IV is Podium B–C (if A is earlier;
above) on the highest part of the mound, the largest Iron Age structure
ever found in Israel. It is still visible today from a distance, even though
it is only the remaining foundation of a palace, or, more likely, part of a
royal citadel. It was constructed of massive boulders on an artificial fill,
creating a rectangular platform some 120 by 250 feet (or 30,000 square
feet). Phases A–C represent three stages of construction as the podium
was expanded, the joins still visible today. Whether it was built according
to a single design in Level IV (V?) or was built in later successive stages is
debated. Since only the foundations of the palace are preserved, the super-
structure cannot be reconstructed with confidence. But upper walls may
have followed the outline of regularly spaced segments in the plan of the
foundation courses. In any case, the palace, however reconstructed, was
only one part of an overall sophisticated design.

First, the palace was set off from the rest of the city not only by its size
and conspicuous elevated position, but it was separated from the small
domestic quarter to the south by a separate enclosure wall several feet
thick, running some 130 feet from the southwest corner of the palace all

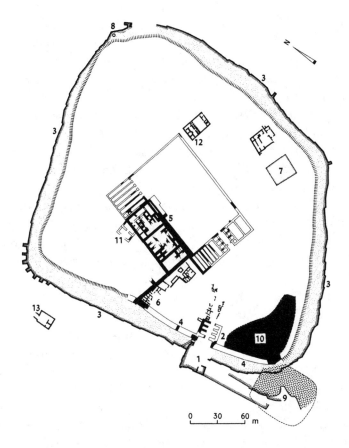

Fig. 5.14. Lachish, Stratum III. 1: outer gate; 2: inner gate; 3: outer revetment wall; 4: main wall; 5: palace-fort; 6: Area S; 7: great shaft; 8: well; 9: Assyrian siege ramp; 10: counterramp; 11: acropolis temple; 12: Solar Shrine; 13: Fosse Temple (Stern 1993, 3:897)

the way to the city wall. This created a sort of *cordon sanitaire*. The isolation, no doubt deliberate, was accentuated by the construction of a vast open-walled courtyard on the other side of the palace, making the entire citadel complex 350 by 350 feet, or circa 122,500 square feet

This courtyard, with its own solid wall and four-entryway gate, enclosed two banks of the large tripartite pillared buildings seen at many other Iron II sites (called annexes by the renewed excavations), usually interpreted as storehouses where taxes were presumably paid in kind and stored for official use or redistribution.

To the southeast the British expedition discovered the Great Shaft, some 80 by 80 feet, dug 75 feet down into the bedrock. It was first thought to be a water system, but it was more likely the quarry for the construction of Palace A–C. Water could have been supplied by a well nearly 150 feet deep at the north end of the mound.

Level IV may have been partially destroyed by the earthquake of 760, as Hazor and Gezer are thought to have been.[20] Stratum III, however, sees the reuse of all the monumental architecture with only minor alterations. Few domestic dwellings had been found in Level IV, and there were relatively few in Level III, mostly south of the palace enclosure wall and along the street leading up from the city gate to the palace. None of these, however, was a classic four-room or pillar-courtyard house.

The site was totally destroyed in the invasion of Sennacherib in 701, witnessed not only by extensive archaeological evidence but also by the well-known monumental Lachish reliefs now in the British Museum depicting the siege and the fall of the city in gruesome detail (below).

Lachish IV–III is without doubt a Judahite royal fortress, as all authorities agree. It was in effect a deliberately planned and provisional garrison town, dominated by the palace-citadel, which itself took up nearly one-fourth of the 30-acre site. To judge from the paucity of private houses, the population was relatively small, perhaps only a few hundred. Much of the open space in the vast palace courtyard (and elsewhere) would have been reserved for storage, trade caravans, or military exercises. Lachish was a highly visible symbol of royal power, and it was meant to be.

Beersheba. Ancient Beersheba is certainly to be located at Tell es-Sebaʿ, a few miles east of modern Beersheba, at the natural southern border on the edge of the northern Negev Desert. Although rainfall here is marginal, the loessal soils can support dry farming, and the tell is situated on a prominent hill overlooking a major wadi, or seasonal river course.

Beersheba was excavated in 1969–1974 by Aharoni and a team of Tel Aviv University archaeologists. The stratigraphic methods have been criticized, and the final reports were never completed. The area within the city walls is only about 3 acres, but more than half of it was cleared. This strategy would be indefensible today, but it did result in the most complete town plan that we have of any Iron II site, except perhaps Tell en-Naṣbeh.[21]

Despite inadequate stratigraphy, the plans of Stratum IV of the ninth century and especially Stratum III of the eighth century are quite clear (fig.

5.15). That is mainly due to the fact that here we have indisputable evidence of town planning so rational that even the missing elements are predictable.

The early tenth century remains (Stratum VI) have been discussed above. Stratum V of the late tenth–early ninth century sees the fortification of the entire site by a solid wall 13 feet wide preserved some 23 feet high, complemented by an exterior glacis, or earthen rampart. A large triple-entryway gate on the southeast overlooks the wadi below and gives indirect access.

Due to the fact that the overlying structures of Stratum III were mostly left intact by the excavations, the town plans of Strata V and IV are unclear, but it seems evident that all the principal elements of Strata III and II, which show direct continuity into the late eighth century, were already in place by Stratum IV at the latest. Beersheba is thus a deliberately planned regional administrative center and barracks town guarding Judah's southern border successfully for at least two centuries.

After the short duration of Stratum IV in the late ninth century, when the fortifications of Stratum V were reused, a more deliberate and extensive town plan becomes clear. In Stratum III, spanning the early to mid-eighth century, we have all the elements in place. These seem to have continued with little change into Stratum II. A new casemate wall enclosing the entire site replaces the old solid wall. The glacis was augmented as needed. The monumental three-way gate was either reused or first constructed. Running around the inside of the casemate wall and parallel to it was a ring road some 6–7 feet wide. Between this street and the city wall to the southwest there was a row of contiguous, small four-room houses (some twenty-five cleared or partially cleared here, at least a dozen elsewhere). The back rooms of these houses were incorporated into the city wall, in fact, constituting the casemates, with direct entry into them via the houses themselves, or in some cases via alleys or narrow lanes. The rectangular houses are even adjusted so that the walls are slightly wider at the back so as to conform to the curvature of the city wall. These features are so consistent that they must have been deliberately conceived and constructed. These houses are evidently barracks for soldiers and possibly their families, where a motive for defending the ramparts would have been the strongest.

A second, inner ring road ran parallel to the outer road. Here the structures are different, with a few larger and more varied pillar-courtyard houses, as well as several much larger buildings, especially one dubbed the

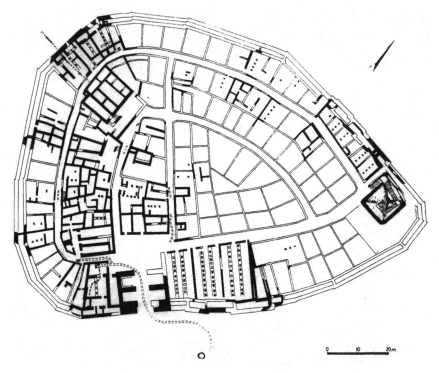

Fig. 5.15. Plan of Beersheba, Stratum III (Herzog 1997, fig. 5.4)

Basement Building by Aharoni and thought to have been a temple that was later dismantled (below). This quarter seems to have housed administrators and their families, as well as some public buildings.

A third parallel road farther toward the center of the town set off yet another district, one that may have featured workshops and perhaps a few storage and commercial buildings.

Flanking the city gate to the south were two installations. To the west was Building 416, which overlooked the large inner plaza of the gate (the latter some 2,500 square feet). The doorway opened onto two large paved corridors that probably served as reception rooms. The large central area was portioned by pillars into two residential suites, augmented by an upper story (as evidenced by a narrow staircase from the entrance hall). At the rear of the house was a small area with its own entrance, probably a kitchen and storerooms. A drain running under the floors collected rainwater from the roof, joining the main drain through the streets to the well outside (below). This was surely the residence of the governor of the fort (below).

On the other side of the gate and connected to it were three of the tri-partite pillared buildings that we have seen at other administrative centers of the ninth–eighth century. Together they extend over an area of more than 6,000 square feet. Found full of hundreds of store jars and other vessels, these were storehouses for provisions, probably also for the receipt of taxes paid in kind, perhaps later redistributed according to need. They were certainly not stables.

The water system in the northwestern quarter was remarkable. A square stairwell leads down 16 feet to a stepped entrance tunnel that opens into a group of five interconnected well-plastered cisterns hewn into the bedrock. A feeding channel led into the cisterns, exploiting the wadi when seasonally flooded. The capacity of the cisterns was at least 5,000 cubic meters of water. Outside the city gate was a stone-lined well more than 70 feet deep, which augmented the town's water supply.

Beersheba IV–III represents a provincial Judahite administrative center and border fortress occupied by some 300 soldiers, commanders, government officials, and their families. The site was destroyed in 701 in the campaigns of Sennacherib and thereafter virtually abandoned.

Tier 3: Cities

Taʿanach. An impressive, high 11-acre mound, Taʿanach, like Megiddo 5 miles to the northwest, is a sentinel guarding a major route from the Samaria hills out into the Jezreel Valley. The publications of the German excavators (1902–1904) are largely useless, and the American excavations (1963–1968) have been only partially published, covering mostly the pottery. Taʿanach I–II have been treated above in our discussion of Iron I. Stratum III–IV belong to the ninth–eighth century. Only Sellin's Nordost-burg, dating to the ninth century, is of much significance. Taʿanach could have been a provincial city of some 1,000 or so people.[22]

Beth-Shean. Tell el-Ḥuṣn, ancient Beth-Shean, is one of the most imposing tells in the entire country, rising high above the eastern Jalud Valley floor, right at its junction with the Jordan River. It is only some 10 acres at the top of the steep mound, but below the vast Hellenistic–Roman city at the base there may be other Iron Age remains.

In the tenth century, Stratum V lower and upper constitute a small Isra-elite settlement. Stratum IV belongs to the ninth–eighth century. Despite extensive excavations by American and Israeli archaeologists, little of the

town plan can be discerned. Mazar's more recent phase P10–9 belongs
to the tenth to mid-ninth century, P8 to the late ninth–early eighth century, and P7 to the mid- to late eighth century. Only fragmentary house
remains have been recovered, with the exception of a fine patrician house
(L. 28636), well known from its destruction in 732. This is an exceptionally
large four-room house, some 2,100 square feet, but without the expected
pillars. The extensive contents provided, among other things, a large
corpus of late eighth-century pottery. An earlier destruction between P8
and P7 may be attributed to the Aramean incursions in the north.[23]

Tel Reḥov. The steep, 24-acre mound of Tel Reḥov overlooks the west
bank of the Jordan River 3 miles south of Beth-Shean. Excavations led
by A. Mazar in 1997–2012 have revealed an impressive urban city of the
ninth–eighth century in Strata IV–III, especially important for their well-
defined destruction layers.

Stratum V, belonging to the mid- to late tenth century, has been
discussed above as a city of the early monarchy, although not markedly
Israelite. After its destruction circa 920, the Stratum IV city was reconstructed according to a well laid out orthogonal plan. In Area B4 there is
a complete change, a double city wall now in evidence. In Area G there is
also a new plan: houses are not of the expected pillar-courtyard type but
are rather ad hoc, with multiple rooms. One house (Building F) is an elite
residence. In Area E a sanctuary with many exotic cult objects was found.

Stratum IV was violently destroyed circa 830, perhaps in the Aramean
incursions (the date is confirmed by C-14 analyses).[24] Thereafter the lower
city was abandoned, and occupation was confined to the 12-acre upper
tell. A rich assemblage of Stratum IV pottery and other objects attests to
wide trade relations with Phoenicia, the Aramean sphere, Cyprus, and
even Greece. This cosmopolitan character contrasts with many other more
demonstrably Israelite sites in the ninth century and seems to testify to
continuing Canaanite or perhaps Aramean cultural influence at some sites
in the north (ch. 4).

Stratum III continues the basic character of the city, although now
reduced to the upper mound. It was destroyed in 732 in the Assyrian campaigns and attested by Assyrian burials. Thereafter the Stratum II city is
reduced to half its former size, still confined to the upper mound.

Dothan. This steep, prominent 15-acre mound is situated on the
border of a broad, open valley some 13 miles north of Shechem. It was
excavated from 1953 to the mid-1960s by Free, but the stratigraphic work

was amateurish, and final excavation reports never appeared. Level 4 belongs to Iron I, ending perhaps 1000 in a violent conflagration. Pillar-courtyard houses, courtyards, and lanes continued and were rebuilt in Level 3, which seems to have been destroyed in the Aramean incursions circa 840–810. Level 2, witnessed mostly by some tombs, was destroyed circa 732, after which there was a gap until the Hellenistic era.[25]

Tell el-Farʿah. Undoubtedly biblical Tirzah, Tell el-Farʿah North was briefly the capital of the northern kingdom before it was moved to Samaria. It was excavated in 1946–1960 by Pére de Vaux. Stratum VIIc represents the rebuilding and expansion of the 10-acre town after its destruction in the late tenth century. It was now a tier-three city of perhaps 1,200, very strategically located in the northern Samaria hill country, at the head of the steep Wadi Farʿah leading down to the Jordan Valley.

Stratum VIIc of the early ninth century (the French phase numbers are, atypically, from the bottom up) is represented by a single building, which de Vaux thought to be an unfinished building left from Omri's brief reign there (but dated later by others). Stratum VIId of the late ninth–eighth century is better known, particularly from a relatively large exposure in the northwestern quarter near the gate (fig. 5.16). The gate is of a two-entryway type, connected to a broad solid wall with an outer revetment. The area inside the gate is divided into two distinct areas. One is immediately inside the gate, connected to it by a large paved court-yard. Off the courtyard to the south is House 148. It is of the four-room type but exceptionally large, some 7,400 square feet. Its size and location confirm that it was the governor's residence, commanding the gate and a large plaza, as well as the gate plaza itself (L. 153). Immediately to the north of House 148 there are three large but poorly attested (unfinished?) buildings of four-room type. To the south is a very large tripartite struc-ture (L. 140) some 12 by 34 meters (ca. 4,500 square feet) whose function is unclear.[26]

To the south of what appears to be an elite quarter, there are several Stratum VIId houses, all of the four-room type, most with pillars (L. 327, 328, 336, 362, 366). The two largest (L. 327, 328) were adjacent, circa 1,470 and 1,200 square feet, respectively, each with a large outer courtyard. The others are smaller (ca. 750 square feet), set off somewhat, and although well designed they are poorly constructed, perhaps using earlier remains. These may be (as de Vaux maintained) the dwellings of lower-class citi-zens. If so, we may see a three-tier social hierarchy at Tell el Farʿah in the

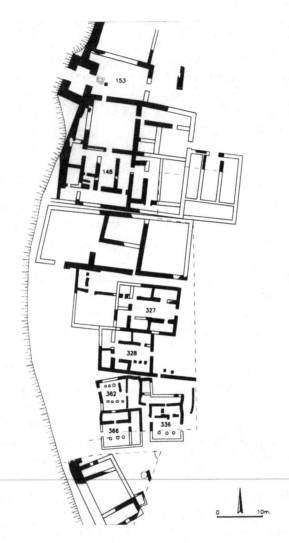

Fig. 5.16. Plan of Tell el-Farʿah North, Stratum VIId (after Herzog 1997, fig. 5:23)

eighth century. The site was destroyed circa 732, after which an Assyrian garrison is founded (Stratum VII$_{e1}$).

Shechem. This prominent 15-acre mound is located 40 miles north of Jerusalem in the pass between Mount Ebal and Mount Gerizim, at the junction of the Jerusalem–Samaria road and the descent into the Jordan Valley. Despite extensive German and American excavations, Iron Age Shechem is not well attested. Stratum IX belongs roughly to the ninth century and may have reused elements of the Middle Bronze casemate wall. Stratum VIII is continuous with Stratum IX but has few remains. Stratum VI belongs to the eighth century and is attested in particular by a pillar courtyard house (House 1727) destroyed in 732 (fig. 5.17).[27]

Hebron. Ancient Hebron is clearly located at modern Hebron, the most prominent site in Judah, some 20 miles south of Jerusalem. Only scant ancient remains under the town have been available for excavation. Above Middle and Late Bronze Age levels are traces of Iron Age occupation that seems to have peaked in the eleventh–tenth century. By Iron II the city may have expanded beyond the 6–7 acres occupied in the Middle Bronze Age, perhaps reusing some elements of the old walls. Its size is unknown, but a population of some 500 seems reasonable.[28]

Khirbet Rabud. Probably biblical Debir, Khirbet Rabud is a prominent 15-acre mound some 4 miles southwest of Hebron. It had been the only Late Bronze Age site in the Hebron hills. The Iron II city was somewhat smaller, represented in the ninth century by Stratum B-II–III and in the eighth by Strata A-II and B-I. In the first phase a massive offsets-insets city wall (Wall 1) was constructed, 4 yards wide, traceable near the surface for nearly 1,000 yards. There may have been a gate on the south of the irregularly shaped mound. Several houses lined the inside of the city walls, but no plan is published.

Tel 'Eton. Possibly biblical Eglon, Tel 'Eton is a prominent 15-acre mound some 7 miles southeast of Lachish. Excavations at an early stage (2006–) reveal major architecture of the ninth–eighth century, brought to an end in 701 (below).[29]

Haror. Tell Abu Hureireh, or Haror, is generally identified with biblical Gerar. A prominent tell on the northern Wadi Gerar, the lower (Bronze Age) city is some 40 acres, the upper Iron Age city much smaller. It seems to have become a small Judean administrative center on the southern border with Philistia, but only in the mid- to late eighth century. It was finally destroyed circa 650, perhaps in an Egyptian raid in the Saite period.

The eighth-century remains in Areas D, E, G, and K include a 150-feet stretch of a plastered mud-brick city wall some 13 feet wide, with uneven outer buttresses and at least one tower. Here and there are additions in ashlar masonry, an unusual occurrence (perhaps Phoenician). A glacis-like revetment augments the defenses. Running along the inside of the wall were small houses and one large storehouse (10 by 21 feet) built up against the city wall. In Phase G3, the last Iron Age phase, these houses

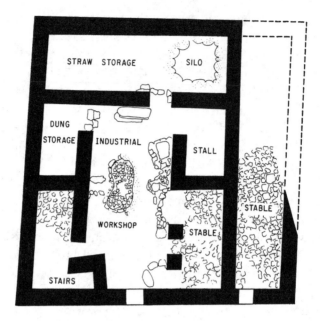

Fig. 5.17. House 1727, Shechem, Strata VIII–VII (Campbell 1994, fig. 3-6)

were altered. The final destruction of this phase is reported to have been violent. A scant Persian occupation follows.

Tier 4: Towns

The multitiered hierarchy of sites proposed here (see fig. 5.1) regards settlements with a population below 1,000 as provincial towns (down to villages of about 300) Based on this threshold, we have perhaps fifteen or so Iron IIB town sites that are known from excavations. Few of these towns, despite their smaller size, have sufficient exposures to allow us to describe them in any detail. There may be, of course, a number of other town sites that have disappeared or have not been located. To these we may add many small villages that are known from surface surveys, of which little can be said.

Yoqneʿam. A typical northern provincial town is Yoqneʿam, a steep 10-acre mound guarding a principal gateway from the hill country of Samaria into the Jezreel Valley. Strata XV–XIV, representing a well-developed, walled town of the tenth century, has been discussed above. By the early ninth century, however, Stratum XIII is only a temporary settlement following the Stratum XIV destruction. Stratum XII then represents a

well-planned and long-lived revival of town life, extending with no inter-
ruptions from the late ninth century to the end of the eighth century.

There is now a unique two-stage (or gallery) defensive wall with buttresses, a renewed water system, well laid out streets and public areas,
and private houses that show some changes within the two phases discernible. Stratum XII persists until the Assyrian destructions in the late
eighth century but appears to have escaped that calamity. Yoqne'am is a
good example of a large town (almost a city) that is devoid of state-level
organization and pursues its own private interests with little government
interference and relative stability.[30]

Tell el-Hammah. Ancient Hamath, Tell el-Hammah is a small but
steep mound in the Jordan Valley 10 miles south of Beth-Shean, the base
about 7 acres, the top only 1 acre. It is near springs, some of them ther-
mal (thus the name). On two upper terraces above earlier levels there are
remains of several eighth-century courtyard houses, as well as a larger
building. The site ends in a late eighth-century destruction.[31]

Khirbet el-Marjameh. One of the best known Judean Iron IIB towns
is Khirbet el-Marjameh. Even though it has not been extensively excavated,
its isolation and its basically one-period character have left its remains
quite visible on the surface. Its biblical name is not clear, but it may be
identified with Baal-shalishah. It is a 10-acre site located on a steep rocky
scarp on the northeastern slopes of Mount Baal Hazor, the highest hill in
the Ephraim mountains, some 1,500 feet above sea level. Strong springs
arising in the ravine below to the south of the site feed the vast oasis of
'Ain es-Samiyeh—the best-watered region anywhere in the central hill
country. The rugged hilltop appears isolated, which is undoubtedly why
it was chosen. However, small intermontane valleys close by with alluvial
soils could easily have been irrigated by the springs.

There are two phases of occupation. The first phase, with ninth-century pottery, sees the construction of a double wall 13 feet wide, with
outer revetments that rest on bedrock (fig. 5.18). On the north side, where
the rocky cliff is steepest, a massive roughly circular tower was built into
the wall, with its own revetment. At one point it measured some 100 feet
across. The inside features at least thirty pillars, dividing the tower-like
structure into numerous small rooms. This building, a citadel of sorts, is
second in size only to the huge bastion of the city gate at contemporary
Lachish. Similar towers, although smaller, are known from other Iron II
sites on both sides of the Jordan.

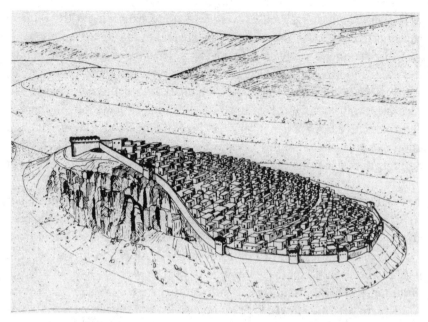

Fig. 5.18. Reconstruction of Khirbet el-Marjameh (drawing by Leen Ritmeyer, in A. Mazar 1982c, 172)

Dating mostly to the later eighth-century phase, when the inner part of the defensive wall went out of use, were densely clustered small houses, arranged along terraces in the bedrock. If the entire area had been built up, as the surface remains suggested, the site could have had a population of 800 or more. It would appear that Khirbet el-Marjameh was a civilian town, albeit one exceptionally well-fortified and probably with a permanent military garrison.

Bethel. Ancient Bethel is certainly to be located at modern Beitin, 10 miles north of Jerusalem. Most of the remains are under the town, but some 4 acres were available for Albright's and Kelso's excavations in the 1930s and 1950s. Inadequate excavation and publication, plus the agenda of traditional biblical archaeology, have left the Iron Age remains unclear.[32]

After a scant Iron I and IIA occupation, there seems to be very little ninth-century occupation. The town revives in the eighth century, but there are no coherent plans, and the pottery is not well stratified. It is similar to that at Khirbet el-Marjameh, 7 miles to the northeast (above).

Gibeon. The town Gibeon is to be identified with el-Jib, a prominent ridge 5 miles north of Jerusalem. American excavations in 1957–1962 revealed little of the Iron Age plan of the site (ca. 5 acres). A massive city wall some 10–12 feet wide enclosed the site.

Two Iron Age water systems were found, the first a round shaft inside the city wall with 79 descending steps cut into the bedrock to a depth of nearly 125 feet to reach the water table (fig. 5.19). Several stamped jar handles found at the bottom reading *gbʿn* confirmed the identification of el-Jib with biblical Gibeon. The second water system, constructed to augment the first, consisted of a tunnel through bedrock under the city wall, with 93 steps leading to a spring outside the wall (fig. 5.19).

More than 60 rock-cut, bell-shaped wine cellars were found, together with wine presses and settling basins. Stamped jar handless read *gbʿn gdr* ("wine of Gibeon"), together with several personal names. The excavator estimates that the caves could have stored some 95,000 liters of wine.[33]

Tel Batash. Biblical Timnah is to be identified with Tel Batash, a 7-acre mound excavated in 1977–1989 by A. Mazar and Kelm. Timnah has prototypes of typical Israelite pillar-courtyard houses as early as Stratum VII of the Late Bronze Age (fourteenth century). A Philistine settlement in Stratum V was destroyed and was followed by a poorly preserved unwalled town in Stratum IV. Dated to the tenth century, Stratum IV has been regarded as representing an Israelite takeover, but Timnah seems to have preserved something of the special character of a border town throughout the subsequent Iron II period, with continuing elements of Judahite and coastal Philistine culture. The subsequent ninth century is not well attested and may witness a gap in occupation.

Stratum III belongs to the eighth century, ending in 701. There is now a massive city wall and four-entryway city gate, with an offset entrance and outer towers. A large complex of private houses is known, but none is of the familiar pillar-courtyard type. A large structure in Area H is likely an administrative building. The Stratum III pottery has close parallels at inland Judahite sites, but it retains some coastal Philistine elements. The population, possibly an ethnic mix, could have been 500 or more.[34]

Tel Ḥamid. Possibly biblical Gibbethon, Tell Ḥamid is a low 10-acre mound 4 miles northwest of Gezer. Stratum VII belongs to the ninth century, dated both by red-slipped and burnished wares, as well as C-14 determinations. It may have been destroyed by the Aramean incursions in the mid-ninth century. Stratum VI, of the late ninth–early eighth century, has a large storehouse (some 2,000 square feet) with pillars, which produced hundreds of store jars. Stratum V succeeds it in the late eighth

Fig. 5.19. Gibeon water shaft (photograph by William G. Dever)

century, perhaps exhibiting now a town wall as well as an iron-working facility. It was destroyed in the late eighth century, its Iron Age history paralleling that of the nearby large city of Gezer.

Beth-Zur. The town of Beth-Zur (Khirbet eṭ-Ṭubeiqah) sits atop one of the highest hills in Judah (some 3,300 feet), on the main road south from Jerusalem to Hebron. The Iron I remains end sometimes round 1000, after which there are sherds from the ninth–eighth century. The major Iron II occupation, however, belong to the seventh century.

There are several other sites in Judah of the ninth–eighth century that would qualify as tier 4 towns, but the excavated exposure is too small at present to add much to the above portrait.

Tel Zayit. Perhaps biblical Libnah, Tel Zayit is a prominent 7.5-acre mound north/northeast of Lachish, on the border with Philistia. This region of the inner Shephelah (the Beth Guvrin Valley) consists of low rolling hills, relatively well watered and with a high water table, ideal for grain cultivation. Excavations by Tappy in progress have revealed a tenth-century public building with an early abecedary display inscription, destroyed sometime in the mid-ninth century. Areas of private houses then follow in, mostly in the seventh century, until the site ends in 586.[35]

Tell Beit Mirsim. Nearly one-fifth of this 7.5-acre mound in the Judean inner Shephelah (foothills) was excavated by Albright in 1926–1932 down to Stratum A_2. First thought to have been destroyed in 586, Stratum A_2 is now correctly dated to the era of Lachish III and Beersheba II (destroyed in 701). It followed a period of unclear occupation in the early eighth century (A_1).

In Stratum A_2 the Stratum B_3 casemate city wall with its two gates, constructed in the tenth century (above), was reused. This city wall is usually considered a typical casemate or double wall. Alternatively, it could be thought of as consisting of the back rooms of a contiguous belt of four-room houses forming a defensible perimeter (as at Beersheba, above). There is a rather poorly built offset-entryway gate to the southeast. The Western Tower may or may not have functioned as a gate (below; fig. 5.20).

Despite the apparent incorporation of many of the houses into the casemate perimeter, in some places there is a sort of ring road running parallel to the city wall and separating banks of continuous houses. (The same phenomenon is seen at other Judean sites, notably Tell en-Naṣbeh, Beth-Shemesh, Khirbet Qeiyafa, and Beersheba.) In some cases, alleys or corridors lead directly from the ring road to the city wall.

Many of the Stratum A_2 houses feature pillars and courtyards, but most do not conform to the standard four-room plan. Neither are they uniform in size. While many share common walls and are oriented toward communal courtyards, there is no street plan that would give the extensive domestic quarters any cohesion. For this reason some consider that there is no evidence for any particular degree of town planning at Tell Beit Mirsim in the eighth century. That view, however, overlooks the fact that the defenses could have been effective despite their ad hoc appearance.

Furthermore, a large structure set into the city wall on the northwest—the so-called Western Tower—may well have been an administrative building or a modest citadel. It features a bank of several rooms surrounding a central court. Its position dominating (and even extending over the city wall) suggests that it was not an ordinary domestic dwelling. This building opens onto a small outer courtyard, on all three sides of

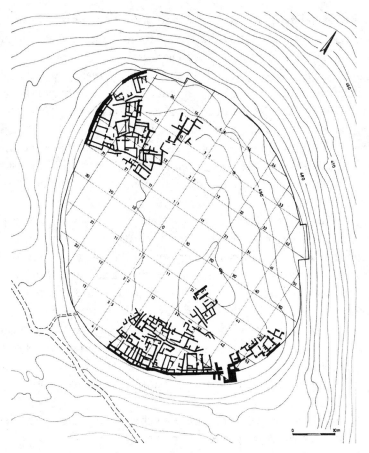

Fig. 5.20. Plan of Tell Beit Mirsim, Stratum A$_2$ (Herzog 1997, fig. 5.29)

which are buildings that are unusually large and somewhat different from
nearby houses and are set off from them by their open spaces. Here in the
northwest quadrant there may be an elite quarter similar to that at Hazor,
although on a much more modest scale.[36]

The southeast quarter, near the gate, contains more ordinary houses.
However, since only about one-fifth of Tell Beit Mirsim A was excavated,
we do not know much about the overall town plan. If most of the 7.5-acre
site was taken up with domestic occupation, the population could have
been up to 700. It seems likely that Tell Beit Mirsim was typical of middle-
level or tier 3 Judean towns.

Tel Ḥalif. Possibly biblical Rimmon, Tel Ḥalif is a small but prominent
mound of 3 acres, 6 miles southeast of Tell Beit Mirsim, where the south-

ern Shephelah borders the Philistine plain. Its strategic location on trade routes and its abundant natural resources gave the site a long history, from the late fourth millennium until modern times.

Stratum VII of the Iron I period, a small Israelite border town, has been discussed above. Stratum VID–B then spans the ninth–eighth century. The casemate city wall had an outer flagstone-paved glacis sloping some 30 degrees. Remains of pillar-courtyard houses included a wide range of domestic objects. One house (F16), destroyed in the 701 campaign of Sennacherib, produced a complete inventory of domestic pottery and implements (below). Stratum VIA, following the destruction, represents a brief reoccupation, stretching into the first half of the seventh century. A partially robbed cemetery near the mound yielded evidence of typical eighth-century rock-cut bench tombs.

Tel Seraʿ. This site, possibly biblical Ziklag, is a fairly steep mound of 4–5 acres located 8 miles southwest of Lachish, on the border with Philistia. Stratum VII extends from the late tenth into the ninth century. There are four-room houses with hand-burnished wares, but the Israelite nature of the occupation is unclear. Stratum VII follows Stratum VIII with no destruction. It is well planned and developed, with several phases of four-room houses, as well as one patrician dwelling 32 by 40 feet. It was destroyed by fire, then succeeded by Stratum VI of the eighth century. Again we see a complex of private houses, some of them incorporating ashlar blocks on the outer faces and in the foundations of the mud-brick walls. A massive destruction ends this stratum in the late eighth century.

Tel ʿIra. Possibly biblical Ramah, Tel ʿIra is a low, irregularly shaped, 6-acre mound 7 miles east of Beersheba, on the border of southern Judah and the Negev Desert. It was excavated in 1977–1978 by Beit-Arieh and is well published. It may be taken as typical of medium-sized Judean towns on the border with southern Philistia in the Iron II B period.

Stratum VIII may have been founded in the late tenth century after a long gap, but it extends into the ninth century. Unfortunately, it is witnessed only by scattered sherds. Stratum VII represents the late eighth- (and perhaps early seventh-) century town. The whole 6-acre site was built up, surrounded by a solid wall 6 feet thick, founded on bedrock. In the area of the four-entryway gate there are casemate segments. A glacis and towers supplement the defenses. There are private houses, some of pillar-courtyard type, as well as a few public buildings, storehouses, and silos.

The Cemetery in Area T has had some twenty bench tombs typical of Judah in the eighth–seventh century, some with evidence of wealth. Given the several public buildings and the open spaces for silos, the population may have been about 500. Dry farming, pastoralism, and trade were probably the major features of the economy.[37]

Tier 5: Villages

Criteria for distinguishing a village from the towns discussed above presuppose that the former are smaller, 1–3 acres, usually more isolated in rural areas, and economically self-sufficient. They may or may not be walled. Most tend to have larger, more ad hoc dwellings, agglutinative in character but showing little planning. Given the dominance of tell-oriented archaeology until recently, relatively few of these small, mostly one-period sites have been excavated. With the advent of settlement archaeology and intensive surface surveys, however, many more of them are now known.

The survey data cannot be as fine-grained as we might like. The basic work of Broshi and Finkelstein breaks down their sites into categories A–E. Categories A and B, up to about 2 acres, would be equivalent to our tier 5 villages. They do not specify categories for all the sites in their ten survey areas, but a rough comparison with our Tier 5 category would yield a total of at least 200 villages in Israel, some 150 or so in Judah. For comparison, the more detailed Southern Samaria Survey showed that nearly 80 percent of all sites mapped were less than 2.5 acres in size, again constituting our villages. These and other estimates, while differing somewhat in method, all yield the same picture of a predominantly rural society in Israel and Judah, not only in the ninth–eighth century but throughout the Iron Age, despite some urban tendencies.[38] Unfortunately, only a handful of Iron IIB villages have been excavated, none of them completely. A few sites may be mentioned.

Tel Qiri. A 2.5-acre low mound near the large tell of Yoqneʿam, Tel Qiri is located at a major pass through the Carmel Mountains out into the Jezreel Valley. It was excavated in 1975–1977 as part of a regional project carried out by Ben-Tor. Stratum VIIB–C belongs to the ninth century, but Strata IX–V, spanning the entire Iron I–II period (ca. 900–600), show so much continuity that building phases can scarcely be separated. Tel Qiri was an unfortified village but was not destroyed or even substantially changed for hundreds of years. The population appears to have been stable and reasonably prosperous, the economy based on agriculture. The houses are small, tightly compacted, sharing some common walls. Interestingly, they are not the usual four-room houses we so often see in villages and towns, perhaps because they needed no pillars. In the courtyards there were many stone-lined silos. There were also a few olive presses. The large number of basalt grinders and pounders in all the houses attests to the processing of agricultural products, as do the abundant flint sickles. Seeds of wheat, pomegranates, chickpeas, and vetch were found. The animal bones were mostly sheep and goat (80 percent), with some cattle (15 percent).[39]

Kinrot. Also known as Tel Chinnereth, this prominent tell on the northwest shore of the Sea of Galilee was excavated by Fritz and other German archaeologists. Stratum II, belonging to the eighth century, succeeds a much larger Bronze Age walled settlement and an Iron I town, now shrunken to some 2.5 acres. There is a row of pillar-courtyard houses near the village wall and gate. A much larger building stands on the other side of the mound, with a cistern. There are a few other scattered, simpler houses.

One of the few archaeological projects that has investigated a larger area characterized by rural settlements is the Naḥal Rephaim project. This project investigated an area of 12 acres on the southwestern outskirts of modern Jerusalem. Most of the remains on the agricultural terraces above the Sorek Valley leading up to Jerusalem from the Shephelah are earlier than our period, but some of the farmhouses scattered along the terraces above the spring are relevant. Here the earlier Bronze Age terraces (Strata II–III) were rebuilt and augmented when new farmhouses were erected sometime in the eighth–seventh century. This no doubt occurred because the population of Jerusalem was now reaching its peak, after an influx of refugees from the north. The scant Iron II remains are said to be similar to other finds on the terraces at nearby Manaḥat, as well as at Givʿat Masura and the farm at Khirbet er-Ras. With nothing available beyond preliminary reports, we can only say that more rural settlements and suburban villages will surely be discovered when archaeologists build the search for them into their strategy, which has heretofore been focused mainly on urban sites.

Faust has recently summarized much of what we now know of house sizes in other villages from surface surveys or small-scale excavations.[40]

Fig. 5.21. Rural Iron II villages

Name	Description	Size (m²)
Khirbet Jemein	A 2.5-acre village in western Samaria. About ten four-room houses were excavated. Most of the houses were built in pairs.	115–135
Beit Aryeh	A 1.5-acre village (Khirbet Hudash) in western Samaria. About ten four-room houses were excavated.	110
Khirbet Malta	A 2.5 acres village near Nazareth. One four-room house was excavated.	120
Khirbet Jarish	A 1.5-acre village in Hebron hill country. One four-room house was excavated.	170
Deir el-Mir	A large village in western Samaria (ca. 2 acres). Several four-room houses were surveyed.	100–140
Ḥorvat Shilḥa	A single four-room structure in a compound in the desert fringe north of Jerusalem.	130
Khirbet er-Ras	Two four-room farmhouses near Jerusalem.	130, 165
Naḥal Zimra	A four-room farmhouse near Jerusalem.	130
French Hill	A four-room (?) farmhouse near Jerusalem.	120
Wadi Fukin	A four-room house in a farm compound in the Hebron hill country.	300
Khirbet ʿEli	A single four-room structure in Samaria.	170

Many more Iron IIB rural sites are known from surface surveys, indicating a substantial population growth from the tenth century. For instance, in the Shephelah 731 sites are now known for the ninth–eighth century. In the Judean hill country, there is an increase from 66 ninth-century sites to 88 by the eighth century, with a rural population of up to 25,000. Some have suggested that between the eleventh and the eighth century the rural population may have doubled every century.[41]

Faust was one of the first archaeologists to document several differences between these villages and farms and the urban sector. For one thing, the rural dwellings tend to be much larger, averaging up to 1,300 square feet, in contrast to 350–750 square feet for urban sites. They also follow the general pillar-courtyard type, but less slavishly and with internal space divided into more smaller rooms. There are large common courtyards but no public buildings. Faust makes a convincing argument that these larger dwellings probably housed extended families, not surprising, since they are farmhouses, and farms favor larger families, more work hands, and heritable lands that can be passed on to generations that remain on the land (fig. 5.22).

From his extensive survey of the data, Faust concludes:

> Based on the size of dwellings in the rural settlement, it seems quite probable that the large structures housed extended families. A family of this type could include father, mother, married sons and their children, unmarried daughters, unmarried aunts, additional relatives who for various reasons remained to dwell in the structure or moved into it, and possibly also servants, slaves, and additional affiliated individuals (along with animals). In rural sites where a relatively large number of structures were uncovered, major differences among the structures were not discerned, and most of them were of similar area and architectural characteristics.[42]

Tier 6: Forts

The final tier of our Iron IIB site hierarchy consists of settlements that are clearly not civilian but military, in other words, forts. Here function, not size, is the criterion. We have nearly twenty-five such forts in the ninth–eighth century, a fact whose significance will soon be clear. Since many are similar and their contents scant, they can be described without much detail.[43]

Israel. We have only four forts in the north. On the Golan Heights, Tel Soreg (possibly biblical Aphek) is a 1-acre fortified site of the ninth–eighth century. Originally a farm on the border with Aram, it becomes an outpost either of northern Israel, or possibly of the Arameans, related to Tel Hadar and 'Ein-Gev on the eastern shore of the Sea of Galilee (below).

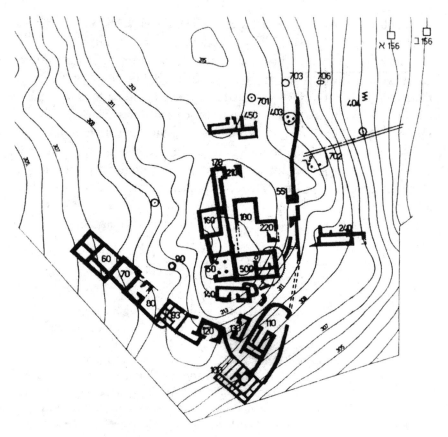

Fig. 5.22. Plan of Khirbet Jemein, Iron II (Faust 2012a, fig. 22)

Jezreel is by far the most impressive ninth-century fort that we know in the north or the south. It is located about 10 miles east-southeast from Megiddo, similarly overlooking the southern reaches of the Jezreel Valley, with splendid views. It consists of an area of about 11 acres enclosed by a casemate wall with corner towers and a three-entryway gate on the south wall. A dry moat dug into the bedrock surrounding the wall outside gave further protection. Few building remains were found in the huge enclosed area. The pottery dates Jezreel broadly to the ninth century. The unique, deliberate plan and the enormous size make Jezreel clearly a royal fort, with provisions for military activities, parade grounds, chariots, and possibly also a part-time royal residence. By the eighth century, however, the fortified enclosure had fallen into disuse, and only a few dwellings were found in the robbed outer walls.[44]

Khirbet el-Maḥruq belongs to a unique type of round tower fortress more common in Judah. The site is strategically located on a rocky precipice overlooking the road down to the Jordan Valley and the modern Damiyeh (Adam) bridge, opposite Tell Deir ʿAlla. An earlier tower of the eighth century is rectangular, 60 by 75 feet, with casemate walls. The slightly later tower is round, some 63 feet in diameter, built of three concentric walls and divided into small cells. It may have extended into the early seventh century.[45]

The final fort in the north is Tell Qudadi, on the north bank of the Yarkon River in modern Tel Aviv. The first phase in the ninth century consists of a rectangular structure at least 46 by 110 feet, with walls 23 feet thick. Inside six rooms were preserved. A later phase, of the late ninth–eighth century, is built with offset-inset walls 8 feet thick. The fort is presumed to have been Israelite, but being right on the border with Philistia it may have been a Philistine outpost.

Judah. Several small tower forts are grouped in the mountainous regions of Judah. There are round towers at Deir Baghl and Khirbet Tabaneh, only a few miles from Khirbet Abu Tuwein (below). Round towers of the ninth–eighth century have also been found at French Hill in Jerusalem.

Khirbet Abu Tuwein, 12 miles southwest of Jerusalem on the slopes of the Hebron hills overlooking the Shephelah, is a square walled fort some 100 by 100 feet (or 10,000 square feet) at an altitude of 2,200 feet above sea level. Around the large open courtyard are many small rooms, most featuring a row of central pillars. The fort dates to the eighth–seventh century. Two similar square or rectangular forts are known nearby, as well as the fort at Ḥorvat Eres on a high ridge west of Jerusalem, with a view all the way down to the coastal plain (fig. 5.23).[46]

A unique fort in the Jerusalem area is Ramat Raḥel, on the road to Bethlehem and Hebron. It is one of the highest peaks south of Jerusalem and part of the ridge surrounding the Rephaim Valley, which was a major approach to Jerusalem in antiquity. The steep slopes to the west give it protection; to the east is the Judean Desert. It has superb views to the north, west, and south; in turn, it is visible from all parts of Jerusalem.

Aharoni excavated Ramat Raḥel in 1954–1962, but final reports never appeared. He found ten Proto-Aeolic (palmette) capitals, as well as elements of carved-stone window balustrades similar to those depicted on Syrian and Phoenician ivories with the "woman at the window" motif. He

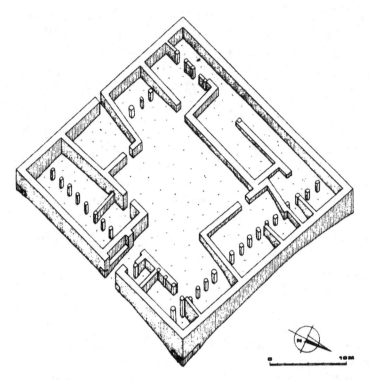

Fig. 5.23. Isometric reconstruction of the fortress at Khirbet Abu Tuwein (A. Mazar 1993, 15)

attributed these to a second building phase, his Stratum VA, of the seventh century. He identified the site with biblical Beth-haccherem, seeing the large architectural elements as part of a large royal palace.

Renewed Israeli excavations (2005–) have shown that Aharoni's palace belongs mainly to the late seventh century (Phase 2) and that in the late eighth–early seventh century (Phase 1) only the western part of the complex functioned, as a tower fortress. Although still in use later, the columns and balustrades probably originated in this first phase (Stratum VB). Even though relatively small, this prominent fortress made a statement about royal power and prestige. It was both a fort and an administrative center, to judge from the numerous stamp impressions on jar handles.[47]

East of Jerusalem, in the Judean Desert down toward the Dead Sea, there are several forts dating from the eighth–seventh century. In the Buqeiʿa Valley west of Qumran is the small rectangular fort at Khirbet Abu Tabaq, measuring about 200 by 100 feet. Nearby is Khirbet es-Samrah, even larger, with evidence of a dozen or so inner rooms. Both forts here in the arid Judean wilderness are situated near runoff terraces and dams, as well as having cisterns. They were evidently meant to be mostly self-sufficient. At Qumran, overlooking the Dead Sea, the earliest occupation consisted of a large square tower. These forts persisted until the fall of the southern kingdom in 586.

South of the Jerusalem–Jericho road near Maʿale-Adumim on a high hill is the fort of el-Khirbe. Early phases belong to the eleventh–tenth century. Phase 2 of the tenth–ninth century features a walled rectangular fort 100 by 70 feet with a large courtyard, many small rooms, and a citadel in the southeast corner. A cistern at the slope supplied water.

There are a number of forts of the ninth–eighth century in the Negev. Tel Malḥata (possibly biblical Baalath-beer) was already fortified in the tenth century (Phase C). A later fortified site (Phase A) of about 4 acres features a wall 12 feet wide with towers, as well as a large triple-colonnaded storehouse. It was apparently destroyed by fire at the time of the fall of the southern kingdom.

The most impressive and the most extensively excavated Negev fort is Arad, a few miles east of Beersheba. The stratigraphy of Aharoni has been much debated, but the outline here follows a reworked, broad consensus.[48] The first fort, on a high hill above the Early Bronze Age city, was constructed in Stratum X of the early ninth century. It was a square building of circa 165 by 165 feet (or 27,225 square feet). In Stratum IX of the ninth–early eighth century, a thick solid wall was constructed, with corner towers and a gate with towers to the east. In the large central courtyard were storage and residential rooms. In the northwestern corner was a tripartite temple, the only one ever found in the country, the significance of which will be discussed below. A deep well at the foot of the hill, with a tunnel leading under the fortress wall, provided water. This fort continued in use in Stratum VIII, with a casemate wall, until the late eighth or early seventh century, when the site was violently destroyed either in the Sennacherib campaigns or by Edomites. Several Hebrew ostraca were said to have been found in Stratum VIII but must belong later, in subsequent Strata VII and VI (seventh century below).

Ḥorvat Radum, 5 miles south of Arad, is another Negev fort situated again on a prominent hilltop. The fort is 70 by 80 feet, surrounded by a thick offset-inset wall and a gate to the east with an offset entrance. In the interior there are casemate-like rooms and a square podium in the center of the courtyard that may be the foundations of a tower. The fort may have been constructed in the late eighth century, but the pottery is seventh–early sixth century. Some Edomite pottery was recovered, as well as five Hebrew ostraca.

Farther south, there is a casemate-walled fortress with corner towers, some 300 by 300 yards, at Mezad Ḥazeva (Stratum V). Pottery of the eighth–seventh century suggests identifying the fort with biblical Tamar.

The southernmost Negev fort of this era is Tell el-Kheleifeh. Glueck famously interpreted the site as Ezion-geber, King Solomon's copper mine. Reinvestigation of his largely unpublished material by Pratico, however, has shown that there are only two phases belonging broadly to the eighth–early sixth century. Phase I is represented by a square casemate fortress with a four-room structure and several other rooms. The mixture of Judahite and Edomite pottery (scarcely published) makes the date of its destruction uncertain. A radical change in Phase II presents a citadel with an offset-inset wall and a two-entryway gate. Again the date is uncertain, but it may extend into the early sixth century (fig. 5.24).[49]

In the eastern Sinai Desert, the fortress at the oasis of ʿAin el-Qudeirat (biblical Kadesh-barnea) continues the now defunct tradition of Negev forts. The eighth-century Middle Fort (Stratum 3) consists of a rectangular enclosure of 26,000 square feet, surrounded by a wall 13 feet thick with eight rectangular walls. The fortress guarded the road from Gaza to the Red Sea, a route that was vital for trade with Arabia.[50]

Another remote eighth-century fort is Kuntillet ʿAjrud, some 40 miles farther south, situated on an isolated hill near springs. The fort resembles other rectangular forts, with casemate walls and corner towers. Built into the gate plaza and offset entrance was a shrine. It had flanking chambers each with a bench and a sort of favissa, the whole plastered. The unique votive offerings and numerous graffiti, which identify Kuntillet ʿAjrud as a sort of caravanserai or fort-cum-sanctuary, will be discussed shortly (fig. 5.25).[51]

In summary, both the northern and the southern kingdoms began to be threatened by neighboring peoples already in the ninth century, particularly after the first confrontation with Assyrian forces under Shalmaneser III at Qarqar in northern Syria in 853. There were also Aramean incursions in the ninth century. By the eighth century, the threat was dire, and the few forts in the north indicate sporadic attempts at defense. Despite this, the northern kingdom was overrun by Assyrian forces in 732–721 (below).

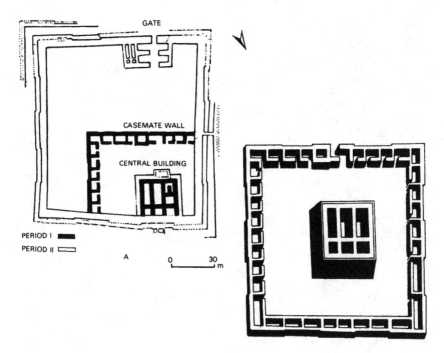

Fig. 5.24. Fort at Tell el-Kheleifeh, Phase II (adapted from Barkay 1992, fig. 9.29)

The far great number of forts in Judah in the eighth century may have helped to stave off an Assyrian invasion there, although only temporarily, until 701 and the campaign of Sennacherib, when most were violently destroyed. It must also be considered that the Judahite forts, especially those in the Negev and Sinai Deserts, could also have had as their primary function protection of trade routes. The aftermath in the seventh century will be considered shortly (ch. 6), along with the political implications.

A General Systems Theory Approach: Summary

Settlement Type and Distribution; Demography

Settlement patterns imply a discussion of demography. Modern demographic studies of ancient Israel and Judah became possible only after the advent of the subdiscipline of settlement archaeology and the beginning of extensive surface surveys by Israeli archaeologists in the early 1980s.

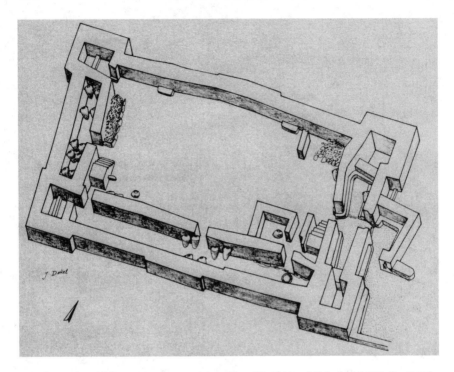

Fig. 5.25. Plan of the major structures at Kuntillet ʿAjrud (Meshel 2012, fig. 2:13)

Earlier estimates of the Iron Age population, little more than guesses, ranged from 400,000 to over 1,000,000. As the result of a number of recent detailed analyses, that number can be reduced to circa 350,000 for both Israel and Judah in the eighth century, when the Iron Age population probably reached its peak. This would be an increase from circa 150,000 in the tenth century. These figures are arrived at by measuring the size of all the known sites, thus calculating what is called the total built-up area, presumably all occupied at a particular time. Then one divides this figure by 100, the presumed number of persons per acre (a coefficient derived from ethnographic studies of modern societies).[52]

Unfortunately, our data are not sufficient at present to enable us to distinguish subphases within the three-century period above. Furthermore, even at best population estimates are largely dependent on surface surveys, which are somewhat problematic. The survey area may be restricted by modern conditions. Numerous small sites may have disappeared due to erosion, cultivation, or modern development. The surface remains and sherds may be visible but scant. The size of the site can be measured, but the size of the ancient settlement at any one period may not be discernible. Sherds may prove that there was occupation at a particular time period but provide no certainty as to its extent over the site. Finally, little of the site plan or the plan of individual buildings, much less the stratigraphy, can be obtained without excavation in depth.

The most comprehensive study for the Iron II period (eighth century) is that of Broshi and Finkelstein, who divide the country into ten regions and subregions based on different natural environments and historical-cultural conditions. Their summary is as follows.

Fig. 5.26. Population estimates for the Iron II period

Region	Number of sites	Inhab-ited area	Total estimated inhabited area	Population
Upper Galilee	84	96	100	25,000
Lower Galilee	54	65	90	22,500
Huleh Valley	23	63	75	18,750
Jordan Valley	66	40	55	13,750
Jezreel Valley	55	95	110	27,500
Samaria				
Mount Gilboa	4	5	5	1,250
Mount Carmel	20	8	12	3,000
northern Samaria	163	200	200	50,000
Samaria (city)	1	60	60	15,000
southern Samaria	190	120	132	33,000
Judah				
north of Jerusalem	100	90	90	22,500
Jerusalem	1	30	30	7,500
Judean Hills	65	105	120	30,000
Shephelah	100	170	200	50,000
northern coast	22	73	88	22,000

central and southern coast

Mount Carmel	ca. 30	32	35	8,750
southern Sharon	19	15	15	3,750
Philistia	47	120	140	36,000
Gaza region	38	30	45	11,250
Beersheba Valley	5	5	6	1,500
TOTAL	1,087	1,422	1,608	403,000

Despite these confident projections, some reinterpretation is required to render these figures appropriate for our Israel–Judah distinction here. For Israel, the northern kingdom, combining the Galilee, Huleh Valley, Jordan Valley, Jezreel Valley, Samaria, and the northern coastal plain give us 604 sites, with a total of about 218,000 population in the eighth century. For Judah, the southern kingdom, combining the Sharon Plain, Judah, the Beersheba Valley (excluding Philistia), and the Shephelah, we have some 307 sites, with a total of about 137,000. That gives us a total population of some 350,000 for Israel and Judah. Although subject to methodological limitations that do not allow us absolute figures, these estimates are fairly reliable for relative numbers, that is, for calculating population change over long time periods.[53] For instance, using the same survey data and methods, we can estimate the population of ancient Palestine over many centuries. Broshi and Finkelstein do this in chart form, giving both total populations and the percentage of people in contrasting lowlands and highlands.

Of particular significance here in using our data base—derived largely from surveys and looking beyond numbers to socioeconomic structure—is a differing view about the percentage of people who lived in rural areas in the ninth–eighth century. Broshi and Finkelstein take their threshold for dividing "lowland" and "highland" as 12.5 acres, but they do not define these regions in terms of rural versus urban. They conclude simply that in the eighth century about 34 percent of the population lived in their lowlands, in settlements of 12.5 acres or more, which would correspond roughly to our cities with populations of 1,000 or more.

Their percentage of the rural (highland) population would thus be 66 percent, which seems much too low, probably skewed by the built-in biases of survey data. To take a different approach, the total estimated population of the ten excavated *cities* in fig. 5.1 is no more than some 12,000. Even adding our fourteen *towns* as nonrural gives us only another 8,000 or so. If we compare that urban population of 20,000—based on excavations that probably includes most of the known ancient sites—with the total population of Israel and Judah, 250,000, we come up with roughly 10 percent of the population living in towns and cities. The remaining 90 percent would have lived in rural areas, in farms and villages. If we add the pastoral element of the population (which Broshi and Finkelstein do not include), usually estimated at about 10 percent in most periods, that would swell the rural population even more. While our figures are also not absolute, they are based on the presumed built-up area derived from excavated sites, not survey data.

More recent analyses, based on both excavated and survey sites, and in this case confined to the Judean Shephelah, yield a somewhat different picture.[54] Faust's detailed study shows that by the eighth century this region had reached its peak, with a population of some 50,000 (Broshi and Finkelstein; cf. Dagan's ca. 108,000) and that nearly 50 percent of the population of Judah was concentrated there, mainly in rural areas. There were only about a dozen excavated sites that could be considered urban at all. However, considering the fact that many small villages, hamlets, and farmsteads may not have survived or were missed even in extensive surveys, the rural population was probably a good deal larger. Again, it would have represented a majority of the population.

The conclusion for our purpose here is that ancient Israel and Judah remained (as they had been in the Bronze Age) predominantly rural societies and economies. To be sure, there were a few cities where truly urban developments are clearly seen on the basis of any criteria, and the small but impressive regional administrative centers by definition are urban, with their monumental architecture. But the analysis here of settlement type, distribution, and demography demonstrates beyond doubt that the Iron Age Israelite ethos was based on *agrarian* life and rural values. That fact will have significance for our further survey of political organization, socioeconomic structure, and religion.

Political Organization

In moving to the next subsystem, political organization, we will not discuss each tier of sites separately, since all settlements of any kind were integral parts of a functioning political system, although of differing influence. Nor will there be detailed presentation of the archaeological evidence, since it has been set forth in the data base above and can simply be summarized here.

First, it is clear that by the mid-ninth century, at the latest, there were political entities that were well developed beyond the inchoate early states that we have seen in the tenth century. There is universal agreement among archaeologists and historians that the northern kingdom of Israel is now flourishing, enough so that it is well known to neighboring peoples and states. At the battle of Qarqar in Syria in 853 a coalition of ten kings of the various petty states in the west met the Assyrian King Shalmaneser III in battle. The Assyrian annals name one "Ahab, king of Israel," who is said to have brought one of the largest forces of any of his cohorts, two thousand chariots and ten thousand soldiers. The slightly later (ca. 840) Dan stela discussed above (ch. 4) is an Aramean victory stela that records an invasion, probably by Hazael, who boasts of killing two kings: Jehoram of Israel (Ahab's son); and Ahaziah of the "house of David" (i.e., Judah). On the Black Obelisk of Shalmaneser III, dated to 841, "Jehu, king of Israel," is named and apparently depicted as paying tribute to the Assyrian king. Finally, the mid-ninth-century stela of Mesha, king of Moab, mentions both David in Judah and Omri in Israel (Ahab's father), complaining that they had oppressed Moab.[55]

Skeptics, reluctant to accept the evidence of early statehood even when we have inscriptional evidence, have argued that none of these inscriptions predates the ninth century. That is not only an argument from silence, but it ignores the fact that the Assyrians never encountered Israel before the mid-ninth century, when their westward advance began. Upon their first meeting, they were impressed enough to acknowledge the state of Israel and to name its king.

Even without textual confirmation, the archaeological evidence that we have surveyed makes it clear that both Israel and Judah were well-organized states by the ninth century. The several tier 1 capitals and tier 2 administrative centers surveyed simply cannot have been planned, constructed, and maintained without a highly centralized government able to command impressive men and material. In addition, we have described some twenty forts in Israel and Judah that were certainly state controlled and designed for its defense. One has only to contrast this array with the acephalous village society and economy of the twelfth–

eleventh century to appreciate how far political development had come by the ninth century.

The growth of the state in both Israel and Judah was clearly accompanied by urbanization, but it is not simply a matter of cause and effect. There are states that never become truly urban, and there are urban societies that do not evolve into statehood. Nevertheless, in this case the administrative centers that we have seen could not have come into existence except as an aspect of centralization: the concentration of resources and authority in an urban environment, even if relatively small-scale. Both the regional centers and the dozen or so settlements with a population of 1,000 or more were the result of deliberate planning, the essential characteristic of urbanization (not size). Some of the cities and all of the regional centers must also have been subsidized by the state in one way or another.

When we come to socioeconomic structure, we shall see that the archaeological evidence demonstrates the existence of a ruling elite—not only kings, some of whose names we know, but also other high-ranking political officials. Most of the tier 1 and 2 sites exhibit palaces, governor's residences, royal storehouses, defenses, and water systems, all of which would have required a coordinated political system to manage. We shall also see trading networks that presuppose a managed economy of sorts.

One argument for late development of statehood in Israel and Judah is the relative lack of written evidence in the tenth and even the ninth century, the assumption being that a centralized bureaucracy would have required detailed record keeping. Again that is an argument from silence, since routine records would undoubtedly have been written on papyrus, which is rarely if ever preserved in the damp climate of ancient Palestine. Now, however, we do have from Jerusalem a hoard of 150 bullae with iconographic motifs that were once affixed to papyrus rolls, dated by the associated pottery to the late ninth century. They were found in the ruins of a building near the Gihon Spring in Jerusalem that appears to have been a counting house or a center for storing and exchanging documents (above).

The expansion of the corpus of Iron II written materials, although it was slow, may provide us with another piece of evidence for political organization. Recent studies have shown that written Hebrew from the beginning could have been used as a tool of political manipulation. The control of the written word—of communication on a wider scene—was a palpable exercise of power. The fact that the earliest inscriptions in the eleventh–tenth century are all abecedaries ('Izbet Ṣarṭah, Tel Zayit) or schoolboy's exercise tablets (the Gezer Calendar) suggests that the view of writing as a political instrument has merit. Whenever it began, writing comes into fuller evidence by the ninth–eighth century (see further below).

One of the most obvious manifestations of political organization is the ability of the state to wage war on a scale unimaginable in less-complex societies. Israel's and Judah's armed conflicts with the Philistines in the tenth century have been discussed above. By the mid-ninth century the northern kingdom faced incursions from the Aramean city-states to the north, especially from Damascus, as well as the beginning of persistent Assyrian campaigns westward to the Mediterranean and down the coast. The conflict with Moab, already noted in the Mesha stela, may have been part of a larger struggle between the rival states on both sides of the Jordan.

The threat of the Assyrian advance westward and invasion of the southern Levant was already evident by the mid-ninth century. That reality no doubt explains the proliferation of more advanced defense systems, consisting of both casemate and solid wall, glacis systems, and multiple-entrance city gates. By the eighth century the fortification systems at various sites can be catalogued as follows.

Fig. 5.27. Defense systems of the eighth century

Site and Stratum	Walls	Gates
Dan II	solid, towers	lower = three-entryway
		upper = two-entryway
Hazor VI–V	casemate (reused)	four-entryway (reused)
Megiddo IVA	solid, offset-inset	three-entryway
Gezer VII–VI	solid, plus casemate	three-entryway
Tell en-Naṣbeh 3A	solid, towers	three- and two-entryway
Tel Batash III	solid	four-entryway
Beth-Shemesh 3	solid, towers	?
Lachish III	solid, double	three-entryway
Tell Beit Mirsim A$_2$	solid	two-entryway
Beersheba III	casemate	three-entryway
Tel Ḥalif VIB	casemate, glacis	?
Tel ʿIra VII	solid and casemate	four-entryway

Further defensive measures taken by both Israel and Judah in the ninth–eighth century included the construction of elaborate water systems at many sites. They were obviously intended to ensure a water supply inside the city in case of a prolonged siege, a favorite tactic of Neo-Assyrian warfare. Again these can be catalogued.[56]

Fig. 5.28. Water systems at various Israelite and Judahite sites

Site	Stratum	Date	Remarks
Hazor	VIII–V	ninth–eighth	stepped shaft 135 feet deep; lateral tunnel 135 feet long
Megiddo	IVA	ninth–eighth	shaft 130 feet deep; lateral tunnel 265 feet long
Gibeon		eighth?	stepped shaft 890 feet deep; supplementary to the spring
Gezer	VII–VI?	ninth–eighth?	stepped shaft 25 feet deep; lateral tunnel 125 feet long
Jerusalem	12	eighth	tunnel from spring 1,750 feet long
Beth-Shemesh	3–2	ninth–eighth	large cistern
Lachish	IV–III?	ninth–eighth	"great shaft"; large well 80 feet deep; unfinished.
Arad	IX–VIII?	ninth-eighth	large well
Beersheba	III	ninth–eighth	square shaft leading to cisterns
Kadesh-barnea	"middle"	ninth?	aqueduct from spring

Another aspect of defense preparations may be seen in the widespread construction of large storage facilities by the ninth–eighth century. Many of these were tripartite pillared buildings, most of which do not appear to be stables for chariotry, as previously thought (above). The following are examples. [57]

Fig. 5.29. Tripartite pillared buildings at various Israelite and Judahite sites

Site	Stratum	Date	Remarks
Hazor	VII	ninth	ca. 100 x 65 feet; columns of dressed stones
Kinrot	II	eighth	ca. 60 x 33 feet
Megiddo	IVA	eighth	seventeen units in four groups; five square pillars; mangers; average ca. 75 x 45 feet
Beth-Shemesh	3 [IIb]	eighth	ca. 60 x 43 feet
Lachish	III	eighth	four, near palace, ca. 70 x 50 feet
Tell el-Ḥesi	VIId–c	ninth	ca. 52x 42 feet
Beersheba	III–II	ninth–eighth	three, adjoining gate, ca. 58 x 34 feet each

The outcome of the attempts in the ninth century to ward off Assyrian advances would ultimately end in failure when the northern kingdom fell in the late eighth century (below). It is worth noting here, however, that after the late tenth century Israel and Judah did succeed in containing the Philistines in the coastal plain and the outer Shephelah, where they remained in check until the late sixth century, when they succumbed to the Babylonians. Here the archaeological evidence of the states' successful political policies in the face of huge odds is indisputable.

The pursuit of imperial ambitions in Transjordan is less clear. The boast of the Moabite king Mesha on his royal stela (noted above) that he reconquered territory that had earlier been seized by Omri would seem to confirm Israelite military presence, if not occupation, in central Transjordan. However, Dibon (Dhiban), where the stela was discovered, presumably the Moabite capital in the ninth century, shows little evidence from excavations of being a royal establishment at the time. Like some of the biblical narratives, Mesha's claims to victory over an Israelite king may have been largely political propaganda.[58]

In Transjordan, most authorities now regard the emergence of modest "tribal states" as not earlier than the late eighth or the seventh century (ch. 4). What David and Omri might have conquered is uncertain, if anything at all. There are, in fact, no destructions known from archaeology in the ninth century that reveal military campaigns. Nor is there convincing evidence that Moab had ever been Israelite territory, even in the Iron I period. The notion of Israel's Moabite wars is derived largely from the later biblical narratives, which seem dubious in the light of the archaeological data, the well-known Mesha stela not withstanding (above).

The pursuit of any Israelite imperial ambitions in Syria is also ambiguous. At best Israel seems to have defended itself against the Arameans with mixed success throughout the ninth century. The Dan stela (above) is an unequivocal witness to Aramean invasions into northern Israel, in this case under Hazael of Damascus. The inscription was a victory stela erected conspicuously in the gate plaza and displayed for some time before it was broken up and the fragments used for building stone. It cannot be dismissed as political propaganda. It is prima facie evidence of an Aramean victory, one that resulted (so it is claimed) in the assassination of the kings of both Israel and Judah. Yet curiously, no evidence of a mid-ninth-century destruction has come to light in extensive excavations at Dan (i.e., in Stratum III). Nor is there any mention of this specific event by the biblical writers. They do note that Hazael campaigned in Israel at this time, but they credit the rebel Israelite general Jehu with the deaths of Jehoram and Amaziah.

The biblical writers do mention one specific event, Hazael's attack and seizure of Gath (2 Kgs 12:18). Recent excavations of Tel Zafit, clearly Philistine Gath, have revealed an enormous, deep dry moat running for a distance of more than a mile around the site, with evidence of towers. This would conform very well with siege tactics known from the Assyrian texts, and it is likely that here we have direct archaeological evidence of the campaign of Hazael. Gath does seem to have been violently destroyed at this time, although the evidence is just beginning to be published.[59]

Again, the biblical narratives, although admittedly late and tendentious, have been taken as primary evidence of wars with the Aramean city-states. The Deuteronomistic Historian describes encounters of Ahab and his successors in both Israel and Judah with Aramean kings known from our sources, such as Ben-hadad and Hazael of Damascus. Joash (805–790) is said to have recaptured towns taken by the Arameans during the reign of his father Jehoahaz (819–804). But the biblical writers have confused the names of the Aramean kings, as we know from the Assyrian annals. There are also contradictions: the biblical writers claim that Ahab fought against Ben-hadad, but the Assyrian sources show that the two were allies.[60]

We shall pursue the matter of the putative Aramean wars further below, but whatever the details, Israel and Judah were playing some political role beyond their own borders. This is an indication of the growth of the two states from the tenth into the ninth–eighth century The dynasties of Omri in the north and David in the south were well known to their neighbors by the mid-ninth century, as we have seen. We have several names of other kings in the north in the ninth–eighth century in Assyrian inscriptions, the following among them.

Omri, 884–873
Ahab, 873–852
Jehu, 842–814
Joash, 805–790
Menahem, 747–737
Pekah, 735–732
Hoshea, 732–724

For Judah, the following are attested:

Ahaziah, 843–842
Hezekiah, 727–698

Instruments of war are not well attested because most would not have survived. We do have, however, some evidence of spears, daggers, arrows, and scale armor. Chariots are presumed, such as those attributed to Ahab by the Assyrian documents, but few traces have been found. The tripartite pillared buildings at Megiddo have been interpreted as stables for chariot horses, but that is still debated.[61]

In summary, Judah and particularly Israel had become mature dynastic states by the ninth century, and they further consolidated their gains into the eighth century. Their ideology can be reasonably well reconstructed with reference to the biblical accounts, as well as on the archaeological and extrabiblical evidence. The ambition of both states was typical of the other rival states and principalities of the time in that region. Their goal was to control as much territory as possible and to ensure defensible borders, to exercise political power in order to maximize resources for imperial projects, and to shape the creation of a national identity that would enhance an ideology of divine kingship.

The archaeological evidence that we have surveyed thus far shows that the Israelite and Judahite states were successful, at least for a time. Israel in the ninth century was by any criteria the most dominant of the petty kingdoms in the southern Levant, able to forestall the Assyrian advance for more than a century. There is, however, further evidence to be extracted from our survey of site formation, demography, and political organization.

Socioeconomic Structure

Ancient Israel and Judah have often been portrayed by biblical scholars as egalitarian societies. But those scholars have bought into a myth created by the biblical writers and have unwittingly perpetuated it. This is the oft-discussed nomadic ideal, which is little more than a romantic longing for simpler times, a nostalgia for a past that never was. To be sure, the agro-pastoral society that characterized early Israelite villages was less complex and therefore more egalitarian in principle, and the ideal—"every man under his own fig tree"—was preserved in the literary tradition and later rationalized by theological concepts of social justice. Yet the reality is that, with the rise of the state and the growth of urbanism, Israelite and Judahite society inevitably became more complex, more diversified, more highly stratified.[62]

The evidence that we have surveyed of life in the town and cities, and especially in the administrative centers, shows clearly that both a middle and an elite class had emerged by the ninth century. An urban society and economy could not have been created nor would it have survived without the development of many varied professions and the differential status that went with them.

The archaeological evidence, although indirect, implies at minimum a number of occupations in which individuals were now engaged. The ruling class or upper echelons of society would have included royalty, political envoys, chamberlains, couriers, governors and district administrators, high-ranking military officers, officials of the judiciary, priestly classes, landed gentry, and noble families, heads of old clans, even if somewhat impoverished. Wealth, power, and prestige accrued to this upper class. But their numbers were small, surely no more than a tiny minority of the population.

The support for these elite classes would have been provided by a much larger middle class. Here again the archaeological evidence is somewhat circumstantial yet quite persuasive. At minimum we must presuppose in the urban centers a number of what we might call vocations, or professions. Among these vocations, based on material culture remains that are well documented, we may include the following: mayors, councilmen, professional military and gendarmes, shopkeepers of many kinds, petty bureaucrats, planners, traders and importers (caravaneers), transporters, purveyors of various goods and services, lenders, tax collectors, accountants, teachers, scribes, healers and medicine men, seers and cult functionaries, magistrates and judges. In addition to these offices and classes of workers, we have good evidence for many kinds of craftsmen and artisans: architects, builders and contractors, road builders, quarrymen, miners, stonemasons, kiln workers (lime for plaster), plasterers, metalworkers, tool makers, weapons specialists, chariot manufacturers, wheelwrights, foresters, woodworkers, papyrus makers, potters, gem cutters, jewelers, ivory carvers, weavers, clothiers, sandal makers, winemakers, brewers, oil producers, millers and bakers, perfumers, beekeepers, tomb diggers, gatekeepers, and watchmen.

These professions (so to speak) were, of course, open almost exclusively to men, and many were organized on an almost industrial scale so as to meet the increasing demands of town and urban life. There were, however, cottage industries. Some women would have continued to make pottery in their own homes, as they had done traditionally. Others probably baked enough bread or wove enough garments to use in barter. There is some evidence that women banded together in sodalities that mediated both economic and social benefits. Some women would have been midwives, wet nurses, or even ritual experts (below).

The practice of the professions that we have just described has left fairly clear traces in the archaeological record, partly because more towns and cities where the middle class resided have been excavated. There is some evidence, however, for a lower class that had less of an impact on material. That would include subsistence farmers and farm workers, construction workers, shepherds on the fringes of settled areas, mercenaries, resident aliens, domestic workers, widowers, pensioners, the ill and afflicted, indentured servants, slaves, outlaws and social bandits, beggars, and thieves. These "people without a history" (as Wolf put it) have left us few traces, but they were undoubtedly numerous.

Most of the economic transactions between all these classes of society would have been based on exchange or barter. By the eighth century we do have sheqel weights, balances, and hoards of silver fragments, so that some "cash" transactions were possible. But there simply was not enough silver in circulation to serve as coin of the realm, nor was centrally managed trade the norm. For their livelihood, most people depended on a redistributive economy, or down-the-line, trade (below).

Even though the above were not professions in the modern sense, they required specialized skills by which individuals could make a living. In some cases, however, there may have been guilds in which people could learn the trade as an apprentice. Most of these associations were undoubtedly voluntary. The central government could intervene in order to attempt to manipulate the system, but for the most part we seem to be dealing with a class of entrepreneurs for whom urban life offered many opportunities— a sort of bourgeois society and economy.

We have sufficiently detailed plans of several urban sites (administrative centers) that allow us to reconstruct the context within which such a middle-class society and economy prospered. Geva's detailed study of Hazor VIII–VA, discussed above, shows distinct residential quarters of the city of 500 or so. The elite structures are near public buildings or in locations of prime real estate. The center, however, is a cluster of small, crowded residences where the middle class lived. Some houses show evidence for oil or wine production, others for weaving. The large storehouses are evidence for redistribution of food supplies.

At Tell en-Naṣbeh, Zorn and Brody summarized evidence for diversified households and means of production, as well as storehouses, silos, and other facilities that would have played a role in the economy. At Beersheba, Singer-Avitz documented several different quarters: a governor's residence, barracks for soldiers and their families, storehouses, shops, an elite quarter possibly for military officers, and a probable shrine.[63]

At Samaria alone we have ample evidence for many of the above professions—perhaps half, if we use a bit of imagination and carry the interpretation of the material culture data to its fullest extent. The dozens of ostraca from Samaria provide fascinating textual confirmation for a number of professions. These are notices of deliveries of commodities, mainly oil and wine, to the palace, presumably in payment of taxes in kind (or, alternatively, to the credit of absentee landowners). These cryptic notes were probably meant to serve as rough drafts for more official papyrus documents, which of course have not survived. On the basis of even a cursory glance, the Samaria ostraca alone would document: a centralized administration, a palace economy, a landed gentry including noble families and royal retainers, absentee estate owners, a hierarchy of rural settlements, a middle class of entrepreneurs, tenant farmers or peasants, freemen, viniculturists, oil producers, road builders, transhippers, accountants (or tax collectors), and storehouse officials.

The Samaria ostraca thus offer us rare, detailed, personal insights into the society and the economy of the eighth century. They would not have been unique, however, and similar documents in the thousands must once have existed.[64] From these documents we can derive a picture of a stratified society in which wealthy landowners acquired and managed large estates, employed numbers of people in various occupations, and prospered sufficiently to pay taxes in kind. It is tempting to see this scenario in terms of land grants to noble families from the state authorities, perhaps with family members serving reciprocally in the administration. (The evidence of corruption will be discussed below.)

The middle-class entrepreneurs whom we have characterized were fairly numerous, to judge from the varied evidence we have of town and city life. They might have made up 15–20 percent of the population. Yet as we have seen, some 80 percent of the population in ancient Israel and Judah lived in the rural areas—villages, hamlets, and farmsteads. Here there must also have been some of the professions that we have noted. For the most part, however, we see a simpler, less stratified, more integrated society and economy. In many cases, the farmers and villagers were secure, relatively prosperous, perhaps in better health. These were not simple lower classes, much less a minority; they were the majority, the *real* ancient Israelites. Since we know these people best from the small towns, villages, and farms that we have surveyed, let us turn to that evidence to broaden our picture of social and economic structure.

We have dealt with overall town and village plans generally, but socioeconomic structure can be better documented by an analysis of house plans and thus of family structure, behavior, and function. It is universally recognized by archaeologists, ethnographers, and historians that domestic dwellings reflect the lifestyle of the lowest common denominator of society, the family. It is here—not in macro-economic theory—that we see the reality of everyday life, too often missed by biblical scholars (and even by many archaeologists).

The "Israelite house" has been analyzed in detail by many scholars since Shiloh's groundbreaking study in 1973 (which coined the term). Of particular importance is a series of pioneering studies by Faust in collaboration with Bunimovitz. A recent volume on household archaeology also features useful essays by several archaeologists.[65]

Distinct houses that characterize the early Israelite village continue in use throughout the monarchy. Often considered stereotypical and therefore a clue to Israelite ethnicity and socioeconomic structure, they have often been described (following Shiloh) as "four-room" or "Israelite" houses. There are, however, numerous problems with this terminology. For one thing, the "rooms" really consist of a central courtyard, plus a u-shaped bank of several smaller rooms. Many houses are three-room structures. There are, however, two consistent features in nearly all cases: the central courtyard and monoliths, or stacked stone pillars (sometimes load-bearing walls), that set off the side rooms and presumably supported a roof and second story (below). Therefore, we shall use the term *pillar-courtyard house* here. The ethnic implications will be discussed presently.

The recent emphasis on household archaeology has produced several studies on food production, particularly the roles of women in grinding grain, baking bread, brewing beer, and weaving. The typical Iron Age pillar-courtyard house would have been well adapted for these and other domestic activities, with its courtyard and tabûn ovens, ample storage areas, and upstairs rooms for looms and other equipment. Several studies have also amplified our understanding of animal husbandry, much of it done by women and girls, and also agricultural practices that followed the seasons of nature. Wheat and barley, olives, grapes, and a few other fruits and vegetables were the bulk of the diet, along with sheep and goat milk and by-products. Meat was consumed only rarely. From all appearances, food production was carried out largely at the domestic level, and it changed only slightly over the entire Iron Age in a society and economy that was fundamentally agrarian.[66]

The houses discussed here are vernacular houses, constructed with native materials, consisting of mud-brick walls above a low stone foundation, usually some 24–30 inches wide, but sometimes only 18–24 inches wide. Several courses of mud-bricks about 1 foot square were laid up to the intended height, then plastered with mud and lime. Roof beams were covered with twigs and mud. The thick yet slightly resilient mud-brick walls could support a second story, where the rooms were small and rested on the partition walls and pillars below. The roof of the first story served as the floor of the upper story, which was then similarly roofed, the mud plaster renewed periodically (as we know from stone roof-rollers sometimes found in the debris).

Most scholars presume a second story, where the family's living quarters were. The first- floor side rooms off the courtyard, often cobbled for mucking them out and sometimes featuring stone mangers, would have made good stables. The back room would have been used for storing foodstuffs, various supplies, and a few tools. The second-story rooms, of the same size and configuration, would have been used as sleeping quarters and as common areas for eating, socializing, and the like (fig. 5.30).The evidence for an upper story consists of several facts. (1) The first-floor side rooms, when the contents of the house are well preserved (as in a sudden destruction), are found filled with dozens of pottery vessels, mostly store jars and other objects for daily use. The courtyard, a food-preparation and cooking area, often contains a *tabûn* (oven), as well as cooking pots, grindstones, and other utensils. There would have been little or no room for people to sleep on the ground floor. (2) One bank of the side rooms is typically set off from the courtyard with pillars, stone monoliths a foot or so square and 5–6 feet high. These monoliths could weigh half a ton or so. They certainly would not have been set so laboriously in place simply to support the roof of a one-story house. They served not only to set off the animal stalls from the central courtyard, but also to support the inner walls of the upper story. Again, the first floor, with animals in the stables, would have been unsuitable as living quarters. (3) Where careful excavation has been done, remains of the upper story, of pottery and objects found there, and the roof above have been observed in the collapsed debris of ruined houses. Of course, not all houses necessarily had a second story, and a second story could have been only partial. (4) Finally, external stairs have been found at a number of sites.

The principal uncertainty concerns the central courtyard: Was it roofed or not? Many scholars think that it was, but that does not seem likely. For one thing, the smoke from dung fires in an enclosed space, even with an open entrance, would have been suffocating. Furthermore, roofing some of these courtyards would have required wooden beams up to 20 feet long, difficult if not impossible to obtain. Finally, where the roof collapse in some houses has been well recorded and published, it shows

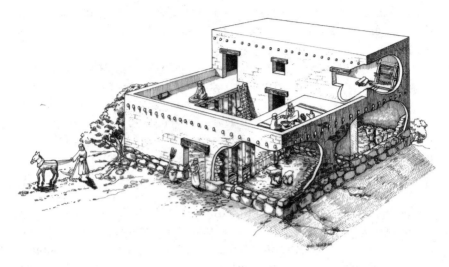

Fig. 5.30. Reconstruction of a typical Iron Age Israelite/Judahite house (drawing by Giselle Hasel)

the fallen remains mostly over the side rooms, not the central courtyard. It is important to note that, if this interpretation is correct, the typical calculation of living space used to estimate family size should be reduced by about one-fourth.

Not only is the typical house terminology imprecise; so is the notion of second-story living space. Few scholars specify whether they are counting one or both stories; here we shall use the term for the upper story only. The concept of living space for our pillar-courtyard houses is largely dependent on ethnographic studies and demographic data, both in latter-day Palestinian villages and in villages in Iran and elsewhere. It is from those data that archaeologists calculate family size, using the plan and function of these peasant villages.

By general consensus, the size of a nuclear family is estimated at no more than five. That is a lower figure than formerly, because infant mortality and early childhood death must be taken into account: we have a father, mother, and two or three surviving children. These data suggest further that about 100 square feet (or 10 square meters) of living space is required for each person. By measuring the size of a typical courtyard house (the upper story, minus the courtyard area), we can then estimate family size.[67]

Older excavations, while they may have recovered large parts of a town or village plan, were deficient in stratigraphy and were often badly published. More recent excavations and reanalysis of the older data have shed much light on the Israelite and Judahite pillar-courtyard houses of the Iron Age.

Some of the best studies focus specifically on the eighth-century Stratum 3 at Tell en-Naṣbeh, where the old excavations cleared 67 percent of the mound and yields data that can now be better quantified. Zorn has reworked the stratigraphy so as to yield important information on demography, family size, and socioeconomic structure. He was able to show that twenty-three pillar-courtyard houses whose plan and contents could be reasonably reconstructed average 625 square feet (although some were up to 900 square feet or more). Assuming a slightly smaller family size than others (4.5), he calculated that the two hundred or so houses at Tell en-Naṣbeh would yield a population of 900. If one utilized instead the total built-up area of 8 acres, the population would have been 800. The comparison of different methods yields very similar results, so the relative figures may be reliable.[68]

Brody, working directly from the original Tell en-Naṣbeh field diaries and the stored material, attempted to reconstruct the contents of a block of five buildings sharing common walls along a street, comprising (he thought) sixteen rooms (fig. 5.31). Three-room pillar-courtyard houses, with the pillars down the center, were the most common type. Because the stone foundations were sometimes under 30 inches wide, Brody argued that they were too flimsy to have supported a second story, an interpretation that is difficult to defend (above). He took the ground floor to be the only living space. In trying to put pots back into their original (?) context, he found that their numbers varied from two or three in a room to more than 40 (plus other domestic objects). But the percentages of ceramic types varied considerably from room to room, a statistic that Brody used to define certain areas as kitchens, eating areas, and the like.

Individual courtyards were not always apparent, so Brody took them to have been shared by several families. Thus he interpreted the sixteen adjacent rooms in this block of buildings as the residence of an extended family consisting of three nuclear families (some fifteen people?). The three clear three-room houses in the complex were then thought to have been occupied by these three families; the remaining buildings were common space.[69]

If one looks closely at Brody's block of buildings, however, such a division is not all that clear. It is possible to see two nearly identical three-room houses, another one less evident, one large open courtyard, and a

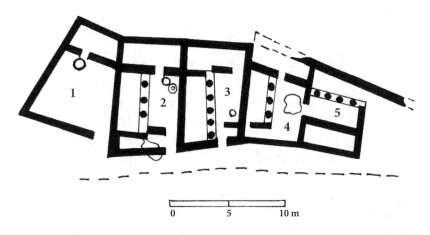

Fig. 5.31. A row of structures at Tell en-Naṣbeh Stratum 3. 1: open courtyard with a stone basin; 2: three-room house with olive-processing vat, basin, and opening to a cistern; 3: threeroom house with vat; 4: three-room house with cistern; 5: adjoining structure, perhaps a stable or for storage; 6: winding street (Brody 2011, fig. 1)

few outbuildings. Other than the differing inventory of the contents of various rooms (not fully reconstructable), there is little reason to see this complex as anything other than the residences of several nuclear families. Brody does not discuss family size, but he seems to adopt the typical estimate of five. His interpretation of house plans may be questionable, but his attempt at inventories is quite valuable.[70]

Faust has done the most innovative recent work on Iron Age socioeconomic structure, particularly in a series of articles on rural villages and farmsteads, then later in a full-scale publication. It was he who first pointed out an average size difference in rural and urban dwellings. The former are larger (ca. 1,300–1,400 square feet) and more ad hoc, and they probably housed an extended family of ten to fifteen people. The urban houses, by contrast, averaging 730–960 square feet, tend to be divided into more smaller rooms, up to eight. These, according to Faust, typically housed a nuclear family of five or six. As he puts it:

> The difference in size between urban and rural four-room houses seems to be a result neither of function (e.g., agricultural needs of the rural populations) nor of circumstance (e.g., more free ground for building in villages than cities). Rather, it is a faithful reflection of the different social units comprising the urban vs. rural sectors of Israelite society

during the Iron Age. On the one hand, the comparatively small size of the urban four-room houses support the common view that they housed nuclear families.... On the other hand, the large size of the rural houses indicates that they housed extended (better: joint) families of at least three generations.[71]

Faust thus sees the difference between rural and urban house size as reflecting both function (i.e., family size) and status. Larger rural houses reflect the need of farm families for more hands—an extended, multigenerational family, including perhaps servants. These are not, however, "lower-class" dwellings. Farm families may be less stratified, more equalitarian, yet at the same time quite prosperous. Urban dwellings may be smaller because they house mostly nuclear families. Yet the small size may conceal wide differences in social standing, welfare, and economic well-being, since urban life tends to be more complex and more favorable to entrepreneurship and thus fosters socioeconomic stratification. Most families functioned as nuclear families, but upper-class families might have had not only larger houses but also larger families.[72]

Schloen followed Stager's pioneering 1985 article on the archaeology of the family, expanding on the model of patrimonialism. For Schloen the extended family, the biblical *bêt 'āb*, is not only the ideal; is the reality in the Iron Age. He argues that Faust's proposed urban-nuclear/rural-extended dichotomy does not exist. The larger houses are not indicative of such a distinction, much less of social class, but simply reflect family size, and smaller houses in urban areas are the result only of restricted space as the population expanded within the confines of the city wall. Schloen's conclusion, after doing his own tabulation of houses at Tell Beit Mirsim, Tell en-Naṣbeh, and Tell el-Far'ah, is that ancient Israel and Judah show a "strong preference for extended families" (i.e., "joint" families) in both rural and urban areas. He proposes that two-thirds of families may have been nuclear but that one-third were typically extended, which would work out to about one-half of the population, given the usual coefficients of living space–family size. The nuclear family would have included four or five individuals; the extended, multigeneration (or joint) family compound would have included fifteen to twenty people.[73]

Singer-Avitz has reanalyzed the plan of Stratum II at Beersheba, somewhat better excavated but also incompletely published. She was able to distinguish three distinct areas of occupation, based on both size and type of residence, as well as comparison of inventories of pottery and artifacts, which were similar but not identical. Eleven four-room houses between the city wall and the outer ring road (the Western Quarter) averaged 650–850 square feet. The back rooms were incorporated into the casemate city wall. These houses would presumably have been barracks for soldiers stationed there and perhaps their families, as suggested by the large number of store jars, cooking pots, grindstones, ovens, and loom weights found (mostly in the front courtyard). Singer-Avitz thinks that these courtyards were roofed, and the common presence of stairs confirms that there was a second story.

The northwestern, northern, and southern quarters of Stratum II feature three-room houses that are somewhat larger. Here there was less evidence for food preparation, suggesting that these were storage rather than residential buildings. The plan of the central quarter was quite different, featuring neither three- nor four-room structures. Located near the gate, and with a smaller corpus of pottery and objects, these may have been more public in character, perhaps guesthouses. In the southern quarter, a large structure with a plaza adjoining the gate has been interpreted as a governor's residence.

Singer-Avitz sees the differences between these residential quarters as primarily functional rather than reflecting socioeconomic distinctions. That would suit our view of Beersheba as a barracks town (which she does not suggest). But a few larger or elite structures, plus the presence of high-ranking military personnel and administrative officers, indicate at least a few elites.[74]

Schloen's model, while sophisticated, does not explain all of the data. For one thing, where we have adequate town and city plans, his ratio of two-thirds smaller houses and one-third larger houses does not work out. At the three sites he surveys, most houses fall within a rather narrow size range (square feet): Tell el-Farʿah: 160–320; Tell en-Naṣbeh: 350–750; and Tell Beit Mirsim: 480–750. Furthermore, Schloen risks the same functionalist or reductionist fallacy for which he criticizes others. Socioeconomic stratification is virtually denied, since his "patrimonial lineages" supposedly dominated all aspects of society, both rural and urban. That would seem to carry a useful theoretical model (somewhat dependent on biblical texts) too far.

Previous studies paid inadequate attention to one of the best-excavated Iron IIB houses we have: House 1727 at Shechem (see fig. 5.17 above). A description of the house and a rough list of its contents is relevant here. Apart from two side galleries (later additions), the house is a typical four-room or pillar-courtyard house, circa 680 square feet in size. The central courtyard was a work area; the two rooms on each side, partly cobbled, and the back room were stables and storage areas. Here meticulous excavation proved that there had been a second story, which collapsed inward in the destruction in 732. The upper five or six rooms would have been the residential quarters for varying domestic activities (as shown by loom weights found there). The living space of circa 680 square feet would have accommodated a typical nuclear family of five or so persons quite nicely. The living space would have been reduced, however, if the central court area had been open. In studies of House 1729 at Shechem, Campbell and Holladay argued that the central courtyard was roofed, but the observations on roof-fall by the Shechem architect G. R. H. Wright (followed by G. E. Wright) suggest otherwise.[75]

We now have an even better example of an eighth-century pillar-courtyard house, this one destroyed with nearly all its contents in 701. House F7 at Tel Ḥalif was carefully excavated and recorded, so it can be faithfully reconstructed. The inventory, presumably complete, is revealing.[76]

Fig. 5.32. Contents of House F7 at Tel Ḥalif

Item	Number	Item	Number
storage jars	19	hammerstones	6
jugs	6	ballistae	1
decanters	3	crucibles	1
amphora	2	whetstones	1
amphoriskoi	1	stone disks	3
flasks	2	stone weights	4
juglets	9	jar stoppers	2
kraters	9	knives	1
bowls	13	arrowheads	3
mortaria	1	nails/rods	1
plates	1	spindle whorls	1
cooking pots	3	spatulas	1

cooking jugs	2	beads	2
lamps	6	seals	1
scoops	1	bullae	1
strainers	1	shells	1
funnels	1	horn cores	1
stands	2	figurines	6
pestles	2	grinders	6
miscellaneous stone	3	clay loom weights	7

Drawing on the extensive presentation and analysis of the nearly complete inventory of this house in Hardin's study, we may summarize the data from House F7 as follows:

Room 4: open courtyard; circa 200 square feet; probably stable
Room 5: probably roofed; circa 230 square feet; food preparation
Room 3: roofed; circa 200 square feet; multipurpose
Room 2: roofed; circa 140 square feet; multipurpose and cult
Room 1: roofed; circa 65 square feet; storage

If House F7 consisted of only a ground floor, the total living space would be about 865 square feet, including the open courtyard, or about 665 without it, that is, roofed living space if the courtyard was open (above). The Naroll coefficient of one person per 10 square meters of living space (or ca. 105 square feet per person) would yield a family unit of nine or ten persons for the larger floor space, or six persons for the smaller floor space. The latter is close to the size of the nuclear family agreed upon by nearly all scholars today, based largely on ethnographic data. Adding the presumed upper roofed story, however, would give us anywhere from 1,300 to 1,700 square feet, providing for an extended family of between 13 and 17 people (below). The latter fits the biblical description of the *bêt 'āb*, the "house of the father," in Stager's view consisting of a man, a woman, perhaps two or three surviving children; a married son, a wife, and a child or two; perhaps even a servant—in total, ten or more people (below).

House F7 at Tel Ḥalif fits Faust's description of a rural extended family:

Based on the size of dwellings in the rural settlement, it seems quite probable that the large structures housed extended families. A family

of this type could include father, mother, married sons and their children, unmarried daughters, unmarried aunts, additional relatives who
for various reasons remained to dwell in the structure or moved into it,
and possibly also servants, slaves, and additional affiliated individuals
(along with animals). In rural sites where a relatively large number of
structures were uncovered, major differences among the structures were
not discerned, and most of them were of similar area and architectural
characteristics.[77]

Here we classified Tel Ḥalif as a tier 4 town (3 acres), but the size of House
F7 makes it possibly more an urban than a rural dwelling. In size, the
living space (clearly the upper floor) would fall toward the upper range of
urban houses: some 650 square feet if the lower courtyard were roofed and
thus usable as floor space. That fits within the estimated 320–750 square
feet for urban houses and/or nuclear families. However, Hardin concludes:

> The F7 dwelling was perhaps occupied by a small extended family that
> included the father, mother, and unwed children as well as the wedded
> sons and their wives and children, and possibly even unwed paternal
> aunts and sometimes even unwed paternal uncles. It also is possible that
> slaves were brought into the dwelling. Two living rooms were suggested
> for the F7 dwelling (Room 2, Room 3: Areas B, C, and D), and it is possi-
> ble that more rooms of a similar type were present in a second floor. Even
> if this is not the case, 79 square meters of interior floor space provide a
> large living area (if the entire floor plan was covered). As is the domi-
> nant pattern in the Middle East, the group probably would have been
> patrilineal and patrilocal, and sons would have brought wives into the
> pillared dwelling. Marriage was most likely endogamous and inheritance
> partible as is common in extended household that are sedentary agricul-
> turalist practicing dry farming. When reconstructed in this manner, the
> occupants of the F7 dwelling—the archaeological household—are strik-
> ingly similar to the Arab extended household or the *za'ila*.[78]

Some degree of social stratification is indicated by the archaeological
data on dwellings, at least among the urban population (although a minority). Economic specialization is also evident from the various professions
that we have adduced. Some scholars (e.g., de Vaux) have tried to use differential house size as an indicator of social status (as at Tell el-Farʿah).
The fact, however, is that house size may be determined by many factors,
including the differences between nuclear and extended families, but also
location, availability of time and resources, and even the vagaries of choice.

Larger houses may be an indication of greater wealth and status, but not necessarily.

In the rural areas, however, we are dealing with a more homogeneous society and economy, more egalitarian and more exclusively focused on agro-pastoralism. Isolated farmers and villagers would necessarily have been mostly self-sustaining, cooperating to produce all the goods and services that they needed. Here the larger houses would likely indicate larger families, or extended families (above). We have good archaeological evidence of such a phenomenon in the farms that we have noted. Here we have terraces, cisterns, silos, storerooms, and presses for olives and grapes. All this suggests what Sahlins has called "the domestic mode of production," in contrast to a state-controlled economy. This has economic, social, and political implications. As Sahlins puts it, such a family-based community is "the tribal community in miniature—politically underwrit[ing] the conditions of society—society without a Sovereign."[79]

This domestic mode of production seems to have characterized villages and smaller towns, but a number of more urban houses also feature oil- and wine-producing installations. Even quasi-industrial production, such as pot making and weaving that went beyond cottage industry, was designed mostly for local consumption. Here, too, the economy was probably not controlled by the central authorities, even if some of its production went for trade or taxes.

Several recent studies of typical Iron Age Israelite and Judahite houses go beyond identifying socioeconomic structure to deal with more specific aspects of ideology and even ethnic identity. Faust and Bunimovitz, in particular, have used socioanthropological theory and cross-cultural comparisons to push the older notion of the Israelite-type house to more sophisticated levels. Assuming that basic house style (our pillar-courtyard house) is indeed typical of Iron II sites that are indisputably Israelite, they have argued that such houses embody a set of identifiable ideals, a shared ethos. This would include universal values that would cut across lines of class, gender, wealth, profession, or social status—a sort of distinctively Israelite mentality, or what we may regard as ethic self-identity.[80] Skeptics, of course, would vehemently deny any such possibility, largely because influenced by postmodernist notions they typically assert that ethnicity is too complex, too subjective, too "fluid" to be identified with material culture, that is, archaeological remains. We shall return presently to the problem of ethnicity.

After a survey of extensive literature, Faust declares that "the present skeptical approach regarding the ability of archaeology to tackle the question of ethnicity is unwarranted." We have simply failed to utilize to the fullest the unparalleled data base that we now have in the archaeology of the southern Levant. In the archaeological record Faust sees several aspects of culture (i.e., ethnicity) in such consistent patterns as house form and function, foodways, certain styles of pottery, burial customs, and an "ethos of simplicity." All these and many other features of Iron Age material culture began early, and they continued as part of "boundary maintenance" during Israel's ethnogenesis.[81]

Dar, who has done extensive survey and excavation in rural Samaria, summarizes the rural society and economy very well.

> The study of twelve tracts belonging to ancient villages in western Samaria makes it possible to sketch the structure of the typical agricultural holding predominating in this mountainous rockbound region. The agricultural economy of western Samaria was based on viticulture and wine production, the growing of olives and the extraction of their oil, the cultivation of cereals and animal husbandry. Auxiliary branches such as lime manufacture and stone quarrying were almost certainly among the region's sources of livelihood. Agriculture was intensive, and exploited every slope and valley to build terraces which were converted to arable and plantations of every size and possible type. Canals and pits were cut among the rocky areas, and in these, various varieties of fruit trees were planted. Every patch of soil was exploited, and sharp gradients or steep slopes did not deter the cultivators from making them part of their agricultural economy. Rainwater and runoff were collected and stored; attempts were made to spread surpluses among the terraces which constituted the main seed-beds in the hill farming of western Samaria.[82]

Dar concludes that a family plot of some 6–10 acres devoted to mixed agriculture could provide a decent livelihood as well as the satisfaction of independence and pleasant surroundings in the open villages and spacious houses. There would even have been a surplus for trade. This, then, was the good life—reflected in the biblical ideal if not always in actual practice.

These material reflections of ethnic behavior are not, of course, unique to Israelite society, any more than the much-discussed collar-rim store jars or four-room houses are. What is most significant is the *combination* of these cultural elements, as well as their consistency across social classes and over a long time span. Many of these ethnic markers are most easily identifiable at the fundamental level of the family, since Israel and Judah were essentially rural societies. Thus we have surveyed domestic houses in some detail.

One aspect of family life has received due attention only recently in the archaeology of the southern Levant: the roles of women. That default is largely due to the fact that the discipline has traditionally been dominated by males, who have been more interested (like biblicists) in the presumably larger issues of political history—the literary Great Tradition that emphasizes the deeds of great men and public events. Thus earlier archaeologists favored the excavation of large tells and urban centers, bringing to light monumental city walls and gates, palaces and temples, elite structures, large-scale production, all reflecting long-term macro-social and -political processes.

A more recent social archaeology—the archaeology of the *family*—is changing all that, led in many cases by women archaeologists and outspoken feminist scholars, both women and men. Among the principals are archaeologists such as Carol Meyers, Michelle Daviau, Beth Alpert Nakhai, Laura Mazow, Jennie Ebeling, Lily Singer-Avitz, and others.[83]

Their publications have focused more on smaller towns and villages, particularly on a broader spectrum of archaeological data that illuminate domestic life, gender roles, household production, individual status, and even the role of women in the larger socioeconomic sphere. The result is that we can now see for the first time the active, multifaceted roles that women in ancient Israel and Judah played—roles long obscured by the one-sided biblical portrayal and long overlooked by both archaeologists and biblical scholars.

If Israelite/Judahite society was centered on the family, women would have been the child-bearers and principal care-givers, often the custodians of family and communal traditions. They would also have been the basic providers: tending animals, storing foodstuffs, grinding grain and baking bread, preparing the family's food, weaving, and making clothes. In particular, they would have served as the real ritual experts, tending family shrines and leading rites of worship, the "religion of hearth and home." All this focused not on national cult or on orthodox theology, "book religion," but rather on the *practice* of religion as the ultimate concern, survival and the security of plenty (the older notion of fertility). These newly documented roles of women are all related to the basically agrarian nature of the ancient Israelite/Judahite society and economy, rural and family-based.

At a macro-level—the analysis of Israelite ideology based on urban and especially political life—there is greater complexity and thus less cohesiveness. Nevertheless, what we have called an agrarian ideology and set of values is reflected there as well, although perhaps more as an ideal than in practice. The widespread adaptation of a basically rural house form—the ideal farmhouse—in an urban setting is but one manifestation of this cultural unity and continuity.

It is at the state level that the Israelite society and economy would supposedly be seen most advantageously, but that is questioned here. In particular, how much did the state actually contribute overall? What degree of control, for instance, did it have over the society and economy? Here the archaeological evidence is not as clear as one would like, so there are legitimate differences of opinion.

Archaeologists dealing specifically with the economy in ancient Israel and Judah have been few and far between. A pioneering study by Holladay in 1995 has generally been neglected, perhaps because it was regarded as too speculative. Holladay did, however, adduce some persuasive archaeological evidence. He argued that the transformation from "acephalous society" to "nation-state" by the Iron II period required a managed economy that involved royal constructions, larger-scale industry, intensified agriculture, a military, long-distance trade, taxation, and the accumulation of wealth by the ruling classes. In particular, Holladay drew attention to the importance of trade with Phoenicia and South Arabia, for which we have some evidence, even if it has been neglected. Despite the existence of considerable state control, he does not think that ancient Israel overall had a redistributive economy. The private sector continued to control much of the means of production until the end of the monarchy, and much of the wealth was in family hands. As Holladay puts it: "It is easy to infer the nuclear family as the basic economic module of the society, and agrarian activity as the dominant element of the economy." A leading Israeli archaeo-botanist has underlined this view, stressing that throughout the settlement period and the monarchy the "household maintained a survival subsistence strategy rather than a market-oriented strategy."[84]

In several later publications Holladay developed the idea of a "smoothly-running, all-pervasive, silver-based market system" in which vast resources were available through state-sponsored trade, especially camel caravan trade with South Arabia. His evidence, however, is derived largely from texts, primarily the biblical and the Neo-Assyrian texts describing large tributes. Holladay thinks that these texts are to be read literally. Thus Hezekiah's tribute to Sennacherib in 701, stripped from the temple, works out to about 1 ton of gold and 24 tons of silver—which he thinks was actually paid. He calculates that the average Israelite family could have been assessed some 50 sheqels, and they were able to pay taxes in one way or another. He goes on to state that, "by the time of Israelite state formation, the entire Levant would appear to have either been on a silver economy … or a more directly monetary choice for people with more gold than silver." There would thus have been a redistributive economy, with officials paid in silver. At the family level, reciprocity (barter) would have been a minor element.[85]

Scholen also emphasizes the economic role of the family, but in his case the family is larger—an extended patrimonial family, in effect a clan. This patrimonial society is such a powerful model in Scholen's work that it leads him to deny the rural–urban dichotomy that most scholars assume: both were patrimonial societies. Schloen thinks, moreover, that there were no real social inequalities between rural and urban groups. In Schloen's view, there was little room for the state; ruling families took its place. As Schloen puts it, there was no "depersonalized exchange" until the Assyrians and Babylonians disrupted the system, after its successful operation for some five or six centuries. Schloen's analysis is sophisticated in theory, but it raises several questions. If most ordinary people were clients of his patrimonial families, is this *not* social inequality? Further, are these ruling families not in turn clients themselves of the state? Schloen seems to envision a sort of "primitive democracy" driven by a king of a market economy. That may be the biblical ideal, but is does not accord well with the reality (below).[86]

One corpus of ninth- (?) or eighth-century inscriptions provides us a rare glimpse into the realities of socioeconomic life in the Iron II period: the 102 ostraca found in the excavations of Samaria in 1916 and 1931–1935. Many of the inscribed potsherds were found in fills under the floor of a later building dubbed the Ostraca House by the earlier excavators or even in later deposits. Thus they are not necessarily in situ in this late eighth-century building, evidently destroyed in the Assyrian destructions in 732. Dating formulae on the texts themselves refer to years 9, 10, and 15 of some king, but no one is named. Thus they can be assigned to the reign of either Joash (805–790) or of Jeroboam II (790–750).

The ostraca record shipments, principally of quantities of oil and wine, to a royal storehouse in Samaria. The disputed *le* prefix—"granted to," "with respect to," "for," "by"—would then denote resident landed gentry, absentee owners who had been granted estates in the nearby countryside and who received regular shipments by managers designated "from." These shipments recorded either profits from the estates or perhaps taxes paid in kind, in which case the designation "to" means paid not to the owners but to the royal tax accountants. Whoever the recipients were, the ostraca were probably working copies that were discarded after the notations were transferred to papyrus records, which, of course, have not survived. The political and socioeconomic implications of the Samaria ostraca have been discussed elsewhere (above). The point here is that by the early eighth century detailed recordkeeping was a mundane activity, well established and accepted, carried out by an efficient bureaucracy and a professional scribal guild.[87]

The most thorough analysis of the ancient Israelite–Judahite economy, well versed in economic theory, the biblical texts, and much of the archaeological data, is Nam's *Portraits of Economic Exchange in the Book of Kings* (2012). In a discussion of the development of modern economic theory since Marx and Weber, he summarizes two views that still prevail in scholarly debates. (1) Formalist (or positivist) economics tends toward emphasizing scientific mechanisms disembodied from social relations and individual initiative, favoring instead capitalist money markets or supply-and-demand effects that appear to satisfy individuals but not necessarily their real wants or needs. (2) By contrast, Polanyi (who elaborated the distinction) located economic reality more in the social arena operating through what he termed three mechanisms: reciprocity, redistribution, and market exchange, all of which could be very complex. Polanyi's early nineteenth-century attempt to apply these to ancient Near Eastern societies had considerable influence, although it was largely neglected by biblicists.

Nam sets out deliberately to apply Polanyi's substantives theories to ancient Israel and Judah in the Iron Age. He disavows Holladay's exaggerated claims for state control, based on the textual evidence, and he looks more toward the archaeological evidence of large state-sponsored projects such as defenses, storage facilities, and water systems, as well as ostraca and seals. He admits, however, that whether the state could have financed such projects is unclear. We can only posit the existence of "some level of market exchange," possibly regulated supply-and-demand, thus forming "an integrated economy." Perhaps it was held together by the old traditions of kinship bonds, loyalty, and honor.

One thing is clear: the centralized urban development and monumental building projects in Iron IIA–B had to be paid for somehow. Although we have scant direct evidence of taxation (the Samaria ostraca above), it must have existed. In addition, a form of corvée conscription would have been necessary to supply labor for these massive public projects.[88]

Faust takes a middle-of-the-road view. He notes considerable archaeological evidence of state control, citing the system of weights and measures, the existence of royal estates, the common public storage facilities, and the evidence of managed trade in the Samaria and Arad ostraca. Overall, the family—the agrarian society—represents the fundamental economic level, yet it must have been integrated somehow into higher levels. To accommodate such arrangements Faust develops a three-tier economic system:

1. A *private economy* characterized by both nuclear and extended families who operated independently.
2. A *lineage economy* that dominated in the rural sector through extended families and clans.
3. A *state* economy at the highest level.[89]

Some of the best evidence for a state-controlled economy does indeed come from the standardized sheqel weights and the royal stamped jar handles. But since these came into use only at the end of the late eighth century, in anticipation of the Sennacherib invasion in 701, we shall defer discussion until chapter 6.

Technology

Much of the archaeological evidence for our next subsystem, technology, has been discussed above. For instance, the emergence of urbanism and the state was made possible only by many technological advances, then in turn it encouraged them further. All of the several dozen professions listed above on socioeconomic structure presuppose technological developments far beyond those seen in the Iron I villages. A few specific examples of such changes will suffice.

The areas of architecture and city planning see great advances in the ninth century. Both the administrative centers and the cities that we have discussed exhibit sophisticated engineering concepts and the mastery of monumental architecture that go well beyond anything seen in the tenth century. The ashlar masonry is especially fine: nothing later ever equaled that in the palace at Samaria. Linking these well-planned towns and cities was an elaborate system of roads.[90]

The ingenious water systems found at a number of sites will not be surpassed until the Roman period. The massive city walls and multiple-entryway gates are marvels of engineering and construction skills. Chariot warfare alone of military technology would rank Israel and Judah as advanced states capable of confronting the powerful Assyrian military machine. At a more mundane level, the intensification of agricultural production required a formidable array of skills in terrace building, in runoff irrigation, in the construction of storage facilities, and in the development of transport systems. A number of other industries will be discussed below in connection with art. All show impressive technological developments.

Metalworking in both bronze and iron now exhibits technological improvements. We have well cast and finished bronze spears, daggers, armor scales, arrowheads, knives, spatula, awls, needles, pins, and other small domestic utensils. The most splendid artifacts are the scepter head and bowl from Dan. The copper for making bronze appears to have come from mines in the Arabah, which reveal an astonishingly productive industry from the tenth century onward. Kilns have not been found, but they must have existed to judge from ceramic tuyeres that we have.

The iron industry is more difficult to document because iron implements are brittle and easily broken, and even in the best of circumstances they rust away and are not preserved. We do have, however, some heavy agricultural tools such as plow points. To judge from the exceptionally well-dressed ashlar masonry found at many sites, as well as carved Proto-Aeolic capitals, there were iron tools, hammers, and chisels. Iron-working installations existed already at Dan and elsewhere in the tenth century. In Strata 3–2 at Beth-Shemesh of the ninth–eighth century, the largest and most advanced ironworks ever found this early in the Near East had an enormous production capacity. The iron ore may have come from the Wadi Wardeh in Transjordan.[91] Gold working is only scantily represented, due to gold's scarcity, but we do have a few fine examples of gold jewelry.

It is in ceramic production that we see Iron II technology in its most common form. (1) By the ninth–eighth century the ceramic corpus is represented by many more forms than the typical tenth-century corpus of store jars, cooking pots, and jugs (fig. 5.33). Now there are dozens of new forms. (2) The streaky red slip and hand burnish on Iron I and IIA vessels is now replaced by heavier slips and more carefully done wheel-burnishing (or spiral burnishing). (3) The repertoire contains more specialized vessels, such as can be seen in the typical repertoires of both north and south. (4) The quality and the sheer quantity of Iron IIB pottery indicates that mass production has now entirely replaced the older cottage industry of women potters in the Iron I villages. Many homes in villages and towns probably still made their own pottery, but there must have been factories in the larger towns and cities where men produced large quantities of standardized wares, possibly under state control. The finest wares without doubt are the well-known ninth-century Samaria luxury wares, which skillfully imitate Phoenician pottery. The chalky clay is finely levigated, with no inclusions (almost like porcelain), the ware eggshell thin and fired in a high-temperature kiln. The dark red slip is artfully removed to create creamy decorative bands. This pottery, as much as any archaeological evidence we have, documents both technological progress and the creation of a distinctive Israelite ceramic corpus that reflects growing national identity. Nevertheless, some of the southern or Judahite distinctions noted in chapter 4 continued, seen, for instance, in such forms as the so-called water decanters.[92]

Improvements in technology are seen in other manufactured products, such as seals and ivory carvings, in the production of cultic items, and in writing materials. These, however, will be discussed elsewhere as aspects of art and religion.

Culture

The remaining subsystem embraces a variety of cultural expressions in material form that are difficult to categorize. This might simply be called culture (or aesthetics) and would consist of art and iconography, writing and literature, religion and ideology, and ethnicity. Of these categories, art and iconography may be taken as especially revealing.

Art and Iconography. Ancient Israel and Judah have usually been taken to be artistically impoverished, at least in comparison to other

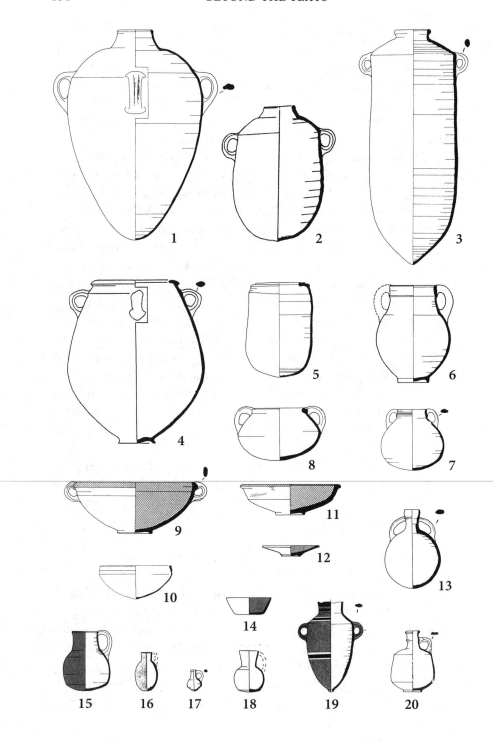

Fig. 5.33. A selection of eighth-century pottery. 1: store jar, Gezer VIA (Gitin 1990b, pl. 15:11); 2: store jar, Arad IX (Singer-Avitz 2002, fig. 36:4); 3: store jar, Gezer VIA (Gitin 1990b, pl. 16:5); 4: store jar, Lahav VIB (Hardin 2010, pl. 16:2); 5: store jar, Gezer VIA (Gitin 1990b, pl. 16:6); 6: jar, Arad IX (Singer-Avitz 2002, fig. 33:1); 7: cooking pot, Beersheba III (Aharoni 1973, pl. 60:78); 8: cooking pot, Arad VIII (Singer-Avitz 2002, fig. 37:12); 9: bowl, Gezer VIA (Gitin 1990b, pl. 20:21); 10: bowl, Lahav VIB (Hardin 2010, pl. 4:6); 11: bowl, Gezer VIA (Gitin 1990b, pl. 20:19); 12: plate, Lachish III (Ussishkin 2004, fig. 26.14:2); 13: flask, Beersheba III (Aharoni 1973, pl. 63:129); 14: bowl, Arad VIII (Singer-Avitz 2002, fig. 37:4); 15: jug, Beersheba III (Aharoni 1973, pl. 64:12); 16: juglet, Tell el-Ḥesi VII (Blakely and Hardin 2002, fig. 20:10); 17: juglet, Arad VIII (Singer-Avitz 2002, fig. 35:16); 18: jug, Lahav VIB (Hardin 2010, pl. 5:8); 19: amphora, Beersheba III (Aharoni 1973, pl. 67:1); 20: decanter, Beersheba III (Aharoni 1973, pl. 62:102)

cultures earlier and later in the ancient Near East. Yet recent studies—especially by the Freiburg school of Othmar Keel and his colleagues—have documented a modest but workmanlike repertoire of artistic works in several media.[93]

We have noted the hundreds of fragments of carved ivory inlays found at Samaria. They were discovered in the burnt debris of the Assyrian destruction but probably originated in the ninth century. They are exquisitely carved, sometimes inlaid with precious stones. They feature a number of iconographic motifs that identify them as belonging to the Phoenician or north Syrian style of ivory carving that is well known in the Iron Age. Many have drilled tabs for attaching them to wooden furniture. Further evidence for this use is provided by several ivory half-panels, obviously intended to be paired. While the wooden furniture has not survived in Israel, chairs from tombs at Salamis in Cyprus have been restored that show how the ivory panels were attached (fig. 5.34). The raw material may have been imported from Syria, where elephants were still extant in the Iron Age. Some have supposed that the ivory carvings themselves were imported from Syria, but it is quite possible that local artisans had mastered the technique. Only a few of these ivory carvings have been found outside the capital at Samaria, undoubtedly because such luxury items were expensive and thus rare.[94]

Another art form that was part of the international scene is gem carving, particularly to create seals for signet rings. In Iron I the iconography tends to be simplistic, mostly consisting of primitive stick figures and representing a parochial style. By the ninth century, however, we begin to have more elaborate designs, often of Egyptian and Syro-Phoenician deri-

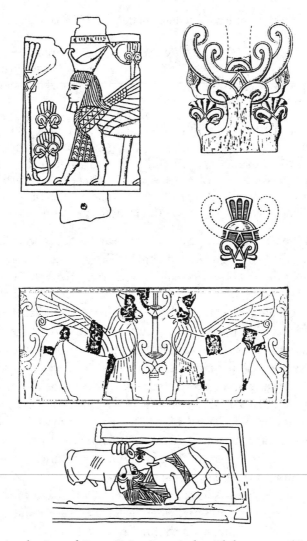

Fig. 5.34. A selection of Samaria ivories, ninth–eighth century (Crowfoot and
Crowfoot 1938, pls. 5, 6, 17)

vation—but nothing distinctively "Israelite." By the eighth century these
seals become quite common, with hundreds of them known. The names
and titles of the owners are of great significance, as well as the iconography,
but the craftsmanship should also be noted. These are very small gem-
stones, brittle and easily broken. Carving them required great patience and
skill, probably with some sort of chest-supported bow drill (and a crystal

lens?). The miniature scene and the writing had to be executed in reverse to make a signet ring. A slight slip would ruin the gem. These Israelite seals may have utilized imported materials and motifs, but most were probably locally made.

Dating the seals and documenting changes over the ninth–sixth century are difficult because more than two-thirds of the known examples here come from the black market and thus have neither documented provenience or context. Even excavated examples may be difficult to use, because seals were often heirlooms and may date decades or even centuries earlier than their find-spots. In general, however, it appears that Phoenician iconography typical in the ninth–eighth century gives way by the seventh century to seals with nothing but personal names, patronymics, and sometimes titles (fig. 5.35).[95]

Another form of carving is sculpture. Figural representations are lacking, especially any examples of life-size humans or animals. We do have, however, sculpted column bases and capitals from a number of sites, especially the so-called Proto-Aeolic capitals from monumental buildings at Samaria, Jerusalem, and a number of administrative centers (above). These capitals seem to anticipate later Greco-Roman Ionic capitals, imitating the crown and drooping fronds of the native palm trees (fig. 5.36). They are found also in Phoenicia (and at Phoenician sites in Cyprus). The vegetation motif goes far back in Mesopotamia, but its adaptation and development in Israel appear to be an aspect of native art.[96]

One unique artistic expression in stone is a deeply incised life-size hand accompanying an eighth-century stone tomb inscription found at Khirbet el-Qom (see below). It looks very much like the Islamic "Hand of Fatima" from centuries later, used to ward off bad luck. Since the inscription invokes the blessing of Yahweh upon the deceased, the hand may represent the extended hand of Yahweh (or, alternatively, the hand of the deceased).[97]

Work in clay went beyond the production of pottery that we have discussed under the rubric of technology. We have as many as three thousand human and animal figurines, most from the Iron II period. These terra-cottas are of several types, either handmade or cast in a mold, sometimes combining both techniques. Those representing humans (or deities; see below) consist of a few early free-form figurines or, more typically, a female holding a frame drum to her breast, a nude full-breasted female with a stylized pillar-shaped lower body and a mold-made head, or a

Fig. 5.35. Iron I and II seal impressions. 1: Khirbet el-Ahwat, eleventh century BCE (Keel 1997, fig. 513:1); 2: Megiddo VIA (Keel and Uehlinger 1998, no. 144a); 3: Tell en-Naṣbeh, seventh century BCE, "Belonging to Jaazaniah, servant of the king" (McCarter 1996, no. 114); 4: Megiddo, uncertain provenience (Keel and Uehlinger 1998, no. 254b); 5: unknown provenience (Keel and Uehlinger 1998, no. 258c); 6: Lachish, uncertain provenience (Keel and Uehlinger 1998, no. 213); 7: unknown provenience, "Belonging to Yahmolyahu" (Keel and Uehlinger 1998, no. 274b); 8: Megiddo, uncertain provenience, "Belonging to Yermiyahu, son of GVS" (?) (Keel and Uehlinger 1998, no. 274d); 9: unknown provenience, "Yehuda. (Belonging to) Hezekiah (the son of) Ahaz the king" (Albertz and Schmitt 2012, no. 5.20); 10: Arad VII, seventh century BCE, "Belonging to 'Elyashib, son of 'Ashyahu" (Keel 1997, fig. 657:14); 11: unknown provenience, "Belonging to the king, mmšlt" (Keel and Uehlinger 1998, no. 276b); 12: unknown provenience (Keel and Uehlinger 1998, no. 288b)

Fig. 5.36. Types of Proto-Aeolic, or palmette, capitals. A: Samaria; B and C: Megiddo; D: Hazor; E: Ramat Raḥel (Barkay 1992, fig. 9.14)

crude handmade female figure with the eyes and nose represented only by a pinch of the fingers.

The drum-player figurines extend from the tenth century, where we have a mold for making them at Taʿanach, to the early sixth century; they are found both in Israel and Judah. The latter two types are often called Judean pillar-base figurines, because they are almost all confined to Judah in the late eighth–early sixth century, and the lower body consists of a pillar or stand with no anatomical features. We possess hundreds of the latter figurines, so common that many people must have possessed them. They are all of nude females. Whether they represent humans (i.e., votives) or a female deity is debated. In any case, they constitute a uniquely Israelite/Judahite art form, with no exact parallels in Philistia, Phoenicia, or Transjordan (see further ch. 6).

We also have Iron II animal figurines. Most are Judahite horse-and-rider representations, occasionally with only the horse, late eighth or seventh century in date. There are a few other terra-cotta animals, such as zoomorphic pouring vessels in the form of a bovine. Some of the few *kernoi*, or trick vessels, feature the head of a bovine or other animal (below).

By all accounts the most interesting piece of ancient Israelite art (although earlier) is a large square terra-cotta offering stand found in a tenth-century context at Taʿanach. The top register features a quadruped carrying a sun disc; the lower three registers and the sides portray winged lions or cherubim. Another stand, found long ago in the same locus by the German excavations, is festooned with bas relief lions. Most of the other Israelite or Judahite cult stands that we have are aniconic (below).

Faience, a glazed frit in a cobalt blue color, was used primarily for jewelry, beads, and pendants. We also have a number of faience amulets representing the Egyptian god Bes or the "Eye of Horus." Gaming pieces can also be made of faience, but they are quite ordinary in style.

Artistic works in bronze are rare, although bronze continued in use well into the Iron Age. We have noted the fine bronze bull from the Iron I period. From the Iron II high place at Dan we have a finely wrought priestly scepter head, as well as a splendid bronze bowl (above).

Painted works must have existed, but they scarcely survive. Some of the female figurines were once painted white, but the paint is fugitive. At Kuntillet ʿAjrud in the dry Sinai Desert, where preservation is good, several large store jars have painted scenes, including scenes of a tree flanked by two rampant ibexes; a lion; a procession of strangely garbed worshipers; a figure on a city wall; and an enigmatic half-nude female seated on a lion throne (below). Some think that a fragmentary painted mural depicts a male seated on a throne, possibly a king.[98]

Jewelry becomes more common now, mostly silver, although we have some earrings in gold and some semiprecious stones.

A final form of cultural expression is music, although its archaeological correlates are often not preserved or not recognized. Several recent studies, however, have sought to distinguish some artifacts that may be related to music and musical performance. Among these items are bronze cymbals, bone flutes, whistles, ceramic drums, and the female figurines apparently holding a frame drum (not a tambourine) to the breast. There have even been a few attempts to re-create versions of what ancient Israelite music may have sounded like, although obviously no musical notation has been preserved.[99]

It can no longer be maintained, whether on biblical or a priori grounds, that ancient Israel and Judah were lacking in artistic traditions. Israel's artistic traditions were indeed modest, especially in comparison with the preceding, sophisticated Late Bronze Age cultures of Canaan. Yet in comparison with Israel's Iron Age neighbors, it is clear that there were unique Israelite cultural expressions that merit attention. If they were usually restricted to the upper classes, the minority, that is unexceptional.

Writing and Literature. Another form of Israelite cultural expression, writing, has already been mentioned in dealing with state control. It could also be discussed under the rubric of technology, since it presumes the mastery of papyrus making. We have mentioned the scant inscriptional material we have from Iron I, especially the abecedaries, as well as a few tenth-century inscriptions. By the ninth century we have a bit more written material, then a relatively sudden upsurge in the eighth–seventh century. Most are inscriptions painted on sherds, but a few are incised.

The question of literacy and its origins is difficult, in large part because of the relative lack of inscribed remains. Most of our data come from the eighth–sixth century. The scarcity may be due to the rarity of writing in any medium before circa 800. On the other hand, we must confront the fact that the apparent scarcity may be due simply to the accidents of excavation, or more likely to the fact that many inscriptions would undoubtedly have been written on perishable materials such as parchment or papyrus. We have only one example of the latter, from dry caves near the Dead Sea. Even ostraca written with ink are perishable or may be unwittingly destroyed when excavated and cleaned carelessly. It has been shown that at sites where ostraca are dipped in water and examined before washing, many more inscribed ostraca tend to be recovered.[100]

One apparent problem is that Israel's neighbors produced monumental inscriptions as early as the ninth century, whereas we seem to have none from Israel or Judah. The well-known Mesha stela found in 1868 at Dhiban in Moab, ancient Dibon, is a case in point (fig. 5.37). It was intact when found by villagers, beautifully executed on a slab of black basalt, containing thirty-four lines in excellent lapidary script, complete with word dividers. It has no archaeological context, of course, but it can be confidently dated to the early ninth century both on paleographic grounds and by the fact that Mesha, the king of Moab, describes his conflicts with Ahab of Israel (ca. 873–852). The detailed descriptions of Mesha's pedigree, his monumental building projects, including a palace and city walls, his military exploits, and his diplomatic relations all attest to the fact that this is a royal inscription. The Siloam Tunnel inscription is our only example of a comparable Israelite/Judahite inscription (ch. 6).

Roughly contemporary is the Tel Dan stela, a mid-ninth-century royal Aramaic inscription (see above and fig. 5.38). Although found in secondary use as part of the eighth-century outer wall of the gate plaza, this large, beautifully executed stone slab must have once been a display inscription in the gate area. It is clearly dated to the mid-ninth century by references to King Joram of Israel (851–842), the grandson of Ahab, and King Ahaziah of Judah (843–842), the son of Jehoram. The stela relates the slaughter of these two kings by the Aramean king, evidently Hazael, in contrast to the claim of the biblical writers that they were killed by an Israelite commander named Jehu, at the instigation of prophets inspired by Yahwistic fervor against the heretical dynasty of Omri.

The reference to a "dynasty of David" (*bêt-dāwîd*) is a recognition of the influence of the Judahite royal house this far north by the ninth century. But the irony is that the only early royal inscription we have from ancient Israel is (1) written in Aramaic, not Hebrew; and (2) it celebrates the humiliating defeat of the northern kingdom. What if we happened to have the contemporary Israelite version (apart from the later and secondary biblical account)?

Whatever the explanation, if any, we have only one or two royal monumental inscriptions from ancient Israel or Judah. One is a fragment of the first line of a dressed stone stela from Samaria, inscribed in a lapidary script of the eighth century Unfortunately, only one word is preserved: *'ăšer*, the relative particle "which." What that word refers to is anyone's guess.[101]

There is another problem to be faced by the historian. We have good evidence of attempts to master the Proto-Canaanite alphabet, even of scribal schools, in the eleventh–tenth century: the 'Izbet Ṣarṭah and Tel Zafit ostraca and the Gezer Calendar. Yet we see little evidence of the expected further advance toward literacy by the ninth century. From that era we have only a few epigraphic discoveries except for one or two debatable ones, such as the seal of "Shema, servant of Jeroboam" found at Megiddo (possibly belonging to the era of Jeroboam II, ca. 790–750).

Fig. 5.37. The Mesha stela (McCarter 1996, no. 71)

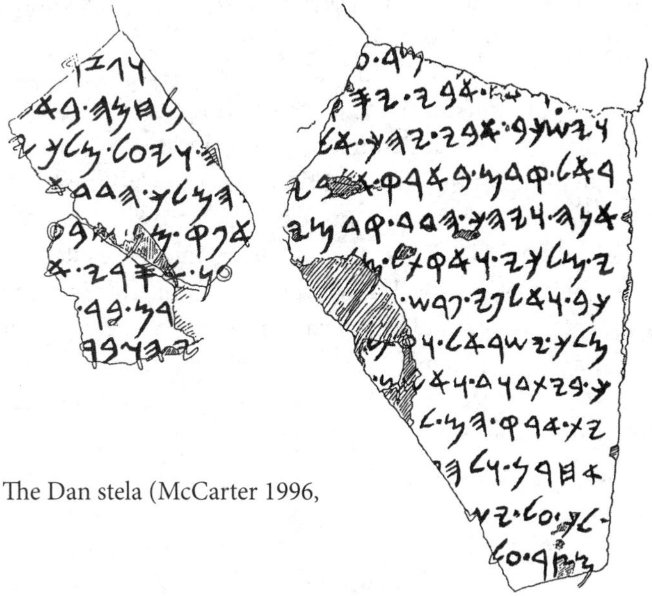

Fig. 5.38. The Dan stela (McCarter 1996, no. 70)

Despite the missing link in the ninth century, by the eighth century we have indisputable evidence of the growth of literacy. This is not simply functional literacy, where people could perhaps read and write their names and list a few commodities. It is real literacy competence, at least for an elite class of scribes who had mastered the alphabet and had also developed some elementary canons of literary production such as syntax. Not surprisingly, most of the texts that we happen to have are administrative documents, since skill in these matters of record keeping would have been fundamental to a developing state apparatus in the Iron II period. In addition, bureaucratic manipulation of writing as a means of communication would have been useful as a tool of the state. The recent discovery of a hoard of some 150 late ninth-century bullae in a building near the Gihon Spring in Jerusalem gives further evidence of a literate bureaucracy, although, unfortunately, the papyri have not been preserved (above).[102]

The Samaria ostraca have been discussed above for the light they shine on socioeconomic structure, but they also have implications for the spread of literacy by the eighth century (fig. 5.39). It is no coincidence that a number of other scattered ostraca exhibit the same characteristics: an agricultural product plus the name of the shipper or recipient. A few eighth-century inscribed sherds from Hazor could be cited, and from the eighth as well as the seventh century there are numerous examples from Arad (below). An eighth-century ostracon found at Tell Qasile even mentions 30 sheqels of gold from Ophir sent to Beth-Horon.[103]

Such economic dockets, undoubtedly very common, are utilitarian and thus may not constitute evidence of widespread literacy, much less of the capacity for the production of literary traditions. But we have other eighth-century epigraphic data that do suggest the latter. The well-known Royal Steward and other tomb inscriptions from the Silwan necropolis in Jerusalem in the late eighth century certainly have literary qualities. The former belongs to a well-defined class of Phoenician burial inscriptions, a sort of widespread literary canon in the southern Levant (below). One should note in particular the beautifully executed script of the Royal Steward inscription, the elegant forms almost cursive although carved in stone, with the consistent use of word dividers. This is clearly the work of a professional scribe and engraver.

The same is true of the nearby and roughly contemporary Siloam Tunnel inscription. We will discuss its political significance elsewhere (ch. 6), but here it is further evidence of literary production. Although

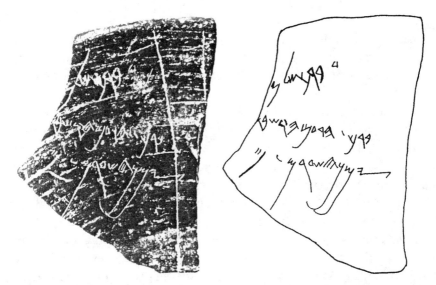

Fig. 5.39. Samaria ostracon: the "barley cheque" (Ahituv 2008, 311). © Copyright Carta, Jerusalem.

certainly commissioned by the king, and thus our only intact Israelite or Judahite royal inscription, the Siloam commemoration plaque was carved by a literate and skilled engraver, not simply a hired craftsman.[104]

In a cave in the cliffs overlooking the Dead Sea near 'Ein-Gedi, an inscription describes Yahweh ruling over the nations in a style that has true literary elements.[105] Two other groups of lengthy eighth-century inscriptions exhibit literary qualities. The first group are the inscriptions from eighth-century tombs at Khirbet el-Qom, biblical Makkedah (below). The best known is Inscription 1 from Tomb I, which contains a blessing formula. This seems to conform to well-known Hebrew formulae, especially in a funerary context—one indeed reminiscent of biblical usage. Here it is significant that this, as well as several other Khirbet el-Qom ostraca, was probably not the work of professional scribes, certainly not urban elites, but of villagers. That would suggest that literacy was fairly widespread by the mid-eighth century.[106]

The second group of longer literary inscriptions comes from Kuntillet 'Ajrud, an isolated eighth-century caravanserai with a gate shrine on the trade routes though the eastern Sinai Desert. Its religious significance is treated below, but here we observe a rather surprising literary tradition in the middle of nowhere. We have not only formulaic blessings and dedications on ostraca, plaster, and stone invoking several deities, but also an abecedary and other practice texts. The script betrays Judahite, Israelite, and Phoenician characteristics. In particular, a theophany is nearly identical to the structure and content of many examples of sophisticated biblical literature, full of nature imagery.

So impressive is the corpus of Kuntillet ʿAjrud epigraphic material that some scholars see evidence of a scribal school there. Whatever the case, a literary tradition is in full view. To be sure, there are a few graffiti, but even these are evidence of the relatively widespread knowledge of writing, although sometimes rudimentary. Graffiti do not exist in a vacuum.[107]

The foregoing survey shows that literacy began as early as the tenth century, but it is not until the eighth century, and especially the seventh century, that we have good evidence of widespread writing, mostly routine record keeping. Yet in remote villages and forts, and even in the Sinai Desert, some people could read or write, and they wrote in Hebrew, which had now become a national language and script. Nevertheless, most scholars agree that less than 5 percent of the population of ancient Israel and Judah were truly literate, even in the eighth century.

The existence of a literate class, even though relatively small, is clearly in evidence in the inscriptions at Samaria and Kuntillet ʿAjrud. Only recently have the implications of these eighth-century inscriptions been explored. Sanders (2009) has documented what he calls "the invention of Hebrew" as a national language and script, beginning in the eighth century. He shows that by now Hebrew writing has been normalized across wide boundaries and, moreover, distinguished from neighboring languages. This does not simply happen: it requires extensive efforts on the part of national institutions. What we see is the deliberate adoption of the alphabet by a *scribal culture* that exercises a broad, tight control that is both bureaucratic and political. In short, written language becomes a tool of the peoples' and the states' self-understanding. As Sanders puts it:

> What we find is not an Israelite state establishing writing but writing being recruited by an Israelite state to establish itself … what the state co-opted for its own purposes in order to argue publicly that it existed…. It helps create its audience by the very means through which it addresses it.[108]

Thus the Hebrew language becomes yet another of the ethnic markers that we shall summarize below.

Religion. Religion played an important role in all early societies, and cultic practices (if not beliefs) are often reflected in material culture remains. In Israel and Judah of the ninth–eighth century we have a number of both public and private cultic installations.

We have already surveyed the Iron I data above. From Iron IIB at Dan on the northern border there is a "high place" (or *bāmâ*) that features a raised platform 60 by 60 feet, with steps leading up to it and remains of a large four-horned altar in the forecourt. An adjoining tripartite structure (perhaps later) had a small stone altar and three iron shovels in one room (fig. 5.8 above). Also in the sacred precinct was a large olive-pressing installation, a house with domestic pottery and an oxhead figurine, a bronze scepter head, a painted offering stand, both male and female figurines of Phoenician style, and a faience die. A much smaller *bāmâ* with five standing stones (*maṣṣēbôt*) was found in the outer plaza of the city gate.[109]

The only other full-fledged Iron II sanctuary we have is the tripartite temple at Arad in the northwest corner of the fortress (fig. 5.40). The temple was constructed in Stratum X of the ninth–eighth century and was then altered in Stratum VIII in what may have been attempts at religious reforms that included abandoning the altar in the outer court and burying the two or three *maṣṣēbôt* of the inner sanctum (below). In the outer courtyard there was an altar of undressed stones, at the foot of which was found a bronze lion weight and two shallow bowls with the letters *qoph* and *kaph*, probably an abbreviation for *qôdeš kôhănîm*, "holy for the priests." Two stylized horned altars flanked the entrance to the inner sanctum, against the back wall of which once stood two (or three?) *maṣṣēbôt*. When the Stratum X temple went out of use in the late eighth century (Stratum VIII), these *maṣṣēbôt* were buried under the floor and plastered over. Among the Arad ostraca was one (no. 15) that refers to the "temple [*bêt*] of Yahweh," which probably refers to this temple rather than the one in Jerusalem. Other ostraca mention the names of known priestly families. The temple is out of use by Stratum VII, perhaps as a result of cult reforms.[110]

No remains of a royal temple in Jerusalem have been found, but that fact means little or nothing, since the relevant areas have never been excavated (below). On the outskirts of Jerusalem, however, a complex of some twenty Iron II *tumuli* on the western outskirts has been found, with perimeter walls and pits containing cooking pots and burned animal bones. These may have been burial sites where ritual feasts were held.

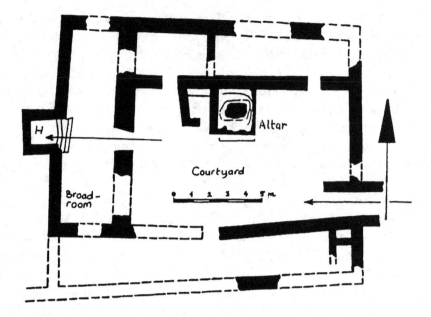

Fig. 5.40. The Arad temple (Keel 1997, fig. 170)

In addition to these monumental remains, we have a number of household shrines of the ninth–eighth century at Beersheba III, Tel Ḥalif VIB, Hazor IX, Kinrot III, Lachish III, Tell en-Naṣbeh 3A, and Tel Reḥov IV. They feature various combinations of small stone altars, cult stands, *kernoi* and other libation vessels, rattles, censers, both zoomorphic and female figurines, miniature furniture and vessels, pots for cooking and feasting, seals, and amulets. All these vessels are appropriate for the family and household cults that we have taken to be characteristic of the varieties of "Yahwism" that characterized Israelite and Judahite religion in the Iron II period (and earlier). The precise theological concepts cannot always be inferred from the archaeological remains, even when extensive. In practice, however, the focus is clearly seen, and it requires no sophisticated theory to comprehend it. It all has to do with *survival*—the ultimate concern of virtually all religions. This entails seeking the favor of the gods by prayers, invocations, and appropriate rituals, placating them by sacrifice, returning their gifts and rendering thanks, invoking their continued blessings by the use of sympathetic magic and feasting, and, of course, aligning oneself with them so as to participate in the "good life," life in accord with nature as the creation of the gods and the arena of their activity.[111]

It is now clear from the archaeological evidence that it was not the orthodox Yahwism of the late literary tradition, sometimes regarded imprecisely as "official" or "state" religion, that prevailed in the Iron II era. It was rather what Albertz has called "poly-Yahwism," the "internal religious pluralism" that is so obvious in the typical family and household cults. Now it is becoming clear that a cult of Asherah flourished, in both domestic and wider contexts, even to the extent of regarding her as Yahweh's consort in some circles. Thus the veneration of Asherah can be understood not as "idolatry" but as one aspect of multifaceted Yahwistic practices.[112]

An increasing number of both biblicists and archaeologists identify the Judean pillar-base figurines that begin in the late eighth century (after the 732–721 destructions in the north) as representations of the old Canaanite mother goddess Asherah (see further ch. 6). That is, these terra-cotta female figurines, of which we have hundreds of examples, are not simply votives or human figurines. They are evidence of a widespread, popular cult of Asherah, no doubt persistent until the end of the monarchy.[113]

Perhaps the most remarkable site with cultic paraphernalia is the eighth-century fortress or caravanserai at Kuntillet ʿAjrud in the eastern Sinai desert (fig. 5.41). Flanking the entrance into the gate are two rooms with plastered walls and benches, each with a *favissa* at the end (above). Among the finds was a large stone votive bowl inscribed "Belonging to Obadiah, the son of Adnah. Blessed be he by Yahweh." Painted scenes on large store jars depict ibexes flanking a stylized phallic-like sacred tree, a large lion, a Phoenicianizing cow suckling her calf, an enigmatic processional scene, and a scene showing two Bes figures and a half-nude female playing a lyre. On the latter there is also a Hebrew text that ends with the formula "May X be blessed," in this case "by Yahweh of Teman and his Asherah." Other inscriptions invoke El and Baal.[114]

It has long been recognized that burial customs, particularly well preserved in the many Iron Age tombs that we have, reflect religious beliefs and ritual behavior. There are few tombs from the north or south in the ninth century (as also in the twelfth–tenth century). By the eighth century, however, we have many tombs, mostly bench tombs, in Judah.[115]

The typical such rock-cut tomb is entered through a stepped passageway (the *dromos*). Off a large central chamber (the *arcosolium*) there are two or three side chambers with u-shaped benches and often a repository for bones underneath (fig. 5.42). These are obviously family tombs

Fig. 5.41. Map, objects, and scenes on pithoi, Kuntillet ʿAjrud (Meshel 1978)

where bones were periodically cleared away for later burials. They are, in effect, "houses for the ancestors." Some are in use for a century or more and contain piles of bones, as well as dozens of ceramic vessels, clay rattles, amulets, figurines, zoomorphic vessels, jewelry, and model furniture.

One eighth-century bench tomb at Khirbet el-Qom (biblical Makke-dah) yielded Hebrew inscriptions that identify several family members. Inscription number 3, although difficult to read because of overwritten letters, might run as follows:

> For ʾUriyahu the governor, his inscription.
> Blessed is ʾUriyahu by Yahweh.
> From his enemies he has been saved

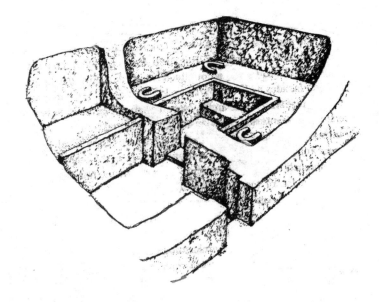

Fig. 5.42. A typical Iron II bench tomb (de Geus 2003, fig. 41)

by his a/Asherah.
(Written) by ʿOniyahu

An inscription from another bench tomb at Khirbet el-Qom identifies one "ʾOphai [swarthy one], son of Netanyahu" in an inscription
carved to one side of the entrance into a side chamber. Over the doorway
is a *di pinto* inscription that may read "ʾUzza, daughter of ʾOphai."[116] Here
we have three generations of what is probably a middle-class Judahite
family. It is significant that the personal names are Yahwistic; even more
significant is the fact that the formula of being blessed by "Yahweh and his
Asherah" parallels the contemporary Kuntillet ʿAjrud inscription noted
above almost exactly.

Another tomb may reflect Yahwistic beliefs (names) and also family
relations, this time those of an upper-class individual. Found in the cliffs
opposite the Siloam Spring long ago, it was eventually deciphered (fig.
5.43). It reads:

This is the tomb of (Shebna-) Yahu, who is over the house. There is no
silver or gold, only his bones and the bones of his slave wife with him.
Cursed be the person who opens this tomb.

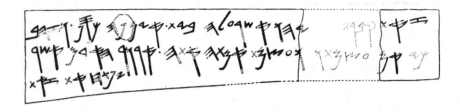

Fig. 5.43. The Royal Steward Tomb and inscription (Barkay 1992, fig. 9.49)

Shebnayahu was evidently a royal chamberlain (mentioned probably in the Hebrew Bible).[117]

Iron II tombs have been discussed recently by several archaeologists, with increasing attention paid to anthropological theory and cross-cultural comparisons. There is a growing consensus that the Judahite bench tomb in particular was conceived of as a "house for the dead," with a concern to perpetuate the memory and symbolic presence of the deceased, who was still part of the family in some sense. The "extended family" extended even further, to past generations.[118]

The multichambered bench tomb has been compared specifically to the typical three- or four-room Israelite house, both seen as the *bêt ʾāb*, the "house of the father." The close clusters of tombs and the frequent secondary burials in the repository thus signify the continuing and powerful metaphor of the patrimonial family. One of the best discussions is that of Osborne, who concludes:

The bench tomb was not merely an ethnic or geographical marker, or simply a convenient way of disposing of the dead (though it was all those things). On the contrary, it was a vital component of Judah's kinship-oriented social structure. The construction and use of these tombs, and the repeated secondary mortuary rituals that were conducted with them, must be seen as some of the most significant practices that generated the self-sustaining household metaphor of society.[119]

In summary, even with few texts the archaeological record for the Iron IIB period is sufficient to provide a consistent portrait of ancient Israelite and Judahite religion, at least in practice. The triumphant national deity was Yahweh, although other gods both male and female were also venerated. Like the other national deities of Israel's neighbors, Yahweh underwrote the nation's successes in holy war, but he punished disloyalty. Covenant with Yahweh was probably an early concept in Israel and Judah, but admittedly we have no direct archaeological confirmation. The whole Sinai tradition, as well as the traditions of the centrality of the Jerusalem temple, may well have been relatively late literary constructs that would have had little relevance for most ordinary people in ancient Israel and Judah. Few people would ever have visited the Jerusalem temple. Fewer still could have read the Pentateuch or the Deuteronomistic History, even if they had been in written form or widely distributed this early. For the vast majority of people, even in urban centers, religious beliefs and practices were focused on family rituals.[120]

The sacrificial system entailed food, drink, and animal offerings accompanied by feasting. Beside sacrifices there were other rituals that had to do with rites of passage, including death and burial. In death one remained united with one's elders and ancestors. Monumental temples were rare, and even public shrines and sanctuaries were infrequent. Most religious rites were simple, informal, family-based—the religion of hearth and home. The essence of this religion was "magic": placating the gods, ensuring the fertility of fields and family, conserving the family and clan heritage. Thus was the nation's destiny fulfilled. To be sure, Israelite religion was not unique but was rooted in Canaanite religion. Yet it was sufficiently different that it can often be distinguished from the religions of Israel's neighbors. Still, there are clear continuities with earlier Canaanite traditions.

Religion, like other aspects of Israelite culture, had evolved by the ninth–eighth century. The tenth-century cult places discussed above were almost exclusively private places of worship. By the ninth century, however, we have the monumental and very visible Dan Strata III–II *bāmâ* and a complex of associated cult installations, including large and small four-horned altars, a bronze-working facility plus a fine bowl and priestly scepter, an olive-oil press, libation facilities, several groups of small *maṣṣēbôt*, a gate shrine, offering stands and vessels, and both male and female figurines. The Arad tripartite temple with its outer altar and bowl inscribed "sacred for the priests," an inner sanctum with two (three?) larger *maṣṣēbôt*, and ostraca mentioning the "temple [*bêt*] of Yahweh" and priestly families is a full-fledged temple, although apparently not public but used largely by the garrison stationed there. The gate shrine at Kuntillet ʿAjrud is in an isolated area, but as part of a caravanserai it was open to everyone coming and going (above).

At the same time that public cult buildings were growing more common with the growth of urbanism, household shrines were flourishing as the rural population grew. The variety of religious practices, few centralized, suggests that attempts to create a national religion were not altogether successful. Some have seen in the alterations of the Arad temple in the eighth century efforts at religious reform by the authorities, but the data, never fully published, are unclear (above).

By the eighth century, we have the first extensive epigraphic evidence of religious beliefs and practices (apart from theophoric names) in the Kuntillet ʿAjrud corpus, reflecting "folk" or nonconformist religion. These texts are roughly contemporary with the earliest versions of the biblical texts and what many scholars have presumed was *orthodox* religion, that is, theology. Yet both the terminologies and the concept of what religion actually *was* must be reexamined in the light of the archaeological evidence.

Only very recently have the cumulative archaeological data been employed in painting realistic portraits of ancient Israelite and Judahite religion, despite our extensive and varied information. Over the years we have had numerous Old Testament theologies and even a few supposed histories of Canaanite and Israelite religions, but most focused almost exclusively on texts, especially the biblical texts, or what van der Toorn has aptly termed "book religion."[121]

These efforts may have produced a portrait of the biblical ideal, and one relatively late at that. But they were largely oblivious to the practice of religion. Throughout the monarchy, when the literary tradition was nascent, it was the religions of the masses of ordinary people that were the real religions of ancient Israel and Judah. Archaeology may not be able to read the minds of the ancients, but it speaks volumes about what people actually did in the name of their religions.

Several recent works by European and American scholars, both archaeologists and biblicists, have not only adduced the archaeological data but have often considered the data as a primary source.[122] While the result has been a much superior, better fleshed-out portrait of ancient Israelite religion in practice, the newer approach still needs clarification on method, not least in the issue of terminology (above). Terms such as *folk* or *popular* religion have been criticized as imprecise, derogatory, or the result of a false dichotomy between *state* or *official* religion. These critiques have not been definitive, but they have suggested a growing preference of terms such as *family* or *household* religion, in keeping with the emphasis on family here.

Ethnicity. We have already dealt with many aspects of what have been called "ethnic markers," as well as noting the skepticism of some about being able to recognize and differentiate these traits on the basis of the archaeological record. The controversy is more acute in dealing with the twelfth–eleventh century, or the prestate horizon, even though the term "Israelite peoples" is attested from the beginning in the late thirteenth century with Merenptah's Victory Stela (above). Some scholars also doubt whether the term *Israelite* is warranted in the north before the ninth century because they favor the low chronology, which dates the origin of an Israelite state that late.

All doubts about ethnicity are removed when we come to the ninth–eighth century, when both the northern and southern states are fully developed. By now their material culture can be compared with contemporary neighboring peoples such as the Philistines, Phoenicians, Arameans, as well as Ammonites, Moabites, and Edomites in Transjordan. These are all related peoples in the Iron Age but sufficiently distinctive that some ethnic distinctions can be made, even without texts, if necessary.

Having looked at site type and distribution, political organization, technology, socioeconomic structure, and other cultural aspects such as art, literature, and religion, we can now draw up an ethnic portrait that does justice to the rich archaeological data that we have. By the ninth–eighth century an Israelite (using the broader term for Judah as well) was one who:

1. Was born and usually lived within the territorial borders of the state.
2. Spoke Hebrew.
3. Lived typically in a variation of a pillar-courtyard house.
4. Used certain styles of local pottery, mostly utilitarian.
5. Had a relatively simple but distinctive material culture.
6. Participated in a basically rural, kin-based, patrimonial society.
7. Was a Yahwist, although not necessarily a monotheist.
8. Was buried in a particular style of family tomb.

It is worth noting that many of these ethnic traits are *not* fluid, such as place of birth, genetic makeup, language, religion, and several other cultural characteristics. In the modern world of travel and communication, people can indeed redefine themselves, but in the ancient world there were many geographical and cultural constraints, few personal options.[123]

It is also significant that all these Israelite cultural traits but one or two (nos. 5 and 6) are unique; they differ markedly from traits of Israel's neighbors. To be sure, there are other important ideological aspects of Israelite ethnicity that can only be elucidated on the basis of texts, but these, too, have their limitations.

In summary, ancient Israelite and Judahite culture is now increasingly well known. The society was stratified, especially with the advent of urbanism and the state. Villages gave way to towns, towns to cities. Life became more complex, more conducive to entrepreneurism. The old independent, egalitarian spirit may have remained the ideal, as seen, for instance, in the adaptation in urban settings for several centuries of the traditional pillar-courtyard dwelling, originally a farmhouse (and also in the biblical texts). Yet inevitably the rise of complex society led to disparities in wealth and status: some prospered, while others did not. It is noteworthy, however, that the archaeological evidence we have, such as town planning and house form and function, suggest that there were relatively few extremes at either end of the scale. The bulk of the population was concentrated in the rural areas—in farms, villages, and small towns. The majority of the population thus constituted a cohesive middle or working class, a sort of bourgeois society. Family lineages were strongly maintained in these kin-based groups. The extended family was the norm, although larger lineages and clans must be supposed. Overall there was a corporate mentality, a social cohesiveness, a resistance to higher-order authority, a conservative tendency in nearly all matters. The traditional patrimonial society naturally flourished here, although on a small scale. There was some degree of stratification, but there were few very wealthy or poor families. This middle class prevailed, but there were both upper and lower classes.

The state controlled political affairs, of course, as well as certain large industries and long-distance trade. It also collected taxes, conscripted young men for military service, and manipulated the middle classes, in both rural and urban areas, using agrarian values to create a pan-national "Israelite" self-identity. But even here, the extended family and the model of a patrimonial society prevailed. The few larger dwellings, and in all likelihood certain clusters of pillar-courtyard houses, reflect the older, rural ethos. Many families were still engaged in various cottage industries, as facilities for weaving, oil processing, and wine making found in many houses attest.

Several archaeologists have analyzed elements of town layout and house form in order to distinguish rural–urban differences, as well as socioeconomic stratification. Various recent interpretations have already been presented. It is difficult to choose between them, largely because the analyses depend on archaeological data that, while extensive, are impossible to quantify, especially when it comes to statistics. For instance, the extended family that all authorities discuss certainly existed, but it cannot be shown either that it predominated or that it was the preferred form of social organization. Nor can it be proven that the larger rural house, or clusters of smaller houses in urban areas, always indicate extended families.

The truth of the matter is that we do not really have sufficient archaeological or ethnographic evidence to decide the matter. What we do know is that there was a socioeconomic continuum along which there existed a nested hierarchy of several forms of communal life. Israel and Judah were class societies but not caste societies. Most people would necessarily have remained in the class into which they were born, especially in the countryside. But there was some room for upward mobility. An enterprising younger son, unlikely to inherit land, could migrate to the city. There, if he possessed entrepreneurial skills and was fortunate, he might attain wealth and even status (although he would still likely have been regarded as an outsider).

The widespread adoption of the patrimonial model of Stager, Schloen, and others does not militate against this interpretation: it presumes it and demonstrates how it might have worked. In fact, a patrimonial form of society had long prevailed in much of the Middle East, as it still does today. It is part of a complex set of both the reality of the environment and the necessity of negotiated arrangements. Thus there developed patrons and clients—a class society, even if it is best understood from the bottom up.

The patrimonial society functions only as long as the power relations and economic arrangements are mutually accepted. That is very much like the General Systems Theory approach here. Equilibrium and stability depend upon the complex interaction of several subsystems, which by definition are hierarchical.

If there is not an absolute dichotomy between upper and lower classes, is there an urban–rural dichotomy? Stager and particularly Schloen think not: their patrimonial society operated in all areas, in both nuclear and extended families. Faust, on the other hand, has developed a model that distinguishes two morphemes of society. One is rural, that of the farms, villages, and (presumably) small towns, where the larger houses indicate that the traditional extended family was the norm. The other was the urban morpheme, where smaller houses predominate and suggest that nuclear families were more common (above).

Faust's view seems preferable, if only on the ground of experience and common sense. The difference in settlement layout and average house size is a fact, and the lifestyle of the two populations must have differed significantly. Again, the problem is quantification. But to suppose that there was no dichotomy between urban and rural areas suggests that an egalitarian model derives from an overarching theory, not the facts on the ground.

The archaeological evidence that we have summarized shows that class distinctions existed and became more pronounced during the ninth–eighth century as the Israelite and Judahite society and economy inevitably became more complex. Biblical scholars have seen that situation as the background for a crisis that provoked the protests of eighth-century prophets such as Amos, Micah, and Isaiah. That view is reasonable, but the topic will be reserved until we come to the biblical connection presently.[124]

Foreign Relations

This is a history of ancient Israel and Judah, not of the entire southern Levant. The interactions of these states with their closest neighbors in Iron II, however, must be discussed at least briefly.[125]

Philistines. Israel's principal neighbors and rivals from the beginning had been the Philistines who had settled along the southern coastal plain in the early Iron I period. They remained there in the ninth–eighth century, evidently held back now from further expansion inland by the burgeoning state of Judah (and farther north by Israel; see ch. 4). The major Iron II sites that developed from the original city-states in Iron I were Jaffa IIIA, Tell Qasile VIII, Ashdod VIII, Ekron III–II, Gath 4, and Ashkelon 16–15. Among other sites, Tell el-Ḥesi VIId–c and Tell Jemmeh G–H/E–F, Tel Haror, and Tell el-Farʿah South are smaller, less urban sites to the south, bordering on the Gaza region.

In the inland Shephelah, on the edge of the foothills of the central edge, Timnah III (Tel Batash) and Beth-Shemesh 2 were Judahite border towns with Philistia, both of which reflect the fact that by now the Philistines were largely acculturated, although ethnic boundaries were still fluctuating and are not always clear.

Some of our best evidence comes from the long-running American–Israeli expedition to Tel Miqne, clearly Philistine Ekron. After the peak of Philistine urban culture in Stratum V of the eleventh century, the unique Aegean character of the city began to diminish. Philistine elements in Stratum III (early ninth century) are less evident; by Stratum II of the eighth century a hybrid Philistine–Judahite coastal culture had emerged. Already in Stratum III the site had shrunk from some 40 acres to only about 10 acres. Only in the seventh century (Stratum I) will the lower city be reoccupied, featuring by then a major olive-oil production facility under the *Pax Assyriaca* (ch. 6).

Ashdod, on the other hand, expands in Stratum VIII to an area of some 65 acres, exhibiting a large area of industrial pottery production, a shrine, and enlarged fortifications. That level seems to have been destroyed by Sargon II in 712, followed by Strata VII–VI (ch. 6).

The Philistine city-states continued to be ruled by local kings, with no apparent attempt to consolidate power in a single authority or location. Ashdod, however, may have been the dominant Philistine site.

Phoenicians. Farther north along the coastal plain (and extending into modern Lebanon and Syria), the Iron I Phoenicians were similarly well settled, and by Iron IIB they had developed a system of loosely coordinated city-states. Few have been extensively excavated and properly published, but those in the south would include Achzib, Akko, Tell Keisan 7–6, Tell Abu-Hawam IIIB–C, Shiqmona B–D, and Dor. Inland from

Akko in the foothills of Lower Galilee, Rosh Zayit is probably to be identified with Phoenician Cabul. A massive fortress 85 by 85 feet, well stocked with store jars, was destroyed perhaps in the mid-ninth century and was deserted for a time before being rebuilt.

Farther north, up the Lebanon and Syrian coast, a number of Iron Age Phoenician sites are known to some degree from excavations at Tyre, Sarepta, Sidon, Beirut, Byblos, ʿArqa, Arwad, ʿAmrit, Tell al Kazel, Tell Sukas, Ras al-Bassit, and Al-Mina. These sites, however, were part of the far-flung Phoenician trade network in the Mediterranean and would have had very little contact with Israel or Judah, except perhaps for Tyre and Sidon, which had long had some relations with Upper Galilee. The transformation of Phoenicia into a territorial power, based on maritime trade, was largely due to Tyre, and its influence would have been felt at the coastal sites in Israel noted above. The principal imports into the northern kingdom were Phoenician-style ashlar masonry and ivories, both conspicuous, for example, at the capital of Samaria in the ninth century (above).

Arameans. The Arameans of the Iron I period, originally seminomadic pastoralists in the Syrian steppe lands, had become settled into several influential city-states by the ninth century in Syria. Chief among them were Tell Fekheriye (Fakhariyah), Tell Ḥalaf, Zincirli (Samʾal), Carchemish, Arslan Tash, Aleppo, Tell Taʿyinat, Tell Afis, Hama, Tell al-Kazel, Qarqar, and Damascus. A number of other sites are known from surveys and ongoing excavations, but few of the sites are definitively published. Although these Aramean sites were flourishing by the early ninth century, the Assyrian advances westward beginning with the battle of Qarqar in 853 triggered a long decline. Many sites were then destroyed in later campaigns in 732–721. The Aramean city-states were often rivals, and an integrated state never emerged.

We have discussed the ninth-century Aramean campaigns into Israel and Transjordan above. The only relevant excavated sites are Bethsaida, Tel Hadar III–I, ʿEin-Gev 3–2, all around the Sea of Galilee, and perhaps the small fortress of Tel Soreq on the Golan Heights. Despite the later biblical writers' description of wars with the Arameans farther north, it appears that there was a détente by the late ninth–eighth century, with a relatively open border to the north and east of the Sea of Galilee. Evidence of shared cultural characteristics with Israel is seen in the tripartite pillared building at Tel Hadar and in the three-entryway city gate at Bethsaida. Some of the Aramean sites in the south were destroyed in the Assyrian destructions beginning in 732, among them Bethsaida, Tel Hadar, and ʿEin-Gev (below).

Transjordan. In the Jordan Valley and on the Transjordanian plateau Israel's neighbors were the peoples of Bashan, Gilead, Ammon, Moab, and Edom (all biblical names). There have been some surveys of the areas of Bashan and Gilead, as well as several excavations in Ammon, Moab, and Edom. But few sites have been excavated in Bashan or Gilead. The current excavations at Tell Abu el-Kharaz near Pella (biblical Jabesh-gilead?), and at Tall Ziraʿa near the Yarmuk Gorge are promising. Pella itself, as well as Irbid and Tell er-Rumeith, are also relevant.[126]

Ammon in the ninth–eighth century began to expand from an early Iron I village culture into a nascent state, a development no doubt aided by the consolidation of the Israelite state within its borders west of the Jordan. Now the settlement area increased beyond the capital area of Rabbath-Ammon (the citadel area of modern Amman), especially on the plateau, north of the Wadi Zarqa to the Madeba plain as far as Heshbon. In the Jordan Valley, Tall as-Saʿidiyeh VII–V, Tell el-Mazar, and Tell Deir ʿAlla IX–VI are probably to be considered Ammonite sites (or on the Gilead/Ammon border).

On the Ammon plateau, partially excavated sites would include Ṣafut, Tell el-ʿUmeiri (Tall al-ʿUmayri), Sahab, Tell Jawa IX–VIII, and Heshbon (the latter two possibly more Moabite). The capital at Rabbath-Ammon has not been accessible to excavations and is known only from soundings around the citadel, the Roman theater, and a few tombs in the general area. The Amman citadel inscription, dating to the ninth century, is a royal building inscription, probably from a temple for the god Milkom, who is named. The few building remains, including ashlar masonry and a Proto-Aeolic column, suggest that the capital was fortified and had some public buildings that would indicate at least a tribal state. Artistic expressions include unique stone statuettes and busts of male and female deities and perhaps of kings.

Tell Jawa provides the best plan of a provincial town, with a casemate city wall, a multiple-entryway gate, and randomly spaced houses with many small interconnected rooms (none of the pillar-courtyard type, as at Tall as-Saʿidiyeh). Tell el-ʿUmeiri is a small village where the Iron I wall was not reused and the pillar-courtyard houses do not continue. At Sahab a pillar-courtyard house was found, dated by the excavator to Iron IIB or C.

On the Ammon–Moab border are the sites of Heshbon and Tell Jalul. Heshbon, only sporadically occupied in Iron I, becomes an impressive town by the ninth century. Its massive water system is the largest in the area, capable of holding five times the annual rain, built in part of ashlar masonry. At Jalul a gateway and paved street suggest a small town. Houses are not of the pillar-courtyard type but resemble them in some ways.

In Moab proper the most important excavated site is Tall Dhiban, clearly the Moabite capital city of Dibon, where the Mesha inscription was found. Two American excavation projects have, however, left the stratigraphy of the site in question. All that can be said is that a platform of some sort may have been the foundation for a large structure of the ninth century.

'Aro'er, on the brink of the Arnon Gorge, has brought to light a fortress in Stratum V, possibly destroyed by Mesha, then rebuilt immediately in Stratum IV. There is a large reservoir at the foot of the fortress.

At Mudeina eth-Thamad there was found a four-entryway gate with both a casemate wall and a lower wall. A C-14 date from timbers of the gate roof suggests a date of circa 800.

Edom is virtually unknown archaeologically in the ninth–eighth century. Buṣeirah (the capital Bozrah) has been excavated to some extent. But the ceramic dates are disputed (as also at Tawilan), and we can only say that the site in the ninth–eighth century may have had a town wall and a palatial structure of some sort. It is not until the seventh century, however, that Edom, isolated and in a marginal region, finally became a tribal state.

The Assyrian Destructions, Circa 740–721. After a period of weakness, the Neo-Assyrian Empire began to expand westward under Tiglath-pileser III (745–727).[127] The Assyrian annals document a campaign against the kingdom of Urartu and the Arameans in the city of Arpad in Syria in 740. Both the Assyrian records and the biblical texts note that Menahem of Israel paid tribute to the Assyrians, as did the rulers of Damascus and a number of other cities in Syria. Faced with a growing threat, Israel and Judah apparently came to blows with each other, and Pekah of Israel even collaborated with Rezin, king of Damascus, to raid Judah. Edomite and Philistine campaigns may also have reduced the Shephelah and the Negev. There is, however, no archaeological evidence for any of these events.

By 734 Tiglath-pileser was campaigning down the Levantine coast to Philistia, specifically attacking Ashkelon and Gaza. In 733–732 there were further campaigns against Damascus, and the stage was then set for a major offensive against the northern kingdom of Israel, undertaken first by Tiglath-pileser III, then pursued by Sargon II (722–705).

Most General Systems Theory approaches to culture and culture change tend to focus on collapse: the failure of the system when various subsystems lose their equilibrium and feed off each other in a downward spiral until collapse is inevitable. Had ancient Israel and Judah lasted a bit longer, they might have collapsed. The northern kingdom in particular had perhaps reached a tipping point in the late eighth century after more than two centuries of intensive development. The population had doubled; cities and towns were crowded; the economy had probably reached its full potential; and there were class conflicts. The end came, however, from an external threat: Assyria. In the following we shall discuss the archaeological and the biblical evidence together for the sake of convenience, but the former will still be considered the primary data.

The Assyrian destruction of the northern kingdom of Israel from 734 to 721 and the fall of its capital Samaria were presumably among the pivotal events in the four-hundred-year history of the monarchy. The military campaigns in the north are described in some detail in 2 Kgs 15:19–17:24, but the only sites specifically mentioned are Ijon, Abel-beth-maacah, Janoah, Kedesh, Hazor (plus the districts of Gilead, Galilee, and "all the land of Naphtali"). The well-known Neo-Assyrian annals of Tiglath-pileser III (and Sargon II) also provide a textual witness. As for the other possible source of information—archaeology—most biblical scholars and even most archaeologists have simply assumed that the archaeological data for eighth-century destructions in the north would, broadly speaking, corroborate the biblical and Neo-Assyrian narratives. Yet that is hardly the case. Again, we shall separate the biblical and the nonbiblical texts.

THE NEO-ASSYRIAN TEXTS. The Neo-Assyrian texts of Tiglath-pileser III's campaigns to Syria-Palestine circa 734–727, as well as those of Sargon II (ca. 722–705), have been exhaustively analyzed. We now also have Tadmor's monumental collation of all the known texts of Tiglath-pileser III, under whom most of the northern destructions occurred.[128]

Excluding Syria, the northern Israelite sites that Tiglath-pileser III claims to have taken (at least in the texts that have come down to us) include Gal'za, Abilakka, and Samaria, as well as the "wide (land of)

Naphta[li]" and all "Israel" (*Bît Ḫumria*). The annals of Sargon II, the conqueror of Samaria in the final phase of the Assyrian campaigns, deal only with that site. For our purposes, we do not need to attempt a detailed reconstruction of the motives, strategies, and chronology of the Assyrian campaigns. Much less are we required to discuss revisionist historians who might be inclined to deny that any such conquest ever took place— presumably regarding them as mere "foundation myths" of the biblical writers and editors.

First, there are sites mentioned only in the Assyrian texts. Gal'za is listed alongside Abilakka as "adjacent to Israel." The location and identification of Gal'za is unknown, but it must have been near Abilakka, which is right on the northern border with ancient Syria.

There are more sites mentioned in both the Assyrian and biblical texts. Abilakka is to be identified with the large tell of Abil al-Qamh at the southern end of the Ijon Valley. There are a number of biblical "Abels," but Tadmor has confirmed that Assyrian *A-bi-il-ak-ka* is to be equated with biblical Abel-beth-maacah (1 Kgs 15:20; 2 Kgs 15:29; see also 2 Sam 20:14–15), as several scholars had previously surmised. The prominent 35-acre site of Abil al-Qamh, on a high promontory overlooking the entire Huleh Basin, still preserves the ancient name in Arabic. The mound is now being excavated, but a thorough survey was made in 1973. In keeping with its mention at the head of the itinerary of the Assyrian forces moving southward from Syria, Abel-beth-maacah was the northern gateway to the southern Levant (i.e., from the traditional boundary of southern Aram). While there is no excavated evidence of a destruction at Abel-beth-maacah, Assyrian forces moving from the Ijon Valley southward into Palestine could not have bypassed the site. The strategic topographical situation alone would have necessitated its conquest, as the Assyrian texts claim.[129]

The "land of Naphtali" noted both in the Assyrian texts and the Bible (2 Kgs 15:29) lies generally to the south of Abel-beth-maacah, extending westward from the Sea of Galilee, to judge from texts such as Josh 19:32–39. But the reading in the Assyrian text is uncertain. The text is broken here, and one suspects that restoring it as Naphtali is based on the reference to Naphtali in 2 Kgs 15:29. In any case, no specific sites in the region are mentioned in the Assyrian texts, although the boundary description of Naphtali in Josh 19:32–39 lists nineteen "towns with their villages." It names, among others, Kedesh, Hazor, and Chinnereth, the first two of which are also mentioned in the list of settlements destroyed by the

Assyrians in 2 Kgs 15:19. No other regions are mentioned in the Assyrian texts, which simply move on to claim that "the entire country of Israel" (i.e., *Bît-Ḫu-um-ri-a*, the usual designation) had been conquered, together with Samaria.

It is the conquest of Samaria, of course, that the texts celebrate, since it was Israel's capital and the major objective of the Assyrian campaigns throughout 743–721. The details of the references to Samaria are well known. Shalmaneser V appears to have laid siege to Samaria in 722 (according to the Bible, although he is not mentioned in the Assyrian sources), but he died that year and was replaced by Sargon II, who actually took the city, probably in the spring of 722. This king styled himself "the conqueror of Samaria" by the power of his god (Assur) and claims to have carried away 27,290 prisoners, then to have rebuilt the city "better than (it was) before." Finally, Sargon II mentions that he settled a new population there from other conquered lands, under an Assyrian governor who imposed the customary tribute upon them. All this is said to have taken place "at the beginning" of Sargon II's rule, that is, in 722 or 721 (see below).

In addition to these major northern sites and regions, all readily identified, a few other sites are mentioned in the Assyrian texts that have not been excavated and are less certainly identifiable. Among them are: (1) Ir[una] (Yiron; modern Yarun?); (2) Merom (Tell el-Khirbe?); (3) Hinatuna (Hannathon; Tell el-Badwiyeh?); (4) Qana (Khirbet Qana); and (5) [Jo]tbah (Khirbet Jefat). All of these, however, are likely to have been somewhere in lower and western Lower Galilee and perhaps were of secondary interest to the Assyrians, even though several hundred prisoners are said to have been taken from this area.

BIBLICAL TEXTS AND POSSIBLE DESTRUCTIONS. In addition to the above-mentioned sites and regions mentioned in both the Assyrian and the biblical texts, there are several sites that the Hebrew Bible describes as having been destroyed that are not mentioned in the Assyrian texts (at least in those that we happen to have). These are Ijon, Janoah, Kadesh, and Hazor, as well as the regions of Gilead and Galilee (2 Kgs 15:29).

Ijon may refer to the Valley of Ijon, as noted above, on the Israel–Aramean border near Abel-beth-maacah; alternatively, it may designate the town by that name, tentatively identified with Tell ed-Dibbin to the north of Abel-beth-maacah in the Ijon Valley (now in Lebanon). The latter has never been excavated, but, like Abel-beth-maacah, it was a gateway town that lay directly in the path of the Assyrian advance (above). Whether the town was Aramean or Israelite is, however, uncertain.

Janoah, the next site mentioned, is usually identified with Yanuḥ, circa 12 miles southwest of Kedesh in Galilee, but nothing is known of the site archaeologically. It is of some strategic importance for control of western Upper Galilee, but it is mentioned only in this one biblical text.

Kedesh (Qadesh), obviously Tell Qades, a prominent 25-acre tell on the Israel–Lebanon border in the ancient territory of Naphtali (see above; see also Judg 4:6), is the largest mound in Upper Galilee. As an important border fortress, it is said to have been defeated by Joshua (Josh 12:22); it features in the battle of Sisera (Judg 4:6); and, finally, much later, it is where Jonathan Maccabeus defeated the army of Demetrius (1 Macc 11:63, 73). The lower tell is currently being excavated and has produced spectacular Hellenistic-Roman remains. The Iron II remains are known, however, only from a small salvage excavation in the place where the modern road divides the site, carried out by Aharoni in 1953. Yet this site was nearly as strategic as Abel-beth-maacah for the Assyrian advance from the north, and that it is mentioned in the biblical list of sites destroyed by Tiglath-pileser III makes good topographical sense.

Hazor is certainly the 180-acre mound of Tell el-Qedaḥ in Lower Galilee, another fortress that features prominently in the Hebrew Bible, from the narrative of Joshua's conquest of "the head of all those kingdoms" onward. Although not mentioned in the extant Assyrian texts, it was the largest, most strategically located mound in the region and lay directly in the path of any Assyrian advance into Galilee and beyond, into the heartland of northern Israel. The city of Stratum VA is represented principally by a massive citadel, incorporating a watchtower on a promontory at the western end of the upper mound (Area B). Apparently the citadel had no surrounding city wall in the preceding Stratum VB. But when the citadel was enlarged and additional buildings were added to the east, an offset-inset wall was constructed. Together with the enormous water tunnel dug in the ninth century, these constructions would have prepared Hazor quite well for the late eighth-century siege that surely had been anticipated (perhaps since the battle of Qarqar in 853).

Yadin describes the citadel as destroyed in a "final, complete" conflagration, "the entire area … covered with a layer of ashes and rubble about 1 m. thick." Area G was also destroyed; Yadin states that "the signs of the terrible destruction manifested in all the excavated areas were still 'fresh' when uncovered, and the next occupants did not trouble to clear the debris." Stratum IV, which followed the destruction, is described as "a temporary unfortified settlement."[130]

In addition to these specific towns, the Hebrew Bible, as noted above, also mentions certain regions. Thus, it refers to "all the land of Naphtali," compared to the possible reference to the same region in the Assyrian texts. All that can be said of this region in terms of specific settlements, however, is that Janoah, already mentioned as destroyed, was in the general area and that this northern tribal region would have lain directly in the Assyrian path of advance southward to Hazor and beyond.

Gilead and *Galilee* are the other regions named in 2 Kgs 15:29. The second is obviously a region of northern Palestine, embracing the general area of the tribal allotments of Naphtali (see above) and Asher to the west. Including both Upper and Lower Galilee, the area would also likely have been a target of the initial campaigns of Tiglath-pileser III. Thus its mention in the Hebrew Bible is realistic, although no specific sites with destructions are known (see below).

Gilead poses a problem, however, because it lies in south-central Transjordan, where Assyrian destructions remain undocumented both textually (outside the Hebrew Bible) and archaeologically. Furthermore, how Israelite this region actually was in Iron II is debatable. Known Iron II archaeological sites both north and south of this area of Transjordan—that is, Wadi Zarqa (the Jabbok)—are rare, and few have been excavated. The recent exhaustive survey of MacDonald lists some fifteen in Gilead proper (i.e., north of Amman, on the border of ancient Ammon).[131]

Irbid in the north, possibly biblical Beth-arbel (Hos 10:14), just southeast of the Sea of Galilee, would have lain closest to the Assyrian territorial interests, although it was peripheral. The site has been investigated only in salvage work and several soundings. Some Iron II tombs are reported, but the layers on the mound after circa 800 are denuded.

Tell er-Rumeith, biblical Ramoth-gilead, still on the border between Jordan and Syria, was excavated by Lapp in 1962–1969. Stratum V, apparently dating to the eighth century, ends in a massive destruction, followed by a gap in occupation until the second century. Perhaps this is evidence of Assyrian campaigns in the area, but that remains speculative.

Pella has been extensively excavated by an Australian team since 1967, but only scant Iron Age remains are reported, and the site, despite its size and strategic location, is not mentioned in the Hebrew Bible.

Tall as-Saʿidiyeh, located on the banks of the Jordan River, possibly biblical Zarethan, was excavated in 1964–1967 by Pritchard. Stratum V, which he dated to the mid- to late eighth century, is reported to have been destroyed, followed by a partial hiatus.

Tell el-Mazar, a small mound nearby, was excavated in 1977–1979 by Yassine. Stratum F, the lowest level, was dated to the eighth century, and its end to the campaign of Sennacherib in 701.

Tell Deir ʿAlla to the south, also in the Jordan Valley, has been excavated on and off since 1960 by Franken and others. Possibly to be identified with biblical Succoth (Judg 8:16), it has produced an intriguing eighth-century sanctuary (Phase IX) that yielded the well-known Aramaic Balaam text. How this stratum ended, however, is not known for certain, but one of the excavators surmises that it ended in the early eighth century (based on some C-14 dates) in an earthquake.

In summary, there is little if any archaeological evidence for Assyrian campaigns in Gilead, despite the reference in 2 Kgs 15:29. Most of this region and other regions in Transjordan, semiarid and sparsely settled until relatively late in the Iron Age, seem to have come under Assyrian influence only in the seventh century, and largely peacefully. One text of Tiglath-pileser III does refer to *Bît Amman*, the northern border of the tribal state of Ammon, and the same king claims to have taken tribute from a certain "Qôs-malah" of Edom. An earlier tribute list (ca. 737) lists a "queen of the Arabs" as paying tribute, but Ammon, Moab, and Edom are not specifically mentioned.[132]

Samaria, mentioned in both the Assyrian and the biblical texts, deserves special attention. This is because the relative wealth of information from all the potential sources—textual and archaeological—ought in principle to supply the convergences that place us on firmer historical ground. Indeed, most scholars have assumed so. Unfortunately, it is not that simple, as more recent research has shown.

Despite the early intuition of authorities such as Albright and Wright that Kenyon's stratigraphy and ceramic analysis were flawed, her reputation as an innovator in field methods was so vaunted that few could offer a plausible alternative to her oft-repeated statements regarding the Assyrian destruction at Samaria (i.e., of her Building Phase VI but Pottery Period V, as Albright and Wright showed). Kenyon claimed that all the buildings below a sterile fill (or "chocolate layer") were destroyed: "everywhere found covered by a layer of debris of destruction; that a 'sooty layer' covered the wall stubs." The floors of the "royal palace" rooms were littered with burnt ivory carvings and other debris. Subsequently, the walls were pulled down, then leveled over with redistributed destruction debris. "Alien pottery" (presumably Assyrian Palace ware) was found in subsequent occupation levels (Phase VII).[133]

Fortunately, we now have Tappy's extensive reworking of Kenyon's 1932–1935 excavation results at Samaria. Tappy has gone through all the original field records and has produced the first comprehensive, persuasive stratigraphic history of the site. He has not only wrung out of the complex data, published and unpublished, every conceivable scrap of information, but he has also fully integrated the pertinent data with both the biblical and the Assyrian texts in a remarkable tour de force. He shows that Building Phase V represents very scant remains, hardly "monumental architecture," that scarcely any diagnostic pottery is published from the crucial loci, and that even Kenyon's famous section drawings are too schematic to be definitive. He tends to agree, somewhat reluctantly, with Forberg's very pessimistic conclusions. Accepting Albright's and Wright's attribution of the pottery of Pottery Period VI (rather than Kenyon's VII) to Building Phase V, Tappy find the corpus astonishingly slight and Kenyon's confident dating precisely to 722/721 not credible. He regards the corpus as mixed and would redate it to the last quarter of the eighth and the early seventh century.

Tappy's overall conclusion after nearly 900 pages of discussion is:

> Ultimately, it is the lack of any stratigraphic bearings that hampers Kenyon's own reporting technique in SSIII.… I have not encountered a blanket of destruction debris across the BPV remains at the site; rather, diverse layers dating from many time periods and extending as late as the Late Roman period have emerged.… Kenyon's archaeological chronology seems tied too directly to generally accepted historical dates (Jehu's coup) and/or presumed historical events (Assyrian military destruction of Samaria).

Speaking generally about the problem addressed this work, Tappy closes with words of caution: "In short, a direct correspondence between archaeological history and political history does not always exist."[134]

LATE EIGHTH-CENTURY ARCHAEOLOGICAL SITES NOT NAMED IN TEXTS. There are at least ten excavated mid- to late eighth-century sites in the north that are not mentioned in the biblical or the Assyrian texts to which we might look for destruction levels between circa 734 and 722/721. We shall examine them briefly from north to south.

Dan has been the subject of long-running excavations that might be expected to have yielded significant evidence. Dan was not only a principal cultural and religious site of the northern kingdom, but it was strategically located on the border with Aram. Indeed, in the Assyrian military itineraries Dan is regularly mentioned at the outset, along with nearby Ijon and Abel-beth-maacah, the strategic importance of which has been noted above (and both are named in the biblical texts). Dan has been extensively excavated since 1966, but little has been published to date. Biran's popular book *Biblical Dan* says of the pertinent Stratum II that the city walls and gate (Areas A and B) and the "sacred precinct" (Area T) were "destroyed." But there is no mention of the domestic areas, and indeed little evidence is presented to substantiate a deliberate destruction in a military campaign. All one can say is that the scant Iron II pottery published from Stratum II does appear to date to the mid- to late eighth century. The gate area is the best candidate for a substantial destruction. This area was found "in ruins," with up to 1 meter of fired bricks and ash overlying the piers and guardrooms. Biran attributes this destruction to Tiglath-pileser III in 732 on the basis of the pottery. While Biran's correlation of the Dan defenses (in particular) with the known Assyrian campaigns is plausible and makes good strategic sense militarily, the evidence thus far is only suggestive.[135]

Tel Kinrot (Chinnereth) is a small but strategically located mound overlooking the northwestern shore of the Sea of Galilee, standing guard over the main route around the sea on the west. It would have been on the natural invasion route south of Hazor. Excavated by Fritz from 1982 to 1992, and other German scholars later, Chinnereth Stratum II is said to have been strongly fortified but destroyed by Tiglath-pileser III in 733, after which it was settled only sparsely.

Beth-Shean is one of the most imposing mounds in Lower Galilee, at the junction of the Jezreel Valley and the Jordan River. It was one of the major sites of the northern kingdom. Stratum IV may date broadly to the eighth century, but it is said to be poorly preserved, and the pottery as published may range from circa 800 to 600 BCE. A gap in occupation follows until the Persian period. The recent excavations conducted by Mazar have yielded somewhat more information, deriving from a large, well-preserved building that was destroyed in a heavy fire, perhaps in the Assyrian campaigns. The debris yielded more than one hundred restorable vessels, plus many other objects.[136]

Megiddo is virtually synonymous with famous battles, and here we might expect to have more persuasive evidence of the Assyrian campaigns (although the site is not named in the texts). Stratum IVA is the pertinent horizon, with its offset-inset city wall, three-entryway gate, water system, three palace complexes, and stables or storehouses (all probably continuing from Stratum IVB of the tenth/ninth century). Megiddo would have been an enviable prize for Tiglath-pileser III, as it was for Thutmose III in the fifteenth century: "The capturing of Megiddo is the capturing of a thousand towns." Surprisingly, Shiloh's authoritative résumé does not mention any evidence whatsoever of an Assyrian destruction, stating only that it occurred. What is clear from the Assyrian texts, however, is that Megiddo became the capital of the new Assyrian province of Magiddu. The new Stratum III two-entryway city gate provides some evidence of the takeover: it was buttressed by several large public and residential buildings that display clear Assyrian architectural features, such as central courtyards. Yet the current excavators specifically note the absence of Assyrian objects (see fig. 5.44 below).[137]

Ta'anach, Megiddo's nearby sister-city, was excavated in the 1950s by Lapp. The Iron II levels are published only in brief preliminary reports, and little can be said except that the scant remains of Period IV apparently belong to the mid- to late eighth century. They are said to have been overlain in one small area by a black ashy layer, tentatively dated by the excavators to 733/732.[138]

Yoqne'am, a steep, 10-acre mound guarding a major pass from the Ephraim hills into the Jezreel Valley, was excavated by Ben-Tor and others in the 1970s as part of a larger regional project. Stratum XII of the eighth century had two heavy defense systems built on the slopes, replacing those of Stratum XIV. The preliminary reports, however, do not mention destructions, but only that the defenses went out of use and that the subsequent Stratum XI had only fragmentary remains.[139]

Tel Qiri is a small, unwalled village just southeast of Yoqne'am, on the lower slopes of the Carmel Ridge overlooking the central Jezreel Valley; it was excavated by Ben-Tor in 1975–1977. No identification is suggested. Stratum VIII belongs to the eighth century and represents a newly founded village. Nothing is reported regarding its end or destruction, but the subsequent Stratum VIB–A shows continuing architectural changes in the domestic architecture and the expanded development of the sort of agricultural industries that would befit a small village. The site would not likely have attracted the attention of invaders.[140]

Tell el-Far'ah (North) is located prominently at the headwaters of the Wadi Far'ah in the hill country of Ephraim. It is the site of biblical Tirzah, which was briefly the first capital of the northern kingdom. The site was excavated by de Vaux in 1946–1960 but has only been partially published. Stratum VIId, belonging broadly to the ninth–eighth century, is a fortified town with a solid city wall, an offset gateway, blocks of well laid out multiroom houses, and a palace. The pottery is reported to be characteristic of other eighth-century sites and includes Samaria Ware. The excavators attribute its destruction to Sargon II, but no details are given. Thereafter, in Stratum VIIe, the town is said to have declined, but Assyrian Palace ware may indicate an Assyrian presence.[141]

Keisan, represented by the large mound of Tell Keisan, was an important seaport near Akko. It has been tentatively identified with several biblical sites, none convincingly. It was excavated on a small scale by French scholars in the 1970s, and, to their credit, they produced a lavish final excavation report. Stratum 6 apparently belongs to the eighth century, but it is described as "a little village on the edge of the kingdom of Tyre," with typical Phoenician coastal pottery and was thus probably not part of the northern kingdom of Israel. It is not likely that the site was in the path of the Assyrian advance down the coast, which concentrated rather on Philistia. There is, however, some Assyrian Palace ware, possibly trade items.[142]

Shechem, in the central hill country some 8 miles south of Samaria, long connected with biblical tradition, was one of the mid-sized towns in the Iron II. Stratum VII belongs to the eighth century, when a casemate wall in Field VI served as a defense. In Field VIII, House 1727 shows particularly clear and detailed evidence of violent destruction by fire. It provides perhaps our most carefully excavated evidence for destroyed domestic structures anywhere, although the pottery and objects are not yet published. The excavators proposed that the "total destruction" was the result of the Assyrian campaign.[143]

Khirbet el-Marjameh, a 10-acre walled halfway between Shechem and Gibeon, was totally destroyed in 732 and abandoned thereafter (see fig. 5.18 above).

Gezer, a 33-acre mound at the juncture of the Judean foothills and the Shephelah near modern Lod, is one of the most strategically located

Bronze–Iron Age sites in ancient Palestine. The site lay on the southern border of the northern kingdom, and after its late eighth-century destruction, it was rejoined with Judah. It thus probably marked the southernmost point of the Assyrian advance toward Judah until the campaigns of Sennacherib in 701. Stratum VI of the eighth century is characterized by a multitowered city wall (the Outer Wall) with some casemate sections, a three-entryway gate with a lower gatehouse in Field III and an adjoining palace (Palace 8,000), and a large area of well laid out private houses in Field VII. Earlier seasons illuminated the wholesale destruction of some domestic areas (Fields II, VII). The 1984 and 1990 seasons brought to light vivid evidence of the breach of the lower city wall near the gate and the fiery destruction of the up-slope casemate wall. In the latter were found quantities of heavily burnt and calcified late eighth-century pottery, iron arrowheads, more than one hundred burned clay loom weights, a carved ivory fan handle similar to one found in the 701 destruction at Lachish, a storage jar fragment reading *yayîn*, and rare examples of clay inkwells. Gezer is unique in being able to boast an apparent eyewitness battlefield sketch, an Assyrian cuneiform tablet showing in detail the attack on the city gate and reading "the siege of Gezer" (*gaz*[*ri*]), found long ago in the ruins of the Assyrian palace at Nimrud.[144]

Tel ʿEton, near Tell Beit Mirsim in the inner Shephelah, has only been partially excavated, but it shows a monumental late eighth-century destruction.

There remain two northern Aramean sites to be mentioned: Bethsaida and Tel Hadar on the northern and eastern shores of the Sea of Galilee, respectively. *Bethsaida* Level 5 exhibits an unparalleled massive triple-entryway gate and city wall, in the external plaza of which was a gate shrine incorporating a stela depicting a moon deity Hauran. A black destruction layer up to 1 meter thick that covered the entire area was attributed by the excavators to the campaigns of Tiglath-pileser III. The small village of Tel Hadar was apparently destroyed by the Assyrians and deserted thereafter. Both of these sites, however, are almost certainly Aramean and thus lie outside our discussion of the northern kingdom. They were probably destroyed after the fall of the Aramean capital at Damascus, during the Assyrian advance southward.

Textual and archaeological evidence for Assyrian destructions in Transjordan is scant, but campaigns claimed against the "Arabs" would have required transit through this area. In the north, Ramoth-gilead (Tell er-Rumeith) and Jabesh-gilead (perhaps Tell Abu el-Kharaz) may have been taken, the area then turned into an Assyrian province (Karnaim).

The Assyrian annals claim that Sargon deported 27,290 from Samaria to Assyria, along with much booty, installing them in Gozan and other sites in Khabur and Syria in the region. In their place, foreign captives were brought into Israel from Cutha in Babylon and Hamath in Syria. To the postdestruction period Faust has assigned the establishment of a number of farmsteads in the Samaria region, in which the material culture does not seem to contain typically Israelite elements. The number of deportees, however, is uncertain. It may have been anywhere from the 27,290 from Samaria (i.e., from the entire region, circa 10 percent of population) to only a few thousand.[145]

There are several sites that illustrate the Assyrian penetration into Philistia. Those mentioned in the Assyrian texts include the major Philistine cities of Ashdod, Ashkelon, and Gath, which have produced some pertinent archaeological evidence. In addition, more data on the subsequent Assyrian occupation of the southern coastal regions comes from excavations at Tel Mor, Tell el-Ḥesi (Eglon?), Tel Haror (Gerar), Sheikh Zuweid, Raphia, and el-ʿArish. All this is significant because it documents that there was an Assyrian presence, if not an occupation, in the south, which could not have occurred, of course, unless the northern access routes had been opened and the former northern kingdom of Israel had been pacified. The reminder of the south, that is, Judah, however, was not overrun until the campaigns of Sennacherib in 701 (ch. 6).

THE POSTCONQUEST HORIZON AND THE ASSYRIAN PRESENCE. The Assyrian presence is apparent in the north, where a wealth of archaeological evidence attests to an actual military occupation and administration. In this context, Stern's recent survey is instructive.[146] Assyrian texts document the establishment of three new administrative provinces in the north—Megiddo, Samarina (Samaria), and Dor—each ruled by an Assyrian governor (*peha* or *šaknu*), together with lower-level officials such as a district official (*rab alani*) or governor of a city (*hazannu*). Large Assyrian-style palaces are known from Hazor III and Megiddo III (above), and indeed Megiddo seems to be a new, planned Assyrian-style city. Also pertinent is a class of distinctive luxurious Assyrian Palace ware—similar to that well attested at Khorsabad, Nineveh, Nimrud, and other Assyrian capitals in the homeland—found in substantial quantities as both actual imports and local imitations. In addition, we now have a relatively large corpus of other clearly Assyrian and Assyrianizing objects, such as seals and seal impressions, metals, stone objects, weight, glass, clay coffins, and so on. We even have a few Assyrian royal inscriptions, notably several fragments of stone stelae in Assyrian cuneiform from Samaria (Sargon II) and Ashdod. Clay tablets in cuneiform include one from Samaria mentioning the Assyrian governor, two legal tablets from Macalister's excavations at Gezer (seventh century), and another legal tablet from Hadid, near Gezer, that contains only Babylonian and Aramaic names, no Hebrew ones. All of the above-mentioned Assyrian material from the late eighth and seventh century has recently been drawn together for the first time by Stern. The point here, as above, is simply that the Assyrian occupation and administration of northern Israel in this period, now well documented, is our best proof that an actual conquest had indeed taken place, however ambiguous the archaeological data (and the texts) may remain.

The Hebrew Bible in the Light of the Archaeological Data

True to our principle of taking archaeology as the primary source for writing a history of Israel and Judah, we have left the biblical texts almost entirely out of consideration thus far. To fail to consider the biblical texts as a source would, however, be irresponsible. Here we shall only summarize the biblical data because it has been dealt with extensively elsewhere in numerous commentaries and biblical histories. Our only concern will be to compare the two sources for the ninth–eighth century, seeking convergences where possible. Again we will employ a continuum from certainty to doubt, locating events where we can. A chart of major political events narrated in Kings may be helpful.[147]

In addition to the places in the right-hand column of figure 5.44 where the Hebrew Bible seems in error and provides no source of reliable information, we must consider omissions. There are several instances where archaeology demonstrates that there are significant gaps and fills them in. For instance, the book of Kings does not mention Ahab's participation in the coalition at the battle of Qarqar in 853, although he appears to have played a significant role. Nor do the writers refer to Jehu paying tribute to Shalmaneser III in 841. Their reasons, assuming that they had sources, are no doubt due to their animosity toward the former, their aggrandizement of the latter. But this illustrates just how biased the biblical writers could be.

Another omission in the Hebrew Bible is any detailed description of Israel's attempt in the ninth century to dominate Moab (2 Sam 8:1–2), possibly because it is assumed that Solomon's vast empire included Moab (1 Kgs 4:21). Neither Omri nor Ahab is mentioned in connection with Moab, but the notice that Moab rebelled after his death assumes that Ahab had controlled Moab (2 Kgs 1:1; 3:4–5). Yet the Mesha stela describes the oppression of Omri and Ahab. To complicate matters further, our third source—archaeology—does not suggest that there ever was an Israelite destruction or, for that matter, even a Moabite kingdom that early. The difficulties can be resolved, however, by supposing that Omri and Ahab did oppress Moab but never had a real presence there and that, in the period of chaos following Ahab's death, Moab broke free. From the biblical texts alone, however, we would know very little.

Perhaps the most obvious disconnect between the biblical texts and the archaeological evidence is in the area of religion. We have seen above the persuasive extrabiblical evidence that, in the family-centered cults that characterized the Iron IIB era, the cult of Asherah was evident and often dominant from the settlement period until the end of the monarchy.

The biblical writers do hint at such a cult, of course, necessarily so in light of their intent to denounce it and legitimize exclusive Yahwism. But the overall impression the historian gets is that the literary tradition, with its ideal of orthodoxy, made every effort to suppress the *reality*. The fact that the term/name ʾăšērâ is so ambiguous in its usage and meanings (and ʿaštōret as well) suggests an attempt to obfuscate rather than clarify. The biblical writers must have known what the names of these old Canaanite deities implied. But they go so far as to tamper with the consonantal texts in some cases, even though it is gaining canonical status as Scripture.[148] Without the archaeological and extrabiblical texts, we would have had little idea of the immense variety of religious beliefs and practices in ancient Israel and Judah.

Fig. 5.44. Biblical narratives analyzed in the light of the archaeological evidence, ninth–eighth century

Proven	Probable; evidence ambiguous	Possible; little or no evidence	Disproven
		1. Site Type, Distribution	
Multitier hierarchy			
Growth of sites			
Increased urbanism but rural sector dominant			
		2. Political History	
Kings of Israel: Omri, Ahab, Ahaziah, Joram, Jehu, Joash, Menahem, Pekah, Hoshea		Jeroboam's fortified cities Other Kings	
Kings of Judah: Ahaziah, Jehoahaz, Hezekiah			
Omri founds Samaria on Shemer's estate	Omri threatens Moab	Elijah anoints Hazel of Syria	Omri ineffectual
		Ahab defeats Hazael Aramean "bazaars"	Ahab weak
Ahab's "house of ivory"	Ahab builds cities	Ahab tries to retake Ramoth-gilead	Ben-hadad king in Ahab's time
Ahab's palace at Jezreel		Jehoshaphat's ships	
Joram as king	Mesha rebels	Moab defeated	
		Elisha anoints Naaman of Aram	
Joram and Ahaziah battle Arameans	Ben-hadad besieges Samaria	Aramaean cease invasions	Hadad replaces Ben-hadad
	Hazel besieges Gath		
Jehu's coup; Ahaziah assassinated	Jehu kills Joram and Ahaziah	Uzziah and Elat	Jehu abolishes Baal worship

Hazael, Ben-hadad, Rezin, Aramean kings	Hazael threatens Jerusalem		
Israel prevails over Aramaeans	Israel defeats Edom		
Hezekiah's Tunnel, "broad wall"	Jeroboam restores Damascus, Hamath		
Menahem pays tribute to Assyria	All kings corrupt; Syro-Ephraimite war		
Assyrian invasions end northern kingdom			Fall of Israel due to apostasy

3. Socioeconomic Structure

Social inequalities	Context of prophets		
Patrimonial	Reform movements	Prophetic groups	
Family the basic unit; *bêt ʾāb*			
Israel stronger than Judah			

4. Technology

City planning
Monumental architecture
Phoenician masonry
Iron working
Many skilled professions

5. Ideology

Literacy spreads	More widespread literacy		
Papyri and seals			
Ivory carvings			
Yahweh national deity; also other deities			Yahwism early or exclusive

	Holy war ideology		
Priesthood		Prophetic movements	Only Jerusalem priests
Local cult sites		Sinai covenant	Jerusalem temple only one accepted
Bāmôt			
Asherah symbols	Temple ideology	Divine kingship	
Maṣṣēbôt		Decalogue	
Horned altars	Avoidance of pork	Circumcision	
Female figurines			Figurines unknown
Iconography			Aniconism
Animal sacrifice			Israelite religion unique
Food, drink offerings			
Attempts to centralize			
	Growth toward monotheism		
Family religion	Women as ritual experts		Fertility religions, pagan
Burials as continuity			
Israelite ethnic identity		Doctrine of "election" widespread	

In addition to political history—which is the forte of the writers of the Hebrew Bible—we might glean further information from narratives that have more to do with the general social and religious situation. Thus the world of the biblical texts—the Iron Age, not the Persian or Hellenistic era—provides a general context for its stories, one that accords quite well with the archaeological picture. Here we have two states with the founding of many cities and towns, a large rural population, a patrimonial society, socioeconomic stratification, an agrarian view of "the good life," and a diverse cult.

There are, moreover, numerous specifics of daily life. A description of such may not have been the intent of the biblical writers, but here and there they do give incidental details that bear examination. A full-scale examination is beyond our purview here (and has been done elsewhere); the chart in figure 5.45 summarizes the data, in this case in the book of Kings only.

In addition to these biblical narratives that purport to be historical, there are numerous places where an archaeologist can instinctively "read between the lines" in various biblical stories. There the biblical writers may inadvertently provide information that correlates well with what we know. Again, confining ourselves to Kings, we note among other things the following:

1. Baking cakes on hot stones (1 Kgs 19:6)
2. Signet rings/seals (1 Kgs 21:8)
3. Pool at Samaria (1 Kgs 22:38)
4. Ahab builds cities (1 Kgs 22:39)
5. No king in Edom (1 Kgs 22:47)
6. Elisha's upper chamber, jars of oil (2 Kgs 4:10)
7. Commerce, administrative officials in city gate (2 Kgs 7:17–19)
8. Tower at Jezreel (2 Kgs 9:17)
9. Jezebel's painted eyes (2 Kgs 9:30).
10. Ahab's seventy sons, rulers of the city, elders, guardians (2 Kgs 10:1)
11. *Maṣṣēbôt* of Baal (2 Kgs 10:26)
12. Jehoash temple with quarrymen, masons, carpenters, builders, silver and goldsmiths, accountants (2 Kgs 12:11–16)
13. Rabshekah's description of "the good life" (2 Kgs 18:31–32)

To be fair, let us consider the situation where the Hebrew Bible is our only source. Do we gain thereby any essential or useful information? We do learn the names of a number of Israelite and Judahite kings unattested in our other sources thus far. For Israel, we have five more to add to the fourteen names that we know otherwise after Israel's first encounters with the Assyrians.

Fig. 5.45. Major Israelite and Judahite kings of the ninth–eighth century (*= also mentioned in Neo-Assyrian, Moabite, or Aramean texts)

Israel	Judah
*Omri (884–873)	*Jehoram (851–843/842)
*Ahab (873–852)	Jehoash (842/841–802/801)

*Joram (851–842/841)   Amaziah (805/804–776/775)
Jeroboam II (790–750/749)   Uzziah (788/787–736/735)
*Menahem (749–738)   Ahaz (742/741–726)
*Pekah (750?–732/731)   *Hezekiah (726–697/696)
*Hoshea (732/731–722)

For Judah during the Assyrian period, the most important king was Hezekiah, and the Assyrian annals do mention him, and in some detail. In the case of Israel, Jeroboam II is the only important king omitted in the Assyrian and other annals. In fact, he is accredited in the Hebrew Bible with doing very little, even though he reigned for some forty years. His one purported deed—restoring the border all the way to Hamath—is doubtful. Knowing his name adds little or nothing to our history. Many of the above are minor kings, and the events described during their reigns are often obscure. In any case, all the northern kings are essentially dismissed as apostates, and in Judah the only two kings given approval are the putative reformers Hezekiah and Josiah.

Everywhere in the biblical narratives the overriding theo-political agenda of the writers makes it difficult to separate fact from fiction. Thus archaeology is still our primary datum. The Hebrew Bible does throw some light on the Iron II religious situation, even if indirectly. The ideal of the biblical writers is certainly exclusive Yahwism. Yet in condemning unorthodox popular religions they give themselves away—so much so that some would now say that the *real* religion of ancient Israel and Judah consisted of everything the biblical writers rejected (if numbers count). Our portrait of Israelite popular (or family) religion today, however, goes far beyond that of the Bible, and moreover it is not dependent upon these accounts in any significant way. The archaeological data are not silent, as a previous generation of biblicists often maintained; they speak volumes.

In conclusion, the biblical texts may add some facts, but most are incidental, and some are not facts at all. In *no* case does the Hebrew Bible *confirm* the archaeological facts or their interpretations. If anything, it is archaeology that may sometimes confirm the biblical version of history—or may not. To be sure, we are thinking of history here in a somewhat restricted sense.

There are many kinds of history and history-writing. Archaeology can write satisfactory (if provisional) histories of (1) political events; (2) technology; (3) socioeconomic; and (4) long-term environmental changes. These would correspond to the Annales historian's *évenements, conjonctures*, and *la longue durée*. As many archaeologists (and a few biblical scholars) have come to realize, archaeology is particularly well suited to complex, long-term history-writing where material culture remains can be definitive.

Broader cultural history, including intellectual, ideological, aesthetic, and religious histories are indeed enhanced by our having pertinent and reliable textual information. That should never be forgotten. But the usefulness of all texts depends upon subjective interpretations that will inevitably differ. The notion of some scholars that the interpretation of artifacts is more subjective, and therefore less decisive than the interpretation of texts, is woefully out of touch with the maturation of archaeology as an independent discipline.

Notes

1. Faust (2012a, 39–41) cites several general studies, such as those of Fox 1977; M. E. Smith 2002; and R. Osborne 2005. He does not, however, distinguish any Iron II categories other than city and village or urban and rural. Herzog's extensive survey of ancient Israelite cities (1997) is not much more specific; Schloen 2001 distinguishes only urban and rural. Here I follow the definition outlined in chapter 4, using size as the principal criterion, although specifying a number of other components as well. For the first, experimental use of the three-tier hierarchy of sites employed here, see Dever 2012, 47–49, 50, 58, 72, 80–84. The model of a city discussed below owes a good deal to Schwartz and Falconer 1994; Falconer and Savage 1995. See also Grabbe 2001b and also other chapters in Grabbe and Haak 2001, such as Nefzger, all with full bibliography but little or no reference to the archaeological data).

2. Statistics enabling us to quantify the carrying capacity of different regions are hard to come by, but see B. Rosen 1986; Zorn 1994; A. Sasson 2010. See also below on economic strategies, especially the continuing dependence on agro-pastoralism in Iron II, despite urbanization.

3. For these surveys, see chapter 4. On demography, see below.

4. For full discussion, see Avigad 1993; Stager 1990; the exhaustive analysis of Tappy 1992, 2001; Franklin 2003. In general, I follow Avigad here. Note, however, that Tappy would date Building Period IV earlier than Avigad, making it longer and dividing it into two phases, circa 815–732. Then building Period V (not VI) would end with the Assyrian destruction circa 722/721. Cf. Avigad 1993, 1303; Tappy 1992, 253.

5. The degree and nature of expansion to the Western Hill is debated. Geva (2006) takes a minimalist view (with Steiner and Ussishkin), seeing a total population of 6,000–8,000 by the late eighth century. Faust (2005) takes a maximalist view (with Barkay and Broshi), arguing for a population of 18,000–40,000. The matter may not be resolved until Avigad's excavations in the Jewish Quarter are fully published. See, meanwhile, Geva 2000, 2003.

6. E. Mazar and B. Mazar 1989.

7. See the summary in Faust 2005, 103.

8. For the history of exploitation of the Gihon Spring, going back to the Middle Bronze Age, see Reich and Shukron 2004. For the engineering of the late eighth-century tunnel, showing how natural features were exploited, see Gill 1994; Lancaster and Long 1999; Sneh, Shalev, and Weinberger 2010. On the famous inscription, see below. Some have argued the construction of "Hezekiah's" tunnel was not short-term in preparation for the siege of Sennacherib in 701 but took longer and may be either earlier or later. See further below.

9. Cf. Reich 2011; Reich, Shukron, and Lernau 2007, 2008. Here a date of the late ninth century is proposed, but Singer-Avitz 2012a argues for an eighth-century date (predictably, on the Tel Aviv low chronology).

10. Arie 2008 uses the Tel Aviv low chronology to down-date Stratum IVA from the late tenth century to the late ninth century, specifically to a destruction claimed by Joash (805–790). He then argues that (1) this stratum was not Israelite but was an Aramean foundation, to which the Dan victory stela belongs; and (2) all phases of the sacred precinct were in use only in this period, thus were also not Israelite. The arguments against the low chronology adduced in chapter 4 would preclude accepting Arie's views. The pottery he publishes is from insecure loci and is clearly mixed; cf. the cooking pots on fig. 10. On the sacred precinct, see further below on religion. See further Herzog 1997, 221–24.

11. Geva 1989, 88. See also the detailed analysis of Herzog 1997, 224–26; Faust 2012a, 46–58.

12. Faust 2003b.

13. Finkelstein, Ussishkin, and Halpern 2006, 630–87. On other tripartite buildings as storerooms, see further below.

14. Finkelstein, Ussishkin, and Halpern 2006, 130–32. Despite their low chronology, the excavators place their Phase H-4–H-3 (IVA) in the ninth century, as I do here. That would leave very little room for Strata VA/IVB. See further Herzog 1997, 226–29; Faust 2012a, 46–58.

15. Ortiz and Wolff 2012. Palace 8,000 west of the city gate, now Buildings A–C, shows that some administrative functions continued into the eighth century. But domestic dwellings now impinge on the area.

16. See the major reworking of the stratigraphy and chronology in Zorn 1994, 1997, 1999; Brody 2011 (based partly on original field diaries). See also McClellan 1984; Herzog 1997, 237–39; Faust 2012a, 72–77.

17. See Faust 2001, 2002a. Cf. Singer-Avitz 2011.

18. See Bunimovitz and Lederman 1997, 2001b, 2003, 2006, 2009; Bunimovitz and Faust 2001.

19. See the new excavation of Ussishkin (2004). Cf. Herzog 1997, 239–42; Faust 2012a, 78–82. On the beginning of Stratum V, see further Mazar A. 1990, 401; Dever 1984b. The former dates Stratum V, the fortifications, and Palace A to the early ninth century; the latter with (Yadin) to the late tenth century (Rehoboam).

20. For both, see Dever 1992b and references. Ben-Tor's renewed excavations did not, however, confirm Yadin's view. On earthquake destructions, pro and con, see further Bunimovitz and Lederman 2011; Cline 2011.

21. On town planning, see Faust 2002a; Singer-Avitz 2011. See also generally Herzog 1997, 244–47; Faust 2012a, 87–94. The water system was excavated after Aharoni's campaigns, in 1993–1995 (Herzog 1997).

22. For the pottery, see Rast 1978. On the tenth-century cult structure, see chapter 4 above.

23. See A. Mazar's final publications, Mazar and Mullins 2007; Panitz-Cohen and Mazar 2009.

24. On the disputed chronology, see A. Mazar 2011; and contrast Finkelstein 2003a; Finkelstein and Piasetzky 2003c, 2011b, all these with references to many earlier publications. Mazar's conventional dates are adopted here; for the rejection of the low chronology, see the extensive discussion in chapter 4.

25. See Master et al. 2005 for the little information that can be gleaned.

26. On the poor or unfinished (?) houses, see Chambon 1984, 39–44; however, the meaning of the inferior construction is not clear. Herzog (1997, 219) inexplicably shows the gate blocked, but it is obvious that the entrance to the city is here and nowhere else. Faust (2012a, 59) republishes Herzog's gate plan, agreeing with him in rejecting de Vaux's interpretation.

27. For an extensive discussion of this house, not published fully, see Campbell 2002.

28. See Chadwick 1992 for a preliminary report of Hammond's excavations.

29. See Faust 2011a.

30. To preliminary reports add Ben-Tor, Zarzecki, and Cohen-Amidjar 2005.

31. Cahill 2006.

32. See reviews of the publications by Dever 1971; Finkelstein and Singer-Avitz 2009.

33. Finkelstein's notion (2002) of a "Saulide Gibeonite confederacy," a "hub" extending its influence all the way up the Jordan Valley in the tenth century, is conjured from nothing we know from the site itself. If it were true, why was it not a target of the Shoshenq raid circa 920? If there was a tenth-century "hub," it was not Gibeon but Jerusalem (which, of course, Finkelstein's low chronology cannot admit). See further chapter 4.

34. Mazar and Panitz-Cohen 2001, 279–81.

35. For preliminary reports, see Tappy 2009.

36. See the extensive analysis of Faust, 2012a, 82–87; cf. Herzog 1997, 242–44. On the Western Tower, add Shiloh 1970, 186; Holladay 1992, 316–17. Herzog thinks that the Western Tower is later (i.e., Stratum A₁; 1997, 244). His notion that it is built over a Stratum A₂ casemate city wall does not seem to have any basis.

37. To preliminary reports, add Beit-Arieh 1999. For discussions of the border of Judah with Philistia in the eighth century, see Finkelstein and Na'aman 2004; Blakely and Hardin 2002; Tappy 2009b.

38. For references to surveys, see ch. 4 n. 50. The most recent discussion of Iron II village sites, especially those known from surveys, is Faust 2012a, 128–77. He defines a typical Iron Age village as (1) a small, dense site (less than 3 acres), often on a hilltop, sometimes walled; (2) with larger pillar-courtyard houses than urban sites (up to 1300 square feet); (3) self-sufficient and specializing in particular agricultural products (such as olive oil, wine) suitable for trade (2012a, 131–32). He does not discuss population, but his 3-acre upper limit would allow for a population of some 300—precisely our threshold here. In the north, Faust maps some fifteen such villages and a similar number in Judah (131, map 2). See his detailed discussion, particularly valuable for his quantification of house type and size, as well as farms. See further below here on socioeconomic structure. Faust does not include Tel Qiri (which he thinks belongs to a different world; 2012a, 234–37, 245) or Tel Kinrot as villages (below). See n. 40 below; see Faust 2012a for bibliography on the village sites in fig. 2; Schloen 2001; Routledge 2009 on family size. Cf. an older work on the Israelite family (Perdue et al. 1997), especially the chapter by C. Meyers, who espouses the "agrarian" model advanced here. See further below.

39. Add to preliminary publications Ben-Tor and Portugali 1987.

40. For details and bibliography (not repeated here), see Faust 2006a; 2012a, 128–77. See also Dever 2012, 142–205.

41. See Ofer 2001; Zertal 2001 and references there.

42. See Faust 2000, 19. See also Faust 2005.

43. For further details, see Faust 2012a, 178–93. Faust recognizes only a few *real* or tower fortresses, in contradistinction to fortified villages in the countryside, some farms, others private estates. He is undoubtedly correct that the perimeter walls at these sites were not designed for military purposes. Nevertheless, Faust discusses of the many sites here only Maḥruq, Deir Baghl, Khirbet Tabaneh, Arad, Ḥorvat Radum, Mezad Ḥazeva, and Kadesh-barnea.

44. Faust 2012a does not discuss Jezreel at all among his sites classified as forts.

45. See preliminary reports in Ussishkin and Woodhead 1992, 1994, 1998. For the pottery, see Zimhoni 1992b; 2004; cf. the use of the ninth-century pottery by Finkelstein (1997 and thereafter) to support his low chronology. The ninth-century pottery at Jezreel is indeed continuous with pottery conventionally dated to the tenth century, as is now generally accepted, but as I have shown in chapter 4, that is largely irrelevant. It has been suggested by some that Jezreel has been

dated to the ninth century mainly on biblical grounds (i.e., Ahab's winter palace), but that is not true. Its stratigraphy, however, is not always trustworthy, even though it is essentially a one-period site, because of very poor preservation. There may be some pre-Omride remains below the three- (or-four?) entryway gate, a corner tower, and on virgin soil—even some ashlar masonry, according to one Field Supervisor (Oredsson 1998). Some reliable stratigraphy may be reflected in the observation that, after the short-lived fortifications had gone out of use, a few domestic dwellings were constructed (Ussishkin and Woodhead 1994, 47). Two other circular tower fortresses in the north are cited by Faust (2012a, 178, 79; Khirbet esh-Shaqq and Rujm Abu-Muheir (surveyed and published in Hebrew by Zertal).

46. See Mazar 1982b for Khirbet Abu Tuwein, as well as the other sites noted around Jerusalem.

47. Lipschits et al. 2011.

48. For reworking of the excavations, see Herzog 1984, 2001; Herzog et al. 1984; Herzog, Rainey, and Moshkovitz 1977.

49. Pratico 1993. Needless to say, Glueck's reconstruction of King Solomon's copper mines must be abandoned. However, there is now evidence of copper production in the southern Arabah during the eleventh–tenth century; see ch. 4 and n. 61.

50. See now the final report, Cohen and Bernick-Greenberg 2007.

51. To preliminary reports, add now Meshel 2012, with many more details than in the numerous (and sometimes sensational) earlier discussions. The site probably served as a combination caravanserai, or way-station, and a fort guarding trade routes along the Darb Ghaza. It is clearly government constructed and supplied. Meshel equivocates on whether 'Ajrud was a caravanserai, a fort, or a religious center. Obviously, it was all three. See further below on religion.

52. For surveys and demographic projections, see references.

53. Broshi and Finkelstein 1992, 54.

54. Broshi and Finkelstein 1992; Dagan 2000; Faust 2013b.

55. On the Dan and Mesha inscriptions, see below and n. 58. On these and the Black Obelisk, see Rainey 2006, 199–213. Some have argued that the figure kneeling before Shalmaneser's throne is not Jehu but only an emissary, but that is irrelevant here. Jehu's name on the inscription is clear.

56. See Fritz 1995, 151–60 for convenient discussion.

57. On the tripartite pillared buildings, see the summaries in Herr 1997, 138; Kochavi 1998; de Geus 2003, 63–74. Opinions on the function are varied, from stables (Holladay 1986), to barracks (Fritz 1995), to marketplaces (Herr 1988), to storehouses (Pritchard 1970; de Geus 2003). Most authorities today favor the latter interpretation. Many of these buildings were found empty, but the three Beersheba examples, adjoining the gate and large plaza, were found full of pottery, including dozens of large storejars. On the Megiddo examples, see further below

and n. 61. Kochavi adds ʿEin-Gev and Tell Malḥata, as well as a few Philistine, Phoenician, and Aramean examples.

58. The earlier excavators of Dhiban claimed that a poorly preserved "podium" was the foundation of Mesha's "royal quarter." But they acknowledged that this was an assumption based on the Mesha stela (Tushingham 1993, 381). More recent excavations undertaken by Routledge, who also examined earlier records, have confirmed that a major building on the summit may indeed date to the ninth century, but its nature and function remain enigmatic (Routledge 2004, 161–68, with plans, sections, and some pottery, all from his Phases 1–5, tenth–seventh century). Routledge attempts to get around the dilemma by arguing that the term "Dibon" in the stela refers not to a capital city but to the larger region; that is, Mesha was a "Dibonite" ruling over a particular tribal entity. See Naʾaman 1999 on royal inscriptions and the book of Kings; and below.

59. See the preliminary reports, convincingly arguing for the correlation of the siegework (Phase 4) with Hazael's campaigns in the late ninth century (Maier 2006; Maier and Gur-Arieh 2011, the latter with references to earlier reports, as well as a detailed discussion of sources on ancient sieges). Ussishkin's attempt (2009a) to refute Maier's interpretation by claiming that the Gath moat is a "natural feature" can safely be ignored (so Maier and Gur-Arieh 2011).

60. Cf. the discussion in Pitard 1987, 100–214 (written before the discovery of the Dan inscription).

61. The classic work of Yadin (1963) on ancient warfare could adduce very little archaeological evidence for Iron Age Israel and Judah. A recent work attempts to assemble more recent data on horses and chariotry (Cantrell 2011); see also Im 2006. A synthetic work on city gates (Blomquist 1999) is concerned more with gate shrines (see below on cult). The so-called stables at several sites are discussed above in n. 57.

62. On the nomadic ideal, see further below. Faust has dealt extensively with the problem of egalitarianism and its possible reflection in material culture remains (2006a, 70–81, 92–107, 194–206; 2012a, 8–21, 31–34, 220–23). He argues that "there is a wealth of evidence indicating that the Israelite society was one with an egalitarian ethos" (2006a, 105). He does distinguish, however, between ethos (the ideal) and behavior (practice). Even so, his overall stress is that village and town layout, house form and function, pottery, technology, and material culture in general all reflect a sort of "democratic" society, one characterized by a preference for simplicity that is the hallmark of Israelite ethnicity.

When Faust comes to deal more explicitly with the archaeological data, however, he does acknowledge that it provides considerable evidence of socioeconomic stratification. Thus he concludes that it is difficult to accept the views of biblical scholars such as Speiser, Mendenhall, Gottwald, and Cross, that the biblical ideal reflects the reality of Iron Age life. As he puts it: "real egalitarian societies do not exist, and it is quite clear that a society as complex as the Israelite society was not egalitarian" (2012a, 222).

Stager (1985a) and Schloen (2001), in advancing the notion of ancient Israel as a patrimonial society, obviously do not espouse an egalitarian ideal—quite the opposite.

On the "nomadic ideal" as fiction, see Dever 1993a; Hiebert 2009. See also above.

63. Cf. Brody 2011; Zorn 2011; Singer-Avitz 2011.

64. On the Samaria ostraca, see Kaufmann 1982 (summarizing a Harvard doctoral dissertation); Rainey 2006, 221–22; Ahituv 2008, 258–312. On the context of the ostraca, see Tappy 1992; 2006. See also further below.

65. The literature on the pillar-courtyard house is vast, but major works are Stager 1985a; Holladay 1992; Netzer 1992; Faust 2001; Herr and Clark 2001; Schloen 2001; Bunimovitz and Faust 2003; Faust and Bunimovitz 2003; Routledge 2009; Hardin 2010; Yasur-Landau 2010; and see chapters and references in Yasur-Landau, Ebeling, and Mazow 2011; add now Faust 2012a.

66. On agriculture generally, see Hopkins 1985; Stager 1985a; Borowski 1987. On animal husbandry, see Borowski 1998; Hesse 1995; A. Sasson 1998, 2010; see below on herding pigs specifically. On grinding grain, see Ebeling and Rowan 2008. On bread baking, see C. Meyers 2001, 2007a; Ebeling and Homan 2008. On cooking generally, see Baadsgaard 2008. On diet, the studies of N. MacDonald 2008 and Shafer-Elliott 2012 are comprehensive. On weaving, see Cassuto 2008. The above topics are also covered in works on daily life, such as King and Stager 2001; Ebeling 2010. See also the extended discussion of Dever 2012, 141–205), with numerous illustrations.

67. Many of the scholars who have discussed these houses (n. 65 above), as well as virtually all survey and demographic studies, have used Naroll's 1962 study. Earlier studies held that an Israelite nuclear family was rather large, but current analyses calculate a family size of anywhere from four to six. Recent treatments of "the archaeology of the family" give access to much of the publications and the data (as Yasur-Landau, Ebeling, and Mazow 2011).

68. Zorn 2011.

69. Brody 2011.

70. Faust (2012a, 111) has also questioned Brody's reconstruction of this block of houses. His objection, however, rests largely on his argument that such compounds do not house extended families, as Stager, Schloen, and Brody think. See further below.

71. Faust and Bunimovitz 2003, 26.

72. Faust 2012a, 159–97.

73. Schloen 2001, 135–36, 147–48.

74. Singer-Avitz 2011.

75. Campbell 1994; cf. Holladay 1992. Stager and others think that the courtyard was not roofed, but others disagree (Shiloh 1970; Herzog 1984; Fritz 1995).

76. Hardin 2010, 125–60. The table in fig. 5.32 here is based on Hardin's 2001 dissertation. In the 2010 publication the contents are discussed and illustrated in

detail, but the table does not appear, apparently because closer analysis yielded slightly different results.

77. Faust 2012a, 160.

78. Hardin 2010, 172.

79. Sahlins 1972, 95, quoted also above in chapter 3.

80. See references in n. 67 above, noting other works. Add now Faust 2012a, 216–29. Some of Faust and Bunimovitz's "ethnic markers" are obvious but represent common sense and are universal, such as the distinction between public/communal areas and private areas. Nevertheless, their shift of the focus of interpretation from the purely functional explanations of many other scholars to ideological factors is welcome, even if debated. See further below on ethnicity and material culture.

81. Faust 2010b, 62; see also 2012a, 216–29.

82. Dar 1986, 253.

83. For the state-of-the-art publication, see the essays in Yasur-Landau, Ebeling, and Mazow 2011, with full references; see especially the introduction by the editors (2011, 1–6). Among biblical scholars (feminist or not), the work of Susan Ackerman stands out, skillfully synthesizing both the textual and the archaeological data on the ancient Israelite family (2003, 2006, 2008). See further below on women and the cult.

84. Holladay 1995, 393; A. Sasson 2010, 117.

85. See Holladay 2006, 2009a, 2009b. See especially 2007, 212 and elsewhere. Here Holladay radically changes his 1995 view that there is no evidence that "these settlements (i.e., four-room house towns) [are] of government redistribution below the palace, military and administrative levels" (1995, 389). Now he assumes that vast reserves of silver would have been readily available from Greece and Sardina, transported by maritime traders, but he gives no details. As for inexhaustible tariffs from overland camel trade in South Arabian spices, that, too, is largely speculation. Finally, the only archaeological evidence we have for extensive silver transactions (sheqel weights, silver hoards) comes from the seventh century. Holladay's fanciful scheme is based largely on an insufficiently critical reading of the texts. They exaggerate. Nevertheless, Holladay does make admirable (and rare) efforts at quantification of the archaeological data. Master (2010) cites some archaeological and textual data for South Arabian trade, but nearly all of it applies to the seventh century, with only the biblical texts to hint at tenth–eighth-century trade, an inadequate witness. On the scarcity of South Arabian texts, see Kitchen 2010.

86. Schloen 2001, passim.

87. Nam 2012, 192–93.

88. Faust 2012a, 31–38, 183–89.

89. On the Samaria ostraca, see also n. 64 above.

90. Older studies of town planning and the use of masonry are Shiloh 1970, 1978. Add now Herzog 1992; Netzer 1992; Faust 2001; 2012a, 68–95. Classic stud-

ies unfortunately neglected are Braemer 1982 and G. R. H. Wright 2000, 2005, 2009. Browsing through Braemer's numerous house plans shows how varied domestic structures are. See below on houses. On roads, see Dorsey 1992.

91. See ch. 4 and nn. 61 and 76 above on the Arabah copper-smelting facilities, although in decline in Iron II. On iron working, see McNutt 1990; on Beth-shemesh, see Bunimovitz and Lederman 2009, 128–31.

92. Wheel-burnishing, which begins in the ninth century and soon dominates, obviously facilitated mass production of pottery. It is usually explained as functional, since burnishing seals the porous surface of a vessel and makes cleaning much easier. Slip and burnish, however, is also a form of decoration, and thus it may have implications for cultural and ethnic identity. Faust has argued that the distinction of unburnished and burnished pottery is evidence of growing social complexity and of diverging male and female roles. Female potters continued to make utilitarian wares, while it was males who produced the highly decorated burnished wares, mostly for feasting (Faust 2002b). On the luxury Samaria wares as derived from Phoenician polished wares, see Holladay 1995, 379–80. For convenient comparisons of north and south, see Amiran 1970, pls. 62–89.

93. Of particular interest is Sylvia Schroer's *In Israel Gab es Bilder* (1987) (*There Was Art in Israel*), which does much to challenge the conventional notion that ancient Israel was devoid of any significant artistic traditions. This pioneering work, however, is rarely cited. See also Bickel et al. 2007. On iconography, especially seals, see also Keel 1997; Keel and Uehlinger 1998. On iconography, see further below and nn. 95 and 114.

94. On the ivories, the standard works are those of I. Winter 1976, 1981. Tappy has shown in a remarkable bit of detective work that the bulk of the ivories were found in disturbed or secondary contexts and cannot be associated directly with the so-called Ivory House (Tappy 2006). Nevertheless, they do help to illustrate the presence of luxury goods in general in the tenth–eighth century. On the difficulty of inferring socioeconomic status from the find-spots of luxury goods in general, see Faust 2012a, 32–35, 169–70 (who, however, scarcely discusses artwork at all).

95. Nearly three thousand Iron Age Israelite (or Hebrew) seals are known. For orientation, see Albertz and Schmitt 2012, 248–49, with reference to basic collections such as Keel 1995, Keel and Uehlinger 1998; Sass and Uehlinger 1993; Renz and Röllig 1995–2003; Avigad and Sass 1997; add now Millard 2012; Lubetski and Lubetski 2012. For the hoard of some 150 anepigraphic seals (symbols only) found near the Gihon Spring in Jerusalem, see above. On iconography, see references in n. 93 above and n. 114 below. See also chapter 6 on seal impressions or bullae.

Older works such as Tigay 1987 on the onomasticon of Iron Age Hebrew seals (many of them anepigraphic) have now been supplanted by Albertz (in Albertz and Schmitt 2012), who catalogues 2,922 seals and seal impressions (2012, 474–609). He reaches the conclusion that "unambiguous allusions to the specific traditions of official Israelite religion—the exodus, conquest, or kingship; Sinai, Zion, or Bethel theology—are non-existent" (2012, 483). Thus, "Up to the seventh century, the Israelite family and household religion manifested almost no unique features but was quite similar to other family and household religions of the Levant" (2012, 495). See further below and nn. 111 and 120.

96. On the Proto-Aeolic capitals, see Franklin 2011; Lipschits 2011. At least twenty-seven have been found at Israelite sites, but none in situ. They probably begin in the tenth century (Megiddo), but they are more common at ninth-century sites. They may be called "volute" (or even "palmette") capitals, from the motif of twin drooping fronds, as though from an original tree motif. Franklin thinks that they were not structural but only decorative.

97. The only study of this unique hand is that of Schroer 1987.

98. See Ziffer 2013, following a reconstruction of the fragments by Pirhiya Beck. On the ʿAjrud paintings' religious significance, see below.

99. The only significant studies are Braun 2002, a musicologist; and Burgh 2006, an archaeologist and musician.

100. On the seventh-century Wadi Murabbaʿat, papyrus, see Ahituv 2008, 213–15. It was Aharoni who pioneered the dipping technique, put into practice at Arad. On literacy in general, as well as the existence of scribal schools, see Rolllston 2006, 2010, with bibliography. The Siloam Tunnel inscription, which we have treated here as a royal inscription, would be another example; see further below. On graffiti, see Naʾaman 2001.

101. See Avigad 1993, 1304; Ahituv 2008, 257.

102. See Reich, Shukron, and Lernau 2008 and references there. On the pottery, see now Singer-Avitz 2012a.

103. On Samaria, see above and n. 64. On the ostraca, add Ahituv 2008, 258–312; Dobbs-Allsopp et al. 2005, 423–97. On the Qasile and Hazor ostraca, see Ahituv 2008, 154–56, 330–32.

104. Some scholars doubt that it is a royal inscription, i.e., commissioned by a king. See Rendsberg and Schiedewind 2010. On the inscription, see Ahituv 2008, 19–25; Dobbs-Allsopp et al. 2005, 499–506.

105. See Ahituv 2008, 233–39.

106. Cf. Ahituv 2008, 180–209, 230–33 and references there.

107. Ahituv 2008, 313–28; cf. Naʾaman 2001 on graffiti.

108. See Sanders (2009, 125, 171), implying the existence of scribal schools. See also Rollston 2006. Schniedewind 2013 speaks of "a linguistic imperialism," clear evidence of political control, but he distinguishes a northern "Israelian" Hebrew (as Rendsburg 2000).

109. On Dan, see now Greer 2013. For the following cult places and practices, I will cite mostly original or primary publications. Subsequent interpretations are too numerous and varied to cite fully. Fortunately, several synthetic discussions can be consulted for differing views and documentation. Some of the most useful general archaeological publications are Holladay 1987; van der Toorn 1996, 1998; Hadley 2000; Nakhai 2001; Zevit 2001; Zwingenberger 2001; Dever 2003d; Herr 2007; Nakhai 2011; Ackerman 2012; Albertz

and Schmitt 2012. Works on women's cults, in addition to the above, include Ackerman 1992, 2003, 2012; E. Meyers 1997; C. Meyers 2013; Nakhai 2011; Albertz et al. 2014, all with full references. On the recent emphasis on family and household religion, see Yasur-Landau, Ebeling, and Mazow 2011 and full references there (as well as Albertz and Schmitt 2012). Works of biblical scholars on Israelite religion are far too numerous to cite; all but a few of the most recent fail to consider the archaeological evidence that is taken here as primary. For a summary and critique, see Dever 2003d, 32–62. Biblical theologies are almost entirely modern apologetical constructs and are thus considered irrelevant here. For a treatise on the archaeological correlates of religious beliefs in general, see the essays in Rowan 2012.

110. Here I follow the reworking of Aharoni's disputed stratigraphy and chronology in Herzog 2001, 2002. The alterations to the Strata X–IX temple and its final abandonment (not destruction) have been reasonably attributed to attempted cult reforms—in the case of Herzog's revised dates during the reign of Hezekiah. Na'aman, however, thinks that the temple was still in use in Stratum VIII and was then destroyed circa 701. It "shows no sign of a cult reform" (2002a, 595). Na'aman, while an excellent historian, had no firsthand experience of the archeological data at Arad. Rainey (1984), like Herzog an Arad staff member, agrees in seeing the dismantling of the Stratum IX temple as part of Hezekiah's reforms. This is not old-fashioned biblical archaeology, only common sense. On the ostraca, see Ahituv 2008, 92–153.

111. See now the comprehensive survey of Albertz and Schmitt 2012, 57–175, which goes beyond that of any archaeologist, even Zevit (2001) or Dever (2005a). These features of widespread communal practice that are largely outside of public cult places (certainly apart from temples) have usually been seen as reflecting folk or popular religion or perhaps nonconformist as opposed to conformist religion. These terms have been criticized as too imprecise, even condescending, so that the term family or household religion is increasingly preferred; see Albertz and Schmitt 2012, 2–16; 45–56, with references.

112. See Albertz 1994 (already in German in 1978); and cf. n. 111 above. The bibliography on Asherah both by biblicists and archaeologists has proliferated beyond our ability to document it here. See U. Winter 1983; Becking et al. 2001; Ackerman 2003; Cornelius 2004; Mastin 2004; Dever 2005a, 176–251; 2014; C. Meyers 2013, all with full references. Much of the discussion has hinged on the interpretation of the term 'šrh in the Khirbet el-Qom and Kuntillet 'Ajrud inscriptions; see below and nn. 114 and 115. Since the figurines proliferate in the seventh century, they will be discussed further in chapter 6.

113. See further below, ch. 6 n. 71. However, the latter category cannot comprehend a number of more specific or more public cult places, such as Dan, Arad, and Kuntillet 'Ajrud.

114. Kuntillet 'Ajrud has been widely discussed since Meshel announced its discovery (1978; cf. Hess 2007, 284). The final publication (Meshel 2012) does

not change much. The notion that it is not a shrine (Holladay 1987, 250) or is a scribal school (Lemaire 2011) can be ignored. It is obviously a combination of a way-station (or caravanserai), a fort, and a desert shrine. The reading "Yahweh … and his Asherah" was contested at first, i.e., "Yahweh and his cult-symbol." The objections were ostensibly on the ground that in classical Hebrew a personal name does not take a possessive suffix; however, one suspects that theological presuppositions were also operative. Yet there are graffiti where grammatical rules may not always apply (and there are other instances). In my case, it is now generally conceded that the Hebrew term *'ăšērâ* here probably does refer to the goddess herself (as also at Khirbet el-Qom). On the inscriptions, see further Ahituv 2008, 313–28; Dobbs-Allsopp et al. 2005, 277–98. See further n. 115 below.

115. The standard work is Bloch-Smith 1992. Most authorities connect the figurines more or less directly with the goddess Asherah, the only well-attested female deity in the Hebrew Bible. Some are hesitant to see the figurines as actual images of the goddess, but few, with the exception of C. Meyers (2007b), interpret them as votives, i.e., human females in the presence of the deity. Some biblicists (McCarter 1987) see the figurines, as well as the ʿAjrud and el-Qom texts, as depicting Asherah as a "hypostasis of Yahweh," i.e., simply a cult image.

On the debated issue of iconography, specifically whether or not ancient Israelite religion was aniconic (as prescribed in the biblical texts), see generally Mettinger 1995; Hendel 1997; Keel 1997; the essays in van der Toorn 1997; Keel and Uehlinger 1998; Becking et al. 2001; Lewis 2005; Ornan 2005; Walls 2005; Dever 2006. There are few studies on Israelite art per se, but see Schroer 1987 as cited above and the several essays of Pirhiya Beck, collected in 2002. See also n. 113 above.

See further below and n. 118. Franklin 2003 claims to have found robbed tombs of some kings at Samaria, and the Silwan necropolis in Jerusalem may also provide some evidence of robbed tombs of elites, perhaps even kings; see Naʾaman 2002a; Zorn 2006. For rare tombs before the eighth century and the wide variety thereafter, see Yezerski 2013a.

116. Dever 1969–1970. Here, too, the literature has burgeoned. For a survey, see Dever 1999. Many of the works cited in nn. 112–13 above deal with the el-Qom inscription (as also with Kuntillet ʿAjrud).

117. Avigad 1953; cf. Ahituv 2008, 44–49.

118. See Faust and Bunimovitz 2008, who liken the typical rock-cut bench tomb that spread in Judah in the ninth–eighth century to the pillar courtyard or four-room house of the period. The multiple burials over a hundred years or so and several generations then represent the continuity of the extended family and its heritage. They explain the new fashion of burials as due to the acceleration of urbanism and all its ills, as well as growing insecurity as the Assyrian destructions began to be immanent. On the wider variety tombs in the north during the eighth–seventh century, after the Assyrian invasions, see further Yezerski 2013a.

119. J. Osborne 2011, 53. The entire discussion, with full bibliography, is stimulating. See also Faust and Bunimovitz 2008.

120. Few biblical scholars treating the topic of Israelite religion (especially biblical theologians) seem to grasp the real-life Iron Age situation portrayed here. If they did, they would realize that they are looking almost exclusively at the texts *about* religion rather than the phenomenon itself. This preoccupation with texts is particularly puzzling, since these same scholars recognize that the biblical texts are a construct that is late and tendentious. Zevit 2001 and Albertz and Schmitt 2012 are refreshing exceptions, but see also Becking et al. 2001. For a critique, see Dever 2005a, 32–62. See n. 95 above and further below n. 121.

121. See van der Toorn 1997.

122. See n. 120 above. Chief among biblical scholars who acknowledge the archaeological data as a primary source is Grabbe 2007b.

123. On ethnicity, see chs. 3–4 above. Most studies have assumed that from the tenth century on (Iron IIA–C) the majority of the population of Cisjordan, apart from the Phoenicia and Philistine coastal plain, were ethnic Israelites. Faust, whose study of Israel's ethnogenesis (2006b) was fundamental, agrees.

124. See Silver 1983; Rofé 1997; Houston 2004; and the essays in Grabbe 2001a.

125. The following summary is based on more detailed descriptions of these sites above in chs. 3–4. On Phoenicia, see ch. 2 n. 44 and ch. 3 nn. 14–16; add now Aubet 2014. On the Arameans, see ch. 2 n. 47; add now Mazzoni 2014; Sader 2014. On the Philistines, see ch. 2 nn. 30–33; ch. 3 n. 8; add now Ben-Shlomo 2014. On Transjordan, see n. 126 below.

126. See references in ch. 2 nn. 47–52; ch. 3 nn. 6–9; add now Bienkowski 2014; Herr 2014; Steiner 2014; Younker 2014.

127. A good summary of the following texts will be found in Rainey 2006, 223–38. The discussion of sites is based on Dever 2007a.

128. Tadmor 1994. See also 1962, on Abel-beth-maacah.

129. The site has been surveyed (Dever 1986), but excavations began only in 2012 under Nava Panitz-Cohen and Robert Mullins.

130. Yadin 1972, 190–94; 1993, 603.

131. B. MacDonald 2000, 195–205. For the possibility that "Galilee and Gilead" are glosses, see Na'aman 1995.

132. Millard 1992.

133. Crowfoot, Kenyon, and Sukenik 1942, 110–15.

134. Tappy 2001, 240–41.

135. Biran 1994, 203–6, 253, 260–70. The recent reanalysis of Arie (2008) does not change the picture. The Stratrum II pottery published (figs. 14–17) is typically mid- to late eighth century.

136. A. Mazar 2001a, 296–300.

137. Shiloh 1993, 1021. For the renowned excavations of Finkelstein and Ussishkin, see Finkelstein, Ussishkin, and Halpern 2000, 468.

138. Rast 1978, 41.

139. Ben-Tor 1993, 807.

140. Ben-Tor and Portugali 1987, 71–73.

141. Chambon 1984, 439–41.

142. Humbert 1993, 866.

143. Toombs 1992, 1185; cf. Campbell 1994.

144. Dever 1985b, 223–26; 1993b, 36–38.

145. Faust 2011c. On deportations, see Younger 1998, who sees several deportations and who also attempts to quantify the various claims in the Assyrian texts by looking at the built-up areas and population of lower Galilee based on the archaeological data. He also speculates on the fate of the deportees in Assyria, as does Knoppers 2004 and Na'aman 1993. See also Na'aman 1995.

146. For the following, see Stern 2001, 14–57.

147. See also Grabbe 2007a, 164–65. The idea of a continuum employed here owes much to Grabbe. On the general problem of utilizing the book of Kings as a historical source, see now the numerous essays in Halpern and Lemaire 2010. See also ch. 1 above.

148. On the confusion of the names Asherah, Astarte, and Ashtoreth, see van der Toorn, Becking, and van der Horst 1999, 99–105, 109–14; cf. LaRocca-Pitts 2001, 187–92, 260–61.

CHAPTER 6

Iron IIC: Judah in the Seventh Century

Introduction

The period we designate Iron IIC is confined principally to the seventh century, set off conveniently by two dramatic destructions: the Assyrian campaigns of Sennacherib in 701 and the Babylonian destructions in 586. After that, the southern kingdom of Judah comes to an end. In the north, in Israel proper, the end had already come with the Assyrian campaigns in 734–721, after which the whole region was incorporated into the Assyrian Empire (ch. 5). Thus was born the legend of the "ten lost tribes of Israel"; our coverage of the seventh century is confined largely to Judah.

The Post-721 Horizon in the South

Following his triumph over Samaria and the northern kingdom of Israel in 721, Sargon II (722–705) campaigned farther south, but apparently mostly down the Philistine coast. First, in his second year he consolidated his hold over Syria by putting down a coalition of the kings of Hamath, Arpad, and Damascus. Then the Assyrian annals say that he subdued the border town of Gibbethon (near Gezer), followed by the taking of Ekron, Ashdod, Gath, and Raphia along the Philistine plain, perhaps in 716. The following several years were devoted to campaigns in Syria and possibly even into the Arabian Peninsula. Then in 712 there is a reference to another campaign against Ashdod. By this time, it is significant that Sargon is claiming to have taken tribute from not only the kings of Philistia but also from the kings of Judah ("the location of which is far away"), as well as the kings of Edom and Moab. By 705 Sargon was dead, apparently fighting rebellion in Babylon.

We shall return to the archaeological evidence for Sargon's dealings with Judah presently, but meanwhile we need to survey the general situation after the fall of Samaria.

The Expansion of Jerusalem

Assyrian deportations must have reduced the population of the northern kingdom drastically. The Assyrian claim to have deported some 27,000 people from the district of Samaria alone, if accepted, would have amounted to perhaps one-tenth of the entire population. Many more would have been killed or deported, leaving the remnant of the population displaced, impoverished, and desperate. It is not surprising that many scholars have suggested recently that, in the wake of the fall of Samaria, thousands of refugees may have moved south to relative safety in Judah. There is now reliable evidence that many of these refugees came to reside in Jerusalem, swelling the size of the occupied area from some 15 acres in the early eighth century to as much as 150 acres by the last years of that century. The population would thus have grown from about 8,000 to perhaps 30,000, according to some authorities.[1]

The principal archaeological evidence for these projections comes from Avigad's excavations west of the Temple Mount in the present Jewish Quarter, as well as other soundings extending as far west as the Armenian Quarter and the Jaffa Gate. In the area designated the Southwestern Hill, the results now published by Geva include large-scale fortifications (beyond the earlier Broad Wall), extensive terracing and filling operations, densely built-up areas of domestic houses thrown up with no evidence of urban planning and even structures identified as "dispersed farmsteads," several dozen tombs outside the city wall, seal impressions (bullae) of high-ranking officials, and pottery and objects such as *lmlk* jar handles typical of Lachish III, clearly destroyed in 701 (below). Jerusalem had thus become a great metropolis—perhaps five times larger than Lachish—and thus the place where the majority of Judah's population may have been concentrated.

Standardization of Weights and Measures

Population growth on this scale places great demands on the local administration, in this case on the Judahite capital's officials. One measure that

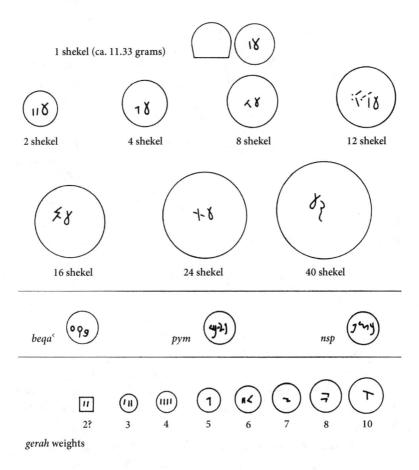

1 shekel (ca. 11.33 grams)

2 shekel 4 shekel 8 shekel 12 shekel

16 shekel 24 shekel 40 shekel

beqaʿ *pym* *nsp*

2? 3 4 5 6 7 8 10

gerah weights

Fig. 6.1. The Judahite sheqel-weight system (Kletter 1999, fig. 6)

indicates an attempt to cope with socioeconomic challenges is the standardization of weights and measures. These measures can be closely dated to the last quarter of the eighth century but are mostly seventh century in date. Since only a handful of the 350 or so weights from known contexts come from the north (ca. 3.5 percent), these weights are characteristically Judahite. Thus they must have come into widespread circulation only after the fall of the northern kingdom in 721.

Kletter, who has published a complete corpus (fig. 6.1), does not regard the Judahite weights as indications of royal measures but only as representing private trade relations. This seems unlikely, however, in view of the highly standardized weights that we actually have. The known examples

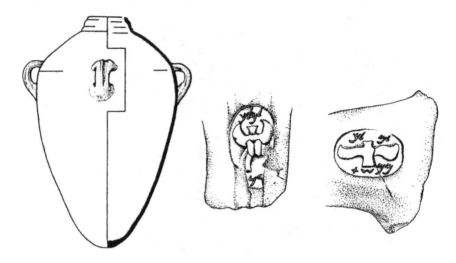

Fig. 6.2. Royal stamped jar handles reading *lmlk*, "belonging to the king" (Gitin 2006, fig. 2:2, 3; McCarter 1996, no. 109)

of denominations of 1 to 40 sheqels, as well as fraction-weights and even smaller *gerah* weights of 1 to 10, are so symmetrical that the official weight of the sheqel can be calculated at circa 11.33 grams. There are variations, to be sure, but these are exceptions that reinforce the rule. The only explanation for such standardization of weights and measures is the regulation of commerce by a centralized government. Private entrepreneurs could scarcely have achieved such regulation. The economic significance of the Judean sheqel weight system will be discussed further below.[2]

The Royal Stamped Jar Handles

A distribution map of the Judahite sheqel weights clearly defines the political borders of Judah in the late eighth–seventh century, as Kletter has shown. Another class of artifacts similarly dated and distributed consists of some 1,700 *lmlk* or "Judean royal stamped jar handles." These are seal impressions on the upper handles of rather stereotypical large store jars, depicting a two- or four-winged scroll and bearing the designation *lmlk* ("for/to the king," or royal) on the upper register. On the lower register there is one of four site names: *mmšt* (Jerusalem?), *śwkh* (Socoh), *zyp* (Ziph), or *hbrn* (Hebron) (fig. 6.2).

The ovoid, four-handled store jars are distinctive in form, and the clays appear to have come from only a few proveniences. An earlier study estimated that the majority of the impressions were made by only a handful of individual seals. Finally, many of the store jars also bear the names of officials. All this, plus the *lmlk*, or "royal," designation and the use of only four place names, suggests that these stamped store jars are evidence of the government's preparations for the anticipated Assyrian invasions of the late eighth century. The store jars were manufactured at designated sites under royal supervision, filled with provisions, then sent to more than seventy sites throughout Judah (almost exclusively).

Vaughn has done the most thorough study of the *lmlk* jar handles. His 1999 summary is worth presenting here in full.[3]

Fig. 6.3. Royal stamped jar handles by site

Site	*lmlk*	Official
Lachish	407	76
Jerusalem	275+	15
Ramat Raḥel	160	17
Gibeon	95	7
Tell en-Naṣbeh	86	5
Beth-Shemesh	48+	13
Tell el-Judeideh	39	17
Gezer	37+	2
Khirbet el-Burj	24	1
Mareshah	19	6
Azekah	18	3
Tel ʿErani	15	1
Gibeah	14	
Khirbet ʿAbbad (Tel Sokoh)	13+	3
Beth-Zur	12	
Arad	10	1
Tel Batash	11	2
Tell eṣ-Ṣafi	6	4
Mevaseret	5	
Hebron	5	
Tell Beit Mirsim	4	2

ʿAroʿer	3	
Ekron	3	
Khirbet Marah el-Jumma	3 or 4	
Khirbet er-Ras	3	
Jericho	2	
Beersheba	2	
Anathoth	2	
Khirbet Qeila	2	1
Khirbet es-Samrah	2	
Tel Ḥalif	2	
Tel Jezreel	2	
Ashdod	1	
Bethel	1	
Bethlehem	1	
Beth-Ḥoron	1	
ʿEin-Gedi	1	3
Eshtaol	1	
Kiryat Ata (Kfar Ata)	1	
Khirbet el-ʿAbhar	1	
Ḥorvat Dorban	1	
Ḥorvat Maʿon	1	
Khirbet Qumran	1	
Khirbet Rabud	1	2
Ḥorvat Shilḥa	1	
Tell ʿIra	1	
Tell ash-Shuqf	1	
Khirbet el-Qom	1	
ʿEin Yaʿel	1	1
Nes Harim	1	
Ḥirbet Jaresh	1	
Adullam	1	1
Khirbet Zawiya	1	
Givat Haaphurit South	1	
Beit Ṣafafa	1	
Dagan 1992, site 62	2	

Dagan 1992, site 66	1	
Khirbat Jannaba et Taḥta	1	
Dagan 1992 unnamed site	1	
unnamed agricultural site	1	
Tel ʿEton	1	
Gedor	1	
Betar	1	
Ḥorvat Shovav		1
Naḥal Zimra		1
Tel Tekoa		1
unknown provenance	355	82
TOTALS	1,716	268

A glance at this chart shows that nearly half of the known examples of the jar handles (842) come from only three regions: Jerusalem, nearby Ramat Raḥel, and the great fortress at Lachish. Another 395 come from ten other strategic sites, including Gibeon, Tell en-Naṣbeh (Mizpah?), Gezer, and Beth-Shemesh.

Despite the evidence for royal administration, until recently there has been little archaeological data to confirm the exact place of manufacture. Now, however, it appears from a computer-generated petrographic analysis of 110 of the store jars that all but two were made in one area in the Shephelah. The name *mmšt* has been interpreted as representing Hebrew *memshalt*, "government." Socoh may be identified with Khirbet Shuweiket er-Ras, at the entrance to the Vale of Elah and the road up to Jerusalem, which has only been partially excavated. Ziph may be located somewhere in the Hebron district. Hebron is clearly Jebel er-Rumeidah, modern Hebron, but again, excavations have been very limited. All these sites, however, appear to be in the Shephelah and the Judahite hill country, where wine and olive production would have supplied important commodities.

Naʾaman's 1986 study could not take into account the material used in Vaughn's work and thus still depended on the obsolete study of Welten (1969). He postulated that there were two closely spaced phases of the use of the store jars, although he did not think that the well-known distinction between the Egyptian-style two-winged sun-discs and four-winged scarab stamps was chronologically significant. Naʾaman regarded both phases of use as short-lived and connected specifically with Hezekiah's preparations for siege. The contents of the store jars were probably wine, to judge from the location of the production centers.[4]

The latest study is that of Gitin, whose argument that the *lmlk* store jars (his type SJO) have a much longer history—up to two hundred years—has far-reaching implications. Gitin divides the store jars into five subtypes, stretching from prototypes (his PSJO types) in the ninth or even tenth century, to post-701 examples continuing in use into the seventh century (perhaps without *lmlk* stamps but with rosette stamps). Nevertheless, it still appears that many, if not most, of the examples do date to the late eighth century and relate to Hezekiah and the anticipated 701 siege.[5]

The Siloam Tunnel

Jerusalem, despite its strategic location, has always suffered from an inadequate water supply. The only natural source was the Gihon Spring, at the foot of the eastern slopes of the Ophel spur. An early Iron Age shaft (called Warren's Shaft, after its discoverer) consists of a sloping tunnel with stairs and a vertical shaft some 45 feet deep, together with another tunnel leading from the spring to the bottom of the latter shaft. It has been identified with the *sinnôr* (or pipe) by which David's troops gained entrance into the city, but this is disputed. Nevertheless, the entrance is inside the line of the city wall, so a tenth-century date is possible.

The major improvement in the eighth century was a meandering underground tunnel cut through the bedrock, some 580 yards long, which conducted the spring water near the base of Warren's Shaft southward to a large reservoir inside the Iron Age city wall. This tunnel is a marvel of ancient engineering. It exploited the natural karsitic features of the bedrock, which produced its convoluted appearance. Periodic vertical air shafts were dug down to the tunnel's level to aid the miners, who worked in the dark in confines where they were barely able to stand. Depending on gravity flow alone, the engineers had somehow to adhere to precise elevations (fig. 6.4).[6]

A magnificent monumental Hebrew inscription found in 1880 just inside the southern end of this tunnel describes how the engineers began at both ends of the tunnel, then broke through to each other by following the sound of the workers' picks. The inscription reads as follows, the top half inexplicably missing:

[The matter of] the breakthrough: And this is the matter of the break-through. While [the hewers were swinging the] axe, each towards his companion, and while there were still three cubits to he[w, there was hea]rd the voice of a man ca[ll]ing to his companion because there was a fissure (?) in the rock, on the right and on the le[f]t. And on the day of its breakthrough, the hewers struck each man towards his companion, axe towards [a]xe, and the waters flowed from the outlet to the pool, one thousand [and t]wo hundred cubits, and a [hu]ndred cubits was the height of the rock above the heads of the hewe[rs].[7]

Miraculously, an adjustment of only a few inches was necessary before the water began to flow. The tunnel was successful, so much so that it is still in use today. At the full daily tide, the water level fills the tunnel almost to the top, making passage difficult if not impossible.

Almost from the moment it was discovered, this tunnel was dubbed Hezekiah's Tunnel because of the references in 2 Kgs 20:20 and 2 Chr 32:4, 30 to Hezekiah's constructing a pool or conduit to bring the waters of the Gihon Spring inside the city wall. Paleographic evidence would support a late eighth-century date for the inscription. Some have doubted that this is a royal inscription, even construing the digging of the tunnel as an ad hoc construction of refugees from the north. Such an ambitious project, how-ever, can only have been undertaken by a central authority, and the elegant script of the inscription qualifies it as a royal monumental inscription. The Siloam Tunnel is thus reasonably understood as another of Hezekiah's efforts at preparing for an Assyrian siege, which shortly after 721 would have seemed inevitable to all.[8]

The Broad Wall

A final witness to preparations for a siege is a stretch of a city wall some 23 feet wide and 700 yards long found by Avigad in excavations in the Jewish Quarter. The wall would have extended westward as far as the Jaffa Gate, but even minimally it suggests that the occupied area of Jerusalem by the eighth century was now at least five times what it had been previously. Avigad dated the wall to the mid- to late eighth century and dubbed it the Broad Wall, assuming that it was the city wall found by Nehemiah and the returnees from Babylon in the late sixth century (see Isa 22:9–11; Neh 2:13–15; 3:24–25).

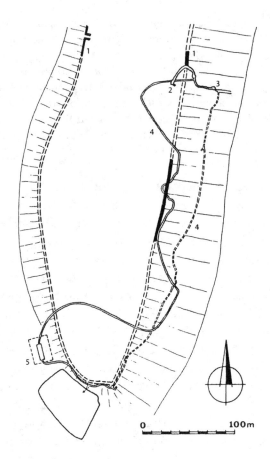

Fig. 6.4. Siloam Tunnel, Jerusalem. 1: city walls; 2: Warren's Shaft; 3: Gihon Spring; 4: Siloam channels; 5: Siloam pool (adapted from Fritz 1995, fig. 56)

The 701 Sennacherib Invasions in Judah

Ever since the beginning of biblical or Palestinian archaeology, scholars have known of an inscription of Sennacherib in which he claims that he besieged Hezekiah "like a caged bird in Jerusalem, his royal city." Furthermore, the Assyrian king declares that he destroyed forty-six walled towns in Judah.

> As to Hezekiah, the Judean, who had not submitted to my yoke, I surrounded forty-six of his strong walled cities and the numberless small towns in their surroundings by laying down ramps and applying batter-

ing rams, onslaughts by foot troops, tunnels, breeches and siege ladders, I conquered them. Two hundred thousand one hundred and fifty people, small and great, male and female, horses, mules, donkeys, camels, oxen and small cattle without number I brought out of them and I counted them as spoil.[9]

Nevertheless, Jerusalem was spared, as the archaeological data show. Several other sites in the vicinity of Jerusalem were also spared, such as Bethel, Tell en-Naṣbeh 3, Gibeon, and Gibeah (Tell el-Ful III).

In summarizing the basic archaeological data for the Sennacherib invasions in 701 at other sites in the following, we shall utilize the multitier site archaeology developed in other chapters (fig. 6.5; see fig. 5.1 for the eighth century BCE).

Fig. 6.5. The seventh-century data base, Judahite sites ranked according to a multitier hierarchy

701	Site, Stratum	586	Acres	Population (est.)
Tier 1	Capitals			
12	Jerusalem 11–10		150	30,000?
Tier 2	Administrative Centers			
III	Lachish II		31	100?
III	Beersheba II?		3	100?
Tier 3	Cities (10 acres and up; population 1,000+)			
3	Tell en-Naṣbeh 2		7–8	100
VI	Gezer V		33	3,000
BII–I	Khirbet Rabud AI–II, B–I		15	1,500
	Hebron		15?	?
C–D	Tell Jemmeh A, B		12 (?)	200
VII	Tell el-Ḥesi VI		4	400
D, E, G	Tel Haror G2		10	1,000
Tier 4	Towns (3–10 acres; population 300+)			
	Bethel		4 (?)	?
	Tell el-Ful III		5	500

		Jericho	?	?
III		Tel Batash II	7	700
2		Beth-Shemesh (gap)	7	400
II		Tel Zayit I	7.5	600
		Tell el-Judeideh	?	?
VI		Tel ʿErani V	?	?
		Mareshah	?	?
		Beth-Zur II	4	400
		Khirbet el-Qom	?	?
		ʿEin-Gedi V	?	?
A_2		Tell Beit Mirsim A_1	7.5	700
I		Tel ʿEton (gap)	?	?
VI		Tel Seraʿ V–IV	4.5	400
VIB		Tel Ḥalif VI A	3	300
VII		Tel ʿIra V–IV	6	600
		ʿAroʿer IV–II	5	500

Tier 5		Villages (2–3 acres; 50–300)
		Jericho farm
		north Rephaim farms
		Aijalon Valley farms
		old town Beersheba
		enclosures near Tell el-Farʿah South

Tier 6		Forts
		Vered Yeriho
?		Qumran
?		Buqeiʿa
3		Ramat Raḥel Phase 2
		Khirbet Abu Tuwein
		Ḥorvat ʿAnim
		Ḥorvat Ṭov
VIII		Arad VII–VI
		Tel Malḥata A
		Tel Masos (fort near mound)

Horvat ʿUza IV
? Horvat Radum
Mezad Ḥazeva IV (Ḥazeva)
I (=I–II) Tell el-Kheleifeh II (=III–IV)
3C–A Kadesh-barnea 2

Tier 2: Administrative Centers

There are only two known late eighth-century regional tier 2 administrative centers in Judah, excepting Jerusalem, the capital, which both the textual sources and the archaeological sources say was spared when tribute was paid by Hezekiah and the siege was lifted.

Beersheba. Stratum II represents the peak development of this exceptionally well laid out border fortress, on Judah's southernmost outpost. The excavators describe its end in a violent conflagration, with a large assemblage of restorable pottery that has close affinities with Lachish III. Only one or two *lmlk* handles were found, however, even though more than half the mound was excavated. Stratum II represents a period of scant reoccupation.[10]

Lachish III. The 701 destruction level of Stratum III at Lachish provides us with the most thoroughly documented prolonged siege and destruction in the entire ancient Near East. The fall of Lachish is witnessed by (1) the archaeological evidence from two extended excavations; (2) the detailed monumental reliefs found in Sennacherib's palace at Nineveh in Mesopotamia; and (3) the Neo-Assyrian annals, which detail the campaigns. Ironically, the Hebrew Bible dismisses the whole incident in one verse, noting simply that Sennacherib had been at Lachish.[11]

Lachish was the most impressive Judahite fortress of all, a steeply built up mound of some 30 acres fortified by a double city wall and an intervening glacis. Both the excavations and the Assyrian reliefs make it clear that the siege was laid at the southeast corner of the roughly rectangular walled town, just east of the massive triple-entryway city gate and ascending ramp. In that area was found a massive stone and mud-brick siege ramp, partly paved so as to give access to the heavy iron-clad wheeled battering rams portrayed on the Assyrian reliefs and constructed with up to 19,000 tons of stones. Inside the city wall, the defenders had mined earlier occupation levels and used the debris to throw up a hasty counterramp. Here there were found hundreds of iron arrowheads; stone ballistae, some weighing up to 400 pounds; parts of bronze Assyrian horse ornaments, helmets, and armor scales; various forms of ammunition; and more than four hundred *lmlk* stamped jar handles.

The city's defenses were breached, probably atop the siege ramp. The gate was destroyed, the inner chambers found filled to the top with burnt mud-brick destruction debris. In several caves on the western slopes there were found mass burials of some 1,500 individuals, including men, women, and children, evidently victims of the Assyrian destruction. Stratum II of the seventh century witnesses a period of abandonment, followed by a much poorer rebuild (fig. 6.6).[12]

Tier 3: Cities

There are only a few late eighth-century tier 3 Judahite cities with 701 destruction layers to be discussed. Jerusalem, easily the largest Judahite city of the time, was not destroyed in 701, as we have seen. That seems to have been the case also with nearby Gibeon (as well as Tell el-Ful/Gibeah III) and Tell el-Naṣbeh 3 (the latter with eighty-seven *lmlk* seal impressions).

Khirbet Rabud. Some 20 miles southwest of Jerusalem is Khirbet Rabud, a unique large mound in the Hebron hills (15 acres) that may be identified with biblical Debir (Kiriath-sepher). The widespread destruction of Stratum B-II is attributed to Sennacherib, with pottery similar to Lachish III and at least one *lmlk* jar handle. Stratum A-I–II, B-1 presents a partly rebuilt, walled town of the seventh century.

Tell Jemmeh. Stratum CD represents a walled town on the southern border with Philistia. The older excavations are poorly published, the more recent excavations more fully published. Several eighth-century building levels end in an apparent destruction, after which Assyrian pitched-brick vault construction and Assyrian Palace ware appears in the seventh century (Stratum AB; see further below on Assyrian policies in the Shephelah).

Tell el-Ḥesi. Nearby Tell el-Ḥesi is also only partially excavated and published. Substrata VIIIa and VII of the more recent excavations are said to have been violently destroyed circa 701. No *lmlk* jar handles were found, however.[13]

Tel Haror. Another border town is Tel Haror, no doubt biblical Gerar.

Fig. 6.6. Scenes from the British Museum reliefs depicting the siege of Lachish (Ussishkin 1982, pl. 86)

There is evidence of a late eighth-century occupation, perhaps Assyrian, but there is no indication of an accompanying destruction.

Tier 4: Towns

A dozen or so smaller sites, towns by our estimate, are known from Judah in the late eighth century. Most are in the south, where the Assyrian destructions are better attested. In the vicinity of Jerusalem, Tell en-Naṣbeh and Gibeon seem to have escaped destruction in 701 (above).

Gezer. After the 732–721 Assyrian destructions in the north, Gezer, on the southern border, is reckoned with Judah. Stratum V is of little importance, except for two Neo-Assyrian cuneiform contracts that bear both Hebrew and Assyrian names. A few *lmlk* jar handles belong to the 701 horizon.

Timnah. Tel Batash, biblical Timnah, is a border town with Philistia exhibiting Philistine material culture in the early phases, but later more clearly ethnic Israelite. Stratum III, of the late eighth century, is said to have been partially destroyed in 701 but not totally devastated until 586 (Stratum II). The eleven *lmlk* jar handles found there belong to the earlier destruction. By the seventh century, Timnah seems to have belonged to the kingdom of Ekron (above).

Beth-Shemesh. The town Beth-Shemesh had been an important administrative center on the border with Philistia in the ninth century, but Stratum 2 sees it decline to a modest settlement characterized by cottage industry. The town was destroyed circa 701, as witnessed by a number of *lmlk* jar handles, followed by a gap.[14]

Tel ʿErani. Another walled Judahite town was Tel ʿErani, where Stratum VI came to an end apparently in 701. Some fifteen *lmlk* jar handles were found in the debris.[15]

Beth-Zur. A late Iron II occupation is evident (Stratum II) in Beth-Zur, but its end seems to be dated to 586 rather than 701 (below). Nevertheless, eleven *lmlk* jar handles were recovered.

Tel ʿEton. Biblical Eglon, Tel ʿEton is a large mound that has only been partially excavated, but an impressive governor's residence appears to have been destroyed at the end of the eighth century. The pottery is quite similar to Lachish III. A single *lmlk* jar handle was found. There seems to be no seventh-century occupation.[16]

Tell Beit Mirsim. Stratum A_2 represents one of the earliest Iron Age destruction levels to be investigated. Albright originally dated it to circa 598, assuming, as others then did, that Lachish III was similarly dated. With the universal recognition more recently that the destruction of Lachish III must be raised to 701, Tell Beit Mirsim A_2 must be similarly dated. Albright describes the destruction in vivid terms, after which the town was greatly reduced. Four *lmlk* jar handles were found in the debris.[17]

Tel Ḥalif. Stratum VIB was a fortified provincial town in the eighth century, destroyed in 701. The evidence is especially clear in House F7, which was found under a heavy fall of mud-brick with its entire contents in situ (below). After an attempt to defend the house, the inhabitants evidently fled. The site was so badly damaged that it was only partially rebuilt in Stratum VIA, then abandoned until the Persian period. No *lmlk* handles were found.[18]

Tel ʿIra. This town was a well-planned and fortified regional center on the southern border with Philistia. Stratum VII, with pottery very similar to Lachish III, is dated by the excavator well down into the seventh century. Only one *lmlk* jar handle was found. The site may have been destroyed, however, in 701. Stratum VI then comes to an end in 586.

Tier 6: Forts

Of the several forts of the ninth–eighth century discussed in chapter 5, only some show evidence of a 701 destruction. Rishon le-Ziyyon, on the coast south of Tel Aviv, was apparently abandoned at the end of the eighth century. Horvat Radum may have been founded in the eighth century, but it more likely ended in the seventh century. The fort at Kuntillet ʿAjrud functioned in the eighth century, but it probably ended in the seventh century. Tell el-Kheleifeh, on the Red Sea, has a destruction at the end of Stratum III (= Pratico's I), but it cannot be dated beyond the mid- to late eighth century. Only Arad appears to have been functioning as a major defensive fort by the late eighth century. A number of smaller forts may have been founded in the late eighth century, such as those at Qumran and its vicinity, but they functioned more clearly in the seventh century. Most of the several other forts listed in figure 6.5 above functioned mainly in the seventh century.[19]

Arad. Stratum VIII represents the peak of the site's development as a fort on the border of Judah and the Negev, after which it declined. The abundant pottery belongs to the Lachish III horizon; ten *lmlk* jar handles were found. Despite the lack of clear evidence of a major destruction circa 701, Stratum VII represents changes in the seventh century.

Excavations over the past century or so have covered much of the Judahite territory, supplemented by recent and very comprehensive surveys. It is unlikely that many eighth-century sites remain unknown to us, except hamlets and farmsteads. Despite this impressive data base, it is clear that Sennacherib's claim to have destroyed "forty-six walled towns" is greatly exaggerated. There cannot have been any such number of fortified sites in the whole of Judah. Here we have been able to cite no more than a dozen or so late eighth-century destructions. Nevertheless, the reduction of Judah by Sennacherib in 701 was apparently devastating.

Faust has challenged the prevailing view of the effects of the 701 invasion, arguing that it was precisely in the seventh century, in the aftermath of the supposed disaster, that Judah reached its maximum population and prosperity. He examines the excavated sites and concludes that only in the Shephelah were there destructions from which many sites did not recover.

He believes that both the Assyrian and the biblical texts support this more modest reconstruction of events. He concludes that, despite some disruptions and no doubt individual tragedies, the overall damage was slight, and the recovery was faster than usually assumed. As Faust describes the post-701 horizon, "The gloomy description of that period is a result mainly of our biased perspective."[20]

Judah's Neighbors

Before turning to developments in Judah in the seventh century, we need to see whether the 701 campaigns had similar effects among Israel's neighbors.

Philistia

As we have already noted (ch. 5), Sargon's well-known campaigns in 712 may account for the destruction of sites in Philistia such as Ashdod VIII, Ekron IIA, Gath 3, and perhaps Ashkelon 15. The clearest evidence for later occupation thus far comes from Ekron, where according to the excavators Stratum IC reveals a prosperous seventh-century Neo-Assyrian vassal-state, even a kingdom of Ekron. (We will return to the significance of this phenomenon below.) In addition, Ashdod VII–VI reveal a prosperous town, probably an Assyrian provincial center, noted for its industrial-level ceramic production. Ashkelon 14 is also a flourishing city, with a population of up to 12,000. It boasts a port, a marketplace and counting house, monumental wine-production installations, large quantities of imported Greek pottery, and ostraca in a Phoenician script, pointing to trade. Tel Batash II, inland on the border with Judah, had probably been a Judahite town in Stratum III, destroyed in 701. Stratum II, of the seventh century, reveals a material culture indicating that the town was a part of the kingdom of Ekron. Tell Jemmeh AB represents another seventh-century Assyrian administrative center, with Assyrian-style buildings and pottery. Nearby Gath, however, seems to be eclipsed now.

There are also seventh-century Assyrian administrative centers in the north now, following the 732–721 destructions, among them Hazor (Ayelet Hashahar), Megiddo, Samaria, Dor, and Gezer (see ch. 5).

It is not only urban sites in Philistia that flourish in the seventh century, but smaller and rural sites as well, as surveys along the coastal plain and the margins have shown. Some settlements in the north along the foot-hills of southern Samaria were newly founded. Other sites to the south, continuing from earlier periods, would include Tell Qasile "VII" and the impressive fortress at Meṣad Ḥashavyahu (Yavneh-Yam; the Hebrew ostracon by that name indicates some Judahite connection). The fortress at Rishon le-Ziyyon, perhaps established in the eighth century, could have been reused in the seventh century under Assyrian control.[21]

Farther north along the coast, a few Phoenician settlements continue into the seventh century, perhaps not having been conquered in the campaigns of Tiglath-pileser III in 712. Among them is Tell Keisan V, probably an Assyrian administrative center, to judge from Assyrian pottery, cylinder seals, and a cuneiform tablet. Akko is apparently extensively rebuilt now and produced several Aramaic ostraca. The cemetery at Achzib continued in use. Shiqmona 3 also belongs to this horizon, as does the small port of Mikhmoret. The question is whether Dor (Phase B5), with impressive fortifications and a two-entryway city gate, was an Assyrian administrative center. It is frequently mentioned in the Assyrian records (*Dur'u*), and it certainly continued to serve as a seaport after the 712 destruction. Yet the material culture is mixed: Israelite, Phoenician, and Assyrian. An iron smithy attests to the site's importance for supplying raw materials to the Assyrians, probably for supplying the needs of the homeland

Transjordan

The Neo-Assyrian annals hint at campaigns of Tiglath-pileser III and Sargon II in Transjordan in the late eighth century (above). The archaeological evidence, however, is scant or nonexistent. We may summarize the inscriptional evidence for the ninth-eighth century as follows.

Fig. 6.7. References to Ammon, Moab, Edom, and Tyre in Assyrian inscriptions

	Ammon	Moab	Edom	Tyre
Shalmaneser III	Baasha (?)			defeat at Qarqar
Adad-nirari III			Edom	tribute
Tiglath-pileser III	Sanipu	Salamanu	Qosmalak	tribute
Sargon II	Ammon	Moab	Edom	tribute

Sennacherib	Pedael	Chemoshnadab	Ayarammu	tribute
Esarhaddon	Pedael	Musuri	Qosgabr	building material
Assurbanipal	Amminadab	Musuri	Qosgabr	troops

Herr and Najar list twenty-six excavated sites from the ninth–eighth century at least partially published.[22] But in spite of their reference to "Assyrian destructions" (at least in Gilead, in the north), there is little supporting evidence at any particular site. It seems likely that the loosely organized tribal states of the hinterland in Transjordan—still in the process of formation as late as the seventh century—did not present any obstacle to Assyrian forces overrunning these territories in the late eighth century. Subsequently, they were incorporated into the far-flung trade network extending from the southern Negev all the way to Arabia, in which southern Transjordan in particular (Edom) played an important role (below).

This expansionist Assyrian imperial policy went back to the ambitions of the great Tiglath-pileser III. His goal had been to reduce a conquered state to the status of a province or petty tributary state, to destroy the urban centers and carry out massive deportations, to rebuild the capitals and administrative centers in Assyrian style and install Assyrian governors, to build new district fortresses to introduce Assyrian economic measures, and to adopt Aramaic as the lingua franca. As Parpolo puts it:

> The inhabitants of the new province became Assyrian citizens; its economy was completely reorganized in line with Assyria's commercial interests; and the seat of the governor, a copy of the imperial court in miniature, became a channel through which Assyrian culture was systematically spread to the country.[23]

Bienkowski, a self-confessed minimalist on Edomite–Assyrian relationships in the seventh century, argues that Ammon, Moab, and Edom were never actually annexed, that is, placed under direct Assyrian rule as official provinces. He bases himself on the absence of the expected Assyrian material correlates, such as deportations, military outposts, Assyrian-style building activities, Assyrian personal names, road networks, and Palace ware and other ceramic imports. Thus Ammon, Moab, and Edom, linked with the southern Negev (below), remained independent, although tributary, states with little or no imperial presence. This is in marked contrast to Assyrian policy elsewhere, such as to the north of Assyria proper. The "great game" of Neo-Assyrian times—complete with spies, assassinations, and fugitives—was played out mostly in the north, and that is where Assyrian resources, communications, and administrative organization were at their most intense. The south, especially in Philistia, may have been different.[24]

Aftermath: Judah in the Seventh Century

In surveying the post-701 horizon in Judah, we shall again employ a multi-tier hierarchy of sites. The following are the main excavated and published sites listed in figure 6.5 (to be supplemented, of course, by survey data).[25]

Tier 1: Capitals

Jerusalem, largely spared by the invasion of Sennacherib, continued as the capital of Judah. By the time of Stratum 11 the city had expanded to as much as 50 acres and may have had a population of up to 30,000 (above); in Stratum 10 it may have been as large as 250 acres, including the city's environs. The old city walls and towers were reused, as well as the water systems. A long stretch of the city wall along the eastern slopes has been exposed, showing reuse of elements of the Middle Bronze Age defenses. On the Temple Mount, the eighth-century citadel and the gate complex on the higher ground continued in use, as the temple itself no doubt did.

The private houses built earlier (eighth century?) in Shiloh's Area G, on the terraced stepped stone structure above the Siloam Spring, also continued in use, although only partially occupied. The House of Ahiel was identified by the name of the owner on several ostraca. The Burnt House gave vivid evidence of the 586 destruction. The House of the Bullae produced a hoard of fifty-one bullae, seal impressions with various Hebrew names and titles, including "Gemariah, son of Shapan," known as a scribe during the reign of Josiah in the late seventh century (see fig. 6.16 and below).

Tier 2: Administrative Centers

There are only two known Judahite sites that would qualify as district administrative centers in the seventh century, perhaps only one of significance, Lachish.

Lachish. Stratum II represents an attempt to reoccupy the site after a period of abandonment following the devastation in 701 at the end of Stratum III. The massive palace/residency goes out of use. The city gate was rebuilt, however, with an outer gate added and below that a sloping entry road. Elsewhere the lower revetted city walls may have been repaired, and portions of a new upper wall were constructed. Yet much of the site lay open and unoccupied, only a few straggling houses still in evidence.

Found in a room near the outer gate in the 586 destruction debris was a hoard of twenty-three Hebrew ostraca, giving dramatic evidence of the last days of Lachish (below). There were also other epigraphic discoveries, including those on wine jars, with date formulae, as well as several bullae (discussed further below).

Beersheba. Stratum II belongs to the early seventh century and reflects an ephemeral attempt to resettle the site after the massive destruction of Stratum III in 701. It is doubtful whether Beersheba any longer functioned as a border fortress or administrative center by this time.

Tier 3: Cities

The lack of functioning administrative centers is complemented by the relative scarcity of cities or urban centers in the seventh century. Fewer than ten are sufficiently well known to be considered here.

Tell en-Naṣbeh. Stratum 3, of the eighth century, appears to have escaped the 701 destructions, like nearby Gibeon and Jerusalem. The inadequacy of the publications, however, make it impossible to say what Stratum 3 elements were still in use in the seventh century.

Khirbet Rabud. This city was an unwalled settlement following the 701 destruction, then completely destroyed in 586.

Hebron. Scant excavation and inadequate publication make it possible only to say that several *lmlk* jar handles reveal a late eighth-century level, followed by scant seventh-century settlement. Hebron may well have been, however, a market town in the southern Judean hills.

Tell Jemmeh. Stratum EF AB (= Phases 7–5) represents the town after the Assyrian takeover in the late eighth century. These levels of the seventh century have produced two unique Assyrian-style buildings (I–II) made with pitched-brick vaulted mud-brick roofs, similar to structures found at Nineveh, Khorsabad, and Nimrud. In one of these buildings a large quantity of imported Assyrian Palace ware was found. Jemmeh may well have been the town of Yurza "on the Brook of Egypt." Captured by Esarhaddon in the early seventh century, it was a major staging point for Assyrian operations in the region and also an important site along the incense trade routes from Arabia to the coast (see further below).

Tell el-Ḥesi. The small, 4-acre acropolis of the large mound of Tell el-Ḥesi belongs to the Iron Age. The massive Stratum VII fortress was destroyed in the late eighth century, then replaced by the modest unfortified town of Stratum VI, possibly destroyed in 701. After that, Tell el-Ḥesi was abandoned until the Persian period.

Tel Haror. Biblical Gerar, Tel Haror had been a major fortified site in the eighth century, perhaps as large as 50 acres It is reported to have been destroyed sometime in the late eighth century, then rebuilt on a more modest scale and finally destroyed again about the mid-seventh century. The cause of destruction is unknown.

Tier 4: Towns

A sizeable number of seventh-century Judahite towns have been excavated and published, most continuing from the eighth century.[26]

Gibeon. One of the northernmost towns in Judah, Gibeon escaped the 701 destructions, like Tell en-Naṣbeh, Bethel, Gibeah, and Jerusalem. The eighth-century water system, the winery, and other installations probably continued in use in the seventh century.

Jericho. Little is known of Jericho in the Iron Age, but it may have flourished toward the end of Iron II.

Beth-Shemesh. The town of Beth-Shemesh had lost its strategic situation as a border site by the seventh century, as the border with Philistia shifted to the west after the Assyrian invasions. Level 1 (old Stratum IIC) is a small, short-lived settlement following the destruction. Attempts to resettle the site are seen in the reuse of the great water system, which, however, was then completely blocked up and the town abandoned.[27]

Timnah. Stratum II at Tel Batash, biblical Timnah, follows a partial destruction of Stratum III in 701. Now the city wall was widened, and some administrative buildings were constructed, along with a number of private houses. Many are of the pillar-courtyard type, some with oil-pressing installations. Stratum II, a prosperous town, was destroyed sometime in the late seventh century, producing a large corpus of ceramic wares of both Judahite and late Philistine types, as well as pseudo-Assyrian Palace ware. Sheqel weights of Judahite type were also found.

Tel Zayit. Little is yet known of this small town (6–7 acres) in the Judahite Shephelah, now being excavated. The late Iron Age remains were mostly destroyed by the Persian occupation.

Tell el-Judeideh. Excavated long ago, Tell el-Judeideh (Tel Goded) has a large structure on the acropolis that may have been built as early as the eighth century or as late as the sixth century. Little more can be said, although the site is on the inland road and near the entrance to the Vale of Elah.

Tel ʿErani. The site Tel ʿErani (Tel Gat) has only been sporadically investigated. Stratum VI, with a defensive wall and two courtyard buildings, seems to have been destroyed in 701, but subsequent occupation is unclear. In Areas A and G, remains of the seventh century may be seen in several Stratum VI pillar-courtyard house. Stratum V continues with domestic occupation of the late seventh century.

Mareshah. Due to scant excavations, Iron Age Mareshah reveals little. Although a magnificent, strategically located mound along the line of the inner Judahite Shephelah (with Azekah, Tell el-Judeideh, and Lachish), all one can say is that after apparently being destroyed in 701 it continued to be occupied in the seventh century.

Beth Zur. Located 20 miles south of Jerusalem, Beth-Zur had been occupied in Iron I, but it was then largely abandoned until refounded sometime in the seventh century. It appears to have persisted then as a small market town until 586.

Khirbet el-Qom. Probably biblical Makkedah, Khirbet el-Qom is located some 7 miles east of Lachish in the Judahite hill country. The site is known mainly for a robbed eighth-century cemetery, but limited exploration of the town site suggests an eighth- to seventh-century occupation of the walled town.

ʿEin-Gedi. This site, also known as Tel Goren, is a unique oasis on the western shore of the Dead Sea north of Masada, near perennial springs. Stratum V represents the founding level in the seventh century. Courtyard houses predominate, some associated with ovens and other installations that were probably used for producing perfume from the abundant balsam plants. Dates were also probably processed. A number of Hebrew seals and impressions were found, including a *lmlk* jar handle and rosette impressions. The site may have been under royal administration.

Tell Beit Mirsim. A typical Judahite hill-country small town, Tell Beit Mirsim was drastically destroyed in 701 (Stratum A2). Stratum A1 represents an ephemeral reoccupation, ending finally in 586.

Tel Seraʿ. Strata V–IV represent the last Iron Age settlement at this small site on the southern border with Philistia. Stratum V yielded evidence of two large citadels, one with its own defense wall. Among the finds were Assyrian-style metal implements (and an industry), Assyrian cult objects, and Assyrian Palace ware. A massive destruction at the end of Stratum IV is attributed to the mid-seventh century.

Tel Ḥalif. Stratum VIA, in the Judean highlands, represents an attempt at reoccupation after the horrific destruction of Stratum VIB in 701. There was, however, some well laid out domestic architecture. This phase may have ended in abandonment rather than destruction. Thereafter the site was deserted until the Persian period.

Tel ʿIra. A few miles east of Beersheba in the northern Negev, Tel ʿIra is a small site where Stratum VI represents a newly established, well-fortified town with a solid wall still preserved up to 6 feet high, a casemate wall in some areas, and a four-entryway city gate with external towers. Domestic four-room houses, as well as larger constructions, were found. A fiery destruction ends the site circa 586.

ʿAroʿer. Some 14 miles southeast of Beersheba, ʿAroʿer is the southernmost town in Judah. Stratum IV represents the founding of the walled town de novo in the early seventh century. Stratum III then gives evidence of an expansion of the settled area into a prosperous town, but without a functioning city wall. Among the finds were female figurines and seals, one of the latter with the name of the Edomite deity Qos, and a bone calendar (?). The pottery includes typical late Judahite Iron II wares, as well as Edomite and Assyrian-style forms. There were a few ostraca with Hebrew names.[28]

Tier 5: Villages

In the nature of the case, few remains of small villages have been preserved for archaeologists to investigate, even though some are known through surface surveys.

1. In the Rephaim Valley, southwest of Jerusalem, several farmsteads can be dated to the eighth–seventh century, with extensive terraces and

rambling houses. Another half-dozen or so hamlets are known in the Jerusalem area (fig. 6.8).[29]

2. In the old town of Beersheba, in limited salvage excavations, there have been found remains of a few structures, indicating a village there.[30]

3. Elsewhere in Judah, Faust has documented a dozen or more farmsteads, but scarcely any coherent plans are available, nor can they be precisely dated for historical purposes. Many of these, as well as a number of farmsteads known in the Samaria region in the north, have only a single building complex. These hamlets and farms could, however, have produced surpluses that would remain almost invisible in the archeological record. Furthermore, these sites help to document social structure throughout the Iron II period, particularly that of families and the rural sector.[31]

Tier 6: Forts

There are many more small forts in the seventh century than in the eighth century, no doubt because of the increased threat of invasion posed by the 732–721 destructions in the north and the 701 destructions in the south. At least a dozen are known in Judah (fig. 6.5).[32]

Vered Yeriho. Located near Jericho, Vered Yeriho is a one-period fort of the seventh century commanding a fine view over the lower Jordan Valley. A nearby domestic site of some 7 acres may well be Iron Age Jericho. The fort is roughly square, some 65 by 80 feet, with several interior rooms, the back rooms resembling the pillar-courtyard houses of the period. There is a double-entryway gate on the east, flanked by towers. Steps lead to an upper story. Among the finds were an enigmatic Hebrew ostracon and a well-preserved iron sword. The fortress was destroyed sometime in the late seventh (or early sixth) century (fig. 6.9).

Qumran. The well-known site of Qumran on the northwest shore of the Dead Sea was, in fact, occupied before the time of the famous scrolls, in the eighth–sixth century The prominent square tower at the north end of the site belongs to this period, probably destroyed in 586. One *lmlk* jar handle and a Hebrew ostracon were found.

The Buqeiʿa. In the Buqeiʿa wilderness, west of Qumran and ʿAin-Feshka, are at least three small forts: Khirbet Abu Tabaq, Khirbet es-Samrah, and Khirbet el-Maqari. All are associated with check-dams and cisterns, and they were evidently intended to be self-sufficient. They may

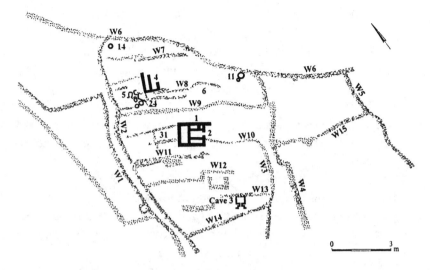

Fig. 6.8. The farmstead and surroundings at Khirbet er-Ras (Edelstein 2000, 40)

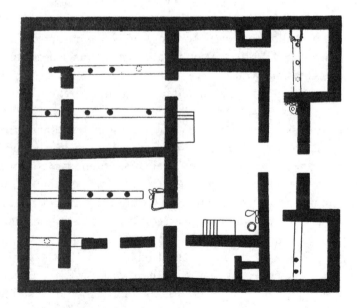

Fig. 6.9. The fort at Vered Yeriho (Eitan 1983, 43)

have been founded in the eighth century, but they flourished primarily in the seventh century. The rectangular or square forts vary from 100 by 100 feet to 150 by 240 feet in size. All three forts appear to have been destroyed in 586. They may well reflect the Judahite state authority in the late Assyrian period. Other small forts in the area include Rujm el-Baḥr, Rujm esh-Shajra, and Khirbet Mazin.

Tell el-Ful. Biblical Gibeah, Tell el-Ful was rebuilt in the seventh–sixth century as a square tower with several rooms. It had not been destroyed in 701 (above).

Ramat Raḥel. At Ramat Raḥel, a fortress on Jerusalem's southern outskirts, the Phase 1 tower is now augmented in Phase 2 (old Va) with a large casemate-courtyard complex structure, turning the whole site into what the excavators describe as "a royal administrative center under imperial hegemony." It seems to persist from the second half of the seventh century into the Persian era. Some two hundred *lmlk* stamps from various contexts suggest to recent excavators that store jars of this type continued in use after 701, but that is debatable. Numerous seals bearing the names of individuals were also found. It appears that Phase 2 was not destroyed in 701 (as also at Jerusalem). It is considered here as a fort, or citadel, because of its natural strategic location and its strong fortification.[33]

Arad. Located on the Negev border, Arad is the most prominent fort in Judah. Stratum VII sees the continuation of the major features of the citadel: the solid wall with its towers and the water system. Most of the Hebrew ostraca found at Arad should be assigned to Stratum VII, despite stratigraphic uncertainties (below). Stratum VII was destroyed in 586, after which the fort has no functions until it was rebuilt in the Roman period.

Tel Malḥata. At Tel Malḥata, east of Beersheba, the walled fort, tower, and rampart, together with a pillared storehouse, continued in use in Stratum A of the seventh century. The fort was then destroyed in 586. The pottery included East Greek wares, as well as large quantities of Edomite-style pottery. An ostracon from this stratum contained Edomite personal names.

Ḥorvat ʿUza. Located 9 miles east of Tel Malḥata, Ḥorvat ʿUza is situated to control the roads linking the northern Negev with the Arabah and Edom in Transjordan. A large, multiroomed fortress with several towers and a gate in Stratum IV comprised an area of some 2,300 square feet. A planned settlement some 1.7 acres in extant was found to the northeast of the fort, probably housing the garrison stationed there. Some thirty-five ostraca were found, in both Hebrew and Edomite scripts, mostly administrative documents dealing with trade, especially grain. After its destruction in 586, the site was abandoned until the Hellenistic period.

Ḥorvat Radum. The fort Ḥorvat Radum is 6 miles southwest of Arad on a spur overlooking the Naḥal Qina, only 1 mile south of Ḥorvat ʿUza. A fort with thick, solid walls and an offset-entryway gate measures some 70 by 80 feet. Inside were several casemate rooms, benches, and a square platform-like structure. The fort may have simply been abandoned in the late seventh/early sixth century. The pottery was scant but includes Edomite sherds. Five Hebrew ostraca were found here and there in the debris.

Mezad Ḥazeva. A small fort in the Arabah, Mezad Ḥazeva is some 12 miles southeast of the Dead Sea. Strata V–IV belong to the eighth–seventh century. The square casemate fort with corner towers and a triple-entryway gate was some 325 by 325 feet. Pottery was scant and generally of uncertain date.

Tell el-Kheleifeh. A small, low mound on the southern Arabah, Tell el-Kheleifeh is located just north of Eilat on the Red Sea. It was excavated and identified with "Solomon's copper mines" at Ezion-geber by Glueck. Later examination of the largely unpublished material concluded that there is nothing earlier than the eighth century in the pottery. The Period I square casemate fortress of the eighth century (?) was replaced in Period II of the seventh century by a much larger fort and enclosure with a three-entryway gate. The old four-room building now stood at the northwest corner. The pottery of this level consisted of Edomite wares and Assyrian-style bowls. Some two dozen seal impressions read "belonging to Qausanal, servant of the king," invoking the name of the Edomite deity Qos. A seal of "Jotham" was dated by Glueck to the reign of Uzziah (788/787–736/735), but it may belong to a later Jotham and could be assigned to Period II.

Kadesh-barnea. The fort at Kadesh-barnea, near the oasis of ʿAin el-Qudeirat in the eastern Sinai Desert, had been established in the tenth century (Stratum 4), then rebuilt in the eighth century (Stratum 3C–A). In the seventh century the upper fort (Stratum 2) was constructed, a rectangular casemate building some 32 by 80 feet, with corner and side towers; the gate has not been located. Inside the enclosure the older cistern was reused, and several small rooms were constructed. The fort was destroyed in a violent conflagration in 586. In the debris there was found a large corpus of pottery, including Edomite wares, as well as several Hebrew ostraca. Two ostraca bore Egyptian hieratic inscriptions, mostly recording numbers and measurements (fig. 6.10).[34]

Supplementary Data from Surveys

In addition to the excavated seventh-century sites summarized above, we have some additional information from several surface surveys, especially those of Dagan and Ofer. Faust summarizes the data by region rather than by site hierarchy, as done here. Nearly all his seventh-century sites, however, are small, although significant in evaluating shifting settlement patterns. Most of the sites are villages or farmsteads. Surprisingly, many of these sites are located in marginal areas such as the Judean Desert and the Negev, where they are newly established. The Shephelah, however, is in decline. The reasons for these demographic shifts will be examined shortly.[35]

A General Systems Theory Summary

As previously, we will employ a General Systems Theory approach to the seventh-century data base, using several subsystems to organize the data and attempt to explain historical changes between the ninth–eighth and the seventh century.

Settlement Type and Distribution; Demography

Several trends are obvious in the changes in settlement type and distribution from the eighth to the seventh century. Most have to do with the nature and pace of the recovery after the 701 destructions. Until recently, scholars assumed that site type and distribution remained essentially the same but that many sites had been so devastated after 701 that they recovered slowly, if at all (above).

Na'aman, for example, argued that Judah shrank in size and population, that "it lacked the resources to resettle the destroyed and deserted areas." In particular, deportations had caused a great shortage of manpower in Judah. Thus the kingdom never recovered. Other scholars essentially agreed. Faust, however, has argued that Judah at this time reached the peak of its development and prosperity, even expanding into marginal areas.

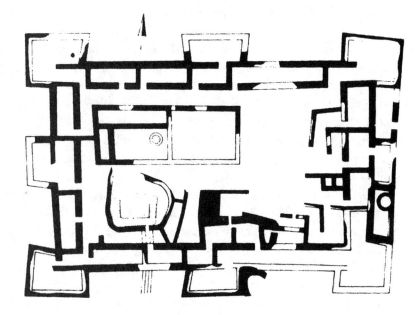

Fig. 6.10. The middle fortress at Kadesh-barnea (Cohen 1993, 844)

His explanation lies in the *Pax Assyriaca*, now more in evidence. Yet that may represent a view to the other extreme.[36] The Shephelah, however, was devastated and played only a minor role thereafter (below).

Recent analyses, based on more comprehensive excavation and survey data, have concluded that the picture is more complex. First, most of the sites in figure 6.5 do represent eighth-century settlements that were reoccupied. But in nearly all of the two dozen sites that we know, we see a possible gap in occupation, then a settlement of diminished size. In particular, former administrative centers such as Lachish and Beersheba virtually ceased to function. None of the many cities and towns listed in figure 6.5 fully recovered.

On the other hand, a few new settlements are founded in the seventh century, such as ʿEin-Gedi. There are also a few new settlements in the Judean Desert and the northern Negev, as Faust has shown, especially ʿAroʿer and Tel Seraʿ. Among the few former sites that gained in size and importance in the seventh century are some sites along the border with Philistia, such as Timnah and Tell Jemmeh, which like Tel Seraʿ (above) became essentially Assyrian-controlled garrisons in the south.

The most striking aspect of settlement type and distribution in the seventh century is the increase in the number of forts: fourteen in Judah, in contrast to only five or so in the eighth century. Most are either in the Jerusalem region, the upper Dead Sea areas, or the south. One explanation might be apprehension after the 701 destructions. On the other hand, during the Assyrian domination such forts would seem not to have been needed or even tolerated. As Assyria weakened, however, by the late seventh century and the Babylonians rose to power, these forts could have come into play, even though they would not have been (and were not) very effective.

Demographic projections are difficult, as always. Earlier scholars had taken seriously figures derived from the Assyrian annals and a few biblical texts suggesting that some 200,000 people may have been deported from Judah following the 701 destructions. Yet according to the authoritative survey of Broshi and Finkelstein, the entire population of Judah in the eighth century had been only circa 110,000.[37]

Zevit did not have access to Faust's work when he wrote, but he supports the minimalist view. He argues that a close analysis of both the Assyrian and biblical texts shows that the point of the elaborate logistics of the Assyrian campaign was not to destroy major sites, much less to reduce the population, but to secure trade routes and quell an Egyptian-backed revolt. Lachish, not Jerusalem, was a test case. As Zevit puts it, "Sennacherib used war to achieve political objectives. He intended to leave loyal allies behind him, not to create enemies." This scenario would make sense of the terse notes in 2 Kgs 18:13 (= Isa 36:1) that Sennacherib "came up against all the fortified cities of Judah and captured them" (as the Assyrian annals also claim), but not that he destroyed them. Zevit concludes that the population of Judah in the seventh century may have been 250,000 or more, despite Assyrian privations. He even asserts that ordinary persons were probably not much affected by the aftermath of the 701 destructions. This would, of course, raise the question of the ʿam hāʾāreṣ, the "folk left behind," those who essentially remained in place, whatever their role or numbers (below).[38]

Newer data and newer views reinforce the notion of Judah in the seventh century as an integral part of the *Pax Assyriaca* in the southern Levant. The shifts in settlement type and distribution we have seen, as well as in demography, support that notion, as do other changes now to be considered.

The Shephelah and Philistia present a post-701 picture that differs from that in Judah. There, too, a peak of population and prosperity had been reached in the eighth century, with perhaps half or more of Judah's population of some 100,000 settled in the Shephelah, according to recent surveys. After the Assyrian destructions, however, particularly devastating there, the region never fully recovered. As Faust puts it, "the Shephelah was devastated.... Recovery was slow and partial, and the settlement in the seventh century did not even resemble the prosperity of the eighth century BCE."[39] The population may have declined by nearly half.

By contrast in the south, Philistia seems to have prospered, no doubt because of the *Pax Assyriaca*, which deliberately fostered trade as an aspect of imperial policy in the conquered territories. The olive-oil industry at Tel Miqne, Philistine Ekron, is a parade example (below). Assyrian-style forts, palaces, distinctive administrative structures, and Assyrian Palace wares, both imported and local at a number of sites, all point to at least some resident Assyrian officials in Philistia.

Several models to explain the economic prosperity have been advocated. One, a bureaucratic model, builds on world-systems and core-periphery theories to emphasize state-sponsored industrial-scale economic production. The other is a patrimonial model that sees a less centralized, "bottom-up" process. One extensively analyzed site, Tell Jemmeh AB (Phases 7–5), suggests that the Assyrians were more flexible and utilized both techniques, perhaps with a gradual decline in imperil domination as Assyrian power declined by the late seventh century.[40]

Political Organization

All the evidence we have points to the fact that Judah in the seventh century was subjugated, reduced to the status of an Assyrian vassal state. It survived by conforming to the new order and by paying tribute when necessary. It was no longer a Judahite kingdom, even though the king and the capital in Jerusalem remained. Much of seventh-century Judah struggled under the reigns of two kings. The hapless Manasseh (698–642), Hezekiah's son, seems to have been ineffective (regardless of the biblical writers' condemnation of him as evil). Josiah (648–609) was able to reassert the authority of Judah in the face of growing Assyrian weakness, but his alleged reforms are debated (below).

It is now clear that not only Jerusalem, but also nearby Ramat Raḥel,

Tell en-Naṣbeh, Gibeon, and Tel el-Ful, were spared in 701. Jerusalem in this era may, in fact, have been a metropolis of 50 acres, with much of that area being extramural neighborhoods. In particular, the surrounding rural areas show a marked increase. Jerusalem and its environs may thus have had a population of up to 50,000. That would mean not only that Jerusalem flourished but that a substantial percentage of the population of Judah lived in that vicinity in the seventh century (above). That is in marked contrast to the days of the early monarchy in the tenth–eighth century, when Jerusalem was at the zenith of its political power. The *Pax Assyriaca* was no doubt the reason for Jerusalem's continued growth and prosperity.[41]

In the countryside, there is good evidence that most regions were now pacified. The former administrative centers continued to be occupied to some degree, but the concentration of political power now shifted to the old Judahite–Philistine border, which virtually disappears. There, under Assyrian control, new administrative centers such as Timnah, Tell Batash, and Tel Seraʿ dominated a coastal culture that illustrates a cosmopolitan mix that contained both Judahite and Philistine elements. Other sites, such as Gezer (perhaps an Assyrian center) and Beth-Shemesh, also reflect the *Pax Assyriaca*. Nevertheless, Judah's effective control was restricted to the central hill country and the Negev south of Jerusalem. The Shephelah and the whole of the former northern kingdom remained firmly in Assyrian hands (above).

Judah did, however, retain some degree of self-identity, even a putative border with Philistia. Kletter has created distribution maps locating all the occurrences of two distinctive classes of material culture object that are clearly ethnic Judahite: the sheqel weights of the late eighth–seventh century and the pillar-base figurines of the same date. In both cases, these artifacts occur only in the hill country and the Shephelah, not in the Philistine plain, a phenomenon that delineates a sort of Judahite border. Even if it is no longer fixed geographically (i.e., it is porous), that border does exist experientially. The ethnic implications of this will be explored below.[42]

In Transjordan, where Assyrian forces had probably overrun the area with little opposition, we see further evidence of the spread of the *Pax Assyriaca*, as, for instance, at Buṣeirah. There sites proliferate, especially in the south, and the Ammonite, Moabite, and Edomite tribal states now emerge fully, apparently with Assyrian tolerance or even support. Much of this collaboration was probably due to the expansion of trade routes (below).

Socioeconomic Structure

The term *Pax Assyriaca*, noted above, is now common in the literature, denoting a period of relative stability and even prosperity throughout the southern Levant as the entire region came under Assyrian hegemony. In particular, Judah and Philistia now cooperated (perhaps under some duress) and became part of a vast area of industrial-level agricultural production. The surpluses of wheat, olive oil, and other commodities were invested by the Assyrians in long-distance trade, both overland and, with Phoenician collaboration, by sea.

The most conspicuous site in this enterprise is Tel Miqne, Philistine Ekron. By the third stage of development, in Stratum IC–B, the city had grown to some 60 acres in size, making it the largest Iron Age city known. The city was well planned and laid out. The fortifications included a double-wall system, a gate, a gatehouse, and some stables. The upper tell had its own defenses, partly of ashlar construction, on the acropolis. A large industrial zone in the lower city, near the city wall, featured several oil-pressing installations, with well-preserved stone crushing vats, remains of wooden beams and perforated stone weights, and a great deal of restorable pottery. Most of the presses were associated with small four-horned altars. It has been calculated that the 115 olive-oil installations required the cultivation of more than 12,000 acres of olive trees and could have produced as much as 1,000 tons of olive oil per year, stored in 48,000 store jars (fig. 6.11).

Gitin, the excavator, concludes that the Assyrians deliberately chose Ekron for its location, natural resources, and the availability of surplus labor (perhaps including deported Israelites). Thus the site's industry was the "direct result of the stability produced by the peace enforced in Philistia and Judah by Assyria in the 7th c. BCE."[43] In addition, the city-state of Ekron probably served as a logistical support base for the Assyrian war effort against Egypt and was a central point in the communications and commercial networks connecting the Assyrian-controlled hinterland of Judah, Edom, and Ammon to the east and the Assyrian-controlled port cities of the coastal plain to the west.[44]

Two other sites in Philistia also apparently enjoyed great prosperity under Assyrian hegemony: Ashkelon and Ashdod. Ashkelon 14, destroyed in 604, revealed a large winery with several buildings, presses, and storage facilities. In addition, there were found a marketplace and shops extending over an area of 5,000 square feet. Finally, a counting house produced weights, parts of a scale balance, and a receipt for grain written in a Neo-Philistine script, paid for in silver. There was also some evidence for large-scale weaving. Stager concludes that what Ashkelon lacked in wheat lands to feed its population of 12,000–15,000, it made up in its commercial economy, dominated by viticulture.[45]

At Ashdod, Strata VII–VI reveal evidence of a prosperous city, with a mixed Philistine–Judean material culture. Evidence of the latter are Judean sheqel weights and a few Hebrew ostraca. An Assyrian-style palace belongs to Stratum VII. Nearby Ashdod-Yam, a small fortified site, was probably an Assyrian administrative center, as was another site recently investigated, Ashdod-Ad Halom.

Faust and Weiss have attempted to summarize the Assyrian-dominated seventh-century economic system in Judah, Philistia, and beyond in terms of zones defined by differing settlement patterns and demographic developments. Philistia, as we have seen, was the most prosperous. To the major sites already discussed one may add many new sites established in the seventh century, such as Mikhmoret near Hadera, Tel Michal and Meṣad Ḥashavyahu near Tel Aviv, and several small enclosed sites (*haserim*) along the coast. The harbors are especially important (along with Ashdod and Ashkelon), since they facilitated trade in collaboration with the Phoenicians.[46]

In contrast with Philistia, much of Judah seems to have been transferred to direct Assyrian rule after 701, so the region remained relatively isolated and underdeveloped. Jerusalem, as we have seen, was a disproportionately large population center in the seventh century, with a population of 30,000 or more. Excavations have been limited, but there is some evidence of trade. A few inscriptions suggest trade with South Arabia.[47]

Somewhat surprisingly, the Judean Desert and the Negev saw an upsurge of settlement, including the forts in the Qumran/Buqeiʿa area (above), as well as at sites such as ʿEin-Gedi, which exploited the natural resources of the area. Many scholars connect this floruit with the expansion of trade with Arabia. On the other hand, the Beersheba Valley, for instance, could have produced as much as 5,000 tons of grain a year—more than twenty times the local needs.[48]

Faust and Weiss's survey provides some valuable details on agricultural production and trade, particularly of wine, olive oil, and grain, and even attempts to quantify production and relative prices. It would appear

Fig. 6.11. Reconstruction of an olive-oil processing installation, Tel Miqne Stratum IB (Gitin 1996, fig. 5)

that Philistia and even Judah, despite some labor shortages, produced sizeable surpluses, now under more economic control by the Assyrians. Trade routes stretched eastward to Arabia, southward to Egypt, and, with Phoenician trade, over much of the Mediterranean.[49]

We have scarcely looked at the northern kingdom after the Assyrian destructions there (ch. 5). Assyrian control was, of course, even more firmly entrenched there by the seventh century. However, there is far less well-published survey work from the north. With the establishment of Assyrian provinces and centers at Hazor, Samaria, Megiddo, and elsewhere (Dor?), much of the population may have been deported or displaced by new peoples brought in.

Assyrian cuneiform documents of the seventh century have been found at Gezer (Stratum V), dated to 651 and 649. They show evidence of Akkadian, as well as West Semitic personal names, and deal with legal rights. At nearby Tel Ḥadid, a complete seventh-century Assyrian legal tablet (698) contains only Akkadian names. It was found in a large building that seems to have had administrative functions.[50]

The countryside in the north is known from villages such as Tel Qiri VI–V, but also from surveys that show that a number of eighth-century farmsteads in the Samaria hill country continued into the seventh century, evidently prospering. By and large, however, the Assyrian-managed economy is currently best witnessed in the south at sites such as Ashkelon and Ekron.[51]

Several studies have summarized the coastal Phoenician culture from the time of the first Assyrian invasions by Tiglath-pileser III in 734. The major Iron Age seaports stretched from the coast of modern Syria all the way south of Tel Aviv. The main Iron II excavated sites in Israel include Achzib, Akko, Tell Keisan 5–4, Shiqmona City 4, Tel Megadim VII (?), ʿAtlit, and probably Dor.

The Phoenicians had been ship-builders and maritime traders far across the Mediterranean even in the early Iron Age. By the seventh century, their maritime trade was at its peak, extending to Egypt, North Africa, Greece and the Aegean, and as far away as Spain. The Assyrians evidently co-opted them to extend their own empire, having subjugated their homeland as early as the late eighth century.[52]

A final aspect of seventh-century socioeconomic structure would be the effect the *Pax Assyriaca* would likely have had on traditional Judahite society, now operating in a very different context. Schloen, who as we have seen has developed the model of a patrimonial society and economy to the fullest, accepts the fact that a managed Assyrian socioeconomic system now put an end to earlier ideals.[53] The reality was that the vanquished northern kingdom of Israel was becoming a distant memory, and tiny Judah, in a survival mode, was a peripheral Assyrian vassal-state, no longer in charge of its own destiny. The results must have been traumatic, with profound implications for most people's lives at every level of the new society. In the countryside, life may have gone on very much as usual, but elsewhere, especially in the urban centers, Assyrian values, lifestyles, culture, and economic measures prevailed. Yet it was out of this crisis that a new order was eventually to emerge (below).

A final aspect of a managed economy must be more fully considered here: the possible growth of a silver-based economy. The case for such an economy has been best made by Gitin and Golani, based on the extensive Assyrian-managed olive-oil industry at Ekron. In Stratum I there were found six hoards of silver fragments (*Hacksilber*, the forerunner of coinage), totaling some 1,420 grams (fig. 6.12). Gitin and Golani regard these not as hoards per se but rather as something like "piggy banks" for accounting, the equivalent of coins. The silver fragments could then be weighed out as payments for various commodities. The authors cite several Assyrian texts describing payments in silver, concluding that by the seventh century, when the Assyrian Empire had expanded to its greatest extent, silver became the generally accepted currency throughout the empire.[54]

There are a number of other Iron Age silver hoards. Five hoards were found at Eshtemoa, east of Hebron, totaling 25,000 grams. Iron I hoards at Beth-Shean totaled 5,222 grams and at Dor 8,500 grams. Another hoard comes from 'Ein-Gedi. These may really be "treasures," but the much smaller Ekron hoard suggests periodic use for exchange. A study of thirty-five silver hoards concludes that "a a kind of coined metal existed in Cisjordan and other parts of the Near East prior to the traditional 'invention' of coinage by the Lydians and Greeks *c.* 600 BC.... The frequency and size of silver hoards from Cisjordan points to a proliferation in the 'monetary' use of silver in that region in the Iron Age."[55]

Kletter has attempted to refute the above conclusion, arguing that "the invention of coinage [is] the symbol and mark of monetary economy." One of his points is that none of the known silver hoards "has been successfully equated with standard measurements known from antiquity."[56] Of course not, since these are unmarked silver fragments. Kletter minimizes his own authoritative study of the Judean sheqel weights, which provides precisely the standard system that was in use in the late eighth–seventh century. Such a highly standardized system makes no sense unless it had actually been used for weighing out silver. Even the sheqel sign indicates a small pouch for carrying silver. A Hebrew ostracon from the 604 destruction at Ashkelon mentions a grain payment of silver, and one from Arad specifies a payment of 8 silver sheqels.

We now have more than 350 stone inscribed sheqel weights from the eighth–seventh century and even fragments of the metal balances used for weighing bits of silver used in business transactions. The numerical signs—of which we have examples of 1, 2, 4, 8, 12, 16, 24, and 40—are Egyptian hieratic symbols. There are also sheqel fraction weights, of which we possess examples of *nesep* (ca. 5/6 of a sheqel), *pîm* (ca. 2/3), and *beqaʿ*

Fig. 6.12. Silver hoard, Tel Miqne, seventh century
(courtesy of Seymour Gitin and Ilan Sultzman)

(Hebrew "half") sheqel weights. There are also smaller sheqel weights marked with signs for 2–10 gerahs, evidently indicating either a system of 20 or 24 gerahs to a sheqel (see fig. 6.1 above).

Kletter's analysis of all the known weights indicates that a sheqel should have weighed circa 11.33 grams, but a parallel "heavy" (possibly royal) system of weights might also have existed. Kletter has shown a remarkably consistent overall standard, so that with the more common 1–8 sheqel weights the deviation is a mere 0.5 percent. The system is obviously Judahite, with only five of the 353 published examples coming from the north. In addition, they all date from the late eighth through the early sixth century—almost certainly reflecting consolidation measures taken in Judah after the fall of the northern kingdom.

The only difficulty with assuming a silver-based economy is that silver might have remained in short supply. Yet as several authorities have pointed out, the Phoenicians were known to have shipped silver from Spain and elsewhere in the Mediterranean to the Levant. It was that supply that enabled the Assyrians to meet the increasing fiscal demands as their empire grew. That is the wider context in which the Ekron and other silver hoards are best understood.

Technology

Technological changes in the seventh century are somewhat diffuse. There are changes in the ceramic repertoire, but they consist mostly of the more frequent importation (and imitation) of Assyrian, Edomite, and even Greek wares, rather than technological innovations. The local ceramic repertoire had long been standardized, and in the seventh century it evolved along predictable lines. At Ashdod there was a whole quarter of pottery workers, with numerous horizontal down-draft kilns.

Seals have already been discussed in chapter 5 as evidence of technology, but by the seventh century typical Judahite seals become simpler, often eschewing any complex iconographic motifs for simple personal names. That may be seen, of course, as a further development of religious aniconism (below).

Glass technology, although difficult, was in evidence already in the Late Bronze Age, although in Egyptian imports. By Iron II, locally made, Phoenician decorated sand-core cast glass bottles appear, imitating their Bronze Age prototypes, although somewhat degenerate.

The large-scale olive-oil processing discussed above would have required some technological innovations in manufacturing large stone presses and vats, as well as constructing elaborate beam-and-weight presses. Mass production of standardized store jars for shipment would also have been required.

We have noted the proliferation of maritime trade under Phoenician auspices. That would have required large-scale ship-building capacity, even though we have little direct archaeological evidence thus far. Several seaports are known, however, such as the ones at Mikhmoret, Akko, and Dor. These, too, presuppose a substantial knowledge of engineering and construction.[57]

Architectural innovations are best seen in Assyrian-style places at Hazor, Megiddo, and elsewhere, often based on the Aramean and Assyrian module of the *bit hilani*, a multiroomed courtyard structure. Distinctive Assyrian-style vaulted mud-brick buildings are known at Tell Jemmeh. At some Philistine sites, and especially at Phoenician sites such as Dor, older ashlar masonry techniques are still in use. Both ashlar masonry and Proto-Aeolic capitals are found in the late seventh-century Building Phase 1 at Ramat Raḥel.[58]

Culture

Under this rubric we have previously discussed literacy, but we have much more substantial evidence by the seventh century.

Writing, Literacy. Elsewhere we have documented the growth of literacy from obscure beginnings in the tenth–ninth century to a reasonably well-documented phenomenon by the end of the eighth century. Although by that period we have literary production and even a monumental royal inscription, much of the corpus consists of ostraca that clearly reflect economic and administrative activities. That is even truer of the seventh-century corpus.

There are a few examples of literary production, notably the Khirbet Beit Lei inscriptions scratched on the wall of a seventh/sixth-century burial cave near Lachish. The readings are difficult and much debated, but in any case there appear to be references to Yahweh as a cosmic deity, one who dispenses justice and mercy. The literary style is very similar to that of many biblical passages in the Pentateuch, the Deuteronomistic History, and the Psalms. A seventh-century graffito found written in ink in a cave near 'Ein-Gedi, although fragmentary, exhibits similar motifs.[59]

Two engraved silver amulets found in a late seventh-century tomb in Jerusalem (Ketef Hinnom) belong clearly to a literary tradition that is close to, almost identical with, the biblical tradition. They bear a striking resemblance to the well-known priestly blessing of Num 6:24–26, but slight variations show how widely such blessings were used (indeed, still are used). Without some degree of literacy, these blessings could not have been so much appreciated. Nevertheless, these two are amulets—in effect, good luck charms for individuals who may have been illiterate, as most persons still were.[60]

The largest corpora of seventh-century ostraca are those from Lachish and Arad. The original twenty-three Lachish ostraca were letters found in one room of the gatehouse in the Stratum II destruction of the city, now clearly dated to the Babylonian campaigns of 586. Some simply list names or give blessing formulas, but many are letters written by one Hoshayahu to his superior officer Yaush, evidently the chief commander of the Shephelah who was in residence at Lachish. A reference to "seeing the fire signals of Lachish" suggests that Hoshayahu was stationed nearby. The political significance of the Lachish letters will be discussed presently, but here we may note the evidence for literacy. Many scholars have noted the similarity of Hebrew vocabulary and syntax in these letters and the contemporary book of Jeremiah. One phrase in letter 6, "to weaken the hand" of someone, is reminiscent of Jeremiah and other biblical texts. Letter 3 is of particular interest, since Hoshayahu complains that he has been falsely accused of "not knowing how to read a letter," whereas no one ever had to instruct him. Other ostraca refer to extensive correspondence, which by this time would have been pro forma in the Judahite administration.[61]

The ninety-one Hebrew ostraca found by Aharoni at Arad are difficult to date stratigraphically due to the faulty excavation and recording methods of the time. Aharoni ascribed them to Strata XI–VIII, ninth–eighth century. Most, however, seem better dated to Strata VII–VI, of the seventh–early sixth century, on both revised stratigraphic and paleographical grounds. The largest group came from one room of the Stratum VI fortress, of the late seventh–early sixth century. They are addressed to one Eliyashib, a superior who seems to be located elsewhere. They contain detailed instructions about the distribution of various commodities, often to the Kittiyim, who may be Phoenician or Cypro-Phoenician mercenaries. There are few pretensions to literary style in these terse commands, but the ostraca do illustrate again how commonplace written correspondence and record keeping were toward the end of the monarchy (fig. 6.13).[62]

There are several other seventh-century ostraca having to do with economic transactions, from Jerusalem, Moza, Ḥorvat ʿUza, Tel ʿIra, Khirbet el-Qom (Makkedah), Kadesh-barnea, and elsewhere.

Another ostracon of the late seventh century was found in the guardroom of a fort at modern Meṣad Ḥashavyahu (Yavneh-Yam) south of Tel Aviv. It is a letter of complaint from an individual who has been defrauded of a garment held in pledge. It was clearly dictated by a commoner to a professional scribe, and it is written in good Judahite Hebrew style and orthography, even though the site is in Philistia.[63]

Two late seventh- or early sixth-century hoards of bullae—clay seal impressions with Hebrew names—have recently been found. The 320 bullae published by Avigad are unprovenanced but probably come from illicit digging (or robbing) in Jerusalem. Yigal Shiloh's hoard of fifty-one, however, is well stratified and dates to Stratum 10 of the early sixth century (586), when the city was finally destroyed. They were found just above the floor of Building 967 (the Bullae House) in the burnt debris.[64]

A few of the latter have iconographic motifs, seals, but most have only personal names of the owners, plus their fathers, eighty-two Hebrew names in all. About half the names have the theophoric suffix -*yahu*. Only thirteen names are unknown in the Hebrew Bible. Some have clear impressions of papyrus fibers on the back. Unfortunately, the fire that baked the bullae and thus preserved them completely destroyed the dozens of papyrus scrolls that they sealed. Nevertheless, the widespread existence of such scrolls, mostly administrative records, is proven. We even have one surviving papyrus fragment, preserved in the dry climate of the Wadi Murabba'at, near Qumran.[65]

In the Avigad and Shiloh corpora there are four bullae with a combination of fathers and sons who are known from the Hebrew Bible: (1) "Seraiyahu (son of) Neriyahu" (biblical Seraiah and Neriah); (2) "Jerahmiel, son of the king" (Jerahmeel); (3) "Berekyahu, son of Neriyahu the scribe" (Baruch and Neriah); and (4) "Gemaryahu, son of Shaphan" (Gemariah and Shaphan). A second bullae of Berekyahu subsequently came to light, like Avigad's, purchased on the market. Doubts have been raised about the authenticity of the latter bullae (and others), but it would be more difficult to fake these fragmentary clay bullae than it would to fake the seals themselves (which would have been required). If these two bullae are genuine, as most epigraphers think, then we have here the signature of Baruch, the scribe of Jeremiah the prophet, who was active during the last years before the fall of Jerusalem, the date of the bullae in the Burnt House. Gemaryahu, the son of Shaphan, is also mentioned in connection with Jeremiah.[66]

As we have seen, the corpus of written material from the seventh century consists of many dozens of stamp seals and bullae. Nearly all contain names, patronymics, and occasionally titles. A few were the possessions of high-ranking officials, even princes and kings, some known to us from biblical or other texts. Most, however, give us the names of folk of lesser rank and vocation. It may be that the ownership of such seals demonstrates that many individuals were virtually illiterate and thus used a seal impression as a substitute for a hand-written signature or title. But unless some people could read, such "signatures" would have been of relatively little value except as symbols.

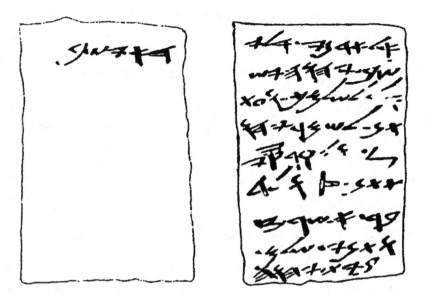

Fig. 6.13. Ostracon number 18 from Arad, mentioning the "house of Yahweh" (Aharoni 1981, 35)

Ironically, the most significant Hebrew document from the late seventh century is the one that we do not have, at least not in the original, that is, the core of the Hebrew Bible. By that time, and perhaps even earlier, the pentateuchal sources, at least the J and E traditions, were being reduced to writing after an oral tradition that may have been much older. More importantly, the composite work that we know as the Deuteronomistic History—the book of Deuteronomy, plus Joshua, Judges, Samuel, and Kings—was probably extant in its first version in the late seventh century. It is commonly thought that the foundation of this great epochal history—essentially the book of Deuteronomy as we now have it—consists of a document claimed to have been found in refurbishing the temple during the Josianic reform. It became a manifesto for supposed Mosaic reforms, then was incorporated into a grand, sweeping epic that recounted Israel's history from Sinai to the fall of Jerusalem. The earliest copies of the biblical texts that we have, however, are among the Dead Sea Scrolls fragments of the Roman period.[67]

In the seventh century we have not only Hebrew inscriptions but also several inscriptions in Phoenician and Edomite scripts. The long early seventh-century dedicatory inscription from Temple IB at Ekron is written in a local script that is a version of Phoenician. It mentions one Padi, the king known from Assyrian texts, as well as a Philistine deity (*ptgyh*). There is also a Phoenician inscription on a potsherd, again naming the king and the deity Baal. There are also a number of short formulas on sherds, several referring to a "shrine of Asherah."[68]

Two Philistine ostraca from Tell Jemmeh in a variant of the local Hebrew script, containing both Philistine and Semitic names, have been found. We have an ostracon from Horvat ʿUza that names the Edomite deity Qos, but it also has Hebrew personal names. An Edomite ostracon from Tell el-Kheleifeh also has the divine name Qos, compounded with personal names. The implications of these multicultural traits will be explored directly.[69]

Art and Iconography. Artistic expressions, always rare in ancient Israel, are scarcely in evidence in seventh-century Judah. For instance, the comparatively rich repertoire of iconographic motifs on seals of the eighth century diminishes by the seventh century (see fig. 5.35). Many of the hundreds of seals and bullae we have feature only Hebrew names, sometimes bearing the owner's name plus a patronymic and often a title. Nevertheless, Keel and Uehlinger have shown that Egyptian-Phoenician iconographic images still appear. The principal themes now include uraei, sphinxes/griffins, ostriches, falcons, lions, bulls/bovines, caprids, snakes, trees, "Lords of animals," worshipers, symbols of royal and court rule, anthropomorphic deities, the child-son deity Horus seated on a lotus blossom, and, in particular, various forms of solar and astral deities (more than 150 examples). As Keel and Uehlinger put it, by the seventh century there had occurred a shift "from provincial reception of Egyptian royal iconography to the integration of religious solar symbolism."[70] Although it is difficult to be sure, most of these seals, made of bone, were manufactured locally. They indicate a kind of syncretism in religious beliefs in which Yahweh was related to other deities.

The anthropomorphic and zoomorphic figurines that will be considered below under the rubric of religion and cult hardly represent notable artistic achievements. In particular, the seventh-century pinched-nose female figurines are quite crude. The mold-made heads of the other Judahite pillar-base female figurines seem to resemble a few Assyrian-style coiffures.

Religion and Cult. There are a number of archaeological finds that illumine the seventh-century Judahite cult. There are a few full-fledged cult installations that can be securely dated to the seventh century. The Dan sacred precinct seems to have gone out of use by the seventh century, as did the Arad temple. The Jerusalem temple probably continued in use until 586, even though we have no direct archeological evidence.

Cave I in Jerusalem, just south of the Temple Mount, excavated by Kenyon, has been much discussed. Belonging to the late seventh century, it appears to have been either a local shrine, or possibly a *favissa* for discarding cult items. Among the contents were more than seventy female and zoomorphic figurines (mostly broken), a terra-cotta rattle, a model shrine, several model couches, a rattle, two miniature stone altars, three offering stands, a few ostraca, and some twelve hundred ceramic vessels, some with the remains of animal bones. There were no human bones, which excludes the cave's use for burials. Some statistics on the ceramic vessels' may be significant: about 9 percent of the vessels are for food preparation (cooking pots and a *tabûn* [oven] were found in the cave); 63 percent are for food consumption; and only 24 percent are for storage. Cave II is not often discussed, but there were a few similar cultic items found there, along with 288 ceramic vessels. More than 70 percent of the latter were for food consumption.

The contents of Cave I in particular have led to several interpretations of what is obviously a cult place. Cave I has been understood primarily as either (1) a functioning cult installation for families or small communal groups; (2) a shrine for feasting to commemorate the dead (the *marzeah* festival); or (3) a facility for stored or discarded cult items, in the latter case a *favissa*.[71]

Only a short distance away, a contemporary assemblage of cult objects was found by Shiloh, in the well-known Stratum 10B Bullae House (Locus 967; see above on the fifty-one bullae). Here there were cooking pots, store jars, kraters, bowls, decanters, juglets, two unusual footed goblets, grinding stones, a dome-shaped weight, a horse-and-rider figurine, and four miniature limestone altars, evidently for burning incense (fig. 6.14).

Another contemporary cult assemblage in Jerusalem was found by E. Mazar in a cave on the eastern slopes of the Ophel (Locus 6015). Again, vessels for the preparation and consumption of food predominated, but there were also fragments of female and horse-and-rider figurines, a rattle, and a store jar incised in Hebrew "Belonging to Yesh'a-yahu."[72]

Whatever the explanation of the uses of Caves I and II, it is worth noting that these cultic installations flourished for some time in the late

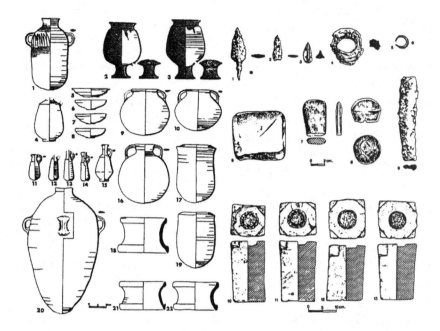

Fig. 6.14. Contents of household shrine from Area G in Jerusalem, Stratum 10B, late seventh century (Shiloh 1986, figs. 5–7, 20)

seventh century, only a few hundred yards south of the Temple Mount—and precisely during the era of the presumed Josianic reforms. In particular, the female figurines are significant, since they are widely seen as representing the goddess Asherah in one way or another, whose cult was a major target of the Deuteronomistic attempts at reform (below). The same may be said of Mazar's nearby cave, even if only for storage or discards. Shiloh's Bullae House, clearly the home of a high-ranking official close to the Temple Mount, is even more revealing, in this case giving us a quite visible family and household shrine (below).

The female figurines are especially noteworthy. The figurines depicting a woman holding a disc to her breast, which originated in the north as early as the tenth century, continued in use in Judah throughout the seventh century, not much changed. The other pillar-base figurines, with mold-made heads or simply pinched-nose faces, began in the late eighth century, but they become much more common in the seventh century. They are distinctly Judahite and clearly differ from contemporary Philistine, Phoenician, or Transjordanian female figurines (fig. 6.15). There is no

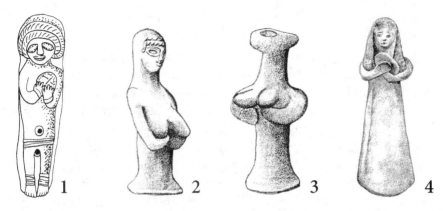

Fig. 6.15. Israelite/Judahite and Phoenician terra-cotta pillar-base figurines. 1: figurine with disc; 2: figurine with mold-made head; 3: figurine with pinched face; 4: typical Phoenician figurine (1: Schroer 1987, fig. 101; 2–4: Vriezen 2001, fig. 13)

doubt that the Judahite figurines represent a nude female, the lower torso not depicted but the breasts prominent. Long called fertility figurines, they have been the subject of much debate. The minimalist school holds that they are votives; that is, they represent human females venerating a deity, as "prayers in clay." An increasing number of scholars, however, view the Judean pillar-base figurines not simply as votives or human representations of women somehow evoking the blessings of the Mother Goddess but rather as actual images of her (i.e., Asherah). Some still maintain that there is no specific divine iconography to be seen here, as in the Late Bronze Age female figurines or those of Iron Age Philistia or Transjordan. But are not the prominently displayed breasts powerful symbols of the fertility and plenty that the gods supply? A functionalist interpretation fails to provide the required explanation.

There are further arguments against the minimalist votive interpretation. These figurines are mass-produced, not personalized in any way. Furthermore, the females are clearly represented as naked—precisely like their ubiquitous Late Bronze Age predecessors, which all scholars recognize as depicting a female deity. Finally, would a Judahite woman present a votive of herself as naked before the goddess? Would she not be more likely to see herself as covered in the presence of the deity, a universal impulse? Furthermore, why would she offer her breasts so prominently, holding them up to the goddess? Should it not be the other way around—*she* praying for nurture? All things considered, both symbolism and common sense suggest that the female figurines of the eighth–seventh century represent Asherah and illustrate cult practices connected with her, especially those having to do with conception, childbirth, and lactation—all stressful and risky in antiquity.[73]

This is not simply speculation based on "mute" objects. Both the eighth-century Khirbet el-Qom and Kuntillet ʿAjrud inscriptions refer in almost identical fashion to "Yahweh and his Asherah" in a context of blessing. Grammatical objections have been raised, but the general consensus seems to have been moving toward reading the term *ʾăšērâ* not as a pole or tree-like symbol but rather as the personal name of the deity. In any case, the symbol would have had no meaning had it not pointed to the reality of the goddess behind it. These figurines are best understood therefore as related to family and household cults where both women and men used them as talismans to aid in conception, safe childbirth, and successful lactation. Most are found in domestic contexts, such as cult corners, dumps, or tombs. They are absent in more public shrines (although these are rarely attested after the late eighth century).[74]

Another category of artifacts that reflect religious beliefs, especially symbolically, consists of seals and seal impressions. More than three thousand are known from the Iron Age, particularly in Judah of the eighth–seventh century (fig. 6.16). They have been studied in detail, both for iconography and in terms of the Hebrew onomasticon, especially the occurrence of theophoric names. Several conclusions may be drawn. (1) By the seventh century, in contrast to the eighth century, nearly all iconographic and other symbols have disappeared. We have mostly the owner's name, a patronym, and sometimes a title. The personal names on the seals that are demonstrably Hebrew (1,978 out of 2,922) are overwhelmingly Yahwistic. Those seals that specify some activity or function are largely concerned with divine mercy, justice, protection, and blessings; the owner's trust and joy in Yahweh; one's familial connection with Yahweh; and praise of Yahweh. It is striking that there are no instances of references to the Deuteronomistic Historians' great themes: Sinai covenant, divine kingship, or Zion and the temple. Typical verbs for these contexts, such as *yṣʾ* ("to lead out"); *ʿlh* ("to lead up"), or several Hebrew verbs for "to choose for," "to give an inheritance" and "to save," do not appear, at least in any theological sense. From an exhaustive analysis of Iron Age Hebrew seals Albertz concludes: "If there was influence of Sinai theophany on the

Fig. 6.16. Seal impressions from Judah

personal names, it must have been quite slight.... It is now clear to us that Hebrew personal names lack reference to Israel's national history."[75]

One remaining implication of the seventh-century seals and bullae needs to be considered. Is the general abandonment of the older Egyptian and Phoenician iconography a sign of the success of aniconoclastic reforms that the Hebrew Bible attributers to Josiah and the so-called "Yahweh-alone" movement of other reformers and prophets? Many biblical scholars have thought so. Nevertheless, the argument is essentially one from silence; the only evidence is circumstantial. The fact is that it is precisely in the seventh century that the Judahite pillar-base figurines proliferate, and at minimum they reflect religious pluralism (below).

The evidence of seals and bullae for cult beliefs/or practices is ambiguous, as Albertz and Schmitt have shown. On one hand, the 404 Hebrew theophoric personal names (out of 675) that are attested are overwhelmingly combined with Yahweh (59.4 percent) or El (13.1 percent). On the other hand, several other deities appear, such as Baal, Mot, Yerah, Shahar, Shalem, Shamash, Edomite Qos, and a few Egyptian deities. There are also a few occurrences of the names of female deities such as Astarte and Anat. The names of all these secondary deities appear in 7.3 percent of the 404 Hebrew theophoric names.

Albertz's exhaustive analysis of seals and bullae with nearly three thousand personal names (675 of them Hebrew) leads him to several conclusions. (1) The distinction between monotheism and polytheism is artificial, and "it would be better to distinguish between different sorts of polytheism." (2) "The primary traditions of official Israelite state and temple religion are almost entirely absent from both biblical and epigraphic names." (3) "Family religion in Israel followed the same basic structure common throughout Syria and the Levant during the first half of the first millennium B.C.E., irrespective of minor differences among cultural groups."[76]

These appear to be startling and perhaps disturbing conclusions, drawn recently by a leading biblical scholar and based now on overwhelming archaeological data, yet they merely confirm the direction in which scholarship on the topic of Israelite and Judahite religion has been moving for more than twenty years. Already in 1994 Dever had published a paper read at a conference in Bern (where Albertz also gave a presentation) documenting the "disconnect" between biblical texts and the artifactual data. There a heuristic distinction was made between official and popular religion, which Albertz and others have criticized but which they and virtually every other scholar must acknowledge in one way or another in the end (even if the term "family/household" religion is adopted for the latter). The religion of the Book and those few elites who wrote it and the religion of ordinary folk *are* different.

There are a number of household shrines dating to the seventh century, as seen previously in the eighth century (ch. 5). In most cases we have only a few presumably cultic items, such as figurines, lamps, chalices, kraters, cooking and serving vessels, small limestone incense altars, and perhaps an occasional fragment of miniature furniture. Most of these items were found scattered in a corner of a room in a private dwelling, with little or no clue to their use or their original context. It may be presumed that they were used in family rituals that had to do with offering sacrifices, seeking blessings, making vows, commemorating life-cycle events, feasting, venerating the ancestors, and the like. These are all well-known rites of family and household religions in ancient Israel and Judah (and elsewhere in the Levant as well). The deity or deities being invoked cannot be directly ascertained, but the presence of Asherah figurines (above) suggests that more than one deity was venerated in domestic cults.[77]

The most intriguing house shrine known thus far is in the Bullae House excavated by Shiloh in Area G in Jerusalem, its destruction well dated to 586. The bullae have been widely discussed, but the accompanying objects have been only partially published. They include, besides pottery, a few items that might have cultic significance, such as two unusual goblets, figurine fragments, and four small limestone incense altars.[78]

Tombs are universally regarded as reflecting religious beliefs and practices. The eighth-century Judahite bench tombs discussed above, with rich evidence bearing on family burial rites, continued with little change throughout the seventh century. Figurines, Bes and Eye-of-Horus amulets, miniature furniture, terra-cotta rattles, cultic vessels, and other exotic items are all in evidence. These artifacts suggest veneration of the ancestors, that is, presenting items from daily life to accompany the dead in the afterlife (if any), and probably communal feasting to recall them and reaffirm family identity with them. As we saw above (ch. 5), such rites are appropriate, since the typical Judahite bench tombs of the eighth–seventh century were no doubt conceived as "houses for the dead."

The amulets in these tombs (many unpublished and unstudied) are indications of magic, the desire to secure the favor of the gods through the use of symbols. We may have some textual evidence on the two late seventh-century silver amulets from Ketef Hinnom on which are engraved a version of the priestly blessing in Num 6:24–26 (above). The text invokes Yahweh's blessings and peace upon the individual who wore it around the neck, almost like a mezuzah. In that case, a quotation from what by now was becoming scripture was not read but worn as sympathetic magic. Van der Toorn has aptly described such practices as "book religion," in which the scriptural text, rather than any other artifact, becomes an icon.[79]

In summarizing the developments in religious beliefs and practices by the seventh century, the following points seem the most significant.

1. With the collapse of Judahite independence, an identity crisis develops that presents a challenge to the religious establishment.
2. Foreign influences included those of Assyria, the Arameans, Phoenicians, Philistines, Egyptians, even Greeks. Old Canaanite traditions reappear. The result is an *enoikismos*.
3. Influenced by Assyrian iconography, there occurs an "astralization" of the cult; Yahweh becomes "Most High God."
4. But alongside Yahweh, Asherah cults prevail and become stronger.
5. There are attempts to ban polytheism, icons, but they fail.
6. Traditional family and household religion supplants the national cult.
7. The stage is set for the development of postexilic Judaism.

We have some evidence for the Philistine cult, such as the Ekron ostraca mentioning a "shrine for Asherah" and the small horned incense altars often found in association with domestic olive-oil pressing installations (above). There is no longer any evidence, however, of the exotic cult paraphernalia known in the early Iron II period, such as the elaborate offering stands from Yavneh-Yam (ch. 5).

Phoenician religion is difficult to document in this era. By the Persian period, however, it is clear that the old Canaanite and West Semitic deities have been adopted. Yet how early this syncretism occurred is hard to say. The seventh-century excavated sites shed only indirect light.

In Transjordan, we have relatively good information, including evidence from some epigraphic data. In Ammon the chief deity was Milkom, perhaps an El-like figure, who is shown in several figurines wearing the Egyptian *atef* crown. On seals he is depicted as a bull with large horns. The female deity Astarte was also venerated as "Astarte of Sidon." No temples are known, but a small household shrine at Tell el-ʿUmeiri features a standing stone (a *maṣṣēbâ*?) and a basin.

In Moab we have some evidence in seals that have personal names compounded with the name of the deity Kemosh, known already in the ninth-century Mesha stela. In Edom proper the chief deity, known from ostraca and seals, is Qaus (Qos). The best evidence, however, comes from the seventh-century Ḥorvat Qitmit and ʿEn-Ḥazeva, both Edomite sites in the Negev where Astarte and at least one other deity are attested.[80]

Ḥorvat Qitmit is a sort of roadside shrine in the immediate vicinity of three northern Negev Judahite sites: Tel 'Ira, Tel Malḥata, and 'Aro'er (south of Arad). The complex consists of two rectangular constructions with courtyards and two circular structures. Among the finds were numerous cylindrical offering and/or incense stands, to which had once been attached painted anthropomorphic and zoomorphic figurines. There were also other similar free-standing figurines. These cultic objects appear to have been originally placed in the courtyard or the small cells of the structures, where benches or platforms and at least one standing stone were found. Cooking pots, ashes, and animal bones suggest that feasting was a part of the rituals. Almost none of the cult vessels have any known parallels, but an Edomite connection is suggested by the proliferation of Edomite pottery, similar to pottery known from Buṣeirah, Tawilan, and Umm el-Biyara, and several ostraca in an Edomite script, one mentioning the deity Qos.[81]

'En-Ḥazeva is located near the fort of Mezad Ḥazeva, some 12 miles southwest of the Dead Sea, in the eastern Negev Desert. Strata 5–4, belonging to the late seventh century, have produced an astonishing array of cult items, most with Edomite connections.[82]

Ethnicity

Defining ethnicity or the basis of material culture remains one of contemporary archaeology's most difficult tasks. Much of the recent discussion is very skeptical, but it must be noted that many if not most of the voices heard are those of anthropologists, biblicists, and others who do not specialize in the archaeology of the southern Levant. We have already argued (in chs. 3–5) that what are called ethnic boundaries are not actually so fluid as to be indiscernible. Place of birth, genetic inheritance, native language, early cultural upbringing—these are all incontrovertible facts, not simply perceptions. The latter can and do change, however, at least in the modern world, and the larger cultural context does indeed influence both individual and national self-identity. With these facts in mind, let us look at general conditions in Judah in the seventh century in order to understand how most people might have experienced life and seen themselves.

First we must note the extent to which Judah under Assyrian hegemony had developed into a polyglot, multicultural society and economy. The many scripts and languages in common use included Akkadian cuneiform, as well as West Semitic Hebrew, Aramaic, and Phoenician, not to mention Neo-Philistine. The fact that the majority of ostraca that we have are in Hebrew suggests that this was the language spoken by most people in the Judahite heartland. But even there, as in the Arad ostraca, there are numerous references to Edomites and even to Cypriots (the Kittiyim; mercenaries?)

Elsewhere, at Ḥorvat ʿUza and Tell el-Kheleifeh, there are ostraca with references to the Edomite deity Qos. At these sites and Tel ʿIra in the northern Negev, there are substantial quantities of easily recognizable painted Edomite pottery. These sites, however, have also produced Judahite-style architecture, pottery, and ethnically specific objects such as sheqel weights and pillar-base female figurines. Mixed with the above artifacts at a number of sites are clear Assyrian ethnic indicators such as monumental architecture, cuneiform inscriptions, and Assyrian Palace ware (or imitations).[83] Finally, a full-fledged Edomite culture is clearly manifest at two seventh-century sites west of the Jordan, well within the borders of Judah: Ḥorvat Qitmit and ʿEn-Ḥazeva (above). Tell el-Khefeilah has even been understood as an Edomite fort. Whatever the explanation, such incursions of Edomites and other ethnic groups into Judah could have been made possible only under the Assyrian policy of pacification and unification. That phenomenon also helps to account for the evidence that, after the fall of Samaria, deportees from (and possibly into) the now-defunct northern kingdom were part of the cultural mix in the south.[84]

Along the Philistine border, the multicultural mix is even more in evidence. Judahite border sites such as Gezer, Timnah, and Beth-Shemesh are good examples of a mix of Assyrian, Judahite, and coastal elements. Neo-Philistine border sites such as Ekron provide even clearer evidence of a multicultural amalgam. Again, all these sites were under Assyrian control, allowing for and even fostering such integration.

The results of such cultural diversity—encountered for the first time in Israelite/Judahite history and in the homeland—would have had far-reaching implications for a people whose self-identity and destiny were now in flux. Most people in Judah would probably have been somewhat confused by the collapse of traditional society and values, certainly apprehensive about the future. In General Systems parlance, everything seemed to be spinning out of control.

On the other hand, such an identity crisis can stimulate creative responses. A closer definition of ethnicity is often stimulated by conflicts with rival cultures: it forces people to distinguish *us* from *them*. We have already seen the dynamics of this process at Beth-Shemesh in the eighth century. It may be that the emergence of the sort of "pan-Israelite" ideology—so clearly reflected in the earliest version of the Deuteronomistic History (which many think belongs to this horizon)—is best explained by the late seventh-century cultural context that archaeology has provided. Was this the crucible in which Israelite identity was finally forged? We will return to this notion presently.

The End: The Babylonian Destructions of 586

Sennacherib ruled from Sargon II's death in 705 until he died in 681. He had greatly facilitated the primary goal of the Assyrians, which was to control the Levantine coast and its lucrative Mediterranean trade, as well as the overland caravan trade with Arabia. That meant dominating the Phoenician and Philistine coast. But the ultimate goal was to reduce Egyptian power in the area. During Sennacherib's final years, he was in conflict with the Egyptian Cushite Pharaohs of the Twenty-Fifth Dynasty. When his son Esarhaddon (681–669) came to the throne he renewed the struggle, apparently in league with Arabian vassals. Esarhaddon then moved down the coast to campaign against Sidon and Tyre in his fourth year (677). In 674 he attempted to invade Egypt but was repulsed by Pharaoh Taharqa. Then in 669 he was prepared to renew the campaign, but he became ill and died on the way. Success came only in 664/663, when his son Assurbanipal (669–627) came to the throne. With Psammetichus installed as a puppet ruler, Assurbanipal seemed poised to stabilize the whole eastern Mediterranean. But by 656, the Assyrian garrisons were expelled, and the Egyptian Twenty-Sixth Dynasty became independent from Assyria.

A decade later, the Elamites of Babylonia were in rebellion, and Assurbanipal's empire began to fall apart. He claimed victory circa 648, but by 644–643 he was battling Arab forces from the South Arabian peninsula. By 630, at the latest, the Assyrian Empire had been rocked to its foundation. Between 614 and 610 the Babylonians, with the help of the Median army, had taken the Assyrian capital of Assur and had converged on Harran on the upper Euphrates to drive back the Assyrian and Egyptian forces.

The Babylonian king Nabopolassar (625–605) never controlled all of Mesopotamia and north Syria. In Egypt, Pharaoh Neco II succeeded his father Psammetichus in 610. Thus there was a brief interregnum in international geopolitics in the last quarter of the seventh century, but the *Pax Assyriaca*—which after all had had a stabilizing influence—was at an end. Egypt would invade Judah (609), but soon thereafter a greater threat would appear with the accession of Nabopolassar's son Nebuchadnezzar (604–562). It was during his reign that the kingdom of Judah was finally ravaged.

The Babylon king undertook campaigns against the Arabs in 598 and, according to the Babylonian Chronicle, even moved against Judah the next year to seize the king of Jerusalem (Jehoiakim). The city is said to have surrendered, and a vassal king was placed on the throne (Jehoiachin). With that, the end was at hand and inevitable.

The biblical texts, which here we are considering separately, focus exclusively on the fall of Jerusalem, which took place in 586, with devastating results. Jerusalem had been besieged for some eighteen months. Finally the city walls were breached; the king (Zedekiah) and his troops fled; the temple and palace were burned; the city was thoroughly looted; and large numbers of the population were deported to Babylon, leaving the "people of the land" behind as a remnant.

The Babylonian Chronicle falls silent at this point, noting only the earlier invasion in 598/597. The Deuteronomistic History, on the other hand, recounts only the final destruction of Jerusalem, nothing else. It is only archaeology that can fill in the gaps, but few modern histories of Israel cite the substantive data that we now have.[85]

Stratum 10 of the recent excavations in Jerusalem dramatically illuminates the 586 destruction of the city. Avigad's defensive tower was found below a deep layer of ashes. Shiloh's houses in Areas E and G—the Ashlar House, the House of Ahiel, the Burnt Room, and the House of the Bullae—were fired; in the collapse were found large quantities of pottery, stone and metal vessels, and the bullae discussed above. The destruction of Mazar's residential quarters is said to have been total. Dozens of iron arrowheads, as well as triangular Scythian arrowheads, attest to the ferocity of the battle. The date was 18 July 586 (the 9th of Ab).[86]

In discussing the multitier data base of Judahite sites in figure 6.5 above, we have noted in most site descriptions the late seventh-century strata numbers. Thus we can merely refer to that list, which includes some forty sites, nearly all of which show signs of disturbance or destruction.[87]

One site to discuss is Lachish, where the ostraca found in Stratum

II destruction debris in the city throw brilliant if chilling light on that city's last days. Letter 4 is a desperate plea for help, probably from nearby Mareshah. The official writing the letter says that he can no longer see the fire signal from Azekah, which must have already fallen, and he is anxiously watching for fire signals from Lachish. The letter was probably never answered, and shortly thereafter it was lost in the ashy destruction debris of the Lachish gate guardroom, where it lay until it was found 2,500 years later.

The several Judahite forts listed in figure 6.5 above, most of which were founded after the 732–721 destructions in the north, were nearly all destroyed in 586, and many were deserted thereafter. The forts in the area of Jerusalem and extending eastward into the Judean desert were undoubtedly overrun by the Babylonian onslaught. The Negev forts, of less strategic importance, were also destroyed and deserted thereafter. They may have been taken by the Babylonians in the course of dominating the southern trade routes or by Edomites taking advantage of Judah's weakness (as possibly in the case of Tel 'Ira VI and Tel Sera' IV; below).

In addition to the destructions of Judahite sites in 586, several sites in Philistia were destroyed by the Babylonians, most slightly earlier, in 604 or 603: Yavneh-Yam (Meṣad Ḥashavyahu); Ashdod VII–VI; Ashkelon 14; Ekron IB; Tel Jemmeh AB (Phases 7–5).[88]

Ashdod VII–VI, although a Philistine site, has affinities with Judah. It may have been destroyed in the late seventh century by Psammetichus I of Egypt, in the contest with the Assyrians.

Ashkelon 14 gives vivid evidence of a Babylonian destruction, dated precisely to Kislev (November–December) of 604. The winery and marketplace, in particular, were devastated in a great conflagration. The crushed body of a thirty-five-year-old woman was found in the debris, along with quantities of local pottery, Egyptian items, and luxury goods. It has been suggested that the pro-Egyptian policies of Ashkelon (and Ekron) may have led to their demise. Nebuchadnezzar II describes how he marched to the site, captured it and its king, plundered it, then "turned it into a heap of ruins" before marching back to Babylon.[89]

Ekron IB was destroyed in the same year, as seen in the Phoenician-style Temple 650 and Auxiliary Buildings 651–655. An intact dedicatory inscription, written in a Phoenicianizing (or Neo-Philistine) script, mentions two kings, Padi and his son Ikausu, both of whom are known in the Assyrian annals. Five caches of silver were also found in the debris. There were also East Greek wares. The population of Ekron, like that of Ash-kelon, was largely deported to Babylon.[90]

A few sites may have been destroyed in the late seventh century in clashes with Edomites or even in Egyptian raids. Tel Masos was perhaps destroyed by Edomites in their struggles in the Negev. Tel Seraʿ IV could have been destroyed by expeditions of the Saite dynasty in Egypt (or by the Babylonians; above).

Phoenician sites along the north coast continue into the seventh century after disruptions in the late eighth century. Among them are Tell Keisan IV, the Akko cemetery, Shiqmona E, and in particular Dor (above). Whether these sites were destroyed in the Babylonian campaigns in 604 or again in 586 is unclear.

In Transjordan there is little or no evidence of late seventh- to early sixth-century destructions. There Ammonite, Moabite, and Edomite sites seem to continue from the period of Assyrian domination to the Babylonian era and thereafter into the Persian period as late as the late fifth century.[91]

Scholars have generally agreed that the Babylonian destructions in 586 devastated most of the urban sites in Judah. The fate of the rural areas, however, has only recently been illuminated. Meanwhile, a few revisionists have put forward the notion of "the myth of the empty land," arguing that this is a biblical construct devoid of any historical value. In this view, Judah was not depopulated or even seriously affected by the Babylonian conquest.

The idea of the empty land gained currency with Barstad's *The Myth of the Empty Land* (1996), although the notion went back to Torrey's publications in the 1950s, and it had been favored by Carrol and Lemche in the 1980s and 1990s. With the work of Lipschitz from the 1990s on, however, the "continuity school" seemed entrenched. Yet the crucial archaeological data had not been analyzed in sufficient detail until Faust's *Judah in the Neo-Babylonian Period: The Archaeology of Desolation* (2012b).[92]

Faust acknowledged the difficulties that had plagued the discussion of the archaeology of the Persian period (late sixth–late fourth century), including inadequate excavation and publication that left the impression of a long "dark age" that may have been misleading. Even more recently, we lack a clearly defined and closely dated corpus of Persian pottery that could prove decisive. Finally, the rural sector has been elucidated only recently, thanks to surface surveys and selective excavations. Despite these limitations, Faust proceeded to a reconstruction of Judah in the post-586 or Persian period, based largely on continuity and discontinuity in material culture in the era following the end of the Iron II period in the late seventh/early sixth century.

Faust's analysis shows not only that there are long gaps in occupation but that distinctive Iron Age cultural traits such as the Israelite pillar-courtyard house, the rock-cut family bench tomb, the ubiquitous pillar-base figurines, and other material culture traits simply disappeared by the early to mid-sixth century. These dramatic changes cannot be coincidental; they demonstrate a discontinuity explainable only by a major disruption of people—a settlement crisis. Such shifts in patterns of settlement type and distribution are among archaeologists' most useful diagnostic tools.

The impression of discontinuity is strengthened by looking at the rural sites, which in principle ought to reflect more continuity, since they would not have been obvious targets of invasions. Yet here the statistics are clear. Of forty-five to fifty rural sites known in Judah, only seven show any degree of continuity from the late Iron Age into the Persian era. It appears not only that most of the urban sites were destroyed and partially abandoned but that the rural population was displaced as well.

After an exhaustive survey of the archaeological data, properly distanced from the biblical perspective, Faust concludes:

> The inhabitants of Neo-Babylonian Judah were scattered from Benjamin in the north to the Negev in the south, but were very limited in number. They clung to deserted settlements, mainly cities but in some cases also to villages; used some farmsteads; and found refuge in abandoned and deserted administrative buildings.... The economy was simple, not far above subsistence level, and probably only included limited regional exchange.[93]

Or again:

> Some people still clung to Iron Age traditions, but due to the collapse of the social order of the Iron Age, many of the traditions gradually faded away.... The world of the sixth century still maintained bits of the Iron Age, but was to a large extent very different.[94]

In Faust's view, the recovery during and after the Persian period took several centuries. The desolation of the Persian era, now well documented, has negative implications for biblical scholars who want to see flourishing "academies" then where the writers of the Hebrew Bible first worked.[95]

The Deuteronomistic History as an
Additional Source for the Seventh Century

All along we have invoked as a possible source the work commonly called the Deuteronomistic History: the book of Deuteronomy, plus Joshua, Judges, Samuel, and Kings. This composite work constitutes a great epic that essentially rewrites Israel's history from Moses in the wilderness to the fall of Jerusalem. Its themes are all more theological than historical: (1) exclusive Yahwism; (2) faithfulness to the Sinai covenant and law; (3) the fulfillment of the promise of the land; and (4) the centrality of the Jerusalem temple.

For more than two hundred years, biblical scholars have seen the core of this work in the scroll claimed to have been discovered in Josiah's day while repairs were being made to the temple. The scroll became the basis for Josiah's attempted reforms—in essence, the ideal of *restoration*. It is this restoration of the old order, the divine order, that offers the only hope for the Deuteronomists in an age of despair, but even more so for the book of Jeremiah, which has its origins at least in oral tradition in the Josianic era.[96]

The question now becomes whether the archaeological context—the historical reconstruction offered here—may possibly provide us with a basis for evaluating the scenario presented by the Deuteronomistic History, as well as by prophetic works such as Jeremiah. In short, what did the biblical writers know, when and how did they know it, and, above all, is it *true*, that is, historically reliable? In the vast literature on the Deuteronomistic History and the Josianic era, the significance of the archaeological data as providing a real-life context has insufficiently been considered.

The archaeological reconstruction advanced in the foregoing discussion leads to the conclusion that for Judah the early seventh century was a time of the eclipse of tradition, multi-culturalism, confusion, despair for the future, and perhaps apocalyptic visions. This was evident during the ascendant reigns of the Assyrian kings Sennacherib (705–681) and Esarhaddon (681–669). Assurbanipal's reign (669–627) continued Assyria's aggressive policies toward vassal kingdoms in the southern

Levant. But as we have seen, by the end of his long reign the Assyrian Empire had been reduced to impotence. At the same time, Egypt was effectively neutralized.

It was precisely in this lull in international affairs in the southern Levant that Josiah, the son of the hapless Manasseh (698–642), came to the throne, and he ruled for thirty years. At this point it may be instructive to evaluate what we may call convergences and divergences in attempting to correlate our two sources for history-writing, comparing the reigns of Manasseh in the early seventh century and the reign of Josiah in the late seventh century.[97]

Fig. 6.17. Possible correlations of seventh-century archaeological data and biblical texts

Proven	Probable; evidence ambiguous	Possible; little or no evidence	Disproven
Hezekiah's conduit; Broad Wall			
Sennacherib's siege of Jerusalem lifted	Sennacherib takes tribute, withdraws	Assyrian troops die in plague	185,000 Assyrian troops killed; Yahweh delivers Jerusalem
Sennacherib at Lachish			
Many Judahite sites destroyed	Libnah attacked	Pharaoh Taharqa invades Judah	
Manasseh paid tribute to Esarhaddon	Manassseh rebuilt "high places," etc.; a vassal	Built city wall; "made son pass through fire"	
Babylon confronts Egyptians in Harran	Egypt withdraws Babylonians attack Arabs, Transjordan		
"Poly-yahwism"; Asherah cult; Yahu-names; Philistia attacked	Josiah's attempted reforms; consulted temple scroll; maintained Judah even if vassal;	Celebrated Passover; extended influence to Shephelah, Samaria	Independent "Yahweh alone movement successful

	Josiah slain in battle, 609	At Megiddo Jehoahaz paid tribute, imprisoned at Riblah, 609
Campaign against Jerusalem, 597; Johoiakim pays tribute	Johoiakim and others deported	
Jerusalem falls and deportations, 586; poorest remain; Jehoiakin released	Jeremiah writes; Ezekial spared and exiled to Babylon	Disaster Yahweh's judgment

For the reign of Manasseh, correlations between our sources are mixed. The Deuteronomist's portrayal of the king as unable or unwilling to resist religious pluralism—an enthusiastic idolater and also an impotent Assyrian vassal—fits the general situation illuminated by archaeology. On the other hand, the one-sided focus of the Deuteronomistic History on Manasseh's supposed heresy occupies almost all of the relatively brief account of his long reign (only eighteen verses; 2 Kgs 21:1–18). In fact, his heresy is virtually all that we learn about Manasseh's fifty-five-year reign. For the "rest of the history of Manasseh," the Deuteronomistic History simply refers to an unknown document, the "Annals of the Kings of Judah."

What may have been one of Manasseh's deciding moments—Esarhaddon's well-documented requirement that he send provisions to his palace at Nineveh—is not mentioned at all in 2 Kings; 2 Chronicles, however, claims that Manasseh himself was arrested and removed briefly from his throne by the Assyrian king. Manasseh's name also appears in records from the reign of Esarhaddon, on which the Hebrew Bible is again silent.

In short, the biblical description of Manasseh's long reign, if roughly contemporary with Assyrian rule as supposed, seems curiously to have been written in a vacuum. There is no apparent awareness of the real political and cultural situation in the seventh century, particularly Judah's status as an Assyrian vassal-state. Is the writers' obliviousness a result of their single-minded ideological bias, or is it an indication of a later (exilic or postexilic) date than supposed for the Deuteronomistic History?

Here archaeology may supplement the biblical text. A large number of Hebrew bullae, unprovenanced but probably from Khirbet el-Qom (or Qeila, biblical Keilah), are unusual in that they contain date formulas. The inscriptions, in a good Hebrew hand of the late seventh- or early sixth-century script, contain variously (1) the date, in an Egyptian hieratic numeral relating to a particular king; (2) the name of a town; and (3) the king's ownership ("belonging to"). The iconographic symbols, if any, are typically Egyptian, as on many seals of the period.

What is significant is the fact that nearly all of the place names on these bullae correspond to places names in the so-called tribal boundary list in Josh 15. This list has long been discussed by biblical scholars, many of whom regard it as late and largely unhistorical. The network of place names is indeed unrealistic for the early settlements of the twelfth century, as we have shown above. Yet it would fit remarkably well in the reign of Manasseh (698–642), who had to pay heavy tributes to Esarhaddon (681–669) and Assurbanipal (669–627) and would no doubt have levied taxes to meet the assessment (attested in the annals of the former Assyrian king). Thus the towns known from these bullae were the capitals of seventh-century administrative districts in Judah. That would make the tribal list of Josh 15 contemporary with what many scholars would take to be the date for the composition of the Deuteronomistic History.[98]

Manasseh's son Amon reigned only one or two years (641–640). The brief account of his reign (2 Kgs 21:19–26; cf. 2 Chr 33:20–25) tells us nothing except that he emulated his hated father. The note that he was assassinated is inexplicable. But attempts have been made to connect this supposed event with the rise of anti-Assyrian parties that attempted to align Judah with rebellions against Assurbanipal in 640.

It is the reign of Josiah (648–609) that is best correlated with the archaeological evidence that we now have. His reputation as a reformer, a restorer of tradition, comports especially well with the more favorable situation that we know obtained with the decline of Assyria that occurred circa 630, just as he was coming into his own (perhaps ca. 620, having ascended the throne at eighteen years of age).

The centerpiece of Josiah's reign in the view of the Hebrew Bible is, of course, his reputed reforms of the Jerusalem temple, its cult, and widespread unorthodox "folk religion" in the countryside. This portrait is obviously in accord with the Deuteronomists' agenda, which is why Josiah, and only he with the exception of Hezekiah among the Judahite kings, earns their approval.

The question is whether the biblical account is realistic or simply propaganda for reformist parties. The Hebrew text of 2 Kgs 23 is not without problems, but in any case the claims for Josiah's specific reform measures are reasonably clear. They are directed against the following: (1) illegitimate priests (non-Aaronide); (2) cult paraphernalia in the temple dedicated to Baal, Asherah, and "all the heavenly host"; (3) "high places" (bāmôt) erected both in the temple and in the countryside, where sacrifices were made to Baal, the Sun and Moon and planets, and "the heavenly host"; (4) the idol and the "weavings" (?) for Asherah in the temple; (5) the chamber in the temples for the "sacred males" in the temple; (6) The Topheth in the Kidron Valley, so that children could no longer be sacrificed to Molech; (7) the horses and chariots of the Sun; (8) Manasseh's altars in the temple and on the roof of the former palace of Ahaz; (9) high places near Jerusalem dedicated to Ashtoreth of Sidon, Kemosh of Moab, and Milkom of Ammon; (10) "sacred poles and pillars"; (11) an altar and high place that Jeroboam had erected at Bethel in the south; (12) the standing stones (maṣṣēbôt) in Samaria in the north.[99]

Numerous studies of these intriguing reform measures attributed to Josiah have been published, but few have paid any attention to possible archaeological correlates—that is, to a possible real-life context in the late seventh century. Most scholars have focused on whether the reform was successful, many assuming that the reforms claimed are simply too fantastic to be credible.[100] The fact is, however, that we have good archaeological explanations for most of the targets of Josiah's reforms. For instance, we know what high places (bāmôt) are, and we have a number of examples of them, perhaps the most obvious example being the monumental one at Dan.

We have many altars in cult places and private homes, large and small. We even have an example of the altar on the roof in the debris of a building destroyed at Ashkelon in 604.

The sacred poles and pillars are easily explained, even in the Hebrew Bible, as wooden images or live trees used to represent the goddess Asherah symbolically. The tree iconography has now been connected conclusively with the old Canaanite female deity Asherah, whose cult was still widespread in Iron Age Israel, in both nonorthodox and conformist circles (above).

The weavings, or perhaps "garments" or even "curtains," for Asherah (Hebrew *bāttîm*) remain a crux. Renderings by the Septuagint, the Targumim, and later Jewish commentaries suggest a corrupt Masoretic Text, but woven garments for deities and tent-like hangings for sacred pavilions are well known in both the ancient and modern Middle East.

The phrase "heavenly hosts" needs no archaeological explanation, since it clearly refers to the divine council well documented at Ugarit and in the Hebrew Bible. The reference to the "horses and chariots of the Sun" recalls examples that we have of terra-cotta horse-and-chariot models from the Late Bronze and Iron Ages. In the Ugaritic texts, Baal is the "Cloud Rider" who flies across the heavens daily as the great storm god, imagery that is even applied to Yahweh in Psalms.

The Topheth in the Kidron Valley (a rubbish dump and place of abomination in any case) is readily explained by the famous sanctuary of Tanit at Carthage, where infant sacrifice was the usual rite, and there the Phoenician god was indeed Molech.

Of the various "pagan" deities condemned—Baal, Asherah, Ashtoreth of Sidon, Kemosh of Moab, and Milkom of Ammon—all are well known, as is their iconography and to some degree their cult practices.

It is not only the description of the specifics of the religious situation in Josiah's time that is realistic in the light of the current archaeological data. The general context of cultural and religious pluralism in the seventh century is an amalgam well illustrated by the archaeological data that we have summarized above, beginning already in the eighth century. That context helps to answer the question raised above about whether the Deuteronomistic Historians' original version fits in the actual historical-cultural setting of the seventh century in Judah. It can be shown in many ways that it does but in other ways that it does not, even though the written version could have been almost contemporary (the question of an older oral tradition cannot be resolved).

It is instructive to set the central themes and ideals of the Deuteronomistic program as summarized above alongside a general description of the realities of life in seventh-century Judah as illuminated by the archaeological evidence here.

Fig. 6.18. Correlations of the Deuteronomistic History and archaeological data	
Deuteronomistic History	Archaeological Setting
1. Exclusive Yahwism	1. Religious pluralism; many foreign deities and cults
2. Faithfulness to traditions of the Sinai covenant and law	2. Revolutionary new secular traditions; Judah reduced to vassal status
3. Fulfillment of the promise of the land	3. The land occupied and governed by Assyria
4. The centrality of the Jerusalem temple	4. Jerusalem marginalized; the temple threatened.

While it cannot be presumed that these unique conditions in Judah caused the rise of the Deuteronomist school at roughly this time, it is reasonable to suppose that they were contributing factors. This was an attempted revolution, a reactionary movement against specific practices considered abuses in the minds of the reformers, all of which can be shown by the archaeological record to have been realities. The Deuteronomists and their allies in Josiah's reform party were not setting up a straw man. They knew what we now know about the realities of life in seventh-century Judah.

An earlier generation of scholars thought that Josiah rebelled against Assyrian authority and had sought to purge the Judahite cult of foreign elements. It is now understood that the target was rather the native Israelite and Judean nonconformist religions, which had always been polytheistic. It is that reality that archaeology has now brilliantly illuminated. Whether Josiah's supposed reform actually succeeded is not the issue here, although the archaeological evidence suggests that it did not.[101]

There are a few other possible convergences between the biblical narrative and the archaeological record. Josiah is said to have been killed at Megiddo, attempting to block an Egyptian relief column trying to come to the aid of Assyrian forces opposing the Babylonian advance, in what we now know to have been the year 609. From extrabiblical texts we know that Pharaoh Neco II in 609–605 had indeed begun to anticipate Babylonian ambitions, exploiting Assyrian fears. He had therefore attempted to neutralize Judah, eventually campaigning there in 605–601. Both the Babylon Chronicle and Josephus preserve memories of these events, even though Josiah is not specifically named. The annals recording the Assyrian destructions in Philistia, shortly after Josiah's death (609), also bear on the situation.[102]

The book of Jeremiah, even though usually taken to be a later composition in its present form, seems to rest on some authentic memories of the late seventh century. The prophet's career, the heart of the story, began in 627, midway through Josiah's reign, just as Assyrian hegemony in Judah was coming to an end.

There are numerous allusions in the book of Jeremiah, contemporary with the mid- to late seventh century, that have the ring of truth about them in the light of archaeology. These include the book's general mood of despair, mixed with faint hopes, the prophecies of doom (if indeed predictions), the vivid descriptions of walled cities and Babylonian attacks, the parallel description of the discovery of the temple scroll and Josiah's reforms, the familiarity with other peoples, such as the Ammonites, Moabites, Edomites, Phoenicians, Medes, Arabs, and especially the Philistines (never mentioned in the relevant passage in Kings), the role of Egypt, and the details of the fall of Jerusalem.

Such details can hardly have been invented by later writers or redactors. They suggest that the original prophet by the name of Jeremiah was an actual historical figure, an eye-witness to many of the tumultuous events of the late seventh century. That does not, of course, rule out the possibility of later additions and redactions in the book bearing his name.

Coming now to Judah's final demise, there are several correlations between biblical accounts of the reigns of Judah's last kings and the archaeological and extrabiblical textual records. Jehozhaz (609) is said to have been imprisoned at Riblah in Syria by Pharaoh Neco (II) in the course of his campaigns against the Assyrians. Jehoiakim (609–598) is said to have rebelled and then become the vassal of Nebuchadnezzar, and the withdrawal of Egypt, defeated by the Babylonians, is noted. The story of Jehoiachin and the first exile of Jerusalemites in 597 accords well with Babylonian records. Jehoiachin is said in cuneiform records to have been released from prison in Babylon and allowed to attend at the king's table, an incident also recorded in an epilogue in 2 Kgs 25:27–30, added in the exilic period.[103]

The reign of Zedekiah (597–586) is described in some detail, and much of the detail has to do with the fall of Jerusalem in 586. While the extant Babylonian records do not cover this event, the biblical version accords well with our general knowledge of this era in Babylonian history.

The Facts of Life—and Death

In summary, archaeology at this point can and does provide an additional tool for source criticism of the Hebrew Bible, although that fact and its potential is only beginning to be recognized. Until recently, both biblical scholars and archaeologists have been too preoccupied with their own specializations to be good partners in a productive dialogue. That may be changing, however. It may be worth noting here that in our survey of correspondences between our two sources (fig. 6.18), the biblical texts are proven wrong in no cases, but they also provide relatively little independent, reliable data. They are secondary sources at best.

The key concept here is the *context of the text*, which by definition can only be supplied by an external source—in this case, archaeological data, including the texts unearthed by digging, legal or illegal. These are now the primary data—more contemporary, more abundant, more varied, more pristine in the sense of being freer from the accumulation of centuries of reinterpretation. The limitations of the biblical narrative in its present, doctrinaire form as a primary source for modern historical reconstructions can easily be seen by noting what that narrative does and does not cover for the seventh century as discussed here. For instance, the narratives in 2 Kings regarding the reigns of the two principal kings—Manasseh and Josiah, their reigns together spanning a total of eighty-six years— never once even alludes to the principal actors on the scene: the Assyrians and the Philistines. Nor are the Arameans, Phoenicians, Ammonites, Moabites, and Edomites ever mentioned. The focus is almost exclusively on evaluating these two kings on the basis of their denial or adherence to the narrow theological agenda of the Deuteronomists.

While the fall of Jerusalem is given much attention, as is to be expected, none of the numerous other Judahite sites shown here to have been destroyed is ever mentioned, not even Lachish, where the archaeological and extrabiblical evidence is overwhelming (above). What the biblical writers and redactors chose to ignore may tell us as much about them as what they chose to include. It is all about ideology. The book of Jeremiah is the exception in the biblical texts, with a documented historical context that gives one some confidence in it as a reliable source at least for some details.

There have been innumerable analyses of the Deuteronomistic History going back more than two hundred years. These approaches vary from historical to literary to theological to social-science and even newer approaches (cultural memory). This is not the place to choose between them, nor are archaeologists necessarily competent to judge. Yet it is pertinent to observe that an *archaeological* approach is now promising, and it may be increasingly decisive if historical context is any criterion.

There would seem to be several ways of offering an archaeologically based evaluation. The Deuteronomistic History may be (1) too late to be a dependable source (i.e., postexilic or even Hellenistic in the date of its composition, as with the revisionists); (2) contemporary with the major events of the seventh century, at least in oral tradition and the first version, but largely unaware of them; or (3) seventh century in date but the product of authors who were so one-sided, so blinded by their radical theocentric agenda that they were oblivious to anything else that was happening. In the latter case, it would not be that the biblical writers were necessarily wrong in what they chose to include but simply that they do not provide material for much of anything except a theocratic history, obviously in need of being supplemented.

The first possibility is still rejected by the majority of scholars, despite the current appeal of postmodern notions. The second possibility is remote: it strains credulity to suppose that the biblical writers were so unaware of the everyday world they lived in, if indeed they had been eyewitnesses. The third option works best in the light of the vastly increased knowledge of the real world of the seventh century that we now have from archaeological sources. Even allowing for the inevitable differences in interpretation, which all honest scholars acknowledge, material culture remains are *realia*, and there is a broad mainstream consensus on what the established facts *mean*, in keeping with the best of current postprocessual and cognitive archaeological theory.

Here our archaeological history of ancient Israel and Judah ends. The northern kingdom of Israel has long since disappeared. After surviving for another century and a half, Judah has been overrun by the Babylonians, and it sinks into a decline from which it never recovers its Iron Age identity. In time, the Persian province of Yehud will provide a fertile ground in which Judaism will grow to replace the old religions of the temple with the religion of the Book. Eventually rabbinic Judaism and the synagogue will emerge, but that presents a different challenge to integrate text and artifact, one beyond our purview here.[104]

Notes

1. See chapter 5 and references in n. 5 there.

2. On the sheqel weights, see Kletter 1999, fig. 7 (although Kletter later denied that this distribution map constituted a real border, at least of a "state"; see 2006, 584–85).

3. See Vaughn 1999.

4. Na'aman 1986. Na'aman disputed the conventional location of Socoh, but he had no alternative. Kletter (2002b) supported the usual identification with Khirbet Shuweikeh but deferred on *mmšt*, against many other scholars (Jerusalem?). He supported Na'aman's two-stage model. Oddly enough, Kletter (2002b) does not cite Vaughn's 1999 study (he may not have seen it, so recently published). In a later publication (2009) he discusses the *lmlk* handles largely with respect to whether or not the capacity of the storejars was based on a standardized system, which he doubts. Again, he does not cite Vaughn. See further below and n. 5.

5. Gitin 2006. Gitin's reworking of the *lmlk* jar handles appears to be widely accepted. More recently, however, there have been attempts to date these store jars as early as the ninth century (Sergi et al. 2012) or as continuing well into the early sixth century (Sergi et al. 2012; cf. Lipschits et al. 2011). There are, however, no clear, well–stratified whole vessels—only sherds, which may easily be intrusive from below. The study of Sergi et al. is important chiefly for showing the place of manufacture.

6. See Sneh, Shalev, and Weinberger 2010 and references there on the construction. The authors think that the tunnel was at least four years in construction, was a response to chronic water shortages, and need not be related only to the threat of Assyrian invasion. See also Reich 2004 and nn. 7–8 below.

7. The translation here is that of Rainey (2006, 253). See also n. 8 below.

8. Recent studies by geologists have thrown light on the engineering and even the date of the tunnel. Sneh, Shalev, and Weinberger (2010) argue that it took at least four years to dig and postdates Hezekiah's time. Others disagree (Shimron and Frumkin 2011), and some would date it much earlier than Hezekiah's time (Reich and Shukron 2011). For a recent attribution to Hezekiah, see Grossberg 2013. Rendsburg and Schniedewind (2010) think that the inscription was not a royal inscription but was engraved in "Israelian" Hebrew by a skilled refugee from the north after the 732–721 destructions.

In spite of all this, two assumptions here seem reasonable. (1) The monumental tunnel itself was surely commissioned and its construction funded by the king.

That no king is mentioned is irrelevant, since part of the inscription is missing. Workmen would scarcely have presumed to carve the inscription under the nose of the king, as it were, even in its somewhat obscure location. On the principle of Occam's razor (above), the most plausible interpretation is the conventional one, attributing the tunnel to Hezekiah, who would have had ample warning of the Assyrian threat since nearly the beginning of his reign (727). See Ahituv 2008, 19–25, who also regards it as a royal inscription. The notion that the inscription is Hellenistic (Davies and Rogerson 1996) is absurd and can be dismissed.

9. The translation is that of Rainey (2006, 245). The archaeological data for the following discussion of the 701 invasion have not been fully analyzed until quite recently—especially now by Faust 2012b. A 2003 volume of the European Seminar (see excursus 1.1) was devoted entirely to the subject, but it did not include a paper by any archaeologist, not even on the crucial and copiously documented site of Lachish. As Grabbe, the editor, put it, "none of the participants devoted much space to the questions of archaeology" (Grabbe 2003c, 311). Nonetheless, Grabbe to his credit did supply a résumé of the data that was admirable for a non-specialist (2003a, 3–20). Some of the participants, along with a few other scholars, raised the question of whether Sennacherib actually did besiege Jerusalem or was simply boasting.

10. Blakely and Hardin (2002) have argued that there were two late eighth-century destructions. Stratum III was destroyed by Tiglath-pileser's III campaign to the *south* in 734. Then Stratum II was destroyed shortly thereafter by Sennacherib (as they also think of two destructions at Lachish, Tell Beit Mirsim, Tel Ḥalif, Tell el-Ḥesi, Tel 'Erani, and Tel 'Eton). Assyrian texts do document a 734 campaign to the south, but to Philistia, mentioning specifically Ashkelon and Gaza. One source does claim to have taken tribute from "Jehoahaz (Ahaz) the Judean." Gezer is said to have been taken, but that city was in Israel (ch. 5), not in Judah. See Rainey 2006, 229–32. Cf. Blakely and Hardin 2002, 41–43, who use the Assyrian sources to demonstrate a vassal status for parts of Judah; however, that does not imply actual destructions. Their reanalysis of the stratigraphy of some Judean sites is provocative, but here we will follow the more conventional scheme. See the rebuttals of Finkelstein 2004; Faust 2008. Master, however, tends to agree with Faust in stating that "Judah's economy was shocked and diminished by Sennacherib's campaigns, but it was not radically altered" (2009, 313).

11. 2 Kgs 19:8, mentioning also a campaign against Libnah (Tel Zayit?); 2 Chr 32:9 mentions only Lachish. Both accounts give extensive coverage to the siege of Jerusalem, particularly its miraculous delivery, consistent with the writers' preoccupation.

12. To the older British reports, add now the sumptuous five-volume publication of Ussishkin (2004). See also the elegant drawings of the Assyrian palace reliefs (Ussishkin 1982).

13. Blakely and Hardin (2002, 32) separate VIII and VII and thus see two late eighth-century destructions.

14. Bunimovitz and Lederman (2009) down-date the end of their Stratum 3 (= old IIa–b) to circa 790, with Stratum 12 ending at 701. Fantalkin (2004) attempts to lower the dates, but apparently only because he, like some of Finkelstein's other colleagues, favors the low chronology generally.

15. Cf. Blakely and Hardin 2002, 32–35.

16. See Blakely and Hardin 2002, 35. Excavations have been renewed under Faust, who has published a large corpus of late eighth-century pottery (2011a). Blakely and Hardin equate Stratum II rather with the 701 destruction. Add now Faust and Katz 2016.

17. Blakely and Hardin have given considerable attention to the stratigraphy of Tell Beit Mirsim, arguing for two late eighth-century destructions and hypothesizing that Albright had originally seen two phases in Stratum A2 (2002, 14–24). See n. 13 above.

18. Blakely and Hardin have now published a sizeable corpus of Tel Ḥalif Stratum VIB and VIA pottery (2002, 24–34). It is very close to that of Lachish III. See also Hardin 2010.

19. Faust (2012b, 21–32) lists a number of these mainly seventh-century forts, such as those in the Jericho/Qumran/ Buqeiʿa area, a few in Benjamin and the highlands, and several in the Negev (2008, 174–77). None of these, however, would have been much of a deterrent to invasions. They are more like watchtowers (below). See fig. 6.5 above, where most forts are listed post-701.

20. Faust 2008, 11 and passim; updated by 2013b, 214–15. Faust's views of minimal destruction may suggest caution; they go against the views of most excavators as well as those of major surveyors such as Dagan and Ofer. They are also opposed by the views of biblical historians such as Halpern, Naʾaman, and others. Faust's picture of seventh-century Judean prosperity does not reflect minimal Assyrian destructions as much as it does the beneficial aspects of reconstruction under the *Pax Assyriaca* (below). See nn. 21, 23–24, 31, 36, 40, 46.

21. See Naʾaman 1993, 1995; Faust and Weiss 2005; Faust 2008, 2012a, 2012b, 2013a. See further below and nn. 23–24, 36, 40, 46.

22. Herr and Najjar 2008, 321. The chart in fig. 6.7 comes from Bienkowski 2000, 48.

23. Parpola 2003, 100. On Assyrian warfare and concomitant policies, see further Mayer 1995; cf. nn. 24, 31, 36, 40.

24. Bienkowski 2000, 52, 53. See nn. 21, 23, 31, 36, 40, 46.

25. On Judah after 701, see the surveys of Stern 2001, 14–57, 130–215; Faust 2012b, 33–72; Ben-Shlomo 2014 for details and references. On the *Pax Assyriaca*, see below and nn. 31, 36, 40.

26. See references in n. 25 above.

27. Cf. Bunimovitz and Lederman 2009, 139–41.

28. See Thareani 2011. ʿAroʿer appears to have been largely a site on the caravan trading routes.

29. Faust 2008, 177–78; for other Iron II farms, see 2012a, 128–77.

30. Panitz-Cohen 2005.

31. See Faust 2008, 179–80; 2012a, 128–77 and references there. See nn. 36 and 46 below.

32. For further discussion and references, see Faust 2008, 175–76; 2012a, 178–89.

33. See now Lipschits et al. 2011, esp. 9. Their citation of *lmlk* handles from the Phase 1 debris as proof that they continued in use after 701 is meaningless, since there was no destruction at that time that would have sealed them. They are almost certainly intrusive sherds in the debris from the Persian period.

34. See Cohen and Bernick-Greenberg 2007. The attempt of Singer-Avitz (2008) to push the founding back to the twelfth century on the basis of sherds of "Midianite" pottery is unconvincing, since this pottery is found in clear Iron II contexts.

35. See Faust 2008, 170–80; cf. Finkelstein and Na'aman 2004. Cf. below and n. 36.

36. Cf. Na'aman 1998, 114–15; Faust 2008. See also above and nn. 20–21, 24–25, 35 above, n. 40 below. On the *Pax Assyriaca*, see Stern 2001, 3–57, 130–215 and further below.

37. Broshi and Finkelstein 1992, 52.

38. Zevit 2006, 362; the discussion of various population estimates, with references, is valuable. On the ʿam hāʾāreṣ, see further below.

39. Faust 2013b, 206.

40. On the Shephelah, Philistia, and the *Pax Assyriaca*, see nn. 20–21, 24, 36 above and specifically Ofer 1994, 2001; Faust and Weiss 2005; Faust 2008, 2012a, 2012b, 2013a; Ben-Shlomo 2014, all with full references. See the latter for the economic models discussed here.

41. See Kletter 1999; Finkelstein and Na'aman 2004; Faust 2008.

42. See Kletter 1999. He concludes that Judah was still a kingdom, if not a state, and that despite some difficulties it is possible to identify a distinctly Judahite material culture. On Judah's expansion into the southern hill country and the Shephelah, see nn. 20–21, 24, 31, 36, 39 above; cf. Faust and Weiss 2005; Sergi 2013.

43. Gitin 1990, 280.

44. Gitin 1996; 2010, 335–47. See further Faust 2011c.

45. Stager 1995, 345.

46. Faust and Weiss 2005. On Phoenician trade, see further below.

47. Faust and Weiss 2005, 75; see below on South Arabian trade.

48. See Finkelstein 1994a, 177; Faust and Weiss 2005, 75–80.

49. On South Arabian trade and Phoenician middlemen, see Holladay 1995, 383–86; 2009b, 208–9; Finkelstein 1994a, 179; Singer-Avitz and Eshet 1999; Bienkowski and van der Steen 2001; Stern 2001, 295–300; Faust 2008, 2012a, 2012b, 2013b. On the Phoenicians as maritime traders, see further below and references in chapters 4 and 5. On Assyrian tax policies, see Holladay 2009a, 2009b. Recent

analysis of seventh-century bullae and the distribution of place names may suggest that the so-called tribal boundary list in Josh 15 belongs rather to the reign of Manasseh (698–642) and reflects the pattern of levies raised for Assyrian-imposed levies. See Barkay 2015.

50. On Tel Ḥadid, see Wolff 2008. On Gezer as an Assyrian administrative center, see Ornan, Ortiz, and Wolff (2013) on the older material, as well as a new Neo-Assyrian cylinder seal (= Stratum V).

51. For the Samaria-area farms, some perhaps worked by foreigners brought in by the Assyrian occupiers, see Faust 2006a; 2012a, 234–54.

52. See n. 49 above and n. 57 below. For the Assyrian horizon, add Stern 2001, 58–101. Faust 2012a, 89–90.

53. Schloen 2001, 360. See also Ben-Shlomo 2014 on a patrimonial economic model.

54. Gitin and Golani 2001. See the critique of Kletter (2004) and the response of Gitin and Golani (2004). Kletter denies that the economy was a silver-based monetary system.

55. C. M. Thompson 2003, 67.

56. Kletter 2003, 149 and 148, the latter quoting Gitin and Golani 2001. For what follows, see also Kletter 1991, 1998. See also n. 54 above.

57. See Linder 1973; Wachsmann 1998; and Ballard et al. 2002, on Iron Age shipwrecks off the Israel coast, with evidence of Phoenician trade goods.

58. On the *bit hilani* model, see Lehmann and Killebrew 2010. On the Proto-Aeolic capitals, see Franklin 2011; Lipschits 2011.

59. Ahituv 2008, 233–36.

60. Cf. Ahituv 2008, 49–55; Barkay et al. 2004. Attempts to down-date these amulets to the Persian (or even Hellenistic) era are unpersuasive.

61. Cf. Ahituv 2008, 56–91.

62. Cf. Ahituv 2008, 92–153.

63. Cf. Ahituv 2008, 156–63.

64. See Avigad 1976, 1986; Shiloh 1986.

65. For the papyrus, see Stern 1993, 3:833. The papyrus has been dated to the eighth century, but there is no context, and a seventh-century date cannot be ruled out.

66. See n. 64 above. On the debate about authenticity, see Vaughn and Dobler 2006. The second Berekyahu bulla came from the Moussaieff collection in London, published by Deutsch and Heltzer 1994, 37–38. Some of the biblical revisionists, such as Carroll and Lemche, have rejected all the Avigad bullae (and others) as genuine—not surprising, in view of their general skepticism about anything connecting the Hebrew Bible to preexilic times. Against the notion that Avigad's 1976 bullae were faked is the fact that they are very close to Shiloh's stratified bullae, which were not discovered until 1982.

67. On the critical use of the biblical literature generally, see the discussion and references in chapter 1 above. A good résumé is Schniedewind 2004. For a

summary with particular reference to the revisionist challenge, see Nicholson 2004. For an authoritative introduction to the book of Kings, our major textual source here, see Cogan 2001, 83–149; pages 103–6 deal with archaeology as a parallel source, mostly with regard to the inscriptions recovered.

68. Gitin 2012. James (2005) and Stager (1996) have argued that the date of Temple 650 and the Padi inscription should be lowered from the early seventh century to the mid- or even late seventh century Gitin's response, however (2012, 244–49), confirms his earlier date.

69. Cf. Ahituv 2008, 66–79.

70. Keel and Uehlinger 1998, 261, 277–81, 369. The term *syncretism*, however, may be misleading, since the "foreign" elements criticized by the biblical writers were actually native to Israelite religions as practiced by the majority (i.e., folk or family religion). See further below.

71. For the original publications, see Franken and Steiner 1990; Eshel and Prag 1995; cf. Keel and Uehlinger 1998, 348–49; Zevit 2001, 206–10; Albertz and Schmitt 2012, 108–12, 462–69. The latter see Cave I as a place for ritual feasting to commemorate the dead, the *marzeah* festival known from some biblical and other texts. They also associate the figurines with an ancestor cult. See further nn. 72 and 75 below.

72. On the foregoing, see the discussion and references in Albertz and Schmitt 2012, 108–12, 462–69. For general discussion of household and family cults, see such standard handbooks as Zevit 2001; Dever 2005a; Hess 2007; Albertz and Schmidt 2012; Albertz et al. 2014, all with full references.

73. These figurines have been discussed in chapter 5, since they began in the late eighth century. The literature is vast and often bewildering. The fundamental study is Kletter 1996 (see also 2001). For other discussions, see Keel and Uehlinger 1998, 325–41; Moorey 2003; Cornelius 2004, Dever 2005a, 2014; C. Meyers 2006, 2007b; Paz 2007; Albertz and Schmitt 2012; Nakhai 2014. For summaries, see Kletter 1996, 10–27, 73–78; Albertz and Schmitt 2012, 230–44. Only Albertz (not Schmitt) and Moorey advocate a votive interpretation; Meyers seems ambivalent. Kletter originally criticized Dever severely, but in the end he concluded that "it seems therefore that the JPFs [Judean pillar-base figurines] are indeed a representation of the Biblical Asherah, this is the simplest and most logical explanation" (1996, 81). Keel and Uehlinger (1992) see the figurines as a deity—the "Naked Goddess" of Syria—but decline to connect her directly with Asherah. Yet Asherah is the only clear female deity in the Hebrew Bible. Anat does not appear, and Ashtoreth/Astarte are conflations.

74. See further chapter 5.

75. Albertz and Schmitt 2012, 267.

76. On the iconography of these seals, see Keel and Uehlinger 1998, 255–354. The most thorough study of Iron Age seals is now Albertz and Schmitt, some 2,922 in all (2012, 505–17, 534–609). Few are illustrated, however, in their corpus, since their interest is in personal names and their significance rather than iconography.

The seventh-century names considered here are overwhelmingly aniconic, a fact that has been interpreted as evidence of cult reforms, i.e., a ban on images (Keel and Uehlinger 1998, 354–59). The latter show, however, that while the Hebrew seals typically lack any iconographic imagery, the local Assyrian seals (including cylinder seals) are now rich in astral images, more so even than in the eighth century. They think that these seals, even though used primarily by the Assyrian overlords, reflect the "astralization of the local cult, in which Yahweh becomes the 'Lord of Heaven.'" Yet the cult of Asherah is now even more important than ever, as seen in some seals (this despite their earlier reluctance to name her in connection with the figurines as other than the Naked Goddess). They point out the fact that Asherah's "enormous popularity" and "Yahweh *and* the Host of Heaven" created a crisis that probably provoked an "*early deuternomistic,' orthodox religious practice*," one that would be realized only in the exile and after (Keel and Uehlinger 1998, 372, emphasis original; see also 277–372).

77. Albertz and Schmitt catalogue forty-two of their Iron IIC household shrines (2012, 502–4), but some of these may be eighth-century, and others are Philistine, Phoenician, Aramean, etc. Yet even their numbers suggest that domestic cults in seventh-century Judah were very common. Of the female figurines alone, we have two thousand or more examples; see nn. 72–73 above. It may be worth noting that by now virtually all of the large four-horned altars of tenth–seventh-century shrines have been replaced by very small, household altars in Judah, which can only have been used for burning incense. Philistine Ekron is the exception; see Gitin 2003.

78. Albertz and Schmitt 2012, 108–12. The bullae were discussed above.

79. On these family tombs, see chapter 5. The *marzeah* feasts, well known at Ugarit and reflected in a few biblical passages, have been understood as part of a funerary cult. Ritual feasting, however, would be appropriate on many other occasions, such as childbirth, life-passage events, the rise of the new moon, or family reunions. In a twelfth-century private house at Tell el-ʿUmeiri in Transjordan, there is evidence of ritual feasting on a grand scale, with thousands of animal bones well preserved (London 2011b). The presence of so many cooking and serving vessels at Iron II household shrines in Israel and Judah suggests similar observances. On the *marzeah* and other funerary rituals, see Albertz and Schmitt 2012, 449–62. See also Lewis 1989. Whether funerary rites at Ugarit and elsewhere included feeding the dead is doubtful.

On amulets, see McGovern 1985; Block-Smith 1992, 81–86; cf. Keel 1995, 702–28; Albertz and Schmitt 2012, 71. See also references in n. 74 above. On magic in general, see Jeffers 1996; Dolansky 2008. On "book religion," see van der Toorn 1996 (although with scant consideration of the archaeological data).

80. See Stern 2001, 118–201, 236–94 and bibliography, 594–96, 605–12. See also the extensive discussion of Philistine and Transjordanian cults in Albertz and Schmitt 2012, 176–219.

81. See Beit-Arieh 1995; cf. nn. 82–83 below.

82. See Cohen and Yisrael 1995. These two uniquely "Edomite" sites in Cisjordan may best be understood as shrines at way stations on the seventh-century camel caravan routes where some traders from Transjordan stopped or even resided. On the difficulties of using the so-called Edomite wares (poorly defined and dated) as ethnic markers, see now Thareani 2010. She sees this pottery as reflecting Edomite tribalists who resided in the Negev, perhaps aided by waning Judahite control of the area by the mid- to late seventh century.

83. On the Assyrian cultural polyglot, see Stern 2001, 14–41 and references in n. 80 above.

84. Faust 2006a, 2012a, 248–62.

85. See, however, the summaries of Lipschits 2005, 72–85, 224–37; Stern 2001, 3–10; add now the authoritative treatment of Faust 2012b (often disagreeing with Lipschits). The evidence of destruction in 586 at all the sites (fig. 6.5 above) is sufficient; we will not discuss it further here.

86. See Faust 2012b, 23–24 and references there.

87. See references in n. 85 above.

88. Tell Jemmeh was probably an Assyrian administrative center in Philistia (Ben-Shlomo 2014). Tel Seraʿ IV, Tel ʿIra VI, and Tel Haror may have been more ethnically Judahite than Philistine.

89. See the extensive presentation of the data in the final report volume of Stager, Schloen, and Master 2011.

90. Gitin 2010, 340–46. On the prevalence of East Greek wares at a number of seventh-century sites, see Stern 2001, 217–27 and bibliography on 625–26; Waldbaum 1994.

91. See the references to Stern 2001 in n. 80 above.

92. For the history of the debate, see Barstad 1996; Faust 2012b, 3–10, 181–89, 249–54. A volume of the European Seminar (Grabbe 1998; see excursus 1.1) devoted much space to the exile. There Carroll, Davies, Jeppsen, Lemche, and Thompson largely dismissed the biblical story of an exile as "mythical." Only Albertz, Barstad, and Becking (Grabbe to some extent) placed much value on the biblical narrative. Significantly, there was no paper by an archaeologist and little attention paid to the data that Faust (2012b) has now documented so decisively.

93. Faust 2012b, 241–42.

94. Faust 2012b, 242.

95. Faust 2012b, 251–54. It is Davies and some other biblical revisionists who reconstruct such academies in the fifth–fourth century to account for their interpretation of the Hebrew Bible as a literary creation of the Persian era. They have never offered any archaeological data that would support their thesis, so they have no real-life context. See Schniedewind 2013 and further n. 103 below.

96. See the discussion and references in chapter 1. Particularly helpful at this point is McKenzie 1991; Römer 2005; see also many of the essays in Halpern and Lemaire 2010 (especially Knoppers, Halpern, and Lemaire).

97. The biblical texts utilized here are 2 Kings, 2 Chronicles, and Jeremiah.

I have not cited commentaries and critical textual studies of the biblical texts. Although they are important for some purposes, the historical claims in the text *as we now have it* are sufficiently clear for our purposes here. See the caveats in chapter 1 above.

98. On the biblical sources, see Schniedewind 2004; Halpern 1991. On the scant archaeological data, see Finkelstein, who concludes of Manasseh that "we do not have even a single stratum firmly dated to his time" (1994a, 171). That is largely due to the fact that nearly all of the archaeological materials come from the very end of the seventh century, in the Babylonian destructions of 586. The end of Tel ʿIra VI may fall mid-century, but that is uncertain. Finkelstein (1994a) does, however, attribute to Manasseh's reign such events as the loss of the Shephelah, the growth of Jerusalem, and the expansion of settlement to the east and south of the hill country (following surveys by Dagan 1992 and Ofer 1994). Nevertheless, the biblical texts do not reflect these events at all, and they no doubt took place independently of any actions of the hapless Manasseh. On the Essarhaddon account, see Rainey 2006, 247; *ANET*, 291. The Assyrian king claims to have received in Nineveh booty from "Manasseh, king of the city of Judah" and other kings, such as all sorts of building materials for his palace, as well as statues of their deities and various luxury goods. In another text some ten years later, Manasseh is required to provide troops for the Assyrian campaign to Egypt (*ANET*, 294). In these cases Chronicles appears to be a better source than Kings (perhaps because it is later and has a better perspective), although still unhelpful.

99. On 2 Kgs 23:1–25, see Cogan and Tadmor 1988, 281–91. The following discussion is based on Dever 1994c; see there for details and references.

100. For instance, Cogan and Tadmor, both eminent authorities, scarcely reference any archaeological data in their commentary; see n. 99 above. Not surprisingly, the revisionists reject the historicity of 2 Kgs 23 on any level. Dever (1994c), however, has used the archaeological data as primary in providing a larger context for the chapter in folk religion of the late seventh century, followed by Uehlinger 2005, who thinks that a "well-grounded minimal" view would allow for at least some success of the attempts at reform.

101. See, for instance, Ackerman 1992. On the notion of foreign elements being adapted in the Judahite cult, see Cogan, who concludes that "the foreign innovations reported of the reigns of Ahaz and Manasseh are attributable to the voluntary adoption by Judah's ruling class of the prevailing Assyro-Aramaean culture" (1993, 403; cf. McKay 1973).

102. Cf. 2 Kgs 23:29; 2 Chr 35:20–24; Cogan and Tadmor 1988, 300–302. The account in Kings does not actually claim any military intervention at Megiddo, so the exact manner of Josiah's death is unclear. On the Assyrian destructions in Philistia in the same year as Josiah's death, see above.

103. The number of deportees is given variously in the Hebrew Bible as 10,000, 8,000, or 3,023 (2 Kgs 24:14–16; Jer 52:28). The Babylonian Chronicle

simply says that Nebuchadnezzar took tribute. For the text concerning Jehoiachin and Evil-Merodach, the son of Nebuchadnezzar, see Cogan and Tadmor 1988, 311 (circa 592, but not actually Nebuchadnezzar's thirteenth year, only some thirty years later).

104. For the post-Babylonian and Persian period, see the basic works of Grabbe 1998; Albertz 2003; Lipschits and Blenkinsopp. 2003; Lipschits 2004, 2005; Lipschits and Oeming 2006; Lipschits, Knoppers, and Albertz 2007; Knoppers, Grabbe, and Fulton 2009; Kelle, Ames, and Wright 2011. On the archaeological data, see the standard work of Faust 2012a. On the transformation of the religions of ancient Israel and Judah into early Judaism, see Brettler 1999; E. Meyers 2011. On how the biblical texts were eventually scripturalized, see Schniedewind 2004, 2013.

Conclusion

In summing up, let us review what this archaeologically based history of ancient Israel and Judah may have accomplished, particularly in light of the objectives set forth in chapter 1. A few case studies may serve as reminders of how the approach has operated and what historical results it has yielded. (Here I revert to the first-person approach.)

Case Study 1: The Israelite Conquest
in the Books of Joshua and Judges

Before the advent of modern archaeology in the mid- to late twentieth century, the Israelite conquest of Canaan could be analyzed only on the basis of the literary tradition preserved in the Hebrew Bible. Yet most of the narrative in its present form is at least five hundred years later than the events in question. Thus there was no external or contemporary witness. Furthermore, the two biblical accounts in Joshua and Judges are radically different, despite having been incorporated back to back in the Deuteronomistic History. Joshua depicts an almost lightning-like, overwhelming military campaign throughout the land, vanquishing the Canaanite population and then parceling out the entire territory among the twelve tribes of Israel. The book of Judges, on the other hand, describes a period of some two hundred years of struggle between the various peoples in the land, a prolonged process of cultural, socioeconomic, and political evolution during which a series of charismatic "judges" arose to provide leadership.

Despite the heroic efforts of conservative and evangelical biblical scholars, these two accounts cannot be reconciled. It is significant that the final redactors of the Hebrew Bible made no effort to do so. There the impasse remained. The "history" of this era that various commentators ancient and modern have produced was largely arbitrary, a matter of personal preference (or theological persuasion).

Archaeology has changed all that. Several recent surveys have charted the changes, from conquest through peaceful infiltration to theories of peasant revolt and now to prevailing models of indigenous origin. However, few have observed that it was not more refined methods of textual analysis that brought about the revolution but rather the mounting archeological data that forced a reexamination of the issue and the texts. That is because one cannot wring out of the biblical texts more information than the authors chose to include, no matter how ingenious or determined the hermeneutics. By the 1980s, biblical scholarship seemed to have reached a dead end, at least in terms of writing more accurate and satisfying histories of Israelite origins. More reliable information was needed.

The breakthrough came in the 1980s when Israeli archaeologists began to publish the results of systematic surface surveys in the West Bank, the heartland of early Israel. These complemented earlier surveys in Lower Galilee, as well as the excavation of small sites such as Tel Masos in the Negev, ʿIzbet Ṣarṭah in the Shephelah, Khirbet Radanna, and Shiloh in the hill country.

For the first time, scholars in several disciplines came into possession of "facts on the ground," in one of the great success stories in the long and frustrating history of "biblical archaeology." There would be, of course, differing interpretations of the new data base, but no one doubted its novelty, its extent, or its promise. By the 1990s, the analysis of the archaeological evidence had begun to trump the analysis of the biblical texts, and archaeologists came to the fore in the ensuing discussion. No more "paraphrases of the Hebrew Bible" (in Garbini's phrase) would be written, except for a few fundamentalist attempts, and even they had to confront the archaeological data. Here was dramatic proof that archaeology had become a primary source for writing Israel's history.

Few, however, saw the implications. To their credit, some of the biblical revisionists did, in their call for new "secular histories of ancient Palestine." But instead of pursuing this insight and striving to comprehend the newer archaeological evidence, the European revisionists fell into caricaturing archaeologists, especially the Israelis and Americans who had been generating the data. Thus a great opportunity was missed in the 1990s and the early twenty-first century.

Here I have tried to move beyond these ideological battles and have attempted to produce a *real* history of earliest Israel, 90 percent of it based on archaeological data. The controversies have not all been resolved to the satisfaction of either archaeologists or biblicists, but there is now a broad enough consensus to present a new, more nuanced, more fully fleshed out portrait of a real "Israel" in the early Iron Age. It is one that differs considerably from the ideal Israel of the Hebrew Bible, as well as one that is surely more convincing to the historian. Our portrait may be provisional, and it will surely change with new archaeological data, but it is different and refreshing.

Some questions remain, of course. Assuming that the archaeological data will be our primary source in the future, where does that leave the study of the biblical texts and their possible contribution to history-writing? Simply put, is it possible to envision several different but overlapping and complementary histories of ancient Israel and Judah? Happily, the answer is yes.

In chapter 1 I outlined several kinds of history. Archaeology provides essentially a history of material culture, of *things*—of artifacts that, like texts, are embodiments of human thought and behavior. These artifacts are encoded symbols that, when decoded, can faithfully reflect certain past realities. Thus archaeology is particularly well-positioned to write histories of the environment and its impact on settlement patterns and demography, of technological change, of long-term socioeconomic and cultural developments, and even of aesthetics to some extent. Texts, however, are required to illuminate political and intellectual history fully, as well as the history of various institutions. In the parlance of the influential Annales school of history, archaeology deals well with *évenements*, especially the *longue durée*, while texts help to elucidate *conjectures* and *mentalitiés*.

This paradigm would suggest a cooperative enterprise in writing history, but matters are not quite that straightforward. In particular, we must ask whether the archaeologically based history put forward here as a model could stand alone: Is it a *truer* history than one based largely on the biblical texts? I would argue that it is, even if the biblical texts are regarded as indispensable in some aspects.

It is widely recognized that the Deuteronomistic History is theocratic history, the entire human venture seen *sub specie aeternitatis*. Thus in the case study presented here, the emergence of the Israelite peoples in Canaan at what we now know as the early Iron Age is to be comprehended as the fulfillment of Yahweh's promise of the land to Abraham and his descendants as the sole legitimate heirs. This denouement is assumed to be inevitable, not to be explained as anything other than miraculous. This is the equivalent of the *deus ex machina* of later classical playwrights when the plot became so convoluted that a gargantuan mechanical deity was wheeled on stage to resolve the dilemma by divine fiat.

For believers and some biblicists, the fact that Joshua evidently did not accomplish the conquest all at once, that the narrative of Judges follows, is no barrier, since acceptance of the narrative is all a matter of faith. Needless to say, this is ideology, not history-writing. The biblical stories may constitute great epic literature; they may be morally edifying (except for the matter of genocide); they may even enhance self-identity. But the biblical narrative in this case is not true *historically*, in the sense that the archaeological record is. The former is revisionist history, while the latter is disinterested and therefore more objective (although not entirely so, of necessity).

To put the issue another way, does the admittedly tendentious nature of the Deuteronomistic History contain *any* useful facts? It does, as we have seen, in the more realistic version of events seen here and there in the account in Judges. Thus we can conclude that it is not so much that the biblical narrative is wrong as it is that it is highly selective in what its writers chose to include and exclude. The archaeological artifacts, by contrast, are contemporary, much more extensive and varied, and unedited, at least until they come into our hands. The archaeological record is thus a much more direct witness to the past.

Biblical scholars have nevertheless been skeptical of such claims since modern archaeology began in the 1950s. Again and again since Noth's day some biblicists have asserted that archaeology is mute, which evidently means that it is anonymous, that it cannot attach *names* to events. Overlooking for the moment the fact that, when archaeology produces texts, it can supply names (such as David and other kings), what essentially would the names of a few individuals add to our history? Does knowing the name of Gideon and something of his personal life, even if confirmed, add anything or explain the complex process of socioeconomic evolution that we now know characterized the formation of Israel in Canaan in the early Iron Age? Or does the story of Samson and Delilah, even if proven to be factual, do anything to elucidate the interaction of Israelites and Philistines in border towns such as Timnah (now excavated) in the twelfth–eleventh century? The point is that the Bible does not "corroborate" the archaeological data or even necessarily comment on it. It is the other way around. The texts purport to reflect the reality, albeit far removed. But the artifact *is* the fact; it does not need external confirmation, only interpretation. Again, the archaeological data are the primary source—so much so that the secondary, textual data may not be a very useful source at all.

The central question is this: Is history made by a few great men (!) and their public deeds, or is history the record of the lives of the masses who in any case remain anonymous? The Hebrew Bible writes its history from the top down (literally); archaeological history is written from the bottom up and is the better for it.

Some biblical scholars, even a few revisionists who are otherwise very skeptical about the historical reliability of the texts, argue that the Hebrew Bible is still useful because here and there it preserves "cultural memories." That is a truism. The question is whether those memories rest on reliable sources, such as older and authentic oral or written traditions, or are simply *invented*. In any case, the memories may be very recent, even roughly contemporary with the time the text is written. In that case, they are too recent to be of much independent historical value, as Wellhausen famously pointed out long ago.

Liverani's fascinating history of Israel recognizes the problem. Thus it begins every chapter of the second half, on "Israel's history" (i.e., the biblical Israel), with the words "the invention of ...." The invention may tell us a great deal about the Persian or the Hellenistic period, depending on one's preference. But unless the memories can be authenticated by an external witness—in this case the much earlier archaeological evidence—they tell us little or nothing about the *real* Israel in the Iron Age (Liverani's "the history of Israel," for which he does adduce some archaeological data).

Davies had similarly attempted to distinguish several Israels, dismissing *biblical Israel* and *ancient Israel* as both ancient and modern ideological constructs. He seems to allow for the possible existence of some historical Israel, but since his is a Persian period Bible, he dismisses the entire body of archaeological evidence for the Iron Age in a single footnote, claiming that it is irrelevant. Is it any wonder that some have called the revisionists nihilists? As Thompson put it, "There is no more ancient Israel. History has no room for it."[1] Archaeology, however, does have room and, if need be, justification for writing new and better histories of ancient Israel.

Case-Study 2: David and His Kingdom

In chapter 1 I reviewed the postmodern malaise that spanned, among other radically skeptical attitudes, the so-called literary turn in biblical studies, which entailed a turning away from history and history-writing. One of the test cases in both biblical studies and archaeology was the historicity of the united monarchy and especially its dynastic founder, King David. Thus in the last generation it has become fashionable to deny the actual existence of such an early state and even of David himself. The emergence of any Israelite state has been down-dated to the ninth century, the Judahite state even later. In addition, Thompson has famously declared that "the Bible's stories are no more factual than the tales of King Arthur."[2]

Stripped of their obviously heroic and fantastical elements, the Hebrew Bible's narratives about David describe the following, presumably historical events.

1. David became king through a combination of charismatic gifts, political machinations, and ability to capitalize on a serendipitous moment in history.
2. He seized the old Jebusite citadel at Jerusalem by a clever ruse, then transformed it into a centralized capital of a new regional kingdom.
3. He established a dynastic state on the shaky foundations of his predecessor Saul's chiefdom. It was a kingdom or empire that eventually extended its sway from the Red Sea to the Euphrates River.
4. He decisively defeated his onetime allay and now nemesis, the Philistines.
5. He co-opted the Phoenicians along the coast and northward by engaging them in trade.
6. He campaigned successfully against the Ammonites, Moabites, and Edomites in Transjordan, even the Arameans of Syria, claiming rule over these territories.
7. He sought to found a dynastic center, a royal compound in Jerusalem, with a palace, administrative buildings, and a monumental temple.

In terms of the *convergences* between texts and artifacts that I have sought in the kind of history-writing that is espoused here, how do the biblical narratives about David fare? First, several of David's characteristics and reputed exploits are characteristic of what we know about other typical oriental despots of the Iron Age (nos. 1–3 above), whose historicity is not doubted. These similarities do not, of course, *prove* that David was a historical figure, but they do suggest that the biblical writers did not simply invent their David as king out of whole cloth.

More to the point, there are several specific convergences, albeit with some qualifications. David's reputed wars against the Philistines were indeed quite successful, as the archeological data adduced in chapter 3 above have shown. He did not, however, defeat them decisively. Still, the claim that he drove the Philistines back to Gezer is realistic in terms of geographical and cultural realities illuminated by the archaeological data. Further, our detailed analysis of the stratigraphy of all the relevant early tenth-century sites above shows definitively that a détente along the border of Judah and Philistia was achieved by the mid-tenth century BCE.

Hiram, king of Tyre (2 Sam 5:11), with whom David is said to have traded, is not a fiction of the biblical writers' imagination; he is well attested, and his inscribed sarcophagus survives in a Beirut Museum.

David's alleged campaigns in Transjordan and even in Syria do not seem realistic in the light of the archaeological data from these regions, and it is doubtful that he ever extended his rule that far. Yet the reference to Hadadezer, king of Zobah, is a detail that rings true; both the individual and the Aramean site are well attested, as are the Arameans themselves in Syria.

David's supposed consolidation of the state at home, however, does fit for instance with the establishment of a string of fortresses in the Negev that date to the tenth century (or possibly Solomonic?).

The archaeology of Jerusalem in the tenth century has been discussed above in detail. Even though there remain some controversies, I have argued that it is reasonable to maintain that the stepped stone structure can be equated with the biblical *millo* (terrace system) that David took over, that Eilat Mazar's "tower of David" can date to the tenth century, and that there is archaeological evidence of fairly extensive occupation in Jerusalem at the time. Even the legend-like tale of David's gaining entrance to the Jebusite city through the *ṣinnôr*, or "conduit," makes sense in the light of extensive exploration of Warren's Shaft and related water systems in Jerusalem (although they have later uses and were probably well known then to the biblical writers).

David's ambitions to turn Jerusalem into a royal citadel, noted above, are neither fantastic nor a late construct of the biblical writers. Just such a complex, fitting the biblical description of a palace, administrative buildings, and monumental temple, is found at several early Iron Age Aramean and Neo-Hittite sites, among them notably at Zincirli (ancient Sam'al). Furthermore, it has been shown that roughly contemporary Neo-Assyrian royal inscriptions, such as the Tukulti-Ninurta Epic, have close parallels to the biblical narratives about David and Solomon as kings.[3] Again, these biblical narratives are hardly fantastic.

It is the most recent excavations at Khirbet Qeiyafa, however, that provide the most impressive external data in favor of an early, Davidic state. Despite a few idiosyncratic interpretations (all by nonarchaeologists), the essential facts are beyond dispute. (1) The date of this essentially one-period site (Stratum IV) falls not later than the early tenth century BCE, both on ceramic and C-14 grounds. All specialists agree, even Finkelstein the contrarian. (2) Khirbet Qeiyafa can be understood only as an exceptionally well planned, constructed, and supplied barracks-town. It is a fortress right on the border with Philistia, overlooking the Vale of Elah with a spectacular view, only 7 miles east of Philistine Gath (even closer to Azekah). Such an impressive, unique fortress can only have been commissioned by a highly centralized administration, presumably in Jerusalem: a state in accord with the usual criteria. (3) The second, jar inscription is well executed by someone literate in early Hebrew (or at least the Paleo-Canaanite script), probably related somehow to a degree of local administration.[4] (4) The personal name on the jar is ʾšbʿl, or Eshbaal. That name is rare, and it never occurs in later passages, or indeed in extrabiblical sources. Of the several clear occurrences, one is in 1 Chr 8:33, which names Eshbaal as one of the four sons of Saul. He ruled for two years in the interregnum and was thus a rival of David as he rose to power (see 2 Sam 2:8, 10, 12, 15). Indeed, David seems to have assassinated all Saul's sons except Jonathan after the ill-fated battle on Mount Gilboa, including Eshbaal (see 2 Sam 2:15–16; 3:7–8; 4:8). It is worth noting that the name Eshbaal in Chronicles, "man of Baal, is changed in all the Samuel passages to a more orthodox Ishbosheth," "man of shame."

The occurrence of such a rare and specific biblical name in a nonbiblical text—and one in a context exactly contemporary with David, who is associated with an Eshbaal —is too much of a coincidence to be overlooked (and too much of an inconvenience for some?). Is it possible that the biblical Eshbaal is actually the same person as Eshbaal at Khirbet Qei-yafa? Probably not, since the Qeiyafa individual is styled son of Beda‘, not son of Saul. But the secure late eleventh- or early tenth-century date of Qeiyafa Stratum IV would suit Saul's reign around 1000 BCE (or better, David's early years). A rather far-fetched possibility is that a descendant of Saul's son Eshbaal, someone with the same name, had been co-opted by a triumphant David and placed in charge at a Judahite border fortress in a show of force majeure.

In any case, the new archaeologically attested name of Eshbaal sug-gests strongly that the writers of the David narratives did not simply invent such an early, authentic name (even more unlikely if they had written in the Persian or Hellenistic era, as the revisionists maintain). There are also other features of the David cycle that seem to betray older, perhaps even tenth-century, sources, as several biblical scholars have argued.[5] Of course, early does not necessarily mean historically accurate, but it does make the case plausible, not easily rejected out of hand. Such arguments are speculative, but they comport with the jurisprudence principle of the preponderance of the evidence; that is, there is no compelling evidence against as a more positivist conclusion.

Finally, those who would deny the existence of historical biblical David must confront the reference to "the house (= dynasty) of David" in the ninth-century Dan stela, further mentioning two other kings known from the Hebrew Bible: Jehoram of Israel and Azariah of Judah. Dismiss-ing the Dan stela as a forgery or trying to read *byt dwd* as anything else is not an argument—especially in the face of the overwhelming verdict of epigraphers (which the revisionists are not).

Our second case study may seem more satisfying to some because it shows that at least the core of the biblical narratives about David and his kingdom can be salvaged as historical, despite claims of skeptics. Here, however, our archaeologically based history may still appear to be mini-malist, even though it is not mute. After all, we *have* David's name—and as a dynastic king—outside the Bible, and some of his monumental build-ing projects and his political policies, his statecraft, are reasonably well attested. That, however, leaves undecided much of the personal drama— the larger-than-life stories about David—that make the biblical narratives fascinating and memorable literature.[6]

My point here, however, is that none of this additional drama is his-tory, nor is it necessary to responsible history-writing. So our history is indeed minimalistic, but that is all the real history that we are likely to have. It is quantitatively better than any more paraphrases of the Hebrew Bible.

Back to Theory?

Some readers may find this archaeological portrait or history insufficiently informed by modern theory—an old-fashioned positivist approach. But in passing we have noted some archaeological theories of the 1970s onward and their inapplicability to our history, such as positivist or processual New Archaeology, postprocessualism, and the so called new pragmatism.

Still more recently (since about 1980) it has become fashionable in the broader discipline of archaeology to advocate other theories, borrowed as usual from cultural anthropology or sociology. These would include the idea of *habitus*, or practice, notions of "lived experience," theories based on structuration or agency, identity and gender issues, and actor-network theory" (ANT).[7] Few southern Levantine (or "biblical") archaeologists have attempted to employ any of these models, and with good reasons. First, they are all based on modern studies of society and individual behavior, where direct observation and quantification may be possible. But it has long been known that archaeologists cannot dig up social structures, much less individuals, only some of their material correlates. Even at best, our data tend to be selective, poorly preserved, difficult to interpret.

Another reason for skepticism about many current theories is that, despite the arcane jargon, there is little that is new here. For instance, *structuration* (an invented term) only means that social structure exists and is pervasive. *Habitus* is simply a Latin catchword for the patterned habits of daily life by which people manage, that is, social context or, more broadly speaking, "culture." Archaeologists have always struggled with these concepts, with varying degrees of success, especially since the advent of social archaeology a generation ago.[8] ANT and related theories simply highlight the obvious: complex networks do govern social and individual action. Furthermore, it is a truism that everything is connected to everything else, and artifacts may indeed be used as agents. Finally, materiality is what has characterized archeology from the beginning, a focus on things.

Sophisticated theories borrowed (often belatedly) from other disciplines, either the social or the natural sciences, may provide working models. But models remain simply theories, a way of manipulating data. They lack explanatory power.

After forty years of experimenting optimistically with archaeological theory (rarely, however, in our branch), some leading authorities have begun to be cynical. Thus Bintliff and Pierce have expressed their doubts in a book with a series of essays under the provocative title *The Death of Archaeological Theory?* (2011). Some contributors argued that an appropriately archaeological theory had never been born, while others declared "good riddance."[9]

It is worth noting that many theorists have been armchair archeologist with little or no field experience. Long hands-on experience, however, has taught most of us that the typical theoretical methods of history-writing are still the most applicable: empathy, the use of analogy, rational arguments, well-balanced judgments, common sense (now making a comeback as self-referential knowledge), a disciplined imagination, and, above all, modesty in recognizing our limitations and those of our data. Archaeology is not a science; it is an art.

What next Great Theory? Probably none. Much contemporary thinking seems to center on the new pragmatism: forget everything theoretical and concentrate on what actually works. The most timely and comprehensive discussion is Preucel and Mrozowski, *Contemporary Archaeology in Theory: The New Pragmatism* (2010). The watchwords are: (1) field practice (professionalism); (2) beyond postmodern paradigms, back to empirical data; (3) a focus on materiality, on material culture; (4) history-writing as the goal; (5) the necessity for interdisciplinary dialogue; (6) eclecticism, a recognition that there are multiple way of knowing the past; (7) above all, the urgency of social relevance. *These* things "work" in the real world. Nevertheless, pragmatism historically has a much longer pedigree, and in essence it raises a fundamental, inescapable epistemological issue: What is truth? Can we know it? If so, how?[10]

One way to address the epistemological issue would be to take an approach related to pragmatism and generally sharing its skepticism about any objective knowledge, that is, investigate a philosophical school of thought known as phenomenology. A phenomenological approach argues that empirically—through the use of our senses—we cannot know how external things and events really are. We can only know how we perceive them and thus experience them, what their appearance is, the *phenomenon*. Thus we should take an existential approach, looking rather at lived experience.[11] This compromise, so to speak, combines the best insights of several other theoretical models, allowing us to make some use of structuration, *habitus*, agency, interconnectivity, entanglement, materiality and thing theory, among other notions. This is, in short, the eclecticism that characterizes most archaeology today.

Such an approach would concede that all archaeological knowledge is conditioned, approximate—a best guess about how people in the past experienced the things they made and used as agents in their natural and social environments. It may be that we can only describe the material culture evidence for these environments. After all, we cannot read the minds of the ancients. This admittedly modestly optimistic approach is the one taken here. That is why ours is a more phenomenological portrait of ancient Israel and Judah, based on the current archaeological data, rather than a definitive history, which will no doubt always elude us.[12]

This archaeological portrait is neither the nonhistory of the revisionists nor the uncritical paraphrase of the Bible adopted by more conservative scholars. It differs by being a secular history, a frankly materialist rather than a naïve idealist history. It is neither old-fashioned positivism nor doctrinaire pragmatism. It understands that, while we cannot know everything through archaeology (the past), we can know enough for our purposes in the present in this world. It represents a *modest optimism* about the past and the present.[13]

Throughout this work has sought to address what is always the critical issue in archaeology: the meaning of things—both an intrinsic meaning and a meaning that, while inferred, is one that makes sense and is one with which we moderns can live. This portrait of ancient Israel's and Judah's history seeks to reinforce the historical foundations of a modest optimism.[14]

On the Possibility of a New Dialogue

It may appear that I have disqualified biblical scholars as partners in a fruitful dialogue by undermining their major resource for making a contribution: the texts of the Hebrew Bible. Yet I have only insisted on our recognizing the limits of these texts for purposes of historical reconstructions—just as we must recognize the limits of archaeological data, which even though expanding exponentially at present are finite. Whatever the case, the dialogue between archaeology and biblical studies that some have confidently predicted since Albright's day has not materialized. Indeed, archaeologists and biblical scholars are now so specialized, so turf-conscious, that they seem oblivious to each other. That is especially clear in Israel, where the prospects would seem best. In America, where the quest began, biblical scholars are preoccupied with new literary critical theory, the new historicism, reader-response criticism, liberation theology, postmodernism, feminist critiques, reception criticism, and anything *except* history. That leaves archaeologists, who are historians of ancient Israel or nothing, with no point of contact—even if they were interested in the dialogue, and that is not always clear. Some Israelis are still quibbling over whether or how to use the biblical texts, despite this issue having long been settled in most circles. A few accuse each other of being too "biblical" or not "biblical" enough. That is a dead end.

Evidently in Europe there is no longer much real interest in archaeology: no centers, very little intent in pursuing fieldwork in Israel, the heartland. Massive tomes still appear as though the archaeological revolution had never occurred.

Even at best, we are too often talking past each other, still bogged down in what are essentially redundant and tiresome monologues. I have campaigned in favor of a dialogue for more than forty years. Now all I can do is to suggest some provisional rules for others to consider.

1. Recognize the limits of our respective disciplines, in particular the limits of our competence as specialists.
2. Respect the other protagonists enough to acquaint ourselves at least minimally with their methods, their concerns, and their data.
3. Develop appropriate and preferable complementary hermeneutics for both disciplines, setting forth in particular our methods and presuppositions.
4. Isolate and neutralize "contrarian" arguments to the left or right and seek a middle-ground consensus.
5. Emphasize what we do know, not what we do not. Extract the maximum information from our sources consonant with critical judgment, but employ Occam's razor in preferring the most parsimonious explanation.
6. Avoid current fads and remain open to new data, new paradigms. The best histories strive for objectivity but remain provisional.

There are several implications of such hermeneutical principles. One is that we do not need any more pontification regarding things about which we know very little. For instance, biblical revisionists and other amateurs have made all sort of pronouncements about what archaeology can and cannot do, about appropriate archaeological theory and method, even about exceedingly complex matters such as comparative ceramic typology. On the other hand, some archaeologists have ventured naïvely into the intricacies of textual criticism and exegesis, engaging in a sort of secular fundamentalism. In both cases, a little learning is a dangerous thing. What we need to do is not to pretend to expertise outside our own discipline but rather learn enough about other's disciplines to conduct an intelligent conversation. Here I have tried to do just that, not to offer any original insights into biblical studies, but to write as an archaeologist *for* biblical scholars, to show what archaeology might contribute.

Let me sharpen the focus by pointing to several other recent efforts. Rainer Kessler of Marburg University has produced a volume entitled *The Social History of Ancient Israel: An Introduction* (2008). But the book is only a history of the handful of biblical writers' *thoughts* about an ideal society, not a history of the *actual* society of the Israelite peoples over time. A volume of essays edited by Francesca Stavrakopolou and John Barton (2010), ostensibly dealing with the "variety" of religious beliefs and practices in ancient Israel, does not feature any contribution by an archaeologist specializing in cult. The focus is almost exclusively on the biblical text—the last place to seek variety, since it is all about orthodoxy.

The recent work of Megan Moore and Brad Kelle, entitled *Biblical History and Israel's Past* (2011), purports to be a guidebook for writing future histories of ancient Israel (it has no other rationale). Yet it does little more than document changes in the viewpoints of leading biblicists and archaeologists over the past generation or so. The authors quote various authorities, pitting them against each other, but they are unable to discriminate between idiosyncratic and mainstream positions. Nowhere do they betray any familiarity with the actual archaeological data. Such guides are worse than useless; they only obfuscate.

A refreshing exception is Lester Grabbe's 2007 work, applauded in chapter 1. He alone of current biblical scholars has produced a useful prolegomenon, precisely because he has done his homework and has managed to comprehend the archeological data to a remarkable degree for a nonspecialist. Further, his work outlines the specifics of what we all know and want to know. It is more works of this kind that we now need, prolegomena to new multidisciplinary histories. My contribution here is a deliberate response to Grabbe's challenge from an archaeological perspective (further below).

Anticipating Critiques

This history hopes to be a harbinger, anticipating future histories of ancient Israel and Judah that incorporate much more archaeological and anthropological data as they become available. As such, it invites and welcomes critical reviews, especially from biblical scholars. It is not difficult to predict what the major complaints will be.

(1) Some will claim that I have ignored or depreciated the Hebrew Bible as a source for writing a history of ancient Israel. I have indeed ignored most of the Pentateuch (or Tetrateuch), since it deals with the prehistory of ancient Israel, beyond our purview here. Only the book of Numbers is relevant, and that only peripherally. The poetic (or so-called devotional) literature, as well as obviously fictional novellas of various sorts, has also been set aside. Chronicles has been regarded as secondary and of relatively little value. The prophetic work has been consulted, but largely as literary rather than historical works, no matter how early, even if contemporary. The Deuteronomistic History—often referred to here simply as "the biblical writers"—has been our major source for obvious reasons.

I have not depreciated the biblical texts, only demonstrated how they compare with the primary archaeological data, showing where they may be limited in scope or skewed in perspective and therefore of dubious value. Where the texts and the archeological record converge, however, I have given the Hebrew Bible its due. Readers will have to judge whether I have been fair on a case-by-case basis.

(2) Second, it may be argued that as a nonspecialist I have made amateur and even mistaken use of the Hebrew Bible. I can only point out that most of my graduate training was in biblical studies and Northwest Semitic languages and literatures. The bibliography will show that I have kept up with the field of biblical studies as it has developed over the past fifty years. Throughout this work, however, I have followed mainstream biblical scholarship, with no pretense to offer any new or original insights. I have not engaged the views of fundamentalists, since that is a waste of

time and effort; their minds are closed. Finally, I have invited dialogue with biblicists, who can correct me where necessary.

(3) Finally, there are those, principally revisionists, who will insist that my views are really not much different from theirs, that is, minimalist. I would only suggest that on some topics, such as the patriarchal era or the Israelite conquest, we are all minimalists nowadays. Yet I differ from the revisionists in degree, if not in kind. They see virtually no real history of an Iron Age "Israel" in the biblical texts, whereas I see some. That is perhaps a small difference, but for history-writing it is one that is crucial.

"Concluding Unscientific Postscript"

With apologies to Kierkegaard, whom I used to read in seminary, I offer a few final observations that may not claim to be entirely objective.

(1) We began with the question that some would say has dominated both the archaeology of Israel and biblical studies for the past twenty years or so: Is it any longer *possible* to write a history of ancient Israel? The answer here is yes—with some reservations, and provided that archaeological evidence is recognized as primary data. The problem may be that we now know too much yet are too skeptical. We are overwhelmed with new data that have already revolutionized our knowledge of a *real* Israel in the Iron Age. We know at least ten times as much as we did when I was a graduate student fifty years ago. This knowledge is empirically grounded, not an ideological construct, and on most of the main points there is a consensus among specialists in archaeology. Yet skepticism prevails. Why?

Archaeologists, for their part, have allowed themselves to be distracted by internal quarrels about details of stratigraphy and chronology, some of them fueled by personality cults. The polarization of the field has led some archaeologists in Israel and elsewhere to shy away from the historical issues and simply concentrate on more data collection, ignoring the fundamental questions of theory (the new pragmatism). In Europe, there is no longer an authoritative spokesman on the archaeology of Israel. In American, a new generation of specialists is impressive but scarcely experienced enough or well equipped enough to have a major voice in the debates.

This malaise is particularly unfortunate, because in Israel we have a well-published archaeological data base that, proportionate to the country's size, is unparalleled anywhere else in the world. Yet few dare to attempt a synthesis of anything beyond their narrow specializations. Several leading archaeologists have become "contrarians," challenging any new discoveries as a matter of course, more interested in displaying their cleverness than in searching for the truth. What, then, is the *point* of all the enormously expensive, long-running, and meticulously conducted and published field projects?

Many biblicists, on the other hand, continue to ignore or caricature archaeology, or, at the other extreme, they make sweeping pronouncements on complex archaeological issues with no effort to read widely, quoting only their favorite authority, almost always a skeptic like themselves. A well-informed, critical yet positivist approach to a possible dialogue, such as Grabbe's *Ancient Israel: What Do We Know and How Do We Know It?* is a rarity (see excursus 1.1).

How is one to explain the overriding skepticism, the negativism, of both our disciplines? The answer is surely to be found in the pervasive influence of postmodernism on all the humanities during the past forty years. I have been severely criticized for mounting an attack on the biblical revisionists, who have obviously, if unwittingly, bought into the postmodernist "incredulity toward all metanarratives." Most archaeologists have ignored the postmodernist threat, but recently leading Americans have acknowledged that, if postmodernism were to prevail, it would mean the end of archaeology, of any claims to reliable knowledge of the past.[15] That leads me to a second observation.

(2) Whatever the possibilities for writing new and more satisfactory histories of ancient Israel, archaeologically well informed, one would hope, can one even justify the attempt? In short, why should we care any longer about the story of a tiny, obscure, culturally undistinguished ancient people in a far corner of the world whose brief appearance on the stage of history ended in disaster and who should by all accounts have been forgotten? The answer is that this is *our* history, at least for those of us who are heirs of the Western cultural tradition.

The wholesale rejection of that tradition is, of course, the hallmark of postmodernism—the Bible *is* the metanarrative. Yet what do they offer in its place? Cultural relativism, endless celebration of novelty, a brave new world where anarchy reigns. The Western cultural tradition does have its faults, to be sure, some of them grievous. But I would argue that it still has some validity because its values of reason, liberty, equality, justice, and progress are unparalleled elsewhere, even if yet to be fully realized. The only alternative to a universal worldview would appear to be Marxism, totally discredited.

One of the foundations of the Western cultural tradition—formerly known as the Judeo-Christian tradition—is obviously the biblical worldview, the essence of which is found in the Hebrew Bible. Yet if the Hebrew Bible is simply a collection of myths, if its stories have no historical basis, its "values" are worthless. There is no escaping the ultimate question of truth, of the *meaning of history*.

Raising such issues will, of course, be dismissed as chauvinism, as moralism. Yet I would argue that the radical postmodernist and revisionist critique has run its course. It has proven sterile, incapable of evolving, of offering anything beyond despair. All claims to knowledge are indeed social constructs, but some constructs are better than others because they are grounded in the reality of human experience and are thus more believable, more satisfying.

The history of ancient Israel envisioned here is not intended to support any theological claims. It is a secular, humanist history of Israel, not an account of God's miraculous intervention in history. Its lessons are simply the presumed lessons of any history—an account of events in history that at best may be found morally edifying. That does matter; it always has; it always will.

(3) Finally, this does not pretend to be *the* history of ancient Israel and Judah. That is why I have styled this work not as a history but a portrait. Our knowledge has increased exponentially in the past generation, due almost exclusively to the progress of archaeology. Even so, we cannot write a definitive history, only a provisional one. Archaeology as a discipline is still in its infancy, and unimaginable new discoveries in future will inevitably alter our views of the past. I can only hope that I have done justice to what we do know at this moment in time, a foundation on which to build.

Several times I have praised Grabbe's *Ancient Israel: What Do We Know and How Do We Know It?* as a prolegomenon to new histories that helped to inspire this work. At the close of a recent international symposium that he convened, published under his editorship as *Israel in Transition 1: From Late Bronze II to Iron IIa (c. 1250–850 B.C.E.); The Archaeology* (2008a), Grabbe provides an admirable critical summary. At the end, he concludes:

Most historians ... would argue that we should use all the data at our disposal, whether textual or artifactual. But this conference has fortified my view that archaeology must be a central core of any history that we write. This puts a burden on historians to listen and archaeologists to deliver.[16]

This book is my response to that challenge. And it echoes the declaration of the distinguished British historian Eric Hobsbawm (himself a leftist) that postmodernists are wrong that there is no clear difference between fact and fiction. "But there is, and for historians, even for the most militantly antipositist ones among us, the ability to distinguish between the two is absolutely fundamental."[17] I have tried to build on the best of the facts that we now have.

Notes

1. Thompson 1995, 698
2. Thompson 1995, 698.
3. Machinist 1976.
4. See the full discussion in Qeiyafa Garfinkel et. al. 2015.
5. For literary analyses of the David cycle, see Schniedewind 1999; Halpern 2001. On possible early sources, see Na'aman 1996b.
6. See especially Halpern 2001.
7. On structuralization, see Giddens 1979, 1981, 1984; on *habitus*, see Bordieu 1977, 1990; on actor-network theory, see Latour 2005; Brughmans, Collar, and Coward 2016. On phenomenology, see Olsen 2013; Merleau-Ponty 2013. For useful analyses and critiques, see Preucel and Mrozowski 2010, 13–18. On "thing theory," see Olsen 2013; for possible applications in Near Eastern archaeology, see Steadman and Ross 2010.
8. For the first full-scale social archaeology in our discipline, see Faust 2012a (who only mentions Bordieu and Giddens in passing; cf. 2006, with somewhat more use of Bordieu). Schloen (2001) explores numerous theories, but he wrote well before the most recent trends, and in the end, he favors only Ricouer (1974, 1984), whose theories are relevant only to textual studies.
9. See Bintliff and Pierce 2011, passim.
10. The skepticism of several archeologists in this volume is reflected in a general mistrust of "theory" after its long run in many disciplines. See, for instance, a recent analysis of the distinguished literary critic (and sometime postmodernist) Terry Eagleton, *Against Theory* (2003). The response is often a return to pragmatism (see further below).
11. Levy's 2010b adoption of the New Pragmatism is rather facile, barely ref-

erencing its founders such as James and Pierce. It skirts the issue of epistemology entirely. What "works" as a criterion for interpreting archaeological data obviously depends upon what one thinks should work—how? for whom? A much more sophisticated analysis is found in Preucel and Mozowski 2010, 1–49. See n. 13 below.

12. Phenomenology may be seen as a form of pragmatism—taking a middle ground between empiricism and rationalism, between skepticism and positivism, between postmodernism and triumphalism. It assumes, with Kant, that we *can* know with certainty, but in the only world we experience, the phenomenal world. That was how Kant sought to resolve the fundamental problem of epistemology; experimental analysis of an objectified world, this tradition focused its attention on "being" itself in the lived world of human experience, on its increasing ambiguity, its santancity and autonomy, its uncontainable dimensions, its ever-deepening complexity (Tarnas 1991, 374). See further nn. 13–14 below.

13. By *modest optimism* I have in mind the notion of Dewey, a renowned pragmatist, who espoused the idea of "warranted assertability." That is, there may be no accessible, absolute facts, but we can nevertheless say something about values; that is, they are not entirely subjective. In our experience, there can be *objective solutions* to problems. Pragmatism, then, cannot simply be dismissed as cultural relativism. "Meaning" exists, even if it cannot be entirely proven. Verification, always the issue, can be claimed existentially. Hilary Putnam, an extremely distinguished philosopher, has dealt a blow to naïve adaptations of cultural relativism in his *The Collapse of the Fact/Value Dichotomy* (2004). The facts may remain disputed, but we can nevertheless assert values by which to live.

14. The literature on the "meaning" of artifacts (as well as texts) is vast, but for archaeology see Shanks and Tilley 1987; Tilley 1999; Renfrew 1994; Hodder 1987; 2006; DeMarrais, Gosden, and Renfrew 2004.

15. For a spirited defense of the Western cultural tradition—but only as it should and could have been—see Gress 1998.

16. Grabbe 2008b, 231.

17. Hobsbawm 1993, 63.

Works Cited

Ackerman, Susan. 1992. *Under Every Green Tree: Popular Religion in Sixth-Century Judah*. HSM 46. Atlanta: Scholars Press.

———. 2003. At Home with the Goddess. Pages 344–68 in Dever and Gitin 2003.

———. 2006. Women and the Worship of Yahweh in Ancient Israel. Pages 189–97 in Gitin, Wright, and Dessel 2006.

———. 2008. Household Religion, Family Religion, and Women's Religion in Ancient Israel. Pages 127–58 in *Household and Family Religion in Antiquity*. Edited by J. Bodel and S. M. Olyan. Ancient World: Comparative Histories. Oxford: Blackwell.

———. 2012. Women and the Religious Culture of the State Temples of the Ancient Levant, Or: Priestesses, Purity, and Parturition. Pages 259–90 in *Temple Building and Temple Cult: Architecture and Cultic Paraphernalia of Temples in the Levant (2.-1. Mill. B.C.E.)*. Edited by Jens Kamiah. Wiesbaden: Harrassowitz.

Adam, A. K. M. 1995. *What Is Postmodern Biblical Criticism?* GBSNT. Minneapolis: Fortress.

Aharoni, Yohanan. 1957. Problems of the Israelite Conquest in the Light of Archaeological Discoveries. *Antiquity and Survival* 2:131–50.

———. 1967. *The Land of the Bible*. Translated by Anson F. Rainey. Philadelphia: Westminster.

———, ed. 1973. *Beer-sheba I: Excavations at Tel Beer-sheba, 1969–1971*. Monographs of the Institute of Archaeology 2. Tel Aviv: Tel Aviv University.

———. 1975. *Investigations at Lachish: The Sanctuary and the Residency (Lachish V)*. Publications of the Institute of Archaeology 4. Tel Aviv: Gateway.

———. 1979. *The Land of the Bible: A Historical Geography*. 2nd ed. Philadelphia: Westminster.

————. 1981. *Arad Inscriptions*. Jerusalem: Israel Exploration Society.

Ahituv, Shmuel. 1978. Economic Factors in the Egyptian Conquest of Canaan. *IEJ* 28:93–105.

————. 2008. *Echoes from the Past: Hebrew and Cognate Inscriptions from the Biblical Period*. Jerusalem: Carta.

Ahlström, Gösta W. 1993. *The History of Ancient Palestine from the Paleolithic Period to Alexander's Conquest*. JSOTSup 146. Sheffield: Sheffield Academic.

Ahlström, Gösta W., and Diana Edelman. 1985. Merneptah's Israel. *JNES* 44:59–61

Akkermans, Peter M. M. G., and Glenn M. Schwartz. 2003. *The Archaeology of Syria: From Complex Hunter-Gatherers to Early Urban Societies (c. 16,000–300 B.C.)*. Cambridge: Cambridge University Press.

Albertz, Rainer. 1978. *Persönliche Frömmigkeit und offizielle Religion*. Calwer theologische Monographien 9. Stuttgart: Calwer.

————. 1994. *A History of Israelite Religion in the Old Testament Period*. London: SCM.

————. 2003. *Israel in Exile: The History and Literature of the Sixth Century B.C.E.* Translated by David Green. Studies in Biblical Literature 3. Atlanta: Society of Biblical Literature.

————. 2010. Secondary Sources Also Deserve to Be Historically Evaluated: The Case of the United Monarchy. Pages 31–45 in Davies and Edelman 2011.

Albertz, Rainer, and Rudiger Schmitt. 2012. *Family and Household Religion in Ancient Israel and the Levant*. Winona Lake, IN: Eisenbrauns.

Albertz, Rainer, et al., eds. 2014. *Family and Household Religion: Toward a Synthesis of Old Testament Studies, Archaeology, Epigraphy, and Cultural Studies*. Winona Lake, IN: Eisenbrauns.

Alter, Robert. 1981. *The Art of Biblical Narrative*. New York: Basic Books.

Amiran, David H. K., and Y. Ben-Arieh. 1963. Sedentarization of Bedouin in Israel. *IEJ* 13:161–81.

Amiran, Ruth. 1970. *Ancient Pottery of the Holy Land: From Its Beginnings in the Neolithic Period to the End of the Iron Age*. Jerusalem: Israel Exploration Society.

Amit, Yairah. 2006. Looking at History through Literary Glasses Too. Pages 1–15 in Gitin, Wright, and Dessel 2006.

Antoniadou, Sophia. 2007. Common Materials, Different Meanings: Changes in Late Cypriot Society. Pages 483–508 in *Mediterranean*

Crossroads. Edited by Sophia Antoniadou and Anthony Pace. Athens: Pierides Foundation.

Arnason, Johann P., S. N. Eisenstadt, and Björn Wittrock, eds. 2005. *Axial Civilizations and World History*. Leiden: Brill.

Arav, Rami, and Freund, Richard A. 1995. *Bethsaida: A City by the North Shore of the Sea of Galilee*. Vol. 1. Kirksville, MO: Truman State University Press.

———. 1999. *Bethsaida: A City by the North Shore of the Sea of Galilee*. Vol. 2. Kirksville, MO: Truman State University Press.

———. 2004. *Bethsaida: A City by the North Shore of the Sea of Galilee*. Vol. 3. Kirksville, MO: Truman State University Press.

———. 2009. *Bethsaida: A City by the North Shore of the Sea of Galilee*. Vol. 4. Kirksville, MO: Truman State University Press.

Arie, Eran. 2008. Reconsidering the Iron Age II Strata at Tel Dan: Archaeological and Historical Implications. *TA* 35:6–64.

Arnold, Bill T., and Hugh G. M. Williamson, eds. 2005. *Dictionary of the Old Testament Historical Books: A Compendium of Contemporary Scholarship*. Downers Grove, IL: Intervarsity Press.

Arnold, Bill. T., and Richard S. Hess, eds. 2014. *Ancient Israel's History: Introduction to Issues and Sources*. Grand Rapids: Baker Academic.

Artzy, Michal. 2003. Mariners and Their Boats at the End of the Late Bronze and the Beginning of the Iron Age in the Eastern Mediterranean. *TA* 30:232–44.

Ash, Paul S. 1999. *David, Solomon and Egypt: A Reassessment*. JSOTSup 297. Sheffield: Sheffield Academic.

Assmann, Jan. 1997. *Moses the Egyptian: The Memory of Egypt in Western Monotheism*. Cambridge: Harvard University Press.

Åström, Paul. 1985. The Sea Peoples in the Light of New Excavations. *Cahiers du Centre d'Études Chypriotes* 3:3–18.

———. 1993. Late Cypriot Bronze Age Pottery in Palestine. Pages 307–13 in *Biblical Archaeology Today, 1990: Proceedings of the Second International Congress on Biblical Archaeology, Jerusalem, June–July, 1990*. Edited by A. Biran and J. Aviram. Jerusalem: Israel Exploration Society.

Aubet, María Eugenia. 2001. *The Phoenicians and the West: Politics, Colonies and Trade*. 2nd ed. Cambridge: Cambridge University Press.

———. 2014. Phoenicia during the Iron Age II Period. Pages 706–16 in Steiner and Killebrew 2014.

Aufrecht, Walter E. 2010. Ammonites and the Book of Kings. Pages 245–49 in Halpern and Lemaire 2010.

Avigad, Nahman. 1953. The Epitaph of a Royal Steward from Siloam Village. *IEJ* 3:137–52.

———. 1976. *Bullae and Seals from a Post Exilic Judean Archive*. Qedem 4. Jerusalem: Institute of Archaeology, Hebrew University of Jerusalem.

———. 1986. *Hebrew Bullae from the Time of Jeremiah: Remnants of a Burnt Archive*. Jerusalem: Israel Exploration Society.

———. 1993. Samaria (City). *NEAEHL* 4:1300–10.

Avigad, Nahman, and Benjamin Sass. 1997. *Corpus of West Semitic Stamp Seals*. Jerusalem: Israel Academy of Sciences and Humanity: Israel Exploration Society, and Institute of Archaeology, Hebrew University of Jerusalem.

Avner, Uzi. 1998. Settlement, Agriculture and Paleoclimate in 'Uvda Valley, Southern Negev Desert, Sixth–Third Millennia BC. Pages 147–202 in *Water, Environment and Society in Times of Climatic Change*. Edited by Arie S. Issar and Neville Brown. London: Kluwer Academic.

Baadsgaard, Aubrey. 2008. A Taste of Women's Sociality: Cooking as Cooperative Labor in Iron Age Syro-Palestine. Pages 13–44 in Alpert-Nakhai 2008.

Bachhuber, Christoph, and R. Gareth Roberts, eds. 2009. *Forces of Transformation: The End of the Bronze Age in the Mediterranean*: Oxford: Oxbow.

Baden, Joel S. 2009. *J, E, and the Redaction of the Pentateuch*. FAT 68. Tübingen: Mohr Siebeck.

———. 2012. *The Composition of the Pentateuch: Renewing the Documentary Hypothesis*. New Haven: Yale University Press.

Bailey, Clinton. 1980. The Negev in the Nineteenth Century: Reconstructing History from Bedouin Oral Traditions. *Asian and African Studies* 14:35–80.

Baker, David W., and Bill T. Arnold. 1999. The *Face of Old Testament Studies: A Survey of Contemporary Approaches*. Grand Rapids: Baker.

Balensi, Jacqueline, Maria D. Herrera, and Michal Artzy. 1993. Abu Hawan, Tell. *NEAEHL* 1:7–14.

Ballard, Robert D., et al. 2002. Iron Age Shipwrecks in Deep Water off Ashkelon, Israel. *AJA* 106:151–68.

Banks, Diane. 2006. *Writing the History of Israel*. LHBOTS 438. New York: T&T Clark.

Banning, Edward B. 1986. Peasants, Pastoralism, and *Pax Romana*: Mutualism in the Southern Highlands of Jordan. *BASOR* 261:25–50.

Barako, Tristan. 2007. *Tel Mor: The Moshe Dothan Excavations, 1959–1960*. Israel Antiquities Authority Reports 32. Jerusalem: Israel Antiquities Authority.

Barfield, Thomas J. 1993. *The Nomadic Alternative*. Englewood Cliffs, NJ: Prentice Hall.

Barako, Tristan J. 2000. The Philistine Settlement as Mercantile Phenomenon? *AJA* 104:513–30.

———. 2003. One If by Sea … Two If by Land: How Did the Philistines Get to Canaan? One: By Sea. *BAR* 29.2:26–33, 64, 66.

Barkay, Gabriel. 1992. The Iron Age II–III. Pages 301–73 in Ben-Tor 1992.

———. 2004. The Amulets from Ketef Hinnom: A New Edition and Evaluation. *BASOR* 334:41–71.

———. 2015. Evidence of the Taxation System of the Judean Kingdom: A Fiscal Bulla from the Slopes of the Temple Mount and the Phenomenon of Fiscal Bullae. Pages 17–50 in *Recording New Epigraphic Evidence: Essays in Honor of Robert Deutsch*. Edited by Meir and Edith Lubetski. Jerusalem: Leshon Limudim.

Barr, James. 2000. *History and Ideology in the Old Testament: Biblical Studies at the End of a Millennium*. Oxford: Oxford University Press.

Barstad, Hans M. 1996. *The Myth of the Empty Land: A Study in the History and Archaeology of Judah during the "Exilic" Period*. SO.S 28. Oslo: Scandinavian University Press.

Barstad, Hans M. 1997. History and the Hebrew Bible. Pages 37–64 in Grabbe 1997b.

———. 2007. The History of Ancient Israel: What Directions Shall We Take? Pages 25–48 in Williamson 2007.

———. 2008. *History and the Hebrew Bible: Studies in Ancient Israelite and Ancient Near Eastern Historiography*. FAT 61. Tübingen: Mohr Siebeck.

———. 2010 History and Memory: Some Reflections on the "Memory Debate" in Relation to the Hebrew Bible. Pages 1–10 in Davies and Edelman 2011.

Barth, Fredrik, ed. 1969. *Ethnic Groups and Boundaries: The Social Organization of Culture Difference*. Boston: Little, Brown.

Barthes, Roland. 1988. *The Semiotic Challenge*. New York: Hill & Wang.

Barton, John. 1996. *Reading the Old Testament: Method in Biblical Study*. 2nd ed. London: Darton, Longman & Todd.

Bar-Yosef, Ofer, and Anatoly Khazanov, eds. 1992. *Pastoralism in the Levant: Archaeological Materials in Anthropological Perspectives*. Madison, WI: Prehistory Press.

Bauer, Alexander A. 1998. Cities of the Sea: Maritime Trade and the Origin of Philistine Settlement in the Early Iron Age Southern Levant. *Oxford Journal of Archaeology* 17:149–68.

Beck, Pirhiya. 1994. The Cult Stands from Ta'anach: Aspects of the Iconographic Tradition of Early Iron Age Cult Objects in Palestine. Pages 352–81 in Finkelstein and Na'aman 1994.

———. 2002. *Imagery and Representation: Studies in the Art and Iconography of Ancient Palestine; Collected Articles*. Edited by Nadav Na'aman, Uza Zevulun, and Irit Ziffer. Journal of the Institute of Archaeology of Tel Aviv University Occasional Publications 3. Tel Aviv: Institute of Archaeology, Tel Aviv University.

Becking, Bob, Meindert Dijkstra, Marjo C. A. Korpel, and Karel J. H. Vriezen. 2001. *Only One God? Monotheism in Ancient Israel and the Veneration of the Goddess Asherah*. New York: Sheffield Academic.

Beit-Arieh, Itzhaq, ed. 1995. *Horvat Qitmit: An Edomite Shrine in the Biblical Negev*. Tel Aviv: Institute of Archaeology, Tel Aviv University.

———. 1999. *Tel 'Ira: A Stronghold in the Biblical Negev*. Tel Aviv: Tel Aviv University.

Beitzel, Barry J. 2010. Was There a Joint Nautical Venture on the Mediterranean Sea by Tyrian Phoenicians and Early Israelites? *BASOR* 360:37–66.

Bell, Carol. 2006. *The Evolution of Long Distance Trading Relationships across the LBA/Iron Age Transition on the Northern Levantine Coast: Crisis, Continuity and Change; A Study Based on Imported Ceramics; Bronze and Its Contituent Metals*. BAR International Series 1574. Oxford: Archaeopress.

———. 2009. Continuity and Change: The Divergent Destinies of Late Bronze Age Ports in Syria and Lebanon across the LBA/Iron Age Transition. Pages 30–38 in Bachhuber and Roberts 2009.

Ben-Ami, Doron. 2001. The Iron Age I at Tel Hazor in Light of the Renewed Excavations. *IEJ* 51:148–70.

———. 2004. The Casemate Fort at Tel Harashim in Upper Galilee. *TA* 31:194–208.

Ben-Shlomo, David. 2003. The Iron Age Sequence of Tel Ashdod: A Rejoinder to "Ashdod Revisited" by I. Finkelstein and L. Singer-Avitz. *TA* 30:83–107.

———. 2006. *Decorated Philistine Pottery: An Archaeological and Archeo-metric Study.* BAR International Series 1541. Oxford: Archaeopress .

———. 2008. Cultural Diversity, Ethnicity, and Power Imbalance in Early Iron Age Philistia. Pages 267–90 in *Cyprus, the Sea Peoples, and the Eastern Mediterranean: Regional Perspectives on Continuity and Change.* Edited by Timothy K. Harrison. Toronto: Canadian Institute for Mediterranean Studies.

———. 2010. *Philistine Iconography: A Wealth of Style and Symbolism.* Fribourg: Vandenhoeck & Ruprecht.

———. 2011. Food Preparation Habits and Cultural Interaction during the Late Bronze and Iron Age in Southern Israel. Pages 273–86 in Karageorghis and Kouka 2011.

———. 2012. *The Azor Cemetery: Moshe Dothan's Excavations, 1958 and 1960.* Jerusalem: Israel Antiquities Authority.

———. 2014. Tell Jemmeh, Philistia and the Neo-Assyrian Empire during the Late Iron Age. *Levant* 46:58–88.

Ben-Shlomo, David, and Gus W. van Beek, eds. 2014. *The Smithsonian Institution Excavation at Tell Jemmeh, Israel, 1970–1990.* Washington, DC: Smithsonian Institution.

Ben-Shlomo, David, and Michael D. Press. 2009. A Reexamination of Aegean-Style Figurines in Light of New Evidence from Ashdod, Ashkelon, and Ekron. *BASOR* 353:39–74.

Ben-Shlomo, David, Itzhaq Shai, and Aren M. Maier. 2004. Late Philistine Decorated Ware ("Ashdod Ware"): Typology, Chronology, and Production Centers. *BASOR* 335:1–35.

Ben-Shlomo, David, Itzhaq Shai, and Alexander Zukerman. 2008. Cooking Identities: Aegean-Style Cooking Jugs and Cultural Interaction in Iron Age Philistia and Neighboring Regions. *AJA* 112:225–46.

Ben-Tor, Amnon, ed. 1992. *The Archaeology of Ancient Israel.* New Haven: Yale University Press.

———. 1993. Jokneam. *NEAEHL* 3:805–11.

———. 2000. "Hazor and the Chronology of Northern Israel: Reply to Israel Finkelstein." *BASOR* 317: 9–15.

Ben-Tor, Amnon, and Doron Ben-Arni. 1998. Hazor and the Archaeology of the Tenth Century B.C.E. *IEJ* 48:1–37.

Ben-Tor, Amnon, Doron Ben-Arni, and Debora Sandhaus. 2012. *Hazor VI: The 1990–2009 Excavations, The Iron Age.* Jerusalem: Hebrew University of Jerusalem.

Ben Tor, Amnon, Ruhama Bonfil, and Sharon Zuckerman. 2003. *Tel Qashish, a Village in the Jezreel Valley: Final Report of the Archaeological Excavations (1978–1987)*. Qedem 5. Jerusalem: Institute of Archaeology, the Hebrew University of Jerusalem.

Ben-Tor, Amnon, and Yuval Portugali. 1987. *Tel Oiri: A Village in the Jezreel Valley; Report of the Archaeological Excavations 1975–1977*. Qedem 24. Jerusalem: Institute of Archaeology, Hebrew University of Jerusalem.

Ben-Tor, Amnon, Annabel Zarzecki-Peleg, and S. Cohen-Arnidjar. 2005. Yoqne'am II: The Iron Age and the Persian Period; Final Report of the Archaeological Excavations (1977–1988). Qedem 6. Jerusalem: Institute of Archaeology, Hebrew University of Jerusalem.

Ben-Yosef, Erez, et al. 2012. A New Chronological Framework for Iron Age Copper Production at Timna (Israel). *BASOR* 367:31–71.

Benzi, Mario. 2013. The Southeast Aegean in the Age of the Sea Peoples. Pages 509–42 in Killebrew and Lehmann 2013a.

Berkhofer, Robert F., Jr. 1995. *Beyond the Great Story: History as Text and Discourse*. Cambridge: Harvard University Press.

Berlin, Adele. 1983. *Poetics and Interpretation of Biblical Narrative*. BLS 9. Sheffield: Almond Press.

Bickel, Susanne, et al., eds. 2007. *Bilder als Ouelle–Images as Sources: Studies on Ancient Near Eastern Artifacts and the Bible Inspired by the Work of Othmar Keel*. Göttingen: Vandenhoeck & Ruprecht.

Bickel, Susanne, Silvia Schroer, and Christoph Uehlinger. 2007. "Die Würde des Originals"—ein Dank an Othmar Keel von FreundInnen und SchülerInnen. Pages xxi–xxvi in *Bilder als Quellen, Images as Sources: Studies on Ancient Near Eastern Artefacts and the Bible Inspired by the Work of Othmar Keel*. Edited by Susanne Bickel et al. OBO. Fribourg: Academic Press.

Bienkowski, Piotr, ed. 1992. *Early Edom and Moab: The Beginning of the Iron Age in Southern Jordan*. Sheffield Archaeological Monographs 7. Sheffield: Collis.

———. 2000. Transjordan and Assyria. Pages 44–53 in *The Archaeology of Jordan and Beyond: Essays in Honor of James A. Sauer*. Edited by Lawrence E. Stager, Joseph A. Greene, and Michael D. Coogan. SAHL 1. Winona Lake, IN: Eisenbrauns.

———, ed. 2009a. *Studies on Iron Age Moab and Neighboring Areas in Honour of Michele Daviau*. ANESSup 29. Leuven: Peeters.

———. 2009b. "Tribalism" and "Segmentary Society" in Iron Age Transjordan. Pages 7–25 in Bienkowski 2009a.

———. 2014. Edom during the Iron Age II Period. Pages 782–94 in Steiner and Killebrew 2014.

Bienkowski, Piotr, and Crystal-M. Bennett. 2002. *Busayra: Excavations by Crystal-M. Bennett 1971–1980*. British Academy Monographs in Archaeology 13. Oxford: Oxford University Press.

Bienkowski, Piotr, and Eveline van der Steen. 2001. Tribes, Trade, and Towns: A New Framework for the Late Iron Age in Southern Jordan and the Negev. *BASOR* 323:21–47.

Bietak, Manfred. 1981. *Avaris and Piramesse: Archaeological Explorations in the Eastern Nile Delta*. Oxford: Oxford University Press.

Bikai, Patricia M. 1987. *The Phoenician Pottery of Cyprus*. Nicosia: A. G. Leventis Foundation.

Bimson, John J. 1981. *Redating the Exodus and Conquest*. 2nd ed. JSOTSup. 5. Sheffield: Almond Press.

Binford, Lewis R. 1982. Meaning, Inference and the Material Record. Pages 160–63 in *Ranking, Resource and Exchange: Aspects of the Archaeology of Early European Society*. Edited by Colin Renfrew and Stephen J. Shennan. Cambridge: Cambridge University Press.

Bintliff, John, ed. 1991. *The* Annales *School and Archaeology*. Leicester: Leicester University Press.

———. 2011. The Death of Archaeological Theory? Pages 7–22 in Bintliff and Pearce 2011.

Bintliff, John, and Mark Pearce, eds. 2011. *The Death of Archaeological Theory?* Oxford: Oxbow.

Biran, Avraham. 1994. *Biblical Dan*. Jerusalem: Israel Exploration Society.

Biran, Avraham, and Joseph Naveh. 1993. An Aramaic Stele Fragment from Tel Dan. *IEJ* 43:81–98.

———. 1995. The Tell Dan Inscription: A New Fragment. *IEJ* 45:1–18.

Blakely, Jeffrey A., and James W. Hardin. 2002. Southwestern Judah in the Late Eighth Century B.C.E. *BASOR* 326:11–64.

Bloch-Smith, Elizabeth. 1992. *Judahite Burial Practices and Beliefs About the Dead*. JSOT/ASOR Monograph Series 7. Sheffield: JSOT.

———. 2002. Solomon's Temple: The Politics of Ritual Space. Pages 83–94 in *Sacred Time, Sacred Space: Archaeology and the Religion of Israel*. Edited by Barry M. Gittlen. Winona Lake, IN: Eisenbrauns.

———. 2004. Resurrecting the Iron I Dead. *IEJ* 54:77–91.

Bloch-Smith, Elizabeth, and Beth Alpert Nakhai. 1999. A Landscape Comes to Life: The Iron Age I. *NEA* 62:62–92, 101–27.

Blomquist, Tina H. 1999. *Gates and Gods: Cults in the City Gates of Iron Age Palestine: An Investigation of the Archaeological and Biblical Sources.* ConBOT 46. Stockholm: Almqvist & Wiksell.

Boling, Robert G. 1988. *The Early Biblical Community in Transjordan.* Sheffield: Almond Press.

Bordieu, Pierre. 1977. *Outline of a Theory of Practice.* Translated by Richard Nice. Cambridge: Cambridge University Press.

———. 1990. *The Logic of Practice.* Translated by Richard Nice. Stanford, CA: Stanford University Press.

Borowski, Oded. 1987. *Agriculture in Iron Age Israel.* Winona Lake, IN: Eisenbrauns.

———. 1998. *Every Living Thing: Daily Use of Animals in Ancient Israel.* Walnut Creek, CA: Altamira.

Braemer, Frank. 1982. *L'architecture domestique du Levant à l'âge du fer: Protohistoire du Levant.* Cahier 8. Paris: Editions Recherche sur les civilisations.

Braun, Joachim. 2002. *Music in Ancient Israel/Palestine: Archaeological, Written, and Comparative Sources.* Grand Rapids: Eerdmans.

Brettler, Marc Z. 1995. *The Creation of History in Ancient Israel.* London: Routledge.

———. 1999. Judaism in the Hebrew Bible? The Transition from Ancient Israelite Religion to Judaism. *CBQ* 61:429–47.

———. 2003. The Copenhagen School: The Historiographical Issues. *AJS Review* 27:1–21.

———. 2007. Method in the Application of Biblical Source Material to Historical Writing (with Particular Reference to the Ninth Century BCE). Pages 305–36 in Williamson 2007.

Bright, John. 1956. Early Israel in Recent History Writing: A Study in Method. SBT 19. London: SCM.

———. 2000. *A History of Israel.* 4th ed. Louisville: Westminster John Knox.

Brody, Aaron J. 2011. The Archaeology of the Extended Family: A Household Compound from Iron II Tell en-Nasbeh. Pages 237–54 in Yasur-Landau, Ebeling, and Mazow 2011.

Broshi, Magen, and Israel Finkelstein. 1992. The Population of Palestine in Iron Age II. *BASOR* 287:47–60.

Broshi, Magen, and Ram Gophna. 1984 The Settlement and Population of Palestine during the Early Bronze Age II–III. *BASOR* 253:41–52.

————. 1986. Middle Bronze Age II Palestine: Its Settlement and Population. *BASOR* 261:73–90.

Brug, John F. 1985. *A Literary and Archaeological Study of the Philistines.* BAR International Series 265. Oxford: British Archaeological Reports.

Brughmans, Tom, Ann Collar, and Fiona Coward, eds. 2016. *The Connected Past: Challenges to Network Studies in Archaeology and History.* Oxford: Oxford University Press.

Bruins, Hendrik J., and Johannes van der Plicht. 2005. Desert Settlement through the Iron Age: Radiocarbon Dates from Sinai and the Negev Highlands. Pages 349–66 in Levy and Higham 2005.

Bruins, Hendrik J., Johannes van der Plicht, David Ilan, and Ella Werker. 2005a. Iron-Age ^{14}C Dates from Tel Dan. Pages 323–36 in Levy and Higham 2005.

Bruins, Hendrik J., Johannes van der Plicht, Amihai Mazar, Christopher Bronk Ramsey, and Sturt W. Manning. 2005b. The Groningen Radiocarbon Series from Tel Reḥov: OxCal Bayesian Computations for the Iron IB–IIA Boundary and Iron IIA Destruction Events. Pages 271–93 in Levy and Higham 2005.

Bruins, Hendrik J., Johannes van der Plicht, and Amihai Mazar. 2003. ^{14}C Dates from Tel Rehov: Iron Age Chronology, Pharaohs, and Hebrew Kings. *Science* 300/5601:315–18.

Bunimovitz, Shlomo. 1986–1987. An Egyptian "Governor's Residency" at Gezer? Another Suggestion. *TA* 15:68–76.

————. 1990. Problems in the "Ethnic" Identification of the Philistine Material Culture. *TA* 17:210–22.

————. 1994. Socio-political Transformations in the Central Hill Country in the Late Bronze–Iron I Transition. Pages 129–202 in Finkelstein and Naʾaman 1994.

————. 1995a. How Mute Stones Speak: Interpreting What We Dig Up. *BAR* 21.2:58–67, 96.

————. 1995b. On the Edge of Empires: The Late Bronze Age (1500–1200 BCE). Pages 320–31 in Levy 1995.

————. 2011. "Us" and "Them": The Distribution of Twelfth Century Cooking Pots and Drinking Cups as Identity Markers. Pages 237–43 in Karageorghis and Kouka 2011.

Bunimovitz, Shlomo, and Avraham Faust. 2001. Chronological Separation, Geographical Segregation or Ethnic Demarcation? Ethnography and the Iron Age Low Chronology. *BASOR* 322:1–10.

———. 2003. Building Identity: The Four-Room House and the Israelite Mind. Pages 411–23 in Dever and Gitin 2003.

———. 2010. Re-constructing Biblical Archaeology: Toward an Integration of Archaeology and the Bible. Pages 43–54 in Levy 2010a.

Bunimovitz, Shlomo, and Zvi Lederman. 1997. Beth-Shemesh: Culture Conflict on Judah's Frontier. *BAR* 23.1:42–49.

———. 2001a. Canaanite Resistance: The Philistines and Beth-Shemesh—A Case Study from Iron Age I. *BASOR* 364:37–51.

———. 2001b. The Iron Age Fortifications of Tel Beth Shemesh: A 1990–2000 Perspective. *IEJ* 51:121–47.

———. 2003. The Final Destruction of Beth Shemesh and the *Pax Assyriaca* in the Judean Shephelah. *TA* 30:3–26.

———. 2006. The Early Israelite Monarchy in the Sorek Valley: Tel Beth-Shemesh and Tel Batash (Timnah) in the Tenth and Ninth Centuries BCE. Pages 407–27 in Maeir and de Miroschedji 2006.

———. 2008. A Border Case: Beth-Shemesh and the Rise of Israel. Pages 21–31 in Grabbe 2008a.

———. 2009. The Archaeology of Border Communities: Renewed Excavations at Tel Beth Shemesh, Part 1: The Iron Age. *NEA* 72:114–42.

———. 2011. Close Yet Apart: Diverse Cultural Dynamics at Iron Age Beth-Shemesh and Lachish. Pages 33–53 in Finkelstein and Na'aman 2011.

Burgh, Theodore W. 2006. *Listening to the Artifacts: Music Culture in Ancient Palestine*. New York: T&T Clark.

Cahill, Jane M. 2003. Jerusalem at the Time of the Monarchy: The Archaeological Evidence. Pages 13–80 in Vaughn and Killebrew 2003.

———. 2006. The Excavations at Tell el-Hammah: A Prelude to Amihai Mazar's Beth-Shean Valley Regional Project. Pages 429–59 in Maeir and de Miroschedji 2006.

Campbell, Edward F. 1994. Archaeological Reflections on Amos's Targets. Pages 32–52 in Coogan, Exum, and Stager 1994.

———. 2002. *Shechem III: The Stratigraphy and Architecture of Shechem/Tell Balâṭah*. ASOR Archaeological Reports 6. Boston: American Schools of Oriental Research.

Cantrell, Deborah O'Daniel. 2011. *The Horsemen of Israel: Horses and Chariotry in Monarchic Israel (Ninth–Eighth Centuries B.C.E.)*. Winona Lake, IN: Eisenbrauns.

Caroll, Robert P. 1993. Intertextuality and the Book of Jeremiah: Animadversions on Text and Theory. Pages 55–78 in Exum and Clines 1993.

———. 1997. Madonna of Silences: Clio and the Bible. Pages 84–103 in Grabbe 1997b.

Carter, Tara, and Thomas E. Levy. 2010. Texts in Exile: Towards an Anthropological Methodology for Incorporating Texts and Archaeology. Pages 205–40 in Levy 2010a.

Cassuto, Deborah. 2008. Bringing Home the Artifacts: A Social Interpretation of Loom Weights in Context. Pages 63–77 in Nakhai 2008.

Chadwick, Jeffrey R. 1992. The Archaeology of Biblical Hebron in the Bronze and Iron Ages: An Examination of the Discoveries of the American Expedition to Hebron. PhD diss. University of Utah Middle East Center.

Chambon, Alain. 1984. *Tel el-Far'ah. 1: L'age du fer.* Paris: Editions Recherche sur les civilisations.

Chaney, Marvin L. 1983 Ancient Palestinian Peasant Movements and the Formation of Premonarchic Israel. Pages 39–90 in *Palestine in Transition: The Emergence of Ancient Israel.* Edited by David Noel Freedman and David Frank Graf. Sheffield: Almond Press.

Chapman, John. 1997. The Impact of Modem Invasions and Migrations on Archaeological Explanation. Pages 11–20 in *Migrations and Invasions in Archaeological Explanation.* Edited by John Charles Chapman and Helena Hamerow. BAR International Series 664. Oxford: Archaeopress.

Chapman, Rupert L., III. 2009. Putting Shoshenq I in His Place. *PEQ* 141:4–17.

Childe, Vere Gordon. 1950. The Urban Revolution. *The Town Planning Review* 21:3–17.

Claessen, Henri J. M., and Peter Skalnik, eds. 1978. *The Early State.* The Hague: Mouton.

———, eds. *The Study of the State.* The Hague: Mouton.

Clancy, Frank. 1999. Shishak/Shoshenq's Travels. *JSOT* 86: 3– 23.

Cline, Eric. 1994. *Sailing the Wine-Dark Sea: International Trade and the Late Bronze Aegean.* Oxford: Tempus Departum.

———. 2011. Whole Lotta Shakin' Going On: The Possible Destruction by Earthquake of Str. VIA at Megiddo. Pages 55–70 in Finkelstein and Na'aman 2011.

———. 2014. *1177 B.C.: The Year Civilization Collapsed.* Princeton: Princeton University Press.

Clines, David J. A. 1993. A World Established on Water (Psalm 24): Reader-Response, Deconstruction and Bespoke Interpretation. Pages 79–90 in Exum and Clines 1993.

Cogan, Mordechai. 1993. Judah under Assyrian Hegemony: A Reexamination of Imperialism and Religion. *JBL* 112:403–14.

———. 1998. Into Exile: From the Assyrian Conquest of Israel to the Fall of Babylon. Pages 242–75 in Coogan 2001.

———. 2001. *I Kings: A New Translation with Introduction and Commentary.* AYB 10. New Haven:Yale University Press.

Cogan, Mordechai, and Hayim Tadmor. 1988. *II Kings: A New Translation with Introduction and Commentary.* AB 11. New York: Doubleday.

Cohen, Ronald, and Elman R. Service, eds. 1978. *Origins of the State: The Anthropology of Political Evolution.* Philadelphia: Institute for the Study of Human Issues.

Cohen, Rudolph. 1976. Excavations at Horvat Haluqim. *'Atiqot* 11:34–50.

———. 1979. The Iron Age Fortresses in the Central Negev. *BASOR* 236:61–79.

———. 1993. Kadesh-Barnea: The Israelite Fortress. *NEAEHL* 3:843–47.

Cohen, Rudolph, and Hannah Bernick-Greenberg. 2007. *Excavations at Kadesh Barnea (Tell el-Qudeirat) 1976–1982.* IAA 34. Jerusalem: Israel Antiquities Authority.

———. 1995. The Iron Age Fortresses at 'En Ḥaṣeva. *BA* 58:223–35.

Cohen, Rudolph, and Yigal Yisrael. 1996. Smashing the Idols: Piecing Together an Edomite Shrine in Judah. *BAR* 22.4:40–51, 65.

Collingwood, R. G. 1946. *The Idea of History.* Oxford: Clarendon.

Collins, John J. 2005. *The Bible after Babel: Historical Criticism in a Postmodern Age.* Grand Rapids: Eerdmans.

Coogan, Michael D., ed. 2001. *The Oxford History of the Biblical World.* Oxford: Oxford University Press.

———. 2006. *The Old Testament: A Historical and Literary Introduction to the Hebrew Scriptures.* Oxford: Oxford University Press.

Coogan, Michael D., J. Cheryl Exum, and Lawrence E. Stager, eds. 1994. *Scripture and Other Artifacts: Essays on the Bible and Archaeology in Honor of Philip J. King.* Louisville: Westminster John Knox.

Coogan, Michael D., and Mark S. Smith. 2012. *Stories from Ancient Canaan.* Louisville: Westminster John Knox.

Cooley, Robert E., and Gary D. Pratico. 1994. Tell Dothan: The Western Cemetery, with Comments on Joseph Free's Excavations, 1953 to 1964. Pages 147–73 in *Preliminary Excavation Reports: Sardis, Bir Umm Fawakhir, Tell el 'Umeiri, the Combined Caesarea Expeditions, and Tell Dothan.* Edited by William G. Dever. AASOR 52. Boston: American Schools of Oriental Research.

Coote, Robert B. 1990. *Early Israel: A New Horizon*. Minneapolis: Fortress.

Cornelius, Izak. 2004. *The Many Faces of the Goddess: The Iconography of the Syro-Palestinian Goddesses Anat, Astarte, Qedeshet, and Asherah c. 1500–1000 BCE*. OBO 204. Göttingen: Vandenhoeck & Ruprecht.

Coughenour, Robert A. 1976. Preliminary Report on the Exploration and Excavation of Mugharat el Wardeh and Abu Thawab. *ADAJ* 21:71–78.

Crawford, Sidnie White, ed. 2007. *"Up to the Gates of Ekron": Essays on the Archaeology and History of the Eastern Mediterranean in Honor of Seymour Gitin*. Jerusalem: W. F. Albright Institute of Archaeology and the Israel Exploration Society.

Cribb, Roger. 1991. *Nomads in Archaeology*. Cambridge: Cambridge University Press.

Croce, Benedetto. 1921. *History: Its Theory and Practice*. New York: Russell & Russell.

Crowfoot, John W., and Grace M. Crowfoot. 1938. *Samaria-Sebaste II: The Early Ivories from Samaria*. London: Palestine Exploration Fund.

Crowfoot, John W., Grace M. Crowfoot, and Kathleen M. Kenyon. 1957. *Samaria-Sebaste III: The Objects*. London: Palestine Exploration Fund.

Crowfoot, John W., Kathleen M. Kenyon, and Eleazart I. Sukenik. 1942. *The Buildings at Samaria (Samaria-Sebaste 1)*. London: Palestine Exploration Fund.

Dagan, Yehuda. 1992. The Shephelah during the Period of the Monarchy in Light of Archaeological Excavations and Survey [Hebrew]. MA thesis. Tel Aviv University.

———. 2000. The Settlement in the Judean Shephela in the Second and First Millennium BCE: A Test-Case of Settlement Processes in A Geographic Region. PhD diss. Tel Aviv University.

———. 2011. Tel Azekah: A New Look at the Site and Its "Judean" Fortress. Pages 71–86 in Finkelstein and Na'aman 2011.

Dar, Shim'on. 1986. *Landscape and Pattern: An Archaeological Survey of Samaria, 800 BCE–636 CE*. BAR International Series 308. Oxford: British Archaeological Reports.

Daviau, P. M. Michele. 2003. *The Iron Age Town*. Vol. 1 of *Excavations at Tall Jawa, Jordan*. CHANE 11.2. Leiden: Brill.

Daviau, P. M. Michele, John W. Wevers, and Michael Weigl, eds. 2001. *The World of the Aramaeans: Biblical, Historical and Cultural Studies in Honor of Paul-E. Dion*. JSOTSup 326. Sheffield: JSOT.

Davies, Philip R. 1992. *In Search of "Ancient Israel": A Study in Biblical Origins*. JSOTSup 148. Sheffield: Sheffield Academic.

———. 1995. Method and Madness: Some Remarks on Doing History with the Bible: *JBL* 114:699–705.

———. 1997. Whose History? Whose Israel? Whose Bible? Biblical Histories, and Modern. Pages 104–22 in Grabbe 1997b.

———. 2007. Biblical Israel in the Ninth Century? Pages 49–56 in Williamson 2007.

———. 2008. *Memories of Ancient Israel: An Introduction to Biblical History—Ancient and Modern.* Louisville: Westminster John Knox.

———. 2013. *Rethinking Biblical Scholarship.* Changing Perpectives 4. London: Routledge.

Davies, Philip R., and Diana Vikander Edelman, eds. 2011. *The Historian and the Bible: Essays in Honour of Lester L. Grabbe.* LHBOTS 530. London: T&T Clark.

Davies, Philip R, and John Rogerson. 1996. Was the Siloam Tunnel Built by Hezekiah? *BA* 59:138–49.

Day, John, ed. 2004. *In Search of Pre-exilic Israel.* JSOTSup 406. London: T&T Clark.

Dearman, Andrew, ed. 1989. *Studies in the Mesha Inscription and Moab.* ABS 2. Atlanta: Scholars Press.

De Groot, Alon, and Hannah Bernick-Greenberg. 2012. *Excavations at the City of David 1978–1985 Directed by Yigal Shiloh,* Vol. 7A: *Area E: Stratigraphy and Architecture.* Vol. 7B: *Area E: The Finds.* Qedem 53–54. Jerusalem: Hebrew University of Jerusalem.

DeMarrais, Elizabeth, Chris Gosden, and Colin Renfrew, eds. 2004. *Rethinking Materiality: The Engagement of Mind with the Material World.* Cambridge: McDonald Institute for Archaeological Research.

Derrida, Jacques. 1976. *Of Grammatology.* Translated by Gayatri Chakravorty Spivak. Baltimore: Johns Hopkins University Press.

Deutsch, Robert, and Michael Heltzer. 1994. *Forty New Ancient West Semitic Inscriptions.* Tel Aviv-Jaffa: Archaeological Center Publications.

Dever, William G. 1969–1970. Iron Age Epigraphic Material from the Area of Khirbet el-Kom. *HUCA* 40–41:139–204.

———. 1971. Review of *The Excavations of Bethel (1934–1960),* by William Foxwell Albright and James L. Kelso. *Or* 40:459–71.

———. 1974. *Archaeology and Biblical Studies: Retrospects and Prospects.* The William C. Winslow Lectures at Seabury-Western Theological Seminary, 1972. Evanston, IL: Seabury-Western Theological Seminary.

———. 1977. Palestine in the Second Millennium B.C.E.: The Archaeological Picture. Pages 70–120 in *Israelite and Judean History*. Edited by John H. Hayes and J. Maxwell Miller. Philadelphia: Westminster.

———. 1981. The Impact of the "New Archaeology" on Syro-Palestinian Archaeology. *BASOR* 242:15–29.

———. 1982. Retrospects and Prospects in Biblical and Syro-Palestinian Archaeology. *BA* 45:103–7.

———. 1984a. Asherah, Consort of Yahweh? New Evidence from Kuntillet ʿAjrud. *BASOR* 255:21–37.

———. 1984b. Gezer Revisited: New Excavations of the Solomonic and Assyrian Period Defenses. *BA* 47:206–18.

———. 1985a. Solomonic and Assyrian Period "Palaces" at Gezer. *IEJ* 35:217–30.

———. 1985b. Syro-Palestinian and Biblical Archaeology. Pages 31–74 in *The Hebrew Bible and Its Modern Interpreters*. Edited by Douglas A. Knight and Gene M. Tucker. Philadelphia: Fortress; Atlanta: Scholars Press.

———. 1986. Late Bronze Age and Solomonic Defenses at Gezer: New Evidence. *BASOR* 262:9–34.

———. The Contribution of Archaeology to the Study of Canaanite and Early Ancient Israelite Religion. Pages 209–47 in Miller, Hanson, and McBride 1987.

———. 1988. Impact of the "New Archaeology". Pages 337–52 in *Benchmarks in Time and Culture: An Introduction to Palestinian Archaeology*. Edited by Joel F. Drinkard, Gerald L. Mattingly, and J. Maxwell Miller. Atlanta: Scholars Press.

———. 1989. Archaeology in Israel Today: A Summation and Critique. Pages 143–52 in *Recent Excavations in Israel: Studies in Iron Age Archaeology*. Edited by Seymour Gitin and William G. Dever. AASOR 49. Winona Lake, IN: Eisenbrauns.

———. 1991a. Archaeology, Material Culture and the Early Monarchical Period in Israel. Pages 103–15 in Edelman 1991.

———. 1991b. Unresolved Issues in the Early History of Israel: Toward a Synthesis of Archaeological and Textual Reconstructions. Pages 195–208 in *The Bible and the Politics of Exegesis: Essays in Honor of Norman K. Gottwald on His Sixty-Fifth Birthday*. Edited by David Jobling, Peggy Lynne Day, and Gerald T. Sheppard. Cleveland: Pilgrim.

———. 1992a. Archaeology, Syro-Palestinian and Biblical. *ABD* 1:354–67.

———. 1992b. A Case-Study in Biblical Archaeology: The Earthquake of ca. 760 B.C. *ErIsr* 23:27*–35*.

———. 1992c. How to Tell a Canaanite from an Israelite. Pages 27–56 in Shanks 1992.

———. 1992d. The Late Bronze-Early Iron I Horizon in Syria-Palestine: Egyptians, Canaanites, Sea Peoples, and Proto-Israelites. Pages 99–110 in Ward and Joukowsky 1992.

———. 1993a. Biblical Archaeology: Death and Rebirth. Pages 706–22 in *Biblical Archaeology Today: Proceedings of the Second International Congress on Biblical Archaeology. Jerusalem, June–July 1990.* Edited by Avraham Biran and Joseph Aviram. Jerusalem: Israel Exploration Society.

———. 1993b. Further Evidence on the Date of the Outer Wall at Gezer. *BASOR* 289:33–54.

———. 1994a. Archaeology, Texts, and History-Writing: Toward an Epistemology. Pages 105–17 in *Uncovering Ancient Stones: Essays in Memory of H. Neil Richardson.* Edited by Lewis M. Hopfe. Winona Lake, IN: Eisenbrauns.

———. 1994b. From Tribe to Nation: A Critique of State Formation Processes in Ancient Israel. Pages 213–38 in *Nuove fondazioni nel Vicino Oriente antico: Realtà e ideologia.* Edited by Stefania Mazzoni. Pisa: University of Pisa.

———. 1994c. The Silence of the Text: An Archaeological Commentary on 2 Kings 23. Pages 143–68 in Coogan, Exum, and Stager 1994.

———. 1995a. Ceramics, Ethnicity, and the Question of Israel's Origins. *BA* 58:200–13.

———. 1995b. Social Structure in Palestine in the Iron II Period on the Eve of Destruction. Pages 416–31 in Levy 1995.

———. 1995c Social Structure in the Early Bronze IV Period in Palestine. Pages 282–96 in Levy 1995.

———. 1995d. "Will the Real Israel Please Stand Up?" Part I: Archaeology and Israelite Historiography. *BASOR* 297:61–80.

———. 1995e. "Will the Real Israel Please Stand Up?" Part II: Archaeology and the Religions of Ancient Israel. *BASOR* 298:37–58.

———. 1996. The Identity of Early Israel: A Rejoinder to Keith W. Whitelam. *JSOT* 72:3–24.

———. 1997a. Archaeology, Urbanism, and the Rise of the Israelite State. Pages 172–93 in *Aspects of Urbanism in Antiquity: From Mesopotamia to Crete*. Edited by Walter E. Aufrecht, Neil A. Mirau, and Steven W. Gauley. JSOTSup 244. Sheffield: Sheffield Academic.

———. 1997b. Archaeology and the 'Age of Solomon': A Case-Study in Archaeology and Historiography. Pages 217–51 in Handy 1997.

———. 1997c. Is There Any Archaeological Evidence for the Exodus? Pages 67–83 in Frerichs and Lesco 1997.

———. 1997d. On Listening to the Text and the Artifacts. Pages 1–32 in *The Echoes of Many Texts: Reflections on Jewish and Christian Traditions; Essays in Honor of Lou H. Silberman*. Edited by William G. Dever and J. Edward Wright. BJS 313. Atlanta: Scholars Press.

———. 1997e. Philology, Theology, and Archaeology: What Kind of History Do We Want, and What Is Possible? Pages 290–310 in Silberman and Small 1997.

———. 1998a. Archaeology, Ideology, and the Quest for "Ancient" or "Biblical Israel." *NEA* 61:39–52.

———. 1998b. Israelite Origins and the "Nomadic Ideal": Can Archaeology Separate Fact from Fiction? Pages 220–37 in Gitin, Mazar, and Stern 1998.

———. 1999. Archaeology and the Israelite Cult: How the Kh. el-Qom and Kuntillet 'Ajrud "Asherah" Texts Have Changed the Picture. *ErIsr* 26:8*–14*.

———. 2000. Biblical and Syro-Palestinian Archaeology: A State-of-the-Art Assessment at the Turn of the Millennium. *CurBS* 8:91–116.

———. 2001. *What Did the Biblical Writers Know and When Did They Know It? What Archaeology Can Tell Us about the Reality of Ancient Israel*. Grand Rapids: Eerdmans.

———. 2003a The Patriarchs and Matriarchs of Ancient Israel: Myth or History. Pages 39–56 in *One Hundred Years of American Archaeology in the Middle East: Proceedings of the American Schools of Oriental Research Centennial Celebration, Washington, DC, April 2000*. Edited by Douglas R. Clark and Victor H. Matthews. Boston: American Schools of Oriental Research.

———. 2003b. The Rural Landscape of Palestine in the Early Bronze IV Period. Pages 43–59 in Maeir, Dar, and Safrai 2003.

———. 2003c. Syro-Palestinian and Biblical Archaeology: Into the Next Millennium. Pages 513–27 in Dever and Gitin 2003.

———. 2003d *Who Were The Early Israelites and Where Did They Come From?* Grand Rapids: Eerdmans.

———. 2004. Histories and Non-histories of Ancient Israel: Theology, Archaeology, and Ideology. Pages 150–206 in Day 2004.

———. 2005a. *Did God Have a Wife? Archaeology and Folk Religion in Ancient Israel*. Grand Rapids: Eerdmans.

———. 2005b. Histories and Non-histories of Ancient Israel: What Archaeology Can Contribute. Pages 29–50 in *Recenti tendenze nella ricostruzione della storia antica d'Israele: Convegno internatioonale, Roma, 6–7 Mar. 7, 2003*. Edited by Mario Liverani. Rome: Academia Nationale dei Lincei.

———. 2005c. Some Methodological Reflections on Chronology and History-Writing. Pages 413–21 in Levy and Higham 2005.

———. 2006. Archaeology and Ancient Israelite Iconography: Did God Have a Face? Pages 461–75 in *"I Will Speak the Riddles of Ancient Times": Archaeological and Historical Studies in Honor of Amihai Mazar on the Occasion of His Sixtieth Birthday*. Edited by Aren M. Maeir and Pierre de Miroschedji. Winona Lake, IN: Eisenbrauns.

———. 2007a. Archaeology and the Fall of the Northern Kingdom: What Really Happened? Pages 78–92 in Crawford 2007.

———. 2007b. Ethnicity and the Archeological Record: The Case of Early Israel. Pages 49–66 in *The Archaeology of Difference: Gender, Ethnicity, Class, and the "Other" in Antiquity; Studies in Honor of Eric M. Meyers*. Edited by Douglas R. Edwards and C. Thomas McCollough. Atlanta: American Schools of Oriental Research.

———. 2009. Merneptah's "Israel," the Bible's, and Ours. Pages 9–96 in Schloen 2009.

———. 2010a Archaeology and the Question of Sources in Kings. Pages 517–38 in Halpern and Lemaire 2010.

———. 2010b Two Views of Ancient Israel: Review of Lester L. Grabbe, *Ancient Israel: What Do We Know and How Do We Know It? BASOR* 357:77–83.

———. 2011. Earliest Israel: God's Warriors, Revolting Peasants or Nomadic Hordes? *ErIsr* 30:4*–12*.

———. 2012. *The Lives of Ordinary People in Ancient Israel: Where Archaeology and the Bible Intersect*. Grand Rapids: Eerdmans.

———. 2014. The Judean "Pillar-Base Figurines": Mothers or "Mother Goddesses"? Pages 129–41 in Albertz et al. 2014.

Dever, William G., and Seymour Gitin, eds. 2003. *Symbiosis, Symbolism, and the Power of the Past: Canaan, Ancient Israel, and Their Neighbors from the Late Bronze Age through Roman Palaestina*. Winona Lake, IN: Eisenbrauns.

Dever, William G., H. Darrell Lance, and George E. Wright. 1970. *Gezer I: Preliminary Report of the 1964–66 Seasons*. AHUCBASJ 1. Jerusalem: Hebrew Union College-Biblical and Archaeological School.

Dever, William G., et al. 1974. *Gezer II: Report of the 1967–70 Seasons in Fields I and II*. AHUCBASJ 2. Jerusalem: Hebrew Union College-Nelson Glueck School of Biblical Archaeology.

———. 1986. *Gezer IV: The 1969–71 Seasons in Field VI, the "Acropolis."* ANGSBA 3. Jerusalem: Hebrew Union College-Jewish Institute of Religion.

Dijk, Jacobus van. 2000. The Amarna Period and the Later New Kingdom (*c*. 1352–1069 BC). Pages 272–313, 464–465 in Shaw 2000.

Dion, Paul-Eugene. 1997. *Les Arameens a l'age du fer: Histoire politique et structures sociales*. Études Bibliques NS 34. Paris: Gabalda.

Dion, Paul-Eugene, and P. M. Michele Daviau. 2010. The Moabites. Pages 205–24 in Halpern and Lemaire 2010.

Dobbs-Allsopp, et al. 2005. *Hebrew Inscriptions*. New Haven: Yale University Press.

Dolansky, Shawna. 2008. *Now You See It, Now You Don't: Biblical Perspectives on the Relationship between Magic and Religion*. Winona Lake, IN: Eisenbrauns.

Dorsey, David. 1992. *The Roads and Highways of Ancient Israel*. Baltimore: Johns Hopkins University Press.

Dothan, Moshe. 1961. Excavations at Azor 1960. *IEJ* 11:171–87.

Dothan, Moshe, and David Ben-Shlomo. 2005. *Ashdod VI: The Excavations of Areas H and K (1968–1969)*. IAA Reports 24. Jerusalem: Israel Antiquities Authority.

Dothan, Moshe, and Trude Dothan. 1992. *People of the Sea: The Search for the Philistines*. New York: Macmillan.

Dothan, Trude. 1982. *The Philistines and Their Material Culture*. New Haven: Yale University Press.

———. 1998. Initial Philistine Settlement: From Migration to Coexistence. Pages 148–61 in Mazar, Stern, and Gitin 1998.

———. 2003. The Aegean and the Orient: Cultic Interactions. Pages 189–213 in Dever and Gitin 2003.

Dothan, Trude, and Alexander Zukerman. 2004. A Preliminary Study of the Mycenaean IIIC:1 Pottery Assemblages from Tel Miqne-Ekron and Ashdod. *BASOR* 333:1–54.

Drews, Robert. 1993. *The End of the Bronze Age: Changes in Warfare and the Catastrophe ca. 1200 B.C.* Princeton: Princeton University Press.

———. 1998. Canaanites and Philistines. *JSOT* 81:39–61.

Eagleton, Terry. 1996. *The Illusions of Postmodernism.* Oxford: Blackwell.

———. 2003. *After Theory.* London: Penguin

Earle, Timothy K., ed. 1991. *Chiefdoms: Power, Economy, and Ideology.* Cambridge: Cambridge University Press.

Ebeling, Jennie R. 2010. *Women's Lives in Biblical Times.* London: T&T Clark.

Ebeling, Jennie R., and Michael M. Homan. 2008. Baking and Brewing Beer in the Israelite Household: A Study of Women's Cooking Technology. Pages 45–62 in Nakhai 2008.

Ebeling, Jennie R., and Yorke M. Rowan. 2008. *New Approaches to Old Stones: Recent Studies of Ground Stone Artifacts.* London: Equinox.

Edelman, Diana Vikander, ed. 1991. *The Fabric of History: Text, Artifact and Israel's Past.* JSOTSup 127. Sheffield: Sheffield Academic.

———. 1996. Ethnicity and Early Israel. Pages 25–55 in *Ethnicity and the Bible.* Edited by Mark G. Brett. Leiden: Brill.

Edeltein, Gershon. 2000. Terraced Farm at Er-Ras. *'Atiqot* 40:39–63.

Ehrlich, Carl S. 1996. *The Philistines in Transition: A History from ca. 1000–730 B.C.E.* SHANE 10. Leiden: Brill.

Ehrich, Robert, ed. 1965. *Chronologies in Old World Archaeology.* Chicago: University of Chicago Press.

Eitan, Avraham. 1983. Vered Yericho [Hebrew]. *Hadashot Arkheologiot* 73:43.

Ellis, John M. 1989. *Against Deconstruction.* Princeton: Princeton University Press.

Emberling, Geoff. 1997. Ethnicity in Complex Societies: Archaeological Perspectives. *Journal of Archaeological Research* 5:295–344.

Epstein, Claire. 1966. *Palestinian Bichrome Ware.* Leiden: Brill.

Eshel, Itzhak, and Kay Prag, eds. 1995. *Excavations by K. M. Kenyon in Jerusalem 1961–1967, IV. The Iron Age Cave Deposits on the South-East Hill and Isolated Burials and Cemeteries Elsewhere.* Oxford: British School of Archaeology in Jerusalem.

Exum, J. Cheryl, and David J. A Clines., eds. 1993. *The New Literary Criticism and the Hebrew Bible.* JSOTSup 143. Sheffield: Sheffield Academic Press.

Falconer, Steven E., and Stephen H. J. Savage. 1995. Heartlands and Hinterlands: Alternative Trajectories of Early Urbanization in Mesopotamia and the Southern Levant. *American Antiquity* 60:37–58.

Fantalkin, Alexander. 2004. The Final Destruction of Beth Shemesh and the Pax Assyriaca in the Judahite Shephelah: An Alternative View. *TA* 31:245–61.

Fantalkin, Alexander, and Israel Finkelstein. 2006. The Sheshonq I Campaign and the Eighth-Century BCE Earthquake: More on the Archaeology and History of the South in the Iron I–IIA. *TA* 33:18–42.

Faust, Avraham. 2000. The Rural Community in Ancient Israel during Iron Age II. *BASOR* 317:17–39.

———. 2001. Doorway Orientation, Settlement Planning and Cosmology in Ancient Israel during Iron Age II. *Oxford Journal of Archaeology* 202:129–55.

———. 2002a. Accessibility, Defence and Town Planning in Iron Age Israel. *TA* 29:297–317.

———. 2002b. Burnished Pottery and Gender Hierarchy in Iron Age Israelite Society. *Journal of Mediterranean Archaeology* 15:53–73.

———. 2003a. Abandonment, Urbanization, Resettlement and the Formation of the Israelite State. *NEA* 6:147–61.

———. 2003b. Judah in the Sixth Century B.C.E.: A Rural Perspective. *PEQ* 135:37–53.

———. 2003c. Residential Patterns in the Ancient Israelite City. *Levant* 35:123–38.

———. 2004a. Mortuary Practices, Society and Ideology: The Lack of Iron Age I Burials in the Highlands in Context. *IEJ* 54:174–90.

———. 2004b. Social and Cultural Changes in Judah during the Sixth Century BCE and Their Implications for our Understanding of the Nature of the Neo-Babylonian Period. *UF* 36:157–76.

———. 2005. The Settlement on Jerusalem's Western Hill and the City's Status in the Iron Age II Revisited. *ZDPV* 121:97–118.

———. 2006a. Farmsteads on the Foothills of Western Samaria: A Reexamination. Pages 477–504 in Maeir and de Miroschedji 2006.

———. 2006b. *Israel's Ethnogenesis: Settlement, Interaction, Expansion and Resistance*. London: Equinox.

———. 2006c. The Negev "Fortresses" in Context: Reexamining the "Fortresses" Phenomenon in Light of General Settlement Processes of the Eleventh–Tenth Centuries BCE. *JAOS* 126:135–60.

———. 2007a. Forum: Rural Settlements, State Formation, and "Bible and Archaeology." *NEA* 70:4–25.

———. 2007b. The Sharon and the Yarkon Basin in the Tenth Century BCE: Ecology, Settlement Patterns and Political Involvement. *IEJ* 57:65–82.

———. 2008. Settlement and Demography in Seventh Century Judah and the Extent and Intensity of Sennacherib's Campaign. *PEQ* 140:168–94.

———. 2010a. The Archaeology of the Israelite Cult: Questioning the Consensus. *BASOR* 360:23–35.

———. 2010b. Future Directions in the Study of Ethnicity in Ancient Israel. Pages 55–68 in Levy 2010a.

———. 2010c. The Large Stone Structure in the City of David: A Reexamination. *ZDPV* 126:116–30.

———. 2011a. The Excavations at Tel 'Eton (2006–2009): A Preliminary Report. *PEQ* 143:198–224.

———. 2011b. Household Economies in the Kingdoms of Israel and Judah. Pages 255–73 in Yasur-Landau, Ebeling, and Mazow 2011.

———. 2011c. The Interests of the Assyrian Empire in the West: Olive Oil Production as a Test Case. *JESHO* 54:62–86.

———. 2012a. *The Archaeology of Israelite Society in Iron Age II*. Winona Lake, IN: Eisenbrauns.

———. 2012b. *Judah in the Neo-Babylonian Period: The Archaeology of Desolation*. ABS 18. Atlanta: Society of Biblical Literature.

———. 2013a. From Regional Power to Peaceful Neighbour: Philistia in the Iron I–II Transition. *IEJ* 63:174–204.

———. 2013b. The Shephelah in the Iron Age: A New Look on the Settlement of Judah. *PEQ* 145:203–19.

Faust, Avraham, and Shlomo Bunimovitz. 2003. The Four Room House: Embodying Iron Age Israelite Society. *NEA* 66:22–31.

———. 2008. The Judahite Rock-Cut Tomb: Family Response at a Time of Change. *IEJ* 58:150–70.

Faust, Avraham, and Hayah Katz. 2016. Tel 'Eton Cemetery: An Introduction. *Hebrew Bible and Ancient Israel* 5:171–86.

Faust, Avraham, and Justin Lev-Tov. 2011. The Constitution of Philistine Identity: Ethnic Dynamics in Twelfth to Tenth Century Philistia. *Oxford Journal of Archaeology* 30:13–31.

Faust, Avraham, and Ze'ev Weiss. 2005. Judah, Philistia, and the Mediterranean World: Reconstructing the Economic System of the Seventh Century B.C.E. *BASOR* 338:71–92.

Finkelstein, Israel. 1984. The Iron Age "Fortresses" of the Negev Highlands: Sedentarization of the Nomads. *TA* 11:189–209.

———. 1986. *'Izbet Sartah: An Early Iron Age Site Near Rosh Ha'ayin, Israel.* BAR International Series 299. Oxford: British Archaeological Reports.

———. 1988. *The Archaeology of the Israelite Settlement.* Jerusalem: Israel Exploration Society.

———. 1990a. The Emergence of Early Israel: Anthropology, Environment and Archaeology. *JAOS* 110:677–86.

———.1990b. Excavations at Kh. ed-Dawwara: An Iron Age Site Northeast of Jerusalem. *TA* 17:163–208.

———. 1991. The Emergence of Israel in Canaan: Consensus, Mainstream and Dispute. *SJOT* 2:47–59.

———. 1992. Pastoralism in the Highlands of Canaan in the Third and Second Millennia B.C.E. Pages 133–42 in *Pastoralism in the Levant: Archaeological Materials in Anthropological Perspective.* Edited by O Ofer Bar-Yosef and Anatoly Khazanov. Madison, WI: Prehistory Press.

———. 1993. Samaria (Region): The Southern Samarian Hills Survey. *NEAEHL* 4:1313–14.

———. 1994a. The Archaeology of the Days of Manasseh. Pages 169–87 in Coogan, Exum, and Stager 1994.

———. 1994b. The Emergence of Israel: A Phase in the Cyclic History of Canaan in the Third and Second Millennia BCE. Pages 150–78 in Finkelstein and Na'aman 1994.

———. 1995a. The Date of the Settlement of the Philistines in Canaan. *TA* 22:219–39.

———. 1995b. The Great Transformation: The "Conquest" of the Highlands Frontiers and the Rise of the Territorial States. Pages 349–65 in Levy 1995.

———. 1995c. *Living on the Fringe: The Archaeology and History of the Negev, Sinai and Neighboring Regions in the Bronze and Iron Ages.* MMA 6. Sheffield: Sheffield Academic.

———. 1996a. The Archaeology of the United Monarchy: An Alternative View. *Levant* 28:177–87.

———. 1996b. Ethnicity and Origin of the Iron I Settlers in the Highlands of Canaan: Can the Real Israel Stand Up? *BA* 59:198–212.

———. 1997. Pots and People Revisited: Ethnic Boundaries in the Iron Age I. Pages 216–37 in Silberman and Small 1997.

———. 1998a Bible Archaeology or the Archaeology of Palestine in the Iron Age? A Rejoinder. *Levant* 30:167–74.

———. 1998b Philistine Chronology: High, Middle or Low? Pages 140–47 in Gitin, Mazar, and Stern 1998.

————. 1998c The Rise of Early Israel: Archaeology and Long-Term History. Pages 7–39 in *The Origin of Early Israel-Current Debate: Biblical, Historical and Archaeological Perspectives.* Edited by Shmuel Ahituv and Eliezer. D. Oren. Beersheba: Ben-Gurion Universityof the Negev Press.

————. 1999a Hazor and the North in the Iron Age: A Low Chronology Perspective. *BASOR* 314:55–70.

————. 1999b State Formation in Israel and Judah: A Contrast in Context, a Contrast in Trajectory. *NEA* 62:35–52.

————. 2000. Hazor XII–XI with an Addendum on Ben-Tor's Dating of Hazor X–VII. *TA* 27:231–47.

————. 2001. The Rise of Jerusalem and Judah: The Missing Link. *Levant* 33:105–15.

————. 2002. The Campaign of Shoshenq I to Palestine: A Guide to Tenth Century BCE Polity. *ZDPV* 118:109–35.

————. 2003a. City-States to States: Polity Dynamics in the Tenth–Ninth Centuries B.C.E. Pages 75–83 in Dever and Gitin 2003.

————. 2003b. The Rise of Jerusalem and Judah: The Missing Link. Pages 81–101 in Vaughn and Killebrew 2003.

————. 2004. Tel Rehov and Iron Age Chronology. *Levant* 36:181–88.

————. 2005a. (De)formation of the Israelite State: A Rejoinder on Methodology. *NEA* 68:202–8.

————. 2005b. High or Low: Megiddo and Tel Reḥov. Pages 302–9 in Levy and Higham 2005.

————. 2005c. Khirbet en-Nahas, Edom and Biblical History. *TA* 32:119–25.

————. 2005d. A Low Chronology Update: Archaeology, History and Bible. Pages 31–42 in Levy and Higham.

————. 2005e. The Settlement of Jerusalem's Western Hill and the City's Status in the Iron Age II Revisited. *ZDPV* 121:97–118.

————. 2006. The Last Labayu: King Saul and the Expansion of the First North Israelite Territorial Entity. Pages 171–87 in Gitin, Wright, and Dessel 2006.

————. 2010a. A Great United Monarchy? Archaeological and Historical Perspectives. Pages 3–28 in Kratz and Spieckermann 2010.

————. 2010b. Kadesh Barnea: A Reevaluation of Its Achaeology and History. *TA* 37:111–25.

————. 2011a. The Iron Age Chronology Debate: Is the Gap Narrowing? *NEA* 74:50–54.

———. 2011b. The "Large Stone Structure" in Jerusalem: Reality versus Yearning. *ZDPV* 127:1–10.

———. 2011c. Jerusalem in the Iron Age: Archaeology and Text: Reality and Myth. Pages 109–201 in Galor and Avni.

———. 2011d. Tall al-Umayri in the Iron Age I: Facts and Fiction, with an Appendix on the History of the Collared Rim Pithoi. Pages 113–28 in Finkelstein and Na'aman 2011.

———. 2013. *The Forgotten Kingdom: The Archaeology and History of Northern Israel.* ANEM 5. Atlanta: Society of Biblical Literature.

Finkelstein, Israel, Shlomo Bunimovitz, and Zvi Lederman. 1993. *Shiloh: The Archaeology of a Biblical Site.* Monograph Series of the Institute of Archaeology. Tel Aviv: Tel Aviv University.

Finkelstein, Israel, and Alexander Fantalkin. 2012. Khirbet Qeiyafa: An Unsensational Archaeologicaal and Historical Investigation. *TA* 39:38–63.

Finkelstein, Israel, Zvi Lederman, and Shlomo Bunimovitz. 1997. *Highlands of Many Cultures: The Southern Samaria Survey; The Sites.* Tel Aviv University Monographs in Archaeology 14. Tel Aviv: Tel Aviv University.

Finkelstein, Israel, and Oded Lipschits. 2011. The Genesis of Moab: A Proposal. *Levant* 43:139–52.

Finkelstein, Israel, and Yitzhak Magen, eds. 1993. *Archaeological Survey of the Hill Country of Benjamin.* Jerusalem: Israel Antiquities Authority.

Finkelstein, Israel, and Amihai Mazar. 2007. *The Quest for the Historical Israel: Debating Archaeology and the History of Early Israel.* Edited by Brian B. Schmidt. ABS 17. Atlanta: Society of Biblical Literature.

Finkelstein, Israel, and Nadav Na'aman, eds. 1994. *From Nomadism to Monarchy: Archaeological and Historical Aspects of Early Israel.* Washington, DC: Biblical Archaeology Society.

———. 2004. The Judahite Shephelah in the Late Eighth and Early Seventh Centuries BCE. *TA* 31:60–79.

———, eds. 2011. *The Fire Signals of Lachish: Studies in the Archaeology and History of Israel in the Late Bronze Age, Iron Age, and Persian Period in Honor of David Ussishkin.* Winona Lake, IN: Eisenbrauns.

Finkelstein, Israel, and Eli Piasetzky. 2003a. Comment on ^{14}C Dates from Tel Rehov: Iron Age Chronology, Pharaohs, and Hebrew Kings. *Science* 302:586b.

———. 2003b. Recent Radiocarbon Results and King Solomon. *Antiquity* 77/298:771–79.

———. 2003c. Wrong and Right; High and Low: [14]C Dates from Tel Reḥov and Iron Age Chronology. *TA* 30:283–95.

———. 2006a. [14]C and the Iron Age Chronology Debate: Rehov, Khirbet en-Nahas, Dan, and Megiddo. *Radiocarbon* 48:373–86.

———. 2006b. The Iron I–IIA in the Highlands and Beyond: [14]C Anchors, Pottery Phases and the Shoshenq I Campaign. *Levant* 38:45–61.

———. 2008. The Date of Kuntillet ʿAjrud: The [14]C Perspective. *TA* 35:175–85.

———. 2010a. Khirbet Qeiyafa: Absolute Chronology. *TA* 37:84–88.

———. 2010b. Radiocarbon Dating in the Iron Age in the Levant: A Bayesian Model for Six Ceramic Phases and Six Transitions. *Antiquity* 84:374–85.

———. 2011a. The Iron Age Chronology Debate: Is the Gap Narrowing? *NEA* 74:50–54.

———. 2011b. Stages in the Territorial Expansion of the Northern Kingdom. *VT* 61:227–42.

Finkelstein, Israel, Benjamin Sass, and Lily Singer-Avitz. 2008. Writing in Iron IIA Philistia in the Light of the Tel Zayit/Zeta Abcedary. *ZDPV* 124:1–14.

Finkelstein, Israel, and Neil Asher Silberman. 2001. *The Bible Unearthed: Archaeology's New Vision of Ancient Israel and the Origin of Its Sacred Texts*. New York: Free Press.

Finkelstein, Israel, and Lily Singer-Avitz. 2009. Reevaluating Bethel. *ZDPV* 125:33–48.

Finkelstein, Israel, David Ussishkin, and Eric H. Cline, eds. 2013. *Megiddo V: The 2004-2008 Seasons*. 3 vols. Winona Lake, IN: Eisenbrauns.

Finkelstein, Israel, David Ussishkin, and Baruch Halpern, eds. 2000. *Megiddo III: The 1992–1996 Seasons*. Tel Aviv: Emery and Claire Yass Publications in Archaeology, Institute of Archaeology, Tel Aviv University.

———, eds. 2006. *Megiddo IV. The 1992–2002 Seasons*. Tel Aviv: Tel Aviv University Press.

———. 2008. Megiddo. Pages 1944–50 in Stern 2008.

Finkelstein, Israel, et al. 2007. Has King David's Palace in Jerusalem Been Found? *TA* 34:142–64.

Fischer, Peter M., and Teresa Burge. 2013. Cultural Influences of the Sea Peoples in Transjordan: The Early Iron Age at Tell Abu Haraz. *ZDPV* 129:132–70.

Flannery, Kent V., and Joyce Marcus. 2011. A New World Perspective on the "Death" of Archaeological Theory. Pages 23–30 in Bintliff and Pearce 2011.

Foucault, Michel. 1980. *Power/Knowledge: Selected Interviews and Other Writings 1972–1977*. Edited by Colin Gordon. New York: Pantheon.

———. 1982. *The Archaeology of Knowledge*. Translated by A. M. Sheridan Smith. New York: Pantheon.

Fox, R. G. 1977 *Urban Anthropology: Cities in Their Cultural Settings*. Englewood Cliffs, NJ: Prentice-Hall.

Frankel, Raphael. 1994. Upper Galilee in the Late Bronze-Iron I Transition. Pages 18–35 in Finkelstein and Na'aman 1994.

Franken, Henk J., and Gloria London. 1995. Why Painted Pottery Disappeared at the End of the Second Millennium BCE. *BA* 58:214–22.

Franken, Henk J., and Margreet L. Steiner. 1990. *Excavations in Jerusalem 1961–1967: II*. Monographs in Archaeology 2. London: Oxford University Press.

Franklin, Norma. 2003. The Tombs of the Kings of Israel: Two Recently Identified Ninth-Century Tombs from Omride Samaria. *ZDPV* 119:1–11.

———. 2004. Metrological Investigations at Ninth and Eighth c. Samaria and Megiddo. *Journal of Mediterranean Archaeology and Archaeometry* 4:82–92.

———. 2011. From Megiddo to Tamassos and Back: Putting the "Proto-Ionic Capital" in Its Place. Pages 129–40 in Finkelstein and Na'aman 2011.

Frei, Hans. 1974. *The Eclipse of Biblical Narrative: A Study in Eighteenth and Nineteenth Century Hermeneutics*. New Haven: Yale University Press.

Freedman, David Noel, ed. 1992. *Anchor Bible Dictionary*. 6 vols. New York: Doubleday.

Frerichs, Ernest S., and Leonard H. Lesco, eds. 1997. *Exodus: The Egyptian Evidence*. Winona Lake, IN: Eisenbrauns

French, Elizabeth. 2013. Cilicia. Pages 479–83 in Killebrew and Lehmann 2013a.

Frese, Daniel A., and, Thomas E. Levy. 2010. The Four Pillars of the Iron Age Low Chronology. Pages 187–202 in Levy 2010a.

Frick, Frank S. 1985. *The Formation of the State in Ancient Israel: A Survey of Models and Theories*. SWBA 4. Sheffield: Almond Press.

Friedman, Richard E. 1987. *Who Wrote the Bible?* Englewood Cliffs, NJ: Prentice Hall.

———. 2010. A Bible Scholar in the City of David. Pages 304–9 in Levy 2010a.

Fritz, Volkmar. 1981a. The Israelite "Conquest" in the Light of Recent Excavations at Khirbet el Meshash. *BASOR* 241:61–73.

———. 1981b. The List of Rehoboam's Fortresses in 2 Chr. 11:5–12: A Document from the Time of Josiah. *ErIsr* 15:46*–53*.

———. 1987. Conquest or Settlement? The Early Iron Age in Palestine. *BA* 50:84–100.

———. 1995. *The City in Ancient Israel.* Sheffield: Sheffield Academic.

Fritz, Volkmar, and Philip R. Davies, eds. 1996. *The Origins of the Ancient Israelite States.* JSOTSup 228. Sheffield: Sheffield Academic Press.

Fritz, Volkmar, and Aharon Kempinski. 1983. *Ergebnisse der Ausgrabungen auf der Hirbet el-mšaš (Tel Masos) 1972–1975.* Wiesbaden: Harrassowitz.

Gaddis, John Lewis. 2002. *The Landscape of History: How Historians Map the Past.* Oxford: Oxford University Press.

Gadot, Yuval. 2003 Continuity and Change: Cultural Processes in the Late Bronze and Early Iron Ages in Israel's Central Coastal Plain. PhD diss. Tel Aviv University.

———. 2006. Aphek in the Sharon and the Northern Philistine Frontier. *BASOR* 341:21–36.

———. 2008. Continuity and Change in the Late Bronze to Iron Age Transition in Israel's Coastal Plain: A Long Term Perspective. Pages 55–73 in *Bene Israel: Studies in the Archaeology of Israel and the Levant during the Bronze and Iron Ages in Honour of Israel Finkelstein.* Edited by Alexander Fantalkin and Assaf Yasur-Landau. CHANE 31. Leiden: Brill.

Gadot, Yuval, and Assaf Yasur-Landau. 2006. Beyond Finds: Reconstructing Life in the Courtyard Building of Level K-4. Pages 583–600 in Finkelstein, Ussishkin, and Halpern 2006.

Gadot, Yuval, and Esther Yadin. 2009. *Aphek-Antipatris II: The Remains on the Acropolis; The Moshe Kochavi and Pirhiya Beck Excavations.* Tel Aviv: Institute of Archaeology, Tel Aviv University.

Gal, Zvi. 1988–1989 The Lower Galilee in the Iron Age II: Analysis of Survey Material and Its Historical Interpretation. *TA* 15:56–64.

———. 1992a *Lower Galilee during the Iron Age.* ASORDS 9. Winona Lake, IN: Eisenbrauns.

———. 1992b Hurvat Rosh Zayit and the Early Phoenician Pottery. *Levant* 24:173–86.

———. 2003. The Iron Age "Low Chronology" in Light of the Excavations at Hurvat Rosh Zayit. *IEJ* 53:147–50.

Gal, Zvi, Yardenna Alexandre, and Uri Baruch. 2000. *Ḥorbat Rosh Zayit: An Iron Age Storage Fort and Village.* IAA Reports 8. Jerusalem: Israel Antiquities Authority.

Gal, Zvi, Dina Shalem, and Moshe Hartal. 2007. An Iron Age Site at Karmiel, Lower Galilee. Pages 119–34 in Crawford 2007.

Galor, Katharina, and Gideon Avni, eds. 2011. Unearthing Jerusalem: 150 Years of Archaeological Research in the Holy City. Winona Lake, IN: Eisenbrauns.

Garbini, Giovanni. 1988. *History and Ideology in Ancient Israel.* New York: Crossroad.

Garfinkel, Yosef, and Saar Ganor. 2009. *Khirbet Qeiyafa*, Vol. 1: *Excavation Report 2007–2008.* Jerusalem: Institute of Archaeology, Hebrew University of Jerusalem.

Garfinkel, Yosef, Saar Ganor, Michael G. Hasel. 2014. *Khirbet Qeiyafa*, Vol. 2: *Excavation Report 2009–2013: Stratigraphy and Architecture (Areas B, C, D, E).* Jerusalem: Israel Exploration Society.

Garfinkel, Yosef, Mitka R. Golub, Haggai Misgav, and Saar Ganor. 2015. The ʾIšbaʿal Inscription from Khirbet Qeiyafa. *BASOR* 373:217–33.

Garfinkel, Yosef, and Hoo-Goo Kang. 2011. The Relative and Absolute Chronology of Khirbet Qeiyafa: Very Late Iron Age I or Very Late Iron Age IIA? *IEJ* 61:171–83.

Garfinkel, Yosef, and Katharina Streit. 2014. Radiocarbon Dating of the Iron Age City. Pages 367–74 in Garfinkel, Ganor, and Hasel 2014.

Garfinkel, Yosef, Katharina Streit, Saar Ganor, and Paula J. Reimer. King David's City at Khirbet Qeiyafa: Results of the Second Radiocarbon Dating Project. *Radiocarbon* 57:881–90.

Geraty, Lawrence T. 1983. Heshbon: The First Casualty in the Israelite Quest for the Kingdom of God. Pages 239–250 in *The Quest for the Kingdom of God: Studies in Honor of George E. Mendenhall.* Edited by H. B. Huffinon, F. A. Spina, and A. R. W. Green. Winona Lake, IN: Eisenbrauns.

Geus, Cornelius, H. J. de, 2003. *Towns in Ancient Israel and in the Southern Levant.* Palaestina Antigua 10. Leuven: Peeters.

Geva, Hillel, ed. 2000. *Jewish Quarter Excavations in the Old City of Jerusalem: Conducted by Nahman Avigad, 1969–1982*, Vol. 1: *Architecture and Stratigraphy: Areas A, W and X-2.* Jerusalem: Israel Exploration Society.

———. 2003. Western Jerusalem at the End of the First Temple Period in Light of the Excavations in the Jewish Quarter. Pages 183–208 in Vaughn and Killebrew 2003.

———. 2006. The Settlement on the Southwestern Hill of Jerusalem at the End of the Iron Age: A Reconstruction Based on the Archeological Evidence. *ZDPV* 122:140–50.

Geva, Shulamit. 1989. *Hazor, Israel: An Urban Community of the Eighth Century B.C.E.* BAR International Series 543. Oxford: British Archaeological Reports.

Gibson, Shimon. 2001. Agricultural Terraces and Settlement Expansion in the Highlands of Early Iron Age Palestine: Is There Any Correlation between the Two? Pages 113–46 in A. Mazar 2001b.

Giddens, Anthony. 1979. *Central Problems in Social Theory: Action, Structure and Contradiction in Social Analysis.* London: Macmillan.

———. 1981. *Power, Poverty and the State.* Vol. 1 of *A Contemporary Critique of Historical Materialism.* London: Macmillan.

———. 1984. *The Constitution of Society: Outline of the Theory of Structuration.* Berkeley: University of California Press.

Gilboa, Ayelet. 2001. Southern Phoenicia in Iron Age I–IIA in the Light of the Tel Dor Excavations: The Evidence of Pottery. PhD diss. Hebrew University, Jerusalem.

———. 2005. Sea Peoples and Phoenicians along the Southern Phoenician Coast-A Reconciliation: An Interpretation of Sikila (SKL) Material Culture. *BASOR* 337:47–78.

———. 2012. Cypriot Barrel Juglets at Khirbet Qeiyafa and Other Sites in the Levant: Cultural Aspects and Chronological Implications. *TA* 39:133–49.

Gilboa, Ayelet, and Ilan Sharon. 2001. Early Iron Age Radiometric Dates from Tel Dan: Preliminary Implications for Phoenicia and Beyond. *Radiocarbon* 43:1343–51.

———. 2003. An Archaeological Contribution to the Early Iron Age Chronological Debate: Alternative Chronologies for Phoenicia and Their Effects on the Levant, Cyprus, and Greece. *BASOR* 332:7–80.

———. 2008. Between the Carmel and the Sea: Tel Dor's Iron Age Reconsidered. *NEA* 71:146–70.

Gilboa, Ayelet, Ilan Sharon, and Elizabeth Bloch-Smith. 2015. Capital of Solomon's Fourth District? Israelite Dor. *Levant* 47:52–74.

Gilboa, Ayelet, and Paula Waiman-Barak. 2014. Cypriot Ceramic Imports at Khirbet Qeiyafa: Provenience, Chronology, and Significance. Pages 391–402 in *Excavation Report 2009–2013: Stratigraphy and Architecture (Areas B, C, D, F)*. Vol. 2 of *Khirbet Qeiyafa*. By Yosef Garfinkel, Saar Ganor, and Michael G. Hasel. Edited by Martin G. Klingbeil. Jerusalem: Institute of Archaeology, Southern Adventist University; Israel Exploration Society; Hebrew University of Jerusalem.

Gilboa, Ayelet, et al. 2009. Notes on Iron II A ^{14}C Dates from Tell el-Qudeirat (Kadesh Barnea). *TA* 36:82–94.

Gill, Dan. 1994. How They Met: Geology Solves a Long-Standing Mystery of Hezekiah's Tunnelers. *BAR* 20.4:20–33, 64.

Gitin, Seymour. 1990a. The Effects of Urbanization on a Philistine City-State: Tel Miqne-Ekron in the Iron Age II Period." Pages 277–84 in *The Proceedings of the Tenth World Congress of Jewish Studies 1989*. Edited by D. Assaf. Jerusalem: World Union of Jewish Studies.

———. 1990b. *Gezer III: A Ceramic Typology of the Late Iron II, Persian and Hellenistic Periods at Tell Gezer*. ANGSBA 3. Jerusalem: Hebrew Union College.

———. 1996. Tel Miqne-Ekron in the Seventh Century B.C.: City Plan Development and the Oil Industry. Pages 219–42 in *Olive Oil in Antiquity: Israel and Neighbouring Countries from the Neolithic to the Early Arad Period*. Edited by David Eitam and Michael Heltzer. HANES 7. Padova: Sargon.

———. 1998. Philistia in Transition: The Tenth Century B.C.E. and Beyond. Pages 162–83 in Gitin, Mazar, and Stern 1998.

———. 2003. Neo-Assyrian and Egyptian Hegemony over Ekron in the Seventh Century B.C.E.: A Response to Lawrence E. Stager. *ErIsr* 27:55*–61*.

———. 2006. The *lmlk* Jar-Form Redefined: A New Class of Iron Age II Oval-Shaped Storage Jar. Pages 505–24 in Maeir and de Miroschedji 2006.

———. 2010. Philistines in the Books of Kings. Pages 301–64 in Halpern and Lemaire 2010.

———. 2012. Temple Complex 650 at Ekron: The Impact of Multi-cultural Influences on Philistine Cult in the Late Iron Age. Pages 223–56 in *Temple Building and Temple Cult: Architecture and Cultic Paraphernalia of Temples in the Levant (2.–1. Mill. B.C.E.)*. Edited by Jens Kamiah. Wiesbaden: Harrassowitz.

———, ed. 2015. *The Ancient Pottery of Israel and Its Neighbors from the Iron Age through the Hellenistic Period*. 2 vols. Jerusalem: Israel Exploration Society.

Gitin, Seymour, and Amir Golani. 2001. The Tel Miqne-Ekron Silver Hoards: The Assyrian and Phoenician Connections. Pages 27–48 in Hacksilber to Coinage: New Insights into the Monetary History of the Near East and Greece. Edited by Miriam S. Balmuth. Numismatic Studies 24. New York: American Numismatic Society.

———. 2004. A Silver-Based Monetary Economy in the Seventh Century BCE: A Response to Raz Kletter. *Levant* 36:203–5.

Gitin, Seymour, Amihai Mazar, and Ephraim Stern, eds. 1998. *Mediterranean Peoples in Transition: Thirteenth to Early Tenth Centuries BCE*. Jerusalem: Israel Exploration Society.

Gitin, Seymour, J. Edward Wright, and J. P. Dessel, eds. 2006. *Confronting the Past: Archaeological and Historical Essays on Ancient Israel in Honor of William G. Devers*. Winona Lake, IN: Eisenbrauns.

Giveon, Raphel. 1971. *Les Bédouins Shosou des documents égyptiens*. Leiden: Brill.

Golani, Amir, and Ora Yogev. 1996. The 1980 Excavations at Tel Sasa. *ʿAtiqot* 28:41–58.

Gonen, Rivka. 1992. *Burial Patterns and Cultural Diversity in Late Bronze Age Canaan*. Winona Lake, IN: Eisenbrauns.

Gottwald, Norman K. 1979. *The Tribes of Yahweh: A Sociology of the Religion of Liberated Israel, 1250–1050 BCE*. Maryknoll, NY: Orbis.

———. 1993. Method and Hypothesis in Reconstructing the Social History of Early Israel. *ErIsr* 24:77*–82*.

Grabbe, Lester L. 1997a. Are Historians of Ancient Palestine Fellow Creatures—Or Different Animals? Pages 19–36 in Grabbe 1997b.

———, ed. 1997b. *Can a 'History of Israel' Be Written?* JSOTSup 245. Sheffield: Sheffield Academic.

———, ed. 1998. *Leading Captivity Captive: "The Exile" as History and Ideology*. JSOTSup 278; ESHM 2. Sheffield: Sheffield Academic.

———, ed. 2001a. *Did Moses Speak Attic? Jewish Historiography and Scripture in the Hellenistic Period*. JSOTSup 317; ESHM 3. Sheffield: Sheffield Academic.

———. 2001b. Introduction and Overview. Pages 15–33 in Grabbe and Haak 2001.

———. 2003a. Introduction. Pages 2–43 in Grabbe 2003b.

———, ed. 2003b. *"Like a Bird in a Cage": The Invasion of Sennacherib in 701 BCE.* JSOTSup 363; ESHM 4. Sheffield: Sheffield Academic.

———. 2003b. Reflections on the Discussion. Pages 308–23 in Grabbe 2003b.

———, ed. 2005a. *Good Kings and Bad Kings.* LHBOTS 393; ESHM 5. London: T&T Clark.

———. 2005b. The Kingdom of Judah from Sennacherib's Invasion to the Fall of Jerusalem: If We Had Only the Bible…. Pages 78–122 in Grabbe 2005a.

———, ed. 2007a. *Ahab Agonistes: The Rise and Fall of the Omride Dynasty.* LHBOTS 421; ESHM 6. London: T&T Clark.

———. 2007b. *Ancient Israel: What Do We Know and How Do We Know It?* London: T&T Clark.

———. 2007c. What Historians Would Like to Know…. *NEA* 70:13–15.

———, ed. 2008a. *Israel in Transition 1: From Late Bronze II to Iron IIa (c. 1250–850 B.C.E.); The Archaeology.* Edited by Lester L. Grabbe. LHBOTS 491; ESHM 7. London: T&T Clark.

———. 2008b. Reflections on the Discussion. Pages 219–32 in Grabbe 2008a.

———, ed. 2010. *Israel in Transition 2: From Late Bronze II to Iron IIa (c. 1250–850 B.C.E.); The Texts.* Edited by Lester L. Grabbe. LHBOTS 521; ESHM 8. London: T&T Clark

———. 2011. *Enquire of the Former Age: Ancient Historiography and Writing the History of Israel.* LHBOTS 554; ESHM 9. London: T&T Clark.

Grabbe, Lester L., and Robert D. Haak, eds. 2001. *'Every City Shall Be Forsaken': Urbanism and Prophecy in Ancient Israel and the Near East.* JSOTSup 330. Sheffield: Sheffield Academic.

Greenfield, Patricia M. 2000. What Psychology Can Do for Anthropology, or Why Anthropology Took Postmodemism on the Chin. *American Anthropologist* 102:564–76.

Greer, Jonathan S. 2013. *Dinner at Dan: Biblical and Archaeological Evidence for Sacred Feasts at Iron Age II Tel Dan and Their Significance.* CHANE 66. Leiden: Brill.

Gress, David. 1998. *From Plato to NATO: The Idea of the West and Its Opponents.* New York: Free Press.

Grossberg. Asher. 2013. A New Perspective on the Southern Part of Channel II in the City of David. *IEJ* 63:205–18.

Hadley, Judith M. 2000. *The Cult of Asherah in Ancient Israel and Judah: Evidence for a Hebrew Goddess.* University of Cambridge Oriental Publications 57. Cambridge: Cambridge University Press.

Haiman, Mordechiai. 1994. The Iron Age II Sites of the Western Negev Highlands. *IEJ* 44:36–61.

Halpern, Baruch. 1988. *The First Historians: The Hebrew Bible and History.* San Francisco: Harper & Row.

———. 1991. Jerusalem and the Lineages in the Seventh Century BCE: Kinship and the Rise of Individual Moral Liability. Pages 11–107 in *Law and Ideology in Monarchic Israel.* Edited by Baruch Halpern and Deborah W. Hobson. JSOTSup 124. Sheffield: JSOT.

———. 1993. The Exodus and the Israelite Historians. *ErIsr* 24:89*–96*.

———. 2001. *David's Secret Demons: Messiah, Murderer, Traitor, King.* Grand Rapids: Eerdmans.

Halpern, Baruch, and André Lemaire, eds. 2010. *The Books of Kings: Sources, Composition, Historiography and Reception.* VTSup 129. Leiden: Brill. Repr., Atlanta: SBL Press, 2017.

Hamilton, Robert W. 1935. Excavations at Tell Abu Hawam. *Quarterly of the Department of Antiquities in Palestine* 4:1–69.

Handy, Lowell K., ed. 1997. *The Age of Solomon: Scholarship at the Turn of the Millennium.* SHANE 11. Leiden: Brill.

Hardin, James W. 2010. *Lahav II: Households and the Use of Domestic Space at Iron II Tell Halif; An Archaeology of Destruction.* Winona Lake, IN: Eisenbrauns.

Harrison, Timothy P. 2009. 'The Land of Medeba' and Early Iron Age Madaba. Pages 27–45 in Bienkowski 2009a.

Harrison, Timothy P., and Barlow, Celeste. 2005. Mesha, the Mishor, and the Chronology of Iron Age Madaba. Pages 179–90 in Levy and Higham 2005.

Hasel, Michael G. 1994. Israel in the Merneptah Stela. *BASOR* 296:45–61.

———. 1998. *Domination and Resistance: Egyptian Military Activity in the Southern Levant, ca. 1300–1185 B.C.* Leiden: Brill.

———. 2004. The Structure of the Final Hymnic-Poetic Unit on the Merneptah Stele. *ZAW* 116:75–81.

Hauser, Alan J. 1978. Israel's Conquest of Palestine: A Peasants' Rebellion? *JSOT* 7:2–19.

Hawkins, Ralph K. 2012. *The Iron Age I Structure on Mt. Ebal: Excavation and Interpretation.* Winona Lake: IN: Eisenbrauns.

Heinz, Marlies, and Sabina Kulemann-Ossen. 2014. The Northern Levant (Lebanon) during the Late Bronze Age. Pages 524–40 in Steiner and Killbebrew 2014.

Hellwing, Shlomo, and Yitzhak Adjeman. 1986. Animal Bones. Pages 236–47 in Finkelstein 1986.

Hendel, Ronald S. 1997. Aniconism and Anthropomorphism in Ancient Israel. Pages 205–28 in van der Toorn 1997.

———. 2001. The Exodus in Biblical Memory. *JBL* 120:601–22.

———. 2006. The Archaeology of Memory: King Solomon, Chronology, and Biblical Representation. Pages 219–30 in Gitin, Wright, and Dessel 2006.

———. 2010. Culture, Memory, and History: Reflections on Method in Biblical Studies. Pages 250–61 in Levy 2010a.

Herr, Larry G. 1988. Tripartite Pillared Buildings and the Market Place in Iron Age Palestine. *BASOR* 272:47–67.

———. 1997. Archaeological Sources for the History of Palestine: The Iron Age II Period; Emerging Nations. *BA* 60:114–51, 154–83.

———. 1999. Tall al-Umayri and the Reubenite Hypothesis. *ErIsr* 26:64*–77*.

———. 2006. An Early Iron Age I House with a Cultic Corner at Tall al-'Umayri, Jordan. Pages 61–73 in Gitin, Wright, and Dessel 2006.

———. 2007. The Late Iron Age I Ceramic Assemblage from Tall al-'Umayri, Jordan. Pages 135–45 in Crawford 2007.

———. 2009. The House of the Father at Iron I Tall al-'Umayri, Jordan. Pages 191–97 in Schloen 2009.

———. 2012. Jordan in the Iron I and IIA Periods. Pages 207–20 in *The Ancient Near East in the Twelfth–Tenth Centuries BCE: Culture and History*. Edited by Gershon Galil et al. Münster: Ugarit-Verlag.

———. 2014. The Southern Levant (Transjordan) during the Iron Age I Period. Pages 649–59 in Steiner and Killebrew 2014.

Herr, Larry G., and Douglas R. Clark. 2001. Excavating the Tribe of Reuben. *BAR* 27.2:36–47, 64–66.

———. 2009. From the Stone Age to the Middle Ages in Jordan: Digging Up Tall al-'Umayri. *NEA* 72:68–97.

Herr, Larry G., and Muhammad Najjar. 2001. The Iron Age. Pages 323–45 in MacDonald, Adams, and Bienkowski 2001.

———. 2008. The Iron Age. Pages 311–34 in *Jordan: An Archaeological Reader*. Edited by Russel B. Adams. London: Equinox.

Herr, Larry, G., et al. 2000. *Madaba Plains Project: The 1992 Season at Tall al-'Umayri and Subsequent Studies*. MPP 4. Berrien Springs, MI: Andrews University Press.

———. 2002. *Madeba Plans Project 5: The 1994 Season at Tall al-ʿUmayri and Subsequent Studies*. Berrien Springs, MI: Andrews University Press.

Herrmann, Siegfried. 1975. *A History of Israel in Old Testament Times*. Philadelphia: Fortress.

Herzog, Zeʾev. 1983. Enclosed Settlements in the Negeb and the Wilderness of Beer-sheba. *BASOR* 250:41–49.

———. 1984. *Beer-Sheba, II: The Early Iron Age Settlements*. Tel Aviv: Tel Aviv University Press.

———. 1992. Administrative Structures in the Iron Age. Pages 68–81 in *The Architecture of Ancient Israel from the Prehistoric to the Persian Periods*. Edited by Aharon Kempinski and Ronny Reich. Jerusalem: Israel Exploration Society.

———. 1993. Gerisa, Tell. *NEAEHL* 2:480–84.

———. 1994. The Beer-Sheba Valley: From Nomadism to Monarchy. Pages 122–49 in Finkelstein and Naʾaman 1994.

———. 1997. *Archaeology of the City: Urban Planning in Ancient Israel and Its Social Implications*. Tel Aviv: Emery and Claire Yass Archaeology University Press.

———. 2001. The Date of the Temple at Arad: Reassessment of the Stratigraphy and the Implications for the History of Religion in Judah. Pages 156–78 in A. Mazar 2001b.

———. 2002. The Fortress Mound at Tel Arad: An Interim Report. *TA* 29:3–109.

———. 2007. State Formation and the Iron Age I–Iron Age IIA Transition: Remarks on the Faust-Finkelstein Debate. *NEA* 70:20–21.

Herzog, Zeev. 2008. Beersheba. Tel Beersheba. Pages 1675–78 in Stern 2008.

Herzog, Zeʾev, and Ofer Bar-Yosef. 2002. Different Views on Ethnicity in the Archaeology of the Negev. Pages 151–81 in *Aharon Kempinski Memorial Volume: Studies in Archaeology and Related Discipines*. Edited by Eliezer D. Oren and Shmuel Ahituv. Beer-Sheva: Ben Gurion University of the Negev Press.

Herzog, Zeʾev, Anson F. Rainey, and Shmuel Moshkovitz. 1977. The Stratigraphy at Beer-Sheba and the Location of the Sanctuary. *BASOR* 225:49–58.

Herzog, Zeʾev, and Lily Singer-Avitz. 2004. Redefining the Center: The Emergence of State in Judah. *TA* 31:209–44.

———. 2006. Sub-dividing the Iron Age IIA in Northern Israel: A Suggested Solution to the Chronological Debate. *TA* 33:163–95.

Herzog, Ze'ev, et al. 1984. The Israelite Fortress at Arad. *BASOR* 254:1–34.

Hess, Richard S. 2007. *Israelite Religions: An Archaeological and Biblical Survey.* Grand Rapids: Baker Academic.

Hesse, Brian. 1986. Animal Use at Tel Miqne-Ekron in the Bronze and Iron Age. *BASOR* 264:195–225.

———. 1990. Pig Lovers and Pig Haters: Patterns of Palestinian Pork Production. *Journal of Ethnobiology* 10:195–225.

———. 1995. Animal Husbandry and Human Diet in the Ancient Near East. Pages 203–22 in vol. 1 of Sasson 2006.

Hesse, Brian, and Paula Wapnish. 1997. Can Pig Remains Be Used for Ethnic Diagnosis in the Ancient Near East? Pages 238–70 in Silberman and Small 1997.

Hiebert, Theodore. 2009. Israel's Ancestors Were Not Nomads. Pages 199–205 in Schloen 2009.

Higginbotham, Carolyn R. 2000. *Egyptianization and Elite Emulation in Ramesside Palestine: Governance and Accomodation on the Imperial Periphery.* CHANE 2. Leiden: Brill.

Hjelm, Ingrid, and Thompson, T. L., eds. 2016a. *Biblical Interpretation beyond Interpretation.* Changing Perspectives 7. London: Routledge.

———, eds. 2016b. *History, Archaeology and the Bible Forty Years after "Historicity."* Changing Perspectives 6. London: Routledge.

Hobsbawm, Eric. 1993. The New Threat to History. *New York Review of Books,* 16 December, 40.21:62–64.

Hodder, Ian. 1986. *Reading the Past: Current Approaches to Interpretation in Archaeology.* Cambridge: Cambridge University Press.

———, ed. 1987. *The Archaeology of Contextual Meanings.* Cambridge: Cambridge University Press.

———. 1999. *The Archaeological Process: An Introduction.* Oxford: Blackwell.

———. 2006. Thing Theory: Toward an Integrated Archaeological Perspective. *Scottish Archaeological Journal* 28:v–vi.

———, ed. 2012. *Archaeological Theory Today.* 2nd ed. Cambridge: Polity.

Hodder, Ian, and Scott Hutson. 2003. *Reading the Past: Current Approaches to Interpretation in Archaeology.* 3rd ed. Cambridge: Cambridge University Press.

Hodder, Ian, et al., eds. 1995. *Interpreting Archaeology: Finding Meaning in the Past.* London: Routledge.

Hoffmeier, James K. 1997. *Israel in Egypt: The Evidence for the Authenticity of the Exodus Tradition.* New York: Oxford University Press.

———. 2005. *Ancient Israel in Sinai: The Evidence for the Authenticity of the Wilderness Tradition.* New York: Oxford University Press.

———. 2007. What Is the Biblical Date for the Exodus? A Response to Bryant Wood *JETS* 50:225–47.

Hoffmeier, James K., and M. Abd el-Maksoud. 2003. A New Military Site on "The Ways of Horus": Tell el-Borg 1999–2001; A Preliminary Report. *JEA* 89:1–27.

Hoffmeier, James K., and Stephen O. Moshier. 2006. New Paleo-Environmental Evidence from North Sinai to Complement Manfred Bietak's Map of the Eastern Delta and Some Historical Implications. Pages 16–17 in vol. 2 of *Timelines: Studies in Honour of Manfred Bietak.* Edited by Ernst Czerny et al. Leuven: Peeters.

Hole, Frank, and Robert Heizer. 1977. *Prehistoric Archaeology: A Brief Introduction.* New York: Holt, Rinehart and Winston.

Holladay, John S., Jr. 1986. The Stables of Ancient Israel: Functional Determinants of Stable Construction and the Interpretation of Pillared Building Remains of the Palestinian Iron Age. Pages 103–65 in *The Archaeology of Jordan and Other Studies.* Edited by Lawrence T. Geraty and Larry G. Herr. Berrien Springs, MI: Andrews University Press.

———. 1987. Religion in Israel and Judah under the Monarchy: An Explicitly Archaeological Approach. Pages 249–99 in Miller, Hanson, and McBride 1987.

———. 1990. Red Slip, Burnish, and the Solomonic Gateway at Gezer. *BASOR* 277–78:23–70.

———. 1992. House, Israelite. *ABD* 3:308–18.

———. 1995. The Kingdoms of Israel and Judah: Political and Economic Centralization in the Iron Age IIA–B (ca. 1000–750 B.C.E.) Pages 368–98 in Levy 1995.

———. 2009a. "Home Economics 1407" and the Israelite Family and Their Neighbors: An Anthropological/Archaeological Exploration. Pages 61–88 in *The Family in Life and Death: The Family in Ancient Israel; Sociological and Archaeological Perspectives.* Edited by Patricia Duchter-Walls. LHBOTS 504. New York: T&T Clark.

———. 2009b. How Much Is That in…? Monetization, Royal States, and Empires. Pages 207–21 in Schloen 2009.

Holm-Nielsen, Svend. 1993. Did Joab Climb "Warren's Shaft"? Pages 38–49 in *History and Traditions of Early Israel: Studies Presented to*

Eduard Nielsen. Edited by André Lemaire and Benedikt Otzen. VTSup 50. Leiden: Brill.

Hopkins, David. 1985. *The Highlands of Canaan: Agricultural Life in the Early Iron Age.* SWBA 3. Sheffield: Almond Press.

Houston, Walter. 2004. Was There a Social Crisis in the Eighth Century? Pages 130–49 in Day 2004.

Humbert, Jean-Baptiste. 1993. Tell Keisan. *NEAEHL* 3:862–67.

Hunt, John D. 1993. The Sign of the Object. Pages 293–98 in Lubar and Kingery 1993.

Iacovou, Maria. 1998. Philistia and Cyprus in the Eleventh Century: From a Similar Prehistory to a Diverse Protohistory. Pages 332–44 in Gitin, Mazar, and Stern 1998.

———. 2013. Aegean-Style Material Culture in Late Cypriot III: Minimal Evidence, Maximal Interpretation. Pages 585–618 in Killebrew and Lehmann 2013a.

Iggers, Georg G. 1997. *Historiography in the Twentieth Century: From Scientific Objectivity to the Postmodern Challenge.* Hanover, NH: Wesleyan University Press.

Ilan, David. 1999. Northeastern Israel in Iron Age I: Cultural, Socioeconomic and Political Perspectives. PhD diss. Tel Aviv University.

———. 2011. Household Gleanings from Iron I Tel Dan. Pages 133–54 in Yasur-Landau, Ebeling, and Mazow 2011.

Im, MiYoung. 2006. Horses and Chariotry in the Land of Israel during the Iron Age II (1000–586 BCE). PhD diss. Bar-Ilan University.

Issar, Arie S., and Neville Brown, eds. 1998. *Water, Environment and Society in Times of Climatic Change.* London: Kluwer Academic

James, Peter. 2005. The Date of the Ekron Temple Inscription: A Note. *IEJ* 55:90–93.

Jamieson-Drake, David W. 1991. *Scribes and Schools in Monarchic Judah: A Socio-archaeological Approach.* JSOT/SWBA 9. Sheffield: Almond Press.

Jeffers, Ann. 1996. *Magic and Divination in Ancient Palestine and Syria.* SHANE 8. Leiden: Brill.

Joffe, Alexander H. 2002. The Rise of Secondary States in the Iron Age Levant. *JESHO* 45:425–67.

———. 2007. On the Case of Faust versus Finkelstein, from a Friend of the Court. *NEA* 711:16–25.

———. 2010. The Changing Place of Biblical Archaeology: Exceptionalism or Normal Science? Pages 328–48 in Levy 2010a.

Johnson, Douglas L. 1969. *The Nature of Nomadism: A Comparative Study of Pastoral Migrations in Southwestern Asia and Northern Africa*. University of Chicago, Department of Geography Research Paper 118. Chicago: University of Chicago Press.

Jones, Sian. 1997. *The Archaeology of Ethnicity: Constructing Identities in the Past and Present*. London: Routledge.

———. 2010. Historical Categories and the Praxis of Identity: The Interpretation of Ethnicity in Historical Archaeology. Pages 301–10 in Preucel and Mrozowski 2010.

Jung, Reinhard. 2010. End of the Bronze Age. Pages 171–88 in *The Oxford Handbook of the Bronze Age Aegean (ca. 3000–1000 BC)*. Edited by Eric H. Cline. Oxford: Oxford University Press.

Kafafi, Zeidan A., and Gerrit van der Kooij. 2013. *Tell Dēr ʿAllā during the Transition from Late Bronze to the Iron Age*. ZDPV 129:121–31.

Karageorghis, Vassos. 2011. What Happened in Cyprus c. 1200 BC: Hybridization, Creolization or Immigration? An Introduction. Pages 19–28 in Karageorghis and Kouka 2011.

Karageorghis, Vassos, and Ourania Kouka, eds. 2011. *On Cooking Pots, Drinking Cups, Loomweights and Ethnicity in Bronze Age Cyprus and Neighboring Regions*. Nicosia: A. G. Leventis Foundation.

Kassianidou, Vasiliki. 2013. The Exploitation of the Landscape: Metal Resources and the Copper Trade during the Age of the Cypriot City-Kingdoms. *BASOR* 370:49–82.

Kaufman, Ivan T. 1982. The Samaria Ostraca: An Early Witness to Hebrew Writing. *BA* 45:229–39.

Keel, Othmar. 1995. *Von Tell Abu Farag bis ʾAtlit*. Catalog vol. 1 of *Corpus der Stempelsiegel-Amulette aus Palastina/Israel*. OBOSA 13. Göttingen: Vandenhoeck & Ruprecht.

———. 1997. *The Symbolism of the Biblical World: Ancient Near Eastern Iconography and the Book of Psalms*. Winona Lake, IN: Eisenbrauns.

Keel, Othmar, and Christoph Uehlinger. 1998. *Gods, Goddesses, and Images of God in Ancient Israel*. Minneapolis: Fortress.

Kelle, Brad E., Frank Ritchel Ames, and Jacob L. Wright, eds. 2011. *Interpreting Exile: Displacement and Deportations in Biblical and Modern Contexts*. AIL 10. Atlanta: Society of Biblical Literature.

Kempinski, Aharon. 1983. From Tent to House. Pages 31–34 in *Ergebnisse der Ausgrabungen auf der Ḥirbet El-Mšaš (Ṭēl Māśoś) 1972–1975*. Edited by Volkmar Fritz and Aharon Kempinski. Wiesbaden: Harrassowitz.

Kempinski, Aharon, and Volkmar Fritz. 1977. Excavations at Tel Masos (Khirbet El-Meshâsh) Preliminary Report of the Third Season, 1975. *TA* 4:136–58.

Kessler, Rainer. 2008. *The Social History of Ancient Israel: An Introduction.* Minneapolis: Fortress.

Khazanov, Anatoly M. 1994. *Nomads and the Outside World.* 2nd ed. Madison: University of Wisconsin Press.

Khoury, Philip S., and Joseph Kostiner, eds. 1990. *Tribes and State Formation in the Middle East.* Berkeley: University of California Press.

Killebrew, Ann E. 2000. Aegean-Style Early Philistine Pottery in Canaan during the Iron I Age: A Stylistic Analysis of Mycenaean IIIC:1b Pottery and Its Associated Wares. Pages 233–53 in Oren 2000.

———. 2003. Biblical Jerusalem: An Archaeological Assessment. Pages 329–45 in Vaughn and Killebrew 2003.

———. 2005. *Biblical Peoples and Ethnicity: An Archaeological Study of Egyptians, Canaanites, Philistines, and Early Israel, 1300–1100 B.C.E.* ABS 9. Atlanta: Society of Biblical Literature.

———. 2013. Early Philistine Pottery Technology at Tel Miqne-Ekron: Implications for the Late Bronze-Early Iron Age Transition in the Eastern Mediterranean. Pages 77–129 in Killebrew and Lehmann 2013a.

Killebrew, Ann E., and Gunnar Lehmann, eds. 2013a. *The Philistines and Other "Sea Peoples" in Text and Archaeology.* ABS 15. Atlanta: Society of Biblical Literature.

———. 2013b. The World of the Philistines and Other "Sea Peoples." Pages 1–17 in Killebrew and Lehmann 2013a.

Kimball, Roger. 2004. *The Rape of the Masters: How Political Correctness Sabotages Art.* San Francisco: Encounter.

King, Philip J., and Lawrence E. Stager. 2001. *Life in Biblical Israel.* Louisville: Westminster John Knox.

Kingery, W. David. 1996a. Introduction. Pages 1–15 in Kingery 1996b.

———, ed. 1996b. *Learning from Things: Method and Theory of Material Culture Studies.* Washington, DC: Smithsonian Institution Press.

Kitchen, Kenneth A. 1973. *The Third Intermediate Period in Egypt.* Warminster: Aris & Phillips.

———. 1986. *The Third Intermediate Period in Egypt (1100–650 BC).* 2nd ed. Warminster: Aris & Phillips.

———. 1992. The Egyptian Evidence on Ancient Jordan. Pages 21–34 in Bienkowski 1992.

———. 1998. Egyptians and Hebrews, from Raʿamses to Jericho. Pages 65–131 in *The Origin of Early Israel—Current Debate: Biblical, Historical, and Archaeological Perspectives*. Edited by S. Ahituv and Eliezer D. Oren. Beer-Sheva 12. Beersheba: Ben-Gurion University of the Negev.

———. 2001. The Shoshenqs of Egypt and Palestine. *JSOT* 93:3–12.

———. 2003a. *On the Reliability of the Old Testament*. Grand Rapids: Eerdmans.

———. 2003b. The Victories of Merenptah and the Nature of Their Record. *JSOT* 28:259–72.

———. 2010. External Textual Sources: Early Arabia. Pages 381–83 in Halpern and Lemaire 2010.

Kletter, Raz. 1991. The Inscribed Weights of the Kingdom of Judah. *TA* 18:121–63.

———. 1996. *The Judean Pillar-Figurines and the Archaeology of Asherah*. BAR International Series 636. Oxford: Tempus Reparatum.

———. 1998. *Economic Keystones: The Weight System of the Kingdom of Judah*. JSOTSup 276. Sheffield: Sheffield Academic.

———. 1999. Pots and Polities: Material Remains of Late Iron Age Judah in Relation to Its Political Borders. *BASOR* 314:19–54.

———. 2001. Between Archaeology and Theology: The Pillar Figurines from Judah and the Asherah. Pages 179–215 in A. Mazar 2001b.

———. 2002a People without Burials? The Lack of Iron I Burials in the Central Highlands of Palestine. *IEJ* 52:28–48.

———. 2002b Temptation to Identify: Jerusalem, *mmst*, and the *lmlk* Jar Stamps. *ZDPV* 118:136–49.

———. 2003. Iron Age Hoards of Precious Metals in Palestine: An "Underground Economy"? *Levant* 35:139–52.

———. 2004. Chronology and United Monarchy: A Methodological Review. *ZDPV* 120:13–54.

———. 2006. Can a Proto-Israelite Please Stand Up? Notes on the Ethnicity of Iron Age Israel and Judah. Pages 573–86 in Maeir and de Miroschedji 2006.

———. 2009. Comment: Computational Intelligence, *lmlk* Storage Jars and the Bath Unit in Iron Age Judah. *Journal of Archaeological Method and Theory* 16:357–65.

Knapp, A. Bernard. 2001. Archaeology and Ethnicity: A Dangerous Liaison. *Archaeologia Cypria* 4:29–46.

Knauf, Ernst Axel. 1991. From History to Interpretation. Pages 26–64 in Edelman 1991.

———. 2000. Jerusalem in the Late Bronze and Early Iron Ages: A Proposal. *TA* 27:75–90.

———. 2008. From Archaeology to History, Bronze and Iron Ages with Special Regard to the Year 1200 B.C.E., and the Tenth Century. Pages 72–85 in Grabbe 2008a.

Knauf, Ernst Axel, and Philippe Guillaume. 2015. *A History of Biblical Israel: The Fate of the Tribes and Kingdoms from Merenptah to Bar Kochba.* Sheffield: Equinox.

Knoppers, Gary N. 1993. *The Reign of Solomon and the Rise of Jeroboam.* Vol. 1 of *Two Nations under God: The Deuteronomistic History of Solomon and the Dual Monarchies.* HSM 52. Atlanta: Scholars Press.

———. 1997. The Vanishing Solomon: The Disappearance of the United Monarchy from Recent Histories of Ancient Israel. *JBL* 116:19–44.

———. 2004. In Search of Post-exilic Israel: Samaria after the Fall of the Northern Kingdom. Pages 150–80 in Day 2004.

Knoppers, Gary N., Lester L. Grabbe, and Deirdre N. Fulton, eds. 2009. *Exile and Restoration Revisited: Essays on the Babylonian and Persian Periods in Memory of Peter. R. Ackroyd.* London: T&T Clark.

Knoppers, Gary N., and J. Gordon McConville, eds. 2000. *Reconsidering Israel and Judah: Recent Studies on the Deuteronomistic History.* SBTS 8. Winona Lake, IN: Eisenbrauns.

Kochavi, Moshe. 1969. Excavations at Tel Esdar. *'Atiqot* 8:14–48.

———. 1998. The Eleventh Century BCE Tripartite Pillar Building at Tel Hadar. Pages 468–78 in Gitin, Mazar, and Stern 1998.

Kofoed, Jens Bruun. 2005. *Text and History: Historiography and the Study of the Biblical Text.* Winona Lake, IN: Eisenbrauns.

———. 2011. Saul and Cultural Memory. *SJOT* 25:124–50.

Kohl, Philip L. 1987. State Formation: Useful Concept or idée fixe? Pages 27–34 in *Power Relations and State Formation.* Edited by Thomas C. Patterson and Christine W. Gailey. Washington, DC: American Anthropological Association.

Kolb, Frank. 1984. *Die Stadt im Altertum.* Munich: Beck.

Kooij, Gerrit van der. 1993. Deir 'Alla, Tell. Pages 338–42 in Stern 1993.

Kratz, Reinhard G. 2015. *Historical and Biblical Israel: The History, Tradition, and Archives of Israel and Judah.* Translated by P. M. Kurtz. Oxford: Oxford University Press.

Kratz, Reinhard G., and Hermann Spieckermann, eds. 2010. *One God–One Cult–One Nation: Archaeological and Historical Perspectives.* BZAW 405. Berlin: de Gruyter.

Kuhn, Thomas S. 1962. *The Structure of Scientific Revolutions*. Chicago: University of Chicago Press.

Laemmel, Sabine. 2013. A Few Tomb Groups from Tell el-Farʻah South. Pages 145–89 in Killebrew and Lehmann 2013a.

Lamon, Robert Steven, and Geoffrey M. Shipton. 1939. *Megiddo I: Seasons of 1935–1934, Strata I–V*. OIP 42. Chicago: Oriental Institute, University of Chicago.

Lancaster, Steven D., and G. A. Long. 1999. Where They Met: Separations in the Rock Mass Near the Siloam Tunnels' Meeting Point. *BASOR* 315:15–26.

Lancaster, William. 1981. *The Rwala Bedouin Today*. Cambridge: Cambridge University Press.

Langgut, Dafua, Israel Finkelstein, and Thomas Litt. 2013. Climate and the Late Bronze Collapse: New Evidence from the Southern Levant. *TA* 40:149–75.

Lapp, Paul W. 1964. The 1963 Excavation at Taʻannek. *BASOR* 173:4–44.

LaRocca-Pitts, Elizabeth C. 2001. *"Of Wood and Stone": The Significance of Israelite Cultic Items in the Bible and Its Early Interpreters*. HSM 61. Winona Lake, IN: Eisenbrauns.

Latour, Bruno. 2005. *Reassembling the Social: An Introduction to Actor-Network Theory*. Oxford: Oxford University Press.

Layne, Linda L. 1994. *Home and Homeland: The Dialogics of Tribal and National Identities in Jordan*. Princeton: Princeton University Press.

Lederman, Zvi. 1992. Nomads They Never Were [Hebrew]. Paper presented at the Eighteenth Archaeological Congress in Israel, Lecturer's Abstracts. Tel Aviv.

———. 1999. An Early Iron Age Village at Khirbet Raddana: The Excavations of Joseph A. Callaway. PhD diss. Harvard University.

Lees, Susan H., and Daniel G. Bates. 1974. The Origins of Specialized Nomadic Pastoralism: A Systemic Model. *American Antiquity* 39:187–93.

Lehmann, Gunnar. 2001. Phoenicians in Western Galilee: First Results of an Archaeological Survey in the Hinterland of Akko. Pages 65–112 in A. Mazar 2001b.

———. 2003. The United Monarchy in the Countryside: Jerusalem, Judah, and the Shephelah during the Tenth Century B.C.E. Pages 117–62 in Vaughn and Killebrew 2003.

———. 2013. Aegean-Style Pottery in Syria and Lebanon during Iron I. Pages 265–328 in Killebrew and Lehmann 2013a.

Lehmann, Gunnar, and Ann E. Killebrew. 2010. Palace 6000 at Megiddo in Context: Iron Age Central Hall Tetra-Partite Residencies and the "Bit-Hilani" Building Tradition in the Levant. *BASOR* 359:13–33.

Lemaire, André. 1984. Date et origine des inscriptions hébraïques et phéniciennes de Kuntillet ʿAjrud. *Studi Epigrafici e Linguistici* 1:131–43.

———. 1994. "House of David" Restored in Moabite Inscription. *BAR* 20.3:30–37.

———. 1998. The Tel Dan Stela as a Piece of Royal Historiography. *JSOT* 81:3–14.

———. 2010. Edom and the Edomites. Pages 225–43 in Halpern and Lemaire 2010.

———. 2011. The United Monarchy: Saul, David and Solomon. Pages 85–128 in Shanks 2011.

Lemche, Niels Peter. 1991. *The Canaanites and Their Land: The Tradition of the Canaanites*. JSOTSup 110. Sheffield: Sheffield Academic.

———. 1997. Clio Is Also among the Muses! Keith W. Whitelam and the History of Palestine: A Review and a Commentary. Pages 123–55 in Grabbe 1997b.

———. 1998a. *The Israelites in History and Tradition*. LAI. London: SPCK; Louisville: Westminster John Knox.

———. 1998b. The Origin of the Israelite State: A Copenhagen Perspective on the Emergence of Critical Historical Studies of Ancient Israel in Recent Times. *SJOT* 12:44–63.

———. 1998c. *Prelude to Israel's Past: Background and Beginnings of Israelite History and Identity*. Peabody, MA: Hendrikson.

———. 2000a. Ideology and the History of Ancient Israel. *SJOT* 14: 165–93.

———. 2000b. On the Problem of Reconstructing Pre-Hellenistic Israelite (Palestinian) History. *JHS* 3:1–14.

———. 2005. Conservative Scholarship on the Move. *SJOT* 19:203–52.

———. 2008. *The Old Testament between Theology and History: A Critical Survey*. Louisville: Westminster John Knox.

———. 2010a. Did a Reform Like Josiah's Happen? Pages 11–19 in Davies and Edelman 2011.

———. 2010b. How to Deal with "Early Israel." Pages 150–66 in Grabbe 2010.

———. 2012. Using the Concept of Ethnicity in Defining Philistine Identity in the Iron Age. *SJOT* 26:12–29.

———. 2013. *Biblical Studies and the Failure of History*. Changing Perspectives 3. Sheffield: Equinox.

Lemche, Niels Peter, and Thomas L. Thompson. 1994. Did Biran Kill David? The Bible in Light of Archaeology. *JSOT* 64:3–22.

Lemert, Charles. 1997. *Postmodernism Is Not What You Think*. Oxford: Blackwell.

Lenski, Gerhard, and Jean Lenski. 1978. *Human Societies: An Introduction to Macrosociology*. New York: McGraw-Hill.

Leriou, Anastasia. 2007. Locating Identities in the Eastern Mediterranean during the Late Bronze Age Early Iron Age: The Case of "Hellenised" Cyprus. Pages 563–91 in *Mediterranean Crossroads*. Edited by Sophia Antoniadou and Anthony Pace. Athens: Pierides Foundation.

Levi-Strauss, Claude. 1963. *Structural Anthropology*. Translated by Claire Jacobson and Brooke Grundfest Schoepf. New York: Basic Books.

Levin, Yigal. 2012. The Identification of Khirbet Qeiyafa: A New Suggestion. *BASOR* 367:73–86.

Levy, Thomas E., ed. 1995. *The Archaeology of Society in the Holy Land*. London: Leicester University Press.

———. 2009. Ethnic Identity in Biblical Edom, Israel, and Midian: Some Insights from Mortuary Contexts in the Lowlands of Edom. Pages 251–61 in Schloen 2009.

———, ed. 2010a. *Historical Biblical Archaeology and the Future: The New Pragmatism*. London: Equinox.

———. 2010b. The New Pragmatism: Integrating Anthropological, Digital, and Historical Biblical Archaeologies. Pages 3–42 in Levy 2010a.

Levy, Thomas E., and Thomas Higham, eds. 2005. *The Bible and Radiocarbon Dating: Archaeology, Text and Science*. London: Equinox.

Levy, Thomas E., Mohammad Najjar, and Erez Ben-Yosef, eds. 2014. *New Insights into the Iron Age Archaeology of Edom, Southern Jordan*. University of California: Cotsen Institute of Archaeology Press.

Levy, Thomas E., Thomas Schneider, and William H. C. Propp, eds. 2015. *Israel's Exodus in Transdisciplinary Perspective: Text, Archaeology, Culture, and Geoscienco*. New York: Springer.

Levy, Thomas E., and Neil G. Smith. 2007. On-Site Digital Archaeology: GIS-Based Excavation Recording in Southern Jordan. Pages 47–58 in *Crossing Jordan: North American Contributions to the Archaeology of Jordan*. Edited by E. C. M. van den Brink and Thomas E. Levy. London: Equinox.

Levy, Thomas E., et al. 2004. Reassessing the Chronology of Biblical Edom: New Excavations and ^{14}C Dates from Khirbat en-Nahas (Jordan). *Antiquity* 78/302:865–79.

Lewis, Theodore J. 1989. *Cults of the Dead in Ancient Israel and Ugarit.* HSM 39. Atlanta: Scholars Press.

———. 2005. Syro-Palestinian Iconography and Divine Images. Pages 69–107 in Walls 2005.

Liebowitz, Harold, and Robert Folk. 1984. The Dawn of Iron Smelting in Palestine: The Late Bronze Age Smelter at Tel Yin'am; Preliminary Report. *JFA* 11:265–80.

Linder, Elisha. 1973. A Cargo of Phoenician-Punic Figurines. *Archaeology* 26:182–87.

Lipínski, Edward. 2010. Hiram of Tyre and Solomon. Pages 251–72 in Halpern and Lemaire 2010.

Lipschits, Oded. 2004. The Rural Settlement in Judah in the Sixth Century B.C.E.: A Rejoinder. *PEQ* 136:99–107.

———. 2005. *The Fall and Rise of Jerusalem: Judah under Babylonian Rule.* Winona Lake, IN: Eisenbrauns.

———. 2011 The Origin and Date of the Volute Capitals from the Levant. Pages 203–25 in Finkelstein and Na'aman 2011.

Lipschits, Oded, and Joseph Blenkinsopp. 2003. *Judah and the Judeans in the Neo-Babylonian Period.* Winona Lake, IN: Eisenbrauns.

Lipschits, Oded, Gary N. Knoppers, and Rainer Albertz, eds. 2007. *Judah and the Judeans in the Fourth Century B.C.E.* Winona Lake, IN: Eisenbrauns.

Lipschits, Oded, and Manfred Oeming, eds. 2006. *Judah and the Judeans in the Persian Period.* Winona Lake, IN: Eisenbrauns.

Lipschits, Oded., et al. 2011. Palace and Village, Paradise and Oblivion: Unraveling the Riddles of Ramat Rahel. *NEA* 74:2–49.

Liverani, Mario. 2007. *Israel's History and the History of Israel.* Translated by Chiara Peri and Philip R. Davies. London: Equinox.

London, Gloria. 1989. A Comparison of Two Contemporaneous Lifestyles of the Late Second Millennium BC. *BASOR* 273:37–55.

———. 2011a. A Ceremonial Center for the Living and the Dead. *NEA* 74:216–25.

———. 2011b. Late Second Millennium BC Feasting at an Ancient Ceremonial Centre in Jordan. *Levant* 43:15–37.

Loud, G. 1948. *Megiddo II: Seasons of 1935–39.* Oriental Institution Publications 62. Chicago: Oriental Institute, University of Chicago.

Lubar, Steven. 1996. Learning from Technological Things. Pages 31–35 in Kingery 1996b.

Lubar, Steven, and W. David Kingery, eds. 1993. *History from Things: Essays on Material Culture*. Washington, DC: Smithsonian Institution Press.

Lubetski, Meir, and Edith Lubetski. 2012. *New Inscriptions and Seals Relating to the Biblical World*. ABS 19. Atlanta: Society of Biblical Literature.

Luciani, Marta. 2014. The Northern Levant (Syria) during the Late Bronze Age: Small Kingdoms between the Supra-Regional Empires of the International Age. Pages 509–523 in Steiner and Killebrew 2014.

Luke, J. Tracey. 1965. Pastoralism and Politics in the Mari Period: A Reexamination of the Character and Political Significance of the Major West Semitic Tribal Groups on the Middle Euphrates, c. 1828–1758 B.C. PhD diss. University of Michigan.

Lyotard, Jean-Francois. 1984. *The Postmodern Condition: A Report on Knowledge*. Minneapolis: University of Minnesota Press.

Macalister, Robert A. S. 1912. *The Excavation of Gezer*. 3 vols. Palestine Exploration Fund. London: Murray.

MacDonald, Burton M. 2000. *East of the Jordan: Territories and Sites of the Hebrew Scriptures*. Boston: American Schools of Oriental Research.

MacDonald, Burton M., Russell B. Adams., and Piotr Bienkowski, eds. 2001. *The Archaeology of Jordan*. Levantine Archaeology 1. Sheffield: Sheffield Academic.

MacDonald, Nathan. 2008. *What Did the Ancient Israelites Eat? Diet in Biblical Times*. Grand Rapids: Eerdmans.

Machinist, Peter. 1976. *Literature as Politics: The Tukulti-Ninurta Epic and the Bible*. Washington, DC: Catholic Biblical Association of America.

———. 2000. Biblical Traditions: The Philistines and Israelite History. Pages 53–87 in Oren 2000.

Maier, Aren M. 2008. Zafit, Tell. Pages 2079–81 in Stern 2008.

———. 2010. "And They Brought in the Offerings and the Tithes and the Dedicated Things Faithfully" (2 Chron. 31:12): On the Meaning and Function of the Late Iron Age Judahite "Incised Handle Cooking Pots." *JAOS* 130:43–62.

———, ed. 2012. *Tell Es-Safi/Gath I: The 1996–2005 Seasons*. AAT 69. Wiesbaden: Harrassowitz.

———. 2013. Philistia Transforming: Fresh Evidence from Tell eṣ-Ṣafi/Gath on the Transformational Trajectory of the Philistine Culture. Pages 191–242 in Killebrew and Lehmann 2013a

Maeir, Aren M., Shimon Dar, and Ze'ev Safrai, eds. 2003. *The Rural Landscape of Ancient Israel*. BAR International Series 1121. Oxford: Archaeopress.

Maeir, Aren M., Alexander Fantalkin, and Alexander Zuckerman. 2009. The Earliest Greek Import in the Iron Age Levant: New Evidence from Tell es - Safi/Gath, Israel. *AWE* 8:57–80.

Maeir, Aren M., and Shira Gur-Arieh. 2011. Comparative Aspects of the Aramean Siege System at Tell eṣ Ṣāfi/Gath. Pages 227–44 in Finkelstein and Naʾaman 2011.

Maeir, Aren M., Louise A. Hitchcock, and Liora K. Horwitz. 2013. On the Constitution and Transformation of Philistie Identity. *OJA* 32:1–38.

Maeir, Aren M., and Pierre de Miroschedji, eds. 2006. *"I Will Speak the Riddles of Ancient Times": Archaeological and Historical Studies in Honor of Amihai Mazar on the Occasion of His Sixtieth Birthday.* 2 vols. Winona Lake, IN: Eisenbrauns.

Maquet, Jacques. 1993. Objects as Instruments, Objects as Signs. 30–39 in Lubar and Kingery 1993.

Markoe, Glenn E. 2000. *Phoenicians.* Peoples of the Past. Berkeley: University of California Press.

Martin, Mario A. S. 2011. Egyptian-Type Pottery at Late Bronze Age Megiddo. Pages 245–64 in Finkelstein and Naʾaman 2011.

Martin, Mario A. S., and Israel Finkelstein. 2013. Iron IIA Pottery from the Negev Highlands: Petrographic Investigation and Historical Implications. *TA* 40:6–45.

Marx, Emanuel. 1967. *Bedouin of the Negev.* New York: Praeger.

Master, Daniel M. 2001. State Formation Theory and the Kingdom of Ancient Israel. *JNES* 60:117–31.

———. 2009. From the Buqeʾah to Ashkelon. Pages 305–17 in Schloen 2009.

———. 2010. Institutions of Trade in 1 and 2 Kings. Pages 501–16 in Halpern and Lemaire 2010.

Master, Daniel M., Penelope A. Mountjoy, and Hans Mommsen. 2015. Imported Cypriot Pottery in Twelfth-Century B.C. Ashkelon. *BASOR* 373:235–43.

Master, Daniel M., et al. 2005. *Dothan I: Remains from the Tell (1953–1964).* Winona Lake, IN: Eisenbrauns.

Mastin, Brian A. 2004. Yahweh's Asherah, Inclusive Monotheism and the Question of Dating. Pages 326–51 in Day 2004.

Matthews, Victor H. 1978. *Pastoral Nomadism in the Mari Kingdom (c. 1830–1760 B.C.).* ASORDS 3. Cambridge: American Schools of Oriental Research.

Mayer, Walter. 1995. *Politik und Kriegskunst der Assyrer*. ALASPM 9. Munster: Ugarit-Verlag.

Mayes, A. D. H. 1983. *The Story of Israel between Settlement and Exile: A Redactional Study of the Deuteronomistic History*. London: SCM.

Mazar, Amihai. 1981. Giloh: An Early Israelite Settlement near Jerusalem. *IEJ* 31:1–36.

———. 1982a. The "Bull Site": An Iron Age I Open Cult Place. *BASOR* 247:27–42.

———. 1982b. Iron Age Fortresses in the Judaean Hills. *PEQ* 114:87–109.

———. 1982c. Three Israelite Sites in the Hills of Judah and Ephraim. *BA* 45:167–78.

———. 1985. *Excavations at Tell Qasile II: The Philistine Sanctuary: Various Finds, the Pottery, Conclusions, Appendixes*. Qedem 20. Jerusalem: Hebrew University of Jerusalem.

———. 1990. *Archaeology of the Land of the Bible: 10,000–586 BCE*. ABRL. New Haven: Yale University Press.

———. 1993. Abu Twein, Khirbet. *NEAEHL* 1:15–16.

———. 1994. The Eleventh Century B.C.E. in Palestine. Pages 39–58 in *Proceedings of the International Symposium, Cyprus in the Eleventh Century B.C.* Edited by Vassos Karageorghis. Nicosia: A. G. Leventis Foundation.

———. 1998. On the Appearance of Red Slip in the Iron Age I Period in Israel. Pages 368–78 in Gitin, Mazar, and Stern 1998.

———. 2001a. Beth Shean during the Iron Age II: Stratigraphy, Chronology and Hebrew Ostraca. Pages 289–309 in A. Mazar 2001b.

———, ed. 2001b. *Studies in the Archaeology of the Iron Age in Israel and Jordan*. JSOTSup 331. Sheffield: Sheffield Academic.

———. 2003. Remarks on Biblical Traditions and Archaeological Evidence concerning Early Israel. Pages 85–98 in Dever and Gitin 2003.

———. 2005. The Debate over the Chronology of the Iron Age in the Southern Levant: Its History, the Current Situation, and a Suggested Resolution. Pages 15–30 in Levy and Higham 2005.

———. 2006a. *Excavations at Tel Beth-Shean 1989–1996 I: From the Late Bronze Age IIB to the Medieval Period*. Jerusalem: Israel Exploration Society and the Hebrew University of Jerusalem.

———. 2006b. Jerusalem in the Tenth Century BC: The Glass Half Full. Pages 255–72 in *Essays on Ancient Israel in Its Near Eastern Context: A Tribute to Nadav Na'aman*. Edited by Yairah Amit et al. Winona Lake, IN: Eisenbrauns.

———. 2007. The Spade and the Text: The Interaction between Archaeology and Israelite History Relating to the Tenth–Ninth Centuries BCE. Pages 143–71 in Williamson 2007.

———. 2008a. From 1200 to 850 B.C.E: Remarks on Some Selected Archaeological Issues. Pages 86–120 in Grabbe 2008a.

———. 2008b. Reḥov, Tel. *NEAEHL* 5:2013–18.

———. 2009. The Iron Age Dwellings at Tell Qasile. Pages 319–36 in Schloen 2009.

———. 2010a. Archaeology and the Biblical Narrative: The Case of the United Monarchy. Pages 29–58 in Kratz and Spieckermann 2010.

———. 2010b. Tel Beth-Shean: History and Archaeology. Pages 239–71 in Kratz and Spieckermann 2010.

———. 2011. The Iron Age Chronology Debate: Is the Gap Narrowing? Another Viewpoint. *NEA* 74:105–11.

Mazar, Amihai, and Christopher Bronk Ramsey. 2008. ^{14}C Dates and the Iron Age Chronology of Israel: A Response. *Radiocarbon* 50:159–80.

———. 2010. A Response to Finkelstein and Piasetsky's Criticism and "New Perspective." *Radiocarbon* 52:1681–88.

Mazar, Amihai, and Israel Canni. 2001. Radiocarbon Dates from Iron Age Strata at Tel Beth Shean and Tel Reḥov. *Radiocarbon* 43:1333–42.

Mazar, Amihai, and Robert Mullins. 2007. *Excavations at Tel Beth-Shean 1989–1996 II: The Middle and Late Bronze Age Strata in Area R*. Jerusalem: Israel Exploration Society and Hebrew University of Jerusalem.

Mazar, Amihai, and Nava Panitz-Cohen. 2001. *Timnah (Tel Batash) II: The Pottery and Other Finds from the Iron II and Persian Periods; Second Final Report on the Excavations between 1977–1989*. Qedem 41.1. Jerusalem: Hebrew University of Jerusalem.

Mazar, Amihai, et al. 2005. Ladder of Time at Tel Reḥov: Stratigraphy, Archaeological Context, Pottery and Radiocarbon Dates. Pages 193–255 in Levy and Higham 2005.

Mazar (Maisler), Benjamin. 1950–1951. The Excavations at Tell Qasîle: Preliminary Report. *IEJ* 1:125–40.

Mazar, Eilat. 2003. *The Phoenicians in Achziv: The Southern Cemetery*. Cuadernos de Arquelogia Mediterranea 7. Barcelona: Universidad Pompeu Fabra.

———. 2007. *Preliminary Report on the City of David Excavations 2005 Near the Visitors Center Area*. Jerusalem: Shoham Academic Research and Publication.

———. 2009. *The Palace of King David: Excavations at the Summit the City of David; Preliminary Report of Seasons 2005–2007*. Jerusalem: Shoham Academic Research.

———. 2011. *Discovering the Solomonic Wall in Jerusalem: A Remarkable Archaeological Adventure*. Jerusalem: Shoham Academic Research and Publication.

Mazar, Eilat, and Benjamin Mazar. 1989. *Excavations in the South of the Temple Mount: The Ophel of Biblical Jerusalem*. Qedem 29. Jerusalem: Institute of Archaeology, Hebrew University of Jerusalem.

Mazow, Laura B. Competing Material Culture: Philistine Settlement at Tel Miqne-Ekron in the Early Iron Age. Ph.D. diss. University of Arizona.

———. 2014. Competing Material Culture: Philistine Settlement at Tel Miqne-Ekron in the Early Iron Age. Pages 131–62 in *Material Culture Matters: Essays on the Archaeology of the Southern Levant in Honor of Seymour Gitin*. Edited by John R. Spencer, Aaron J. Brody, and Robert A. Mullins. Winona Lake, IN: Eisenbrauns, 2014.

Mazzoni, Stefania. 2014. Tell Afis in the Iron Age: The Temple on the Acropolis. *NEA* 77:44–52.

McCarter, P. Kyle, Jr. 1987. Aspects of the Religion of the Israelite Monarchy: Biblical and Epigraphic Data. Pages 137–55 in Miller, Hanson, and McBride 1987.

———. 1996. *Ancient Inscriptions: Voices from the Biblical World*. Washington, DC: Biblical Archaeology Society.

———. 2008. Paleographic Notes on the Tel Zayit Abecedary. Pages 45–59 in Tappy and McCarter 2008.

———. 2011. The Patriarchal Age: Abraham, Isaac and Jacob. Pages 1–34 in Shanks 2011.

McClellan, Thomas L. 1984. Town Planning at Tell en-Nasbeh. *ZDPV* 100:53–69.

McGovern, Patrick E. 1985. *Late Bronze Palestinian Pendants: Innovation in a Cosmopolitan Age*. JSOT/ASOR Monograph Series 1. Sheffield: JSOT.

———. 1986. *The Late Bronze and Early Iron Ages of Central Transjordan: The Baqʿah Valley Project, 1977–1981*. University Museum Monograph 65. Philadelphia: University Museum, University of Pennsylvania.

McKay, John W. 1973. *Religion in Judah under the Assyrians, 732–609 B.C.E.* Naperville, IL: Allenson.

McKenzie, Steven L. 1991. *The Trouble with Kings. The Composition of the Books of Kings in the Deuteronomistic History*. VTSup 2. Leiden: Brill.

————. 2005. Historiography: Old Testament. Pages 418–25 in Arnold and Williamson 2005.

McKenzie, Steven L., and Stephen R Haynes., eds. 1993. *To Each Its Own Meaning: An Introduction to Biblical Criticisms and Their Application.* Louisville: Westminster John Knox.

McNutt, Paula M. 1990. *The Forging of Israel: Iron Technology, Symbolism, and Tradition in Ancient Society.* JSOTSup 108; SWBA 8. Sheffield: Almond Press.

Meiri, Meirav, et al. 2013. Ancient DNA and Population Turnover in Southern Levantine Pigs: Signature of the Sea Peoples Migration. *Scientific Reports* 3:3035. doi.org/10.1038/srep03035.

Mendenhall, George E. 1962. The Hebrew Conquest of Palestine. *BA* 25:65–87.

————. 1973. *The Tenth Generation: The Origins of the Biblical Tradition.* Baltimore: Johns Hopkins University Press.

Merleau-Ponty, Maurice. 2013. *Phenomenology of Perception.* Translated by Donald Landes. London: Routledge.

Meshel, Ze'ev. 1978. *Kuntillet 'Ajrud: A Religious Centre from the Time of the Judean Monarchy on the Border of Sinai.* Jerusalem: Israel Museum.

————. 2012. *Kuntillet 'Ajrud (Ḥorvat Teman): An Iron Age II Religious Site on the Judah-Sinai Border.* Jerusalem: Israel Exploration Society.

Mettinger, Tryggve N. D. 1995. *No Graven Image? Israelite Aniconism in its Ancient Near Eastern Context.* ConBOT 42. Stockholm: Almqvist & Wiksell.

Meyers, Carol L. 1992. Temple, Jerusalem. *ABD* 6:350–69.

————. 1997. The Family in Early Israel. Pages 1–47 in Perdue et al. 1997.

————. 2001. Kinship and Kingship: The Early Monarchy. Pages 165–205 in Coogan 2001.

————. 2007a. From Field Crops to Food: Attributing Gender and Meaning to Bread Production in Iron Age Israel. Pages 67–83 in *The Archaeology of Difference: Gender, Ethnicity, Class, and the "Other" in Antiquity; Studies in Honor of Eric M. Meyers.* Edited by Douglas R. Edwards and C. Thomas McCollough. Atlanta: American Schools of Oriental Research.

————. 2007b. Terracottas without Texts: Judean Pillar Figurines in Anthropological Perspective. Pages 115–30 in *To Break Every Yoke: Essays in Honor of Marvin L. Chaney.* Edited by Robert B. Coote and Norman K. Gottwald. Sheffield: Sheffield Phoenix.

———. 2013. *Rediscovering Eve: Ancient Israelite Women in Context*. New York: Oxford University Press.

Meyers, Eric M., ed. 1997. *The Oxford Encyclopedia of Archaeology in the Near East*. 5 vols. New York: Oxford University Press.

———. 2011. Exile and Return: From the Babylonian Destruction to the Reconstruction of the Jewish State. Pages 209–35 in Shanks 2011.

Millard, Alan R. 1992. Assyrian Involvement in Edom. Pages 35–39 in Bienkowski 1992.

———. 1995. The Knowledge of Writing in Iron Age Palestine. *TynBull* 46:207–17.

———. 2004. Amorites and Israelites: Invisible Invaders—Modern Expectation and Ancient Reality. Pages 142–60 in *The Future of Biblical Archaeology: Reassessing Methodologies and Assumptions*. Edited by James K. Hoffmeier and Alan Millard. Grand Rapids: Eerdmans.

———. 2005. Writing, Writing Materials and Literacy in the Ancient Near East. Pages 1003–11 in Arnold and Williamson 2005.

———. 2012. Hebrew Seals, Stamps, and Statistics: How Can Fakes Be Found? Pages 183–91 in Lubetski and Lubetski 2012.

Millard, Alan R., James K. Hoffmeier, and David W. Baker, eds. 1994. *Faith, Tradition, and History: Old Testament Historiography in Its Ancient Near Eastern Context*. Winona Lake, IN: Eisenbrauns.

Miller, J. Maxwell. 1991. Is it Possible to Write a History of Israel without Relying on the Hebrew Bible? Pages 93–102 in Edelman 1991.

Miller, J. Maxwell, and John H. Hayes. 1986. *A History of Ancient Israel and Judah*. Philadelphia: Westminster.

———. 2006. *A History of Ancient Israel and Judah*. 2nd ed. Louisville: Westminster John Knox.

Miller, Patrick D., Jr., Paul D. Hanson, and S. Dean McBride, eds. 1987. *Ancient Israelite Religion: Essays in Honor of Frank Moore Cross*. Philadelphia: Fortress.

Miller, Robert D. 2005. *Chieftains of the Highland Clans: A History of Israel in the Twelfth and Eleventh Centuries B.C.* Grand Rapids: Eerdmans.

Mittmann, Siegfried. 1970. *Beiträge zur Siedlungs- und Territorialgeschichte des nördlichen Ostjordanlandes*. ADPV. Wiesbaden: Harrassowitz.

Momiglianio, Arnaldo. 1966. *Studies in Historiography*. New York: Harper & Row.

Monson, John. 2000. The New ʿAin Dara Temple: Closest Solomonic Parallel. *BAR* 26.3:20–35.

———. 2005. Solomon's Temple. Pages 929–35 in Arnold and Williamson 2005.

Moor, Johannes. C de., ed. 2001. *The Elusive Prophet: The Prophet as a Historical Person, Literary Character and Anonymous Artist.* OTS 45. Leiden: Brill. Repr., Atlanta: Society of Biblical Literature, 2005.

Moore, Megan Bishop. 2006. *Philosophy and Practice in Writing a History of Ancient Israel.* LHBOTS 435. New York: T&T Clark International.

Moore, Megan B., and Brad E. Kelle. 2011. *Biblical History and Israel's Past: The Changing Study of the Bible and History.* Grand Rapids: Eerdmans.

Moorey, P. Roger S. 2003 *Idols of the People: Miniature Images of Clay in the Ancient Near East.* Schweich Lectures of the British Academy 2001. Oxford: Oxford University Press.

Moran, William L. 1992. *The Amarna Letters.* Baltimore: Johns Hopkins University Press.

Morris, Ian. 2000. *Archaeology as Cultural History: Words and Things in Iron Age Greece.* Oxford: Blackwell.

Mountjoy, Penelope A. 2013. The Mycenaean IIIC Pottery at Tel Miqne-Ekron. Pages 53–75 in Killebrew and Lehmann 2013a.

Na'aman, Nadav. 1981. Economic Aspects of the Egyptian Occupation of Canaan. *IEJ* 31:172–85.

———. Hezekiah's Fortified Cities and the LMLK Stamps. *BASOR* 261:5–21.

———. 1992. Israel. Edom and Egypt in the Tenth Century B.C.E. *TA* 19:71–93.

———. 1993. Population Changes in Palestine Following Assyrian Deportations. *TA* 20:104–24.

———. 1994a. The Canaanites and Their Land: A Rejoinder. *UF* 26:397–418.

———. 1994b. The "Conquest of Canaan" in the Book of Joshua and in History. Pages 218–81 in Finkelstein and Na'aman 1994.

———. 1994c. Hezekiah and the Kings of Assyria. *TA* 21:235–54.

———. 1995. The Deuteronomist and Voluntary Servitude to Foreign Powers. *JSOT* 65:37–53.

———. 1996a. The Contribution of the Amarna Letters to the Debate on Jerusalem's Political Position in the Tenth Century BCE. *BASOR* 304:17–27.

———. 1996b. Sources and Composition in the History of David. Pages 170–86 in Fritz and Davies 1996.

——. 1997. Cow Town or Royal Capital? Evidece for Iron Age Jerusalem. *BAR* 23.4:43–47.

——. 2000. Three Notes on the Aramaic Inscription from Tel Dan. *IEJ* 50:92–104.

——. 2001. Hebrew Graffiti from the First Temple Period. *IEJ* 51:194–207.

——. 2002a. The Abandonment of Cult Places in the Kingdoms of Israel and Judah as Acts of Cult Reform. *UF* 34:585–602.

——. 2002b. In Search of Reality behind the Account of David's Wars with Israel's Neighbors. *IEJ* 52:21–24.

——. 2006. *Ancient Israel's History and Historiography: The First Temple Period*. Winona Lake, IN: Eisenbrauns.

——. 2008. In Search of the Ancient Name of Khirbet Qeiyafa. *Journal of Hebrew Scriptures* 8.21. http://www.jhsonline.org/Articles/article_98 .pdf.

——. 2009. The Contribution of Royal Inscriptions for a Re-evaluation of the Book of Kings as a Historical Source. *JSOT* 24/82:3–17.

——. 2011. The Exodus Story: Between Historical Memory and Historiographical Composition. *JANER* 11:39–69.

——. 2012a. Five Notes on Jerusalem in the First and Second Temple Periods. *TA* 39:93–103.

——. 2012b. Hirbet ed-Dawwara: A Philistine Stronghold on the Benjamin Desert Fringe. *ZDPV* 128:1–9.

——. 2013. The Kingdom of Judah in the Ninth Century BCE: Text Analysis versus Archaeological Research. *TA* 40:247–76.

——. 2014. The Interchange Between Bible and Archaeology: The Case of David's Palace and the Millo. *BAR* 40.1:57–61.

——. 2016. Tell Dor and Iron IIA Chronology. *BASOR* 376:1–6.

Nakhai, Beth Alpert. 2001. *Archaeology and the Religions of Canaan and Israel*. ASOR Books 7. Boston: American Schools of Oriental Research.

——. 2003. Israel on the Horizon: The Iron I Settlement of the Galilee Pages 131–51 in *The Near East in the Southwest: Essays in Honor of William G. Dever*. Edited by Beth Alpert Nakhai. AASOR 58. Boston: American Schools of Oriental Research. AASOR 58. Boston: American Schools of Oriental Research.

——, ed. 2008. *The World of Women in the Ancient and Classical Near East*. Newcastle: Cambridge Scholars Publishing.

——. 2010. Contextualizing Village Life in the Iron Age I. Pages 121–37 in Grabbe 2010.

———. 2011. Varieties of Religious Expression in the Domestic Setting. Pages 347–60 in Yasur-Landau, Ebeling, and Mazow 2011.

———. 2014. The Household as Sacred Space. Pages 53–71 in Albertz et al. 2014.

Nam, Roger S. 2012. *Portrayals of Economic Exchange in the Book of Kings.* BibInt112. Leiden: Brill.

Naroll, Raoul. 1962. Floor Area and Settlement Population. *American Antiquity* 27:587–89.

Naveh, Joseph. 1987. *Early History of the Alphabet: An Introduction to West Semitic Epigraphy and Palaeography.* 2nd ed. Jerusalem: Magnes.

Netser, Michael. 1998. Population Growth and Decline in the Northern Part of Eretz-Israel during the Historical Period as Related to Climate Changes. Pages 129–45 in Issar and Brown 1998.

Netting, Robert M. 1977. *Cultural Ecology.* Menol Park, CA: Cummings.

Netzer, Ehud. 1992. Domestic Architecture in the Iron Age. Pages 193–201 in *The Architecture of Ancient Israel: From the Prehistoric to the Persian Periods.* Edited by Aharon Kempinski and Ronny Reich. Jerusalem: Israel Exploration Society.

Nicholson, Ernest. 2004. Current "Revisionism and the Literature of the Old Testament. Pages 1–22 in Day 2004.

Niditch, Susan. 1996. *Oral World and the Written Word: Ancient Israelite Literature.* Louisville: Westminster John Knox.

Nielsen, Flemming A. J. 1997. *The Tragedy in History: Herodotus and the Deuteronomistic History.* JSOTSup 251. Sheffield: Sheffield Academic.

Niemann, Hermann Michael. 2015. *History of Ancient Israel, Archaeology, and Bible: Collected Essays.* AOAT 418. Milnster: Ugarit-Verlag.

Noll, K. L. 2001. *Canaan and Israel in Antiquity: An Introduction.* BibSem 83. London: Sheffield Academic.

Noth, Martin. 1960. *The History of Israel.* 2nd ed. Translated by Peter R. Ackroyd. New York: Harper & Row.

Novick, Peter 1988. *That Noble Dream: The "Objectivity Question" and the American Historical Profession.* London: T&T Clark.

Oestigaard, Terje. 2007. *Political Archaeology and Holy Nationalism: Archaeological Battles over the Bible and Land in Israel and Palestine from 1967–2000.* GOTARC ser. C 67. Götenborg: Göteborg University, Dept. of Archaeology.

Ofer, Avi. 1993. Judea: Judean Hills Survey. *NEAEHL* 3:815–16.

———. 1994. "All the Hill Country of Judah": From a Settlement Fringe to a Prosperous Monarchy. Pages 92–121 in Finkelstein and Na'aman 1994.

———. 2001. The Monarchic Period in the Judean Highland: A Spatial Overview. Pages 14–37 in A. Mazar 2001b.

Olsen, Bjorn. 2013. *In Defense of Things: Archaeology and the Ontology of Objects*. Archaeology in Society Series. New York: Alta Mira.

Olyan, Saul M. 1988. *Asherah and the Cult of Yahweh in Israel*. SBLMS 34. Atlanta: Scholars Press.

Oredsson, Dag. 1998. Jezreel: Its Contribution to Iron Age Chronology. *SJOT* 12:86–101.

Oren, Eliezer D. 1985. "Governors" Residencies in Canaan under the New Kingdom: A Case Study of Egyptian Administration. *JSSEA* 14:37–56.

———. 1987. The "Ways of Horus" in North Sinai. Pages 69–119 in *Egypt, Israel, Sinai: Archaeological and Historical Relationships in the Biblical Period*. Edited by Anson F. Rainey. Tel Aviv: Tel Aviv University.

———, ed. 2000. *The Sea Peoples and Their World: A Reassessment*. University Museum Monographs 8. Philadelphia,: University Museum, University of Pennsylvania.

Ornan, Tallay. 2005. *The Triumph of the Symbol: Pictorial Representations of Deities in Mesopotamia and the Biblical Image Ban*. OBO 213. Göttingen: Vandenhoeck & Ruprecht.

Ornan, Tallay, Steven Ortiz, and Samuel Wolff. 2013. A Newly Discovered Neo-Assyrian Cylinder Seal from Gezer in Context. *IEJ* 63:6–25.

Orser, Charles E., Jr. 1984. The Archaeological Analysis of Plantation Society: Replacing Status and Caste with Economics and Power. *American Antiquity* 53:735–51.

Ortiz, Steven M., and Samuel R. Wolff. 2012. Guarding the Border to Jerusalem: The Iron Age City of Gezer. *NEA* 75:4–19.

Osborne, James F. 2011. Secondary Mortuary Practice and the Bench Tomb: Structure and Practice in Iron Age Judah. *JNES* 70:35–53.

Osborne, R. 2005. Urban Sprawl: What Is Urbanization and Why Does It Matter? Pages 1–16 in *Mediterranean Urbanization 800–600 BCE*. Edited by Robin Osborne and Barry Cunliffe. Oxford: British Academy and Oxford University Press.

Panitz-Cohen, Nava. 2005. A Salvage Excavation in the New Market at Beer-sheba: New Light on Iron Age IIB Occupation at Beer-sheba. *IEJ* 55:143–55.

Panitz-Cohen, Nava, and Amihai Mazar, eds. 2009. *The Thirteenth–Eleventh Century BCE Strata in Areas N and S*. Vol. 3 of *Excavations at Tel Beth-Shean 1989–1996*. Jerusalem: Institute of Archaeology, Hebrew University of Jerusalem.

Pardee, Dennis. 2002. *Ritual and Cult at Ugarit*. WAW 10. Atlanta: Society of Biblical Literature.

Parpola, Simo. 2003. Assyria's Expansion in the Eighth and Seventh Centuries and Its Long-Term Repercussions in the West. Pages 99–111 in Dever and Gitin 2003.

Pauketat, Timothy R. 2001. Practice and History in Archaeology: An Emerging Paradigm. *Anthropological Theory* 1:73–98.

Paz, Sarit. 2007. *Drums, Women. and Goddesses: Drumming and Gender in Iron Age II Israel*. OBO 232. Göttingen: Vandenhoeck & Ruprecht.

Peilstöcker, Martin, and Aaron A. Burke, eds. 2011. *The History and Archaeology of Jaffa 1*. Monumenta Archaeologica 26. Los Angeles: Costen Institute of Archaeology Press, University of California.

Perdue, Leo G., et al. 1997. *Families in Ancient Israel: The Family, Religion, and Culture*. Louisville: Westminster John Knox.

Petersen, David L. 2002. *The Prophetic Literature: An Introduction*. Louisville: Westminster John Knox.

Petit, Lucas P. 2012. What Would Egyptian Pharaoh Shoshenq I Have Seen If He Had Visited the Central Jordan Valley? *PEQ* 144:191–207.

Pfoh, Emanuel. 2008. Dealing with Tribes and States in Ancient Palestine: A Critique on the Use of State Formation Theories in the Archaeology of Israel. *SJOT* 22:86–113.

———. 2016. *Syria-Palestine in the Late Bronze Age: An Anthropology of Politics and Power*. London: Routledge.

Pfoh, Emanuel, and Keith W. Whitelam, eds. 2013. *The Politics of Israel's Past: The Bible, Archaeology and Nation-Building*. Sheffield: Sheffield Phoenix.

Pigott, V. C., Patrick E. McGovern, and M. R. Notis. 1982. The Earliest Steel from Transjordan. *Masca Journal* 2:35–39.

Pitard, Wayne T. 1987. *Ancient Damascus: A Historical Study of the Syrian City-State from Earliest Times until Its Fall to the Assyrians in 732 B.C.E.* Winona Lake, IN: Eisenbrauns.

Porter, Benjamin W. 2013. *Complex Communities: The Archaeology of Early Iron Age West-Central Jordan*. Tucson: University of Arizona Press.

Pratico, Gary D. 1993. *Nelson Glueck's 1938–1940 Excavations of Tell el-Kheleifeh: A Reappraisal*. Atlanta: Scholars Press.

Preucel, Robert W., ed. 1991. *Processual and Postprocessual Archaeologies: Multiple Ways of Knowing the Past*. Carbondale: Southern Illinois University Press.

Preucel, Robert W., and Ian Hodder. 1996. *Contemporary Archaeology in Theory*. Oxford: Blackwell.

Preucel, Robert W., and Stephen A. Mrozowski, eds. 2010. *Contemporary Archaeology in Theory: The New Pragmatism*. 2nd ed. Oxford: Wiley-Blackwell.

Pritchard, James B. 1970. The Megiddo Stables: A Reassessment. Pages 268–76 in *Near Eastern Archaeology in the Twentieth Century*. Edited by James A. Sanders. Garden City, NY: Doubleday.

Propp, William H. C. 2000. Monotheism and Moses: The Problem of Early Israelite Religion. *UF* 31:537–75.

Provan, Iain W. 1995. Ideologies, Literary and Critical: Reflections on Recent Writing on the History of Israel. *JBL* 114:585–606.

Provan, Iain W., V. Philips Long, and Tremper Longman III. 2003. *A Biblical History of Israel*. Louisville: Westminster John Knox.

Prown, Julius D. 1993. The Truth of Material Culture: History or Fiction? Pages 1–19 in Lubar and Kingery 1993.

Putnam, Hilary. 2004. *The Collapse of the Fact/Value Dichotomy and Other Essays*. Cambridge: Harvard University Press.

Raban, Avner. 1998. Near Eastern Harbors: Thirteenth to Seventh Centuries BCE. Pages 428–38 in Gitin, Mazar, and Stern 1998.

Rainey, Anson F. 1984. Early Historical Geography of the Negeb. Pates 88–104 in Herzog 1984.

———. 1996a. *Canaanite in the Amama Tablets: A Linguistic Analysis of the Mixed Dialect Used by the Scribes from Canaan*. 4 vols. Leiden: Brill. Repr., Atlanta: Society of Biblical Literature, 2010.

———. 1996b. Who Is a Canaanite? A Review of the Textual Evidence. *BASOR* 304:1–15.

———. 2001. Israel in Merenptah's Inscriptions and Reliefs. *IEJ* 51:57–75.

———. 2003. Arnama and Later: Aspects of Social History. Pages 169–87 in *Symbiois, Symbolism and the Power of the Past: Canaan, Ancient Israel and Their Neighbors from the Late Bronze Age through Roman Palaestina*. Edited by William G. Dever and Seymour Gitin. Winona Lake, IN: Eisenbrauns.

———. 2006. See Rainey and Notley 2006.

———. 2007. Whence Came the Israelites and Their Language? *IEJ* 57:41–64.

———. 2008a. Inside, Outside: Where Early Israelites Come From? *BAR* 34.6:45–50.

———. 2008b. Shasu or Habiru? Who Were the Early Israelites? *BAR* 34.6:51–55.

Rainey, Anson F., and R. Steven Notley. 2006. *The Sacred Bridge: Carta's Atlas of the Biblical World*. Jerusalem: Carta.

Rappaport, Robert. 1977. Maladaptaton in Social Systems. Pages 49–73 in *The Evolution of Social Systems*. Edited by J. Friedman and M. Rowlands. London: Duckworth.

Rast, Walter E. 1978. *Ta'anach I: Studies in the Iron Age Pottery*. Cambridge: American Schools of Oriental Research.

Redford, Donald B. 1986. The Ashkelon Relief at Karnak and the Israel Stela. *IEJ* 36:188–200.

———. 1992. *Egypt, Canaan, and Israel in Ancient Times*. Princeton: Princeton University Press.

———. 1996. A Response to Anson Rainey's "Remarks on Donald Redford's *Egypt, Canaan, and Israel in Ancient Times*." *BASOR* 301:77–81.

Redmount, Carol A. 1998. Bitter Lives: In and Out of Egypt. Pages 79–121 in Coogan 1998.

Reich, Ronny. 2011. *Excavating the City of David: Where Jerusalem's History Began*. Jerusalem: Israel Exploration Society.

Reich, Ronny, and Eli Shukron. 2004. The History of the Gihon Spring in Jerusalem. *Levant* 36:211–23.

———. 2011. The Date to the Siloam Tunnel Reconsidered. *TA* 38:147–57.

Reich, Ronny, Eli Shukron, and Omri Lemau. 2007. Recent Discoveries in the City of David, Jerusalem. *IEJ* 57:153–69.

———. 2008. The Iron Age II Finds from the Rock-Cut "Pool" Near the Spring in Jerusalem: A Preliminary Report. Pages 138–44 in Grabbe 2008a.

Reich, Ronny, and Eli Shukron. 2006. On the Original Length of Hezekiah's Tunnel: Some Critical Notes on David Ussishkin's Suggestion. Pages 795–800 in vol. 2 of Maier and Miroschebji 2006.

Rendsburg, Gary A. 2000. Notes on Israelian Hebrew. *JNES* 26:35–45.

Rendsburg, Gary A., and William M. Schniedewind. 2010. The Siloam Tunnel Inscription: Historical and Linguistic Perspectives. *IEJ* 60:188–203.

Renfrew, Colin. 1979. Systems Collapse as Social Transformation: Catastrophe and Anastrophe in Early State Societies. Pages 481–507 in *Transformations: Mathematical Approaches to Cultural Change*. Edited by Colin Renfrew and Kenneth L. Cooke. New York: Academic Press.

———. 1994. Towards a Cognitive Archaeology. Pages 3–12 in Renfrew and Zubrow 1994.

Renfrew, Colin, and Paul Bahn. 1991. *Archaeology: Theories, Methods, and Practice*. New York: Thames & Hudson.

Renfrew, Colin, and Ezra B. W. Zubrow, eds. 1994. *The Ancient Mind: Elements of Cognitive Archaeology*. Cambridge: Cambridge University Press.

Renz, Johannes, and Wolfgang Röllig. 1995–2003. *Handbuch der althebraischen Epigraphik*. 3 vols. Darmstadt: Wissenschaftliche Buchgesellschaft.

Ricoeur, Paul. 1974. *Conflict of Interpretations: Essays in Hermeneutics*. Evanston, IL: Northwestern University Press, 1974

———. 1984. *Time and Narrative*. Chicago: University of Chicago Press.

Rofé, Alexander. 1997. *Introduction to the Prophetic Literature*. Biblical Seminar 21. Sheffield: Sheffield Academic.

Rollston, Christopher A. 2006. Scribal Education in Ancient Israel: The Old Hebrew Epigraphic Evidence. *BASOR* 344:47–74.

———. 2010. *Writing and Literacy in the World of Ancient Israel: Epigraphic Evidence from the Iron Age*. ABS 11. Atlanta: Society of Biblical Literature.

———. 2015. The Incised Ishba'l Inscription from Khirbet Qeiyafa: Some Things That Can and Cannot Be Said. *Zwinglius Redivivus*, 21 June, http://tinyurl.com/SBL9025a.

Römer, Thomas C. 2005. *The So-Called Deuteronomistic History: A Sociological, Historical, and Literary Introduction*. London: T&T Clark.

Rosen, Baruch. 1986. Subsistence Economy of Stratum II. Pages 156–85 in Finkelstein 1986.

Rosen, Steven A. 1988. Finding Evidence of Ancient Nomads. *BAR* 14.5:46–53, 58–59.

Rosen, Steven A., and Gideon Avni. 1993. The Edge of the Empire: The Archaeology of Pastoral Nomads in the Southern Negev Highlands in Late Antiquity. *BA* 56:189–99.

Routledge, Bruce. 2000. Seeing through Walls: Interpreting Iron Age I Architecture at Khirbet al-Mudayna al-'Aliya. *BASOR* 319:37–70.

———. 2004. *Moab in the Iron Age: Hegemony, Polity, Archaeology*. Philadelphia: University of Pennsylvania Press.

———. 2009. Average Families? House Size Variability in the Southern Levantine Iron Age. Pages 42–61 in *The Family in Life and in Death:*

The Family in Ancient Israel; Sociological and Archaeological Perspectives. Edited by Patricia Duchter-Walls. London: T&T Clark.

Rowan, Yorke M. 2012. Beyond Belief: The Archaeology of Religion and Ritual. Pages 1–10 in *Beyond Belief: The Archaeology of Religion and Ritual.* Edited by Yorke M. Rowan. Archaeological Papers of the American Archaeological Association 21. Hoboken, NJ: Wiley.

Rowton, Michael B. 1974. Enclosed Nomadism. *JESHO* 17:1–30.

———. 1976. Dimorphic Structure and Typology. *OrAnt* 15:17–31.

———. 1977. Dimorphic Structure and the Parasocial Element. *JNES* 36:181–98.

Saadé, Gabriel. 1979. *Ougarit: Metropole cananeenne.* Beirut: Impremerie Catholique.

Sader, Hélène. 1987. *Les états araméens de Syrie depuis leur fondation jusqu'à leur transformation en provinces assyriennes.* Beirut: Steiner.

———. 1992. The Twelfth Century B.C. in Syria: The Problem of the Rise of the Aramaeans. Pages 157–63 in Ward and Joukowsky 1992.

———. 2010. The Arameans of Syria: Some Considerations on Their Origin and Material Culture. Pages 273–300 in Halpern and Lemaire 2010.

Sagona, Claudia. 2008. *Beyond the Homeland: Markers in Phoenician Chronology.* ANESSup 28. Leuven: Peeters.

Sahlins, Marshall D. 1968. *Tribesmen.* Edgewood Cliff, NJ: Prentice-Hall.

———. 1972. *Stone Age Economics.* London: Tavitock

Saidel, Benjamin A. 1997. New Insights into Ancient and Modern Pastoral Nomads. *RSR* 23:349–53.

———. 2008. The Bedouin Tent: An Ethno-archaeological Portal to Antiquity or a Modern Construct: Old World and New World Nomadism. Pages 465–86 in *The Archaeology of Mobility: Old World and New World Nomadism.* Edited by Hans Barnard and Willeke Wendrich. Los Angeles: University of California Press.

———. 2009. Pitching Camp: Ethnoarchaeological Investigations of Inhabited Tent Camps in the Wadi Hisma, Jordan. Pages 87–104 in *Nomads, Tribes, and the State in the Ancient Near East: Cross-Disciplinary Perspectives.* Edited by Jeffrey Szuchman. Oriental Institute Seminars 5. Chicago: Oriental Institute, University of Chicago.

Saidel, Benjamin, and Eveline J. van der Steen, eds. 2007. *On the Fringe of Society: Archaeological and Ethnoarcheological Perspectives on Pastoral and Agricultural Societies.* BAR International Series 1657. Oxford: Archaeopress.

Salzman, Philip C., ed. 1980. *When Nomads Settle: Processes of Sedentarization as Adaption and Response*. New York: Praeger.

Sanders, Seth L. 2008. Writing and Early Iron Age Israel: Before National Scripts, Beyond Nations and States. Pages 97–112 in Tappy and McCarter 2008.

———. 2009. *The Invention of Hebrew*. Chicago: University of Illinois Press.

Sass, Benjamin, and Christoph Uehlinger. 1993. *Studies in the Iconography of Northwest Semitic Inscribed Northwest Seals*. OBO 125. Göttingen: Vanderhoeck & Ruprecht.

Sasson, Aharon. 1998. The Pastoral Component in the Economy of Hill Country Sites in the Intermediate Bronze and Iron Age Sites: Archaeoethographic Case Studies. *TA* 25:3–51.

———. 2008. Reassessing the Bronze and Iron Age Economy: Sheep and Goat Husbandry in the Southern Levant as a Model Case Study. Pages 113–34 in *Bene Israel: Studies in the Archaeology of Israel and the Levant during the Bronze and Iron Ages in Honour of Israel Finkelstein*. Edited by Alexander Fantalkin and Assaf Yasur-Landau. CHANE 31. Leiden: Brill.

Sasson, Jack M., ed. 2006. *Civilizations of the Ancient Near East*. 4 vols. New York, 1995. Repr. in 2 vols. Peabody, MA: Hendrickson.

Schäfer-Lichtenberger, Christa. 1996. Sociological and Biblical Views of the Early State. Pages 78–105 in Fritz and Davies 1996.

Schiffer, Michael Brian. 1987. *Formation Processes of the Archaeological Record*. Albuquerque: University of New Mexico Press.

———. 1996. Formation Processes of the Historical and Archaeological Records. Pages 73–80 in Kingery 1996b.

Schloen, J. David. 2001. *The House of the Father as Fact and Symbol: Patrimonialism in Ugarit and the Ancient Near East*. Studies in the Archaeology and History of the Levant 2. Winona Lake, IN: Eisenbrauns.

———. 2003. The Iron Age State as a State of Mind: A Response. Pages 263–92 in *One Hundred Years of American Archaeology in the Middle East*. Edited by Douglas R. Clark and Victor H. Matthews. Boston: American Schools of Oriental Research.

———, ed. 2009. *Exploring the* Longue Duree: *Essays in Honor of Lawrence E. Stager*. Winona Lake, IN: Eisenbrauns.

Schneider, Thomas. 2010. Contributions to the Chronology of the New Kingdom and the Third Intermediate Period. *Egypt and the Levant* 20:373–403.

Schniedewind, William M. 1996. Tel Dan Stela: New Light on Aramaic and Jehu's Revolt. *BASOR* 302:75–90.

———. 1999. *Society and the Promise to David: The Reception History of 2 Samuel 7:1–17*. Oxford: Oxford University Press.

———. 2000. Orality and Literacy in Ancient Israel. *RSR* 26:327–32.

———. 2004. *How the Bible Became a Book: The Textualization of Ancient Israel*. Cambridge: Cambridge University Press.

———. 2010. Excavating the Text of 1 Kings 9: In Search of the Gates of Solomon. Pages 241–49 in Levy 2010a.

———. 2013. *A Social History of Hebrew: Its Origins through the Rabbinic Period*. New Haven: Yale University Press.

Schreiber, Nicola. 2003. *The Cypro-Phoenician Pottery of the Iron Age*. CHANE 13. Leiden; Brill.

Schroer, Sylvia. 1987. *In Israel Gab es Bilder: Nachrichten von darstellender Kunst im Alten Testament*. OBO 74. Göttingen: Vandenhoeck & Ruprecht.

Schwartz, Glenn M., and Steven E. Falconer, eds. 1994. *Archaeological Views from the Countryside: Village Communities in Early Complex Societies*. Washington, DC: Smithsonian Institution Press.

Sergi, Omer. 2013. Judah's Expansion in Historical Context. *TA* 40:226–46.

Sergi, Omer, et al. 2012. The Royal Judahite Store Jars: A Computer Generated Typology and Its Historical and Archaeological Implications. *TA* 39:64–92.

Shafer-Elliott, Cynthia. 2012. *Food in Ancient Judah: Domestic Cooking in the Time of the Hebrew Bible*. London: Acumen.

Shai, Itzhaq. 2006. The Political Organization of the Philistines. Pages 347–59 in Maeir and de Miroschedji 2006.

———. 2011. Philistia and the Philistines in the Iron Age IIA. *ZDPV* 127:119–34.

Shamir, Orit. 2007. Loomweights and Textile Production at Tell Miqneh-Ekron. Pages 43–49 in Crawford et al. 2007.

Shanks, Hershel, ed. 1992. *The Rise of Ancient Israel*. Washington, DC: Biblical Archaeology Society.

———. 2010. The Devil Is Not So Black as He Is Painted. *BAR* 36.3:48–58.

———, ed. 2011. *Ancient Israel: From Abraham to the Roman Destruction of the Temple*. 3rd ed. Washington, DC: Biblical Archaeology Society.

Shanks, Michael, and Christopher Tilley. 1987. *Social Theory and Archaeology*. Cambridge: Polity.

Sharon, Ilan. 1994. Demographic Aspects of the Problem of the Israelite Settlement. Pages 119–34 in *Uncovering Ancient Stones: Essays in Memory of H. Neil Richardson*. Edited by Lewis. M. Hopfe. Winona Lake, IN: Eisenbrauns.

Sharon, Ilan, and Ayelet Gilboa. 2013. The SKL Town: Dor in the Early Iron Age. Pages 393–468 in Killebrew and Lehmann 2013a.

Sharon, Ilan, and Annabel Zarzecki-Peleg. 2006. Podium Structures with Lateral Access: Authority Ploys in Royal Architecture in the Iron Age Levant. Pages 245–67 in Gitin, Wright, and Dessel 2006.

Sharon, Ilan, et al. 2005. The Early Iron Age Dating Project: Introduction, Methodology, Progress Report and an Update on the Tel Dor Radiometric Dates. Pages 65–92 in Levy and Higham 2005.

Shaw, Ian, ed. 2000. *The Oxford History of Ancient Egypt*. New York: Oxford University Press.

Sherratt, Susan. 1998. "Sea Peoples" and the Economic Structure of the Late Second Millennium in the Eastern Mediterranean. Pages 293–313 in Gitin, Mazar, and Stern 1998.

———. 2003. The Mediterranean Economy: "Globalization" at the End of the Second Millennium B.C.E. Pages 37–62 in Dever and Gitin 2003.

———. 2013. The Ceramic Phenomenon of the "Sea Peoples": An Overview. Pages 619–44 in Killebrew and Lehmann 2013a.

Sherratt, Susan, and Amihai Mazar. 2013. "Mycenaean IIIC" and Related Pottery from Beth Shean. Pages 349–92 in Killebrew and Lehmann 2013a.

Shiloh, Yigal. 1970. The Four-Room House: Its Situation and Function in the Israelite City. *IEJ* 20:180–90.

———. 1978. Elements in the Development of Town Planning in the Israelite City. *IEJ* 28:36–51.

———. 1986. A Group of Hebrew Bullae from the City of David. *IEJ* 36:16–38.

———. 1993. Megiddo. *NEAEHL* 3:1003–24.

Shimron, Aryeh E., and Amos Frumkin. 2011. The Why, How, and When of the Siloam Tunnel Reevaluated: A Reply to Sneh, Weinberger, and Shalev. *BASOR* 364:53–60

Shryock, Andrew. 1997. *Nationalism and the Genealogical Imagination: Oral History and Textual Authority in Tribal Jordan*. Berkeley: University of California Press.

Silberman, Neil Asher, and David Small, eds. 1997. *The Archaeology of*

Israel: Constructing the Past, Interpreting the Present. JSOTSup 237. Sheffield: Sheffield Academic

Silver, Morris. 1983. *Prophets and Markets: The Political Economy of Ancient Israel.* Boston: KluwerNijhoff.

Singer, Itamar. 1986. An Egyptian "Governor's Residency" at Gezer? *TA* 13:26–31.

———. 1988. Merneptah's Campaign to Canaan and the Egyptian Occupation of the Southern Coastal Plain of Palestine in the Ramesside Period. *BASOR* 269:1–10.

Singer-Avitz, Lily. 2002. Arad: The Iron Age Pottery Assemblages. *TA* 29:110–214.

———. 2008. The Earliest Settlement at Kadesh Barnea. *TA* 35:73–81.

———. 2010. The Relative Chronology of Khirbet Qeiyafa. *TA* 37:79–83.

———. 2011. Household Activities at Tel Beersheba. Pages 275–301 in Yasur-Landau, Ebeling, and Mazow 2011.

———. 2012a The Date of the Pottery from the Rock-Cut Pool Near the Gihon Spring in the City of David, Jerusalem. *ZDPV* 128:10–14.

———. 2012b. Khirbet Qeiyafa: Late Iron Age I in Spite of It All. *IEJ* 62:177–85.

Singer-Avitz, Lily, and Yoram Eshet. 1999. Beersheba: A Gateway Community in Southern Arabian Long-Distance Trade in the Eighth Century B.C.E. *TA* 26:3–75.

Skjeggestad, Marit. 1992. Ethnic Groups in Early Iron Age Palestine: Some Remarks on the Use of the Term "Israelite" in Recent Research. *SJOT* 6:159–86.

Smith, Mark S. 2001. *The Origins of Biblical Monotheism: Israel's Polytheistic Background and the UgariticTexts.* New York: Oxford University Press.

———. 2006. In Solomon's Temple (I Kings 6–7): Between Text and Archaeology. Pages 275–82 in Gitin, Wright, and Dessel 2006.

Smith, Michael E. 2002. The Earliest Cities. Pages 3–19 in *Urban Life: Readings in the Anthropology of the City.* Edited by George Gmelch and Walter P. Zenner. 4th ed. Prospect Heights, IL: Waveland.

Sneh, Amihai, Eyal Shalev, and Ram Weinberger. 2010. The Why, How. and When of the Siloam Tunnel Reevaluated. *BASOR* 359:57– 65.

Soggin, J. Alberto. 1985. *A History of Ancient Israel: From the Beginnings to the Bar Kochba Revolt, A.D. 135.* Philadelphia: Westminster.

———. 2001. *Israel in the Biblical Period: Institutions, Festivals, Ceremonies and Rituals.* London: T&T Clark.

Sparks, Kenton L. 1998. *Ethnicity and Identity in Ancient Israel: Prole-gomena to the Study of Ethnic Sentiments and Their Expression in the Hebrew Bible*. Winona Lake, IN: Eisenbrauns.

Stager, Lawrence E. 1982. The Archaeology of the East Slope of Jerusalem and the Terraces of the Kidron. *JNES* 41:111–21.

———. 1985a. The Archaeology of the Family in Ancient Israel. *BASOR* 260:1–35.

———. 1985b. Merenptah, Israel and Sea Peoples: New Light on an Old Relief. *ErIsr* 18:56*–64*.

———. 1985c. Respondent. Pages 83–87 in *Biblical Archaeology Today: Proceedings of the International Congress on Biblical Archaeology, Jeru-salem, April 1984*. Edited by Janet Amitai. Jerusalem: Israel Explora-tion Society.

———. 1990. Shemer's Estate. *BASOR* 277:93–107.

———. 1995. The Impact of the Sea Peoples in Canaan (1185–1050 BCE). Pages 332–48 in Levy 1995.

———. 1996. Ashkelon and the Archaeology of Destruction: Kislev 604 BCE. *ErIsr* 25:61*–74*.

———. 1998. Forging an Identity: The Emergence of Ancient Israel. Pages 123–76 in Coogan 1998.

———. 2003. The Patrimonial Kingdom of Solomon. Pages 63–74 in Dever and Gitin 2003.

———. 2006. Biblical Philistines: A Hellenistic Literary Creation? Pages 375–83 in Maeir and de Miroschedji 2006.

Stager, Lawrence E., J. David Schloen, and Daniel M. Master. 2008. *Ash-kelon 1: Introduction and Overview (1985–2006)*. Winona Lake, IN: Eisenbrauns.

———. 2011. *Ashkelon 3: The Seventh Century B.C.* Winona Lake, IN: Eisenbrauns.

Stavrakopolou, Francesca, and John Barton, eds. 2010. *Religious Diversity in Ancient Israel and Judah*. London: T&T Clark.

Steadman, Sharon R., and Jennifer C. Ross, eds. 2010. *Agency and Identity in the Ancient Near East: NewPaths Forward*. London: Equinox.

Stech-Wheeler, Tamara; et al. 1981. Iron at Taʿanach and Early Iron Metal-lurgy in the Eastern Mediterranean. *AJA* 85:245–68.

Steel, Louise. 2004. *Cyprus before History. From the Earliest Settlers to the End of the Bronze Age*. London: Duckworth.

———. 2014. Cyprus during the Late Bronze Age. Pages 577–94 in Steiner and Killebrew 2014.

Steen, Eveline J. van der. 2004. *Tribes and Territories in Transition: The Central East Jordan Valley in the Late Bronze and Early Iron Ages; A Study of the Sources.* Leuven: Peeters.

———. 2010. Judah, Masos and Hayil. Pages 168–86 in Levy 2010a.

———. 2013. *Near Eastern Tribal Societies during the Nineteenth Century: Economy, Society and Politics between Tent and Town.* New York: Acumen.

Steiner, Margreet L. 2003. The Evidence from Kenyon's Excavations in Jerusalem: A Response Essay. Pages 347–64 in Vaughn and Killebrew 2003.

———. 2014. Moab during the Iron Age II Period. Pages 770–81 in Steiner and Killebrew 2014.

Steiner, Margreet L., and Ann E. Killebrew, eds. 2014. *The Oxford Handbook of the Archaeology of the Levant c. 8000–332 BCE.* Oxford: Oxford University Press.

Stendahl, Krister. 1992. Biblical Theology, Contemporary. *IDB* 1:418–32.

Stepansky, Yosef, Dror Segal, and Israel Carmi. 1996. The 1993 Sounding at Tel Sasa: Excavation Report and Radiometric Dating. *'Atiqot* 28:63–76.

Stern, Ephraim. 1990. New Evidence from Dor for the First Appearance of Phoenicians along the Northern Coast of Israel. *BASOR* 279:27–33.

———, ed. 1993. *The New Encyclopedia of Archaeological Excavations in the Holy Land.* 4 vols. Jerusalem: Israel Exploration Society and Carta; New York: Simon & Schuster.

———. 2000. *Dor, Ruler of the Seas: Twelve Years of Excavations at the Israelite-Phoenician Harbor Town on the Carmel Coast.* Rev. ed. Jerusalem: Israel Exploration Society.

———. 2001. *The Assyrian, Babylonian and Persian Periods, 722–332 BCE.* Volume 2 of *Archaeology of the Land of the Bible.* New York: Doubleday.

———, ed. 2008. *The New Encyclopedia of Archaeological Excavations in the Holy Land 5: Supplementary Volume.* Jerusalem: Israel Exploration Society; Washington, DC: Biblical Archaeology Society.

———. 2013. *The Material Culture of the Northern Sea Peoples in Israel.* Winona Lake, IN: Eisenbrauns.

Sternberg, Meir. 1985. *The Poetics of Biblical Narrative: Ideological Literature and the Drama of Reading.* Bloomington: Indiana University Press.

Stiebing, William H. 1989. *Out of the Desert? Archaeology and the Exodus/Conquest Narratives.* Buffalo, NY: Prometheus.

Stone, Bryan J. 1995. The Philistines and Acculturation: Culture Change and Ethnic Continuity in the Iron Age. *BASOR* 298:7–32.

Strange, John. 2000. The Late Bronze Age in Northern Jordan. Pages 476–81 in *The Archaeology of Jordan and Beyond: Essays in Honor of James A. Sauer*. Edited by Lawrence E. Stager, Joseph A. Greene, and Michael D. Coogan. SAHL 1. Winona Lake, IN: Eisenbrauns.

Szuchman, Jeffrey, ed. 2009. *Nomads, Tribes, and the State in the Ancient Near East: Cross-Disciplinary Perspectives*. Oriental Institute Seminars 5. Chicago: Oriental Institute of the University of Chicago.

Tadmor, Hayim. 1962. The Southern Border of Aram. *IEJ* 12:114–22.

———. 1994. *The Inscriptions of Tiglath-Pileser III, King of Assyria*. Jerusalem: Israel Academy of Sciences and Humanities.

Tainter, Joseph A. 1988. *The Collapse of Complex Societies*. Cambridge: Cambridge University Press.

Tappy, Ron E. 1992. *Early Iron Age through the Ninth Century B.C.E.* Vol. 1 of *The Archaeology of Israelite Samaria*. HSS 44. Winona Lake, IN: Eisenbrauns.

———. 2001. *The Eighth Century B.C.E.* Vol. 2 of *The Archaeology of Israelite Samaria*. HSS 50. Winona Lake, IN: Eisenbrauns.

———. 2006. The Provenance of the Unpublished Ivories from Samaria. Pages 637–56 in Maeir, and de Miroschedji 2006.

———. 2009. East of Ashkelon: The Setting and Setting of the Judaean Lowlands in the Iron Age IIA Period. Pages 449–63 in Schloen 2009.

Tappy, Ron E., and P. Kyle McCarter Jr., eds. 2008. *Literate Culture and Tenth-Century Canaan: The Tel Zayit Abecedary in Context*. Winona Lake, IN: Eisenbrauns.

Tarnas, Richard. 1991. *The Passion of the Western Mind: Understanding the Ideas That Have Shaped Our World View*. New York: Ballantine.

Tarragon, Jean-Michel de. 1980. *Le Culte a Ugarit: D'apres les textes de la pratigue en cuneiform alphabetiques*. CRB 19. Paris: Gabalda.

Thareani, Yifat. 2010. The Spirit of Clay: "Edomite Pottery" and Social Awareness in the Late Iron Age. *BASOR* 359:35–55.

———. 2011. *Tel 'Arner: The Iron Age II Caravan Town and the Hellenistic-Early Roman Settlement; The Avraham Biran (1975–1982) and Rudolph Cohen (1975–1976) Excavations*. NGSBA 8. Jerusalem: Nelson Glueck School of Biblical Archaeology.

Thompson, Christine M. 2003. Sealed Silver in Iron Age Cisjordan and the 'Invention' of Coinage. *Oxford Journal of Archaeology* 22:67–107.

Thompson, Thomas L. 1974. *The Historicity of the Patriarchal Narratives: The Quest for the Historical Abraham*. Berlin: de Gruyter.

———. 1987. *The Origin Tradition of Ancient Israel: The Literary Formation of Genesis and Exodus 1–23*. JSOTSup 55. Sheffield: JSOT Press.

———. 1991. Text, Context, and Referent in Israelite Historiography. Pages 65–92 in Edelman 1991.

———. 1992. *Early History of the Israelite People: From the Written and Archaeological Sources*. SHANE 4. Leiden: Brill.

———. 1995. A Neo-Albrightian School in History and Biblical Scholarship? *JBL* 114:683–98.

———. 1996. Historiography of Ancient Palestine and Early Jewish Historiography: William G. Dever and the Not So New Biblical Archaeology. Pages 26–43 in Fritz and Davies 1996.

———. 1997. Defining History and Ethnicity in the South Levant. Pages 166–87 in Grabbe 1997b.

———. 1999. *The Mythic Past: Biblical Archaeology and the Myth of Israel*. New York: Basic Books.

———. 2014. *Biblical Narrative and Palestine's History: Changing Perspectives in Biblical Interpretation*. Changing Perspectives 2. London: Routledge.

Tigay, Jeffrey H. 1987. Israelite Religion: The Onomastic and Epigraphic Evidence. Pages 157–94 in Miller, Hanson, and McBride 1987.

Tilley, Christopher, ed. 1990. *Reading Material Culture: Structuralism, Hermeneutics, and Post-structuralism*. Oxford: Blackwell.

———. 1991. *Material Culture and Text: The Art of Ambiguity*. London: Routledge.

———. 1993. *Interpretive Archaeology*. Oxford: Berg.

———. 1999. *Metaphor and Material Culture*. Oxford: Blackwell

Toombs, Lawrence E. 1992. Shechem (Place). *ABD* 5:1174–86.

Toorn, Karel van der. 1996. *Family Religion in Babylonia, Syria and Israel: Continuity and Change in the Forms of Religious Life*. SHANE 7. Leiden: Brill.

———, ed. 1997. *The Image and the Book: Iconic Cults, Aniconism, and the Rise of Book Religion in Israel and the Ancient Near East*. Leuven: Peeters.

———. 1998. Goddesses in Early Israelite Religion. Pages 83–97 in *Ancient Goddesses: The Myths and the Evidence*. Edited by Lucy Goodison and Christine Morris. London: British Museum Press.

—————. 2002. Israelite Figurines: A View from the Texts. Pages 45–62 in *Sacred Time, Sacred Place: Archaeology and the Religion of Israel.* Edited by Barry M. Gittlen. Winona Lake, IN: Eisenbrauns.

Toorn, Karel van der, Bob Becking, and Pieter W. van der Horst, eds. 1999. *Dictionary of Deities and Demons in the Bible.* Leiden: Brill.

Tov, Emanuel. 2012. *Textual Criticism of the Hebrew Bible.* 3rd ed. Minneapolis: Fortress.

Trigger, Bruce G. 2006. *A History of Archaeological Thought.* 2nd ed. Cambridge: Cambridge University Press.

Tushingham, A. Douglas. 1993. Dibon. *NEAEHL* 1:350–52.

Uehlinger, Christoph. 2005. Was There a Cult Reform under King Josiah? The Case for a Well-Grounded Minimum. Pages 279–316 in Grabbe 2005a.

Ussishkin, David. 1982. *The Conquest of Lachish by Sennacherib.* Publications of the Institute of Archaeology 6. Tel Aviv: Institute of Archaeology, Tel Aviv University.

—————. 1985. Levels VII and VI at Tell Lachish and the End of the Late Bronze Age in Canaan. Pages 213–28 in Palestine in the Bronze and Iron Ages: Papers in Honour of Olga Tufnell. Edited by Jonathan N. Tubb. University of London, Institute of Archaeology Occasional Publication 11. London: Institute of Archaeology.

—————. 2000. The Credibility of the Tel Jezreel Excavations: A Rejoinder to Amnon Ben-Tor. *TA* 27:248–56.

—————. 2003. Solomon's Jerusalem: The Text and the Facts on the Ground. Pages 103–15 in Vaughn and Killebrew 2003.

—————, ed. 2004. *The Renewed Archaeological Excavations at Lachish (1973–1994).* 5 vols. Monograph Series of the Institute of Archaeology of Tel Aviv University 22. Tel Aviv: Tel Aviv University.

—————. 2007a. Megiddo and Samaria: A Rejoinder to Norma Franklin. *BASOR* 348:49–70.

—————. 2007b. Samaria, Jezreel and Megiddo: Royal Centres of Omri and Ahab. Pages 293–309 in Grabbe 2007a.

—————. 2009a. On the So-called Aramaean "Siege Trench" in Tell es-Safi, Ancient Gath. *IEJ* 59:137–57.

—————. 2009b. The Temple Mount in Jerusalem during the First Temple Period. Pages 413–482 in Schloen 2009.

Ussishkin, David, and John Woodhead. 1992. Excavations at Tel Jezreel 1990–1991: Preliminary Report. *TA* 19:3–56.

———. 1994. Excavations at Tel Jezreel 1992–1993: Second Preliminary Report. *Levant* 26:1–48.

———. 1998. Excavations at Tel Jezreel 1994–1996: Third Preliminary Report. *TA* 24:6–72.

Ussishkin, David, et al. 2007. Has King David's Palace in Jerusalem Been Found? *TA* 34:142–64.

Uziel, Joe. 2007. The Development Process of Philistine Material Culture: Assimilation, Acculturation and Everything in Between. *Levant* 39:165–73.

Vanhoozer, Kevin J., ed. 2003. *The Cambridge Companion to Postmodern Theology*. Cambridge: Cambridge University Press.

Van Seters, John. 1975. Abraham in History and Tradition. New Haven: Yale University Press.

———. 1983. *In Search of History: Historiography in the Ancient World and the Origins of Biblical History*. New Haven: Yale University Press.

Vaughn, Andrew G. 1999. *Theology, History, and Archaeology in the Chronicler's Account of Hezekiah*. ABS 4. Atlanta: Scholars Press.

Vaughn, Andrew G., and Carolyn Pillers Dobler. 2006. A Provenance Study of Hebrew Seals and Seal Impressions: A Statistical Analysis. Pages 757–71 in Maeir and de Miroschedji 2006.

Vaughn, Andrew G., and Ann E. Killebrew, eds. 2003. *Jerusalem in Bible and Archaeology: The First Temple Period*. SymS 18. Atlanta: Society of Biblical Literature.

Vieweger, Dieter, and Jutta Haser. 2007. Tall Zira'a: Five Thousand Years of Palestinian History on a Single Settlement Mound. *NEA* 70:147–67.

Vriezen, Karel J. H. 2001. Archaeological Traces of Cult in Ancient Israel. Pages 45–80 in *Only One God? Monotheism in Ancient Israel and the Veneration of the Goddess Asherah*. By Bob Becking, Meindert Dijkstra, Marjo C. A. Korpel, and Karel J. H. Vriezen. New York: Sheffield Academic.

Wachsmann, Shelley. 1998. *Seagoing Ships and Seamanship in the Bronze Age Levant*. College Station: Texas A&M University Press.

Waldbaum, Jane C. 1980. The First Archaeological Appearance of Iron and the Transition to the Iron Age. Pages 72–73 in *The Coming of the Age of Iron*. Edited by Theodore A. Wertime and James D. Muhly. New Haven: Yale University Press.

———. 1994. Early Greek Contacts with the Southern Levant, ca. 1000–600 B.C.: The Eastern Perspective *BASOR* 293:53–66.

Walls, Neal H., ed. 2005. *Cult Image and Divine Representation in the Ancient Near East*. ASOR Book Series 10. Boston: American Schools of Oriental Research.

Ward, Graham. 2003. Deconstructive Theology. Pages 76–91 in Vanhoozer 2003.

Ward, William A., and Joukowsky, Martha S., eds. 1992. *The Crisis Years: The Twelfth Century B.C.; From beyond the Danube to the Tigris*. Dubuque, IA: Kendall/Hunt.

Weinfeld, Moshe. 1972. *Deuteronomy and the Deuteronomic School*. Oxford: Clarendon.

Weinstein, James M. 1981. The Egyptian Empire in Palestine: A Reassessment. *BASOR* 241:1–28.

———. 1997. Exodus and Archaeological Reality. Pages 87–103 in Frerichs and Lesco 1997.

Weippert, Helga. 1988. *Palästina in vorhellenistischer Zeit*. Handbuch der Archäologie. Vorderasien 2/1. Munich: Beck.

Weippert, Manfred. 1971. *The Settlement of the Israelite Tribes in Palestine: A Critical Survey of Recent Scholarly Debate*. SBT 21. London: SCM.

Whitelam, Keith W. 1991. Between History and Literature: The Social Production of Israel's Traditions of Origin. *SJOT* 5:60–74.

———. 1996. *The Invention of Ancient Israel: The Silencing of Palestinian History*. New York: Routledge.

Whitley, David S., ed. 1998. *Reader in Archaeological Theory: Post-processual and Cognitive Approaches*. London: Routledge.

Williamson, H. G. M., ed. 2007. *Understanding the History of Ancient Israel*. Proceedings of the British Academy 143. Oxford: Oxford University Press.

Wilson, Robert R. 1980. *Prophecy and Society in Ancient Israel*. Philadelphia: Fortress.

Windschuttle, Keith. 1997. *The Killing of History: How Literary Critics and Social Theorists Are Murdering Our Past*. New York: Free Press.

Winter, Irene J. 1976. Phoenician and North Syrian Ivory Carving in Historical Context: Questions of Style and Distribution. *Iraq* 38:1–22.

———. 1981. Is There a South Syrian Style of Ivory Carving in the Early First Millennium B.C.? *Iraq* 43:101–30.

Winter, Urs. 1983. *Frau und Göttin: Exegetische und ikonographische Studien zum weiblichen Gottesbild im Alten Israel und in dessen Umwelt*. OBO 53. Fribourg: Vandenhoeck & Ruprecht.

Wolf, Eric R. 1966. *Peasants*. Englewood Cliffs, NJ: Prentice-Hall.

———. 1969. *Peasant Wars of the Twentieth Century*. New York: Harper & Row.

———. 1982. *Europe and the People without History*. Berkeley: University of California Press.

Wolff, Samuel, and Alon Shavit. 2008. Ḥamid, Tel. Pages 1762–63 in Stern 2008.

Wood, Bryant G. 1990. *The Sociology of Pottery in Ancient Palestine: The Ceramic Industry and the Diffusion of Ceramic Style in the Bronze and Iron Ages*. JSOTSup 103. Sheffield: Sheffield Academic Press.

Wright, G. R. H. 2000. *Historical Background*. Vol. 1 of *Ancient Building Technology*. Technology and Change in History 4. Leiden: Brill.

———. 2005. *Materials*. Vol. 2 of *Ancient Building Technology*. Technology and Change in History 7. Leiden: Brill.

———. 2009. *Construction*. Vol. 3 of *Ancient Building Technology*. Technology and Change in History 12. Leiden: Brill.

Wright, G. Ernest. 1952. *God Who Acts: Biblical Theology as Recital*. SBT 8. Chicago: Regnery.

Wyatt, Nicolas. 2008. The Mythic Mind Revisited: Myth and History or Myth versus. History, a Continuing Problem in Biblical Studies. *SJOT* 22:161–75.

Yadin, Yigael. 1963. *The Art of Warfare in Biblical Lands in the Light of Archaeological Discovery*. London: Weidenfeld & Nicolson.

———. 1972. *Hazor: The Head of All Those Kingdoms (Joshua 11:10)*. London: Oxford University Press.

———. 1993. Hazor. *NEAEHL* 2:594–606.

Yadin, Yigael, et al. 1958. *Hazor I: An Account of the First Season of Excavations, 1955*. Jerusalem: Magnes.

Yasur-Landau, Assaf. 2010. *The Philistines and Aegean Migration at the End of the Late Bronze Age*. Cambridge: Cambridge University Press.

Yasur-Landau, Assaf, Jennie Ebeling, and Laura Mazow, eds. 2011. *Household Archaeology in Ancient Israel and Beyond*. CHANE 50. Leiden: Brill.

Yezerski, Irit. 2013a. Typology and Chronology of the Iron Age II–III Judahite Rock-Cut Tombs. *IEJ* 63:50–77.

———. 2013b. Iron Age Burial Customs in the Samaria Highlands. *TA* 40:72–98.

Yoffee, Norman. 1988. Orienting Collapse. Pages 1–19 in Yoffee and Cowgill 1988.

———. 2005. *Myths of the Archaic State: Evolution of the Earliest Cities, States, and Civilizations*. Cambridge: Cambridge University Press.

Yoffee, Norman, and George L. Cowgill, eds. 1988. *The Collapse of Ancient States and Civilizations*. Tucson: University of Arizona Press.

Yon, Marguerite, Maurice M. Sznycer, and Pierre Bordreuil, eds. 1995. *Le Pays d'Ougarit autour de 1200 av J.-C.: Histoire et archeologie; Actes du collogue internationale, Paris, 28 juin–1e juillet 1993*. Paris: College de France.

Younger, K. Lawson, Jr. 1998. The Deportations of the Israelites. *JBL* 117:201–27.

———. *A Political History of the Arameans: From Their Origins to the End of Their Polities*. ABS 13. Atlanta: SBL Press.

Younker, Randall W. Ammon during the Iron Age II Period. Pages 757–69 in Steiner and Killebrew 2014.

Yurco, Frank. 1986. Merneptah's Canaanite Campaign. *JARCE* 23:189–215.

———. 1997. Merneptah's Canaanite Campaign and Israel's Origins. Pages 27–55 in Frerichs and Lesco 1997.

Zertal, Adam. 1986–1987 An Early Iron Age Cultic Site on Mt. Ebal: Excavation Seasons 1982–1987: Preliminary Report. *TA* 14:105–65.

———. 1991. Israel Enters Canaan-Following the Pottery Trail. *BAR* 17.5:28–47.

———. 1993. Samaria (Region): The Mount Manasseh (Northern Samarian Hills) Survey. *NEAEHL* 4:1311–12.

———. 1994. "To the Land of the Perizzites and the Giants": On the Israelite Settlement in the Hill Country of Manasseh. Pages 238–50 in Finkelstein and Na'aman 1994.

———. 1998. The Iron Age I Culture in the Hill-Country-A Manassite Look. Pages 220–50 in Gitin, Mazar, and Stern 1998.

———. 2001. The Heart of the Monarchy: Pattern of Settlement and New Historical Considerations of the Israelite Kingdom of Samaria. Pages 38–64 in A. Mazar 2001b.

———. 2004. *The Manasseh Hill Country Survey 1: The Shechem Syncline*. CHANE 21. Leiden: Brill.

———. 2007. *The Manasseh Hill Country Survey 2: The Eastern Valleys and the Fringes of the Desert*. CHANE 21.2 Leiden: Brill.

———. 2012. *El-Ahwat, Fortified Site From the Early Iron Age Near Nahal 'Iron, Israel: Excavations 1993–2000*. CHANE 24. Leiden: Brill.

Zevit, Ziony. 2001. *The Religions of Ancient Israel: A Synthesis of Parallactic Approaches*. London: Continuum.

———. 2006. Implicit Population Figures and Historical Sense: What Happened to 200,150 Judahites in 701 BCE? Pages 357–66 in Gitin, Wright, and Dessel 2006.

———. 2008. The Davidic-Solomonic Empire from the Perspective of Archaeological Bibliology. Pages 201–24 in *Birkat Shalom: Studies in the Bible, Ancient Near Eastern Literature, and Post-biblical Judaism; Presented to Shalom M. Paul on the Occasion of His Seventieth Birthday*. Edited by Chaim Cohen et al. Winona Lake, IN: Eisenbrauns.

Ziffer, Irit. 2013. Portraits of Ancient Israelite Kings? *BAR* 39.5:41–51, 78.

Zimhoni, Orna. 1997a. Clues from the Enclosure-Fills: Pre-Omride Settlement at Tel Jezreel. *TA* 24:83–109.

———. 1997b. *Studies in the Iron Age Pottery of Israel: Typological, Archaeological, and Chronological Aspects*. Tel Aviv: Tel Aviv University.

———. 2004. The Pottery of Levels V and IV and Its Archaeological and. Chronological Implications. Pages 1643–1788 in vol. 4 of Ussishkin 2004.

Zorn, Jeffrey R. 1994. Estimating the Population Size of Ancient Settlements: Methods, Problems, Solutions, and a Case Study. *BASOR* 295:31–48.

———. 1997. An Inner and Outer Gate Complex at Tell en-Nasbeh. *BASOR* 307:53–66.

———. 1999. A Note on the Date of the "Great Wall" of Tell en-Nasbeh: A Rejoinder. *TA* 26:146–50.

———. 2006. The Burials of the Judean Kings: Sociohistorical Considerations and Suggestions. Pages 801–20 in Maier and Miroschedji 2006.

Zuckerman, Sharon. 2007. Anatomy of a Destruction: Crisis Architecture, Termination Rituals and the Fall at Canaanite Hazor. *JMA* 21:3–32.

Zwickel, Wolfgang. 1994. *Der Tempelkult in Kanaan, und Israel: Ein Beitrag zur Kultgeschichte Palastinas von der Mittelbronzezeit bis zum Untergang Judas*. FAT 10. Tübingen: Mohr Siebeck.

Zwingenberger, Uta. 2001. Dorfkultur der frühen Eisenzeit in Mittelpalästina. OBO 180. Göttingen: Vandenhoeck & Ruprecht.

Biblical Index

Place Name Index

Subject Index